CW00556430

January 8 2019

For Bishop Allan

from [signature] and

[signature]

With cordial wishes

HUMAN COMES FIRST

HUMAN COMES FIRST

The Christian Theology of N.F.S. Grundtvig

Edward Broadbridge
Translator and Editor

Introduction: Niels Henrik Gregersen
Contributions by Hans Raun Iversen, Brian Degn
Mårtensson, Michael Schelde, Vanja Thaulow,
Steen Tullberg, and Ole Vind

*"Human comes first, and Christian next,
for that is life's true order"* (1837)

Aarhus University Press |

Human Comes First. The Christian Theology of N.F.S. Grundtvig
© Edward Broadbridge, and Aarhus University Press
Illustrations selected and annotated by Michael Schelde and Edward Broadbridge
Language Consultants: Hanna Broadbridge, John Nicholson

Typeset by Narayana Press
Cover design by Jørgen Sparre
Printed in Denmark by Narayana Press 2018

A recording of all the texts is available free at www.unipress.dk

This book is number three in the series N.F.S. Grundtvig: Works in English
Series editors:
Niels Henrik Gregersen, Ove Korsgaard
ISBN 978 87 7184 135 0
ISSN 2246-7025

Published:
vol. 1.   The School For Life. N.F.S. Grundtvig on Education for the People (2011)
vol. 2.   Living Wellsprings. The Hymns, Songs, and Poems of N.F.S. Grundtvig (2015)
vol. 3.   Human Comes First. The Christian Theology of N.F.S. Grundtvig (2018)

Forthcoming:
vol. 4.   The Common Good. N.F.S. Grundtvig as Politician and Contemporary Historian
vol. 5.   The Advance of Learning. N.F.S. Grundtvig's Philosophical Writings

Published with the financial support of international and Danish foundations as well as individual donors. For a full list see p. 12

Aarhus University Press
Finlandsgade 29
8200 Aarhus N
Denmark
www.unipress.dk

INTERNATIONAL DISTRIBUTORS

Oxbow Books Ltd.
The Old Music Hall
106-108 Cowley Road
Oxford, OX4 1JE
United Kingdom
www.oxbowbooks.com

ISD
70 Enterprise Drive, Suite 2
Bristol, CT 06010
USA
www.isdistribution.com

Contents

IV LETTERS AND SPEECHES 443

Introduction: Michael Schelde & Edward Broadbridge

Illustrations

Cover: P.C. Skovgaard's drawing of Grundtvig, 1847 in Frederiksborg Castle. The handwriting is Grundtvig's own. It includes the famous lines: "Freedom for Loki as well as for Thor". The Royal Library, (fasc. 382(1) Grundtvig Archive, Royal Library, Copenhagen).

1. Grundtvig's birth and baptism 1783

*D 8de Septbr: som var en Mandag effter D; 12 Trin: Kl. 3 effter
Middag blev min kjære Hustrue Catharine Maria Bang lyckelig
forløst med en Søn, som den 10de dereffter blev af mig hjemme-
døbt og kaldet Nicolaj Frideric Severin Grundtvig. Jordemo-
deren Madame Carstensen bar ham da –*

On 8th Sept., which was a Monday after the 12th Sunday after Trinity,
at 3 o'clock in the afternoon my dear wife Catharine Maria Bang was
safely delivered of a son, who on the 10th inst. was baptised by me
at home and named Nicolaj Frideric Severin Grundtvig. The midwife,
Madame Carstensen, carried him.

Foreword

Grundtvig is primarily a theologian and pastor. He graduated from the Faculty of Theology at the University of Copenhagen in 1803, was ordained in 1811, and remained a priest until his death, though occasionally without a parish. From 1839-72 he was pastor of Vartov Church in the heart of Copenhagen, which is the building most closely associated with him.

'Human comes first, and Christian next' is a famous Grundtvig quotation, and aptly summarises the starting-point for his theology. For the first time in English *Human Comes First* presents his key theological ideas as articles, book chapters, sermons, and letters. From his extensive production a central selection has been undertaken by the translation committee comprising in alphabetical order: Edward Broadbridge, Niels Henrik Gregersen, Anders Holm, Hans Raun Iversen, Uffe Jonas, Ove Korsgaard, Kim Arne Pedersen, Michael Schelde, and Ole Vind.

This is the third book in the five-volume series 'N.F.S Grundtvig. Works in English', which seeks to give an insight into the time when Grundtvig was writing as well as to bring a present-day perspective to Grundtvig. His thinking belongs to a specific period and was written into a particular context, but at the same time many of his ideas have become historically significant, with an impact far beyond the 19th century – and far beyond the Danish border. Niels Henrik Gregersen's introduction to *Human Comes First* draws a line right up to today's theological debate. The individual introductions are written by Grundtvig scholars, who place the texts in their contexts. The conversation on current theological issues is firmly supported by the Grundtvig Study Centre through the publication of books on Grundtvig's theological ideas and through regular conferences with contemporary relevance.

The Grundtvig Study Centre was established on 1st January 2009 to continue the work of the former Centre for Grundtvig Studies from 1988. It has taken the initiative for the present translations and is also responsible for an ongoing critical edition of Grundtvig's Works (in Danish) as they were published in his lifetime, see www.grundtvigsvaerker.dk. The Centre supports research focusing on all areas of interest in Grundtvig studies, including comparative research initiatives that offer new perspectives on Grundtvig's ideas, supportive knowledge exchange, and the dissemination and understanding of his work.

A timeline, extensive footnotes, a bibliography of works in English, a few selected illustrations, and a comprehensive index provide readers with a scholarly basis on which to build.

Edward Broadbridge is the translator and editor of the volume, with John Nicholson and Hanna Broadbridge as language consultants. The main introduction has been written by Niels Henrik Gregersen and there are chapter contributions by Hans Raun Iversen, Brian Degn Mårtensson, Michael Schelde, Vanja Thaulow, Steen Tullberg, and Ole Vind.

Human Comes First has been supported financially by a number of foundations and individuals. The Grundtvig Study Centre wishes to thank the following:

Aarhus Universitets Forskningsfond
Konsul George Jorck og Hustru Emma Jorcks Fond
Carlsen-Lange Stiftelse
N.F.S. Grundtvigs Fond
Grundtvigsk Forum
Svend Grundtvigs og Axel Olriks legat
Members of the Board of The Danish Interest Conference (Church and Life)

Andres Albertsen, Edward Amundson, Doug Bro, Carol Christiansen, Hans Clausen, Robert Hansen and Cathy Mahowald, Joy Ibsen and Don Lenef, Bridget Jensen, Bridget Lois Jensen, Janet Jensen, Sonja Knudsen, Lee Mitchell Martin, Fred M'Gee, Daniel and Alice Mikel, Aryn Mikel, Leland and Virginia Molgaard, Carla and Joel Mortensen, Mark Nussle, John Rasmussen, Bert Schou, John and Polly Snider, Lora Lee Pedersen-Thousholt, Sonja Walker.

Michael Schelde, Director of the Grundtvig Study Centre, Aarhus University.

Editor's/Translator's Note

Edward Broadbridge

Sentence length

Whereas Grundtvig's hymns are immediately understandable except for a few archaic words, his theological writings, like all his prose, are by modern standards convoluted. With an *average* sentence length of 110 words, they are no longer read below university level, and even there only by theologians and aficionados. Take for instance the chapter 'On our Third Article of Faith'. This contains 4,012 words in a mere 33 sentences with only 28 paragraphs, so most sentences fill a whole paragraph. The average sentence length is thus 121 words! The longest sentence runs to 235 words and contains 27 commas. To make Grundtvig accessible to the modern reader, I have disentangled the complex syntax and rewritten a single paragraph of Danish as 7 or 8 sentences in English. However, in each of the five volumes in the series I have left (and noted) a single English sentence in its original Danish length and syntax – see footnote 76 in this volume.

Specific editorial usage

To give a sense of the original power of Grundtvig's theological writing I have occasionally used italics for emphasis, and, hopefully, for easier reading.

Grundtvig consistently uses 'England' when referring to the United Kingdom, a usage which is still widespread and which I have retained for historical reasons.

I have capitalised the twin sacraments in the Danish Lutheran Church thus: 'Baptism' and 'Holy Communion'. Similarly 'Church' and 'State' are for the most part capitalised. The German language still uses capital letters for all nouns; this was also the custom in Denmark until 1948. So when Grundtvig writes about the truth of the word (*ordets sandhed*), he may in fact be speaking about the Truth of the Word (*Ordets Sandhed*)! Most likely he is referring to the latter. Following this usage, I have capitalised 'the Devil', 'Heaven' and 'Hell' as well as 'the Articles of Faith'.

Where Grundtvig always speaks of Man and Mankind, I have deliberately made these concepts gender-neutral, using 'human beings', 'humankind', or simply the first person plural – except in the case of 'Natural Man'. However, since female pastors were not allowed in the Danish Lutheran Church before 1948, Grundtvig's references are always to male pastors, so I have retained this usage. For historical, biblical (and psychological?) reasons we still envisage the Devil as male, which is in direct contradiction to what I have just written. Are not the snake in Paradise and the Tempter in the desert also gender-neutral?[1]

I have translated the Danish word *Alter-Bogen* with the English 'Altar Book', which is the US Episcopal translation, whereas the Church of England uses 'Service Book'. The 'Altar Book' contains the liturgy for the services of the Evangelical Lutheran Church in Denmark.

One idiosyncratic translation I have retained throughout: Grundtvig is fond of assuring his readers that "it is clear as sunlight" – where 'daylight' would be the obvious choice, but would miss his veneration of the sun as a favourite metaphor.

I follow Grundtvig's paragraph demarcations for the most part, until by modern standards they seem overstretched, i.e. over a whole page.

Footnotes occupy roughly a seventh of the complete text, since Grundtvig himself makes so many references, and the modern reader needs a good deal of contextual information. On the assumption that readers may wish to pick and choose among the chapters, some important footnotes are repeated.

Folkekirken in translation

Until 1849 the Evangelical Lutheran Church in Denmark – to give it its correct modern name – was the State Church of Denmark, regulated by the absolute monarch and his civil servants. With the new democratic constitution of 1849, this church was given absolute priority, since its membership included almost the entire Danish population. It was renamed The People's Church (*Folkekirken*), a usage which Grundtvig employed and which I have retained. Other modern translations vary:

The Folk Church: E. D. Nielsen (1955)
The Danish Church: K. Stevenson (1993) M.S. Lausten (2002)
The Church of Denmark: G. Wainwright (1993) and A.A. Allchin (1997)
The National Church: S.A.J. Bradley (2008)

---

1. The American scholar Judith Plaskow has written: "...feminists, although we continually confront human evil in the form of patriarchy and other destructive structures of hierarchical relation, have not yet fully addressed the theological question of evil as a feminist issue" (quoted in Arthur Roy Eckardt, *On the Way to Death*, Transaction Publishers 1996).

Folkekirken in the Danish Constitution

The relevant paragraphs and sections, introduced in 1849 and last revised in 1953, read as follows:

§ 4 The Evangelical Lutheran Church shall be the Established Church of Denmark, and, as such, it shall be supported by the State.

§ 6 The King shall be a member of the Evangelical Lutheran Church.

§ 66 The constitution of the Established Church shall be laid down by Statute.

Section 67 [Right to Worship] The citizens shall be entitled to form congregations for the worship of God in a manner consistent with their convictions, provided that nothing at variance with good morals or public order shall be taught or done.

Section 68 [Church Contributions] No one shall be liable to make personal contributions to any denomination other than the one to which he adheres.

Section 69 [Regulation of Other Religious Bodies] Rules for religious bodies dissenting from the Established Church shall be laid down by Statute.

Section 70 [Freedom of Religion] No person shall for reasons of his creed or descent be deprived of access to complete enjoyment of his civic and political rights, nor shall he for such reasons evade compliance with any common civic duty.

Biblical Quotations

All biblical quotations are from the *New International Bible* (UK), unless otherwise noted.

My thanks go to all the contributors listed below, as well as to Klaus Nielsen, Liselotte Larsen, and Else Riisager at the Grundtvig Centre for help with translation and bibliographical information.

Notes on Contributors

Translator and Editor

Edward Broadbridge (b.1944) BA London, MA Aarhus, taught English and Religious Studies at high schools in Denmark 1967-2008. Among his many theological translations are books on Ruth, Luke, Paul, and Titus of Bostra, as well as translations of 50 Danish hymns, *Hymns in English* (2009). He is also a librettist for Danish composers, a writer/director of children's musicals, and an official interpreter for the Danish legal system. His translations of Grundtvig began with *A Grundtvig Anthology* (1984) and include the first major appraisal of Grundtvig in English, *Tradition and Renewal* (1983), as well as *Grundtvig as a Political Thinker* by Ove Korsgaard (2014) and most of the essays in *Building the Nation. N.F.S. Grundtvig and Danish National Identity* (2015).

His translation of *N.F.S. Grundtvig – A Primer* by Anders Holm is forthcoming.

He is the translator and editor of the 5-volume series, N.F.S. Grundtvig. Works in English (2008-20).

Language Consultants

Hanna Broadbridge (b.1945) MA Aarhus English & Japanese, married Edward in 1967 and has been a teacher of English in Denmark 1971-2010 and lecturer in English at the Royal Academy of Education 1978-2003. She has been an external examiner in English at all the Danish universities 1998-2015. She is an official interpreter for the Danish legal system and represents the European Churches (minus the Roman Catholic Church) in the Education Committee of the Council of Europe.

John Nicholson (b.1938) MA Oxon, married his Danish wife in 1966 and moved to Denmark in 1977. In England he worked in probation and prison after-care, in Denmark in refugee resettlement. In both countries he has designed and facilitated programmes for adult learning, including applied theology and Christian spirituality. He was a committee member of the Ecumenical Association of Academies and Laity Centres in

Europe. For over 30 years he was active in retreat conducting and retreat development in Denmark. He was a language consultant on the above-mentioned *Hymns in English* and on the two previous volumes in this series.

Introductions

Niels Henrik Gregersen (b.1956) MA & PhD Copenhagen Theology, held various faculty positions at Aarhus University 1986-2004, and from 2000 to 2004 was Research Professor in Theology and Science. Since 2004 he has been Professor of Systematic Theology at the University of Copenhagen. Among his edited or co-edited English publications are: *From Complexity to Life: On the Emergence of Life and Meaning* (Oxford University Press, 2003); *The Gift of Grace: The Future of Lutheran Theology* (Fortress Press, 2005); *Incarnation: On the Scope and Depth of Christology* (Fortress Press, 2015) and *Reformation Theology for a Post-secular Age: Løgstrup, Prenter, Wingren, and the Future of Scandinavian Creation Theology* (Vandenhoeck & Ruprecht, 2017).

Hans Raun Iversen (b.1948) MTheol Aarhus (1976), Doctor of Divinity Uppsala (2016), was Associate Professor in Practical Theology at Aarhus 1974-82 and at Copenhagen 1982-2018. He has conducted over 20 courses on Grundtvig's theology and specialises in church research – emphasising relationships between church and people in Denmark and the influence and perspectives of Grundtvig. He has published extensively in Danish. Among his publications in English are *Church, Society and Mission. Twelve Danish Contributions to International Discussions* (Copenhagen, 2010) and *Spirit and Life-Form. The Home, the People and the Church in Grundtvig's Time and Today* (Montreal, 2013).

Brian Degn Mårtensson (b.1979) gained an MPhil Aarhus (2013) on the relation between sense and sensibility in N.F.S. Grundtvig's educational and political philosophy. He has given lectures in many countries and writes on Grundtvig, Kierkegaard, philosophy, and education (especially the German tradition of pedagogics), as well as on the new 'pedagogy of the competitive state'. He has been a member of the digitalization and annotation staff of 'Grundtvig's Works' at the Grundtvig Centre since 2017.

Michael Schelde (b.1954) MTheol, MA Aarhus, PhD Copenhagen in Adult Education *Religion, Church and Enlightenment*; has since 2009 been the Director of The Grundtvig Centre at Aarhus University & Vartov, overseeing the digitalization of Grundtvig's works and the first comprehensive English edition. He coordinates all activities at the Centre, including the bi-annual Grundtvig conferences, and has co-edited two books on Grundtvig. He is planning a French translation of Grundtvig's educational writings, as well as a Chinese version of Grundtvig's theological works, translated by Wen Ge (PhD Aarhus).

Vanja Thaulow (b.1977) MTheol Copenhagen (2005), was Pastor of Majbølle-Vigsnæs parish on Lolland 2007-11. She has been a member of the digitalization and annotation staff of 'Grundtvig's Works' at the Grundtvig Centre since 2011, and is currently studying for a PhD in Theology at Aarhus University on Grundtvig's theological polemics in the period 1810-25, and polemics as a genre.

Steen Tullberg (b.1968) MTheol Copenhagen (1999), is a former head of the Philological Department at the Søren Kierkegaard Research Centre, which produced the complete works of Kierkegaard in Danish (1997-2013). He has been a member of the digitalization staff of 'Grundtvig's Works' at the Grundtvig Centre since 2013. His publications are primarily on the Danish and German reception of Kierkegaard, including 'Denmark: The Permanent Reception – 150 Years of Reading Kierkegaard' in *Kierkegaard's International Reception, vol. 1, Northern and Western Europe* (Ashgate, 2009).

Ole Vind (b.1944) MSc (1972), DPhil Copenhagen on Grundtvig and the History of Ideas (1999), has been a teacher at Grundtvig's People's High School, north of Copenhagen, since 1976. He writes regularly about intellectual history, the history of ideas, and the People's (Folk) High Schools. He has also published extensively on Grundtvig, including the chapter 'The Gordian Knot: Grundtvig and British Liberalism', in *Building the Nation. N.F.S. Grundtvig and Danish National Identity* (Montreal, 2015).

Timeline – Grundtvig as a pastor

1800 7 November. Begins study of Theology at Copenhagen University

1802 26 December. Preaches for the first time in Udby-Ørslev parish

1803 25 October. Gains Theology degree

1806 26 October. Preaches in Bøstrup Church

1807 15 February. Preaches again in Bøstrup Church

1808 1 September to 28 November. Chaplain for Langeland Territorial Army

1810 17 March. Gives dimissory sermon in Trinity Church, passes with Honours

1811 13 January. Applies to become curate to his father, Johan Grundtvig

24 March. Passes *Cathechet* exam with honours and becomes a 'church teacher of faith'

24 May. Passes Bishop's exam (in audience with the bishop) and can now be ordained

16 June. Ordained by his brother Otto as his father's personal curate in Udby-Ørslev

1813 5 January. Father dies, and later his mother moves to Præstø

27 October. Moves back to Copenhagen

1815 5-8 January. Preaches in Frederiksberg Church

26 December. Preaches in Frederiksberg Church and then declares he is resigning from the priesthood, partly because of the lack of support for his 'old-fashioned' preaching

1821 2 February. Becomes by royal decree parish pastor of Præstø-Skibbinge

15 April/Palm Sunday. Installed in Præstø-Skibbinge

1822 6 November. Becomes by royal decree curate at the Church of Our Saviour, Copenhagen

1 December. Installed at the Church of Our Saviour

1826 8 May. Following an audience with the King, sends resignation from his curacy in protest against losing a libel case to Professor H.N. Clausen and his general lack of support

26 May. The King accepts his resignation

1831   24 November. Applies to the King for permission to form a free congregation
        at Frederik's German Church (which in 1901 became Christian's Church), which
        originally served the German population in Copenhagen

1832   28 January. Application rejected by the government

        11 February. Application again rejected by the government

        1 March. Allowed by royal decree to hold evening service at Frederik's German
        Church

        4 March. Preaches for the first time at Frederik's German Church. Remains at
        this church until 1839 but without the right to perform public church ceremo-
        nies

1839   25 March. Applies to the King for the pastorate at Vartov,[2] which is not a parish
        church

        28 May. Application granted

        9 June. Installed as pastor at Vartov

        21 July. Preaches for the first time at Vartov

1854   7 May. P.O. Boisen (1815-62), his son-in-law by his daughter Meta (1827-87),
        becomes his curate at Vartov

1856   June. While Vartov is being rebuilt, services are held at Christiansborg Palace
        Church

1858   January. Worship at Vartov is resumed

1861   29 May. On the 50th anniversary of his becoming a pastor, he is awarded the
        honorary title of Bishop of Zealand and is celebrated at Vartov; a medal is
        minted in his name

1867   14 April. During the Palm Sunday service at Vartov, he suffers a major break-
        down in front of his congregation of over 400. He manages to complete the
        service, and is subsequently taken into medical care. His letter of resignation
        the following day is ignored

        He resumes his pastoral role at Christmas

1872   1 September. Preaches his last sermon, and dies the following day

---

2. The Vartov complex, next to City Square, Copenhagen, was built in 1722-55 as a hospital for the poor, the orphaned,
    the sick, and the elderly, but ceased operation as such in 1934. It was then used by the municipality until 1947, when
    it was taken over by Kirkeligt Forum, now Grundtvig's Forum. The present buildings house among others: Vartov
    Church, the Grundtvig Centre, the Grundtvig Library, the Grundtvig Academy, and Grundtvig's Forum. Also situ-
    ated here are the Søren Kierkegaard Centre, the Danish Cultural Institute, and offices for the Copenhagen People's
    High School Association, the Danish Library Association, and a museum and a music association. The complex
    also houses two youth centres, the Vartov Kindergarten, and Copenhagen's Philatelic Club.

2. Udby Church and vicarage today

The country church set in the South Zealand landscape dates from c. 1150 and has fine frescos from 5 different periods. To the left can be seen the vicarage where the Grundtvig family lived and where he was born and baptised. Among the items in the Grundtvig Memorial Museum here are his writing-desk, his armchair, and the bible in illustration 6. (see www.oerslevkirke.dk). Photo: Michael Schelde.

Church and Culture in Living Interaction – Grundtvig the Theologian

Niels Henrik Gregersen

In depicting the contours of N.F.S. Grundtvig's theological universe, we shall trace his progress from a sensitive Romantic poet and historian into a theologian of classic calibre and scope. In his own 19th century context, Grundtvig (1783-1872) developed a theological vision with two ellipses: the primacy of God as the source, medium, and goal of all reality, and the primacy of humanity for understanding and living the Christian faith. "Human comes first, and Christian next/for that is life's true order", as he argued in a poem.[3] All human beings are created in the image and likeness of God prior to becoming (or not becoming) Christian, and every Christian is called to become a full human person.

Grundtvig understood himself as a theologian *of* the Church – and so he was. Yet he was also a theologian *for* his contemporary culture. It is thus a special signature of Grundtvig's theology that he anticipates a cultural situation in which some are Christians, others Muslims, Jews, and believers of other faiths, and still others are Naturalists. In his lifetime, Danish society changed from being an absolute monarchy into a more democratic society, in which a number of religious and cultural forces were present. In *Nordic Mythology* (1832) Grundtvig explicitly addresses his potential reader as being "Christian or heathen, Turk[4] or Jew", or even "Naturalists of spirit", all of whom are aware of the deep mystery of humanity.[5]

Grundtvig's theological writings show him to be a champion of what he himself called an "old-fashioned Christian faith"; yet he moves effortlessly between unfolding the message and mission of the Church and engaging the wider public culture. For

3. The poem 'Human comes first, and Christian next' (1837) is no. 123 in *Living Wellsprings. The Hymns, Songs, and Poems of N.F.S. Grundtvig*, trans. & ed. Edward Broadbridge (Aarhus: Aarhus University Press 2015), 249-251.
4. i.e. Muslim.
5. See 'Nordic Mythology' (1832), in *The School for Life. N.F.S. Grundtvig on Education for the People*, trans. Edward Broadbridge, eds. Edward Broadbridge, Clay Warren, and Uffe Jonas (Aarhus: Aarhus University Press, 2011), 60-61.

Grundtvig, the Church is a part of the shared human realm, but only one among other voices in society; he himself was active in other areas of life than theology – as a historian and poet, a hymnwriter and translator, an educator and even as a politician. However, underlying these came his theological concerns, guiding him in his endeavours to create a more inclusive human society with greater individual freedom for all.

From 1811 to his death in 1872 (six days short of his 89th birthday), Grundtvig was a pastor in the Danish Evangelical-Lutheran Church, though with lengthy interruptions.[6] Programmatically, he preferred the spoken word to the written language, and he was known as a charismatic speaker also outside the pulpit. In articulating his theology he used poetry more fluently than his more dense prose, and his undisputed influence in Danish church and culture is therefore primarily due to the more than 1,500 hymns from 1810 onwards, in addition to his many popular songs and national poems.[7]

Alongside his published authorship of 37,000 pages (and numerous unpublished papers), Grundtvig was a public figure in Danish culture who debated many of the questions of the day – from the religious, educational, and political situation to the fundamental question of the role of ordinary people in the transition from elitist to democratic culture. In brief, Grundtvig was what we today would call a public intellectual.

In what follows, we shall briefly note facets of Grundvig's influence in Golden Age Denmark (c. 1800-70). We shall then delineate certain important stages and turning-points in his theological biography, in order, finally, to discuss Grundtvig's relevance in the context of today's international theology. For his personal biography see the introductions to vols 1 and 2 in this series.

1. Grundtvig's intellectual context

Even though Grundtvig came to the capital as a pastor's son from the village of Udby in south Zealand, he soon became a household name in the Copenhagen establishment. Copenhagen was then the centre of what has been termed 'Golden Age Denmark'. On its streets or on private occasions, notabilities such as the writer Hans Christian Andersen, the philosopher Søren Kierkegaard, the discoverer of electromagnetism H.C.

---

6. See the Timeline, pp. 19-20.

7. In the current *Danish Hymnbook* (2003), 253 of the 791 hymns have Grundtvig's signature, some written by himself, others as Danish versions of hymns from the Greek, Latin, English, and German Church traditions. Also in the latest, and always popular, *People's High School Song-Book* (18th edition, 2006) Grundtvig has more hymns and songs than any other contributor.

Ørsted, and the theologian Grundtvig, came across one another, each with their likes and dislikes of their Copenhagen fellows.[8]

Theological Debates

Until around 1830, Grundtvig was more infamous than famous. His difficulties began early on. In 1811 he received an official reprimand from the governing body of the University of Copenhagen for his dimissory sermon of 1810, *Why Has the Word of the Lord Disappeared from His House?* In this he harshly criticised the majority of the Danish pastors for being more interested in human affairs than in the Word of the Lord. Likewise, in *The Church's Retort to Dr. H.N. Clausen, Professor of Theology* from 1825 (Text 1), Grundtvig demanded that the university's leading Professor of Dogmatics, H.N. Clausen, should resign his office, since his theology was in conflict with the beliefs of the Church. In response, Clausen sued for libel; Grundtvig was fined, and his publications put under lifelong censorship. This requirement of a prior *imprimatur* of his writings was not lifted until 1837. By then Grundtvig had already gained a widespread and far more positive reputation, not only among his many followers in the countryside but also in Copenhagen circles, including the royal house.

Grundtvig spoke up also after 1825, though now in a more moderate tone. Since the 1820s, the Danish government (backed by church officials) had been persecuting the new revivalist groups, and from 1840 Baptists were even imprisoned for not baptising their children. Grundtvig publicly defended these 'godly assemblies' as well as the Baptists, even though he did not personally agree with all their theology (Texts 2 & 7). His argument was twofold: Theologically, freedom of conscience is essential in matters of religion; and politically, the revivalist groups do not impose a danger to the order of the state. Only with the Danish Constitution of 1849 was religious freedom given to all citizens, and the State Church was now transformed into a People's Church with voluntary membership, based on baptism.

In his arguments for religious freedom, Grundtvig was initially influenced by German Enlightenment philosophy, but later on he was persuaded by English liberalism. He read periodicals such as *The Westminster Review* (1824-27) and the *Edinburgh Review*

---

8.   Bruce H. Kirmmse, *Kierkegaard in Golden Age Denmark* (Indianapolis: Indiana University Press 1990) offers an excellent overview of the intellectual circles in Copenhagen at the time. On Kierkegaard's relation to Grundtvig, see Anders Holm, 'Nicolai Frederik Severin Grundtvig: The Matchless Giant', in *Kierkegaard and His Danish Contemporaries. Tome II: Theology*, ed. Jon Stewart (Farnham: Ashgate 2009), 95-151. Holm shows how Kierkegaard was more concerned about Grundtvig than the other way round, also due to the painful fact that Kierkegaard's elder brother P.C. Kierkegaard became a leading Grundtvigian. Though Grundtvig clashed with Ørsted in 1815, he later became more friendly towards him, seeing him as a 'Naturalist of spirit'. The relation between Grundtvig and Hans Christian Andersen is difficult to pinpoint, and an understudied area.

(1820-27), and in 1829-31 he was able to make three trips to England, supported by the Danish King (Texts 44-46). The experiences in England convinced Grundtvig to trust the empirically-oriented common sense traditions in the vein of John Locke and John Stuart Mill rather than speculative philosophy. While Grundtvig set his own tone and made his own judgments in matters of theology, Grundtvig the politician sided with the English tradition, distancing himself in particular from the French variety of Enlightenment philosophy: "In all parliamentary matters [I] think of the English", he said.[9]

Grundtvig as a Politician

Grundtvig lived in a tumultuous but also highly creative epoch of European history. Politically, his life spanned the era of absolutist European kingdoms over revolutionary times up to the formation of modern democracy, instituted in Denmark by the 1849 Constitution. Grundtvig's newly-awakened interest in politics saw him become not only a member of the Constitutional Assembly which drew up the new constitution, but also an actual Member of Parliament for most of the period 1849-58.

The Danish Constitution of 1849 established a parliamentary democracy, but formally it was still called a 'constitutional monarchy', that is, a monarchy framed by a parliamentary system. Grundtvig himself sought to retain a sense of 'covenant' or living bond between the King, the national father of Denmark, and Parliament, the living voice of the Danish people.[10] At the same time, he was fully aware that it meant the end of the older concept of the four estates: clergy, nobility, citizenry and peasantry. "The age of the estates is over, now it is time for the age of the people," he said in a parliamentary session in 1849.[11] In 1866, at age 82, he allowed himself to be elected into the Upper House (*Landstinget*) in order to prevent a revision of the 1849 Constitution to the disadvantage of the peasants. Much to his dismay, Grundtvig did not succeed.

As a member of parliament, Grundtvig was active in furthering the freedom of faith also within the Danish Church. 99% of the Danish population were baptised members of the Evangelical-Lutheran Church, now officially called The People's Church (*Folkekirken*) in the Danish Constitution (§ 3, today § 4). Already in the 1830s, however, Grundtvig was concerned about the so-called parish-tie. In 1833 Grundtvig wrote to

---

9. N.F.S. Grundtvig, 'Parliamentary Speech on Danish Church Freedom' (*Tale til Folkeraadet om Dansk Kirkefrihed*. Copenhagen: Wahlske Boghandels Forlag 1939), 7, quoted in Ove Korsgaard, 'How Grundtvig Became a Nation Builder', in *Building the Nation. N.F.S. Grundtvig and Danish National Identity*, eds. John A. Hall, Ove Korsgaard, and Ove K. Pedersen (Montreal: McGill-Queen's University Press 2015), 192-209 (193).

10. See Tine Damsholt, 'Hand of the King and Voice of the People': Grundtvig on Democracy and the Responsibility of the Self", in *Building the Nation* (2015), 151-168.

11. N.F.S. Grundtvig, *Danskeren II (The Dane)* (Copenhagen: F.H. Eibe 1849), 81, quoted in Ove Korsgaard, *N.F.S. Grundtvig – as a Political Thinker* (Copenhagen: DJØF Publishing 2014), 23.

the king (Text 45) on this issue, and he also discussed the problem in other writings from the 1830s to the 1850s (Texts 5 & 10). Grundtvig and his allies wished to establish a freedom clause within the Church so that any individual member could 'break the parish-tie' that bound them locally, and worship elsewhere. They succeeded through Parliament in breaking the parish-tie in 1855, thus paving the way for the revivalists to remain within the over-all framework of the People's Church; all members were now free to join the pastors and congregations congenial to their own religious views. In the same manner, Parliament allowed for the establishment of free schools alongside the public schools run by the government.

The Fight against Slavery

While the trading of slaves was officially forbidden in 1792, owning slaves was still an option in the Danish colonies until 1848, such as in the Virgin Islands in the Caribbean, a Danish colony until 1917. Likewise, until 1847, Danish criminals could be condemned to life-long slavery in the castle of Kronborg at Elsinore. Due to his strong view of the value of the human person as a "unique creature of dust and spirit", Grundtvig was opposed to the idea of slavery. Under the personal influence of Quakers such as G.W. Alexander and Elizabeth Fry, he became part of a three-person committee in 1839 to put an end to slavery; later the committee brought in two other intellectuals, including Professor H.N. Clausen and the liberal clergyman, D.G. Monrad, who drafted the Danish Constitution of 1849. The Committee Against Slavery dissolved itself in 1848 when its task had been completed.[12]

Grundtvig and the Danish People

Also in terms of nationhood, Grundtvig's long life spanned an era moving from a larger unified Danish-Nordic kingdom (at his birth in 1783) to a diminished Denmark with the independence of Norway in 1814, and a further reduction with the loss of Schleswig and Holstein to Prussia in the war of 1864. As a result, Denmark was no longer a multi-lingual state comprising the Danish, Norwegian, and German languages but a smaller, mostly monolingual, country with a relatively unified Danish-Icelandic-Faroese culture. In this process, Grundtvig became an important nation-builder by bringing the peasantry into the cultural and political centre of Danish society. One thing is shar-

---

12. On Grundtvig's engagement in the slave cause, see Knud Eyvin Bugge, *Grundtvig og slavesagen* (Aarhus: Aarhus University Press 2003), with an English summary pp. 201-208. The subject will also be dealt with in *The Common Good. N.F.S. Grundtvig as Politician and Contemporary Historian*, trans. & ed. Edward Broadbridge, co-ed. Ove Korsgaard (Aarhus: Aarhus University Press 2019).

ing political power 'from above' in the parliamentary system of the *state*, another thing is the *nation* understood as a lived culture 'from below', i.e. a culture held together by internal communication within the Danish people, even among political opponents.[13]

For Grundtvig it was particularly important to expand education to all classes, and to make sure that education was not only a top-down 'teaching' but also a bottom-up 'learning'. Alongside his historical and political authorship, Grundtvig's educational writings became highly influential, not only in the Danish People's (Folk) High School movement in Denmark, but also during his lifetime in Norway and Sweden: The first People's High School in Denmark was established in 1844, in Norway in 1864, and in Sweden in 1868. In the 20th century, the idea of a People's High School – learning for life rather than to pass examinations – spread to other countries including the USA, and even China.[14] Grundtvig feared that the 'dead school' system educated middle-class people to become a cultural elite and to dissociate themselves from ordinary people by thinking and communicating mostly in German, or by using artificial language such as what Grundtvig called "dog Latin".[15] In his well-known poem, *Enlightenment* (1839), Grundtvig prioritized the light shining on ordinary people over the learned world of elitist scholars:

> The sunrise on the peasant shines
> but on the scholar never,
> enlightening the agile man
> in all his bright endeavour ....
>
> ... Enlightenment must be our joy,
> regard to small things giving,
> but always with the people's voice
> enlightenment for living.[16]

There is an irony here compared with Grundtvig's own life. Even though he himself routinely criticised what he called the 'black school' of Latin and German education, he himself studied many languages, not only the Old Icelandic language and Old

---

13. Francis Fukuyama is a contemporary political theorist who has pointed to the role of Grundtvig and Grundtvigianism for the formation of a national culture conceived in broader terms than that of the political system of power, see Fukuyama, 'Nation Building and State Building', in *Building the Nation* (2015), 29-50.

14. See Clay Warren, 'The International Reception of N.F.S. Grundtvig's Educational Ideas' in *The School for Life* (2011), 352-369. On China, see Wen Ge, *The Deep Coinherence: A Chinese Appreciation of N.F.S. Grundtvig's Public Theology* (PhD thesis, Aarhus University, August 2013), 237-241 (with bibliography).

15. N.F.S. Grundtvig in *Nordic Mythology* (1832), *The School for Life* (2011), 61.

16. N.F.S. Grundtvig, 'Enlightenment' (1839) in *The School for Life* (2011), 255-256.

English, but also Greek, Latin, and German. Like most other learned Danes of the time, he was particularly well-read in German literature and philosophy. His life of studying and writing with such intensity meant that he was not much of an outdoor man who enjoyed the sunlight falling on the agile citizens for whom he was writing.

2. Stages in Grundtvig's Theological Development

Although Grundtvig studied theology at Copenhagen University from 1800-03 he had no intention of becoming an ordained pastor. He started his working life as a private tutor, then became a high school teacher, and he made his first forays into the public realm as a translator, editor, and interpreter of Nordic myths and sagas – as part of his work as a historian.

At university Grundtvig was taught the metaphysical school of philosophy of G.W. Leibniz (1646-1716) and Christian Wolff (1679-1754), but over time he also familiarised himself with the philosophy of Immanuel Kant (1724-1804).[17] During his early student days he adopted the triad of God, virtue, and immortality as being sufficient for belief. He admired the comedies of the Danish-Norwegian Enlightenment writer, Ludvig Holberg (1684-1754), while distancing himself increasingly from his own father's Lutheran Orthodoxy. German philosophy, however, was not first and foremost channeled to Grundtvig through the transcendental thinkers such as Kant and Johann Gottlieb Fichte (1762-1814). More important to Grundtvig was the Romanticist strand of German idealism which he met later as a student of theology. Rather than assume a category thinking based on the structure of a transcendental Ego, the Romanticists gave precedence to concepts of intuition and anticipatory feelings (*Ahnung*) as well as to the poetic imagination (*Einbildungskraft*). Figures such as Friedrich Schiller (1759-1805) and F.W.J. Schelling (1775-1854) were of particular inspiration to Grundtvig, especially in his 'mythological period' from 1805-10. The idea of a poetic imagination remained central to his philosophical writings in 1816-19, though with the amendment that it not only has its origin in the creativity of the 'genius', but is receptive before it becomes creative.

Chronology and Continuity: Grundtvig's Path Dependencies

Grundtvig research has often focused on the critical junctures in Grundtvig's theological development, and particular interest has been devoted to his spiritual crises and theological breakthroughs. First comes his personal breakdown around the new

---

17. See his recollections in N.F.S. Grundtvig, *Mands Minde 1788-1838 (Within Living Memory 1788-1838)* (Copenhagen: Karl Schønberg's Forlag 1877), 274: "Our professors at that time were not really abreast with their age, so our theologians knew very little about Kant, and our philosopher taught in strict allegiance to Leibniz and Wolff".

year 1810-11, leading to his return to the Biblical orthodoxy of his father from 1811-14, followed by his subsequent philosophical period 1816-1819, in which he was also highly active as a historian and translator. In 1825 he experiences his so-called 'matchless discovery' of the role of the confession and the baptismal Creed in the oral tradition of the Church. Finally in 1832, on his return from England, he writes the introduction to *Nordic Mythology* in which he argues for the shared humanity of Christians and non-Christians alike in the context of his creation theology.

In Grundtvig scholarship there is overall agreement that the return to Lutheran Orthodoxy in 1811-14 is merely a parenthesis in his theological journey, whereas 1825 and 1832 mark the two major turning-points in his development. There is a difference of emphasis among scholars between the more Church-oriented interpretation of Grundtvig, focusing on 1825, and the more Culture-oriented interpretation which marks 1832 as a major new stage in Grundtvig's theology, pointing forward as it does to his later educational ideas and political activities.[18] Overall, however, there is in fact an astonishing *continuity* in Grundtvig's theological development; even as he broadened and nuanced his theological views, there is a persistent presence of earlier stages in his later views, as he continues to accommodate new insights into his ever more comprehensive theological vision.

Just as his Enlightenment motifs continue well after 1825, so do the roles of mythology and history after Grundtvig's 'mythological excitement' of 1805-1810. While he kept silent on mythology between 1811-1814, following his Lutheran conversion, the mythological programme was soon taken up again in his philosophical and historical work, including lengthy translations of Saxo's chronicle of Danish history, *Gesta Danorum*, and Snorri Sturluson's Old Icelandic work on Norway, *Heimskringla*. Even Grundtvig's 'biblical period' from 1811-14 is later enhanced in the numerous biblical references and allusions running through his works. In the present volume, for example, the editor has been able to identify no fewer than 322 biblical references. Something similar applies to Grundtvig's indebtedness to German Romanticism. In the years after 1810, he criticised Schiller's anthropological optimism, and distanced himself from the harmonious view of the striving forces of reality in Schelling's philosophy of nature. Nonetheless, the Romantic tone, and much of its vocabulary, is present throughout his later writings.[19] The same applies even more to this so-called

18. The gravitation around respectively 1825 or 1832 is represented by Hal Koch, *Grundtvig*, trans. L. Jones (Yellow Springs, Ohio: Antioch Press 1952) and by Kaj Thaning, *N.F.S. Grundtvig*, trans. D. Hohnen (Copenhagen: Danish Cultural Institute 1972). A.M. Allchin, *N.F.S. Grundtvig: An Introduction to His Life and Work* (Aarhus: Aarhus University Press 1997; repr. 2015) takes a mediating position.

19. See the nuanced analysis in Flemming Lundgreen-Nielsen, 'Grundtvig and Romanticism', in *N.F.S. Grundtvig: Tradition and Renewal. Grundtvig's Vision of Man and People, Education and the Church, in Relation to World Issues of Today*, eds. Christian Thodberg and Anders Pontoppidan Thyssen, trans. Edward Broadbridge (Copenhagen: The Danish Institute 1983), 19-43.

'Church view' of 1825. The central role of baptism and Holy Communion developed also after 1832, as we see in the consummate work of his maturity, *Basic Christian Teachings* (especially Texts 14-16).

All in all, we must conclude that on Grundtvig's theological journey the pathways tried out and trodden in his early life were never absent from his later views. Rather, the earlier 'stages' were refined and developed in new contexts, often in tension with the original sources that influenced his own theological vision. For everything in Grundtvig reveals his particular stamp as a theologian and contemporary thinker.

1802-1810: The Romantic and Mythological Period

As early as 1802, Grundtvig attended a lecture series by the Romantic philosopher, the Norwegian Henrich Steffens (1773-1845), who happened to be his cousin. The nine lectures on the philosophy of nature presented in the spirit of Schelling were published in Danish in 1803 as *Introduction to Lectures on Philosophy*. In a poem written after Steffens' death, Grundtvig described his cousin as the "lightning-man" who appeared in Copenhagen "like an angel from the heavens" rolling away the stone of Enlightenment, much like the stone at Christ's grave.[20] Grundtvig was forever grateful to Steffens, since he offered him a way out of the confines of Enlightenment Christianity. Although Grundtvig initially found Steffens' views confusing,[21] he nonetheless experienced a Romantic awakening to such an extent that his early works, 1806-10, linger on a symbolic understanding of Christianity, a sort of *Religion as Art,* in which the Nordic myths seem to be assigned a revelatory character of their own. The scholarly discussion is whether the early Romantic Grundtvig approached the Nordic myths as constituents of a self-sufficient religious system, or only as analogous witnesses and intimations to the Christian faith.[22] The answer depends not least on the interpretation of Grundtvig's early work, *On Religion and Liturgy* from 1807, in fact the first theological treatise from Grundtvig's hand.[23] Here he gives full rein to his fervour for Romantic language in an interpretation of the religion of Jesus as the "reconciliation of the finite with

---

20. See 'Henrik Steffens' (1845), no. 145 in *Living Wellsprings* (2015), 300-02.
21. See, for example, Grundtvig's both appreciative as well as critical evaluation of Steffens in *Verdenskrønike af 1812* (*World Chronicle of 1812*), in *Udvalgte Skrifter* (*Selected Writings*), ed. Holger Begtrup (Copenhagen: Gyldendal 1909), vol. 2, 384.
22. Sune Auken, *Sagas Spejl. Mytologi, historie, kristendom hos N.F.S. Grundtvig* (*Saga's Mirror. Mythology, History, Christianity in N.F.S. Grundtvig*) (Copenhagen: Gyldendal 2005) opts for the former interpretation. For the latter interpretation, see Flemming Lundgreen-Nielsen, 'Grundtvig and Romanticism' in *Tradition and Renewal* (1983). Lundgreen-Nielsen summarises his interpretation as follows: "in a great many ways Grundtvig came close to romanticism in the first two decades of his writing career, but he never became a proper romantic" (33).
23. N.F.S. Grundtvig, 'On Religion and Liturgy' in *The Advance of Learning. N.F.S. Grundtvig's Philosophical Writings* (Aarhus: Aarhus University Press, forthcoming 2020).

the eternal" by way of poetry and philosophy. Nonetheless, it is still "by Christ" that the atonement and peace between humanity and God takes place.This suggests that while the young Grundtvig gives poetry and philosophy an elevated epistemic role for religion, he refrains from seeing poetry and philosophy as a self-absorbing ontology. This is even the case where Grundtvig describes Christ in a more symbolic form. In a poem from 1808, he places the Nordic Odin on a par with Christ:

> High Odin, White Christ!
> Settled is your former clash,
> both are sons of the All-Father!
> With our cross and sword afire,
> here we consecrate your pyre:
> Both of you have loved our Father.[24]

Although he later regretted the comparison, the young Grundtvig obviously wished to overcome the conflict between the Nordic myths and Christianity, while also distancing himself from the horizontal pantheism of Romantic thinking: Life and death are not on the same level as competing powers in a friendly tension; they are enemies, and life will ultimately conquer death. The Romantics opened the horizon to the invisible world, but they did not clearly acknowledge the priority and independence of the spiritual world, in which God is the life-giving creator and spiritual relations are expressions of the divine Spirit. Here Grundtvig the theologian remained indebted to the neo-Platonic tradition, even in the midst of his mythological excitement.

1810-14: Lutheran Orthodoxy and Piety

While Grundtvig's theological stance was ambivalent in the mytho-poetical years 1805-10, the aforementioned dimissory sermon of 1810, *Why Has the Word of the Lord Disappeared from His House?,* is quite straightforward. It witnesses to Grundtvig's conversion from a mythologising amalgam of poetry, philosophy, and theology back to an 'old-fashioned Lutheranism' with an emphasis on the biblical message and the clarity of the gospel. "Faith comes from hearing, and the Word of God is what should be heard," Grundtvig proclaimed with Paul and Luther. Grundtvig's criticism of the majority of his contemporary pastoral colleagues is that that they do not themselves "believe the doctrine they are called to preach".[25] This can be interpreted as a sign of Grundtvig's Lutheran Orthodoxy, but it is at the same time a typical Pietist complaint

---

24. No. III in *Living Wellsprings* (2015), 225.
25. N.F.S. Grundtvig, 'Dimisprædiken' (Dimissory Sermon) in *Udvalgte Skrifter* (note 21), vol. 2, 11-20 (20 and 17).

about the infidelity of the age. Until his father's death, Grundtvig served devotedly as his father's curate in Udby from 1811-13.

1814-1824: The Philosophical Period and the Idea of Universal History

Grundtvig's theological return to the Lutheran faith of his childhood led to a three-year pause in his editing and interpreting of the Nordic myths. When the mythical themes re-appear, they do so in the context of Grundtvig's new concept of a Christian philosophy developed in four volumes of the journal *Danne-Virke*, which he wrote singlehandedly between 1816-19.[26] In this philosophical period, he programmatically criticized the view that human consciousness in general, and the transcendental Ego in particular, are the cornerstones of all philosophy, as argued by Kant and Fichte. In contrast, Grundtvig contends that human understanding takes its point of departure in the human senses (particularly touching, hearing, and seeing) and in the human sense of spiritual relations (beauty, truth, and goodness). Crucially, these are experienced *prior* to the evaluations of the human mind. Since human beings, in body and mind, are part of a greater world – a microcosm of dust and spirit reflecting a wider macrocosm of aesthetic and spiritual relations – we are exposed to real sensory things and real spiritual relations, which are only *subsequently* reflected in our human subjectivity. The passive reception of things-in-relation is thus the basis for the productive power of human imagination.

In the period 1812-17, Grundtvig also makes extensive use of ideas from another German thinker, Johann Gottfried Herder (1744-1803), whom he had already drawn on in his earlier mythological period. Though critical of Herder's ambivalent theological stance,[27] Grundtvig shares the idea that each natural language brings with it a particular horizon, at once rooted in the experiences of particular people in world history but also shaping and refining their perception of reality. Herder's *Ideas on the Philosophy of the History of Mankind* (1784-91) was an important impetus to Grundtvig's own thinking of the universal history of humankind, based on the particularities of peoples, languages, and nations. Over the years 1812, 1814 and 1817, Grundtvig produced no less than three world histories.

Later in his life, Grundtvig expanded his vision of world history, which before had been largely confined to European history and the Middle East. From 1847 he further developed his earlier idea of seven basic communities of the Christian Church, going

---

26. These articles from *Danne-Virke* form the cornerstone of volume 5 in this series, *The Advance of Learning. N.F.S. Grundtvig's Philosophical Writings* (Aarhus; Aarhus University Press, forthcoming 2020).

27. See Grundtvig's *Verdenskrønike (World Chronicle)* from 1812, *Udvalgte skrifter (Selected Writings)*, vol. 2, 329-330.

from (1) the original Hebrew church to (2) the Greek church, and from here to (3) the Latin, (4) the English, and (5) the German church onwards to (6) the Nordic church. In his most universalist poems, *The Seven Stars of Christendom* (*Christenhedens Syvstjerne*) from 1854-55, Grundtvig hypothesises that the seventh and most fulfilled church would be established in India. Also this preference for India shows how Grundtvig remained a Romantic. While the Enlightenment thinkers used to look to China, the Romantics more often had India as their preferred other.

1825 onwards: Grundtvig's Church view

In its briefest expression, Grundtvig's so-called Church view (*den kirkelige Anskuelse*) consists of the thesis that the fundamental expressions of the Christian Church over the ages are the sacraments of baptism and Holy Communion: "the Font and the Table" (*Badet og Bordet*). The positive meaning of the Church view is that any Christian, simply by confessing and accepting in faith the baptismal Creed, is included into the body of Christ. Hence, the membership of the one and only Christian Church is given by Baptism; the rest must be left for the free working of the Holy Spirit in the lives of individual Christians. Baptism stands out as the beginning of the Christian life (faith), to be subsequently nourished by the preaching of the Word (hope), and to find its fulfilment in the Lord's Supper (love). Grundtvig's 'matchless discovery' in 1825 is that it is the baptismal Creed, not the Bible, which has served as 'the rule of faith' in the Christian Church since the days of the Apostles.

By the early 1820s, Grundtvig had developed a softer tone in his relation to the State Church, but around 1824-25 he once again became agitated, due partly to personal disappointments about the reception of his own work, and partly to the persecution of the revivalist Pietists.[28] Although he shared neither their negative view of culture nor their overheated appeals to conversion, he nonetheless saw them as expressions of "old-fashioned Lutheran Christianity", and hence as fellow-Christians.

Grundtvig vented his pent-up anger on the young Professor of Dogmatics at Copenhagen University, H.N. Clausen, a proponent of the father of neo-Protestantism, Friedrich Schleiermacher (1768-1834). Like Schleiermacher, Clausen wished to establish a Protestantism which gave equal weight to Martin Luther and John Calvin, and in 1825 he published a massive historical and programmatic work, *Catholicism and Protestantism: Their Constitution, Doctrine, and Ritual.* Grundtvig's verdict on the book was uncompromising:

---

28. See Anders Pontoppidan Thyssen, 'Grundtvig's Ideas on the Church and the People 1825-47', in *N.F.S. Grundtvig: Tradition and Renewal* (1983), 226-34.

Professor Clausen's Christianity is completely false and his protestant church a temple of idols where falsehood is proclaimed as truth and the attempt is made to revoke the irrevocable divide between truth and falsehood as between light and dark, yes and no, affirmation and denial, claim and counter-claim" (Text 1, p. 73).

Against Clausen's desire to construct an amalgam of Lutheran and Calvinist theology by minimising their differences, Grundtvig argued that the nature of the Church is not something to be socially constructed, nor to be defined by academic theologians who want to build a "self-made church-in-the-air". Rather, Christianity is defined by its actual *history* – as inaugurated by Christ, continued by the Apostles, and practised throughout the history of the Church. The rule of faith is found in the Apostolic Creed, and "has been transmitted unbroken through Baptism from the days of the Apostles, from generation to generation and from one people to another".[29]

More precisely, three aspects constitute Christian baptism from its inception: "the renunciation of the Devil, the confession of faith, and the forgiveness of sins."[30] Grundtvig is thus referring to an uninterrupted oral tradition which precedes the written New Testament, and he appeals to existing continuities in the historical Church, despite the theological differences between Catholics and Protestants. His source here is the early Church father Irenaeus (c. 140-202), who cited "the rule of faith" with a substance close to that of the later Apostolic Creed.[31]

In his rejoinder to Clausen Grundtvig appeals not only to the historical Church, but also to a Church from below, existing in local congregations, belonging to different cultural epochs underneath the differences between papal powers, Protestant denominations, and particular schools of academic theology. Christians become Christians by their faithful response to the living Word of the Lord, beginning with baptism, and no Christian should therefore be burdened by the new "exegetical papacy" of a professor who wishes to act as "the Church's exegetical pope" (p. 78). Vis-à-vis Clausen, Martin Luther appears in a favourable light:

... it is certain that no one was stronger than Martin Luther in raising up the simple child-like faith of the Christian Church above all academic wisdom. No one showed more clearly his trust in the Church's immutable foundation than by linking the

---

29. N.F.S. Grundtvig, *Om Christendommens Sandhed (On the Truth of Christianity)* (1826-27), *Udvalgte Skrifter (Selected Writings)*, vol 4, 519-723 (535).

30. Ibid., 618. In a later *Postscript* (1865) to this work, Grundtvig derives the rule of faith from the mouth of Jesus himself ("the Spirit of Christ and the eternal Word of His mouth"). Grundtvig presents this (very!) strong historical claim as his own view, given for the enlightenment (*Oplysning*) of the Christian community, though he also makes clear that it is an offer open to "their free consent", and not a binding view, see *Udvalgte Skrifter (Selected Writings)*, vol. 4, 726.

31. Irenaeus, *Against Heresies* I.10.1.

Apostles' Creed insolubly to Baptism and, in his *Small Catechism*, making this the basis for childhood faith and childhood teaching wherever there were people who agreed with him (p. 78).

However, Grundtvig's overall relationship to Luther is more complex than indicated here. From one perspective Grundtvig saw Luther as the "unrivalled Church reformer", a man who brought about a new way of life that was "fruitful in Christian enlightenment" (pp. 93-94). But he also had his reservations. Most importantly, written Scripture cannot be the final arbiter in theological matters. The principle of *sola scriptura* features neither in Luther's *Small Catechism* nor in the *Augsburg Confession*, the only two confessional documents from the Reformation acknowledged in the Danish Evangelical-Lutheran Church.

In place of the scriptural principle, Grundtvig developed the view that while the oral confession to the baptismal Creed constitutes the "Word of Life" (*Livs-Ordet*) in the Christian Church, the Bible is to be used as the "Word of Light" (*Lys-Ordet*) only, that is, as a testimony in which Christians find comfort and confirmation of their Christian life already established by baptism. The Bible also offers a deep and penetrating illumination of the human condition, so Grundtvig's Church view assigns to the Bible a central role for the education of the Christian community. Yet he also insists that the written word is secondary to the oral word of promise and faith in the Christian Church – the Living Word. Just as the Holy Spirit precedes the written testimony of the Bible, so does the oral tradition of the Church precede the resulting holy Scripture.

A second critique of Luther is that he and his followers adapted too quickly to the state church, thus allowing it to be imprisoned in the Babylonian captivity of worldly government. In passing, this argument led Grundtvig to a similar, critical view of the First Ecumenical Council in Nicea from 325 CE – not because of the Nicene Creed itself, but because the council was headed by Constantine who was still a heathen emperor! Another problem was that the Greek Orthodox church had allowed the Nicene Creed to *replace* the Apostolic Creed as the baptismal formula.[32] According to Grundtvig, this was a breach with the older view in the Greek church, as found in Irenaeus. Grundtvig's 1827 translation of Book 5 of Irenaeus' *Against Heresies* shows his eagerness to find his way back to the roots of Greek theology – before the Greek tradition became divided into the speculative theology of the Alexandrians after Origen and the ritualistic tradition within the Byzantine church that tended to make any church tradition a matter of faith.

Underpinning Grundtvig's both positive and critical view of Luther was his universal-historical view of the Christian Church. In his distinctive interpretation of the

---

32. N.F.S. Grundtvig, *Skal den lutherske Reformation virkelig fortsættes* (*Should the Lutheran Reformation Really be Continued*), *Udvalgte Skrifter (Selected Writings)*, vol 5, 296-301. Not included in the excerpts in Text 3.

seven churches of Christendom in the Book of Revelation, the Reformation had been the expression of the German church (the fifth community) which was now, according to Grundtvig's intimation, moving forward to the Nordic countries (the sixth community). Due to his emphasis on the Apostolic church, Grundtvig naturally attached a special role to the original Hebrew church, since no later church will reach such a zenith of faith. Nonetheless, the explication and understanding of the Christian faith is growing over time, from childhood to maturity, and from intuition to wisdom. By looking back on Luther as the highest representative of the German church, Grundtvig can describe him as the Reformer who reached a new clarity of the gospel, whilst elsewhere he describes him as another Moses looking into the promised land without being able to enter it. Grundtvig can thus celebrate Luther as a giant in the development of the Christian church; yet he can also call himself "Luther the Little", for Luther has arisen again in Grundtvig himself in his own life and place – now as a member of the sixth community:[33]

> When Luther the Little,
> who in me arose,
> sat quietly believing
> and opened the Book,
> I then saw a taper
> go up from the word,
> then light-angels little
> did play in the heart,
> from above they were singing
> we'll come to the forest,
> from heaven on high we came here.

To the question, *Should the Lutheran Reformation Really be Continued* (Text 3), Grundtvig gives a resounding 'yes'. The insights of the Reformation must be retained but also purified from their built-in confines. For, as we have seen, Luther is at fault in disregarding the oral testimony of faith in the baptismal Creed, in overlooking the testimony of tradition throughout Church history, and in believing that all theology should be tested on the basis of written Scripture.[34]

---

33. Stanza 68 in N.F.S. Grundtvig, *New Year's Morning (Nyaars-Morgen*, 1824), trans. Kristian Schultz Petersen (Copenhagen: Vartov 2009).

34. No wonder, therefore, that Grundtvig was regularly accused of being a Roman Catholic in disguise. Already in December 1825 he responded to this criticism as "childish talk"; he sought to restore and renew old-fashioned Christianity but did not assign particular authority to later councils of the Church, or to Papal decrees, see *Theologisk Maanedsskrift (Theological Monthly)* 1825, 248-278 (274).

Grundtvig's appeal for a self-critical continuation of the Lutheran Reformation was occasioned by the 300th anniversary of the Augsburg Confession of 1530, and it is here that we find Grundtvig's own summary of his view of the Church:

1. The oral Confession of faith at Baptism is independent of all Scripture, and, being the unanimous testimony of the Church concerning its faith ... it is what all Christians believed from the beginning.

2. Being the sole condition of membership of the Christian Church Community this Confession of faith is the Church's unalterable rule of faith and foundational law, which in its indissoluble union with Baptism marks the only secure boundary between the Church and the world or between true Christianity and what is not true Christianity.

3. The oral Word at the Sacraments and especially the Confession of faith is the foundational rule for all interpretation of the Bible in Christendom, by which every theologian who wishes to belong to the Christian Church shall and must be guided.

4. The Bible has never been the rule of faith in the Christian Church, neither from the beginning nor by its nature. (pp. 103-04).

What we find here is the insistent voice of an evangelical theologian committed to the unchangeable nature of the Apostolic Church – Grundtvig himself being at one and the same time a catholic (in the sense of universal and ecumenical) and a Lutheran theologian. In what follows, however, we find Grundtvig also emphasising positive features of modernity, since he makes clear that the Holy Spirit is a divine influence not constrained to the preaching and sacraments of the Church:

1. A border sharper than ever before should now be drawn between what all Christians must believe and confess and what must be left to the free working of the Spirit and the individual Christian.

2. Therefore the University, or Theology, should enjoy far more freedom than Luther intended without laying claim to the least authority over the faith and the Church which the Reformers in their view logically had to allow them (p. 104).

Thus, while Grundtvig's view calls for an absolute certainty about the foundation upon which the Church stands and falls, considerable space is left for free explorations of how Christian lives are to be led in contemporary times and contexts – always open to the free workings of the divine Spirit. Similarly, there is, and should be, ample space for theological diversity and experimentation in all scholarly matters. Only the confession to God in the baptismal Creed belongs to the *esse* (essential nature) of the Church; other things that might be beneficial for the church, belong to its *bene esse*; and still other things belong to the *adiaphora* (indifferent things) that present-day Christian congregations, and their members, can either adopt or simply omit.[35]

This combination of a concision in basic matters of faith, and a corresponding openness to variation in the many penultimate matters of life is typical of the generous orthodoxy of Grundtvig's Church view. One thing is what constitutes "authentic Christianity", another thing is whether this authentic Christianity is true or not. On the latter point there should be an open discussion, and even a debate between those adhering to authentic Christianity, and those challenging the truth of Christianity. In the years 1826-27, immediately following *The Church's Retort*, Grundtvig wrote two books composed as a twin work, the first *On Authentic Christianity*, and the second *On the Truth of Christianity* in which philosophical and historical issues are discussed at length between defenders of the faith and critics of Christianity.[36]

1832 onwards: Grundtvig's Creation Theology and Cultural Agenda

On the shoulders of his Church view, Grundtvig began to develop a more general outlook on the shared conditions of human existence. Here the theme of *creation theology* becomes ever more prominent and lays the groundwork for a new cultural programme, based on a sense of a shared humanity in a shared cosmos. He gave up the assumption that the rediscovery of authentic Christianity can on its own solve the shared cultural problems of his age: politics, nationhood, and education. The Church is no longer a ruling power in society, but more a transactional agent in a wider cultural circulation of drives and ideas.

In his lengthy Introduction to *Nordic Mythology* (1832), Grundtvig states his view of humanity as a "divine experiment of dust and spirit". He begins by distinguishing human beings from the higher animals, mere imitative creatures, whereas creativity and openness to development are specifically human characteristics. The destiny of

---

35. Even though Grundtvig always stood by his Church view as being ecclesiologically normative, his opinions on the ecclesial order of the Danish Lutheran Church fluctuated over time. See the analysis by Anders Pontoppidan Thyssen, 'Grundtvig's Ideas on the Church and the People', in *N.F.S. Grundtvig: Tradition and Renewal* (1983), 87-120, 226-292 and 344-370.

36. See N.F.S. Grundtvig, *What Constitutes Authentic Christianity?*, trans. E.D. Nielsen (Philadelphia: Fortress Press 1985) for the twin books: *Om den sande Christendom* and *Om Christendommens Sandhed* (1826), from *Udvalgte Skrifter* (*Selected Writings*), vol 4, 442-518 and 519-723.

humanity is to bring dust and spirit *together*, thus uniting heaven and earth under the guidance of divine Providence down the ages. In the end humanity will grow into the divine consciousness itself, out of which human beings were created in the first place:

> For man is not an ape, destined first to ape the other animals and then himself until the world's end. Rather is he a glorious, incomparable creature, in whom divine powers through thousands of generations proclaim, develop, and enlighten themselves as a divine experiment, in order to show how spirit and dust can permeate one another and be transfigured into a common divine consciousness.[37]

Grundtvig finds the special role of humanity explicated in what he calls the 'Mosaic-Christian' perception of life, which he takes to be shared between not only Jews and Christians, but also with "Naturalists of Spirit", by which he probably meant the Romantics of his day, such as the scientist H.C. Ørsted. Grundtvig is thus pointing to a sort of cultural alliance between spokespersons of different religious and philosophical views, who nonetheless share the sense of the mystery of the origins, development, and fulfilment of humanity:

> The belief that natural humankind is created in the image of God, and through the breath of life from God possesses all that is required to reach its great destiny as children of God – on that point everyone with spirit must surely agree.[38]

The motto, "Human comes first, and Christian next" is a central expression of Grundtvig's creation theology. The Danish can also be translated, "Be first a human, and then be a Christian in accordance herewith," thus pointing to the demand to fulfil our human destiny in faith, hope, and love. At the same time, however, Grundtvig has a keen sense of the great Fall in the history of humanity, and in the biography of individuals. He is well aware that the traditional talk of sin and its basis in a human fall "sounds a bit flat", and he points to other terms more attuned to naturalistic understandings of humanity, such as 'error' or 'aberration'.[39] For Grundtvig, the real difference between Christians and the Naturalists of spirit is concerned neither with the conjunction of

---

37. *The School for Life* (2011), 66.
38. Ibid. 61. Grundtvig articulates his theological anthropology in male-gendered terms, as was customary in his time. It should be noted, however, that in other places he speaks about the "sons and daughters", for example in his sermons, see Text 41 (p. 441). In his later hymns, Grundtvig goes much further by drawing a parallel between the Son of God and Mary as God's begotten Daughter. Thus in the hymn "Earth and heaven, be united" from 1868: "Love, God's once-begotten Daughter,/is both fair and beautiful,/she is ever smile and laughter,/and the Son's bride dutiful,/heav'nly groom and earthly bride,/ever shining at God's side", see *Living Wellsprings* (2015), 256.
39. *The School for Life* (2011), 61.

dust and spirit nor with the failings of human beings to fulfil their destiny. Rather, the divisive issue is whether the damage to human nature can be healed "by natural means", such as self-improvement, or solely by the divine grace in Jesus Christ:

> Christians believe that through the Fall human nature has become so corrupted that all true healing is impossible; they celebrate Baptism as a true *rebirth*, in which the believer is spiritually recreated. The task of the Church, both individually and in general, is to raise this new person to a divine union with the Saviour and Divine Man, Jesus Christ.[40]

This and many other passages show how Grundtvig's Church view is still operative after 1832, and he frames his argument for our shared humanity in theological terms. Human beings are sinners through minimalizing, diverging from, and corrupting their full humanity as it was intended by God from the beginning. At the same time, human beings are always *more than sinners*. Faith, hope, and love are at work amongst Christians, but traces of the image of God are also present in the lives of non-Christians, even though they do not know Christ as their saviour.

Grundtvig thus establishes a balance in his Christian anthropology between the original *imago dei* and the subsequent development of the self-centred *imago sui*. However, he adds that human beings are also to be understood from their embeddedness in the created cosmos, as an *imago mundi*. We are microcosms of the wider macrocosm, both as sensory and as spiritual beings. In this manner Grundtvig adopted central aspects of the theology of the Eastern Patristic writers, in particular the anthropology of Ireneaus, but also that of a later Eastern father such as Maximus Confessor (c. 580-662).

While some Grundtvig scholars such as Kaj Thaning have interpreted Grundtvig's idea of "Human comes first" as a secular programme for a culture that entails a clear *separation* between church and culture, it is probably more correct to say that Grundtvig worked for a living *interaction* and *interpenetration (levende Vexel-Virkning)* of church and culture. He did so in a cultural context where the people of the Danish Church and the people of the country of Denmark no longer coincided, since the Danish people consisted of both Christians and adherents of other beliefs.

A particular consequence of Grundtvig's cultural agenda was his distinction between *faith matters* and *school matters* (meaning matters of opinion). Even theology, as we saw, is a school matter compared to the life of the congregations, in which Christians respond in faith to the words of God in confessions, hymns, prayers, and the

---

40. Ibid. 61.

sacraments. In a brief article, 'Is Faith Truly a School Matter?'[41] from 1836, Grundtvig answers negatively: "Faith is not a matter of schooling at all – thank God". The public schools may well introduce pupils and students into the history and meaning of the church but Grundtvig did not support the established practice of pastors who performed a compulsive catechesis in the public schools. The mechanical exercise in the catechism was for Grundtvig a failed and backward-oriented teaching method. Gently opening a child's eyes to heaven is in general a good thing, also at school, but "whipping him into heaven does not work at all". Grundtvig even continues by saying that it is "a sin to say that Christ bade us do so – He who himself did not come to judge but to save, and who told us to be like He was in this world."[42] Here we see how Grundtvig conducts a secular argument in tandem with a theological argument in which he refers to the purpose of education – all due to the incarnation of God's Son within this very world of creation.

After 1832 Grundtvig was thus able to rearticulate his Church view of 1825 alongside his new universal outlook on a human and natural world shared by Christians and non-Christians alike. He is now able to meet the secular world on its own terms, but he does so out of the fundamental conviction that the secular world is God's own world creation, and God is forever *united* with this world. There is no purely secular world in Grundtvig, nor does he speak of a purely spiritual world without a firm anchorage in God's creation. On the twofold axis of his Church view and his more expansive creation theology Grundtvig continued to develop new aspects of his theology in unexpected ways. His majestic *Song-work for the Danish Church* and his *Basic Christian Teachings* are the consummation of his later theological work, in poetry and prose.

1837-70: Song-Work for the Danish Church

Grundtvig began writing hymns early on. Immediately after his nervous breakdown in 1810, he wrote an uplifting hymn on the three wise men, *Lovely is the midnight sky*, and in 1826, at the millennial celebration of Christianity's arrival in Denmark via the German missionary, Ansgar, he composed another of his most beloved hymns, *We welcome with joy this blessed day*.[43] Indeed, the positive tone of Grundtvig's early hymns, in which grace and nature are intertwined, anticipates his later creation theology. This hymnal tone is one of the reasons why foreigners sometimes call Grundtvig and the Grundtvigians "the happy Danes" in contrast to the "gloomy Danes" in the Pietist

---

41. Text 4 in *The School for Life* (2011) 121ff.
42. Ibid. 122 and 125.
43. Nos. 12 and 53 in *Living Wellsprings* (2015).

tradition. Be that as it may, Grundtvig was critical of the "still waters" of hymns written in a dogmatic and moral style; he wanted to write hymns more "like a running stream," i.e. using a narrative form with energy and flow.[44]

Inspired by a powerful tradition that included Luther, Kingo, Brorson, and his friend Ingemann, Grundtvig conceived of his hymns as songs of praise written for the contemporary Danish church. Being in his own words "very unmusical" he wrote them as poems, quite often with published tunes in mind, and always to a strict metre. He sent out the subscription request for *Song-Work for the Danish Church* on October 30th 1836, one day before the 300th anniversary of the Danish Reformation in 1536. Published from 1837 and finalised in 1870, the *Song-Work* contains 401 hymns (by 1870: 1,585 hymns), some original by Grundtvig, some translations, and some written on material from the aforementioned five church-epochs prior to the Nordic church.

Grundtvig's ambition was no longer to point solely to baptism etc. as the *basso continuo* of Christianity. He now wished to show how each of the five ecumenical churches had contributed something novel and specific to the development of Christianity, something useful for the contemporary enlightenment of Christian self-understanding and perception of reality. From the Hebrew community, examples range from new versions of the Psalms of David up to New Testament hymns. More important was his rediscovery in 1837 of the liturgical tradition of the *Greek* church, sometimes referred to as Grundtvig's "Greek awakening". The Greek tradition led him to expand the liturgical repertoire of his Church view from 1825, not least by adding stronger Trinitarian motifs and doxological elements. The Greek tradition also brought a greater emphasis on resurrection motifs. His hymns on the resurrection and ascension of Christ are far more plentiful in number than his hymns on the cross. In a sermon given on Good Friday 1843, Grundtvig advises his fellow Christians not to mourn for more than half an hour or so! The concept of the quiet week up to Easter Sunday is a remnant from the Middle Ages, and Christians should joyfully celebrate the great divine work of the sacrifice of love accomplished by Christ rather than sit in gloomy despondency.[45]

From the Latin church Grundtvig is inspired by powerful expressions of a cosmic Christology that absorbs the depth of human suffering. In *Hail, our reconciling saviour!*,[46] Christ is described as the one "in whom all things coinhere" (*den dybe Sammenhæng*, lit. the deep connection). From the body of Christ rent asunder on Calvary springs the overwhelming divine love that melts the icebergs of human hearts. In Grundtvig's

44. N.F. Grundtvig, *Poetiske Skrifter* (*Poetic Writings*), ed. Svend Grundtvig (Copenhagen: Karl Schønberg 1880), vol. 1, 299-300. See Christian Thodberg, 'Grundtvig the Hymnwriter', in *N.F.S. Grundtvig: Tradition and Renewal* (1983), 160-210 (162).

45. Grundtvig, *Prædikener i Vartov. Kirkeåret 1842-43* (*Sermons in Vartov for the Church Year 1842-43*), eds. Jette Holm, Elisabeth A. Glenthøj in collaboration with Christian Thodberg (Copenhagen: Forlaget Vartov 2007), vol. 5, 181-186.

46. No. 20 in *Living Wellsprings* (2015), 93.

version of the hymn, reworked from Arnulf of Leuven (c. 1200-50), the Christian is not called to choose between God's world or this world, as in the original, more Augustinian, hymn. In Grundtvig's view, this world is already God's world! Thus, by loving this world with a warming heart, we will meet the self-sacrificing incarnate Christ, resurrected and present in the midst of all reality:

> As for me You once have striven,
> May I love life in you given;
> May my heart for You alone beat,
> So my thoughts alone in you meet,
> In whom all things coinhere.[47]

In Grundtvig's *Song-Work* we thus find new expressions of Grundtvig's ecumenical awareness.[48] One thing is "the Font and the Table", including the faithful response to the words of Christ; this constitutes the common thread throughout the history of the Church. Another thing is the new interpretations of faith, hope and love that emerge in the course of history, alongside new ways of intensifying the response to God in doxology and praise. The contemporary Church as well as individual Christians stand on the shoulders of earlier Church communities, and can reap the harvest of experience and wisdom from earlier epochs of Christianity. The ecumenical dimension is about accumulating insights from a variegated Christian tradition.

Grundtvig's new songs and hymns are intended to enable contemporary Christians to channel and spread their praise of God, and to reorient their lives accordingly. For *fruits* are expected to come from new experiences and expressions of faith. As Grundtvig already wrote in *Nordic Mythology* (1832), it is "by the fruits" that we will recognize the difference between Naturalists and Christians.[49]

Basic Christian Teachings: 1855-61

The same practical interest is evident in *Basic Christian Teachings*, written when Grundtvig was in his 70s: "... we must endeavour in all our speech and writing about the kingdom of God to arouse and sharpen attention to the fruits of the Spirit and the effects of Christianity" (Text 19, p. 292).

In philosophical terminology, Grundtvig the theologian is interested in both the *semantics* of the Christian faith, i.e. its interpretation and understanding, and in the

---

47. Ibid. 94. The 'coinherence' is Broadbridge's translation of "the deep connection".
48. See A.M. Allchin, 'Grundtvig Seen in Ecumenical Perspective', *Grundtvig Studier* 1989-90, 105-20.
49. *The School for Life* (2011), 61.

pragmatics of faith, i.e. its life practices. Throughout his theology, Grundtvig employs not only a descriptive or assertive language, expounding the Christian message to his fellow-Christians; he also speaks in an inviting style, involving a directive tone and advising how to live as Christians in a contemporary context. In Grundtvig, theology is not only knowledge about Christian history and thought; it is also *know-how*, about how to live as a Christian. We must "take possession [of the Christian message] in faith, hope, and love in order to harvest its fruits in righteousness, peace, and joy" (Text 27, p. 370). Thus, to be faithful is also to be fair, righteous, and proportionate; to live in hope is also to give comfort to others, encourage them, and make peace; likewise, love is about the joyful flourishing of life towards the fulfilment of all relations in everlasting life.

For Grundtvig, faith, hope, and love are not mere inner mental states; they are dynamic "life-expressions", as he says in *Basic Christian Teachings*. Moreover, faith, hope, and love are nourished by the three corresponding external "signs of life", or characteristics, of the Church: confessing the faith, preaching and praying, and the praise of God in hymns and songs. These "signs of life" are related to baptism, the words of Christ, and Holy Communion, through which the Holy Spirit is at work in the community. Finally, these life expressions must have their 'fruits' or 'effects' in the social kingdom of God, also *beyond* the Christian community.[50]

Basic Christian Teachings (Texts 13-20) takes its point of departure in Grundtvig's recapitulation of his Church view of 1825, followed by an expanded version of his threefold expressions of Christian life based on the 'signs of life' of the church, and their fruits in the wider society (Texts 21-27). What is at stake here is the relation between human existence in general and Christian existence in particular.

In the chapter on "Inborn and Reborn Human Life" (Text 23), we find a more or less systematic attempt to coordinate Grundtvig's theology of creation and his new 'Church view' with its expansive focus on faith, hope, and love. What is the difference, and what is the likeness between the humanity that is *inborn* with creation, and the Christian existence *reborn* with water and Spirit at baptism? Grundtvig answers thus:

... between our inborn and our reborn human lives there is a world of difference. They differ in quality, breadth, and degree with regard to their vitality. They differ in the truthfulness, love, and goodness with which human life expresses itself in human speech. And yet it is the very same human life that we are speaking of, with the same laws and original characteristics, and the same energies and hallmarks. Thus in its darkest, poorest, and murkiest form it is nevertheless of the same basic nature as in its richest, purest, and clearest form. To put it in a nutshell, the thief

---

50. See the introduction to *Basic Christians Teachings* by Hans Raun Iversen, p. 233-38.

on the cross who shared the same human life as God's only Son, our Lord Jesus Christ, and to whom he cried, "Remember me, when You come into Your kingdom", received the truthful, uniquely powerful and loving answer, "Truly I tell you, today you shall be with me in Paradise." (p. 324-25)

The difference between inborn and reborn humanity is one of quality, but also one of scope, degree and intensity. Thus the thief on the cross and God's own Son on the cross share *exactly the same human nature*. Grundtvig supports this view in his theological anthropology. Even after the Fall, no human being is *only* a sinner, for the image of God (*imago dei*) was never *fully* destroyed. If that were to happen, no communication whatsoever would be possible between God and humanity. Yet the Bible mentions many such examples:

> The so-called Bible Story can only be true on the condition that human life, before and after the Fall and before and after the Rebirth, is extremely homogeneous and basically the same. If Adam's human life in the image of God had been entirely *destroyed* by the Fall, then God could not even *speak* to the fallen Adam, nor could Adam answer Him (pp. 327-28)

On this point, Grundtvig takes issue with Luther's anthropology, insofar as Luther argues that the *imago dei* was totally lost with original sin; on these premises, no faith, hope, or love is possible apart from the rebirth of Baptism, in which the Holy Spirit offers the gift of faith. By contrast, Grundtvig argues that the Spirit of God is at work also outside, and prior to, the Christian Church.

> However long it has been overlooked and however boldly it is often denied, it remains as clear as it is certain that the faith, hope, and love of the old being must be uniform with that of the new being. (Text 25, p. 350).

Grundtvig's emphasis on the possibility of a natural faith, a natural hope, and a natural love *prior* to Baptism, also explains the central role he assigns to the renunciation of the Devil at Baptism. This is an aspect of Grundtvig's theology which modern readers may find strange, yet there is a logic to Grundtvig's argument which runs as follows: (1) The baptismal candidate is *not yet* baptised, is *not yet* reborn by the Holy Spirit, and is *not yet* included in the body of Christ. (2) The baptismal candidate must renounce the Devil and all his deeds as a *logical precondition* for becoming aligned with the God of light and love. (3) This requirement only makes sense if the baptismal candidate *is already capable of doing so* due to his or her inborn humanity:

What we can and must say 'yes' to with our renunciation at Baptism must be no more than what we can, with God's help, honestly and sincerely say yes to before the rebirth and renewal that has its source in Baptism (Text 15, p. 257).

In other words, the renunciation of the Devil is the unavoidable counterweight to the positive confession of the Father, Son, and Holy Spirit. We face here the *principle of contradiction* that Grundtvig always cherished: In order to commit oneself to the Truth, one must renounce the Devil as "the father of lies" (John 8:44).

The renunciation at Baptism is only a special case for Grundtvig's general view that human freedom is part of the *imago dei*, also in spiritual matters. Grundtvig is certainly not a Pelagian presupposing an autonomy of will; rather, like another modern Protestant such as John Wesley (1703-91), he understands human freedom as being circumscribed and assisted by the presence of the divine Spirit. Grundtvig offers a variety of positive examples of faith, hope, and love outside the context of the Christian Church. In many cases he refers to Bible stories, especially regarding faith and hope in his sermons (Text 32), but he can also bring in ordinary life experiences when pointing to the persistence of the *imago dei* after the Fall and outside Christian congregations. Examples are marital love and the love of parents for their children. Here too Grundtvig's principle applies: "Human comes first":

Thus the love between parents and children and the love within marriage between a man and a woman in the old being, insofar as it existed and insofar as it stretched, must have been altogether uniform with the love between the heavenly Father and His earthly children and with the love in the marriage between Christ and His Church in the new being's life. (p. 351).[51]

Grundtvig's general idea is that as human beings we must know about love relations "from below" before we can speak about divine love as a comprehensive "love from above". It is important to note, however, that Grundtvig is not speaking of human love as a mere analogy to divine love. Rather he speaks of human love in the world of creation as being "altogether uniform" (*aldeles eensartet*) with God's love for humanity. The love of parents towards their children is, in other words, of the same character as the love of God the Father for *his* children. Similarly, deep partnerships of love are instantiations of (i.e. exemplify) the same kind of love that comes forth in the relationship between Christ and his Church. What then is the difference between human and divine love, when we take into account that Grundtvig can also speak of a "world of difference" (p. 324) between inborn nature and reborn nature, just as he can also say

---

51. Text 25, Christian Marriage, p. 343ff.

that divine love is an "unparalleled power and love" beyond comprehension (p. 276)? Nowhere does he give a systematic answer to this question. The best interpretation, in my view, is to say that divine love has a universal scope, thus not confined to the love within the family only, or to the favoristic love of one's husband or wife. Moreover, divine love is unparalleled and of another quality by not being conditioned by degrees, since divine love expresses itself in the full vitality of divine life.

The important point is that for Grundtvig also *social life* is part of the image of God. This comes as no surprise when we read his interpretation of the Trinity. He defines the word 'Trinity' as the name for the *divine communion of Father, Son, and Holy Spirit*. Already in mid-19th century Europe we find in Grundtvig a proponent of a social doctrine of the triune God:

> It is the name of the everlasting communion in which the Father, Son, and Holy Spirit enjoy and employ the one true divinity in the order and relationship which their proper names, 'Father', 'Son', and 'Holy Spirit' express (Text 27, p. 365).

Like many Greek Church fathers, Grundtvig speaks of the Father as having a superior position in the triune life, since the source of divinity resides in the one called by the proper name: 'The Father', while the proper name of 'The Son' is logically subordinate in being the principle of receptivity in divine life. Grundtvig is no doubt historically correct in arguing that this understanding of 'subordination' is fully in line with orthodox theology, and is not a subordination which implies that Christ is only *semi-divine*. Rather, the Son is fully divine, and without his eternal Son even the Father could not be the eternal Father: "God could not be the eternal Father if He did not have an eternal Son, and yet He must be the eternal everything – which He is!" (p. 366). The Holy Spirit is fully divine too, also in the sense of being fully self-aware, and is thus able to take initiatives in accordance with the Father's advice and the Son's deeds.

Grundtvig supports his social view of the *imago dei* by also pointing to the incarnation of God's Son. The incarnation implies that God and humanity not only communicate with one another through language, but share one and the same human condition of living in the world of flesh. Fully in line with Martin Luther,[52] Grundtvig argues that divinity and humanity are so intimately interwoven in Jesus Christ that it is impossible to take his humanity apart from his divinity, or to view divinity without God's inclusion of humanity. In short, the incarnation in Christ presupposes a shared humanity between Jesus and all manner of sinners:

---

52. Martin Luther, *Confession concerning Christ's Supper* (1528), in *Luther's Works* (Minneapolis: Fortress Press 1972), vol 37, 218-230.

If this were not so, God's only Son could just as little have willed Himself to be and become a real human child born of a woman as any woman-born *human* child would or could have been a real divine child, born of water and spirit. For then divinity would have excluded humanity, and humanity in turn divinity, and there would no longer be any spiritual or heartfelt reciprocal feeling, no inclination, no interaction (p. 325)

Grundtvig goes on to say that this remains the divisive issue between Muslims and Christians. Muslims declare "divine and human nature so different in kind that no living contact between them was conceivable. They deny the possibility of the incarnation of God's Son and the fusion of divine and human nature in the personality of our Lord Jesus Christ ..." (p. 325). Union, or no union, is the religious question dividing Christians and Muslims, according to *Basic Christian Teachings*. Similarly, a redemption by grace versus a self-redemption by the inborn sparks of light, was the dividing issue between Christians and the Naturalists of spirit in *Nordic Mythology*.

Having argued that faith, hope, and love are part of human nature as created by God, and also a consequence of the incarnation, Grundtvig also develops a new reflection on the Church to avoid its self-understanding being decoupled from local Christian congregations. In *Basic Christian Teachings* Grundtvig is uncomfortable about using the general term 'Church' as being self-evident. At its deepest level, the Church (with a capital C) is "the Holy Spirit's presence in the entire holy Church as being the holy catholic gathering of the people, and in the fellowship of the saints with the forgiveness of sins, the resurrection of the flesh, and the life everlasting" (Text 17, p. 274). This is certainly a 'high' concept of Church, entailing what the whole ballast of the Christian faith is ultimately about. In more ordinary settings, however, Grundtvig's advice is to eschew self-congratulatory uses of 'Church' and instead use more down-to-earth concepts such as 'congregations' or 'gatherings'.[53] Otherwise church leaders tend to forget the Holy Spirit while highlighting their ecclesial power structures. By using the term 'Church' indiscriminately, we can all too easily become "a loophole for the Pope and all those who as 'Lords of the faith and the Church' wished to set themselves up in place of the Holy Spirit, or at least be assumed to have the Holy Spirit all to themselves and thus be the sole medium between the Spirit and the Church" (p. 275).

Grundtvig's ecclesiology is complex. It seems that he both wants to keep together, yet make a distinction between his 'high view' of the Church with a Capital C, and his more modest, almost congregationalist view of the local gatherings of people as the

---

53. The same argument as in Martin Luther, *On the Councils and the Church* (1539), in *Luther's Works* (Minneapolis: Fortress Press 1972), vol 41, 143-145.

concrete place for the life-signs of the Church, and the life-expressions of Christians. Christian community should appreciate on the one hand that the love of God in the final end "surpasses all natural human love", while acknowledging on the other that human faith, hope, and love, also outside the Church, exemplify expressions of divine love. Any Christian congregation, and any individual Christian ...

> ... must first know the natural life and culture of their own people from its best side. Although carnality continues to be dominant, in our best side there is so much spirituality and cordiality that we can gain from it the living measure which can teach us to appreciate the unparalleled power and love in the spirit of God's people and the heart of the Christian brotherhood" (p. 276)

We are here placed in the living interaction between church and culture that may be seen as Grundtvig's particular contribution to theological reflection. On the one hand, he is firm in his conviction that Christian existence offers a life of trust, hope, and love which far exceeds what can be offered on the market of cultures and religions. Hence, being part of the Christian community can never be the same as being part of a particular people – such as the Danes. Christianity and culture never can, and never should, become identical (Text 9). At the same time, life expressions of faith, hope, and love, as well as ideals such as truth, goodness, and beauty, emerge also outside Christian congregations. The Christian therefore has to support any expression of shared humanity, regardless of religious world-views, "for on earth one can never find humaneness without culture" (Text 9, p. 194). It would be curious if Christian congregations, living in different cultural atmospheres, had nothing to learn from the cultures of which they are part. Being a Christian also means being a learner.

Grundtvig in the Context of Contemporary International Theology

Where does Grundtvig belong in contemporary theology, and what is his potential relevance today? A first observation is that Grundtvig's theological vision does not sit well with the oft-used dichotomy between conservative and liberal theology; for he was both a conservative and a liberal. The question is, how is such combination possible?

Grundtvig the theologian was very much aware of the identity of the Christian faith, and he was likewise concerned about the authenticity of the one and only Christian Church. With his Church view in place by 1825, he could now relax somewhat as to the penultimate matters of faith, such as the different ways of organizing Christian congregations and the varieties of biblical interpretation in historical-critical scholarship (see Text 6). In a sense, it was precisely Grundtvig's 'conservatism' concerning the triad of Baptism, the Word, and Holy Communion that allowed him a high degree of flexibility with regard to many other day-to-day theological matters. As we have seen, some things are *necessary* and other things are *beneficial* for the development of the Church, but most things are open to free use and exploration, or can simply be omitted. These tenets of Grundtvig's Church view can speak to our current ideas of an evangelical catholicity based on the claim that Luther and the other magistral Reformers did not plan to create a *new* church but to reform it in continuity with the 'one, holy, catholic, and apostolic' Church.[54]

We have seen that Grundtvig's *Song-Work* of 1837 built on the concept of a growth in understanding, clarity, and wisdom during the history of the Christian Church. And yet he was not a progressivist, for he did not believe that later churches were *per se* livelier than earlier churches. Often on the contrary. Nonetheless, growth is always possible if contemporary churches use the insights of earlier theological epochs, just as Grundtvig himself drew on Irenaeus and Luther. Much like the leading Roman Catholic voices around the Second Vatican Council 1962-65, Grundtvig called for a *ressourcement* of Christian theology.[55] Deliberately, he went back to the Patristic, Mediaeval, English, and German sources of Christian hymns and liturgy – putting these resources into new songs attuned to his contemporary context of Christian life and culture. As we have seen, he also returned to the Bible, absorbing the texts in his own manner, without setting up wedges between the Bible, the living tradition of the Church, and his own time.

There are deep theological reasons for such a 'transhistorical' awareness in Grundtvig's theology. First of all, it is the same Christ and the same Spirit who are at work in the Hebrew church as in his own age – and indeed in ours. Secondly, for Grundtvig eternity is here and now; it is illogical to suppose that eternal life has a beginning 'after death,' for this "could only lead the Congregation to think that it was not until *after* death that Our Lord would grant us a share of eternal life, even though He had promised all his faithful that He would open a life-source in them with His Spirit that would be a wellspring to an everlasting life." (p. 274). Third, Christ's sharing of eternal life *takes place at every Church service*, particularly in Holy Communion, where Christ gives his eternal life to those who partake in the meal. Accordingly, Grundtvig understands the 'real presence' of Christ as not confined to bread and wine; the presence of Christ and the kingdom of God takes place in the community of believers too. This view has a remarkable affinity with the Eastern Orthodox view of the divine

---

54. Carl E. Braaten and Robert W. Jenson eds., *The Catholicity of the Reformation* (Grand Rapids, MI: Eerdmans 1996), vii.
55. See Gabriel Flynn and Paul D. Murray eds., *Ressourcement: A Movement for Renewal in Twentieth-Century Catholic Theology* (Oxford and New York: Oxford University Press 2011).

liturgy.[56] In his mature theology, we may say, Grundtvig transformed his Church view into a Liturgical view.

The 'liberal' aspects of Grundtvig's theology come to the fore in his emphasis on human freedom. In political matters, there should be "Freedom for Loki, as well as for Thor", for a free society must give space to both critics and supporters of the establishment culture, including Christian churches. Freedom must reign in spiritual matters too. From the 1820s onwards, we find in Grundtvig a call for freedom of conscience and religious expression even at a time when this is not yet an established right in Danish society.

Human freedom also plays a significant role within church life, and overall freedom has a special room in Grundtvig's theology. Grundtvig was enough of an Augustinian and Lutheran to know that a self-salvation via human freedom is at odds with human experience, and will lead us astray. We thus saw how his emphasis on the overwhelming power of divine grace was part of his controversy with the Naturalists of spirit in 1832. Human freedom, he believed, is a divine gift, and an *inborn* gift to humanity prior to Christian existence, and even outside the compass of the Church. The freedom to move in the direction of the Truth (Christ), the Life-force (Spirit), and the Love of God (Father) is accompanied by a human freedom to reject the powers of evil. 'Wanting', however, is not the same as 'having the power' to turn one's wants into reality. For Grundtvig, salvation and the flourishing of life require a creative encounter between the longings of the human heart and the life-giving power of grace, so that the affective basis of the human will can be empowered, and the deepest longings of the human being find anchorage, peace, and joy.

Regarding the concept of the human heart, Grundtvig often refers to the *female* aspects of being human. In a sermon from 1848, he argues that in order to be a full human being, Jesus Christ must comprise both male and female characteristics: "the Lord could not be the perfect human being without in fact being man *and* woman ... Only the perfect human being is created in God's image and according to His likeness; only in the perfect humanity, both male *and* female, can God's power be revealed and perfected" (Text 33, p. 406).

Grundtvig makes a similar argument concerning the life expressions of faith, hope, and love. Considering that faith, hope, and love are the essence of Christianity, he even says that "two-thirds of Christianity, namely faith and love, are 'feminine'. Since faith is the first and love the greatest, hope, which is the masculine element in between, can be no more than an empty spiritual death and impotent fantasy if its feminine elements are missing" (Text 32, p. 401). This is indeed a remarkable view of

---

56. See the classic exposition in St Germanus of Constinople, *On the Divine Liturgy: Ecclesiastical History and Mystical Contemplation*, ed. and trans. Paul Meyendorff (Crestwood, N.Y: St Vladimir's Seminary Press 1984).

a 19th century theologian, even though some might argue nowadays that it rests on gender stereotypes. However, Grundtvig's view of the feminine can more graciously be interpreted as an argument in favour of a *gender fluidity* so that any Christian – male and/or female – should embrace a fuller gamut of the human expressions of faith, hope, and love, and thereby expand the scope and vitality of Christian existence.

Apart from the breadth of Grundtvig's view of the Christian faith, the most original contribution of his theology is his cultural agenda, developed in the context of his creation theology after 1832. Indeed, a school of theological thinking has developed around Grundtvig's cultural agenda known as *Scandinavian Creation Theology*.[57] This school of thought aims to use Luther in the context of Grundtvig's theology. While both Luther and Grundtvig appreciate the world of nature as God's unpolluted creation, they differ markedly in their theological anthropology. In spiritual matters, Luther's views of humanity are defined by his allegiance to Augustine's doctrine of original sin. Grundtvig, on the other hand, speaks of the *imago dei* as present in all human beings. From this perspective, it is a natural expectation that the life expressions of faith, hope, and love are, at least occasionally, lived out among human beings independent of any relation of faith to Christ. Thus, Christians belong to a specific community but are not thereby lifted up above other people. All human beings share a basic human nature – of body, soul and spirit. All human beings share bodies and feelings – hand, mouth, and heart – and are guided by similar spiritual values and powers: vitality, truth, and the beauty of goodness. Likewise, in any given context, Christians share with non-Christians quite a few cultural forces of the time, basic ambitions, hopes, and often also national identities.

Certainly, church and culture are not the same for Grundtvig, but he would still insist that there are usually overlapping concerns between most people living in the same place, even despite conflicts between ideologies and religions.[58] Otherwise, in situations of conflict, it may be tempting to withdraw from society, and establish counter-cultural religious groups and parallel societies. In today's theology some argue, for example, that congregational life may be seen as a *polis*, an oasis of peace in a world of conflict.[59] However, the price to be paid for such a view is that the majority culture, or particular groups within society, are defined as enemies. Grundtvig's approach was altogether different: "we wish both the Church and the State well."[60]

---

57. See Niels Henrik Gregersen, Bengt Kristensson Uggla, and Trygve Wyller eds., *Reformation Theology for a Postsecular Age: Løgstrup, Prenter, Wingren, and the Future of Scandinavian Creation Theology* (Research in Contemporary Religion vol. 24) (Göttingen: Vandenhoeck & Ruprecht 2017).

58. We find a similar view in Miroslav Volf, *Flourishing: Why We Need Religion in a Globalized World* (New Haven and London: Yale University Press 2016).

59. Examples are Stanley Hauerwas, *After Christendom?* (Nashville: Abingdon Press 1991), or John Howard Yoder, "How H. Richard Niebuhr Reasoned: A Critique of Christ and Culture", in *Authentic Transformation: A New Vision of Christ and Culture*, eds. Glen H. Stassen, D. M. Yeager & John Howard Yoder (Nashville: Abingdon Press 1996), 31-89.

60. *The School for Life* (note 2), 125.

3. Grundtvig in Udby Church 1811

In 1810 Grundtvig's father, Pastor Johan Grundtvig, asked his son to become his curate. Reluctantly, Grundtvig was ordained and moved back to his childhood home in Udby to serve his father until his death in 1813. His decision to leave his career in Copenhagen brought on a deep spiritual crisis in December 1810, but also helped to make him a Bible believer and an "old-fashioned Lutheran Christian", opposed to both rationalism and romanticism. The illustration is a section of a photogravure from a painting (1900) by Carl Thomsen in which Grundtvig sits, Bible in hand, at the altar-rail in Udby Church. To help himself out of the crisis he wrote his first hymn, 'Lovely is the midnight sky' (no. 12 in *Living Wellsprings*, 2011).

As we have seen above, this does not mean that Grundtvig gives his assent to all regulations from the state; he was also a critical voice in society. But his theology of culture means that Christians should firstly acknowledge that they are *more* than Christian, simply because human beings have multiple identities – as family members, workplace colleagues, interest groups, congregations etc. – and also constantly use public utilities such as water, the internet, and libraries. According to Grundtvig, nobody can or should claim to be "merely a Christian" without also taking part in the cultural circulation, the need for survival, and the striving for life to *flourish*, also economically. Secondly, the Christian should unhesitatingly acknowledge the humanity of other people, as willed by God, upheld by God, and strengthened by God. Theologically speaking, my neighbour cannot be defined as a stranger or an enemy; while it is true that human beings are sinners, no human being is nothing *but* a sinner.

What is particularly promising in Grundtvig's cultural agenda is that he is an encouragement to contemporary theologians to be *bilingual*, as he was in his approach to the public issues of his time, such as education and freedom. Grundtvig could speak about secular matters in effective secular terms, but he did not subdue his Christian voice to a 'purely secular' language, just as he avoided approaching common cultural concerns from a 'purely Christian' view. He was programmatically bilingual in addressing the common problems of society while speaking from the viewpoint that he called the 'Mosaic-Christian' perspective.

Grundtvig can hardly be said to be a political theologian in the sense of presenting a Christian solution to the many unprecedented and pressing issues of his time. Rather, he was a theologian active as a politician, and a public theologian addressing his audience in a language which is both secular *and* religious. Not an either-or, but a both-and.[61]

---

61. I wish to thank Edward Broadbridge for improving my original English, and for his perceptive comments and encouragement.

I

THE CHRISTIAN CHURCH AND
THE PEOPLE'S CULTURE

1. The Church's Retort to Professor of Theology Dr H. N. Clausen (1825)

Introduction by Vanja Thaulow

The Church's Retort to Professor of Theology Dr H.N. Clausen is a central work in Grundt-vig's theological writing, since it is here that he first presents the view of the Church for which he later became known. Our extract covers roughly two-thirds of the book.

Grundtvig had long sought to write a defence of Christianity that took issue with the rationalist theological environment dominant in Copenhagen at the time, but he did not find the right approach until 1825, when, inspired by Irenaeus, he made the 'matchless discovery' that the foundation of Christianity was not to be found in the Bible but in the Church. Its core lay in the fellowship that it had shared from the very beginning around the Apostolic Creed and the sacraments of Baptism and Holy Communion as instituted by Jesus.

Grundtvig presented this realisation for the first time in a sermon on 31st July 1825. He found good cause to pursue his views further when the young Professor H.N. Clau-sen (1793-1877), 10 years his junior, published the voluminous *Catholicism and Protestant-ism: their Constitution, Doctrine, and Ritual* on 3rd September 1825. Clausen, who had trav-elled in Europe and been inspired by among others, Friedrich Schleiermacher, argued that whereas Catholicism built on the Church, Protestantism built on Scripture, with the New Testament in particular being its core and norm. At the same time he pursued the new historical-critical method of exegesis which subjected the biblical material to critical, rational study, for only through reason could the revelation become accessible to man. Grundtvig was particularly incensed by Clausen's demand for the academic freedom to pursue this rationalist path and to set less store by the Church's Confes-sional Books,[62] which, according to Clausen, were 'man's work' and not binding for theologians and pastors alike.

Grundtvig called his retort a *Fejde-Brev*, literally a 'Feud Letter', and presented Clausen as a false teacher. Either he must solemnly apologise for his unchristian and reprehensible teaching, or he must resign his university chair and discard the name of 'Christian'. This difference of opinion was primarily to do with their views of 'the Church'. One of Grundtvig's strongest objections was that Clausen's understanding

---

62. The Confessional Books of the Evangelical Lutheran Church in Denmark are the Apostles' Creed, the Nicene-Constantinople Creed, the Athanasian Creed, the Augsburg Confession, and Luther's *Small Catechism*.

was not 'historical' – indeed, that word appears over 20 times in the text. In building a Church with the help of his own reason and a "broomstick through the air", Clausen was simply creating a "self-made castle-in-the-air"; Grundtvig, the historian, leaned towards the Church's historical tradition, towards the Apostles, the Church Fathers and the many witnesses to the Truth of the Gospel over the years.

Grundtvig found it equally problematic that Clausen built his church solely on Scripture, which in his case he took far too literally. As *theologians* the reformers could indeed raise Scripture to an article of faith, but as *pastors* they had to take for granted both the Church *and* the faith and insist that Scripture could not truly be understood without the help of the Holy Spirit. It was also a fatal contradiction of Clausen to regard the Bible as the Church's article of faith while on the other hand criticising it and questioning its authenticity.

When *The Church's Retort* was published on 5th September 1825, it created a great stir. The first print-run of 500 copies sold out within days, and a second and third soon followed. Grundtvig had expected a theological polemic, but to his surprise Clausen sued him for libel, thereby making the issue a civil rather than a theological matter. Grundtvig complained in vain to King Frederik VI, and at a meeting on 8th May 1826, he realised that the King supported Clausen. Sorely troubled, he decided to resign his living at the Church of Our Saviour. He found it impossible to continue as a pastor if he were not to be allowed to fight against false teaching – as his pastoral vow and his conscience prompted him. In October 1826 the judgement went against him. He was found guilty of insulting language, his statements were declared "null and void", and he was forced to pay Clausen's expenses, plus a fine of 100 silver *rigsdaler*[63] to the Poor Law authorities of Copenhagen. Worst of all, he was placed under lifelong censorship, a punishment which was nevertheless rescinded after 11 years, on 27th December 1837.

In the following years Grundtvig showed no regrets over publishing *The Church's Retort* (see Text 4, *On the Clausen Libel Case*), but in time he modified this position. When he looked back on *The Church's Retort* much later in life he called it "an unreasonable caper and a preposterous venture". In the intervening years he had realised that something more than polemics was needed to arouse the Christian Church.

Foreword

It cannot come as a surprise to any serious reader of Professor Clausen's new book, *Catholicism and Protestantism: their Constitution, Doctrine, and Ritual*, that I challenge its author not as his reviewer but as the opponent of his Church view. With this book he places himself at the head of all the enemies of the Christian Church and the despisers

---

63. 1 *Rigsdaler* in 1844 was worth c. 2 modern *kroner* ($0.30), but a large farm could be purchased for c. 1,800 *Rigsdaler*.

of the Word of God in our country. It is true that the Professor has no reputation as a writer, nor in my view any leadership abilities, but his position as a pastoral teacher and his standing as a biblical scholar among our young Theology students give him an importance in the Danish Church that it would be irresponsible to ignore. To indicate this and to remind readers that for my part the conflict is neither personal nor academic but purely a Church matter, I call this challenge 'the Church's retort' as an appeal to the reading public as much as to the judgement of universal Christianity. This is the pastor-teacher in the Christian Church challenging the Professor of Theology, who is a teacher of pastors in the faculty of Theology. I demand that as an honest man he either makes a formal apology to the Christian Church for his unchristian and offensive teachings, or he resigns his office and discards the name of 'Christian'. This is my irrevocable declaration in the name of the Christian Church and Congregation,[64] and if Professor Clausen refuses to do either of these, then – on behalf of the only true historical Church which was and is and shall be, and whose doctrine is clearly revealed and known through its history – I declare him to be a false teacher who abuses the name of 'Christian' in order to confuse and seduce the Church as best he can in his endeavour to undermine what he professes to serve and affirm!

At heart I would be glad if this declaration were never effected. However, I cannot withdraw my allegation without excluding myself from the Church, for the Christian Church is not an empty, debatable flight of fancy but an obvious reality, a well-known historical fact; it will not give an inch to all the protests in the world, let alone be destroyed by them. What has demonstrably been Christianity from the beginning, is, and will continue to be Christianity not only until the end of the world but throughout all eternity. For this reason no one must claim for Christianity what it demonstrably neither is nor ever can be – unless true, genuine Christianity is itself a falsehood, which is a clear denial of the truth. Nor is this an idle battle of words, for the Christian Church is a grand and matchless reality to which numerous great events over two thousand years are inseparably linked by their effects. Through its witness to these events, good or bad as they may be, the Christian Church undeniably has sole rights, and it cannot claim these except by excluding those who protest against them and who, by falsely claiming its name, wish to gain glory in the eyes of the ignorant and the ill-informed.

The question is only whether I myself am a false teacher or a blind zealot, who passes off what is uncertain and ambiguous either as the basic teaching of the Christian Church or in order to attack it. This I must leave to the judgement of the Church

---

64. Grundtvig follows Paul's distinction between *vaos*, Church as sanctuary and institution, and *ekklesia*, Church as Congregation (etymologically the 'called-out'): The sacraments signify this double role in that at Baptism one is admitted to the true Church, and at Holy Communion one is then granted unity with Christ's Congregation – "His real, spiritual body".

and its Congregation here and hereafter, and place the Professor's book beside the Church's Creed in order to declare that they cannot be reconciled!

I realise that the step I am taking is unusual in our day. For many it is laughable, for many others indefensible, but it is nonetheless deliberate and absolutely essential if with my present insight I am not to be a traitor to the Church in which I have received my hope of salvation and a call to spread and defend the great gospel which I am entrusted to preach. Whatever the judgements and consequences of such a step, it is enough for me to know with absolute certainty that I have done my unavoidable duty. All reasonable judges will find this duty quite different from the time when priests and theologians, since the days of the Nicaean Council, denounced one another for their views or debatable doctrines; for even though I cannot acquit myself of doing such things in my youth, I shall not pursue them here. As soon as a council, a pope or a faculty of Theology arrogates the interpretation of Scripture to itself and excludes the teachers in the Church who interpret it differently – without demonstrably contesting or contradicting the original Christianity that is known to the *whole* Church – the kingdom of Heaven is subjected to violence, and those who do the violence are "raiding" it.[65] For the main question is not whose theological opinion is the most defensible, but with what right an individual theologian or a whole theological group publishes its interpretation of Scripture as the only correct one without being able to prove it indisputably in broad daylight!

At its own risk every state has the right to define a particular rule for interpretation, to be followed by all teachers whom it wishes to reward, protect, or merely tolerate within its borders. It is thus our own affair whether we can agree to subject ourselves to such a rule for the Church, for Scripture, and for our conscience. If not, we must surrender the protection and amity of the state and, as evangelists in the name of Jesus, teach what we should and suffer what we must. The university, on the other hand, has no *power* over the Church or its Congregation, which it is called to serve, to teach, and to counsel, free of any other authority than that which the Congregation grants it by following its counsel and doctrine. This the Church must accept so long as theology truly builds on its foundational Creed, or at least does not deviate palpably from it. Should the latter nevertheless happen, the Church must persuade and admonish, and if that does not help, it should exclude the theologian or the theological group from the Church, which has in fact already *happened*, since by opposing the Church it has excluded itself! It has become difficult to apply this form of self-defence, due to the civil consequences that the temporal authority has attached to such an exclusion; solely for that reason it has long been avoided in our day. But it must *not* be avoided, and all that the Church can do is to ask the authority sincerely and fervently to issue

---

65. Mt 11:12.

a civil edict on tolerance so that exclusion for any who have not otherwise broken a civil obligation shall have no further civil consequences!

In the above-mentioned book, Professor of Theology H.N. Clausen has declared in the clearest and strongest terms that he will not tolerate any other source of knowledge or rule of faith in the Christian Church than Scripture, and with equal firmness he has declared Scripture to be unsafe and contradictory! From this it inevitably follows that he not only rejects the original Creed of the Christian Church, but declares the Christianity that has been known for many hundreds of years to be altogether *un*known and *un*recognisable. Since he nevertheless wishes to be called not only a Christian but also a Christian interpreter of Scripture who can teach others what on his own admission he does not know – namely, what is true Christianity – he must either be deliberately setting out to deceive his readers and listeners, or he must have been blind to the most obvious of truths. Which of these is the case he must now decide for himself, inasmuch as the clear and irrefutable truth is here and now set before him. What is true of him is of course true of all those who own up to his obviously false teaching yet pretend to be, under whatever other name, 'Christian' teachers.

The external consequences here have nothing to do with the matter at hand. Even if false teachers everywhere had the power to exclude us true teachers from what they falsely call the Christian Church, the separation would make no difference. For together with the Christian fathers we comprise the only true Christian Church on earth, which is always at its most recognisable when it is being persecuted.

The reason why I have not taken this step before in a time that abounds with false teachers is in particular that only recently did I come to the clear realisation of what constitutes the unshakeable and unchangeable foundation of the Christian Church. While this still remained unclear to me, every distinction I made between the basic doctrines and other doctrines remained somewhat arbitrary. Moreover, I constantly felt that however sure I was of my own interpretation of Scripture and however many genuine Christian teachers I shared it with, I ought never to pronounce any judgement of church separation upon them, since without any open denial of the truth, such a judgement could be declared invalid, even though it was not so. Now, however, I am making this move with an assurance that I believe will be obvious to all, in the knowledge that our foundational doctrine – whether or not I or others may fail in its application – is unshakeable, and can never again be overlooked for as long as there is a Christian Church. For when our foundational Christian doctrine is clearly acknowledged, the door is shut to false teachers and none can open it, whereas it is open to all believers, and none can close it.[66]

66. Rev 3:7-8.

Praise be to the God and Father of our Lord Jesus Christ,[67] who opened our eyes when clarity was needed and who has wondrously led our Christian Fathers in so many ways as He led His people through the desert.[68] He has guarded their feet from the dark hills,[69] so that we in truth can say that we belong to the only true, universal, Christian Church, under a Christian authority and with a place in civil society. This is a little too comfortable, however, so the only request we must blend with our gratitude to the matchless royal house of Denmark is that the civic restraint on the Church's enemies may be lifted to the extent that is conducive to civic order. We also request that the Church's defence is left to itself, or rather to its invisible King and builder,[70] who is together with His Church "always to the very end of the age",[71] and for whom it is no more than a game "to make His enemies a footstool for His feet".[72]

I am fully aware that there will be cries of 'Alas!' and 'More's the pity!' at my heresy, which is the name given to every protest that the Church makes against its false friends. However, we must also admit that this kind of heresy has not been seen recently, in fact not since the book was written from which I have learned this: namely, Irenaeus' blessed book in defence of the Church,[73] which only now can be understood and put to good use!

Christianshavn,[74] on the Feast Day of Irenaeus 1825.

***

I shall treat as little as possible the abundant material for endless dispute to be found in a book whose author not only seeks to put new wine into old leather bottles[75] but wishes to put gunpowder into old buildings in order to blow them sky-high. The pieces will then be captured in their pure, ethereal radiance in a book whose author makes an honour out of being if not an autocrat then at least an independent owner-occupier in the borderless kingdom of self-contradiction. Being far too down-to-earth to venture

---

67. 1 Pet 1:3.
68. The book of Numbers recounts Moses' wanderings in the Sinai and Paran desert.
69. Ex 19:12.
70. Heb 3:4.
71. Mt 28:20.
72. Ps 110:1.
73. Irenaeus (c. 130-c. 200 CE). Born in Smyrna (now Izmir, Turkey), Irenaeus is one of the first great Christian theologians, and a major influence on Grundtvig's thinking. His book *Against Heresies* (c.180) in defence of the Church is a detailed attack on Gnosticism. He became Bishop of Lugdunum (now Lyon, France) where he died. His feast day is 28th June.
74. From 1823-27 Grundtvig lived at Prinsessegade 52, Christianshavn, near the Church of Our Saviour, where he was pastor from 1822-26.
75. Mt 9:17; Mk 2:22; Lk 5:37.

up to these sub-celestial yet super-terrestrial regions I shall simply prove from my low but steadfast plane that the Church which the Professor commends is not the Christian Church but a self-made castle-in-the-air. It therefore relates to the Church as wind does to Spirit or as state and history do to a mirage on earth. Such proof should of course not be necessary, for the Professor himself has taken the trouble of providing it. But since he has taken the impermissible freedom of attributing his own views to Christ, the Bible, and Luther, and since he boldly claims that his castle-in-the-air is the only true Evangelical Christian Church, it is not gratuitous in these enlightened times of ours to demonstrate incontestably that this is not true.

Following the book's title one might expect a survey of the constitution, doctrine, and ritual of Catholicism and Protestantism as they have actually been and still are practised. But already in the Preface (p. viii) we hear that although with regard to Catholicism the Professor has limited himself to those sources to which the Church ascribes canonical validity – since negligence of this has created great confusion in our view of the nature and principles of Catholicism – Protestant *doctrine* by comparison allows for a far freer treatment. One can draw on it as much as one likes (though not without some confusion) when it comes from a mind that protests against Catholicism or even against the entire historical Christian Church. On this point the Professor immediately adds the naïve explanation "that the Catholic Church rests solely on its historical foundation, but that Protestant doctrine neither stands nor falls on the witness of history". From this it is clear that with regard to 'Protestantism', the Professor seeks to employ the boundless indeterminacy of that word to make fools of his readers and complicate matters utterly. He deliberately confuses his own and others' opinions of how Protestants *should* have protested with the story of how the church of Luther, Zwingli, and Calvin – with its doctrinal creeds (symbols) and catechisms as its historical foundation – can in reality only stand or fall with the witness of history! If the Professor truly regards this procedure as honest, then he is in dire need of more light over his moral concepts; for it is either the acknowledged *Church* protestantism he is referring to, or it is not. If it is, then he must confine himself solely to what is known and accepted as regards doctrine, constitution, and ritual. If he is referring not to our *acknowledged* protestantism but only to his own and his good friends' *version* of it, then he must steer clear of all the ritual and canon law of historical Protestantism as well as its doctrine. Otherwise he is attempting to smuggle in a foreign doctrine under priestly vestments, or to foist his own protestantism onto the Church and its Congregation, even though it has recognised another kind. If this is not the case, why has he not included his own liturgical proposal in the book itself as evidence of the ritual of the Protestant Church? Or if the Professor's private opinion as to how the Augsburg Confession should be altered is more than a suggestion, can his audacity actually make it what it is not, namely the doctrine of our Congregation? In vain does he therefore talk backwards and forwards (pp. 303-35) about the difference between the Confessional Books of Catholicism and Protestantism; for in so doing he merely says how the Protestant Church *ought* to be, if he is to do it the honour of being its member! It is beyond question that what the Protestant Churches have recognised in their creeds and catechisms they have indeed *recognised* – and they must be seen most assuredly to have done so until they solemnly disavow it!

It is truly most obliging of Professor Clausen to have taken this trouble on his own, but since he does not have the Congregation's authority to do so, such a disavowal naturally applies only to himself. All his zeal against the spiritual tyranny that the Congregation is claimed to demonstrate by shackling those who wish to be teachers of a specifically defined doctrine only shows that he is seriously considering leaving our Congregation if it fails to agree with him. It simultaneously shows how little it should agree with him as it has *already* done. If the Professor wishes to persuade us that we should reject our forefathers' Christian faith and creed, it is of little help to prove that this faith and creed demand a humility and self-denial that is very unpleasant for flesh and blood; for we knew this before he was born, and both Luther and our forefathers have constantly impressed this upon us. Instead he must show us either that such a humility and self-denial are a sin and in conflict with what we owe God and the Truth, or that the doctrine of the Christian Church is false and is in no way worthy of the humility and self-denial that it costs to believe it and follow it. If he cannot do either – as I together with the Christian Church frankly claim – then he must not call us irrational when we hold firm to our forefathers' faith and creed; and since he rejects both of these, we must allow him to convert to another religion that he finds more suitable to his nature. For us to dismiss – without any proof and solely on the word of Professor Clausen – a faith and creed which in the Christian case has the experience of ourselves, our forefathers, and millions of others over eighteen centuries as well as a wondrous witness of history behind it ... this cannot be called rational by anyone except a foolish fanatic who sets his own airy fantasies high above the sober, reliable witness of experience.

We now come to one of the Professor's worst self-contradictions. For however grandly he talks about his Protestant Church as one that does not stand or fall with the witness of history – which is understandable if it is floating in air – and however disparagingly he refers to the historical Church which considers it not only best to stay on earth until one goes to Heaven but will also have nothing to do with any flights of fancy, he nevertheless christens his church-in-the-air with well-known, earthly, historical names such as 'Christian' and 'Evangelical' and appeals to Christ, the Bible, and Luther. He does so in order not to drag them down but to raise them up, not to disgrace but to honour his castle-in-the-air. And since the historical witness of experience is the only one that honours Christ, the Bible, and Luther – who have always had the world and its wisdom against them – it must be precisely these praiseworthy witnesses that the Professor otherwise fails to recognise. They are in fact the very same witnesses that he seeks to couple to his castle-in-the-air in order to give what is otherwise quite invisible a touch of form and standing in the eyes of earthly people.

There is admittedly nothing new in this, for all the heretics did the same as best they could from the very founding of the Church. But not everything old is good. Lies and drivel also have a long history, even though Truth is always seen to be a day older, since a lie cannot possibly be voiced before it has something to counteract, something true that it has to deny. The older the Church has become, the stronger and more perceptible has been the testimony of its experience. When it was discovered during the 'church storms' of the 18th century that there was a high wall to be climbed over, the attempt was made, as is the case in wartime, to crawl *under* it by declaring the testimony of experience 'invalid'. When it was then realised that this was too gross a self-contradiction, since experience was otherwise being *deified*, it was decided to pursue a middle way and, out of a deep-seated love of peace and sympathy for its grey hair, the 'Christian Church', as it was called, was offered a strange peace proposal. If the Church would surrender to the enemy, the enemy would allow himself to be baptised and called 'Christian' with the reservation that he would be allowed to tear down everything he did not like in the Church and divide the testimony of its experience so that he took the good and left the bad to the Church, which was the lion's share! This is the famous agreement and concordat that the Christian Church is supposed to have made with its arch-enemy: false, mortal Rationality. Through thereby protesting against itself it has indeed become genuinely 'protestant'! But since everything that protests against itself thereby *revokes* itself, it is easy to see that either the Christian Church must be stormed and destroyed – which the enemy would excuse with the lie that it was with its own permission – or the whole narrative was only a strategem whereby the enemy sought to lull the churchwarden to sleep while he performed his masterstroke of tearing down what the Church has built up.

We shall allow it to remain undecided whether or not Professor Clausen knows the proper context of this matter: whether he truly fancies that such a Church that protests against the Creed and entire history of the Christian Church can still remain 'Christian', or whether he simply *calls* it so in order to pull the wool over anyone's eyes that he can. However, we cannot be persuaded that his protestant castle-in-the-air has been, is, or ever can be the only true Christian Church, recognised and recommended by experience; nor can it acquire the least little share of its divine and human testimony, sealed with the noblest blood of heroes – for we can prove it is not.

For this reason we shall first allow Professor Clausen to build his protestant church-in-the-air as he so wishes, and then compare this figment of his imagination with the true Church of Jesus Christ on earth. It will then become clear as sunlight that the Church of Christ is neither built to Professor Clausen's design, nor, without an-nihilating itself totally, can the Professor's design be regarded as the ideal which it must endeavour to arrive at or become a likeness of. [76]Once that is done, the Christian Church and Professor Clausen will have nothing more to do with one another – un-less he wishes to proclaim an open dispute; once the entire Congregation knows that Professor Clausen's Christ is an altogether airy, deaf-and-dumb, impotent, impersonal person who does his best to do nothing by allowing Professor Clausen and whoever else to believe in His name and do what they themselves like ... once in other words it knows that he is a person totally and essentially different from the Church's Christ, who is both heavenly and earthly, divine and human, almighty, present in His spiritual power, one person with the Father, Himself, and His Congregation, who Himself in both spirit and word will do His Father's will[77] in and through His believers ... once its Congregation knows all this, the Church can simply leave it to the individual's own judgement *which* Christ they wish to worship: the one who has done great and wondrous things for His Church so that it has become known honourably to the very ends of the earth, or the one who, unlike Christ, has never done anything but attempt, though always in vain, to disrupt His work and interrupt His activity.

The Professor begins by stating that 'the Church' is a community for the promo-tion of general religiosity.

Let us not quarrel with the Professor over this curious subject as to what the name 'Church' even means. However, if it is his view that the word 'Church' has come to us as the name of every community that seeks to promote general religiosity, then he is very much mistaken. For everyone knows that it is far from being unknown in Church history that the monastic orders were not called 'churches', even though they were undeniably independent communities for the promotion of general religiosity. Nevertheless, so as not to quibble over a word to no avail, we shall allow the Professor to think what he likes about 'the Church', provided that he admits that the Christian Congregation (*Ecclesia Christiana*) is a faith community with a Creed which it sets before all those who wish to be its members and only allows them to be so through Baptism and Holy Communion, once they have learned the Creed. It considers to be apostates those who hereafter renounce the faith or refuse to say the Creed, and it declares them to be false Christians (heretics) if in their obvious departure from the Creed they stubbornly claim the right to be called 'Christian'. On the other hand, if the Professor will not even admit this, but stubbornly claims that his protestant church – his church-in-the-air where one may believe what one likes or where the creed

---

76. I have followed Grundtvig's syntax in this next sentence to give an example of his style – the sentence in Danish runs to 235 words.
77. Jn 10:37-38.

runs into the self-contradiction: "I believe I know not what" – if he claims that this is the true Christian Church, then we must turn the sentence round and say what he is forced to concede or make himself a liar, that "There is for the time being a faith community that calls itself the only true Christian Church into which no one is admitted to membership by Baptism and Holy Communion, nor do they have to learn the so-called Apostles' Creed, nor do they exclude themselves by refusing to say the Creed, nor are they prevented from starting a new Church whose members are in no way bound either by faith or doctrine to any Creed." It is from this Church – into which through Baptism and Holy Communion after reciting the Creed Professor Clausen became a member – that he has undeniably excluded himself in his present book. So, if he nonetheless claims to be a member of 'the Christian Church', he must prove that the faith community on which he has turned his back so scornfully has falsely acquired and bears the name of 'the Christian Church'. Otherwise, he must allow himself to be declared a member of the Heresy Society outside the Church, whose only shared belief is that the Church has gone astray and that their protest is sufficient if not to tear it down, then at least to shame and condemn it!

The Professor's description of his Christian Church is as an earthly institution bound to the universal forms of the sensual world but which by its nature (as a castle-in-the-air) shuns all contact with the earth and the body (p. 4). If we wish to see this, we should first read his oh-so-beautiful introduction (pp. 7-8): "In Christ God revealed Himself to the generations of the earth so that the finite form can be absorbed into the infinite form. For the first time a pure, refined universalism in which oriental height and depth were united with occidental clarity and softness, and the light of thought with the warmth of feeling and the tinge of fantasy; in the oldest Confessional Books the teaching expressed the faith that is lodged in every human being, but in only a few does it develop into clear consciousness. It thereby gave this faith a firmness, a definition, and an application; it granted full satisfaction to the complete human being; and it ensured against all the errors and distortions that arise from a one-sided spiritual activity. Down through the centuries this teaching was proclaimed as the promised and expected revelation of God, and its utterance was confirmed by the testimony from God; for the connection from this teaching to the series of world events demonstrated clearly the guiding hand."

The most peculiar element in the Professor's book is its boundless praise of the vague 'nature' of the Church (his pure universalism) and his consequent attempt to say everything that can be said without actually saying the least word about the *foundation* on which it is built. Serious readers unaware of this will certainly be surprised at this description of Christ and His teaching, but if they look very closely, they will find a brief remark that both of these are worth almost nothing. Like Professor Clausen himself, Christ is no more than the infinite in a finite form (soul and body); Christ's teaching, like the Professor's, is a statement of the faith that is lodged in every person (presumably faith in its own reason); and God's witness to the truth of this teaching is the same as Muhammed's, namely the connection to the series of world events which clearly shows the guiding hand.

The Professor continues: "Thus in the fullness of time the conditions were granted and the religious idea released from the visual images of nature worship, freed of its human bonds, purified of the additives of wisdom and self-interest, its throne visibly raised in the midst of the pious – and the effect did not fail to materialise. Humans followed the divine voice and their inner desire; Christ left the earth, but His Spirit remained in His teaching; it drew them together and united them in a collaboration higher than any other. A Church formed itself in Christ's name in which Christ would continue to speak to His followers; out of this the Christian faith, as the animating principle, was to flow into all earthly relations. Thus it is the nature of the Christian Church to work in the spirit of Christ for the same goal, in the same way as the divine model was active on earth. As the organ through which Christ's plan will in time be realised, the Church must embrace Him with the greatest conviction and as far as possible adopt *His* concerns and activity; its effect is more complete the less active it is, the less it flows from the Church as an independent community; its nature is one of preparation, of mediation, and must limit itself to paving the way for the power that is at work in Christ's teaching, which in itself must be sufficient if it comes from God and is supported by God."

It goes against the grain with me to have to make a copy of the Professor's nonsense, but who would otherwise have believed me if I had told them that, according to his assertion, the nature of the Christian Church was to be so little active and so utterly aimless that he would find nothing extraordinary about it except a dead man's spirit in the power of whose teaching it should trust, but whose teaching it must allow the good people to guess at?

This last line does not appear expressly here but merely lies in the Church's 'aimlessness'. However, if we ask the Professor where we find this teaching of Christ which is *from* God and supported *by* God with a power that renders the Church's activity not only superfluous but also harmful, then of course we must look for the answer in the Professor's description of his protestant church, on which he generously confers all the Christian Church's titles; I shall make an honest attempt to inform the reader as to what we find there.

After the Professor has accompanied Catholicism and thus, following his explanation, the historical Church – the only true Christian Church – to its resting-place, he raises a brand-new subject (p. 298) which he is pleased to call, pure and simple, "the Protestant (i.e. contradiction's own) Church". In the Professor's account – and he should know best what only exists in his own imagination – this derives from the same dogmatic point as the Catholic (historical-Christian) Church: from belief in the revelation in Christ. But it immediately diverges from this point to distinguish (p. 299) with critical stringency between the written word and the oral tradition.[78] To be sure, he admits (p. 301) that Christianity has been transmitted by oral teaching before written Scripture; indeed most of the holy books are the fruits of the oldest Christian tradition. Nor can the possibility be denied that a number of the sayings of Jesus and the Apostles could have been preserved in the writings of the Holy Fathers, where they can still be read in their original purity. Equally, it must be granted that provided the authenticity of such teachings and sayings were demonstrable, the Church would be duty-bound to acclaim them with religious awe. However, the Professor continues thus (p. 311): "Even in the case where a specific teaching that was completely disregarded could be traced with every certainty through the tradition back to Jesus or the Apostles, the Church would not be entitled to place it alongside those that are transmitted in the holy books. For if it dare not ascribe this to accident but must see a higher dispensation behind its not being incorporated into Holy Scripture, then there is nothing to be done except acquiesce in the divine hint; and it is incumbent upon the Church to respect the limit that has once been set by the guiding finger."

Well now, that truly shows a proper belief in Scripture, the reader might say! To which I must answer No! It is a quite extraordinary belief, the grossest literalism I have ever seen in writing! What a blind faith in Scripture it must be – for no other reason than the command of the Protestant Church in Christ's name – to defy the living Word that issues demonstrably from the mouth of Christ and cannot be proved without special guidance from God!

So in the Professor's protestant church the written word is *everything*, and even the oral word of Jesus cannot change it one jot – including presumably Professor Clausen's oral word and written letter. This is a major mistake, for in such a church miracles can happen that none would believe, and even the impossible is made possible!

To be sure, we can read (pp. 303-4) that the written word is the only form in which doctrine has been maintained in its demonstrable integrity, so that it sounds to us as it sounded to the Christians in the first centuries. It is the only source of knowledge and rule of faith given to us by God; it is the true sanctuary of Protestantism, the bulwark of the evangelical faith, of holy reverence, of unlimited trust, of undaunted faith, by which it points to Scripture as its light and leader; it is the dogmatic characteristic of the Protestant Church. Scripture is the sufficient and complete vehicle for doctrine, to which nothing can be added, just as nothing can be taken away; it is enough in itself, its own interpreter, and in itself clear and evident to every seeing eye. To be sure, we read all this, and here of course the reformers must hold up a light for Professor

---

78. This is Grundtvig's core criticism of Clausen.

Clausen; but we only have to turn over the page and we abandon all the reformers – and the Professor himself is so good as to hold up a light for us all. For now we hear (p. 306) that 'the Protestant', who is continually handling and being occupied with the Holy Books, cannot conceal the following facts: repetitions that could have been avoided are as frequent as holes that should have been filled; Scripture is silent where we would have preferred it to speak; it speaks obscurely and indistinctly where the eye is most eager for a guiding light; and veils rest over certain passages and individual books with regard to their authenticity, their text, and their interpretation, veils which no era has managed to lift.

This would be sufficient to show the tangible self-contradictions the Professor with his frightening superstition believes he can marry with his protestant church. It is undoubtedly sufficient to divest us of any desire to be incorporated into it; and it is also sufficient to demonstrate that this is not the Church that the reformers sought to enlighten through Scripture. But there is more where this came from: immediately on the following page (p. 308) we read that not a single word has been delivered to us by Jesus Himself, nor any word expressly sealed with His highest authority! His words and deeds are not listed for us in any continuous, complete account; two of his biographers[79] do not even belong to the Apostolic eye-witnesses; the accounts of the four evangelists can only with difficulty be made to harmonise chronologically, where much is uncertain and many obvious differences and contradictions remain; by far the majority of the largely dogmatic share of our Holy Book is written by one of the Apostles who neither saw his teacher and master with his own eyes nor heard him with his own ears;[80] throughout the books the dogmatic and moral, the real and the allegorical-unreal, the literal and the figurative, the universal and the local and the temporal, the Christian and the Jewish are mixed together; the individuality of the Apostles shines through manifestly in the treatment of the Christian dogma and already gives us an illustration of the theological differences which have since characterised the Christian Church. Thus, it is only through a knowledge of philology and a critique of philosophy that it becomes possible to fill out what is missing, illuminate what is obscure, and define what is vague. Finally, in a number of cases proof of the authenticity of the Holy Books does not lead us further than to a higher or lesser degree of probability that the actual text of these books has not avoided the fate to which every other book is exposed over the course of time; and biblical criticism and hermeneutics reveal problems that will doubtless never cease to be the subject of dispute in the Christian world.

All readers will undoubtedly by now have realised that this protestant church is a

79. i.e. Luke and Mark.
80. i.e. Paul.

quaint castle-in-the-air that Professor Clausen has been pregnant with, and that there can hardly have been so foolish a belief in this world as that a book can be its read-ers' source of knowledge and rule of faith yet at the same time its shoe-brush! It can be both genuine and false, clear and obscure, complete and incomplete, definite and indefinite, divinely true and clearly false; so it is falsehood pure and simple that the Apostles tell us about Jesus' assurance that the Spirit of Truth would remind them of all His words.[81] Pure falsehood! For did not the most dogmatising Apostle, Paul, solemnly testify that he had both *seen* and *heard* Jesus?[82]

This is supposed to be the divine ideal which the Christian Church under God's guidance has gradually endeavoured to approach, and in Professor Clausen's head has completely achieved! It is supposed to be Christ's view, like Professor Clausen's (p. 307), that perfect unity of faith can only be imagined among human automata, where spiri-tual life is strangled! As with the Professor's 'reason', Christ Himself is supposed to regard it as blasphemy to attribute the aim of annihilation to the divine revelation; and it is equally as biblical as it is Christian (pp. 343-44) whether one regards Christ as God or as a limited human being; whether one sees human deeds as the effects of the fully active divine power or the product of human freedom; whether one hopes for eternal life solely through God's mercy or through the strict law of acquisition as a reward for human virtue; whether one interprets the coming life as communion with God or in the tempting colours of sensual pleasure; and whether one considers faith or deeds to be the path to being justified *for* God! It is thus presented in the clearest terms that, regarding the relation between God and humankind, truth and falsehood are equally biblical and equally Christian. From this it follows that the Bible and Christianity are not true but completely false, not divine but in fact a devilish revelation, for it cannot be denied that God is the God of Truth who hates all lies and falsehood and that only the Devil, the father of lies,[83] could fabricate the notion that truth and falsehood are one and the same thing!

In truth, we see here that it was wise of the Christian Church – which in reality has been, is, and (this is our faith) will endure to the Last Day – that it asks all those who wish to be baptised: "Do you renounce the Devil and all his works and all his being?" For as long as it continues to do so and to declare the Devil the father of lies, no one can claim that it is directing its members to the ideal in which truth and falsehood lovingly embrace one another.

The Professor himself must admit that there really *is* a Church on earth that calls itself 'Christian' and incorporates through Baptism and Holy Communion only those

81. Jn 15:26.
82. Acts 9:1-9.
83. Jn 8:44.

who renounce the Devil and confess their faith in God the Father, Son, and Holy Spirit, according to the three Articles of Faith which scholars call the Apostles' Creed. And it is quite true that it would have ended its days on earth if, following the Professor's proposal (pp. 833 and 837), we no longer bound ourselves to an always unequivocal Baptismal formula or had not made faith in, and confession of, the three Articles the condition for the adoption and effect of Baptism. But what should tempt the Church to follow such obviously inimical advice? What should tempt it to commit suicide, to end, and bring shame on, an honourable life? What could be the *reward* for Professor Clausen's approval?

I realise that the Professor will not admit that this church, which in the name of Jesus Christ demands full unity of faith of all its members, is the *Christian* one; for his reason calls such a demand 'blasphemy'. But it will be hard for him to kick against the pricks,[84] and impossible with the least appearance of justice to deprive it of its Christian *name*, which it has borne with honour and shame – the honour of God and the shame of the world – from the beginning of the name of Christ to this very day.

I am also well aware that with his deliberate disregard for all intervening history, the Professor is transmitting himself and his protestant church (p. 68) back to the birth of Christianity; but on such a very historical question the by-passing of the entire history that alone can answer it, is, and always will be, a ridiculous pipedream that cannot change one iota in the real world; and that is solely what we must do if we consider it worthwhile to trace the *history* of Christianity. I hear the Professor saying that Church history is a dark, wild labyrinth of contradictory accounts, interpretations, and claims based upon them, from which we must turn to Christ as the only Lord and Master, and to Scripture as the sole self-sufficient rule and guideline. But if we deliberately disregard the entire intervening period which is actually the only real path through time, how do we come to Christ and Scripture except on a broomstick through the air? I know the Professor thinks we can do what we like with history, pass over it completely, and construct the Church *a priori*. We can call on it for help, build on it, and assess it; but we cannot really do so without a clear contradiction. This is undeniably the mark of falsehood! The Christian Church, having promised to lead believers to a realisation of the truth, has always avoided falsehood like the plague, for it only ever brought death with it.

Nevertheless, imagine for a moment that we *accepted*, on the testimony of the Church Fathers, that a Christ *had* existed and that the New Testament was written by His *Apostles*. Imagine this had happened without giving any credence whatsoever to the testimony of the same Church Fathers as to what the Church believed and confessed, for whose enlightenment and edification the New Testament was written according

---

84. Acts 26:14.

to their witness. Imagine, as no one actually can, what we would thereby have gained? Would that be *proof* that Jesus Christ was credible and that the New Testament was a true, divine revelation? That is what the Professor assumes, but it is on a par with the grossest superstition that with no other cause than one's own will one assumes a human being to be the Son of God and a book to be a divine revelation. If we are to have *cause* to believe, we must return to *history* and regard the Gospels and the Acts of the Apostles as a true story which shows that Jesus is worth believing in! And that the Apostles are witnesses to His Spirit, whose enlightenment on spiritual matters is *credible*. I realise that it is not the Professor's intention, on the basis of his own reason, to have Jesus made a divine name and the Bible a phantasm of his own wise thoughts. But this clearly means only making fun of Christ, the Bible, and the entire Christian Church. For we must neither worship an idol who is worth nothing in this world and from whom we can gain no benefit, nor must we attach the words 'a divine revelation' to a book which cannot enlighten us on a matter of importance and cannot be used as a source of knowledge or a rule of faith.

From all this it is clear that Professor Clausen's Christianity is completely false and his protestant church a temple of idols where falsehood is proclaimed as truth and the attempt is made to revoke the irrevocable divide between truth and falsehood as between light and dark, yes and no, affirmation and denial, claim and counter-claim. It is equally proven that Professor Clausen has no right to call the church he will establish 'biblical and Christian' when he is demonstrably contradicting the Word of the Bible and refuses to find any rule of faith within it; on the contrary he declares that the authenticity of the New Testament is doubtful, the text unsafe, and its interpretation a bone of contention!

The only question that remains is whether the historical Christian Church into which we are incorporated through Baptism and Holy Communion has a better claim to call itself 'Christian', and whether it is worth remaining within it or renouncing it in the name of truth. In the latter case we must either remain spiritually homeless or we must set about building ourselves a church that is only a little more justifiable than Professor Clausen's, one that is recognisable not for itself but only for its contradictions. It affirms nothing of itself but only opposes (protests against) something else. It will fall of its own accord as soon as its oppositional element is removed, which is the obvious mark of falsehood and of no value in its own right. Truth, on the other hand, only protests against falsehood out of necessity, and when that is removed, it shines in all its splendour and reveals all of its abundance.

It goes without saying that 'the Christian Church' which was first known under that name also has the *claim* to that name, and an exclusive claim at that. Anyone who disputes our name must prove that we stole it from them, in other words that they bore it before us. Another question is whether the Church of which we are members may rightfully call itself 'Christian', for that depends on whether it is the same church that was first known *under* that name. The question would be as unanswerable as it is unavailing if 'Christian' were in its origin an empty name which was not a term in itself but only had any meaning as a contrary term. In that case it would be like the names James, Peter, and John; all who constantly answer to those names have a more or less equal claim to them. But that is not the case with the first known 'Christian' Church, as we can see from its history and its *apologia*; these justify its protest against heathenism and heresy through its distinctive faith and teaching, which cannot be changed or made compatible with idol-worship. It cannot be denied that this distinctive character, upon which the oldest Christian Church was built and by which it was known not just for its enemies but especially for its friends, must be found in every church that rightly can be called 'Christian'. I claim that it is found in *our* Church, and indeed is found in every Church which makes the Apostles' Creed the sole condition for incorporation into the fellowship and which ascribes to the sacraments of Baptism and Holy Communion the power of salvation, as it also does to the Creed. I argue this point not just as a theologian or a Church scholar but primarily as a believing member of the universal Christian Church which in the Apostles' Creed and the Sacraments not only distinguishes itself from Jews, Turks,[85] and heathens but first and foremost ensures for its members the forgiveness of sins and salvation in the name of Jesus Christ. It is incumbent upon Professor Clausen and every other Protestant to refute this claim of the Church if he intends to deprive our Church of its name as being 'the only true universal Christian Church'.

There is no room here for evasive answers or deliberate disregard of history, or airy transport to the birth of Christianity. For we cannot deny that a Christianity *has* been born on earth, since it not only lies behind us in history but is also what is alive for us today, wherever we hear faith in Jesus Christ being confessed and the Sacraments administered in His name. So the Christian Church is a fact of life that cannot be blown away by airy dreams or upset by loose talk that is no more than hot air! All Church scholars know that it would be easy for me to present large amounts of evidence to prove that our Creed is truly the same as the one that was placed on the tongue of the Christian Church from the very first moment it opened its mouth in vociferous defence of its spiritual riches against proven enemies and false friends. But a Church that commands all its members to die rather than betray its Creed must be deemed honest to that Creed until it is clearly proved to be false; such a Church must never call witnesses to its honesty but only turn to them as a last resort against the fabrications which are used to make its honesty seem suspicious.

This is how we face Professor Clausen and all those who wish to pass off their

---

85. i.e. Muslims.

dreams as the Christian revelation and the figments of their imagination as Christianity. We face them with the immutable fact that there *has been* and still *is* a Christianity on earth, recognisable from everything else by its unparalleled Creed. In every tongue[86] and under every wondrous shape and form it has preached and continues to preach faith in Jesus Christ, crucified and risen again, as the certain and only way of salvation for sinners, a way that through Baptism and Holy Communion leads to the kingdom of God and the Land of the Living.

One can doubt the truth of whether this obscure secret path leads to fellowship with the God who is light beyond all darkness and who alone has true immortality and eternal life – one can doubt it, and without any obvious self-contradiction one can deny it! But it remains a truth as clear as sunlight that this way is exclusively the *Christians'* way, and that the Creed which forms the narrow door to the Church is the unchangeable and, we believe, immovable foundation for both faith and doctrine in the Christian Church. One can only *doubt* this if one is willing to doubt one's own eyes – for only a desperate liar would gainsay it! One must stop to consider with what means one will *contest* the foundational doctrine that the Sacraments and the corresponding Creed are the only features that have been shared by all Christians, in every walk of life, in every Church, and at all times. They are what has made the Church recognisable to friends and enemies alike and held it together. They are the undeniable hallmark and bond of fellowship in the Church. They are the foundation that until now has matched the charge that the Lord laid on the rock,[87] which despite the gates of Hell and the power of Death was to bear His Church 'always to the very end of the age'! With what means can one contest this foundational doctrine? How can we *only in our minds* set the Church on the ground where it has demonstrably stood and undeniably stands for as long as a single person, such as I myself, adopts this Creed? How can one contest that of my own free will I declare myself through the Sacraments to be linked to all true believers who have been, are, and shall be born, reborn in the same faith, of the same Spirit, with the same Baptism, to the same hope?[88] One cannot use *reason* to contest a fact which divine, omniscient, and almighty Reason itself can only explain but never overturn, and cannot dispute without self-contradiction! Nor in the case of the New Testament can one contest what it in every way presupposes, rests on, and builds on, since it is undeniably no more than the testimony of the Christian Church which makes this book the light of the Church. Scripture is addressed expressly to the already believing and baptised Church and does not wish to teach it anything new but only to strengthen and maintain it in the Christian faith which, as mentioned, is presupposed!

---

86. Acts 2:4, 11.
87. Mt 16:18.
88. Eph 4:4-5.

Truly, it is high time that all of us who wish to be Christian in the Spirit and in truth[89] must unite alone in building the rock which over time has defied the stormy blasts and the roaring waves. We must limit ourselves as a faith community and Church to the crib in Bethlehem, as history teaches. We must victoriously defend it against all the powers of the World and Hell, so that we can withdraw to the choir of the church, so to speak, and offer each other and all those Christians who have fallen asleep in the Lord our hand over the font and our mouth at the altar in the one bread and the one chalice.[90] As brothers we must set aside all disputes on questionable subjects, and if we are strong, then we must not abuse our power to burden the helpless but use it to bear their weaknesses! So, Christians, wherever you build, it is time for us again to unite around all that is Christian, as lay and learned, and as different in our way of thought as was shared by Justin Martyr and Irenaeus, Ansgar and Luther, Reinhard and Balle;[91] for undeniably all of them are fundamentally *Christian*. We must unite around this and tolerate in each other all compatible theological diversity, but not deviate a hairsbreadth for open enemies or false friends. We must solemnly separate ourselves from those who by rejecting the Church's original Creed and divine Sacraments would separate themselves from us and would prefer to retain the name of 'Christian' only under the mask of 'friendship' – and only in order to seduce the Church and obtain by underhand means the lustre of the Church's great testimony which they refuse to believe! As history indisputably proves, this is what the earliest Christians did while the persecutions lasted, and we only need to put ourselves in their place (reminders of which are plentiful) in order to realise that this is what the Christian Church should do at all times. For what cannot go through fire is not gold! No Church can know, gather, and confess everything in writing; and none of us can die in the name of Jesus Christ merely on our interpretation of Scripture or the word of any human being who does not have God's visible testimony. This divine testimony contained the original Creed for the Church Fathers, inasmuch as they did not give false witness but sealed the testimony with their own blood. This divine testimony contains the Creed for us in the Apostolic Writings[92] and in the entire wondrous history of the Church. However, there is no *rule of interpretation* except that Scripture must be understood according to the Creed and cannot be understood except by believers with the Holy Spirit: there

---

89. Jn 4:23-24.
90. 1 Cor 10:17.
91. Justin Martyr (aka St Justin, 100-165) was an early Christian apologist and the foremost interpreter of Logos theory in his time. For Irenaeus, see note 73. The Benedictine monk Ansgar (801-65) is credited with bringing Christianity from Bremen to both Sweden and Denmark and is therefore known as 'the apostle of the North'. He is also credited with building the first Danish church in Hedeby. Martin Luther (1483-1546) was the German theologian whose writings inspired the Protestant Reformation; Franz Reinhard (1753-1812) was a German Lutheran theologian; Nicolai Balle (1744-1816) was Bishop of Zealand, Denmark 1783-1808.
92. The 'Apostolic Writings' comprise the whole of the New Testament.

is no other rule of interpretation but this one, the divine and human testimony of the Apostolic Church and of history. The Church must keep to this rule and let the university otherwise go free. It must let the university theologians and scribes deliberate and dispute with one another if they so wish, provided they allow that the Holy Bible is enlightening and edifying for all Christians according to the measure of the faith and wisdom that the Lord grants, and provided that they do not seek to sow division between Scripture and the fundamental Creed of the Church. If they do so, they exclude themselves from both the Church and the Faculty of Theology.

This is how we salute all the spiritual universalism and academic freedom that a Church, as a faith community, can accept, without declaring itself, in obvious self-contradiction, to be abolished and a completely false and mendacious community! The learned and the lay who cannot accept this necessary restriction and who thus in no way wish to be Christian must *discard* the name of 'Christian', whereas conversely we grant them all other names, even the most high-sounding, that they wish to give themselves. If they wish to be called 'Protestants', let be! They may do so, and we surrender to them every claim to a name that unquestionably best suits those who prefer not to share anything more definite than the protest against the Christian Church and every faith community that seeks to confess its faith and stand by its creed. If they wish to be called 'Rationalists', let be! We certainly cannot sign away our reason, either as it is in God or as it is figuratively in us. But we have nothing to boast about, and we therefore willingly leave that boastful name to our opponents, just as the Church Fathers, without committing themselves to folly, allowed their opponents the name of 'Gnostics'![93] If, out of some unfathomable humility, they wish to call themselves 'Lutherans', we who belong to the Church will not quarrel with them; for we are not baptised in Luther's name and our forefathers did not teach us that Luther rather than Christ was crucified for us. But at the university we must defend our Father in Christ and prove that all the 'protestants' against the historical Christian Church who appeal for His acceptance are either reeling around in a fearsome historical darkness or are surrounded by falsehood. In either case they are disgracing the blessed memory of our glorious Lord and abusing His rightfully famous name in Christianity to gloss over what He loathed with all His heart.

It is quite certain that whatever the Reformers, with Martin Luther as their great leader in the battle against the papacy, may have claimed as theologians about Scripture as the rule of faith, they nevertheless as pastors and teachers in the Church always *assumed* both the Church and the faith, and *agreed* that Scripture could not truly be understood without the help of the Holy Spirit: in other words believing Christians

---

93. Gnosticism taught that *gnosis*, intuitive knowledge, is the soul's way to salvation from the material world. It was practised in various cults in late pre-Christian and early Christian times.

could not possibly *deduce* their faith from Scripture until they understood it. It is equally certain that in the Augsburg Confession, which Luther and Melancthon[94] did not protest against, our Church bound its teachers to the Apostles' Creed (Article III) and to the one true, historically Christian, unchangeable catholic Church (Articles VII and XXI). Finally, it is certain that no one was stronger than Martin Luther in raising up the simple childlike faith of the Christian Church above all academic wisdom. No one showed more clearly his trust in the Church's immutable foundation than by linking the Apostles' Creed insolubly to Baptism and, in his *Small Catechism*,[95] making this the basis for childhood faith and childhood teaching wherever there were people who agreed with him.

It would therefore be most agreeable of Professor Clausen and all such protesters against the Church's foundation if they would allow our temporal High Priest of the Order of Melchisedek[96] – whom the Lord Himself made pope after His death because in real life he refused to be so – to rest in peace in the open coffin before the altar, since no one can rightfully contend with this true Apostolic successor. But if they really wish to conjure up his shade to bear witness to what his life most vigorously denied, then the Christian Church, which is not built on his[97] word, must let it happen and can only encourage its learned members to honour in love the evangelical Moses[98] with a heroic struggle for his body!

We must of necessity admit that all the reformers saw errors in the *original* shape of the Christian Church and, knowingly or unknowingly, they laid the groundwork for the new exegetical papacy under which the entire Christian Congregation now sighs. All Christian scholars must unite to destroy it completely, since we have reached the point where even the youngest professor at our university, like the most senior one, *summus Theologus*, wishes to be the Church's exegetical pope! At their command the historical Christian Church must be destroyed and a new one built of nothing but second-rate theological books and exegetical copy-books protesting against one another. The Christian Church is to confess it believes unanimously in these self-constructed castles-in-the-air – but it is not sure what they are!

Nonetheless, in honour of the truth we must admit our own error, which, on our exodus from the darkness of the papacy and from our spiritual Egypt, was so excus-

---

94. Philip Melancthon (1497-1560) collaborated with Luther in moulding the Protestant Reformation, and is seen as its intellectual leader as well as the first systematic theologian.

95. Luther's *Small Catechism* was published in 1529.

96. Gen 14:18-19: "Then Melchizedek king of Salem brought out bread and wine. He was priest of God Most High, and he blessed Abram." Cf. Heb 5:10: "You are a priest for ever in the order of Melchizedek." And Heb 7, according to which Jesus is made King of Righteousness and King of Peace after His death. Luther taught that Melchizedek was a historical figure who was an archetype of Christ. In this sentence the reference is to Peter.

97. i.e. Peter's.

98. Again, Peter.

able. Then, in the light of history which only the children of darkness scorn, we must separate Martin Luther from those who refuse to agree with him and claim that with him and those who faithfully followed him the error was fundamentally insignificant and ended in a mere formality. For when our Church built on the evangelical history and the Creed which the Apostles themselves as members of the Church confess to in their writings, then it was building indubitably on the Apostles' Creed and interpreting the words of Scripture for our teaching accordingly. Their error was merely that the authenticity of the New Testament does not prove *itself* but is proved only through the Church's open testimony, which is therefore the only true and defensible groundwork.

This was not so easy to make out in the early dawn, and at a time when on the basis of the loosest rumours everything which passed itself off as such was assumed to be 'Apostolic'. It was not easy for believing Christians to accept that with a modicum of approbation the authenticity of the Apostolic Writings was called into question, for they rested on such clear and extremely credible historical testimony. Here we can see the difference between Luther's and Clausen's attitude to Scripture as the only source of knowledge and rule of faith: Luther assumed that the New Testament was genuine, the text safe, and the words ascribed to the Son and the Holy Spirit a genuine and harmonious Word of God; in his historical acceptance he found a sure rule with which to interpret the dogmatic material. Clausen on the other hand claims that the authenticity of the book is doubtful, the text unsafe, the evangelical story totally unreliable, the calling of Paul the Apostle invalid, and all the Apostles' testimony that they were speaking the words of God and Jesus false or spurious; he also finds nothing of the Word of God in the New Testament and no rule of interpretation for what he does find. The difference is undoubtedly that with the greatest honesty Luther complied with the Scripture's Spirit and Word, and that Clausen, to put it mildly, plays the rashest and most inexcusable of tricks with Scripture as a vapid source of knowledge and a completely invalid and indeterminate rule of faith. With these words I hope to have made such a clear distinction between Luther's and Clausen's faith in the Bible and interpretation of Scripture that not even the youngest student will be able to confuse the two; for they are far more irreconcilable than fire and water! ...

2. On Godly Assemblies (1825)

Introduction by Brian Degn Mårtensson

In 1825, with Denmark still an absolute monarchy, the question of religious freedom and tolerance became ever more relevant with the rise of revivalist movements holding 'godly assemblies' and the growing number of lay preachers speaking at them. Grundtvig's distaste for this phenomenon found expression in his attack on the so-called 'Kerteminde sect' on Funen, started by Rasmus Klink around 1800 and at first a private undertaking without greater ambition. However, under the leadership of smallholder Christen Madsen the movement spread to other parishes, including Ellinge, where there was soon a conflict between the temporal and spiritual authorities which ended with Madsen and a number of other leaders being jailed and fined.

In this article, published in *Latest Picture of Copenhagen* (Nyeste Skilderie af Kjøbenhavn) on 8th and 12th February 1825, Grundtvig also referred specifically to the Haugian movements in Norway, where in 1795 lay preacher Hans Nielsen Hauge had started the biggest revivalist movement in the country's history.[99] His speeches and letters were disseminated throughout the land and helped to reduce illiteracy significantly. His infringement of assembly laws and his attack on the clergy landed him in prison in 1804, but subsequent legal proceedings, ending in 1814, found him not guilty on most charges and sentenced him to a fine. Although Hauge was a broken man after spending much of those 10 years in prison, his movement also gained ground in Denmark, the other half of the joint kingdom of Denmark-Norway until it split in 1814.

As Grundtvig affirms, the times were conducive to revivalist movements throughout Western Europe, deriving, as with pietism, from a greater emphasis on 'authentic' personal faith – bordering on fervency! The tendency can rightfully be seen in relation to the preoccupation of the Romantic Movement with an inner, emotional life, but it must also be regarded – as in the case of the Quakers – as a result of the cultural interaction between Europe and the rest of the world

---

99. Hans Nielsen Hauge (1771-1824) led a revival of pietism in Norway and was influential in the country's early industrialisation. He travelled throughout most of Norway and parts of Denmark holding revival meetings, often after church services, and openly flouting the Conventicle Decree of 1741 which prohibited any religious meetings not authorised by the state church and held under the supervision of a state-approved pastor. Like Luther, Hauge advocated a priesthood of all believers. He was imprisoned 14 times between 1794 and 1811, after which he became an influential industrialist, setting up factories and mills and advocating for the common people.

Grundtvig's tone is at first cautious as he seeks to discuss the question more generally. He gives the revivalist movement credit for its 'awakening' of the people, but he ends by calling the godly assemblies 'surrogates' and by advocating a combined Lutheran and liberal attitude in which the individual forges the link to God rather than being browbeaten into doing so by the state or by religious 'scribes'. The most *they* can do is to encourage and inspire. In this matter he took the same line as Kierkegaard, who set great store by the inherent, liberal consequences of Lutheranism. Grundtvig emphasises that the assemblies represent a movement 'of the people' and of the common man's self-assumed right to gather with his fellow-minded brothers for spiritual edification.

* * *

It is common knowledge that in recent times round and about on Funen the common people have expressed a desire for 'godly assemblies' outside the Church. Several pastors have complained about this to the temporal authorities and have taken a number of their parishioners to court. That such a thing could happen would always be a matter of sadness for me, but now I feel the sadness more intensely and the call more deeply to plead the cause of conscience and love, after having read the extract of the court records. In these a number of people in Ellinge[100] parish were not accused of the least *offensiveness*, but on the contrary were given the most honourable testimonies to their character, partly by the pastor, their accuser! In the most calm and decent way, they had gathered a few times for their mutual edification, but after a complaint from the pastor they received a prohibition from the police against their meeting. Since they believed, and not without some justification, that the basis of the complaint was their negligence in regard to the regulations laid down in the statutory decree of 1741, they had approached their pastor and asked him to be present at their meetings. Whether or not he really did strengthen them in their resolution and, as they claim, made a promise to come to their gatherings, the court could not decide from lack of valid evidence, but it did consider it perfectly reasonable that with his ambiguous words he had given them cause to believe this to be so. Nonetheless, those who had attended the gatherings were charged, and since it was only with violating a statutory ordinance, the court decided not to instigate an investigation into the *true* nature of the religious devotions but considered itself entitled to declare the charged to be adherents of the fanatical 'Kerteminde sect' etc.

The higher courts, before whom the case is to appear, must decide to what extent the behaviour of the pastor and the court is lawful, and I shall govern all remarks

---

100. The parish of Ellinge is in the deanery of Kerteminde on East Funen.

that are pressing upon me in order not to damage, through my personality perhaps, the case whose spokesman I am. Being assured that our paternal government wishes to see the difficult question of the godly assemblies discussed impartially as regards their civic relations I shall here, as an honest Danish subject, contribute my mite and nothing else.

There can be justified disagreement on the extent to which the basic principle of mitigation in our Criminal Law deserves to be invoked here. But just as it is undeniable that in our day the mildest view has found the greatest acceptance, it goes without saying that the Criminal Law should not be invoked more stringently unless it is absolutely imperative. The 1741 ordinance clearly has no intention of placing obstacles in the path of godly assemblies but on the contrary seeks to remove them by as far as possible preventing disorder and taking away from our pastors all justified grounds for complaint. This being so, the question is whether the common good in this case requires a greater legal stringency whereby these godly assemblies outside the Church, simply by their *existence*, are deemed to be criminal acts which, if they cannot be prevented by the threat of the law, must be seriously punished.

In answering such a question in an age that has held tolerance, even at times boundless tolerance, as its watchword, I find myself in a state of some embarrassment. I am easily tempted without further ado to answer firmly No, and merely appeal to the universally recognised truth that what one believes and where one seeks to practise one's self-improvement is something that one owes solely to God and one's own conscience. So it is down to the question of whether, under the pretext of a specific faith or specific devotions, people have committed a *crime* or disturbed the public *order*. However, it is unacceptable to take the question so lightly. For on the one hand the state has never 'acknowledged' tolerance to such an extent, and on the other hand experience teaches us that even the keenest advocate of tolerance often claims, in a peculiar contradiction, that the state ought to tolerate the most blatant *lack* of faith and the scorn for all forms of self-improvement, not least scorn for expressing a faith or performing a devotion that is considered incorrect or exaggerated.

We are best served here by choosing the longest path and by beginning with the question: If the state regarded the godly assemblies as damaging, could it reasonably, through the Criminal Law, make them less frequent and less damaging? If, as I believe, this question should be answered in the negative, then the authorities must realise that it is no use counting up all the damage that may be caused if it is impossible to *prevent* such assemblies. They should instead sharpen their attention on making such matters as tolerable as possible. If we turn for an answer to *experience*, which alone can teach us what is reasonable, then we know that from the earliest days of Christianity and until the Haugian movement in Norway, every attempt by the temporal authorities to suppress by force the manifestations of a burgeoning religious element has not only been futile but has clearly contributed to strengthening and spreading it. This of course does the greatest damage to the state when it sets itself up in *opposition* to the faith that always moves mountains! I really do believe that if the authorities were as seriously convinced of the damaging effect of gatherings outside the church as they are of tavern-going, drinking, gaming and wild living, then they should answer the church zealots as they answer the moral ones: "If you can change our citizens for the better, we would highly appreciate it: to work for this is your call and your duty. But we have to take people as we find them, allow the stone to lie that we cannot lift, and not waste the state's energy on moving it." That, I believe, is how the wisdom of the authorities must disarm the alarmists, even if it regarded the penchant for godly assemblies to be as great a plague as the prevailing desire for passing the time corrupting oneself in taverns and dives. Indeed, if it were possible – though no one would argue the case – that the *godly* assemblies might be even more abominable to the rational authorities than the most *ungodly* ones, wisdom would dissuade them from declaring open warfare on an element which, whatever it consisted of, clearly proved that it was among the most powerful that was fermenting in human society. In an age of great impropriety and among the most wanton circles even a Napoleon must admit his impotence to oppress the movements of such an element!

However, even though I believe that this observation should be sufficient to show that a state ought much rather to soften than sharpen its legislation with regard to the godly assemblies, I cannot and will not refrain from regarding the case from the other side and asking the question: "How should statecraft have advised the authorities, who believed that the godly assemblies could be restricted by the Criminal Law?" Whether I regard the question in general or in these particular circumstances, I cannot help but think that an authority gifted with statecraft, far from hating and fearing, should be appreciating and congratulating itself on all the godly assemblies which can justifiably be called precisely that throughout the whole of Christendom.

Perhaps universally there will be less agreement with me than there must be concerning my first statement, but agreement is not necessary, since in politics the first principle (of leave well alone) must carry the day. I venture to hope that having listened to me just as calmly as I am speaking, the local authorities will not call my opinion 'unjustified'. I believe that they are best advised to regard every godly assembly that they themselves have not called to be a social recreation in which a section of the people seek encouragement and refreshment, as others do in play-going, card-playing, string-plucking, feasting or whatever else the children of humankind can delight in by sharing one another's company.

Without going any further into these forms of recreation, I venture to claim that in their general development none of them offers the state less risk and more gain than gatherings whose purpose is mutual self-improvement! No one can deny that they can also bring about disorder and even, when a spirit smites them, give rise to criminal acts; nor can it be otherwise, since everything in the world depends on how it is used. But would anyone seriously argue that even the most decent of recreations cannot in general happen without some form of disorder – without there being bad natures causing evil thoughts and intentions? Should we not admit that of all social gatherings the godly assemblies give rise to the *least* wickedness? And what does experience teach us, the great and the small experience, the daily and the historical? Does it not say: "It is a serious question whether the majority of those who place their happiness in godly assemblies become better *people* thereby, but there is no question that at least for a time they become better *citizens*! Do they not give back to the state part of the energy that is otherwise wasted away in noisy joys and common delights? Their earnestness and outward modesty, their disgust with the wild world's being, and their ongoing concern for transcendental objects – these are the distinctive features of people who are mockingly called 'the Holy Joes'. Such features are found not only in the best people at their gatherings but probably even more so among the worst. All are a benefit to the state, which thereby has far fewer criminals and far more decent, hard-working, useful citizens. Imagine, for instance, what the Quakers have meant, and to some extent still mean, to England and North America, or take stock of the approval that the Haugians in Norway acquired from friend and foe alike as soon as there was sufficient peace and calm to discuss their cause impartially. Then judge whether my claim is not substantiated that even if the state thought it *possible* to suppress the godly assemblies by force, it should never consider it *wise* to do so."

So much for the general, now for the particular circumstance. It goes without saying that what is impossible and unwise in the general sense is the same in the particular. Circumstances can contribute so much to hindering or facilitating insight into the handling of matters of state, and I am sure that the present circumstances are qualified to make that claim obvious. When would it be less possible to suppress a religious movement by force than when from top to bottom there was the realisation, clearer than ever before, that so long as faith and all its manifestations are within the legal boundaries of the state, no person must ever seek to decide over others in such circumstances? Fundamentally, is this not a matter of conscience rather than a matter of state? And does it not arise at a time when this right is generally recognised, and, we must add, at a time when, despite prevailing reason, one is far more inclined to hold firm to one's opinion? For this reason alone I cannot imagine when it would ever be *less* wise to use force against the godly assemblies! And when, I must add, did the state ever need them more? Whether the state needs religion as such, it has yet to decide in many places, following its precipitate denial round and about; but all would admit that the state needs equanimity, frugality, obedience, modesty, decency, and what in general we call virtue and good nature. These it cannot *itself* produce; it can only covet these from the Church and legislate for them accordingly.

We live in a time when all those who are wise in matters of state must fear for its debility and internal dissolution, for its lack of honesty and decency, for its pursuit of gain and pleasure at all costs, for its dissatisfaction with the present, and for its desperate contemplation of what the future will bring – which is all too obvious. And we live in a time when there is an awakening of the religious element which alone in the experience of history can create a tolerable balance in human life. When this element is not satisfied, and perhaps not even addressed, by the Church, what else should the state wish for when it has the following choice: either that this powerful and beneficial element should die out again or that it should seek nourishment where it can find it? If the Danish government 100 years ago was so rich in experience as not to oppose the godly assemblies despite them seeming unnecessary or perhaps even dangerous, it should now, being animated by the same paternal mildness, regard them in an even more favourable light. For a living religiosity is so obvious a *need* among us. When the religious element that quickened our forefathers awakes, it can only be to find itself in many places *foreign* to the Church. For better for worse, in joy or in sorrow, it is a fact that in the last century theology – and the extension of theology in serving the Church – has undergone so great a change that whoever professes an old-fashioned Christianity finds it difficult to be edified by the new theology and is easily offended by it. During this time of change the Church has clearly lost almost all its influence over the people, which was all the more necessary since the cold and compulsory book-language that predominated in the Church might just as well have been Latin to the common people. And how can it be otherwise now – when old-fashioned Lutheran Christianity is awaking among the people – than that they must painfully discover what a towering difference there is in both content and form between Luther's sermons and those of nowadays! Out of this and with stringent necessity arises the desire for godly assemblies outside the Church.

As far as I am informed, for an old-fashioned Lutheran Church these godly assemblies on Funen are just such surrogates, where Luther's sermons are mostly what hold the floor. It is not difficult to understand why an unpleasant tension has therefore so easily arisen between a pastor and his parishioners. Nevertheless, the consequences could not have been more damaging to the state than when the pastor, simply by declaring his parishioners to be heretics and fanatics, had them charged and then punished. What must the common people think when they consciously drew on their Christianity, on their edification in the Danish Bible, on the writings of Luther and other famous teachers, and then heard themselves called a 'fanatical sect'? Truly, if in general it is wise to treat the godly assemblies leniently, then I can only deem that in such a case where basic religious principles are at stake and the laws of the state sacrosanct and the assemblies impossible to criticise by law without splitting hairs, there is no question as to which side the temporal authority should take, once the case has been impartially presented and properly illuminated. This, however, is extremely difficult in an age when learned theologians have washed their hands of old-fashioned Lutheran Christianity and its devotions to such an extent that they themselves, let alone the majority of their disciples, would not recognise it again! That is why they are quick to call it a dangerous fanaticism for the state, when it is no more than a glimmer of what our forefathers and Luther called 'Christian faith and common sense'. The state has experienced its beneficial effects so often over the centuries that it cannot consider this faith 'dangerous'!

In all fairness we cannot expect or request our county prefects or our county judges to understand better than our pastors how to distinguish established Danish Christianity from fanaticism. That is why it can easily come about that the government constantly hears only one side of the story, and partly because of its own involvement in the case and partly because of its lack of genuine knowledge about Church history can only regard the godly assemblies in an unfair light. This is the observation that has moved me to pick up my pen over the case, and with all possible impartiality to present it in its true context. I wish to do so publicly so that others can add to what is missing here and protest against what they consider incorrect. In this, if in anything, it is for me solely a question of what is right, what is wisest, what it is best to do. For in this matter I am defending something that at heart I do not appreciate at all. It is just that as a human being I want to see lenient treatment, and as a historian I wish to recommend this to the favourable attention of the state.

Whether I am serious in saying that I do not appreciate the godly assemblies that the common people are setting up for the purpose of mutual self-improvement is immaterial for the state, since it is not my opinion but my *reasoning* that must be considered. However, anyone who has read my writings on history will hardly doubt that in my honest view such godly assemblies are only poor surrogates for Church life, and no more than feeble nurseries for true piety, humility, and love. Church history has taught me that a certain sickly pietism at such gatherings can so easily be paired with warped ideas, scorn for the teaching profession, and ultimately for Scripture itself. I have therefore never recommended them but rather have deplored them; indeed, in the years when I as a pastor was *outside* the Church I have with exaggerated anxiety perhaps even shunned everything that has the slightest such appearance. But the question here is not what we regard as serving the growth and preservation of true Christianity, where each of us must judge according to our faith and intellect. The question is only how we as educated servants of the state who best know the religious element should advise the state to act when the desire for such godly assemblies expresses itself. Should we advise it to apply the sword or to sit back and wait? I counsel the latter, in the full conviction, based on human history, that it is a counsel that no state would ever regret following. If there are any with equal conviction of the opposite, let them counsel it as openly and cheerfully as I have done. But do not believe that anything is proved by larding one's speech with empty phrases and abusive words, with obscurantism, fanaticism, 'the terrible monster', and such-like. This is not a question of where true, enlightened Christianity is to be found – an inquiry that following Danish law would hardly be pleasant for all our pastors. This is solely a question of what is wisest for the state: to pour oil on the wound or throw it into the fire?

It will doubtless be objected: Is not fanaticism also a dangerous and terrible thing which the temporal authority ought to combat most seriously and seek to prevent without asking what is the point?

To this I must answer that it is a great mischief when specialist words change their meaning in the course of time and creep into our legal language; and that is unfortunately the case with the word 'fanaticism'. Whatever constitutes murder, theft, fraud, and the like, we know what they *are*. But 'fanaticism' can be endlessly disputed because unfortunately it is a specialist word that has no specific meaning and can therefore be used in many different senses. There is nothing that can reasonably be done about this except to exchange the word for another one in the law which, like murder and theft, has a fixed definition, or to examine what the word meant when it was put into the law and what it means when it is used in the sense of a civil offence. If on the historical path we now examine what has been called 'fanaticism' (borrowed from *fanum*, meaning 'temple of idols'), we find that it was first used to denote the fury of the rabble of heathen priests who sought with fire and sword to eradicate the Christians, because the growth of Christianity emptied the tables and decreased the sacrifices. Since then the teachings of Muhammed have also been called 'fanatical' because they were to be spread by the sword, while during the Reformation they called 'fanatic' those who contrary to Scripture disregarded the temporal authority and under pretence of divine inspiration claimed the right to turn civil order upside down as they pleased. In its latest sense the word has naturally acquired legal significance and it is a superfluous question to ask whether the state should 'tolerate' fanaticism. For obviously the state cannot tolerate what the *law* calls fanaticism, since it is an evil or a madness which under the appearance of holiness preaches rebellion. In law fanaticism does not denote a particular kind of godly direction that the state regards as punishable, but all unruly excess against civil order, all disturbing political directing of the religious element.

On the other hand, during and after the pietistic ferment of the previous century it became increasingly common to call every excess of the religious element that expressed itself with any perceptible power 'fanaticism', so its meaning became *wild, obdurate* passion whether or not its direction was political, in fact without the slightest question of whether the civil order was thereby threatened or fortified. In a time that more or less agreed on religious sobriety it would have made no appreciable difference, even though it is always a dangerous matter to expand legal expressions into the indefinite. But in an age such as we have experienced, it could only have the saddest consequences when interpreters of the law understand 'fanaticism' as everything that the ruling party in language matters decides to call such, or to stamp with the name of wild, obdurate, dangerous passion. For then the state is in danger of lending an arm to what was no better than the persecution of heretics in the past, and indeed could end up punishing as so-called 'fanatics' those who in a political sense were the most calm and most sober in their expression of the faith, as well as the devoutness its own laws praised and most strongly recommended. For in the nature of the case, as soon as we no longer regard its political direction as being characteristic of fanaticism but include wild, obdurate, religious passion, then the word no longer has a specific meaning and no longer designates something that can be the object of legal inquiry. Instead it becomes something that only has theological and philosophical reality, and it can therefore as little be defined, acknowledged, and distinguished legally as what we have otherwise called 'heresy' and 'infatuation'. These words continually change the object according to a way of thought, faith or lack of faith, wisdom or stupidity of those who use them, since everyone naturally calls something 'heresy' if it clearly conflicts with his own faith, and 'infatuation' if it surpasses his thinking without rhyme or reason. If the time came – and it did – when it became the linguistic fashion to call practically everything intangible 'infatuation', then all old-fashioned Christian 'superstition', all zeal in its preaching an 'infallible Word of God', and all powerful expression of the belief that Christ is spiritually with His Church in its preaching until the end of the world, together with the conviction that it matters not whether human beings gain the whole world if they damage their souls in the process – if there came a time when all this was called 'fanaticism', and was not only called it then but is to this day by so many, what would the consequence be if the legal definitions of fanaticism were more or less what at any one moment is deemed to be so? For then the state would begin to contradict *itself*, and would be forbidding and punishing the expression of what its own laws enjoined and recommended!

Clearly the state must either uphold the Catholic principle of allowing its priests and bishops to determine what is called 'fanaticism' and is punished as such – whereby the foundation is laid for a new hierarchy with all its persecution of heretics and other horrors – or it must hold firm to the Protestant principle that whatever terms of abuse the religious parties use against each other, 'fanaticism' in the eyes of the state (and without asking the advice of bishops and priests) is defined as being *politically* in conflict with the Word of God! So I say loud and clear: If pastors want the temporal arm to form the faith and devotion of their parishioners according to the pastors themselves, and when they shout 'fanaticism' without being able to show any politically dangerous direction, then at heart they are papists, however solemnly they protest against the name. The authority that is wise in statecraft will surely be deaf to their complaints!

4. The Lutheran Service

'The Lutheran Service' was painted by Johan Lund in 1843 and hangs in the Hall of the Ministers of State (*Statsrådsalen*) in the Danish Parliament in Copenhagen. It is one of a series of five depicting the history of religion in Denmark. Set in the 17th century, the painting depicts many of the elements associated with the Lutheran service, including the two sacraments: a baptismal font in the bottom left corner and the taking of Holy Communion (both bread and wine). Also present are a wedding couple with their pastor, as well as a boys' choir with their conductor to illustrate the importance of hymnsinging in the Lutheran service. Photo: Petra Theibel Jacobsen.

3. Should the Lutheran Reformation Really Be Continued? (1830)

Introduction by Steen Tullberg

Should the Lutheran Reformation Really Be Continued? was written after Grundtvig's second trip to England, from June to September 1830. His stay there clearly influenced his writing, as did the violent disturbances on the European mainland that he witnessed from England that summer – the July Revolution in France, and the subsequent unrest in Brussels, Braunschweig, Saxony, Hesse, and Hamburg. The work was first published in J.C. Lindberg's *Monthly Journal of Christendom and History* from December 1830 to April 1831, and saw Grundtvig return to the subject of church politics following the lifelong censorship imposed upon him after losing a libel case in 1825 to Professor H.N. Clausen (1793-1877).[101] It was also coloured by his 'matchless discovery' that year that the *original faith* is to be found in the Creed and in the institution of the sacraments of Baptism and Holy Communion. These are *independent* of the State Church, so it should therefore be possible for people to secede from it and form independent congregations.

Grundtvig begins by arguing that if the Reformation is to continue, it is essential to identify the unchanging 'core faith' of the Church and to cut out all that is extraneous to it. He limits his study of the Lutheran Reformation to the Church itself and to its relation to the State and the School (i.e. University Theology), from which the three text excerpts below are taken.

In the first section on the Church, Grundtvig defends Luther against what he considered the creeping contemporary rationalism typified by Clausen. He contends that Luther, far from wishing to restructure the Church, sought only to *re-form* it back to its original state. He therefore purified it of all that contradicted the primal Spirit of Christianity and all that was hindering its spiritual growth. Grundtvig wants Luther's process of purification to be continued, and he criticises pontificating theologians and self-satisfied 'modern' pastors who threaten the 'old-fashioned' Christians – amongst whom he wished to be counted. He therefore takes a tough line: he and his kind can no longer share the Church with those who refuse to acknowledge the confession of the Creed as the condition for acceptance into the Universal Church.

---

101. See Texts 1 & 4. The censorship was lifted in 1837.

In the second excerpt Grundtvig argues that the Church's close relation to the State must be *severed*, since that was their original situation. Such a separation will primarily allow for 'freedom of conscience', which Grundtvig equated with 'freedom of faith' and 'freedom of worship'. The Roman Church under Emperor Constantine I (c.280-337) became a 'matter of state', and in the Middle Ages the state became a *church* matter, with the reformers endeavouring to establish a link between church and state that guaranteed the freedom and stability of both. In the event, most of the individual reformed churches became Protestant *national* churches, where the prince again made himself lord of the faith and no citizen was exempt from church membership and attendance. Only in England had the Anglican Church allowed for secession from the episcopal church and the establishment of free, *non-conformist* churches – a move which Grundtvig admired and advocated.

In the third excerpt Grundtvig discusses the relation between faith and theology, with both praise and criticism of Luther from a historical perspective. He praises Luther for translating the Bible into the mother-tongue of the German people, for enlightening them about the unchanging Christian faith, and for safeguarding the Church against the Pope's fallacies. But the great reformer also made mistakes, which Grundtvig largely attributes to his historical situation; at the time, Luther had to stand firm on Scripture alone (*sola scriptura*) as the basis of faith and doctrine in order to protect true Christianity. While Grundtvig agrees with Luther's second principle that faith is central to Christianity (*sola fide*), he takes the Creed and the twin sacraments of Baptism and Holy Communion rather than Scripture as the rule of this faith.

Grundtvig summarises his criticism in four points: 1) Luther underestimated the *oral* tradition and made no exception here for the two Sacraments and the Creed; 2) Luther did not accept that a tradition had been handed down that was *irrespective* of Scripture; 3) Luther overlooked the witness of Church *history* if it did not tally with Scripture; and 4) Luther made the Augsburg Confession an article of faith. Against these Grundtvig argues that 1) The oral Creed at Baptism is independent of "all Scripture"; 2) This Creed is the condition of membership of the Church of Christ and is itself the rule of faith; 3) Together with the other Words of Institution at Holy Communion this Creed is the fundamental principle for all interpretation of the Bible; 4) The Bible cannot be a rule of faith; 5) A sharp distinction must be drawn between what all Christians *must* believe and what each is *free* to believe; and 6) Theology should enjoy greater freedom than Luther would allow, without it having the least dominion over faith.

Grundtvig defends his view that the oral tradition, handed down by Jesus personally in the institution of Baptism and Holy Communion, is the lifeblood of the faith. Even though the Bible is the greatest book in the world, it cannot grant either the forgiveness of sins or the life everlasting. Neither the Confessional Books,[102] such as the Augsburg Confession, nor any worldly decrees must impose limits on Theology, which should enjoy a total freedom within the boundaries that Baptism sets. Theology exists not just for the Church but also for enlightenment in general. It must keep abreast of the times and of all learning concerning Man, society, or the world at large. Therefore the Lutheran Reformation must *certainly* be continued – for the sake of the Church, the State, the School – and also for Grundtvig personally: "The Lord is my witness when I say that I honour and love Martin Luther, and that I wish him to be honoured and loved by my children."

***

Extract I

I. On the Lutheran Reformation in the Christian Church Itself

... In my eyes it is as clear as sunlight that Martin Luther was an unrivalled Church reformer, by the grace of God. For he realised that what the Christian Church lacked was in no way a new faith or anything new of any kind, but only life and light in the *ancient* faith and organisation; and he was found to be just as capable as he was willing to redress this need. The Lord has not built His Church from dead stones but from living ones; nor does it need 'building extensions', which always turn into dens of robbers! Nonetheless, over time His Church had become almost stone-dead, and the spark of life that remained was misused in order to produce incense on the altars of idols – until Martin Luther arrived! Then it was as though one man had awakened spiritually from his torpor, had risen from the dead, and had let Christ shine for him. He was given the great commission – which he so faithfully carried out – to waken the sleeping, raise the dead, and teach them to see light in the *Lord's* light, to live on the bread that came down from *heaven*, and to take the chalice of salvation from the hand of Him who is the *source* of light. Such a reformation is a revitalisation, like life from death, and clearly something that can only take place in Christ's Church. This is without doubt what befell Martin Luther, and it is equally certain that in him the Apostles again began to speak of God's wondrous deeds with the voices of the nations. With Luther's hymns the churches again began to praise the Lord in their native language, where they best could express themselves with spirit. With Luther, Holy Scripture again became the Christian textbook for the Lord's people, as it had once been determined. And from Luther's time the faithful who followed him began a new way of life, perhaps not so pure and powerful as in

---

102. For the Confessional Books of the Evangelical Lutheran Church in Denmark, see note 62.

the days of old, but nevertheless recognisably purified, active, pleasing, and fruitful in Christian enlightenment.

This, then, was 'the Lutheran Reformation'; and if we ask whether it should be continued, we as Christians must answer immediately and spontaneously, 'Yes of course!' For life in the Lord's Congregation must not merely be sustained, but must grow in purity and power until it becomes like His own life on earth. The light must not merely be lit but must be transformed from glory to glory,[103] and shine over the whole earth. The more we consider the matter, the clearer it becomes how much we need a *continuation* of the Lutheran Reformation in the strictest sense, for Christian life in human eyes has never been closer to extinction, or the Christian light closer to being snuffed out by itself, than at the end of the 18th century. Whether or not in the 19th century something really *is* alive and flaring up, as we think to be the case, something that can lay claim to the great and honourable name of 'the light and life of the Lord', only time will tell. What I do know is that the Christian hope which lives in *me* has risen like a corpse from the bier. The light that gladdens my eye, even when I look away to the inevitable Valley of the Shadow of Death, has risen for me like a setting sun from the bosom of the sea. I also know for certain that – call it what one will and laugh at it as loudly as one may – I have in the Church of Our Saviour[104] made Joshua's words my own: "You can serve whichever other gods you like, I and my household, we will serve the Lord."[105] This Lord was conceived by the Holy Spirit and born of the Virgin Mary, and we will serve Him as our Christian fathers did, as Martin Luther and Ansgar,[106] Augustine and Irenaeus, Paul and John did. In short, when the heavens shine with His Father's glory and He is seen to be coming again to judge the quick and the dead we will serve like the old disciple who shall not die but shall gladly sing: 'Come, Lord Jesus!'

This is certainly true, and we have not forgotten it. Nor do we hide the fact that Luther held a 'clean-sweep' festival in the Church! What is more, even though we cannot approve of everything that happened as a result, least of all the yelling at the tops of their voices by the Church masses, we nevertheless realise that a clean sweep of the old leaven was necessary before we could properly hold Easter, the Festival of Resurrection for which we shall forever thank our Lord. On the other hand, we cannot possibly persuade ourselves to regard the clean sweep by the self-styled and

---

103. 2 Cor 3:18.

104. From 1822-26 Grundtvig was pastor at the Church of Our Saviour (*Vor Frelsers Kirke*) in Copenhagen.

105. Jos 24:15.

106. The Benedictine monk Ansgar (801-65) is credited with bringing Christianity from Bremen to both Sweden and Denmark and is therefore known as 'the apostle of the North'. He is also credited with building the first Danish church in Hedeby.

newly-fledged Reformers as being the *main* achievement of the Reformation, since in the nature of things this is in clear conflict with our common sense.

For if the arch-*Catholics* were right to regard the Christian Church as a great stone chamber which as a matter of course christianised and sanctified everything that entered it by permission of its self-styled doorman (the Pope), then the arch-*Protestants* were also right to regard the clean sweep as being their main achievement and themselves as being happy to christianise and sanctify everything that they wished by introducing it to their clean-swept, well-aired, empty, and capacious stone chamber. However, since the arch-Catholics are clearly in the wrong, so no less of course are the arch-Protestants! For the Christian Church that we speak of and dispute over is at heart nothing other than a human community or congregation with a specifically defined, wonderful faith, from which emerges an incorruptible hope of salvation. So wherever something *real* is the first consideration, reason teaches us that a clean sweep can never be the first reality but takes all its value from that first consideration, which of course must not be swept out completely but must in the course of the sweeping find room, become visible, and take effect without hindrance.

Extract 2

II. On the Lutheran Reformation in the Church's Relation to the State

When we speak about the 'Reformation', it is doubly necessary to say clearly what we mean by it, partly because it is a spiritual matter that has nothing visible or tangible corresponding to the actual *word*, and partly because 'reformation' is a foreign word which is in daily use among people and has therefore not acquired a fixed meaning. On the contrary, it has been as much misused by book-writers as any word that has the misfortune to fall into their claws and be left to its fate! In fact we have reached the position these days where, if we hear a person talking about 'reforming', the word tells us nothing about their *intention* except that they want a *change*. Everyone who wishes to 'reform' claims that they want *improvement*, but that does not lift the veil at all, since we all know that improvements are a very good idea but that the word is quite indeterminate. It only means something when we hear what it is that *needs* to be improved, and then what is the *nature* of that improvement. Not everything that is called 'improvement' is by any means so – as Europe has painfully discovered – and will doubtless continue to do so. It therefore came as no surprise that the indignation aroused by the self-styled 'reformers' eventually gave rise to a prejudice among many against all 'reformation' as being no more than a cloak for whoever wishes to turn the established order upside-down. Since the word 'reformation' cannot be dismissed, for it expresses a real and important event in the history of Christianity, we are forced to buy clarity at the cost of brevity and note that whatever one is pleased to call 'reformation' is derived from a Latin word meaning a renewal or a rebirth of an originally given relation or arrangement; it was in this sense that it was used by Martin Luther and his first disciples. Thus, in the history of the Church and the State the Lutheran Reformation can never mean anything but Luther's attempt to bring the Christian Church back to its *original* nature in every respect.

Before we can speak clearly about whether the Lutheran Reformation in the Church's relation to the State should be continued or not, we must first know what that relation was *originally*, what *changes* it had undergone, and to what extent Luther succeeding in *renewing* it. For it is only then that we can distinguish which side the Church should take in this matter and embrace whatever outcome is given to it by the Church's invisible head, the almighty King of God's Heaven.

Fortunately it is well known and cannot be contradicted without obvious stupidity that, as a faith community that merely occupied itself with spirit and eternity, the Christian Church was originally completely separate from the temporal state, though far from taking up a hostile position towards it; for wherever the Church spread, it gave birth to a litter of heavenly citizens which the temporal state had to congratulate itself on as models of subservience and mildness, honesty and decency, and all civil virtue. Unbelievers nowadays are therefore in complete agreement with us that from the point of view of the Roman authorities, the cruel persecutions which the Christian Church had to endure in its earliest days were as unwise as they were unjust. For even if we can neither acquit the first Christians of being over-zealous nor approve of the obduracy with which they who worshipped a human being as God resisted everything that otherwise tasted of Roman idol worship and emperor deification, conscience, as they say, is still not something that can be forced. Moreover, virtuous conduct is so advantageous for a state that only foolish or callous tyrants would rage against peaceful, upright subjects who apart from a few whims that harmed nobody were the best citizens in the state.

It is equally well known that although in those days the Church not only had to maintain and help itself but in most cases was fighting the temporal authority and the state religion priesthood, as well as the general public, nevertheless its history over the first three hundred years is very much its highest badge of honour. So it was not easy to understand how the Church could acquire a relationship with the temporal organisation of the state that was even more serviceable to it.

Nonetheless, relations did change when the Roman emperor Constantine[107] declared himself the protector of the Christian Church. What it would gain from this could also be predicted, for even before he was baptised, the emperor claimed the front seat at the great Council of Nicaea, where the question under discussion was who could be regarded as Christian believers and who as heretics. It was no surprise that the heathen emperor was not thinking of the Christian Confession of faith at Baptism! Being unbaptised, he may not even have known of it, much less possessed the spirit to gain an ardent understanding and a suitable appreciation of it. All he had to constitute the main question was what he had acquired from conversations with individual bishops and his reading of the Bible.[108] Here we can immediately identify a major reason why Christianity does not sit well as a state religion, for the head of any state is used to decreeing laws, and if he considers himself head of the Christian Church he is time and again tempted to *decree* what Christians should believe, which is fundamentally unacceptable. The first step may have seemed tolerable, since the memory was still fresh of what all Christians *had* believed and the emperor had no wish to decree a new faith but only to clarify further how the faith should be understood. But once the emperors joined in the writing of creeds, they sometimes wished to go further, and it was already a great shame that anyone should be *excluded* from the Church despite having the Christian faith. Exclusion became a matter of state that had civil consequences, and of course punishment followed. In this way the Church Community lost a great share of its freedom and purity, since in order to avoid punishment or the loss of the emperor's favour with all its civil consequences, many who had turned their backs on the Church naturally preferred to feign their faith or ensure that it was changed to the emperor's liking. This happened already in the time of Constantine and became patent under his son Constantius,[109] who commanded that the Arians should be counted as true believers.[110]

---

107. Emperor Constantine I (272-337) converted to Christianity and built the Church of the Holy Sepulchre in Jerusalem over the cave where Jesus is said to have been buried and resurrected. To rule his eastern empire Constantine also built the city of Byzantium, which remained the eastern capital until 1453. From 450 the city was also known as Constantinople, and even before 1453 it was known in Turkish as Istanbul.

108. The First Council of Nicaea was a council of Christian bishops convened by Constantine I in 325 in Nicaea, now Iznik in north-east Turkey. All 1,800 bishops were invited (c.1,000 in the east and 800 in the west), but only some 300 (with their priests and deacons) attended, despite free travel and lodging. The total number of attendees could have been up to 2,000. It was presided over by Bishop Hosius of Corduba. Constantine himself was not baptised until some 11 or 12 years after the council, delaying his Baptism so as to be absolved from as much sin as possible in the belief that in Baptism all sin is forgiven fully and completely.

109. Emperor Constantius II (337-361).

110. Arius (c.250-336), from whom the term 'Arian' derives, was a Christian theologian in Alexandria who opposed the nature of the Trinity and argued that Christ did not *always* exist, but was created by God the Father (see Jn 14:28 – 'the Father is greater than I'). The Council of Nicaea in 325 deemed this a heresy, and this was confirmed by the Council of Constantinople in 381.

After the time of Julian[III] matters took a turn for the worse, as the emperors forced their heathen subjects to be baptised and thus filled the state church with unbelievers. They must have regarded the church either as a prison which they longed to see demolished or an institution which they had to work towards transforming into a temple for idols where no questions were asked about faith, hope, and love but only about ceremonies and external functions.

The latter, as we know, was very successful, but if we are scandalized by the worship of saints and the cultivation of images, by Purgatory and all the idolatry that poured in, we should not forget that it was all naturally and necessarily linked to making Christianity the state religion in the ancient Roman sense and to making Christianity compulsory in the Roman kingdom. So the only surprise is that the Christian faith did not go *under* in all that idolatry and superstition. This would doubtless have happened in the east if the Christian Church had not acquired a new external enemy who returned its share of its spiritual freedom – and that was the Muhammedans. For wherever *they* gained power, Christianity ceased to be the state religion and no one was forced into the Church any longer. Some were actually enticed out of it and under these otherwise unfavourable circumstances, it maintained itself at the same level to which it had sunk under the state compulsion.

This did not last long, however, for we know that it was not in the east that Luther arose. I add for my own part that no Luther *could* have arisen there, where the Baptismal Covenant had been tampered with, and the Spirit thus crippled. It was among the proselytes from *Rome* that the Reformation was hatched and took effect, so it is to Rome that we must now turn our gaze.

The Bishop of Rome, who occupied the only Apostolic throne in the west – in other words the only leader of a Church which the Apostles themselves had founded – had opposed any change to the Baptismal Covenant already through the emperors' guardians of the Church; and fortunately the western empire collapsed so early that the state's compulsion could not bear such sorry fruits. The immigration of heathen peoples and the mission to the heathens, during which the Church again for a period maintained an internal peace and freedom under external hardships, also helped to retain the fundamentally Christian feeling and to delay any degeneration. But misfortune could not fail to materialise, since the church-state relation continued to be conjoined and confused. The heathen-Roman principle of making the Church merely a *state* organisation was rejected, but an Israelite principle was adopted to make the state a *church* organisation. The consequence was the same in church terms except that the fundamentally Christian content of the Church's organisation long remained unchallenged. Wherever Christianity spread and gained the favour of the local govern-

---

III. Emperor Julian II (c.331-63).

ment, those who were *unwilling* were also forced to be baptised. Particularly during the crusades the lesson was learned that entire peoples could be baptised with a sword over their heads, whereby of course Christianity in every way lost and heathenism won.

This is not the place to undertake a study of whether, following the peculiar circumstances of the Middle Ages, the papacy was a civil benefit which, as it degenerated, could only destabilise itself, since it did not derive any support from the temporal ascendancy. Here we are only dealing with the Christian Church, which undoubtedly was always forced to take a deep sigh under the papal yoke.

What we call 'the papal yoke' is of course only what a temporal arm used in order to force Christians to share a church community with the enemies of their faith and to accept changes in the Church which it pleased the Pope and the clergy to introduce. All the excesses and other misfortunes that papal power brought with it were a burden not so much on the Church as on the state, a burden that afflicted everyone whether they were Christian or not.

As we know, long before Luther's time many had loudly complained about this yoke, and it was even thrown off by the Hussites in Bohemia.[112] But in this regard it was not until the 16th century that a new order began, when entire peoples protested against the heavenly vice-regentship which the Pope and the legislative authority in the Church, the clergy, had appropriated to themselves.

This was undoubtedly the prime and essential step towards a reformation of the Church's civil situation, since it first had to argue – against the self-styled vice-regent of the Lord – that the kingdom of Christ was not of *this* world. Only then could the Church Community become a question of freedom. No one should be *coerced* into the Church and no person or rank should set itself up as its lord. However, this reformation was never completed, except in a sense in the North American states; everywhere else, we still find the Church and the State more or less entangled in each other.

Another question is whether the Reformation nonetheless was *completed* as far as was necessary and as the times allowed. And if that were the case, whether a continuation is *necessary* now – or at least whether it is timely. For although the original position of the Christian Church in the world must be the model that we look to, it depends on the circumstances of the Church and the State whether such a total *renewal* should be necessary or even desirable at the present time.

The inalienable *freedom* of the Christian Church lies in its faith not being changed or opposed in the Church Community; in other words no one in the Church sets himself up as master over the faith, or denies or disputes it. For a time this was achieved

---

112. In the early Bohemian Reformation the Hussites followed the teaching of Czech reformer Jan Hus (c.1369-1415) in pursuit of social and religious justice. The Catholic Church convicted Hus of heresy and he was burned at the stake in 1415. To this day he is revered as a national hero in the Czech Republic.

in reality wherever the Lutheran Reformation was implemented and was successful in the best possible way, given the conditions of the time. For only one tyrant, Henry VIII,[113] set himself up as 'head of the Church in England' and claimed mastery over the faith, just like the Roman emperors. When the princes who followed Luther also called themselves 'heads of the Church', they clearly did not mean that they had the right to control the faith of the *people*, but only that of the *clergy as citizens of the state*, as well as to control the external *form* of worship in agreement with the proper use of the Sacraments and the free proclamation of the gospel.

In the Lutheran church parish it was not the princes who *coerced* anyone; it was the preachers who *persuaded* both the people and the princes to agree on a new order of things by which Luther's *Catechism*[114] became the rule for the people's faith, the Augsburg Confession[115] became the rule for the clergy's doctrine, and the inclination of the prince, guided by scholarly advice only, the rule for the rest of the Church. Since Luther's *Catechism* limited itself to the basic Christianity that had carried the Church since the days of the Apostles, and since the Augsburg Confession in no way contradicted but only continued it in further detail, the Christian Church still retained its inalienable *freedom* and was not a state church in the old Roman sense but an Apostolic Church in alliance with the state.

There could not be the least objection to this, for every people that constituted a temporal state was, and continued to be, in agreement on both the foundations of Christianity and the Lutheran view of Scripture. Yet since this was nowhere the actual *case*, the relation carried with it from the very beginning an impairment which in time would come to light and have dangerous consequences for the Christian Church. The more homogeneous the people were that made up the state, the less was the danger and the longer the error could remain unnoticed; and it was undoubtedly a great step forward that Christendom no longer constituted a 'universal state church', nor that the whole of the West constituted a deformed church-state as it did under the papacy. Instead it now comprised, alongside the Papal Church, a number of Protestant *national* churches. The only matter of regret was that the choice between these, and indeed between all the religious denominations that arose at the time of the Reformation, was not allowed to be free everywhere, or at the least in the Protestant

---

113. Wishing to divorce his first wife, Catherine of Aragon, in order to marry Anne Boleyn, Henry VIII asked the Pope for a special dispensation but was refused, since the Catholic Church opposed divorce. He then sought and acquired a divorce from the Archbishop of Canterbury, married Anne in 1533, was excommunicated by Pope Clement VII six weeks later, and made himself 'the only supreme head in [sic] earth of the Church of England' by an Act of Parliament in 1534.

114. Luther's *Small Catechism* was published in 1529.

115. The Augsburg Confession is the primary confession of faith in the Lutheran Church. It was agreed at the Diet (Council) of Augsburg on 25 June 1530 by Lutheran princes and representatives of 'free cities', and comprised 21 Chief Articles of faith and 7 statements concerning abuses of the Christian faith in the Roman Catholic Church.

countries, where they should clearly have granted all the religious freedom that they themselves operated with.

Extract 3

*III. On the Lutheran Reformation in the
Church's Relation to the University*

... Let us now bear in mind that at the beginning of the 16th century Italy was the principal centre of learning. Yet in the obscurity of the Middle Ages under the papal yoke, the Church and its clergy, the spiritual episcopal authority and the temporal episcopal power, the Church's agreed testimony, and the secret news from the monastic cells – in other words the most reliable history and the loosest gossip with the most tangible lies – were all thrown together in a heap. Over this heap the stupid monks made the sign of the cross as though it had all fallen out of the sky. In this situation it would have been the height of injustice to demand of the German reformers that they should not only implement a justifiable *divorce*, but should also locate it clearly and fundamentally in their scholarship! It followed inevitably that even though a German reformer like Martin Luther, through a marvel that can only be explained by the wisdom of the Holy Spirit, built creditably on the immutable foundation of the Church, nonetheless in his polemical treatises against the papacy and all that pertained to it he often went astray in the new heathen-based scholarship with which he had concluded an alliance against the dominant superstition and ignorance.

It is from this viewpoint that we should take stock of the Lutheran Reformation in the Church's relation to university theology. This took the form of the Bible being opened again for the whole Church, for enlightenment in the immutable Christian faith, and as a safeguard against all fairy-tales, pipe dreams, and falsehoods concerning the original Apostolic Christianity.

If we then ask whether the Lutheran Reformation should be continued in *this* regard too, my answer is without the slightest reservation and with the greatest conviction, 'Yes! What else? It should be continued like everything else that has to do with the Christian Church, "from glory to glory", so that we discern more clearly what flows from the immutability of the Christian faith and under what conditions the Bible can serve as the book of Christian enlightenment for which it has self-evidently been granted us.'

As regards 'Theology', we are in the same position with the Lutheran Reformation as we are with the State and the Church, for we not only approve of it in its time but also rejoice over it, because its intention is Christian and comprehensive and is the best that could happen to the Christian Congregation in the circumstances. But we cannot possibly consider it a fully completed work, since it in no way brought the Church back to its *original* state. We cannot even deny that the foundational Alexandrian[116] doctrines which the reformers only more or less paid homage to contrast both with Martin Luther's Christian practice and with the foundational law of the Christian Church!

Unlike his modern imitators, Luther never drew a line through the history of the Church, which alone can teach us what Christians have believed and what is the only true Apostolic Christianity. On the contrary, he frequently *appealed* to it, and the *Magdeburg Centuries*[117] is a vociferous testimony as to how eagerly his disciples endeavoured to show, while his spirit was over them, that they disallowed everything which in the course of time had crept into the Christian Church and needed to be removed in order to bring it back to its original immutable form. Nevertheless, we must admit that even Luther:

a. rejected the oral testimony to the faith, without drawing any clear distinction between what he rejected and the Creed as confessed at Baptism with the Words of Institution at both Sacraments;
b. argued that everything which claims universal authority in the Church must be provable from Scripture;
c. disregarded the testimony of Church history concerning what was in the Church from the beginning if he did not find it corroborated in the Bible;
d. declared the entire development of the order of salvation as found in the Augsburg Confession to be a collection of Articles of Faith which all true Christians should accept.

I believe that all the scholars in Luther's so-called 'church' who had any voice would agree that this is the case, but we are in total disagreement over the justification of these points. There are those who side with Luther in general; the majority allow him only three out of the four points, in that they totally reject the universality of the Augsburg Confession. Even though for a long time I was inclined towards the majority view, I now think that Luther was clearly mistaken on all four points. While I cannot conceal the fact, either for myself or for others, that so few scholars are on my side, I nevertheless claim that fundamentally not only Luther himself but the entire Christian Congregation with the Lord and the Holy Spirit, the Word and Scripture, are on my side. May God therefore always let me be so assured of Heaven (until I come there)

---

116. As formulated by Clement of Alexandria (c.150-c.215), who emphasised the divine nature of Christ, and Origen of Alexandria (185-255), whose rule of faith is akin to the Apostles' Creed.
117. The *Magdeburg Centuries* is a history of the Church over thirteen hundred years, ending in 1298 and published from 1559 to 1574. It was compiled by several Lutheran scholars in Magdeburg, and is the basis of all modern church history. The work demonstrates the continuity of the Christian faith, which shows "perpetual agreement in the teaching of each article of faith in all ages".

as I shall assuredly be proved right on this point by all those who faithfully bow the knee in the name of Jesus and who with cheerful voice confess that He is the Lord, to the honour of God the Father! The Lord is my witness when I say that I honour and love Martin Luther, and that I wish him to be honoured and loved by my children; those who know me will be aware that this is no small thing. I therefore wish to offer a thousand times more than I already have done an *apology* to Luther, even though my attentive readers know that this too is no small thing. However, where what is at stake is faith in our Lord Jesus Christ, the defence of His Church, and the well-being of His Congregation, I must not and shall not, not even for the sake of Martin Luther, conceal any truth. I know that when we meet in Heaven he will say to me, "Basically, I do not need to thank you, because you were only doing your duty, but nevertheless you deserve a thank-you from the spirit of Martin Luther!"

I am very well aware that such outpourings of the heart on paper only cause laughter or embarrassment for most readers, and my natural bias towards them is also part of the 'Lutherness' that I confess. But there are nonetheless cases when, despite the pen's innate incompetence to carry much weight and despite all the mouths that yawn and all the smile-lines that crease up around the world, one must not refrain from defining with the pen what actually cannot *be* defined; and I feel that to be the case here. So I have not the heart even to show my weapons against the shadow of Luther without solemnly assuring that I feel he is as innocent as we people of a sinful descent can ever be of what clings to us from the best-concealed flaws of our time. In the history of our Church I therefore still regard our heroic, highly-enlightened, childlike Martin Luther with the same admiration, love, and fundamental agreement as I did in attempting with all my strength not to dig him up (in vain, naturally!) but to raise him to life from the dead. No reader could therefore consider this assurance so tedious or futile as it was necessary for the author to write; nor can it possibly have been wasted on any reader, since it is well-known that I neither lavish praise on those I do not like nor shrink from knocking down a scholar, even though round and about he enjoys a much greater reputation than Luther does now!

I therefore maintain against all radicals and everything that has favoured them in times past:

a. that the oral Confession of faith at Baptism is independent of all Scripture, and, being the unanimous testimony of the Church concerning its faith, it is the most valid testimony to that faith that can be given: it is what all Christians believed from the beginning.

b. that being the condition of membership of the Christian Church Community this Confession of faith is the Church's unalterable rule of faith and foundational law, which in its indissoluble union with Baptism marks the only secure boundary between the Church and the world or between true Christianity and what is not true Christianity.

c. that the oral Word at the Sacraments and especially the Confession of faith is the foundational rule for all interpretation of the Bible in Christendom, by which every theologian who wishes to belong to the Christian Church shall and must be guided.

d. that the Bible has never been the rule of faith in the Christian Church, neither from the beginning nor by its nature.

e. that a border sharper than ever before should now be drawn between what all Christians must believe and confess and what must be left to the free working of the Spirit and the individual Christian.

f. that therefore the University, or Theology, should enjoy far more freedom than Luther intended without laying claim to the least authority over the faith and the Church which the Reformers in their view logically had to allow them.

4. On the Clausen Libel Case (1831)

Introduction by Vanja Thaulow

The pamphlet *On the Clausen Libel Case* was Grundtvig's final contribution to the controversy that played out around his vitriolic attack on Professor H.N. Clausen in *The Church's Retort* (1825, see Text 1). Clausen had brought a case against him and Grundtvig was found guilty of using unseemly language, though not of libel. He was given a lenient fine but placed under lifelong public censorship, hence the police permission appended at the beginning of the piece. In high dudgeon over this and other perceived injustices Grundtvig wrote a letter to his bishop in which he resigned not only his living at the Church of Our Saviour but also his "entire teaching office in the Danish Church".

Between 1826-1831 his friend J.C. Lindberg (1797-1857) took up the battle for 'old-fashioned Lutheran Christianity'. Lindberg repeatedly attacked Clausen and his followers for taking the academic freedom to teach a theology that was at odds with the tenets of the Christian faith as found in the Church's Confessional Books.[118] Clausen remained, in Grundtvig's words, a "false teacher" – and in a dangerous position as teacher. In their day all future clergymen studied Theology to Masters level at the University of Copenhagen, where Professor Clausen taught from 1822-74.

In January 1831 Clausen had had enough of the attacks and wrote to the university authorities to complain about these quasi-libellous condemnations from Lindberg – a "Church terrorist". He asked the government to set up a commission to settle the matter once and for all, but the government dragged its feet and in mid-October Clausen therefore published the critical pamphlet, *On the Position of the Libeller and the Libelled in Denmark*.

Grundtvig was stung into action and on 2nd November responded with *On the Clausen Libel Case*. He stated that he had no regrets over publishing *The Church's Retort* and reasserted his argument that if the rationalist theologians and pastors refused to align their teaching with the Christian faith, a "Church separation" would be inevitable. However, six years on from his defeat in 1825, Grundtvig now argued *not* that Clausen should be excluded from the State Church but that he himself and the "old-fashioned believers" should be allowed to go their own way and set up "a little, historically-based Christian church". Time would tell who was the stronger: the Ap-

---

118. For the Confessional Books of the Evangelical Lutheran Church in Denmark, see note 62.

ostolic Church or Professor Clausen's church. If Clausen insisted on his academic freedom, then Grundtvig insisted on the Christians' freedom of conscience. As in Text 3, *Should the Lutheran Reformation Really Be Continued?*, Grundtvig added a personal note to clinch his argument. He had two sons, whom he wished to study Theology, but "I dare not send them in their unreflecting youthful years to Professor Clausen's School of Theology".

In the event Grundtvig lost not only the libel case and the argument to exclude Clausen and his like from the Church. He himself had also resigned his own pastorate, yet had failed to win his petition to leave the State Church and start his own *free* church. The petition was finally rejected in February 1832, but Grundtvig's fight for Church freedom was far from over.

∗∗∗

May be printed. Copenhagen Police Court 1st November 1831. Holm.

Professor Clausen has recently had some pages printed entitled *On the Position of the Libeller and the Libelled in Denmark*. They force me to take up my pen, if for no other reason than to declare categorically that the Professor is seriously misguided if he attributes my lengthy silence to a feeling that *The Church's Retort* should be an error of judgement. However heavy the consequences have been for me to bear, I cannot possibly regret taking the step which nothing under the sun could have prompted me to do except the full and firm conviction that it was my irremissible duty.

It is doubtless true that if the case had merely been between Professor Clausen and myself, or was solely about a book of far more distinguished significance than his about Catholicism and Protestantism, then public discussion of it would already have gone on for far too long. But it is clear that the case first and last is about the faith, the conscience, and the hope and comfort in life and death of countless people living now and in the future. For this reason Professor Clausen ought to shrink as I do from the personal vexations that can neither be avoided nor find their proper limit until the government becomes sufficiently informed about the true context of the case and is moved to apply the effective reconciliatory measures that Providence has placed in its grasp. When I wrote *The Church's Retort*, I could not possibly see the consequences, but I did not doubt for a minute that they would be unpleasant for myself as well as for a number of others. I also considered it highly likely that in the course of the libel case both the Professor and I would lose our jobs. Despite the case costing me considerably more and the Professor considerably less than I had supposed, it is not in order to complain about that which makes me draw the comparison, but only to show how unjustified the Professor is in raising a cry of woe as though he, the unrepentant, had borne the entire burden, while I, the offender, the defamer, the lampooner, had got off with an insignificant fine. To what extent the judgement of the High Court of Justice also legally could justify the Professor commenting on me in such an unworthy way I do not need, thank God, to investigate. My literary career has been long and demonstrable, and my circumstances in life sufficiently manifold for me to know that the Danish public, however it may judge *The Church's Retort*, will in cold blood only regard with indignation the Professor's designation and treatment of me as a mean lampooner and defamer.

What I will do instead, because it is essential, is, with all the calmness that a clear conscience can provide and all the clarity I can summon, to present the facts of the matter as they are in *truth*. In so doing I hope that it will become clear to all that Professor Clausen has no reason to complain so loudly over anyone but himself, nor does it lie within my or my fellow-Christians' power to keep silent until our modest and submissive request to the government has been heard.

The fact that Professor Clausen wrote a book which I considered unchristian was very much part of the natural order, and in my eyes of such insignificance that I could never for a moment be tempted for *that* reason to put pen to paper, let alone raise an outcry – as though *this* book was more dangerous than thousands and thousands of others tarred with the same brush and in my opinion any the more *influential*. Since I am no fool, what I said in *The Church's Retort* comes from the heart: it was purely and simply the Professor's position as the teacher of future clergymen and his reputation among students of theology that infuriated me, and this of course has nothing to do with him as a person – which I had not the slightest intention of damaging or slandering. My protest was against the compulsion of conscience and oppression that can only harass the true adherents of the state religion when a respected teacher of future clergymen, who has publicly acknowledged the most intense dissatisfaction with the teaching of the State Church and its outward condition, is allowed to be continually active in that direction. All that the Professor and so many others tell us about 'academic freedom' sounds fine, and I believe I have demonstrated that I am as honest and close a friend of it as anyone in the country; but one fact is constantly forgotten on which the whole question depends, a fact that I shall therefore stress so that it can no longer be forgotten by those willing to remember more than just what pleases them.

It is my full and firm conviction that whatever the law of the land allows, Christians in Denmark must accept all the freedom that the government is willing to grant or recognise in the State Church, provided they are free to *leave* it. Christian freedom consists solely in being allowed to confess the faith, spread it spiritually, and worship God accordingly. It does not mean that Christians can bring it into churches and schools that are maintained and equipped at the expense of the state. However, if Christians are not allowed to leave the State Church and are furthermore compelled to use the services of the pastor in whose parish they live as their 'spiritual adviser', then it is as clear as sunlight that either we must keep an account to ensure that teachers in the State Church – and above all the teachers of future clergymen in the university – should direct their teaching according to the Christian faith, or Christians have lost their inalienable freedom. If I were ever to live outside Copenhagen, for instance, where there was a parish pastor of the Clausen-kind who, following his master's instructions, viewed the Bible as clearly self-contradictory, the real living presence of Jesus Christ in His Church impossible, a genuine redemption by Him from sin and death unjustifiable, and every church built on confessional books a temple of idols, then the Danish pastoral vow[119] would be meaningless. In this case I could personally be given permission to find another father confessor and have my children taught about their Baptismal Covenant and confirmed in it by another pastor. But if there had only been 'Clausen-pastors' in the area, even I would have been in the greatest embarrassment, since my Christian conscience would not allow me to lead my children into temptation. It is easy to see that the believers among our peasant farmers, whose souls are just as precious and whose conscience is just as sensitive as mine, were otherwise ill-used.

Moreover, I have sons whom I wish to study Theology, God willing, assuming they themselves have both the desire and the ability. Even though I more than most could work towards preventing the danger, I dare not send them in their unreflecting youthful years to Professor Clausen's School of Theology, nor can I advise fellow-Christians to send him *their* sons. It is in the nature of things that if I were in Professor Clausen's place and he were in mine, he would come to the same conclusion. He continues to complain that we charge him 'in his office as Professor', that we are trying to destabilise him in his discharging that office, and that we are endeavouring to destroy the trust of both old and young that he needs in order to work successfully. This is very strange talk, for it cannot be otherwise for as long as we are tied to the Church in which he is a teacher of future clergymen yet cannot accept that the faith we confess, because we love and treasure it above all things, will die out among us. This will surely be the case if Professor Clausen's office is crowned with a successful outcome, for he himself has solemnly declared that he teaches in full agreement with his published book. On the other hand, as soon as the government either completely abolishes the ban on leaving the State Church, or allows me and other old-fashioned Christians to leave it and worship our God in the good old Christian, Lutheran way without any church link to Professor Clausen and his school, then I have nothing at all against him becoming

---

119. In the Danish Lutheran Church the pastoral vow is taken by new priests who have been 'called' (i.e. already selected) by a specific congregation. It is spoken and signed after the so-called 'Bishop's exam' (an episcopal interview) but before actual ordination. With minor modifications the present pastoral vow dates from 1870, when it replaced the Latin oath of 1685.

Summus Theologus[120] in the State Church and enjoying all the trust he will be granted and all the success in his work that can befall him. If all the inhabitants of Denmark except ten would rather be Clausenists than old-fashioned Christians, then in a church sense it has nothing to do with me as long as the ten were allowed to form a little, historically-based Christian church among themselves and let time decide who was the stronger – either the Church from the days of the Apostles, or the protest against it.

If there was any ecclesiastical error in *The Church's Retort*, it would be that I only petitioned for a free exit from the State Church for those who, like Professor Clausen, declared themselves dissatisfied with it because of its legally established teaching. I should have proposed that those who like me were well satisfied with the teaching of the Confessional Books but implacable towards that of Professor Clausen could take the other exit possibility. But as long as I remained in holy office in the State Church it seemed inappropriate to express the thought that Professor Clausen's protest should have more validity than the Confessional Books. It may be remembered that as soon as I had resigned my office, I made no secret of stating an alternative, even though at the time I still considered it more logical that the Professor, and not I, should leave the Danish State Church.

I have thus put my house in order and explained that, for the sake of my conscience and the spiritual freedom of my fellow-Christians, as an old-fashioned Christian I had to do what I was called and duty-bound to do through my oath of office as a pastor in the State Church. In the name of that Church in which I had received Baptism and ordination I asserted that Professor Clausen should either recant or stand outside the Church to which I belonged!

But how does Professor Clausen put his house in order? Has he attempted to prove that he and I were basically in agreement on faith and doctrine, so that it was only my foolishness or my dishonesty when I claimed the opposite in *The Church's Retort*? Or has he admitted that he and I cannot possibly be teachers in one and the same State Church without it thereby contradicting itself, i.e. spiritually abolishing and destroying itself? Was it therefore merely a question of whether the Danish State Church would retain one of us or reject us both? Or does he unite with me in his plea to the government that however it applied its discretion, it would allow those teachers who protested against the teaching that it upheld the freedom to leave, and outside the State Church to teach according to their convictions in a way that was compatible with civil order? No, none of this at all! Not even a sound has the Professor made that there was a conflict between our faith and teaching, or that the case itself should be investigated by expert and impartial judges. On the contrary, bourgeois as he is, he has welcomed everything in such a secular, even unscholarly, manner, by advertising

120. 'the leading theologian'.

in the newspapers that he was compelled to judgement to disavow the dishonourable accusations that Pastor Grundtvig had made against him. Next came a proper libel action, after which these and other 'insulting discharges' should be deemed dead and meaningless and should not damage the honour, the good name, and the reputation of the plaintiff.

If it had been me who had been found not guilty, I imagine that I would have succeeded in proving that the so-called 'insulting discharges' were, legally speaking, well-founded in the Professor's *own* discharges on the teaching and constitution of the State Church, whose servants we are both supposed to be. But there was nothing to be done, and since in my view the move could not be avoided, I resigned my office and did not even read my opponent's contribution, let alone respond to it or have my friends do so for me. My view of the libel case as my *own* case I neither wish to offer nor to defend; I have done the former a long time ago in my questions to Denmark's legal experts, and I will not do the latter because I believe there is something wrong about it. True it was impossible for me with my personality to act differently, but another in my place would have done much better than me by raising himself above all other considerations and making use of all his legal advantages. For if the Professor had been unable to acquire the desired mortification in the case,[121] it would logically have taken a far more serious turn. Since it had never been my main intention to diminish Professor Clausen's honour and esteem in society, but only in the Church, I could do no better, given the wrong turn that the case took, than to let the Professor win it and then see what it actually was that he had won.

It is now as clear as sunlight that I may well be right about my claim that Clausen's teaching was incompatible with that of the State Church and old-fashioned Christian faith, which is what *The Church's Retort* is all about, even if in my rashness I had used 'extremely inappropriate terms' about the Professor's behaviour. But despite this being as clear as sunlight for me and a number of others, it seemed for a long time to be concealed from the Professor. For with every new protest against his inner clerical calling to the Danish State Church, he appealed in triumph to the judgement whose premises expressly state that the *question of his teaching* has not been examined in the least. As we can see from his latest writing,[122] the Professor has at last realised that the judgement of mortification he has been given, and a hundred similar ones, did not basically help him at all, since the accusation of false teaching continues vociferously, unpleasantly, and effectively to separate him from the trust of old-fashioned Christians.

---

121. Mortification (Lat. *mors* = death) is a legal term denoting that the court declares something null and void, in this case the use of 'extremely inappropriate terms' to which Grundtvig here admits.

122. i.e. *On the Position of the Libeller and the Libelled in Denmark.*

Now that he has finally realised this – something that I thought no student, let alone a professor, could overlook – is it not a matter of remorse for him that both for the case's and for his own sake and mine he hung a libel charge round my neck that may well damage me but will never benefit him? Does the man who set such store by his office regret that his thoughtlessness separated me from mine? And as the warm advocate of academic freedom does he not regret that the pointless trial severed a respected writer from the freedom of speech that he truly had not abused?[123] No, not at all: the Professor finds the only wrongs done were that I was not punished harshly enough, and that the government will allow either myself or another, subsequent to the date of judgement, to claim that his teaching is indeed wrong and intolerable in the Church to which old-fashioned Christians and Lutherans are bound. At the most he can admit that, beyond the mortification finding, an answer might be required from a professional man to the question "whether in the book under attack on Catholicism and Protestantism any freedom has been employed that is incompatible with the academic theologian in his function of writer". If the Professor had petitioned for this instead of taking me to court, that would indeed have been worthy of his office and might have brought us closer to the goal than we can realise, but in itself it would have been insufficient. In the first place it would depend on whether the academic theologian was a private teacher or an officially appointed teacher of future clergymen, and in the second place it makes a great difference whether as in Prussia there are five universities for fathers to choose among or, as in Denmark, there is only one. Thirdly, the question is not about what freedom a government is willing to give teachers of future clergymen to criticise the doctrine of the church which they are set to transmit, but how *much* freedom can be allowed them (without the greatest injustice and forced conscience) as long as the King's subjects remain tied to the State Church?

Is it not strange that Professor Clausen, who is so sensitive about what he calls his 'academic freedom', never mentions the *freedom of conscience* which is of much greater and unconditional importance and is the desire of millions, whereas his is the desire of barely a hundred? And is it not a quite peculiar claim that people should have their faith challenged by those who are set to nourish and defend it, just so that they do not lose face in their 'academic freedom'? And what shall I call the trait in the Professor whereby he constantly ignores the genuine paradox in our faith of which he is well aware, and which generates the same conviction in him as in us: namely, that either a Church separation must take place, or one of two things must perish: Luther's faith or the gloss of teaching!

---

123. This refers to the censorship placed upon Grundtvig's publications following judgement against him in the libel case.

I, who am called a zealot, have diligently sought to demonstrate that even if the head of the State Church[124] were to enforce silence on his opponents, enlightened Christians must urgently pray that they are granted permission without any civil disadvantages to *leave* the State Church. But although he wants our mouths gagged on church matters, does the humane, liberal Professor Clausen offer even a hint that we must of course be allowed to walk out and take with us the faith that we could not bear him to call 'superstition'? So I really do not know how Professor Clausen will bring continuity and consistency into his thought all the while he refuses to argue what seems constantly to float obscurely around his head: namely, that when he was appointed to teach future clergymen he did not think he was obliged in any way to follow the teaching of the State Church, but could become our pope, with an equally valid but much greater authority than the Pope in Rome. As a result the common people and laymen in general must without a grumble permit him and those whom he graduates to do as they like with their own faith, while we so-called educated people are allowed to make modest objections against one thing or another. However, if we dare to declare his teaching to be wrong, unchristian, anti-Lutheran, and therefore intolerable in the Church to which we belong, then the government, acting as his temporal arm, must close our mouths and seal up our pens, because his learning is hallowed by his office, and his work will necessarily be paralysed if he is not believed! In my eyes, only such an argument – which the Professor would doubtless never acknowledge – could give his, as far as I know, unique behaviour in Christianity any firmness or consistency.

If he will take some good advice, then like me he should voluntarily resign his post so that the government can see whether it is just our *personalities* that have created this incompatible difference of opinion or whether it goes so deep that freedom of religion, which was always our desire, is now absolutely necessary. However, if as before the Professor still finds his office far too great a sacrifice to inflict on his own scholarly, and our people's, freedom of conscience, let him grasp the only remaining means to gently rescue both of these. Let him tell the government the truth: that he cannot possibly find peace until the hyper-orthodox and the old-fashioned Christians leave the Church that he is in the process of reforming. And let them do so without regard for the historical form that was laid down by Luther but which according to the Professor's absolute declaration is the foundation of the Catholic Church and in no way the Protestant. This would pave the way for the giant step that the Professor recommends. It would safeguard him against the attacks from Grundtvig that he complains about without justification, and also, even in the eyes of his opponents, safeguard the high esteem that I myself am proud to acknowledge among many men of honour who neither share my faith nor approve of my ideas but who respect as a

---

124. i.e. the King.

basic principle in me what all honest, noble, and genuinely powerful natures must have in common: never to wriggle out of their words or shun self-sacrifice, but always to grant the same freedom that they demand for themselves and always in their spiritual struggle to scorn the body blow from behind!

5. An Impartial View of the Danish State Church (1834)

Introduction by Steen Tullberg

An Impartial View of the Danish State Church was published amid the reverberations of *The Church's Retort* (1825), in which Grundtvig had castigated the 'rationalist' university theologians with their new-fangled biblical exegesis and had argued for an 'old-fashioned' Apostolic Christianity which took Church *history* into consideration. The book's main features represent his views on freedom within the Danish Church, which to this day is known for being accommodating. *An Impartial View of the Danish State Church* is a major work that helped to lay the foundation of this freedom.

In the intervening period between the two books Grundtvig changed his views. In 1825 it was Professor Clausen[125] who ought to leave the Church on account of his false teaching; then it was Grundtvig himself who should be allowed to leave and seek freedom of worship in a free congregation outside it. Finally, he argues here that there should be room for both Clausen *and* himself in an accommodating State Church that embraced both of them in a wider diversity of doctrine and liturgy – on condition that all forms of *compulsion* were abolished and people were allowed to "break the parish-tie" that had bound them to their local church and pastor from time immemorial. Thanks largely to Grundtvig's efforts both in and out of Parliament the law was finally changed to this effect in 1855.

No other prose writings by Grundtvig in the years after his England trips (1829, 1830, and 1831) carry their mark so directly and indirectly as this one. In his introduction Grundtvig actually uses the English word 'establishment' about the Danish State Church, and he refers a number of times to the Anglican Church and its social organisation. The 'impartial view' in the title refers to the *social* organisation of the Danish Church, which is dominated by two more or less equally powerful groups: the rationalist theologians, heirs of the Enlightenment, and the old-fashioned Christians who have inherited "the faith of our fathers" which has stood Denmark in good stead for close on 1,000 years. To further this faith the parish-tie must be broken and congregations should even be allowed to choose their own hymns for worship!

---

125. In 1825, in response to a major work on church history by Professor H.N. Clausen, Grundtvig published a vitriolic attack, *The Church's Retort*, which brought down a libel case on his head. When he lost and was placed under lifelong censorship, he resigned his living. After 11 years the censorship was lifted by the King in 1837. See chs. 1 and 4 above.

Grundtvig goes on to argue that pastors who adhere to the 'old-fashioned' faith should follow the Altar Book with no significant variations; yet even if *all* pastors were to do so, the parish-tie would still be a severe limitation on freedom of worship. Grundtvig accepts the link between Church and State but maintains that all pastors should be granted doctrinal and liturgical freedom if they are to be useful to the State, for this "will bear wonderful fruit for virtue, for the education of the people, and for all learning". The promotion of learning and popular education is an important element in Grundtvig's defence of a free State Church, which is better served by the beneficial effects of the "faith of our fathers" than mere encouragement to moral edification. He criticises the shallow intellectual enlightenment of the 18th century and compares it unfavourably with the true enlightenment that an understanding of Christian history brings.

As an indispensable medium for universal popular education, Grundtvig turns to the village schools, which will need "pastors with a scholarly training" to maintain the people's respect for genuine learning by allowing them to reap its fruits. He also recalls the great colleges he has seen in England and proposes a joint Nordic university along similar lines, thus linking his theological ideas expressed here to his educational ideas expressed in the People's High School.[126]

***

Foreword

'Impartial' is a big word to use in this world, if it is to be anything other than hot air or a pleasant expression for an ugly thing – for indifference to everything except one's little self. Nonetheless I cheerfully call this study of the Danish State Church 'impartial', for I know that whoever reads my book attentively will find that it has no bias towards anything in the civil realm apart from opponents of my faith, and this must be regarded as an unintentional and easily forgivable offence. However, I can exact no credit from this impartiality, since it is a necessary result of the many trials and experiences that I would rather have been without, of a nature I have not myself created, and of an advantageous standpoint for which I cannot thank myself but only His Majesty's[127] grace. Being of a somewhat poetic and very bookish nature I have always preferred the idyllic life of the hermit in the bosom of my family, with a small circle of friends, to the bustle and all-consuming activity on the great stage.

---

126. See vol. 1 in this series, *The School for Life* (2015).
127. King Frederik VI reigned from 1808-39 and was a supporter of Grundtvig, not least in his grants for the three trips to England in 1829, 1830 and 1831.

So it was clearly only vociferous scorn for the pride and joy of my thought and the sanctuary of my heart – combined with the beleaguered position in which I saw my fellow-believers – that occasionally drew me out of my Elysium[128] and drove me out of my dream-world peopled by lifelike shadows of our forefathers and shining with the glory of the past. For a long time therefore the present was a foreign world where I discovered on my visits, as travellers often do, a number of things that the residents had overlooked, and was also taken aback by a good deal of what was well-known to them. I had expected to see much that turned out not to exist, because a distant resemblance to something in my own world had deceived me; and I got into particular trouble when I treated living people as if they were dead. In other words, I treated their shadows just like any other shadows, not paying attention to the obvious difference it makes whether the shadow is of a corporal body or not!

I think it was in England – where the past and the present meet romantically yet at the same time in a very real way – that I first learned the difference between shadows with and without bodies. Then I became almost as good here in Denmark at distinguishing between *present and past time*. In the act of comparing, I also learned to pay suitable regard to the undoubted advantage it is for both objects and people to exist in reality – outside our brains! This is a quality the lack of which all histori-cal and poetic glory strives to make good in vain. It is through these eyes that I now observe the Danish State Church as it *really* is and – with as little self-sacrifice as is hardly worth mentioning – envisage what it *could* be: hopefully, a gloriously active establishment for centuries to come. Even the doubtful outcome of the deliberations of the moment does not worry me, since my present position predicts that whatever is considered the most advisable thing to do with the State Church, it will assuredly grant me and my nearest and dearest the right to hold on to the faith of my forefathers and the unchanged means of grace which are indispensable to it.

So the only thing that disturbs me somewhat is the unrest that a lengthy period of irresolution creates and nourishes in all the sensibilities involved in matters of the Church. Their number is actually much larger than most people in the capital[129] believe. Knowing how superficially liturgical matters are usually dealt with in our country, I genuinely fear that in their evaluation of all the contradictory statements that must follow any general request to the clergy, the Royal Danish Chancellery[130] would conclude that there was nothing to be done.

Moreover, I myself have a deep longing to settle down with a clean conscience to the pursuits that suit me best and to contribute my mite to Nordic enlightenment,

128. In Greek mythology Elysium is a western island kingdom where the specially chosen gods can live a carefree, eternal life.
129. i.e. Copenhagen.
130. The Royal Danish Chancellery was the central governing organ in Denmark from the 12th century until 1848.

which is my preferred interest – and indeed the North in general. So for better for worse I could not help presenting the subject of our Church yet again as honestly, peacefully, and clearly as is in my power. I realise it is no surprise that a book of this kind from an aging writer will remain unread by those for whom it is written, and that what seems as clear as sunlight to the writer can be very obscure for other sensible people. What then? Whoever is put to the book always hopes for something from the pen. My voice on Church matters is echoed on so many sides that it is not too bold to claim that all serious men who have no wish or prospect of being a little parish pope may find it best to break the parish-tie,[131] whether the benefit be great or small. It is clearly a heavy burden, and if it is further tightened it can do irreparable damage.

However, even in the worst case, not one of my contemporaries can deprive me of the writer's last hope: to be read and praised by posterity. If I must settle for that, it does me no great injustice. For I have actually written about the Church the way I would talk about it to coming generations, who are strangers to the petty interests of the moment past for them. Such will not matter if in their eyes the State Church has already achieved the form that I wish for it, and they simply seek to know the thoughts of a man of the time, an experienced pastor and man of learning, concerning the gradual progress of this Church and its relation to Christianity, to freedom of conscience, to enlightenment, and to the understandable needs of civil society!

The Ruling Church

Christianity – or, if preferred, the faith of Christianity's forefathers and the society that it creates – is a demonstrable fact from the past which cannot be other than what it has been. So whoever rewrites it is only shirking his responsibility and making himself look ridiculous by pasting its name onto his own handiwork. The State Church is not a church state but simply a state organisation (establishment) that the government is entitled to do with as it pleases – without any bishop, pastor, or professor having the right to murmur a protest, provided there are no breakages in freedom of conscience! For the latter is both the fundamental principle of all religion and the inalienable right of every blameless citizen. This is my starting-point, and in this regard my sole subject-matter. I am thus a declared opponent of not only the High German habit of calling new things by old names but also the hierarchical ghost which in recent times, like a poorly exorcised pope, returns to haunt Protestant Christianity. It seeks to dupe us into believing that the clergy should always be the soul of the State Church, the government its worldly arm, and the jurists its fingers – in other words that it ought

---

131. The parish-tie as set down in the Danish Law of 1683 limited parishioners' worship to their parish church. Grundtvig fought long and hard to break this tie, and was finally successful through a Parliamentary Law in 1855.

to be a church state in a civil state. The consequence would be that the people should either endeavour to be doppelgängers, or that the spiritual and temporal soul (cf. the pope and emperor) should again patrol the body of the state. I am well aware that such offensive phrases are no longer in use, but instead it is merely noted 'the Church should be emancipated'. This seems very modest but clearly amounts to the same thing, and it really is high time that we put an end to this scholastic humbug of empty or at least undefined and ambiguous wording and look at the matter as it is in reality.

What has given this masked ghost from the Middle Ages a kind of respect is also clearly a similar case of humbug. For on the one hand it confuses the Church with the University schools, and on the other the clergy with the idea of the Church as faith and conscience. This confusion is such a tangible error that even the weakest intelligence can understand that faith and conscience, as well as thought, can be 'duty-free', precisely because the clergy's are *not* so![132] Indeed, civil freedom depends on the clergy being *tied*, so that in civil terms they cannot move, for a state-church clergy will oppose tooth and nail a genuine freedom of belief and religion as long as civil society can exercise itself as a corporation. It is the firm conviction of this 'corporation brotherhood' that true freedom of religion means that the true religion (with its management clergy) is free of duty and tax, if possible, but in particular free of all powerful opposition. For, it claims, such opposition always creates a sect that tears apart the body of the Church and eventually torments the soul out of the Church's life. Since every clergy holds its religion to be the true one, it has not the least sympathy with the sects, which are presumed in advance to be refractory towards the true religion and to employ words like 'religion' and 'freedom of conscience' as a cloak for clergy-hatred, megalomania, infatuation, and fanaticism.

I myself have had the opportunity to experience how ingrown this idea is in our country. For I have always earnestly believed that it is madness to seek to control another's faith and conscience, and foolishness to say to people who call our religion false, "You should be ashamed of yourself! You know that we have the one true religion, so can you not see that the religion you confess is in opposition to it and is therefore false infatuation and fanaticism?" I have always had these unappreciated but obvious truths stamped on my mind, yet I could never accept the religious freedom of my 'opponent' without making short work of it and resigning my pastorate, for only then would I become 'impartial'. So I do not blame the clergy for following their instinct; but I do demand that the jurists should prevent them from doing civic damage by tying their hands, with or without ceremony. I use the word 'hands' deliberately, for if one must not muzzle the mouth of a treading ox,[133] then even less

---

132. The clergy are not 'duty-free', in that they have taken the pastoral oath and are bound by it to preach the Gospel.

133. Deut 25:4, "Do not muzzle an ox while it is treading out the grain." Also quoted in 1 Cor 9:9 and 1 Tim 5:18.

so is it the case with the pastor who must preach! The clergy should always have a free voice, as Molesworth[134] discovered in Denmark to his great annoyance, since he had taken pride in staking his honour on there being no sign of any such thing! The clergy must have the right to call theirs the only true religion of salvation, and, as this implies, to claim that all else is superstition, infidelity, infatuation, fanaticism, sectarianism, whatever it wishes, even the right to suggest the state eventually goes to hell with all the heretics, because it does not burn them in time! The clergy have the right to all this on their responsibility to God, conscience, and the facts, but not to touch a hair on any heretic's head. They have no power to separate anyone from so much as a fingernail of his citizenship just because he calls another religion true and that of the clergy false and follows his own and not theirs. Nor do they have the power to stop the spreading of information in any way, which is undoubtedly the case when the so-called 'heretics' are not allowed to produce theoretical or practical proof of the truth and benefit of their religion.

When the clergy complain about sects, a statesman in Christendom can never be without an appropriate response that goes to the marrow. For St. Paul says specifically, "No doubt there have to be differences among you to show which of you have God's approval."[135] So it clearly belongs with the Cross, before which no righteous pastor must flinch! I should also be surprised if all the statesmen of our time cannot see that church sects may inflict on the great Church-State a mortal wound – as the Protestant sects did on the great Church-State of the Middle Ages at the Reformation. The civil state, far from being dissolved by them, must rather thank those sects (Lutherans, Episcopalians, and Calvinists) for its independence, and they are certainly in no danger from the ruins collapsing as those of the great Church-State did among the Protestants. For it is as clear as sunlight that it is only when the ruins collapse that the civil state is entirely emancipated. And yet, they cannot collapse while there are sects, as we can see in England, whose history I take the opportunity to regret is not better known among us than that of Germany. It is also clear from both the Quakers and the Methodists that the smaller sects are relatively speaking as beneficial to the civil state as the larger sects were at the Reformation; they will never do any damage unless the government takes the side of the dominant church and treats its best friends as enemies just because they are enemies of the Church-State that the government itself

---

134. In 1694, the British ambassador to Denmark from 1689-92, Robert Molesworth (1656-1725), published *An Account of Denmark as it was in the year 1692*, an innovative work in political science. He criticised the absolute monarchy of Denmark as opposed to the British electoral system, but agreed that although the Danes were a 'mediocre people' they could all read and write!

135. 1 Tim 1:9.

wishes to be well rid of. Now that the 'High Church'[136] is apparently reeling without frightening anyone but its beneficiaries, no statesman believes that the enemy is at the door just because a little sect makes the same demand on a smaller scale for freedom of conscience as the Protestants did on a larger scale at the Reformation, with the Augsburg Confession[137] being their keenest defender.

Whatever the view of eyes elsewhere, we in Denmark must open ours, since for fifty years the government has clearly favoured all church-sects and for that reason has been in opposition to the clergy's sectarian nature without thereby causing the least civil inconvenience worth mentioning. At the same time, its great result has been the complete internal dissolution of the Church-State, making it possible for it to be blown down – and with no power to raise itself up again. We learned from our neighbours in North Germany about the indulgence of heretics, of which the 18th century was so proud ('tolerance'), and we lose nothing by letting others quarrel about their originality. This tolerance was a slippery customer, for it all depended on who was exercising it. Friedrich II[138] 'tolerated' the tearing down of the faith that he himself derided, so that was no surprise. In the 'Lutheran' countries they tolerated the old pastors continuing to preach until the words stuck in their throats at death and were of little consequence. To my knowledge, German tolerance refused to proceed further than this. But after some reservations *Danish* tolerance went so far as to give even me – a declared and not entirely harmless opponent of the heterodox sect that had become dominant behind the scenes – both the permission and the opportunity to do my best for that Lutheran sect which in the eyes of the law is orthodox, but in the eyes of the clergy wholly blameworthy.[139] So at present none of us really knows which sect is the strongest in our State-Church, whereas we all know that no one is in charge! This is an anarchic situation that points to the dissolution of the State, by which I mean of course the 'Church-State'. Clearly, if the government were to take sides among the quarrelling sects, it should be for the one that I belong to, which has

---

136. The Church of England distinguishes in the use of ritual, liturgy, and accoutrements in worship (though not in faith) between its High Church (Anglo-Catholics, high on the above), its Broad Church (moderate on the above), and its Low Church (low on the above).

137. The Augsburg Confession is the primary confession of faith in the Lutheran Church. It was agreed at the Diet (Council) of Augsburg on 25th June 1530 by Lutheran princes and representatives of 'free cities', and comprised 21 Chief Articles of faith and 7 statements concerning abuses of the Christian faith in the Roman Catholic Church.

138. Friedrich II (the Great; 1712-86) was King of Prussia from 1740 until his death.

139. i.e. what Grundtvig calls 'the old-fashioned Lutherans'.

not only the Altar Book,[140] the liturgy, and the law of the land, but also the constitution[141] behind it. I do not think it is in any way advisable to give either this or any sect a monopoly on the kingdom of heaven. Heaven lies in a quite different place, namely in the freedom of conscience, in relation to which even the most Christian of sects, once they became dominant, have become such Jews[142] that it has normally cost lives.

If the government has no need to take sides, it will not need to abolish the State Church, nor even give one of the parties a position outside it, as has been the case with the Dissenters in England.[143] What future circumstances may force upon us naturally nobody knows, but at the moment, the dictates of which must always be the concern of the State, it is so far from being necessary that it would barely be possible. For the abolition of the State Church would be just as little to the people's liking as it was in the state's interests, and since the main parties appear to be of roughly equal strength, none of them would willingly retreat. So the government would have to force through a separation, in practice actually take sides, not just with the pen but also with the whole hand.

On several occasions in recent times I have both claimed and endeavoured to show that the government can avert the dreadful storm gathering in the Church's skies by simply loosening a tie which should never have been bound in the first place, namely the parish-tie. For it ties the layman's faith and conscience to the parish pastor, and all thinking men must agree with me that if no more is required to bring the Church into a desirable relationship with the State, then the task is child's play. The fact that this is not yet the case shows that the advisability of the move has either been put in doubt or has encountered a difficulty where circumvention was preferred. However, the question which the government is putting to the clergy of the whole country at the moment – whether and to what extent a change in the liturgy and the Altar Book is advisable – shows that the matter is regarded as of sufficient importance to be taken very seriously. I must not spare any endeavour to let my fatherland harvest the benefit

---

140. The first Altar Book (or Liturgy Book) in Denmark was compiled and published in 1556 by Bishop Peder Palladius (1503-60). Born in Ribe, Palladius was a student of Luther and Melancthon in Wittenberg and later became the first Lutheran bishop of Zealand as well as Professor of Theology at Copenhagen University. He is best known for promoting Luther's teaching in Denmark, not least through his visitations to all 390 parishes in his diocese between 1538-43, reflections on which are collected in his *Visitation Book*. The Altar Book for Denmark in use at this point was from 1830 and had replaced the Altar Book for Denmark and Norway of 1812, since in 1814 Norway left Denmark for a union with Sweden.

141. The royal constitution of the absolute monarchy in Denmark (*Konge-Loven*) was introduced by Frederik III in 1665 and lasted until the democratic constitution introduced in 1849.

142. i.e. so miserly, a not atypical attitude in Grundtvig's time.

143. Dissenters in the 16th to 18th centuries dissented from, and did not conform to, the established Church of England under the Acts of Uniformity (1559 and 1662). They included the Anabaptists and the Quakers. They were later called 'non-conformists' and by the end of the 19th century included Presbyterians, Congregationalists, Baptists, and Methodists.

of the lengthy attention that nature and circumstances have partly tempted and partly forced me to offer Church matters, and of the rather rich experience that my peculiar career has not only enabled me to gather but also made it impossible for me to avoid.

A good conjecture as to the benefit of my advice would also call forth the awareness that although in Church matters I am indissolubly wedded to the past, I nevertheless prefer a step forward than a step backward. Moreover, my advice contains a word of praise for the Church policy that through a strange accident almost cost me my civil existence. When the advice does not come from someone who by nature is a very poorly endowed person, such a strange and rare encounter must deserve a certain curious attention. If this is granted me, I do not doubt for an instant that the breaking of the parish-tie will be found both necessary and beneficial. Indeed my genuine surprise will be shared to see how peculiarly Providence continues constantly to watch over us, or, if preferred, how Fortune favours Denmark. This is not without reason, for the King and the people have a good heart that sincerely desires to do what is right – where no mere intelligence can fathom it.

The Faith of our Forefathers

If we wish to understand the present and look with prudence into the future, then we must both know the past and observe the present as it truly is, whether we like it or not. For if we begin by disappointing ourselves, we are sure to be disappointed by all our expectations.

So when we consult history we immediately see that the present Church crisis is far from being something new but is equally far from being unimportant. For it is one of the great turning-points in the position of the earth towards Heaven in a given place; from here it will be decided for centuries whether Church life will die out or open up onto a new path.

For me as an individual, religion is a faith and conscience question, i.e. my own affair. It does not concern anyone else unless he either wants to hear me talk about it or I press myself upon him. I have not the slightest right to do the latter except where a close and loving relationship can allow me, as a father or friend. But religion has a social side that history teaches us about, giving us a testimony so important that no wise or well-qualified statesman can lose sight of it. We hear both Greek and Roman writers complaining that with the decay of their forefathers' faith came also the degeneration of their customs and the drying-up of the wellsprings from which the people imbibed their heroic courage in the moment of danger and the strength for all that self-denial and mutual sacrifice of their own immediate desire and advantage. These are essential if civil society is to be strong externally and calm internally, beneficial and gratifying from generation to generation. Even if we as individuals fail to recognise ourselves in the faith and worship of these ancient forefathers, we cannot deny that while they flourished, those peoples took giant strides towards what in their view was earthly happiness. Nor can we conceal from ourselves the fact that those who prophesied that the decay of popular belief would bring about the dissolution of the civil state had good reason to do so and were proved to be more accurate than they themselves would have wished.

So when at the turn of the present century a number of men in Europe predicted a sorry future for the countries in the new Christianity, it was certainly not only our statesmanship that found it ridiculous. Nor in any way has the first generation of the 19th century confirmed the bold claim of the 18th that we had found the 'philosopher's stone' which, as the unshakeable foundation of civil society in its full power and glory, made religion completely superfluous, if not in individual instances, then at least in general. Most governments are therefore striving again to tighten the religious bonds that in the previous century were loosened. In Denmark they are strongly supported in this by us who are born more recently and who, as they say, are 'infatuated' by our forefathers' faith; and yet on the other hand we are proving a little tiresome for them with our fervour for what cannot just be conjured up.

This then is the situation all around Protestant Christendom. In Germany and England, as well as in Denmark and wherever our forefathers' faith is subject to the same conditions as popular belief in Greece and Rome once was, any sensible person would declare all attempts to revive it totally futile; and he would also prophesy the same *consequences* of its cessation which the ancient states manifested as they went to earth. Even if in Athens they had made Epicurus[144] drink the same bowl as Socrates,[145] no one can fool himself into believing that the ancient gods would thereby have been *revived*. And no state in Christianity would do more to keep the old faith alive than was done for temples and priests in Greece and Rome for century after century, yet all in vain. Leaving our forefathers' faith aside, since all our wisdom had its wellspring in Greece and Rome, it would be folly to expect that this wisdom should work greater miracles to strengthen and govern civil society among the Scythians and Barbarians[146] than it did in its homeland!

There is no reliable historical basis for lumping our forefathers' faith together with that of the Greeks and Romans, since it has twice done greater things than theirs and

---

144. Epicurus (341-270 BCE) was a Greek philosopher who identified good with pleasure and evil with pain. According to Seneca, the gate to Epicurus' garden carried the sign: 'Stranger, here you will do well to tarry; here our highest good is pleasure.'

145. Socrates (c.470-399 BCE), a Greek philosopher, was convicted of corrupting the youth of Athens and dishonouring the gods; he was forced to drink poison.

146. Col 3:11. The Scythians lived north of the Black Sea and were considered wild and ungovernable; 'Barbarian' in the NT means non-Greek, and therefore uneducated.

it is possible, indeed reasonable, to believe that it may well do so a third time if it is allowed to do its best.

For when we call Christianity in Denmark the 'faith of our fathers', we do not mean to say that it is a figment of their imagination or an invention of their heart. We mean that although it came as a 'foreign guest'[147] it has for a millennium taken such deep root in the heart of our people, in our language and our way of thinking, in our home lives and public institutions, that our people know of no other 'faith of their fathers'. Even our scholars argue about what the people of the North actually believed before the days of Ansgar[148] and Olav the Holy.[149]

As we know from Saxo,[150] the heroic ballads, and our ancient laws,[151] the life of the people and civil society in Denmark under the Valdemars[152] was the first heroic outcome of the Christian faith in Denmark. I call it greater than any 'folk' belief because it was practised among a 'foreign'[153] people whose strange beliefs the foreign faith replaced in a heroic deed that truly has something of the supernatural about it! Our astonishment increases when we realise that it was not only in Denmark and the North but also in Germany, England, France, and Italy – in fact wherever Christianity met German or Nordic peoples – that it became the religious element in a far more developed and creditable civil society than had been the case with the faith of old.

If we have seen *one* miracle, we are not so surprised to see a *second*; so it is easy to overlook the matchless effect of the Christian faith at the Reformation. Yet that does not make it any the less miraculous. For after the crusades it seemed that despite its previous miracles the Christian faith and its unparalleled universal (catholic) power would go the way not of all flesh but of all spirit on earth: in other words, after an active life it would go home to the gods. For gradually the great idea lost its power, the idea of the new Christendom as a divine Church-State, in which the spirit expressed

---

147. Ex 2:22.

148. The Benedictine monk Ansgar (801-65) is credited with bringing Christianity from Bremen to both Sweden and Denmark and is therefore known as 'the apostle of the North'. He is also credited with building the first Danish church in Hedeby.

149. In 1014 the Norwegian warrior Olav Haraldsson (995-1030) helped the Anglo-Saxon King Ethelred II in his war against the Danes by pulling down London Bridge; this may have been the origin of the famous song 'London Bridge is falling down'. Olav returned to Norway with four English bishops and christianised the country. He was crowned King Olav II of Norway in 1015 and was canonised as Olav the Holy.

150. Saxo (c.1160-post 1208) worked as a scribe for the great Bishop Absalon (1128-1201). Saxo's *Gesta Danorum* (Deeds of the Danes) was handwritten in elegant Latin in 16 volumes. The early volumes contain mainly legendary material, but references to documented events become more and more common in later volumes. *Gesta Danorum* was first published in 1514. Grundtvig's Danish translation was published in 3 volumes in 1818-22.

151. 'Our ancient laws' include the Jutland Law of 1241 covering Jutland and Funen, and the first national 'Danish Law' of 1683.

152. The reign of 'The Valdemars' spanned nearly a century: Valdemar I (the Great, reigned 1157-82), and his two sons Knud VI (reigned 1182-1202) and Valdemar II (the Victorious, reigned 1202-41).

153. i.e. the Danes, who lived by pre-Christian laws.

its deep secrets in the tongues of all peoples,[154] and in which the peoples retained their independence, the kings found their crowns, and earthly life found its sanctification in every direction. This matchless idea of the centuries (for all its quixotic echoes) gradually diminished, and the holy mother-church in Northern Europe, where it suppressed everything that was 'of the people' including their mother-tongue, was soon seen as a nightmare that was difficult to remove, but no less grievous to endure. The North in the 15th and at the beginning of the 16th century therefore displays an impotence, a coarseness, and a corruption of its customs, coupled with a scorn for faith and clergy that portended the worst. And yet, only a generation later, the churches were resonating with the Word of the Spirit on the tongues of the people as the multitude sang the praises of the same Christ whose Roman vice-regent[155] children pointed their fingers at in Luther's catechism.[156]

I assume that readers are aware that this wonderful resuscitation of our forefathers' Christian faith merges into the new epoch in the history of the State and the School that has brought fame in particular to both Germany and England without thereby making Denmark less happy or enlightened. Nor can my hope be called quixotic that in a renewed enthusiasm for this faith of our fathers the religious indifference that spread through the 18th century and reached its peak at the beginning of the present century may find a spiritual counterweight that averts its natural consequences for civil society and grants it a new epoch that is as happy as it is honest, especially in Denmark and the North!

I am not blind to the far greater difficulties that our forefathers' faith endures than in Luther's day in seeking to benefit the life of the people and the state as a whole. Having been a passionate supporter of both for a generation now, I know better than most the slippery and fragile nature of their relationship. My eye for historical parallels is also practised enough to recognise in our generation the stage of development at which the faith of the people in all the ancient states lost its influence on life. This happened when the temples became what they still are in China and Italy – dilapidated hospitals for the clergy – while the philosophers struggle in vain to replace the faith of the people with their ruminations. For this reason I am also too well-informed to imagine for a moment, as do so many others, that these pathetic musings, far less rooted in and formulated by the people as they are, should be better suited to replace our forefathers' faith now than before. Although poetically speaking I am a priest of

154. Acts 2:1-4.
155. i.e. the Catholic Pope.
156. Grundtvig refers here to a verse often reprinted under an engraving of Luther on the back of the title-page in the *Small Catechism*, which read: "Hear me, Pope, I shall be your plague while you live! When I am dead, you shall perish. So says Luther; beware!" Grundtvig uses the verse as a motto in a number of his writings, including the second edition of *An Impartial View of the Danish Church*, where he replaces Luther's name with his own.

the ancient gods of the North, I am not enough of a romantic to believe that they really can *enliven* our country. So either I must give up my patriotic hope that the common life of our people will continue as a powerful presence leading to a Nordic enlightenment, or I must cling to the hope that the faith of our fathers which has animated all my views, wishes, and strivings will – along with freedom, which is the natural environment of the spirit – perform a third heroic deed: namely, the rebirth of civil life and popular learning to create a singular, joyous contrast to the spiritual death and dissolution that all the omens have prophesied.

Of course I cannot require that any others than those who share my belief should also share my hope of its effects. But it is just as easy to let the faith of our fathers continue to do however much or little it can after its matchless feats, as it is wise for the State to promote by all possible means the effects of a faith which after a millennium of unquestionable witness, constitutes the only well-founded hope for the development of civil society and humanity in general.

Nonetheless, a government has two paths to tread: it can either dismiss the faith of our fathers from the State Church and allow it the freedom to manage as best it can on its own and with its own strength, or it can open up a free sphere of activity for it *within* the State Church.

With regard to the former, my view is that our forefathers' faith – or rather all the individuals for whom it is a question of salvation – would be best served by this solution, since they must find all Church relations with opponents of this faith disagreeable, and even the greatest possible freedom within the State Church is linked to many obstacles to the growth of Christian life. But it would be dishonest of me to argue that our forefathers' faith would in this way be most beneficial to the life of the people and to the State as a whole. That faith would indeed always present the State with its most diligent, faithful, and obedient citizens, but in an open quarrel with the State Church it would lose most of its influence on the people as a whole and for internal and external reasons be far less beneficial for the study of literature learning in general. If a wise government refuses to allow our forefathers' faith a free field of activity, it will lead to the abolition of the State Church. It would then inevitably become the emptiest theatre in the land, or a dearly-bought shadow of the square and cloisters in Athens at the time when all the philosophical branches strove only to say or hear something new.

However, no matter what other governments may do, we can be sure that the Danish government wishes to retain a State Church and the faith of our fathers within it, just as it has solemnly accepted this resolution in the Royal Law.[157] The only question

---

157. The Royal Law of 1665 confirmed the absolute monarchy, which remained in force until the introduction of democracy in 1849.

is what is needed to ensure that their faith can continue its life and activity in the State Church. The government appears to feel that something must be done, since it is asking the clergy for advice!

It is my absolute and repeated conviction that if the faith of our fathers is to live and work in the State Church, then the parish-tie must be loosened and everything else be kept more or less as it is – or be made even freer. And when I say 'as it is', I am referring not to words on paper but to what has been the actual case for a generation now: that the pastors in their teaching no longer feel bound by the Confessional Books or by the *ministerialia*[158] to the Altar Book but use them freely to support their defence of Holy Scripture and universal truth.

Against this voice I would not expect to hear any objection except from my own fellow-believers. For although the legal passages remain unaltered, the government has openly favoured both liturgical and dogmatic freedom to the point that the faith of our fathers remonstrated loudly against this abuse of freedom. Those pastors who demand all manner of freedoms must accept that the parishioners, for whose sake they exist and by whom they are paid, have at least as much right to freedom of conscience as they themselves.

However, despite my assumption that my fellow-believers among our pastors will be those who most criticise this proposal, the government nevertheless seems to be persuaded that they could remain free dogmatically yet bound liturgically. In response to my suggestion to loosen the parish-tie I have had so much to put up with from the dissenters' side that it is there they will doubtless find the greatest freedom dearly bought, since no one must dominate proceedings. Thus it is not impossible that the most votes among the clergy could be gained by pursuing the middle way: not to loosen the parish-tie, but rather to bind the pastors to a somewhat altered Altar Book and then let them teach more or less what they like. Yet this would be sad for all parties and a death sentence for the faith of our fathers, which I think 'the one above' would never ratify. It could be disastrous for the land in which it was passed into law.

The Altar Book and the Parish-tie

I shall try to prove three things here: first that if the pastors of the faith of our fathers are to remain bound to the Altar Book, nothing in it of note can be changed; second, even if every pastor followed the Altar Book to the letter, those who confess our forefathers' faith could not sow a freedom of conscience without breaking the parish-tie; third, pastors of every confession need dogmatic and liturgical freedom in equal measure in order to give the State the service it requires and must expect of its church.

---

158. i.e. the pastoral duties laid down by the Ministry.

My first argument – that pastors of our forefathers' faith should be bound to an Altar Book that is more or less the same as at present – is based on my belief that among Lutheran Christians liturgy and teaching are very closely connected, and that the Word in the Sacraments, which is the core of disputes about the liturgy, is not merely a matter of taste but is the source of hope and comfort for all the faithful. Whoever wishes to deprive them of that, whether they know it or not, will actually deprive them of their religion.

Opponents of the faith of our fathers will of course call this a fanatical claim, and it must indeed sound strange to the majority in our times. For the liturgical matter in the disputes is usually treated only in the 'court of good taste' with the expressed or silent assumption that only the ignorant common people could think that they were being given a 'new faith' just because the 'formulae' were being altered at Baptism and Holy Communion. But whether it sounds strange or familiar, pleasant or grating, it is true! And it would be realised too late, if we were to conceal the fact that the sacramental means of grace cannot be altered if our forefathers' faith is even to be *tolerated* in the State Church. There are doubtless many who would deny that if the sacramental means of grace were removed the Christian Church would immediately disappear. But it is *certain* that it would lose all attraction for those who in the Church seek divine comfort when faced with sin and death and worldly toil: that is for sure all the true adherents of the faith of our fathers – and it is those we are speaking of here. So I allow it to stand entirely on its merits whether it would be worth maintaining a State Church for people who felt no need of divine comfort from sin and death and worldly toil or believed that they could read their way to it by themselves.

If the sacramental means of grace are the Church's treasure or the Church's blessing, then no one can deny that there are 'special words' upon which their authenticity depends. However much they may be disputed and however many these words may be, it is equally clear that if in one of the Sacraments I am deprived of words that I believe are part of its authenticity, my conscience is violated. In my view that is the same as depriving me of the Sacrament itself. Instead of pursuing here the very difficult question as to how much sacramental words could be altered without violating something very essential, let me ask every thinking man, lay or learned, whether one is not sure of retaining the essential if one retains the entirety, and whether one can truly, on someone else's opinion, give up something to which one believes one's temporal and eternal well-being is bound.

We are dealing here with each individual's faith and comfort, soul and salvation, and it is no use speaking in general and imprecise terms. The question must be taken straight from life in order to stand in its proper light and demonstrate that what is altered in teaching-primers, hymnbooks and indeed in all sorts of books is a trifling matter compared to changes made in the sacramental words of grace in the Altar

Book when it is to be followed absolutely at every celebration of Baptism and Holy Communion in our State Church.

If we set aside what are known with a dignified expression as the 'formulae for Baptism' and concentrate on a person with our forefathers' faith who regards Baptism as "the water of rebirth and renewal in the Holy Spirit" that grants him forgiveness of sins and makes him a child of God with the inherited right to eternal life, then that is the Baptism that is performed according to the Altar Book; that is the Baptism upon which he bases his hope of salvation; that, he takes for granted, was authentic, performed according to Christ's institution; that, his soul assures him, has the power to comfort and strengthen in life and death; and that is his assurance, either because he believes the testimony of his Lutheran forefathers as to what they had experienced, or because within himself he has traced the divine effects of the Baptism with which he was baptised.

Since it so happens that I am one of these – as well as being a pastor – I should deprive this of all that is vague and indefinite to point to myself and confess honestly what I could and could not accept by way of change to the Baptism ritual if I had a child in church; and what I could and could not change, if I had to baptise children. No-one has greater competence than I with regard to the history of Baptism and the Altar-Book, nor in distinguishing the faith of the fathers that I share with many from my own dogmatics and exegesis, which I may not have in common with anyone else. Greater *competence* than I have cannot possibly be found among any of my fellow-believers: neither with the doctors who are ignorant of Church history, nor with the "scribes" whose faith and theology are commonly so fused together that they cannot see any difference between them.

How accommodating should I then be if I went as far as my conscience will allow? I know that the year I was born quite a few changes were made to the Baptism ritual and that I was baptised without the 'renunciation of the Devil' and with a new preamble by Bishop Balle[159] without my being aware that it has made any difference to the effect of Baptism on our forefathers or me. So as a father myself I should not of course pick a quarrel with anyone who baptised the child according to a different preamble provided that it was true to the faith and to Baptism and omitted what I do not consider very important. But if the sign of the cross were omitted, I should immediately be on the alert, for I sense that it means more than I understand, and I know that it is an ancient ritual at Baptism, if not contemporary with it. And if the slightest change were actually to be made to the Baptismal Covenant or to Baptism

---

159. Nicolai Edinger Balle (1744-1816) became Professor of Theology at Copenhagen University in 1772 and then Bishop of Zealand in 1783. He published his *Textbook of the Evangelical-Christian Religion Authorised for Use in Danish Schools* in 1791, which became the authorised schoolbook on the Catechism.

itself, I would protest; if that did not help I would baptise my child myself, in the way I was baptised. This would not only be my heart's desire, to prevent the Church fellowship between myself and my child from suffering any damage, but a matter of conscience, since it must not just be a whim of fortune whether the truly *altered* ritual would have the same divine effect on my child as I believe the uncorrupted version had on me and my forefathers, indeed on countless people from time immemorial.

If one wished to pacify me with the assurance that in ancient times the Baptismal Covenant underwent many changes without it making any difference, then it would fail completely to have any effect on me, for I know from Church history that that is a very thin pretext, and I realise that it must be empty of all truth, if not a sheer fraud, with regard to Baptism and the faith of our fathers throughout the thousand years that we Danes have professed them. Anyone who wishes may make this argument, but he must really not demand that I give *credence* to his claim or countenance that the Baptism I was given should be *corrupted*, when I believe that I am reborn to eternal life. For it is clear as sunlight that if my Baptism on the word of Christ is to be an exalted means of grace, then it must be carried out *according to Christ's institution*, and it would no longer be carried out thus if done in a different way. If I am to be comforted by being told that my *own* Baptism was not performed on the basis of Christ's institution, then I am simply being openly mocked, as is my Baptism and the faith of our fathers.

If, alone as a *father*, I cannot consent to the least change in reality of the Baptismal Covenant and keep my conscience clean, and if I had to declare as a real change the turning of "the Devil" into an impersonal and undefined 'concept of sin'; and if I have to omit an element of the Creed, or agree to the fragmentation of 'in the name of the Holy Spirit' into its constituent parts, then as a pastor with the faith of our fathers I should have to regard the matter even more stringently. For on the one hand I should have to declare the bond broken between us and our Lutheran forefathers of old, when we reject their Creed and Baptismal Covenant, and on the other hand I should have to decline to carry out any Baptism at which it was not, as in the old form, solemnly declared that it was the water of rebirth and renewal that Christ has instituted which grants the believer forgiveness of sin and the right to inherit eternal life. And finally I would have to shrink at any change about which a father had misgivings for his own child's Baptism, since, out of regard for the conscience of the weak in faith, we have a strict order from the apostle Paul which I believe to be a commandment of God.[160]

---

160. 1 Cor 8:7-12.

None of the changes in Baptism that the Clausens[161] and their party propose can be accepted if supporters of the faith of our fathers are to retain their freedom of conscience and the pastors are to follow a new Altar Book. So we are barely inside the church door before we see that the disagreement over the liturgy is actually an irreconcilable dispute about 'the faith' that is impossible to settle because honest people can just as little deny their faith as profess that which they repudiate. We need go no further, for at the entrance and exit of the Church[162] it is only the first step that counts, and if the State Church pastors cannot agree on the words to be used at Baptism, then all other agreement would be immaterial. However, it goes without saying that since the dispute about Baptism has to do with "faith, hope, and the conditions for salvation", it must therefore call forth disagreement about every expression about Church life, but in Holy Communion, as a mysterious uniting with "the crucified and risen Saviour", the dispute must reassume its irreconcilable quality. Indeed, even though as a communicant I am not at all set on a conflict over the great shibboleth of a 'true body' and 'true blood', I can only call it a violation of conscience to abolish a word in the Sacrament whose use is harmless but whose omission is suspicious and can offend many an honest Lutheran.

Since my opponents will agree that if no changes are made to Baptism and Holy Communion the rest is not worth discussing, I have presented the valid reasons for my first claim that no change worth mentioning should be made to the Altar Book, if pastors with the faith of our fathers are compelled to follow it and people of the same faith are obliged to remain within the State Church.

My second claim was that even if all our pastors were compelled to follow the old Altar Book word for word, only through breaking the parish-tie could followers of the faith of our fathers gain the absolutely essential freedom of conscience. To make this clear we can take confirmation: here not only do liturgy and doctrine clearly meet, but the contrary teaching of the pastor is even more intolerable for a believing father than a liturgical deviation.

'Confirmation' should be a solemn confirmation in the Baptismal Covenant and therefore in the faith of our fathers. Essential to this are the prescripts of the Altar Book, that is, a repetition of both the main questions asked at Baptism. So there is no conceivable reason for their frequent omission unless it be the opinion of the pas-

---

161. Archdeacon H.G. Clausen, father of Professor H.N. Clausen (see Texts 1 and 4), administered Baptism with his own self-appointed changes, which he proposed should be adopted by the entire Danish Lutheran Church. First, he omitted the sign of the cross. Then in the Creed preceding the sacrament he rejected the phrase "descended into Hell" and altered the words "Do you renounce the Devil and all his works" to "Do you renounce sin and all evil displeasing to God?" Grundtvig argued that if Clausen's proposal were accepted, then logically the Holy Communion ritual would also have to be changed, and this was quite unacceptable.

162. i.e. at Baptism and at death.

tors concerned that the Devil need not be renounced because he does not exist, or that belief in the Father, Son, and Holy Spirit is either a superstition or a trifle. It is clear, however, that pastors who teach this to their confirmands cannot, without being deeply ashamed of themselves, solemnly ask the children, "Do you renounce the Devil; do you believe in God the Father, Son, and Holy Spirit; and will you remain in this your Baptismal Covenant until the blessed ending of your days?" It is equally clear that I cannot have my own Baptismal Covenant in view as a living reality and intend to remain faithful to it until the end of my days and still send my children for confirmation to a pastor whom I know will not confirm them in this covenant but must, following his own opinion, enjoin them to abandon it! To make such a demand on me is not only unjust but so unnaturally brutal and outrageous that no person of honour can bear the thought. For it would be a monstrous demand that I should betray my faith and my hope of salvation in my underage children, something which is not even demanded of Jews in Turkey![163]

Of course, no one is demanding this of me, and indeed I live in a parish where the parish-tie is more or less broken already. But if I were a peasant farmer, then it could easily happen under the present circumstances that my parish-priest demanded it of me without there being any real chance of rescue. So I am quite sure that when our paternal government stops for a moment to consider what a torture-rack the parish-tie is at the present time for a father's or mother's heart where the faith of our fathers is alive, then that tie is sure to snap, even if the pastors on Funen protest even more strongly against breaking it than the lords of the manor in Jutland protested against the abolition of adscription.[164]

I am therefore certain that this tie would have been broken long ago, if it had not always been foreign to our capital city with regard to confirmation and had therefore in its actual character escaped the government's attention.

I have now demonstrated that if the government cannot and will not oblige all the pastors in our State Church to follow the Altar Book in the sacramental means of grace and to teach our confirmands in accordance with their Baptismal Covenant, then breaking the parish-tie is the only means whereby we who respect the faith of our fathers can have true freedom of religion and conscience in the State Church. This for me is the main point, since it has to do with the question of salvation. So I gladly leave it to the government's mature deliberation as to how it will maintain the faith of our fathers in its well-earned and constitutional right[165] to endure and propagate itself throughout the country. However, it would be neither honest nor patriotic of

163. i.e. of Jewish believers in a Muslim country.
164. The abolition of adscription in 1788 freed the peasant farmers and workers from the estate where they were born and worked for the local landowners. It had been introduced in 1733.
165. i.e. according to the Constitution (the Royal Law) of 1665.

me to keep silent on the weighty reasons that make it advisable not to *limit* but to confirm and *extend* pastoral freedom, which with the breaking of the parish-tie loses its only harmful encumbrance and gains a benefit that the distant future will most clearly reveal.

Whoever has worked untiringly with heart and soul for a number of years for a noble goal that at an early stage occupied and enthused him knows best how crushing it would be finally to have to give up his efforts and as far as possible himself destroy their fruits. So we all sympathise with Emperor Joseph II[166] in his deep grief even though we disagree profoundly with him on the enlightenment and good fortune of his people whom he sought to promote and on the goodness of the means he employed. Bearing in mind the judgement of posterity, which I should hate myself for despising, I nevertheless venture to ask: What were Joseph's efforts worth compared to those of Frederik VI[167] for genuine civil freedom and equality and for popular education and the advance of learning in every possible direction? Even if I had no strong personal reason to wish His Majesty all the happiness that can make a king with a 'grey-haired crown'[168] reap the first fruits of his spring sowing, it is only with deep sadness that I must raise the possibility that the noble royal hand should itself contribute to upsetting its famous work. And if circumstances forced me to it to ask for, and explain, the need for this, then I would consider myself born under an unlucky star.

Will this prove to be the end of all our Church ferment and tension – which no human power or wisdom could prevent, since it appears to be based on the immutable laws of natural and historical progress? Will it prove to be the end of the ferment and tension which it was not my choice to promote and increase but rather my unavoidable lot? Will the keen supporters of the faith of our fathers, once they are separated from the State Church, lose nearly all their civil and scholarly influence? Will the 17th century be repeated in the 19th, with all the restrictions on the instruments of the Spirit, as though they were tethers that would now become fetters? If this *were* to be the case, then I cannot see other than that Denmark's famous lucky star would have waned, never to rise again. For every navigation mark in the river of time would

---

166. Joseph II (1741-1790) was Holy Roman Emperor from 1765 until his death. He reigned as an absolute monarch during the Enlightenment and sought to introduce enlightened legislation such as the abrogation of aristocratic and clerical privilege, the abolition of the death penalty, religious tolerance for Jews, Protestants, and Orthodox Christians, and emancipation of the serfs in his vast domains. He required all parents to send their children to secular public schools, or to pay higher taxes. With the nobility and the clergy set against him, the peasantry disillusioned about the lack of land reform, and his own health failing, he revoked his reforms in 1790 and died a disappointed man.

167. Frederik VI (1768-1839) was Prince Regent from 1784 and King of Denmark from 1808-39, a reign of 55 years. In 1834 his government introduced Provincial Advisory Assemblies in Holstein, Schleswig, Jutland, and the islands (Zealand, Funen etc.) to discuss a new form of government. As a result the first democratic constitution was approved by law in 1849. Frederik VI was the penultimate absolute monarch and was succeeded by his cousin, Christian VIII.

168. Prov 16:31.

have deceived us, if in both cases the Spirit among us were to end its course without reaching its goal!

That is why I must always regard as an inspiration from Denmark's good genius[169] that the benign, bright thought that arose in my soul – the breaking of the parish-tie – will on the one hand guarantee the faith of our fathers against unpleasant civil consequences, and will on the other lift all reservations by creating teaching and liturgical freedom *within the law*. For half a century now our government has favoured this, and among pastors of our forefathers' faith as much as among all the others it will bear wonderful fruit for virtue in general, for the education of our people, and for all scholarly learning.

The task of seeking to unite the civil peace of the faith of our fathers with the general freedom of conscience and a steadily increasing enlightenment has occupied me over a number of years – and me more than most of my contemporaries. It was the situation of the English that I knew best – with their forefathers' faith supreme in their State Church and full religious freedom outside it. However, the stagnation of their Established Church and the wild disorder outside it with the whole disparity between religion, literature, and learning was an obstacle for me, and English idiosyncrasy alone could not explain why everywhere else something similar might be *feared*. Only when I saw that this faith of our fathers could just as easily be secured with the *breaking of the parish-tie* as by the departure of the Dissenters, did I find the calm to compare our State Church as it is at the moment with the English one. I swiftly discovered that the main cause of England's spiritual crisis, in which both the Established Church and the universities are threatened with destruction, must be sought not in the freedom of religion that has clearly delayed the crisis and still mitigates against it, but in the disordered way in which that freedom has arisen and in the paralysis that cannot escape a State Church which must maintain its position over and against all manner of sects.

The chaos in *our* State Church would actually be an incalculable advantage if only the people's freedom of conscience did not drown in that of our pastors, with every parish pastor becoming a little pope, and their congregations, for whom it would be impossible to change their faith as often as their pastor, becoming either totally indifferent or becoming prey to all kinds of infatuation. If we simply *break* the parish-tie, the pastors' free position will mean that *all* religious views will be represented in the State Church and will interact with each other under the most favourable circumstances. The uniform scholarly training of our pastors and their equally dependent and legal relation to the government and to the people will, as far as possible in this world, not only prevent but to the utmost degree decrease the dangerous consequences

---

169. 'Genius' in early Romanticism is a term akin to 'peculiar essence'.

of opposition to religion. In the Age of Reason this opposition cannot possibly just disappear except in an indifference to heavenly matters, and this is as much the curse of the State as of the Church.

So, a free State Church, with a free national congregation, is my deepest wish for our fatherland. I am sure that this will contribute greatly to saving it from the deep shocks that threaten Christianity as well as furthering a high standard of education and learning, broad yet calm, and historically progressive. Europe will be obliged to confess there is something 'genuinely Danish' that deserves the applause of all and must be envied where it cannot be imitated! It is quite possible that such a State Church can only thrive in Denmark, where hardly even at the inception of Christianity was the sound of arms heard! Nor is it likely that it could be established anywhere else on earth. So when the breaking of the parish-tie sees the victory wreath placed upon this new edifice, the castle of Glintner built by Forsete,[170] who straightens out all disagreements, we and our most recent generations must admire and gratefully kneel down before the loving Providence who like a female Norn,[171] a Queen of Destiny, has granted Denmark kings after the people's heart! At the great moment when the people's spirit hovered between life and death, Providence gave us a jubilee king so peace-loving that even the toughest warriors who had rested under Denmark's heart could not look him in the eye without plunging their swinging swords into their sheaths as he, with 'the sword of righteousness' that suffices all men, cut the knot that had never linked hearts together but had strapped on belts of opposing spirits to our national grief and common ruin.

A Free State Church

I shall not deny myself or my friends in spirit the joy of hearing what the 'genius' of Denmark whispers when we listen and sing quietly of the happiness in a country where even the most heated spiritual struggles, though honestly engaged, are mere jousting and combat in Valhalla.[172] They end without bloodshed, they do not disturb the peace, and the Valkyries[173] shed their weapon-skins and go to the table as heroines yet tender Danish women. Nor could I conceal this treasure that belongs to the King and pleases the people. But I must point out that nothing worse could befall the free

---

170. In Snorri's Edda poem *Grímnismál*, the building 'Glintner' in Asgaard, is the golden-walled, silver-roofed home of the god Forsete, a mediator and peace-keeper.

171. In Nordic mythology the Norns are the goddesses of human and divine destiny.

172. In Nordic mythology Valhalla is 'the hall of the slain' where Odin welcomes dead warriors to his home.

173. In Nordic mythology a Valkyrie (from Old Norse *valkyrja* 'chooser of the slain') is one of a host of female figures to choose who may die in battle and who may live. Selecting half of those who die in battle (the other half go to the goddess Freya's afterlife field Fólkvangr), the Valkyries bring their chosen to the afterlife hall of the slain, Valhalla, ruled over by Odin.

State Church than to be regarded as a delusion of the imagination, lovely to behold but existing only in the Realm of Possibility, and I must remind everyone that a 'free State Church' is not an ideal but an actual reality among us. We have had it now for half a century, not 'black on white' perhaps but far more importantly 'in fact and in truth'. The question is not about establishing it, but about abolishing or ratifying it! If it is seen as a great misfortune, we must consider whether its abolition would merely make matters worse. I have shown that it cannot be abolished without a decision either to ban the faith of our fathers or to compel all the clergy in their means of grace to follow our old Altar Book and teach our youth Luther's *Catechism*. Since they shun the former and are incapable of the latter, the worm's path in the kingdom of thought will lead us to the same goal as the bird's path, provided we follow it as respectable citizens. There is, however, a middle way between the thought flying high or crawling on all fours or fives. It is the human way, with eyes wide open to the wonder that we ourselves are, and to the indisputable testimony of lengthy experience: in brief, the path of world history. If we follow this path to our free State Church, we shall not be tempted to wish for this freedom to be abolished. On the contrary, we shall wish for its extension first and foremost to all Danish men and women – for the simple reason that lay-people have as much soul as the learned and often a more sensitive conscience – and then to all our clergy in as ample a form as they might justly wish and the government wisely grant.

We have noted earlier how, in the Age of Reason or Enlightenment, popular belief in Greece and Rome lost its beneficial influence on civil society. The temples became monoliths over the grave of faith, and the priests became itinerant Egyptian mummies depicted from top to toe in hieroglyphs they themselves could not read – just as travellers tell us is still the case in China. However, in days of old there was a little corner where the Church in the Age of Reason acquired its strangest history, and where popular belief animated the people even while the temples were burning! That little corner was Palestine, and there we could surely learn the conditions needed for the living activity of both faith and the Church in the Age of Reason. Whether we consult the four evangelists or Josephus,[174] we immediately note that after the Exile there was a freedom in the synagogues which in Roman times went so far as to allow that the high priests were commonly Sadducees,[175] that is, people who freely admitted that they believed neither "in spirits nor angels nor the resurrection of the dead".[176] They had a quite different concept of the scriptural canon, which they limited to the

174. Titus Flavius Josephus (37-c.100) was a Romano-Jewish scholar whose works include a few references to Jesus, some of which are disputed.
175. The Sadducees were a Jewish sect active in the time of Christ and identified by Josephus with the upper class of Jewish society. They were pro-Hellenisation and their social roles included maintenance of the Temple in Jerusalem.
176. Acts 23:8.

Pentateuch (the five books of Moses), while between them and their contraries, the Pharisees,[177] there were so many intermediates that even the learned argued about the *number* of sects, let alone about their opinions. Under this 'church' constitution Jesus arrived and the Galilean fishermen preached the gospel. It is clear as sunlight that this could not possibly have happened in a State Church like the Anglican, or like ours in the 17th century, since Jesus' speeches to the high priests and the scribes would have amounted to defamation of character, and his disciples' preaching in the synagogues to a fanatic attack on the exclusive privilege of the priests.

I do not mention this in order to argue that our State Church should enjoy as much freedom as the Hebrew one, since the degree of freedom in time and place depends on its usefulness, that is, its desirability, and on a people's stage of development and other circumstances. But all the same it is worth noting this, for it is obvious that the compulsory church under which the Christian religion could not possibly have originated can equally impossibly have been its *Spirit*. When protests are made 'on be-half of Christ' against the breaking of the parish-tie using the argument that freedom could be extended to such a degree that 'artisans' would be preaching the word in the Church – in other words it would be as bad as the time when Jesus and His apostles were allowed to preach – then that is just absurd!

If we come back to the North with this information and regard our own Church organisation then and now, we see at the beginning of our recorded history what we call 'the faith of our fathers' to be a *foreign guest*. From the free 'state church' of the Holy Land it trod many a weary mile over hill and vale through fire and water before it arrived in the high North with a messenger from Christ's governor in Rome or, as we of the faith pointing to the 'apostle of the North'[178] can cheerfully state, 'from the King on High Himself'. However, Denmark did not thereby acquire a 'State Church', but was incorporated into the great Church-State which had curiously formed itself on the Mosaic model between the Scythians and the Barbarians. Throughout the Middle Ages it could not be otherwise, for just as in days of old the Church was father to the State, so in the Middle Ages did it become its 'holy mother', not by coincidence but because faith in the reign of the imagination and feeling acquires all its influence precisely *through* them.

At the Reformation it should have been otherwise, for that was when 'reason' came into play in governing the kingdom of faith, and so in a way we *did* gain a 'State Church'. But this was only in regard to the Pope in Rome and in no way to Christ and

---

177. The Pharisees were a religious and political party active in the time of Christ whose beliefs constituted the liturgical and ritualistic basis for Rabbinic Judaism.

178. The Benedictine monk Ansgar (801-65) is credited with bringing Christianity from Bremen to both Sweden and Denmark and is therefore known as 'the apostle of the North'. He is also credited with building the first Danish church in Hedeby.

the Spirit. The Middle Ages continued in Denmark in such a way that for a long time Martin Luther was regarded by our State Church as an unrivalled *German* pope who knocked the wicked Romans off their perch, clipped the wings of the bishops, sent the lazy monks packing, liberated the Bible, and brought the mother-tongue back to a place of respect and honour. A new esteemed and reverent clergy applied itself to academic studies and good habits. Both large and small read their texts honestly, and preached the gospel so strikingly and clearly that the Church Congregation could feel their souls being comforted and could not but sing the loveliest songs of praise that they had learned!

And so we come to what I have not injudiciously called the three great miracles of the 17th century that distinguished our State Church from all others: the Danish Law, the Altar Book, and Kingo's *Hymnbook*.[179] Even these taste of the Middle Ages far more than of our 'new times' – and that is their 'miracle'! For they cannot be *imitated* in an age such as ours, which in regard to both the Church and the country have been 'replaced by the *community*'.

If we are surprised that these miracles of pen and ink nonetheless fail on a small scale - or rather, constantly fall short, so that we separate into constituent parts what we had imagined to be indissolubly joined – it is probably because we underestimate the basic truth that 'people make books and not books people'. No profession knows better than we writers how tempting is the thought that with our pens we can reshape the world for a century or two, and to think that the famous books of the past in this regard are rather disappointing; until, that is, we realise the devices that writers of old employed to make their books perform miracles! For they used the innocent trick of only writing about what had *already* existed, of only ratifying what was *already* held good! This of course became every man's knowledge until it later fell out of favour. Such a miracle from the 17th century is of no use to us in the 19th, unless it be for *new* miracles to be enabled today! Above all we must not misunderstand and think that they had actually effected what they only demonstrated.

If we realise that the Altar Book and the Hymnbook, like the law of the land, only sought to reveal what had been living among the people and had been valid for the country, partly since the Reformation and partly since time immemorial, then we might well be surprised that so much of what still lives on continues to appeal to a large number of our people. Yet it would never occur to us to create freehand counterparts to such books - which appear to have written themselves! As regards the 'Danish Law', our historical Danish jurists know far better than I where the lion's share belongs. But

---

179. The Danish Law was the code introduced in 1683 by Christian V (1646-99), who also commissioned Thomas Kingo (1634-1703) to publish a new hymnbook. His first attempt was deemed a failure and a commission of Copenhagen theologians and parish pastors published *The Authorised New Church Hymnbook* in 1699. Such was Kingo's influence on the final book, however, that it came to be known as 'Kingo's *Hymnbook*'.

since I probably know more than they do about the Altar Book and the Hymnbook, I cannot conceal that the only innovation I have discovered in the Altar Book is the address to the communicants. For the Collects are all in the Altar Book of Palladius, and the Precepts for both the marriage ceremony and Baptism are Martin Luther's. Kingo's hymns are new, but only insofar as the *Iliad* and the *Odyssey* were new for the Greeks, for they came first from the mouth of the people. The hymns are the Danish Christians' own view of faith, and the Bible story as executed by Kingo is accepted by Danish Christians for what it is. And yet it is very strange that the hymnbook that Kingo and his good friends compiled was not officially sanctioned, so in the 'decreed new Altar Book' Kingo's hymns were only a makeweight for the old 'spiritual songs' which even before the Reformation were partly in the mouth of the people.

Although the time came in the 18th century when a good number of laity and clergy thought the Altar Book and the Hymnbook were as outdated as the Danish Law was for our jurists, it proved even more impossible to replace them with new and comparable books. And yet the jurists managed to produce a suitable new lawbook! When 'reason' takes control, there is nothing that divides the people more than 'faith and taste'. Indeed, history teaches us that in the Age of Reason faith was generally so unimportant and taste so unpoetic that the Church was superfluous and the hymns were ridiculous. We have seen that the only ancient people who continued to seek the Church in the Age of Reason could not agree on either faith or scripture,[180] while the Reformation teaches us that nor could the Germans and the English. So we Nordic people must be an unnatural exception from everyone else if in the Age of Reason we could place so little emphasis on faith without fighting over it until we were pulled apart, like the Germans and the English, or accommodating one another, like the Hebrews. In short, it was a miracle that we 'stupid Danes'[181] lived up to our name at the Reformation and acquired a new Altar Book, a new Hymnbook, and a new Textbook that followed on literally as in the Middle Ages!

It may be true that it was the Germans and not us who 'discovered the gunpowder',[182] but however exceptional it is as a means to disintegrate and divide, we can possess just as much reason as its inventors when it comes to connecting and uniting. In that context a shot of gunpowder is no more than a stroke of the pen, and posterity will surely find that the Danish Church Reformation was indeed praiseworthy – apart from the mistakes induced by the Germans' example. Bishop Balle, for all his orthodoxy, was a reconciling man who in good conscience granted the clergy all the freedom that the

---

180. i.e. the Jews as they became Christians.
181. In *Virtuoso Number Two* (1793) the Danish playwright P.A. Heiberg (1758-1841) has a German character, Spatzier, escape scot-free from his tricks, after which he exclaims, "Ha ha ha/die dummen Dänen!" The phrase may already have been extant. Nowadays it is used mostly by Danes imitating Germans mocking Danes.
182. i.e. initiated the Reformation.

government requested and the people could manage. So when he nevertheless wrote a new Textbook,[183] published a new Hymnbook, and proposed a new Altar Book for general usage, it only shows that his head was German but his heart was Danish. It is the greatest tribute to the management of the Church that the government let his Textbook more or less make its own way, left the use of his Hymnbook to the individual 'congregations', and embraced his Altar Book in acknowledgement of his passion for the faith of our fathers linked to the greatest leniency towards the heterodox.

With regard to this 'faith of our fathers' we must always remember that despite its well-earned name, it was originally a 'foreign guest' which abused its right to asylum and rewarded the most hospitable people under the sun with ingratitude! It would not govern us a moment longer than we wished, or demand a degree more latitude that its friends had the right to grant it. While it would be as un-Danish as it would be ungodly either to outlaw this guest of a thousand years or strangle it with false caresses, it would equally be just as un-Christian as it would be unjust to force the learned and the unlearned to simulate a faith they did not voluntarily acclaim and to silence their opponents or others who held a different conviction concerning spiritual and eternal matters. The impossibility of *enforcing* this new religion becomes clear when we consider how all the philosophical sects in Greece were the rational products of their original beliefs. Similarly in the North, all the beliefs that might deviate from the Christian faith would be rational products of our heathen forefathers, and cannot possibly become null and void unless the generations that held them died out spiritually. Experience has shown, and will continue to show, that the good friends of this 'foreign guest' have in no way died out with Bishop Balle, as had been predicted; some of them just needed to go through the Purgatory that tests their youthful friendships, while others needed to grow out of the cradle at which pious mothers had sung songs about what must never be forgotten.

Experience has also shown that not all our compatriots are good friends of 'the guest', so it would have been foolish to imagine that the heterodox should die out either with Archdeacon Clausen or others we could name. Since the government does not want the people to divide up into sects, as in Germany and England, but is willing to accommodate both the supporters of the faith of our fathers and the freedom of religion and conscience for our philosophical schools, there is no alternative to making the State Church sufficiently commodious to include even opposing viewpoints. This cannot possibly be achieved with Textbooks, Altar Books, and Hymnbooks that have the most intelligent parties, or even all the parties except one, against them. It

183. Nicolai Edinger Balle (1744-1816) became Professor of Theology at Copenhagen University in 1772 and then Bishop of Zealand in 1783. He published his *Textbook of the Evangelical-Christian Religion Authorised for Use in Danish Schools* in 1791, which became the authorised schoolbook on the Catechism.

can only be done by allowing, as the government has steadfastly sought to do, all these instances to be as free as possible – and also, which has unfortunately so far escaped their notice, by breaking the parish-tie.

If this is the only way to ensure freedom of conscience without the dissolution of the State Church, then I venture to say that it is the only way in which a State Church, even when the outcome is as free as it is in England, can retain the people's favour and be of benefit to the State.

If we take an impartial view of our State Church in the middle of the previous century, when all the clergy followed chapter and verse in the Ritual Book, the Altar Book, and Pontoppidan's *Exposition*,[184] we must admit that it is not an encouraging sight. The country pastor (by far the most important for the State) was commonly a bogeyman for the peasants, whom they used literally to frighten their naughty children, while for respectable people he was 'God's Word from the country' and often somewhat 'stiff' in every sense. Sermons in both city and country were long and boring, the worship was sleep-inducing, and educated people generally agreed that the State Church was 'a necessary evil'. Was not the reason for this that most of the clergy were neither Lutheran nor Calvinist, neither Halle nor Moravian pietists,[185] and that the intellectuals, who along with Holberg wanted religious freedom, both hated and despised the State Church that stood in its way and echoed a faith that in most cases they could hear came from pastors who had learned it by heart from their own preaching? These are indeed weighty reasons that must be considered!

Nor must we forget in the Age of Reason that we look in vain among learned and lay alike for a high opinion of the Church or a deep feeling for its vital necessity in its previous stages of development. Yet even what may be justly described as a 'necessary evil' must ward off something that is worse. A State Church that is only deemed a benefit by those to whom it gives 'a living' and is regarded by educated people as standing in the way of something better must be called by any statesman an unnecessary and dangerous evil that must be made good as soon as possible. If we did not already

---

184. The Service Book covers the whole Lutheran service, while the Ritual Book covers the individual rituals. Pontoppidan's *Exposition*, as it came to be known, was published in 1737 by the Danish pietist theologian Erik Pontoppidan (1698-1764) as an exposition of Luther's *Small Catechism* (1529). Its original title, *Truth that Leads to Godliness*, was taken from Titus 1:1 and the exposition consisted of some 750 numbered questions followed by correct answers. It was used to prepare candidates for Confirmation.

185. The founder of the Pietist movement in the German Church was Philipp Jakob Spener (1635-1705), who believed that Christian life was being strangled by Lutheran orthodoxy and conceived Christianity as involving a change of heart and the pursuit of a holy life. His influential book *Pia desideria* or *Earnest Desire for a Reform of the True Evangelical Church* (1675) gave rise to the term 'Pietist', originally a pejorative term. Support came from theologians in Leipzig, Dresden and not least Halle, where a famous orphanage was founded in 1695 and where Spener himself founded the new University of Halle. After his death the movement gathered strength and spread from Halle through Middle and North Germany to the Nordic countries. Among its other successes were the revival of the Moravian Church in 1727 and the establishment of Protestant missions.

know this, the tottering Church of England could teach us that in the Age of Reason there was no need for anything other than a prescribed Liturgy, a Textbook, and a Hymnbook to make the State Church just such an evil. In England, as we know, there has been such religious freedom outside the State Church throughout the last century that we must assume there were not many who opposed the faith of their fathers. We also know that a large number left because of the liturgy, and what with the Thirty-Nine Articles[186] and the Psalms of David we can see how heavy the burden must have been. This is clear from the lethargy that is so contrary to their brisk enterprise round and about that it must be deemed 'unnatural', so much the more since English intelligence is far from being inimical to the Church. It cannot be the fault of the English liturgy, hymnbook, and doctrine, for they are of no less value for people with their forefathers' faith, and they mean the same to the English as the Altar Book, the old hymns, and the Augsburg Confession do to us. They are masterpieces from the past which we do not attempt to emulate, let alone surpass, since nowadays we have far less feeling for the essential and the universal and far greater preference for our own 'individual' outlook and the 'eggs' we ourselves have hatched than for older things.

No indeed, in differing from previous generations in our 'plain good sense' with all its virtues and faults, its desire for progress, variety, and changeability for better for worse – therein lies our natural and essential characteristic. It is not just that a number of our people openly dismiss and dispute the faith of our fathers – especially when it is enforced – but also that even when we do retain it and are far less at home in one another's hymns and doctrines than in those of the past, we nevertheless find ourselves unpleasantly limited and oppressed by them, especially when we are *bound* by them. This cannot be changed by any skill or power, for we can as little 'get behind' our own age as our forefathers could 'get in front' of theirs. If one wanted to make everyone happy by binding oneself to something that no one could seriously object to since it was vague and indefinite, then it would torment if not the soul out of life then the life out of the soul, which is the same thing. It would be the State's own fault if the clergy were good-for-nothings and the State Church was an object of derision for the reckless and one of annoyance for the serious, who were concerned about what it cost and what it wasted. Even in England, where canonicates and bishoprics are attractive, very few wise heads 'went astray' among the working priests in the last century, and even their good abilities were to be found everywhere else but in the Church, where all is tailored, weighed, and apportioned. It came as no surprise that the same thing happened to us in Denmark in the last century, when the Liturgy, the Altar Book,

186. The Thirty-Nine Articles of Religion are the defining statements of doctrines of the Church of England established in 1563. They were not adopted in the American Church until 1801, and do not appear in Prayer Books there until after about 1808.

and Pontoppidan's *Exposition* were the dead things to whose service all pastors' lives should be dedicated, and at whose altar all should be sacrificed.

We must pay special attention to Pontoppidan's *Exposition*, not because I believe that it is any worse to be bound by his book than Balle's *Textbook*, but in particular because our forefathers really *were* bound to the former as we are *not* to the latter, and also because while Pontoppidan's *Exposition* was dominant, no people were more bound to a catechism than we Danes. For, God be praised, it was 'the First and the Last',[187] and only a handful of pastors regarded Balle's *Textbook* with the same admiration and were willing to die for it in the spirit. For before Pontoppidan's *Exposition* received canonical status, pastors could choose between all the orthodox expositions or write their own, a fact which undoubtedly helps to enliven teaching. As it was, they were bound, and bound moreover to a somewhat pietistic book that many of them would much rather have preached against! The situation was clearly desperate, so it was no wonder that the capable shunned the cassock or wore it with dismay and sighs.

But, one might well ask: Were the pastors better or the churches livelier or the State Church more beneficial when a blind eye was always turned to unlimited freedom?

A pause for consideration is required before we dare to answer 'yes'. But when we summarise the whole period of freedom, as we must, I answer 'yes' with no reservations whatsoever: the Danish State Church in 1833 was livelier and richer in pastors who discharged their offices diligently and was therefore more beneficial to the State than in 1783. Yet no one has the right to claim any appreciable development until the parish-tie has been broken and the pastoral vow abolished or softened.[188] The latter may not deter or trouble the conscience-free, the layman, or the light-minded, but they always have one or other of these effects on the serious and the conscientious who cannot make them rhyme with their convictions. I say this all the more frankly since I myself was one of the few fortunate people in this regard who took the pastoral vow with *total* conviction. It only hurt me insofar as I took it more seriously than the government or the courts found legitimate under the freedom that existed at the time – but 'hurt' I was nevertheless. So in my view the first improvement that the ritual[189] requires is that the pastoral vow is altered to a promise in Danish to administer the Sacraments "with the Words of Institution", and that doctrine should be both according to Holy Scripture and graced with discipline and good habits. This is an

---

187. Rev 22:13.

188. In the Danish Lutheran Church the pastoral vow is taken by new priests who have been 'called' (i.e. already appointed) by a specific congregation. It is spoken and signed after the so-called 'Bishop's exam' (an episcopal interview) but before actual ordination. With minor modifications the present pastoral vow dates from 1870, when it replaced the Latin oath of 1685.

189. The Book of Ritual at this point was still *Church Rituals for Denmark-Norway* from 1762. Denmark and Norway were a united kingdom from 1524-1814.

upright undertaking and will mean that the State need only call to account those who bring shame and misfortune to it. After many centuries of experience and with the current state of learning, this can hardly be called a 'constraint' for a serious, honest, well-read man. I say 'hardly' deliberately, for I know of no pastor in Denmark who has refused to use, or even shrunk from using, the Words of Institution at Baptism and Holy Communion. On the other hand, the Quakers for example could not make that vow without the express reservation that if they wished, they would not administer the Sacraments. In a free State Church with no parish-tie this could be tolerated as a rare exception, whereas an administering of the Christian Sacraments without the Words of Institution is an insult and a perversion that cannot be allowed in a State Church, which the supporters of our forefathers' faith must regard without aversion.

I must constantly repeat that without the breaking of the parish-tie pastoral freedom will destroy the State Church by either driving out or rooting out the supporters of our forefathers' faith, without whom it would be the worst theatre in the country. Equally importantly, I must add that if the State Church is to find favour in the eyes of the people – which is the main concern since it exists for the sake of the people – then somehow *compulsory* hymn-singing must also be abolished. For it has contributed incalculably to a decrease in church attendance and makes the service boring, especially for the ears that enjoy singing. If it continues, it will of necessity generate so many private gatherings that the Church will become redundant where it might in particular be beneficial. We are not speaking here of a new hymnbook, since we have already had two new hymnbooks in the space of half a century[190] and may God preserve us from a third, even if it were I myself who was allowed to make it, if both the present and future generations had to be bound by it. No, what we are speaking about is a way by which churchgoers get to sing their 'life-hymns'. This is not such an easy task, as we are in a State Church where a certain stiffness is necessary for the sake of good order, nor can it directly be the churchgoers who choose the hymns; that must be left to the pastors. But how poorly their taste has represented the churchgoers is sadly testified to by the introduction of Balle's *Hymnbook* to the islands.[191] Again of benefit here can be the breaking of the parish-tie, without which in my view the State Church will perish. For it is an essential consequence of free relations that on both sides people learn for their own sake to accommodate one another; the knot that remains is simply how much freedom the pastors can be allowed to share with their congregation.

---

190. The two new hymnbooks were *Hymnbook or a Collection of Hymns Old and New* (1779), and *Evangelical-Christian Hymnbook for Use in Church and Home* (1798). All the 560 hymns were cut to the same pattern of max. 8 verses, and in a number of churches the pastor and the parish clerk would stop singing, while the congregation continued, following Kingo's beloved hymnbook of 1699.

191. Initially, Balle's *Hymnbook* was distributed on the islands of Zealand and Funen, but not in mainland Jutland.

If it is in the State's interest that all religious views among the people which are reconcilable with the social order and good habits can be represented and addressed by the State Church, it can have nothing against the people being allowed in an orderly fashion to follow their taste for such hymns, provided that the pastors with all discipline and honesty guarantee their compatibility with Holy Scripture. The greatest obstacle to extending freedom is then perhaps the privilege of Vajsenhuset.[192] Once the Danish government understands its importance, which is much more the case in Denmark than in Germany and England, there is no question but that it will go the same way as all the other relics from the Middle Ages that resisted the demands of the times. This privilege has among other things brought about so many tiresome printing errors in books that can least bear them that it would be a great benefit if they ceased.

Impossible to implement yet conceivably also of great benefit would be the granting of permission for any pastor to add a supplement to the *Hymnbook*, once the parish-tie *has* been broken. The said pastor would vouch for its purity, just as is the case with cantatas at church festivals and private songs at weddings, official funerals, and the like. In this respect at least those pastors with the faith of our fathers would be able to accommodate the simple, warm wish of their audience to sing again the old well-known hymns of the people that they have been deprived of through the poetical imprudence and distorted view of hymns in the 1790s. If, for instance, the Faeroese,[193] who still sing their old folk-songs at celebrations and gatherings, were forced to use a collection of 'Festive Songs' from the 1790s, they would doubtless slip away or fall asleep. The new *Hymnbook* actually relates to the old one, and as a Zealander I have made so many attempts with my countrymen both young and old that I venture to say: If we want people to go to church happily then we must give them back their beloved hymns! What a great loss they have been, and just because the honourable Bishop Balle was too gullible and had less energy than the Jutlanders and Norwegians to ward off the pastors' importunity with a royal ordinance. The Jutlanders and the Norwegians indeed! May I not as a Zealander be saddened by the thought that they can sing 'O blessèd Easter Day' and 'As the golden sun advances',[194] whereas Kingo's

---

192. In 1727 King Frederik IV set up an orphanage in Copenhagen, The Royal Vajsenhus (pron. Vie-sen-whose, lit. 'waifs' house') as a home and school. The establishment also included a factory, an apothecary, and a printing and publishing works to which in 1740 Christian VI granted sole rights to the Danish bible and the Danish hymnbook, a privilege that despite Grundtvig's protest it has retained to this day. The school also still flourishes, with c.400 children, mainly of single parents.

193. From 1035-1814 the Faroe Islands belonged to the kingdom of Norway, as did Greenland and Iceland. In 1814 the Treaty of Kiel granted all three to Denmark. Norway became fully independent in 1905, Iceland in 1944. Greenland and the Faroe Islands are today both self-governing but not fully independent of Denmark, whose monarchy they share.

194. 'O blessèd Easter Day' and 'As the golden sun advances' are hymns from 1689 by the great hymn-writer, Thomas Kingo (1634-1703), nos. 232 and 227 respectively in the current *Danish Hymnbook* (2002).

and my closest friends must manage with what neither he nor I can be bothered to read? But since there are circles round and about in Denmark where Kingo's hymns are thought to be just as flat and tasteless as we think them great and unrivalled, fairness demands that where Kingo's *Hymnbook* has continued in use, pastors should also have the right to use a supplement. Once the parish-tie is lifted, no one will have the right to complain about this.

There are doubtless many other small things that could contribute to extending and embellishing the Danish State Church so that it visibly became what our government has aspired to: a model of its kind, a model of impartiality in matters of faith and freedom of conscience, as well as devoid of all the spiritual and temporal privileges which in the Age of Reason can only make a State Church as useless as it is detested in the country. But 'Rome was not built in a day', and since time immemorial it has been such a great joy for Denmark for every important question to take a long time to solve that I am loathe to wish for any more haste over a matter that I consider wise and beneficial, unless, in contrast to the breaking of the parish-tie and a little freedom around hymn-singing, it were absolutely essential. This is in order for the process of fermentation to be calmed down to a quiet, beneficent development of a new church character that is in keeping with the times and the needs of the people. I am not asking for rapid progress, but I do fear any kind of crab-walk backwards – and my heart bleeds over all the despair. So I venture to say that even if a majority of our pastors preferred to be tied again by the strange desire for popehood that continues to dog our profession rather than set their parishioners free, nevertheless the clear realisation of 'the abomination of desolation'[195] that would follow from this weighs far more heavily in the State's scales than the voices of many pastors motivated solely by prejudice, or what is worse!

The Indispensability of the State Church

Many thousands in our day ask: 'But what is the use of a State Church?' Even its sensible defenders admit that it must be completely transformed if it is not to be a national scourge! The argument that it prevents sects from being formed is a legend from the Middle Ages which its wise friends ridicule in their admission that it is precisely an Established Church that *creates* every sect. Once that church is dismissed, the sects have no civil status. Thus in North America we never hear one faith community accuse another of being 'a sect', but we do hear them all praising freedom of conscience! The idea that priests in a State Church are models of decency, while heretical priests are fanatical and spineless, is an old story told by our State Church priests which succes-

---

195. Mt 24:15 et al.

sive governments in Denmark have swallowed. But to their shame the history of the Church teaches us the complete opposite. For if we compare the best priests in Israel with Jesus, whom they sentenced to death, and with His apostles, whom they flogged, or if we compare the Christian Church's bishops and priests while it was being proclaimed a den of robbers with the Christian Church that becomes the Holy of Holies in the Roman Empire with the emperor becoming Pontifex Maximus,[196] then every sensible state would ask for 'sect-priests'. Doubtless even the English bishops would wish that the morals of the Established Church were as good as they were among the Quakers, Methodists, and Presbyterians!

Common sense also tells us that priests who are not paid or maintained by the state but must settle for the standing they have, as pious men and diligent carers are for their own sake compelled to do much more to achieve a good appearance than state priests. And when the latter declare that this demonstrates a shameful hypocrisy, the wise statesman must answer thus: 'What remains inside and outside the State Church when all *appearances* are removed is left to the heart's connoisseur to know and judge, but we statesmen, who can see no further than anyone's teeth[197] and cannot assess their will at the moment of action, must ask at least for 'a good appearance'. We should of course be delighted if the remainder lived up to that description so that the lustre is genuine!'

Such an address meets us much more pointedly among the informed Dissenters in England than among the somewhat ignorant clergy-tormentors in Denmark, but it is by no means less well-founded. We must assume such an address if we are to draw up a balance sheet for the genuine usefulness that our State Church represents in the Age of Reason; for in this age it is a great betrayal today to build on an assumption which tomorrow, with a little enlightenment from London or Paris, is seen to be nothing but misguided prejudice. Nor must we place too much emphasis on the service that State Church pastors perform by enjoining blind obedience to the authorities. On the one hand pastors do not do this unless the authorities are willing to let them be rulers of conscience, and on the other hand everywhere the time is almost past when pastors could browbeat people by making Hell hot for them! Those pastors who truly have the faith of our fathers will in no uncertain terms impress upon their congregations obedience to all legal authority as a matter of conscience, but they will do so even more certainly *outside* the State Church than inside, and at the same time we must remember that this only avails their fellow-believers, i.e. only a few, while the majority

---

196. Pontifex Maximus (Lat., 'the greatest bridge-builder') was the title used first by the pre-Christian Roman religious leader, and assumed later by the Christian pope.

197. The Danish proverb translates as 'You cannot see people further than their teeth'. Grundtvig was a great believer in proverbs, which he claimed contained 'the wisdom of the people'. In 1845 he even published a collection of 15,000 well-known as well as rare Danish proverbs entitled *Danish Proverbs and Sayings*.

these days will show no more obedience than they have to, or than they believe to be to their advantage.

However, this is the starting-point for the great desire of every state in our time to have a church in which the faith of our fathers remains, with the right to that freedom of activity of which it is capable and with the opportunity to extend a corresponding ineffably beneficial enlightenment to the state. When therefore they claimed in the 1790s that if priests were necessary at all, it was solely for the sake of 'the School',[198] they were saying more than they realised, and they developed the idea very lazily, for they were thinking superficially and were themselves in need of schooling. It is well-known that the still influential Enlightenment of the 18th century could not find a more recalcitrant eulogist in all the world than I myself. But I must agree with that age that every planned eclipse of enlightenment in the Age of Reason is a work of artifice that brings upon us double shame because it can only be unsuccessful. By neglecting enlightenment in our day we reject the only powerful means we have to prevent the natural consequences of that conceit and obstinacy which we cannot eliminate and which the language of power can only make worse.

These faults, natural to the Age of Reason, and combined with arrogance, lack of faith, and the false enlightenment originating from the latter, were what broke up the great states of old. The clearer it is that all the states of Christendom are threatened by the same dangers, the more eagerly should we work towards a thorough enlighten-ment to demonstrate that nobody won but everybody lost with the dissolution of these states – even thieves and villains, because there were too many of them in the trade and they soon exhausted their lines of supply. An enlightenment that goes hand in hand with the State religion is therefore also being considered even in England, although one important realisation is lacking in this attempt: namely, that the State has never had nor ever will have a *religion*. For 'the state' is only a personification, and not a real person, which one *has* to be before one can believe anything, let alone be trusted by the people. 'State religion' is therefore an artificial phrase, and our State clergy have overlooked this because on church matters they always confuse the state with them-selves. Wherever the authorities try to force the people to accept the so-called religion of the 'State clergy', or force its own religion on learned and lay alike, being told that this is 'enlightening', it will hardly *please* the people, nor will posterity ever allow that such 'enlightening' was wise. So the enlightening that they believe should surround the State religion with a halo will always be both unpopular and unhistorical – a pure delusion to conceal the emptiness of what it *should* surround.

---

198. 'The (university) School' covers all higher learning, and forms the third branch of Grundtvig's concern for 'Church, State, and School'(see vol.5 forthcoming in this series on Grundtvig's philosophy).

If on the other hand 'state religion' means the same as 'the faith of our fathers', which in the Middle Ages was the 'holy mother' or at least the 'loving wet nurse' of civil society, then it is very true that the forefather-faith of Christianity has the great advantage over all heathen folk-belief that it generates a corresponding enlightenment which is worth far more than gold to the State in the Age of Reason. If, however, the State wants to benefit from this enlightenment, it must in no way seek to impose this forefather-faith on its people but must allow it to work freely in its Church alongside its opponents, in other words it must behave like the Danish government for the last half-century. Any *compulsion* makes the faith of our fathers unpopular as well as ineffective, since all compulsion in matters of faith conflicts with its spirit, for "where the Spirit of the Lord is, there is freedom".[199] A faith that is deprived of its spirit is a death's head that scares away children, but men it only embitters. So however fervently all wise statesmen might wish the faith of our fathers to be in the hearts of all our people, they will realise that compulsion is divisive; they must limit themselves to protecting it within our State Church against those diametrically opposed who would outlaw it. But wherever else what has happened to us has also occurred – with faith being seen as a minor matter and enlightenment as a major matter in our State Church – there is room for the faith of our fathers to develop an enlightenment as beneficial and honourable for civil society as all experience shows the enlightenment which is conceited and self-willed to be destructive and thus dishonourable. To the same degree that the faith of our fathers has truly been cherished by the people, its modest historical enlightenment will have a mollifying and educative effect on its opposite. For the faith of our fathers is of a historical nature, and from its historical effects it can call up all necessary testimonies to its authenticity and heavenly origin. In the Age of Reason a training in history is a universal advantage, both for the age itself and as a support for the bourgeoisie in their old age; as we know, shared advantage makes for firmest union, especially in our time.

The State, therefore, by offering civil protection to pastors who preach the faith of our fathers in its church, retains them as friends; and by letting them look after themselves spiritually, it obliges them to remain at their posts. In this way the State does both the faith of our fathers and itself the greatest service. Simultaneously, it facilitates a training in history the depth of which rests on the people's natural capacity and whose civil usefulness grows to the same degree as the State rests on a sound historical basis, and that training will always be of great benefit. This was the sentiment in Denmark, where there has been a love of history from time immemorial and where we have therefore only the best to expect of it. It is also the deeper reason why the freest 'State Church' deserving of the name has arisen here and now needs only a

---

199. 2 Cor 3:17.

helping hand with the breaking of the parish-tie in order to raise itself to a brilliance that the Danish government can enjoy and Europe admire. The understanding of history which the faith of our fathers develops will be concerned not only with our people's history and the immediate needs of the State, but also with universal history, with the defence of our faith, and an understanding of Holy Scripture. We know that Holy Scripture is written in two renowned languages of classical times and is the great stumbling-block not only between Jews and Christians but also between pastors of our fathers' faith and all other scribes of Christianity. Thus, as long as the faith of our fathers remains in living interaction with the world, Holy Scripture will maintain and promote the universal learning which, even limited to its Christian context, does the faith of our fathers undying honour and is the only thing that can lead to a full explanation of the world and mankind.

So if a state protects the pastors of its forefathers' faith alongside all manner of other scribes, then it ensures as far as possible a beneficial, indeed indispensable, education of its people, while simultaneously facilitating the deepest understanding of universal history, which is the great concern of the entire human race. As long as the human spirit remains equal to the task and Providence does not lose sight of the world, this will bless and benefit every state that truly nurtures it to its breast and upholds it in its Church.

However differently the Bible is interpreted and explained with regard to the faith of our fathers, its historical side is nevertheless clear, attractive, and rich in thought for learned and lay alike; and its ethical teaching is similarly pure and pithy. By commenting on the major truths of natural religion – of a living, omnipotent, just, and merciful God without whose care no sparrow falls to earth[200] – it is also so enriching that no state can ask for a better literary basis for educating its people, provided that the pastors' disputes can be kept in balance so that no side becomes all-powerful. For in that case it will only rest on its laurels and fob the people off with a Bible story and a book of doctrine (*liber sententiarum*[201]), which sometimes will be the opposite of the Bible and will always offer "stones for bread".[202] In both cases our State Church has clear and cautionary examples from the middle of the previous and the beginning of this century.

Our people's education was thus far from being hostile to the Bible, for it was limited to Luther's *Catechism* and Pontoppidan's *Exposition*, and it was obvious that wherever the faith of our fathers was not at hand to aid us, this education was so

---

200. Mt 10:29.
201. Lat., lit. 'Book of Moral Sayings'. A number of such books were written in the Middle Ages, the most famous being *The Four Books of Sentences* (*Libri Quattuor Sententiarum*), a systematic compilation of authoritative statements on biblical passages written by Peter Lombard in the 12th century.
202. Mt 7:9.

lean, so tasteless and unfruitful, indeed so deadening and burdensome, that if such orthodoxy had remained in power until now, it is likely that all would have been lost. How lethargic, dead, and apathetic the orthodox clergy were can best be seen from the spiritual opposition that the heterodoxy faced in print in the days when everyone believed that the pen would carry the victory, for had Balle not been there, the Bible would literally have had to defend itself![203]

If we turn the page and look at Henke's and Thonboe's *Bible Stories* alongside Campe's *Guidelines*,[204] then we see clearly that in the course of a generation people would even have forgotten that the Bible existed if *that* set of pastors had become autocratic. We could see how deeply they slept and how little they were able to cope spiritually when they were called to account for their soundness and scriptural knowledge. If Professor Clausen[205] had not grown up under their unparalleled failure and taken care of them a little, we should have taken the whole State Church away from them without striking a blow and it would have passed quietly away before we realised it!

Now, however, the dispute has turned serious and entered the public realm – to the benefit of the State and our forefathers' faith. For both of these it is extremely important that the dispute is kept alive, if possible until the end of the world! Both sides have benefitted from the move towards a genuine biblical and fruitful education of the people, towards a more complete canon law and biblical exegesis, and towards the advance of general learning. This is enough to show what we have lacked and how far self-defence and a competitive spirit can drive scholarly opponents. But if we force the keen supporters of the faith of our fathers out of the Church using a liturgy by Clausen or something resembling a parish papacy, or if we compelled Clausen's followers to teach according to the Creed and baptise according to the Altar Book, we would be putting an end to the most beneficial education with the highest aspirations that ever began to grow in Christendom before it even had time to make itself known, before it could secure the deep respect that we dare to hope will guarantee its progress for many centuries to come.

Our village schools,[206] which England is now in all seriousness beginning to envy us, are undoubtedly an indispensable medium for popular education. But even when

---

203. The reference is to Balle's periodical, *Christian Weekly on the Dictum: The Bible Defends Itself* (1798-1810), which in turn had been a response to *Jesus and Reason*, a weekly published between 1797-1801 by Otto Horrebow (1769-1823).

204. The German rationalist H.P.C. Henke (1752-1809) published *Selected Bible Stories for Early Youth* (1796); Peter Thonboe (1769-1806) published *Bible Stories as an Introduction to Religious Instruction in Schools* (1804). J.H Campe published *Guidelines to the Teaching of the Christian Religion for More Cultivated Youth* (1800).

205. For 'Clausen', the professor's father, see note 161.

206. Grundtvig's Danish word, *almueskole*, denotes peasant schools, or the common people's schools. In his day these were to be found in the small towns and villages – as opposed to the civic schools in the large towns and cities.

this achieves a living balance at a civic school[207] or a people's high school[208] – a balance which to its detriment it currently lacks – biblical scholars will still be required to give education a religious slant that it must not be without. Similarly, pastors with a scholarly training will be key intermediaries who can maintain the people's respect for genuine learning by allowing them to reap its fruits.

I have often envied England its glorious colleges, where in a pleasant environment men of learning can dedicate their whole life to the studies that please them. If Nordic academic learning one day attains the living balance that I sincerely hope for it, with a great common university for the three Nordic kingdoms, then it will certainly gain such grand apartments for study.[209] But even then the academic world would have as great a need of a thousand vicarages if our well-read citizens are to influence the universities in the same popularising way that they influence our people with their learning! For experience teaches us that however necessary it is for some to be imprisoned in a study for the sole purpose of 'spending time with the dead', and however important it is to keep studying for sound knowledge to be maintained and the ensuing scholarship to grow, nevertheless such things have a very damaging effect on the life and health of the soul. So without powerful remedies the stiffness and coldness felt in the feet, known as pedantry and apathy, will be the surest portent of death. At this point our pastors, who have a time-honoured claim to the spiritual art of healing, must come to the rescue; indeed we can hardly imagine a better earthly antidote than the one which well-read country pastors drink in on a daily basis, in living contact with nature and under spiritual and heartfelt interaction with country people. If we add to this what a *nursery* for learning and culture vicarages as a whole must be under these conditions, where 'wife and children' belong almost as necessarily to the house as they are excluded from the colleges, then one must be a philistine in most need of a pastor if one calls into question the importance, indeed the spiritual necessity, of such a free State Church.

Conclusion

If we gather all this together, we can see that a State Church in which the faith of our fathers continues to be active and engender a corresponding enlightenment is of the

---

207. Grundtvig's Danish word, *borger-akademi*, denotes civic schools in the large towns and cities, attended by children of the middle-class and above.

208. After spending three summers in a row in England in 1829-31 Grundtvig began to formulate his ideas for a 'people's high school'. See further in *The School for Life* (2011).

209. Grundtvig is referring here to the actual rooms that professors had at universities in England. He was particularly impressed by his stay at Trinity College, Cambridge in the summer of 1831. However, his dream of a pan-Nordic university in Gothenburg was never realised.

greatest importance in the Age of Reason. It can be practised throughout Christendom if only the authorities either produce a revolution in the Church-State, or cleverly maintain it as it is but break the parish-tie in time for the supporters of our forefathers' faith in the midst of the confusion to allow that freedom of conscience in the State Church that they are otherwise forced to look for *outside* the Church.

This is a brand new realisation for which the Danish government alone should take the honour, for only its genuine discretion and impartiality has made it possible. It is a realisation for which Denmark should therefore reap the first and thus the best fruits. Over the past fifty years our government's singular steadfastness has favoured the church revolution and at no point given rise to the suspicion that it would eradicate or expel the faith of our fathers from the State Church. So we pastors who hold that faith must continue to discard our inherited prejudices and apply our shrewdness to give it a free sphere of activity in the State Church without, as our forefathers did, using its name to control the people's faith and conscience. It took a long time and we were hard put to realise what lay before our very eyes, for blood is never so thin that it is not thicker than water, and the impulse to hierarchy is never so small in Denmark that we would not prefer to conquer than to risk submission. Better to triumph once and for all than be at war until Judgement Day without using the most brilliant victories to win more than permission to retain what we have! Under such circumstances virtue clearly needs incentives so powerful that we will hardly exercise it before we must make 'a virtue of necessity'!

I cannot otherwise explain why I could not just as well twenty years ago have sung the praises of a Church-State loosening and shown how, to be not just harmless but inexpressibly beneficial, it only needed to become complete with the breaking of the parish-tie. For it is as clear as sunlight that when the tie that has bound the Protestant clergy to the Confessional Books breaks, then the Church-State arrangement is broken too, inasmuch as, spiritually speaking, every parish pastor becomes his own master, and that is for the best! It is good for the authorities, who no longer have a clergy to deal with as the representatives of the faith of our fathers but only with a number of ecclesiastical civil servants, and it is good for the pastors themselves if they wish to live and work in the Spirit. All that is needed is for it also to be good for the people and for the State. It would be in no way good for them if instead of the dead pope there were just as many living 'popes' as there are parish pastors! For though they may be so few that the authorities can easily overlook them, they will become freer to exercise their beliefs and to exert harder pressure on the consciences within their narrow circles. Wherever this covert popery is not strangled at birth under the breaking of the parish-tie, it will either generate the most terrible indifference to all religion among the people or, to the greatest detriment, it will give new birth to the Church-State and cause disunion in civic life. The latter would clearly be the case in the North, where the reply of the faith of our fathers would force the little popes to unite under a little ecclesiastical Napoleon. Following this, there would be a restoration of the dead pope, knights' tournaments in the dog days,[210] and so on and so forth. With the breaking of the parish-tie on the other hand it will accord with the State's interest and the people's will that parish pastors who are no longer living popes will never be bound to any dead pope who prevents them from being living pastors. For power-seeking pastors this is doubtless a desperate situation, since not even the highest dignitaries in the State Church offer them the slightest favourable prospect, while for lethargic and sleepy pastors it is equally desperate, since the dead pope is indispensable to them both as a shield and an excuse. But it is in the interests of the authorities, the people, and enlightenment in general that the lethargic and the power-seeking feel ill-at-ease in church, while for capable, active, and popular pastors such a free State Church will be a little Heaven on earth. It may never be without "thorns and thistles",[211] but it will be a mirror of the world of the spirit that no people who come to know it would want to lose for double the cost of such a State Church.

I am well aware that – as in North America where freedom of conscience already exists and there is no State Church – such a development would not move the people to want one like it. The danger of losing what they already have would seem certain, and the advantage distinctly uncertain. But where there is an *old* State Church, as in Denmark, and where despite all government endeavours it is as yet only Calvinists, Catholics, Jews, State Church pastors, and Copenhageners who enjoy something like freedom of conscience, nothing at all is attempted, but much is gained by what gives all these people this freedom, even if it were the only beneficial consequences thereof. The Danish government has long realised that universal freedom of conscience in our day must be brought about somehow or other.

Once our breaking of the parish-tie shows that this can be granted without abolishing the State Church or creating sects in opposition to it, the English will immediately regret that they did not understand this in time. I imagine that even in North America they will imitate an arrangement that as far as possible on earth links all the advantages of spiritual freedom and civic order. Admittedly it is a precondition here that the government has the more or less exclusive right of nomination to church livings, so the reform in England must take a number of steps before such a free national State Church would be conceivable there. But in this regard the reform in Denmark also has such a clear lead that there are few areas left where, by choosing only a pastor from one and the same 'school', a private person could counteract the intention behind the breaking of the parish-bond. It follows by nature that in a free

210. i.e. the hot and sultry days of summer.
211. Hos 10:8.

National State Church reasonable regard must be taken for the people's well-being, so the religious viewpoint that conspicuously lacks a Church representative in a particular area is if possible given one. This is also in the State's interest, which requires that pastors are never permitted to pass away in 'sinful security' but must, when they find themselves surrounded by 'old school friends', be sure to appoint, when the next living falls vacant, someone who is a thorn in their own eye.[212]

And now, to conclude! What books need more than people – so as not to be misunderstood and unappreciated but to accomplish their purpose in being published – is obviously good fortune and success. Even though, unlike the heathens of old, I in no way regard good fortune and success as gods, I do believe along with the Christians of old that they come from above, so I cheerfully pray for them to descend on these pages. They are dedicated to a paternal government, to civic unity, spiritual freedom, and historical progress. Human enlightenment is a poor yet not unworthy sacrifice on the altar of the fatherland when governed paternally. This is our peaceful, considerate, equitable Denmark of loving memory and with a history that shows it is not cowardice that pleads the cause of peace, nor the spirit of rebellion that pleads the cause of freedom!

It would be my greatest joy if I could convince both friends and enemies among the clergy that they must never seek domination over other people's faith but only permission to serve those whom they please and to argue only about who serves best. But I will also count myself happy, even against the wishes of both parties, if what happens best serves Denmark and the State Church as well as the faith of our fathers, enlightenment, truth, and love!

---

212. Num 33:55; Mt 7:5.

6. The Christian Church and German Theology (1837)

Introduction by Brian Degn Mårtensson

In 1835-36 widespread controversy followed the publication in Germany of David Strauss' two-volume work *The Life of Jesus Critically Examined* (*Das Leben Jesu, kritisch bearbeitet*). Its markedly mythical view of the gospels as developed from Hegel's philosophy was described by Grundtvig as "the preparation for a Homeric tempest" in theology, which indeed proved to be the case. The ensuing fiery dispute on the nature of the gospels and the life of Jesus led to Strauss even publishing corrections to his work, as well as to a series of contributions culminating in a split between right and left 'Hegelians'. A number of Strauss's functional perspectives were passed down through the history of ideas and influenced Karl Marx, amongst others.

Grundtvig begins his article, published in *Nordic Church Times* no. 50 in 1837, by emphasising that he is unfazed by the dispute: Christianity is too strong a faith and the Church too firm an institution to be moved by such polemics. In a poetic sense, however, he welcomes the debate precisely for those reasons, and he compares it to three other recent religious divisions: between rationalists and super-naturalists, between Protestants and Catholics, and between syncretists and Lutherans. Again he promotes the liberal, Lutheran view that has been characteristic of his writing thus far. He sees the dispute as theologically deficient, in particular in its fundamental premise: the polemicists of the 19th century have misunderstood the nature of faith and Scripture, which were already clarified in the third century. He rejects the Hegelian view and all 'scholasticism', while looking to a civil peace and scholarly freedom in which "the human spirit would develop all its powers and resources in the great struggle for the crown of life".

***

The Christian Church is an unshakeable fact, and German theology a shallow conception of Christianity, so the relation between them is fundamentally the same as the rock to the wind, or Jesus' actual life to the book by Strauss,[213] which blows wind around the rock. However, when a house is built on such firm foundations that it can defy every tempest, and when it is so well supplied with warmth that one can live

---

213. Dr David Strauss (1808-74), applied the concept of myth to the Gospels and denied the divine nature of Jesus.

there with open windows and doors, then there is no denying that fresh air does it good, especially since the Lord has made sure that wherever the wind has free access, the light also has its highway. So for the last three centuries German theology has truly contributed a great deal to the purification and enlightenment of the Christian Church. From this we can reasonably conclude that in both the present and the future the same theology will contribute much to proving how firmly the Church stands, and to keeping it light and airy. If we are to benefit from this, we must of course not run with the wind over the rooftops and straight through the house as though the wind were the Holy Spirit. Instead we must remain where we are, and use the freedom to draw breath in fresh air and in the enlightenment this provides for spirited activity: We must say as it is written: God is not in the wind that passes by His face, but is "in the gentle sound" of the voice from heaven.[214]

If for a moment we view German theology from this firmly-grounded position, it resembles the preparation for a Homeric tempest in which the winds from all four corners of the world have been awakened but have not yet rubbed the sleep out of their eyes. It is only from the completely opposite direction that the weather experts can see there is stormy weather hanging over their heads, while the multitude still believe that the winds only wish to play with one another! For the 'sea of the people' is the battlefield for the winds, and so long as they are not strong enough to rouse it, the reading public remains merely a playground for them. Even the most contrasting books that we can see on our shelves are not in conflict with one another and only seem to be so when we read them imagining what would happen if their writers met in real life and tested them on one another's brows! If we wish to know what a polemic entails, we should not make a point of asking how artistic are the books in question and how wittily are they addressed, but only what is their backbone! What is the life-spirit and power behind them in their writers and supporters? For experience will always confirm that in the real world it is not the gloss and thunderclap that decide the outcome but the life-spirit and the inherent power.

Recently we have seen three polemics crossing swords among the reading public for theology: one between the so-called rationalists and super-naturalists, another between Protestants and Catholics, and the third between syncretists and Lutherans. All three are actually ancient quarrels from the 16th century, but their forces are distributed in a very different way in the 19th century, so rationalism or naturalism, which amount to the same thing, are now so superior to everything else in Germany as they were inferior in the 16th. We only have to see what theological renown such natural

---

214. 1 Kings 19:11.

rationalist Lilliputians as Semler, Løfler, Henke, Røhr, Zimmermann, Bretschneider[215] etc. have acquired and then ask ourselves whether this could have happened if they had not been the mouthpiece, or rather the quill-pusher, for millions who through them voiced their opinion and of course considered themselves absolutely splendid! Otherwise how can any knowledgeable person explain the astonishing attention that Strauss has received with his totally Turkish[216] view of gospel history? Or how can one explain the curtseys that even his opponents have made towards him except it be because of the quietly dominant anti-Christian mood that one expects to break out into open warfare soon against all piety, faith, and genuine fear of God? It must also be this premonition of an impending storm that stirs up the troubled waters around Strauss's book, which as a declaration of war and open polemic from the big wide world can only be regarded as *awful*, for as a genuine attack on historical Christianity now in its nineteenth century it is more embarrassing than ridiculous.

For eighteen hundred years the Christian Church has been unshakeable, and the Christian faith has performed matchless deeds, including teaching to read and write all the Germans who now rail against it! Over these eighteen hundred years such a multitude of books has been written partly to contest and partly to rescue the natural credibility of the gospel history that if books could have rendered it doubtful, this would have happened at least 1500 years before Strauss was born. So if we take the 1600-year-old allegorical exposition of the Bible story that Origen[217] propagated at the high school in Alexandria, which was the only seat of learning at the time, it strives no less than the mythical interpretation to undermine the Bible's historical credibility. For a century Origen was this oracle of learning for the Greek clergy that Strauss is unlikely to be for the German clergy. Finally the Diocletian persecution[218] allied to this was such a test for the Christians' faith that if books could shake it, their power would inevitably have destroyed it. These matters belong to the 3rd century of the Christian Church, and if as a scholar in the 19th century one is looking to cross swords with it, one must obviously not pitch into the ancient Book of the Church and its learned interpretations. Its absurdities have been displayed and exulted over thousands of times without us ever seeing a stone moved in the singular building from which it came. The Bible clearly has an unparalleled power to defy the times; indeed even when in the name of a hostile world and on an excellent pretext one actually seeks to declare

215. These were all German theologians: Johann Semler (1725-91), Josias Løffler (1752-1816), Heinrich Henke (1752-1809), Johann Røhr (1777-1848), Ernst Zimmermann (1786-1832), Karl Bretschneider (1776-1848).

216. i.e. non-Christian.

217. Origen (185-254 CE) was a biblical commentator and Christian philosopher in Alexandria and Caesarea.

218. Emperor Diocletian (284-305) instituted the final persecution of Christians in the Roman Empire with his edict in 303 enforcing traditional religious practices of Rome in connection with the Imperial cult. As many as 3,500 Christians were executed.

war on the Church, it is a poor, threadbare basis to invoke the obscurity of the Book of the Church and the stupidity of its interpreters. This is because, even from its early days and in the hands of unlettered men, obscurity is not a cause for shame, and even less is it an offence in the Church to own and use such a book which, without being convicted of any historical falsehood, affirms and illuminates the Church's ancient revered faith, well-tested in the fire.

If the hostile world wants a good pretext to assess whether now is a better time than before to destroy the Christian Church and wipe off the face of the earth the strange people who take pride in having citizenship in heaven, it should trouble itself not with an old book that it can leave unread or theological systems and exegetical tricks it can laugh at. It should instead look at something that all Christians have to acknowledge if they are not to exclude themselves from the Church and thereby renounce their inheritance of sainthood in the light that it has promised them. Either Strauss is so ignorant that he does not even know on what the Christian Church stands and falls, or he dare not tackle the living and prefers to score a cheap point at the expense of the dead. This is mere humbug! It is ridiculous to watch a whole crowd of German theologians march into the field on this declaration of war to demonstrate how justifiable the gospel story is when it is only being disputed by a pen and can be corrected and improved a little by its learned friends! Since it is doubtful whether a single one of them has found anything false by way of myth or legend in the gospel story, at least as Strauss pointedly remarks at the beginning and end, they undoubt-edly have the smiling prospect of a brilliant victory and thus a surge of renown. But the campaign will soon be over and a number of theological bookworms with their corresponding works would be all that could be carried off in triumph, provided that the campaign was linked to the Church in Protestant Germany.

On the other hand, now that the little flock of old-fashioned Lutherans is the only one that has a more or less honest leg to stand on, the future would look dark for Christians if the prevalent anti-Christian sentiment were ready to break out into proper persecution. Since that is hardly the case, however, until the political upheaval threatening Germany erupts, the Christians will probably maintain their respite. Even the persecution they must presently suffer under the name of 'Lutherans' at the hands of the so-called 'Evangelical Church' will doubtless soon make way for a tolerance that is clearly just as advisable for Prussia as it is conspicuously fair. I therefore assume that for the time being the German theologians are allowed to cavort around with one another not only with useless weapons among an increas-ingly indifferent reading-public but also with the living Word that stirs the people at large. Under this assumption the open feud that Strauss has proclaimed rather than initiated will doubtless contribute a great deal to clearing the ecclesiastical air and to showing what in the course of eighteen centuries has actually borne and protected the Church. Already Ulmann[219] for one has pointed out that this firmly entrenched building will require far more than pen-nibs to upset it, and has argued that people are not so eager to relinquish their shared faith and the consequent source of its blessing just because scholars quarrel over genealogies or over how well or badly the childhood stories of Jesus in Matthew and Luke tally. Indeed, it is most likely that today or tomorrow a clever giant will force Mr. Strauss and all his patrons to see that it is in the School of Theology that they have discharged their weapons and wasted their powers with no more than a couple of roof tiles flying off the Church! If they wish to *change* it, they must begin again and prepare themselves for a quite different kind of opposition.

For this to happen, the Christian-minded German theologians must first overcome the childish horror of 'the Church' which has lain in almost every Protestant since the Reformation. If Mr. Haase[220] now wishes to make the renunciation of every infallible external Church a shibboleth, he has a long way to go. The problem is not what the hares but what the lions will do. When they feel a need for 'the Church', they will not be scared away by the Pope, who creeps off into a mousehole when he is in a fix. We can already see that the so-called 'invisible' Church which Protestant theologians wish to set up to replace the real Church as we know it is an empty conception, a castle in the air. We are close to forgetting that a Church is neither more nor less than a *faith community*, which as such is infallible when its faith is divinely true and 'real' not just in the physical sense in the *eyes* of all but also in the *ears* of all, when it openly stands for its faith through all its members.

If the discerning German theologian gets this far, he will see precisely that the Christian Church stands for its faith in Baptism, and that this Creed contains for Catholics or Protestants not a single word about the Pope or any papistry. This is all the more reason why, since papistry contradicts the Creed, it should be excluded from the Church. Moreover, if it promotes itself to being a third Article of Faith, it has already condemned itself, since no Church that establishes a Baptismal Covenant with its members on the forgiveness of sins and the promise of eternal life can add conditions for salvation without refuting itself. A Church can only counsel its members as to what it considers fitting for retaining one's faith, fighting the good fight, and finishing the race. With this discovery the Protestant theologian will naturally gain the courage to glorify 'the holy, catholic Church' in spite of any Catholic and will find himself liberated from all responsibility for the School of Theology that must defend itself and its biblical interpretation as best it can without this affecting the Church's members as such. For not even in Baptism have they confessed a faith in or about

---

219. Karl Christian Ulmann (1793-1871), Baltic German theologian.
220. Adolf Theodor Haase (1802-70), German evangelical theologian.

Scripture, i.e., handed its interpretation freely to priests and scribes provided they do not thereby seek to dispute the common faith.

I can well imagine how a Christian theologian in Germany will rejoice in heart and soul when he sees how systematically he can organise and how easily (with objective validity) he can develop the relationship between church and school, between faith and theology in the Christian Church. Then faith becomes unchangeable but theology becomes constantly progressive with all the scholarly freedom that any Christian could desire. It only remains to say that if a Christian parish or church does not alter its creed and Baptismal Covenant, they can boldly defy both the Pope and the Turk,[221] whatever happens in their theological schools.

The next problem we meet in Protestant Germany is the sad fact that in most places they have either *altered* the Creed or, at the least, omitted the renunciation of the Devil, which is also part of the Baptismal Covenant. Presumably the German theologian who makes this discovery belongs to the old-fashioned Lutherans who have preserved what they once had in order to be sure that at least no one took their crown away. At all events both he and all believers among the people will at once see that any alteration to the Baptismal Covenant is a great error that must be rectified as soon as it is discovered. Once the Protestant Christian theologians in Germany learn to let the Church stand on its original foundation as the rock on which Christ has set it, the division between all the Protestants who do not trust their own common sense and all the Catholics who believe in Christ rather than the Pope will naturally disappear. Instead there will clearly be a holy, catholic Church, whose scattered members do not disturb society just because temporal princes set various conditions on the Church's activity or because the Schools of Theology dispute interpretations of the Bible or their own relation to the Church. Those who remain papists or Protestants against the holy, catholic Church will be recognised by their obvious alteration to the Baptismal Covenant.

In these circumstances it is doubtless of little significance what advantage Dr Strauss may derive from his protest against historical Christianity, though since German theology is still far from wiping away its cobwebs, it is hardly wrong to place him in this new category in relation to little people like us who have realised what serves our peace and our growth in the grace and knowledge of the Lord.

If Dr Strauss were to come to us with such a book, we would immediately point out that of all his objections to the history of the gospel, only those directed against the possibility of the resurrection and the ascension affected the Christian Church, and that he would have to admit that, lacking the incidental circumstances, he did not have the evidence to prove these absolutely impossible. However hard it might be

---

221. i.e. the Muslim.

to accept this, he would realise that he had to do so and would never again attempt to present such self-evident and irrefutable proof of the absolute impossibility of either the resurrection or ascension of Christ. He himself would have to admit that such proof must be presented to them before all Christians on that basis would have to renounce a faith that with its open and hidden effects over eighteen centuries had provided such a matchless assurance.

If he wishes to continue the dispute, he must change both weapons and position and deny the apostolic authenticity of our Baptismal Covenant, partly by separating it from its historical witness and partly by catching us in a lie. For the historical Christ cannot possibly be the founder of the Church if by altering our Baptismal Covenant we can *leave* His Church and establish a new one of our own making!

Let us impress upon him the solemn assurance of the entire Church that Baptism is the most authentic historical evidence that we are aware of, and let us ask him if he genuinely finds comfort in this truly historical question from presenting a contrary case that did not seriously weaken, let alone upset, the witness of the holy, catholic Church to which we belong.

Since, with his allegation that Scripture is spurious, he would deprive himself of the only source from which he could hope to find objections to the apostolic authenticity of our Baptismal Covenant, his only option would be to withdraw it and claim that, even if neither the spuriousness of Christianity nor the impossibility of the resurrection and ascension of Christ can be strictly proven, our historical Christianity was nevertheless *just* as spurious and could have had just as little effect as, from a mythical viewpoint, it had on the truly spiritual union of the divinity and humanity.

To this we would of course answer that without accepting any allegation that conflicted with our faith, we would for the time being allow scholarship to determine to what degree he was right. He himself would have to realise that even if he established such a mytho-Christian Church tomorrow, it would take eighteen centuries before it could prove itself to have made greater achievements than the *historical* Church. If, as we sincerely hope, our historical Church continued its activities at the same time, it would always be eighteen centuries ahead.

By this I do not mean to say that Dr Strauss or any other more capable giant who was truly enthused by the idea would be frightened out of the great race. On the contrary, I hope that in our time the naturalism of Christianity will be given a church form as being the only way to establish civil peace during a time of spiritual dispute. A historical decision can be reached on the important question as to whether it is our Christ or we ourselves who have confused a deep and true view of nature with a supernatural story. If such a mytho-Christian Church could be established and have any historical effect, the Hegelians must be in charge of it, for they acknowledge the historical facts as the essential starting-point and only wish to explain them through scholarship, not ignore them completely. All Church activity without a historical basis is mere somersaulting, while the story of Christ is too well attested and verified to be rejected in our enlightened times without great recklessness or an indifference to the truth. The Hegelians have also wisely realised that this story does no *damage* to naturalism, since the true matter in dispute between naturalism and old-fashioned Christianity is not what happened in days of old – and had to happen if humanity were to achieve its goal – but according to which *laws* it happened and in what relationship we stand to the historical facts to achieve that goal. So everything that the evangelists tell us about Christ may not only be true, but may be the true development of humanity and the necessary condition for learning, without us having to think that there is either anything new in human nature or any supernatural transformation of it. We can imagine human nature being equipped from the outset with the cure for all its flaws and we can imagine it capable of preparing for redemption and transfiguration.

German theologians of all colours should give up the scholasticism that hangs around them and grant one another the same freedom they themselves wish to enjoy, so that under whatever form there is true religious freedom. Were they to do so, we would glimpse a future that the past could never rival when in civil peace and scholarly freedom the human spirit would develop all its powers and resources in the great struggle for the crown of life. We must be allowed to search for this in whatever way we please, since it is something we all need. No prince is so powerful nor wise person so rich that they can grant this to their neighbour.

7. On Religious Persecution (1842)

Introduction by Brian Degn Mårtensson

The Baptist movement had its origins in Amsterdam, where the first 'Baptist' Church rejected baptism of infants in favour of baptism only of believing adults. By 1840 the movement was growing in Denmark, much to the distaste of Bishop Mynster of Zealand,[222] who demanded the compulsory baptism of infants by the State Church. Among others, Pastor Peter Kierkegaard of Pedersborg (Søren's elder brother) refused to obey his bishop, and received support from Grundtvig in this pamphlet from 1842, which argues for a wide-ranging freedom of conscience on the grounds of spiritual tolerance, political practicality, and Christian solidarity. Grundtvig was inspired not only by English thinkers such as John Locke and his own experiences on his England trips, but also by the visit to Copenhagen of the Quaker and prison reformer Elizabeth Fry and her brother Joseph John Gurney. With his reasonable competence in English, Grundtvig had been appointed their interpreter on their visit to the Copenhagen prisons the previous year. In a letter home dated 30th August 1841, Mrs Fry wrote: "We found Baptist ministers, excellent men, in one of the prisons, and many others of this sect suffered much in this country, for there is hardly any religious tolerance."[223] Grundtvig had also spoken words of comfort to the prisoners, as Joseph John Gurney noted in his journal: "They were also addressed by the celebrated pastor, Grundtwig (sic), a truly spiritual man, who seems to depend on a divine influence in his preaching. It was evident to us that the unction accompanied his words, though we could not understand them."[224]

Even more clearly now, Grundtvig argues that human freedom and human duty are the basis for true faith, and that religious persecution creates division and disagreement while rarely leading to a change in attitude. This was his own personal experience in the dispute with Professor Clausen (see Texts 1 & 4), where he himself had suffered censorship: the authorities "managed to close all the pulpits in the capital to me and sought to limit all my prospects of pastoral activity". Finally, he asserts that Lutheran

---

222. Bishop of Zealand, Jacob Mynster (1775-1854).

223. *Elizabeth Fry, A Quaker Life*, ed. Gil Skidmore (Altamira Press 2005) p. 223. For further discussion of her influence on Grundtvig, see ch. 19 in volume 4 of this series, *The Common Good: N.F.S. Grundtvig as Politician and Contemporary Historian* (forthcoming).

224. 'Unction' here means 'spiritual fervour'. *Memoirs of Joseph John Gurney*, vol. 2. ed. Joseph Braithwaite (London 1854) p. 278.

Christianity contains an implicit message of tolerance, and that, following the Augsburg Confession, any persecution must be a remnant of Roman Catholicism, since it is in conflict with the Evangelical Lutheran State Church. Now aged 59, Grundtvig had acquired something of a reputation, as well as royal support, so his own experience carried not a little weight. In both this and in *On Godly Assemblies* (Text 2) we can see that Grundtvig was not enamoured of these occasionally 'sensationalist' sects, but that he admired their spiritual energy. They should be tolerated in the greater interest: there must be "Freedom for Loki, as well as for Thor".

***

The reason I have not taken up my pen before now to make my voice heard concerning the current persecution of the Anabaptists is simply that I believed my view to be so well-known! It was not until I read the article in *Berling's Times*[225] (No. 46) on 'The Religious Freedom of the Baptists' that I became aware that many people undoubtedly regard the matter in so distorted a light that they cannot see it has to do solely with: How Christian, how Danish, how praiseworthy and how beneficial is religious persecution? For to what degree religious freedom should be a specific and basic component in the constitution of every civil society, and how far it is desirable in any state to retain church uniformity in spite of all disagreement on matters of faith and salvation, is a universal historical and philosophical question which can be disputed until the end of the world; but that is not what I wish to deal with here. What concerns me now is the extent to which Christianity, the Augsburg Confession,[226] or human experience, counsel religious *persecution*. This is such a plain and simple question that even though a comprehensive answer is more than challenging for our 'ordinary common sense', it is no more challenging than that we must at least assume that it involves all those who have learned their Church history and are pastors in a State Church that subscribes to Christianity and the Augsburg Confession. Since I myself am one of these pastors, I can no longer avoid presenting the matter in its proper light by arguing the following:

I. It is religious persecution when Anabaptists or others are imprisoned and punished merely because they practise and propagate a form of worship that deviates from the State Church.

---

225. Founded by Ernst Berling in 1749, this daily newspaper, now known as *Berlingske*, is amongst the oldest newspapers in the world.

226. The Augsburg Confession is the primary confession of faith in the Lutheran Church. It was agreed at the Diet (Council) of Augsburg on 25 June 1530 by Lutheran princes and representatives of 'free cities', and comprised 21 Chief Articles of faith and 7 statements concerning abuses of the Christian faith in the Roman Catholic Church.

2. Religious persecution contradicts the Christian faith and Creed as well as the Augsburg Confession, which the royal constitution of Denmark[227] declares to be the foundation of the State Church.

3. Experience teaches us that religious persecution does not diminish but increases division and disagreement in the kingdom.

If I could only manage to convey these plain truths with a mere one-tenth of the clarity they have for myself, then I am sure that the Danish government would either abolish the punitive laws against religious sects as such or let them remain dead and impotent. It is in no way the *wish* of the Danish government to practise religious persecution, since, in preferring to follow the Danish way of thinking, it inclines more to indifference than to strictness, and manifests itself in the care with which at least from above it seeks to alleviate the severity of the law.

I take the case to be settled beforehand that it really is 'religious persecution' if Anabaptists or others are summonsed and convicted without being charged with a misdemeanour under the guise of worship or with a proselytisation that infringes the civil freedom and rights of others; for it cannot be proved more clearly than it proves itself. Only with the strictest formalism can it be claimed that such people are judged and punished not for their deviant form of worship but merely for an actual violation of a specific statute in the law, an explicit decree, or public notice. If the judge is accused of brutality, he can defend himself with the fact that the persecution is legal, but of course the persecution does not thereby cease to be what it is; and by being undertaken according to the provisions of the law it becomes only a correct, *legal* persecution. On the other hand, as will be seen, I at once grant that there may well be something that such people call 'religious persecution' without justification, when those in question commit some civil misdemeanour under the pretext of it belonging to their form of worship, or because they were striving to force their religious opinions onto others or were cajoling minors. In the first case the law ought to punish them doubly hard in my view; and in the second, it should hardly be allowed for adherents of the state religion let alone others to use religious force. In the case of the Anabaptists I should also add that if they continue to insist on baptising on open ground, they could be punished for this without it being a form of religious persecution; for that is the same as with Catholics if they flout the law with their public processions in the streets. But for as long as this has not been announced to them and they are still punished for house-gatherings or for immersions that seem openly offensive to our custom and under our skies, they are for friend and foe alike martyrs for what should be a matter

---

227. The royal constitution of the absolute monarchy in Denmark (*Konge-Loven*) was introduced by Frederik III in 1665 and lasted until the democratic constitution was introduced in 1849.

of conscience for all, and they complain rightly of religious persecution. We are free to say that Anabaptists have relatively few or no grounds to complain as long as the adherents of the State Church are themselves pursued by the law and punished merely for holding 'godly assemblies' outside the appointed time, place, or manner that is lawful, or in greater numbers than one of Christian VI's decrees determines; but even though the persecution of these poor people can be called much stricter and more incomprehensible, the case of the Anabaptists remains just as much one of persecution.

Over many centuries the Pope in Rome and his clerics have claimed that religious persecution is a Christian activity – either a Christian duty or an act allowed by Christianity. Since we are all children of papists, none of us can be surprised that a little papistry has still stuck to us, especially those of us who belong to the priesthood. But among Protestants I do not know of any who have argued that it could be proved from the New Testament or from the spirit of Christianity that we should persecute with fire and sword, or fines, imprisonment and the like, those who pursue another form of worship. It is much more the case that there is a general assumption among us that all such persecution is fundamentally in conflict with the spirit and letter of Christianity. It is only for certain reasons of state that even Protestant authorities are forced to some extent to close their eyes to the message of Christianity and copy the Roman authorities, just as many of the baptised emperors and later the popes in Rome and many other so-called Christian authorities did.

With regard to the argument that no temporal authority can possibly organise everything in the state on the basis of Christianity, no one is more willing than me to grant this to be so. Christianity can only be required of those who voluntarily profess it, and to judge from experience it cannot even be assumed in all of them! Moreover, it is very damaging to any kingdom to decree what it knows beforehand cannot be obeyed. However, if we agree that even the most Christian authority, to be wise, must avoid *prescribing* many obviously Christian rulings, we cannot afterwards come and say that it is incumbent upon, or appropriate for, a Christian authority, precisely *as* such, to prescribe such an unchristian thing as religious persecution. Nor must we say that the royal constitution *obliges* the Danish government to pursue religious persecution. If it obliges the government to anything at all on the matter, then it is clearly the opposite, unless it should happen that the Augsburg Confession conflicted with the Christian faith and Creed, since according to the royal constitution both of these must be strictly enforced and protected. However, if they were in conflict, it would clearly be an impossibility to enforce them both, and as we know, with an 'impossibility' there is no legal commitment. On the assumption that religious persecution is a contradiction of Christianity, there is not even a shadow of disagreement, since it is undeniable that the Augsburg Confession expressly protests against *all* religious persecution.

If anyone therefore wishes to argue that the Danish government is either duty-bound or has the right to religious persecution, this cannot be ascribed to Christianity or the royal constitution, but springs from another source that forces or entitles it to ignore both of these.

It would also be the most desperate claim to argue that the State Church should be this 'source' that stood above Christianity and the royal constitution, so that as its head and first bishop our King should have the duty or entitlement to anything that contradicted these two. For the Danish State Church is no more than an arrangement for retaining and transmitting the Christian faith and Creed and the Augsburg Confession; it disappears together with all its legal rights as soon as they are mentally discarded. So even if all the *clergy* argued that religious persecution was an integral part of its formidable power of enforcement and protection, the Danish State Church would have to secede by law from both the Christian faith and the Augsburg Confession before it could be compelled by anything that conflicted with these.

I for my part do not deny either the Danish or any other government the right, at its own risk, to change and transform its State Church as often as it thinks appropriate, and if it also found it most appropriate to organise its Church so that like the papal church it demanded religious persecution, then from a civil point of view there is nothing more to say than that on the basis of experience it was making a strange mistake.

If it became clear to the Danish government that what has entangled it against its will in a religious persecution is neither Lutheran Christianity nor the royal constitution but only the natural desire of the state clergy to be free of rivals, then it would doubtless follow its inclination to do to the ecclesiastical, or rather the clerical, penal code against so-called 'heretics and fanatics' what it has done to them as regards 'public confession and compulsory Communion, the iron collar and sacrilege, cohabitation and divorce'.[228] Nor is it gratuitous to note that religious persecution has never diminished division and disagreement in a kingdom but only increased it.

Peace and unity are not only the greatest inclination of the Danes but also the condition for the solidity and vigorous activity of every society, so for the sake of peace and unity a wise government should be ready to sacrifice its entire State Church if it had to, let alone a handful of Anabaptists. Even if experience had taught us that religious persecution was either a necessity or at least a worthy and useful means to maintain or bring about peace and unity, that would not make it 'Christian'; but then nor is the kingdom of Christ in this world, and a government could well

---

228. A decree from 1617 required that adulterers should confess their sin at the chancel door or before the altar in the presence of the congregation and be punished with a fine. After a third offence the man could be condemned to death and the woman whipped and excluded from the community. In principle, though not practice, these punishments remained on the statute book for a first offence until 1812 and for a third offence up to 1866. Whipping was converted to imprisonment in 1751 and public confession was abolished in 1767.

defend a severity that would be to the benefit of all and in the case of Denmark an absolute necessity.

As far as I can see, for too many years the argument that under no circumstances should Church matters be allowed to disturb the civil peace was the reasoning of the Danish government – and presumably it still remains so. If I still disagreed with this, as I did in my youth, and believed that even at the cost of peace and unity a govern-ment in its administration of the state should follow the spirit of Christianity and the basic Lutheran principles, then all the same, like Bishop Balle[229] I would vote as I have always done against all religious persecution as being unchristian and anti-Lutheran (papist). However, in our day and age, when we have had enough of storm and strife and quarrel and division and need seriously to safeguard and even nurse the scrap of peace and unity that still remains, I can at once envisage that I would be better off sparing myself the trouble; and if I still could not calm down then I could emigrate to England, where civil strife on Church matters is the order of the day.

On the other hand, since not only the history of England and the whole world but also even of Denmark teaches us that, far from procuring civil peace and unity, religious persecution is much more likely to destroy them utterly, I must be absolutely sure to make my voice heard. Or rather, I would do so were it not that there is a far different and vociferous voice, like that of many waters, which despite all experience claims that stone-dead orderliness and drab monotony are the sources from which all civil peace and unity spring and that therefore these must be enforced and championed to the utmost, regardless of all else. Even if one had the wisdom of Solomon to work out that there is nothing more conceited under the sun than the application of stone-dead orderliness and drab monotony to human life, which by nature is so manifold and so impressionable, it would still make no difference here. For the statesmen of our time do not believe that the State is only a form under which human life with all its great energies should develop into a beautiful harmony as completely and freely as possible; they are accustomed to asserting that this human life, whether it can or not, must accept the stone-dead orderliness and drab monotony which the State demands and which, being a higher entity, it has every right to demand. We ask in vain what is this 'State', which is neither the government nor the people, neither a human arrangement for the common good nor a divine arrangement for spiritual development and the triumph of truth, yet it demands that all this be sacrificed? What kind of a 'nothing' or evil spirit is it, and from where does it derive its equally intangible and unrestricted right whereby no divine or human right can exist? No answer is forthcoming, and

---

229. Nicolai Edinger Balle (1744-1816) became Professor of Theology at Copenhagen University in 1772 and then Bishop of Zealand in 1783. In 1791 he published his *Textbook of the Evangelical-Christian Religion Authorised for Use in Danish Schools*, which became the authorised schoolbook on the Catechism.

we must be glad that we do not receive the expected answer that the 'State', which demands all other forms of sacrifice, also demands the sacrifice of such futile speculations and useless, alarming, in fact pernicious, questions. It is equally pointless to seek illumination via natural history (biology) as to how this unreasonable and, for human life, intolerable concept of the 'State' has arisen and been unnaturally hatched in the Egyptian baking-ovens, raised in the Roman robber-state, made up heavily in the papal writing-rooms, justified in the German universities, and deified by the Chinese mandarins, so that it is as totally strange in the North as it is in England or Greece and cannot do more damage here than in its native soil or in places where through the Poor Laws it has acquired for itself the right to public assistance. No, we must assume that either it is just a joke that at best is witty, or it is one of those over-imaginative, misleading, alarming views that the 'state' too must oppose and suppress for the sake of its self-preservation or its perfection.

If we wish to delve further into the problem, we can ask: What was the point of the council in Jerusalem persecuting Christianity on the basis of what they called the 'divine right of the state and the law'? Or to what end did Rome do the same on behalf of its eternal existence and unparalleled uniformity? What use was it that the Holy Roman Empire persecuted Luther and all the Protestants for the sake of its holy order, its weekdays and Sundays, its survival, and its own instituted order? It is like talking about the snow that fell last year, which no sensible person is concerned with this year unless it be to calculate how many inches high it would have lain if it had been spread equally on a given surface. There is simply no point in asking what was the use of Spain and Portugal suppressing the Reformation and all free expression of human life through censorship and the Inquisition, or whether the peace and unity that these two kingdoms enjoy in reward should be envied. There is no point in doing so because those who daydream about a state with perfect order and uniformity will find great deficiencies in this respect in Cardinal Ximenes[230] and Philip II,[231] deficiencies which to be honest only German Protestants (who in *principle* should have been strangled at birth!) have learned to remedy, but are now being helped every day (they believe) to prevent every such revolution for ever!

If we stick to what we all know, however, just pause to think about it, and ask how far in our day and age we have created peace and brought about unity, then it should perhaps be obvious that at least in Denmark at the moment religious persecution is not the means we are tempted to choose.

The first thing I remember 50 years ago was that Denmark and Norway were famous throughout Europe for peace and unity, and rightly so, for although even in those days

---

230. Cardinal Ximenes (1436-1517) was made grand inquisitor and cardinal under Ferdinand in 1507.
231. Philip II of Spain (1527-98) was a champion of the Counter-reformation.

there was serious disagreement *about* our State Church, and also *within* it, people could nevertheless speak and write whatever they liked about the Church and its clergy and have as little or as much to do with them as they wished. So it made not the slightest difference to civic peace and unity, especially when Bishop Balle, however badly he himself was knocked about, would not hear a word about religious persecution or temporal force in matters of faith. This was in the early days of press freedom and the French Revolution, in its boyhood so to speak, so the government and the constitution of 1660 was hauled over the coals in the clubs and in the papers. But this had no effect on the people, and all those who had any religion found that it was much better to live under the *Danish* government than the French, which persecuted *all* religion. Here and there in Norway, on Funen, and in Jutland the 'godly assemblies'[232] were held, but they passed off as quietly as in Stormgaden,[233] and no one paid any heed to them, so they were closer to passing peacefully away than waking up others.

In the transition to the new century, when the man with the iron rod ascended the throne in Paris,[234] certain local judges and prefects who were passionate either about 'free thinking' or about a 'police force' – at the request of certain pastors – began to take Christian VI's decree on the godly assemblies[235] off the shelf where it had long rested in peace among the others that still remain there. They could use it to persecute 'the Holy Joes' in Jutland[236] and primarily in Norway, where the young peasant Hans Hauge[237] was creating a stir and running down the clergy – not, as was the custom among respectable people, because of their clerical incompetence but because of their temporal tendencies. In this persecution, matters came to such a head that the Norwegian peasantry, which until then had fully respected the Danish government, rose up in discontent and bred a resentment which, if the divorce had not soon gone

---

232. The 'godly assemblies' comprised gatherings of revivalist Christians, especially among the common people, from c.1790-1840. They were highly critical of the established Lutheran church and held their own religious services, often with itinerant preachers. They were part of the popular movement that led to the end of the Absolute Monarchy in 1848. Their influence also led to the breaking of the parish-tie in 1855 and to the law of 1868 allowing for the establishment of Free Churches with or without affiliation to the established Church. These latter developments were both strongly supported by Grundtvig. See Text 2.

233. Grundtvig's own footnote: "where the Moravian Brethren had their assembly hall".

234. Napoleon I made himself Emperor of France in 1804.

235. In 1741, to combat the rise of 'godly assemblies' Christian VI issued a decree that only the parish pastor was allowed to hold them; they were ended by Christian VIII in 1839.

236. The 'Holy Joes' lived in Jutland (as opposed to Zealand), which was traditionally more faith-oriented.

237. Hans Hauge (1771-1824) was a Norwegian lay preacher and a leader in both Norway and Denmark of the revivalist movement that led to the 'godly assemblies'. See note 99.

through,[238] would have brought it about in a quite different form; and if the persecution had not ceased on the same occasion, Professor Hjelm[239] would doubtless never have proposed an even worse persecution on behalf of the Norwegian State Church, for then the uprising would have been buried in its mother's womb.

In Denmark, where the persecution was nowhere near so rabid and the people far more resistant, the movement, God be praised, has still not created resentment against the government or placed the State Church in obvious danger. But it has gradually given rise to godly assemblies spreading throughout the country, even on Zealand, where the predisposition towards them is very thin and has finally brought about disturbances against the Anabaptists; if they are persecuted even more strictly, it can only give the whole movement a political character and a particularly hostile attitude to the State Church.

This is how far we have come with just the modicum of religious persecution that has been exercised, and which nevertheless, just as it reached its peak, was stopped by our present King Christian's keen eye and determined pronouncement that when pastors called upon the temporal authority to take revenge on the godly assemblies, they should be investigated as to how good they *themselves* were as the directors of souls! How much further we might have come if this had happened some twenty years ago – and if the godly assemblies had found the requisite spiritual support, or the exit from the State Church had reached the extent that I would have allowed it and was sorely tempted to join!

There is no need to say that it ill becomes me and that it is a hazardous matter on such occasions to speak about myself; for I have long been aware of this. But if anyone could have told me how to illuminate a point, great or small, in the history of the Danish State Church or any other story without discussing or mentioning it I would gladly have followed his directions. Since for a whole lifetime my relationship with the Danish State Church has been the same as every other 'personal curate' and young 'Vartov pastor',[240] it is ridiculous to mention it in any other story but that of the State Calendar. I cannot possibly believe anyone else's word on this, since my own experience tells me that, be it to my honour or shame, my relationship with the Danish State Church since 1810 has been rather odd and remains so to this day, and I really believe that I only needed tomorrow to arrive before I *left* the Danish State Church in

---

238. Denmark and Norway were one kingdom from 1523 to 1814, when they 'divorced'. The kingdom was forced to split by the Treaty of Kiel at the end of the Napoleonic wars, when Norway was ceded to Sweden. A constitutional assembly rejected the treaty and declared Norwegian independence on 17th May 1814, now the 'national' day. Crown Prince Frederik was elected King of Norway, but a Swedish invasion forced Norway into union with Sweden, though it retained its liberal constitution and separate institutions, except on foreign policy. This union was in turn dissolved on 7th June 1905, when Norway finally became an independent nation.

239. Claus Hjelm (1797-1871) was a Norwegian Professor of Philosophy and a High Court judge.

240. i.e. Grundtvig himself.

order to persuade even the greatest disbelievers of this! Thirty years ago, with a certain anticipation, I took the Danish Bible and the Augsburg Confession *off* the shelf, and for that reason the clergy of the time wished to have me excommunicated. Even though they failed, they managed to close all the pulpits in the capital to me and sought to limit all my prospects of pastoral activity. Since this was to last for seven years, would it not have been reasonable in the circumstances to hold godly assemblies with the not so few people who wished to hear me preach? And would it not have been reasonable to assume that if I and my supporters had been persecuted, the godly assemblies would have spread faster and wider and created a far graver situation for both our parish pastors and the government than is the case right now?

Then, fifteen years ago, with a certain anticipation I defended 'the Christian faith and Creed' from time immemorial as well as the Augsburg Confession against one of our pastoral teachers in the State Church. I was punished for doing so with a libel case and censorship.[241] As a result, I found any pastoral benefice in such a disconsolate State Church intolerable. My deepest wish was to walk out, together with those who would follow me and hold firm to what the royal constitution said, believing it should be strictly enforced and protected. Since this painful situation lasted over ten years, it is almost incomprehensible that no withdrawal actually took place! Had it happened, I would have been doubly hated by the state clergy and considerably more dangerous for the State Church than Anabaptism, and I would probably have caused a civil division and discord that Denmark would not have recovered from in our eventful times!

Without the impact of many fortunate yet incalculable circumstances, this is how far the request of the state clergy could and would have led us away from civil peace and unity. And this is how far we nevertheless will proceed, if we continue to persecute the Anabaptists instead of letting both them and the godly assemblies more or less look after themselves. We can then break the parish-tie as regards the Sacraments and allow those who have scruples about infant Baptism or the sprinkling of water to postpone their children's Baptism until they can answer for themselves and then have them baptised in the State Church.

It would be easy to prove that such a peaceful approach to the question of faith, conscience, and salvation is both a Christian and a Lutheran one and in agreement with Balle's *Textbook*. But what use is it in the Danish State Church to appeal by law to either 'the Christian faith and confession' or 'the Augsburg Confession', or to Balle's *Textbook*? Have not fifty years' experience taught us not only that there is a huge difference in what bishops, pastors, and professors think and say about these things but also

241. Following a vicious pamphlet attack on Professor of Theology H.N. Clausen, Grundtvig was found guilty of libel and placed under publishing censorship from 1826-37. In protest he resigned his pastorate in 1826. He was allowed to hold evensong sermons at Christianskirken but forbidden to administer Baptism and Holy Communion. See chs 1 and 4.

that at every given occasion the courts declare that they cannot deal with reality but only with form? For the sake of the strict orderliness and drab monotony of the State Church is it really worth sacrificing civil peace and unity in life, which we hardly have enough of? Or can we perhaps also manage with it written down on a piece of paper?

It is true that Anabaptism is still of little significance, but on the one hand religious persecution is *never* insignificant and on the other hand, for as long as it lasts, it will either itself become more significant or it will make withdrawal from the State Church more significant day by day, which amounts to the same thing. For even though it is a ghost from the 16th century, and has to the best of my knowledge no roots in Denmark as regards ecclesiastical or natural history, and has so far had very poor spokesmen, its very persecution has caused it to grow visibly. So what will happen, when only half of those who are dissatisfied with the State Church in its current legal form or its desperate state of imminent internal dissolution join the Anabaptists or realise that they must do just as much as them for what *they* call their faith and conviction concerning salvation?

Is this not seriously worth thinking about for jurists and theologians before it is too late? Does no one realise that there are bright heads with theological degrees and even pastoral vestments who regard infant Baptism as being of no avail and the *Bible* as the only creed one should confess? Is there anyone who thinks that not one of these people can become an Anabaptist to match the courage of the Mønster brothers?[242] Might not just one of them wish to become a martyr for as good a cause as can be found in Denmark, where people are threatened more than they should be, but rarely take a knock? Can it be that people in the 19th century in Denmark are by no means so indifferent to faith and salvation as they were in the 18th? Do people not realise that, with the continuing persecution of the Anabaptists, pastors who have any faith must feel forced to risk just as much for the State Church as the Anabaptists for theirs, if they are not to stand in a scornful light? I am aware that all these questions are not nearly as clear to everyone as they are to me! My historical nature and studies, together with my whole inner and outer life, have consistently led me to this observation and conclusion for a whole generation now. But why do people never heed what I give good reasons for, and why can they not even think that without any freedom at all either inside or outside the State Church they will inevitably drive me or my pastoral friends, if for no other reason, to demonstrate that we are serious about the faith we have preached, about the freedom we have counselled, and about the power which we claim *every* spirit, not to mention God's *own* spirit, has to defy all temporal entities that seek to rule it!

---

242. Grundtvig's own footnote: "The engraver P. Mønster and his brother A. M., who studied embroidery, were among the first Baptists in Copenhagen. In 1840-42 they were arrested and fined."

But back to the heart of the matter, to which I here give my vote and would give ten thousand votes if I had them against persecution of the 'godly assemblies' and the 'Anabaptists'! I say this not because I have the least sympathy with either of them but because it is clear as sunlight to me that all religious persecution is unchristian, anti-Lutheran, and quite unnatural. Given the internal dissolution and confusion in our State Church it is also so clearly unjust and unreasonable that nowhere else and at no other time (though that is saying much) has it done so much harm as it would do here. Only by a miracle has it so far been prevented from turning the best friends of the State Church into its enemies, throwing the government's loyalist supporters into the arms of the opposition, and destroying the most peaceful and friendliest life of any people that has flourished on earth!

Despite our rarely agreeing, I vote with the *Copenhagen Post*,[243] just as it has voted with me, in never taking into account the objections of the state clergy on such occasions; it is best never to ask them their opinion, since it only leads them into a temptation so great that it has never been overcome in this world. For instance, to the best of my knowledge the majority of our qualified doctors have never recommended the free practice of what they call 'quackery', nor has any chartered guild with a majority of votes recommended the abolition of their charter, however much it might affect civil society and hasten the demise of the guild. How can one expect a clergy that has a licence to rule – and has even portioned out the residence so that each has his part – ever vote for church peace? In this respect the Danish state clergy are no exception, and they gave the Copenhagen clergy sufficient guarantee the other year in Roskilde when they came close to recommending the breaking of the parish-tie to the same degree as in the capital. For the entire clergy of Copenhagen nevertheless voted *against* the proposal, despite the saying that 'common destiny is sweet' and despite the obvious advantage it is for a State Church as a whole that one can walk in whichever door one wishes! Our state clergy have not been able to live with even a scrap of sacrifice of the individual pastor for the sake of the whole clergy and the State Church, nor live with it in a time when it knows it is obviously contradicting itself in not dissolving the parish-tie, when it is stamping out all piety in the State Church among the people, and when it is bringing about the creation of sects! How can it then vote for a freedom that undeniably damages the exclusive charter of the entire clergy and may have far more unpleasant consequences for the individual than sharing its supporters, confirmands, and penitents with a fellow-pastor?

No indeed, it was *against the will* of the state clergy that Christianity took the freedom

---

243. The *Copenhagen Post* was founded in 1827 by A.P. Liunge (1798-1879) and was at first a cultural paper, but became a radical opposition paper until its demise in 1856. It is credited with introducing Marx and Engels to Denmark in 1845.

of coming into being in Jerusalem and throughout the Roman empire; it was *against the will* of the state clergy that Martin Luther took the freedom of making reforms; it was *against the will* of the state clergy that Luther gained a footing in Denmark and took possession of the State Church; it was *against the will* of the state clergy that freedom of worship was introduced in England, and *against the will* of the state clergy that the Duke of Wellington and Robert Peel emancipated the Irish Catholics. So wherever one waits for freedom until it is *recommended* by the state clergy, one must wait until the millennium!

On the other hand, as soon as anyone *seizes* the freedom that the clergy refuse, as in the case of the Anabaptists, then the die is cast; then no one waits any longer, and the choice is between religious *freedom* in some guise or other or religious *persecution*. His Majesty has clearly let it be known that he wants freedom in a decent, peaceful form, and the state clergy have very clearly demonstrated that they seek to *avoid* freedom in all forms. So it is quite clear, as the *Copenhagen Post* remarks, that if His Majesty does not decide the case in a reasonable way according to his own view and that of his legal experts, we shall have a religious persecution that is as unreasonable and self-contradictory as the declaration of the Langeland pastors,[244] but truly not, as in their case, one to laugh at or forget in a hurry! However, the same gentle Providence that has so far watched over Denmark will hardly withdraw its solicitude for us in this dangerous moment, but with the will of the state clergy it will save the Danish State Church and preserve Denmark's reputation as the home of peace!

---

244. In 1841 the pastors at the Langeland Convention had declared that there should be unity of religious faith in Denmark, sanctioned by the State. The *Copenhagen Post* (10th Nov. 1841) protested that this was not the business of the State, and that the right to freedom of worship for however small a minority was sacrosanct. Grundtvig agreed with this position: the State had no right over freedom of conscience or the freedom to practise one's religion.

5. Grundtvig in his vestments

The painting from 1843 by Christian Jensen is in the Hirschprung Collection in Copenhagen. It depicts Grundtvig, aged 59, in his vestments and bearing the Knight's Order (*Ridderkorset*). This was given to him by King Christian VIII and Queen Caroline Amalie on the occasion of their own Silver Wedding in 1840, for which Grundtvig wrote a song. Thanks not least to his 1838 series of public lectures on contemporary history, later entitled *Within Living Memory*, Grundtvig was now a national figure and well-respected for his Vartov ministry, not least by the Queen.

8. On the History of the Church (1847)

Introduction by Ole Vind

Grundtvig's writings include several versions of world history, which he narrated as a continuous 'universal history' from the earliest times to his own contemporary Europe. The genre was common during the Enlightenment, promoting as it did a characteristic belief in human progress down the ages. In this world history Grundtvig shared the overall optimism of a steady evolution towards a further developed, better organised, more enlightened society on earth.

What distinguishes Grundtvig's philosophy of history from that of his contemporaries such as Hegel is his view that *Church* history constitutes an integrated and critical part of *world* history. The history of the Church testifies to a development over 1,800 years of history, with the Lutheran Reformation marking the provisional culmination of true Christian spirit and enlightenment – exceeded only by Grundtvig's own Nordic church. Church history has thus developed alongside *political* history and, in Grundtvig's highly original view, is carried by the same major peoples that have played a decisive role in world history: the Jews, the Greeks, the Romans, the English, the Germans, and the Nordic peoples.

A seventh people, probably to be found among converted Hindus, will complete the purpose of Divine Providence, as prophesied in Revelation.[245] God has chosen them to ensure the return to a regained paradise for all peoples before the Judgement Day that will end all history on earth. Like the six other major peoples, Hindus possessed a living mythology from ancient times, as revealed in the Sanskrit texts that were being made available in Europe in Grundtvig's time; moreover, they lived closer to the *original* paradise, traditionally sited on the Euphrates river. Christianity could thus return to its source and convert the Jews in the process, this being a traditional portent of the end of history.

In such a development Grundtvig saw the progressive work of the Christian spirit in upholding the original, oral creed at Baptism and Holy Communion. This had been his criterion for true Christianity since his 'matchless discovery' of the tenet motivated him to write *The Church's Retort* in 1825. A sign of this progress was the growing sense of the importance of a people's *language*, and thus an emphasis on the importance

---

245. Rev 2-3. Grundtvig treats the subject in greater depth in his poem *The Seven Stars of Christendom* (1860).

of reading the Bible (in their own language), on the power of the sermon, on *singing* God's praise, and on Christian enlightenment and education.

On the History of the Church divides Christianity into the old and the new, with the old lasting from its zenith in the Apostolic Church in Jerusalem through the Greek Church to the Roman Church, where it falls to its lowest point. As in his world history, Grundtvig sees the revival beginning with the demise of the Roman Church and the rise of the Germanic-Nordic peoples: the Anglo-Saxons, the Germans, and the Nordic kingdoms.

Grundtvig's unorthodox view was never taken seriously by theologians, and in his own circles it was regarded as more of a 'poetic' vision. Nevertheless, his dream of a seventh church in India and his hope of a Christian mission to India secured sufficient support among his followers for the joint-Nordic foundation in 1867 of the Santal Mission to north-east India, now part of Danmission.

On the History of the Church is central to any understanding of Grundtvig's original philosophy of history, in which three characteristics are clearly present: a trust in the Bible and its prophecies; an optimistic view of human progress; and the belief that Luther and the Reformation are only a provisional culmination of the path towards further Christian advancement – which includes Grundtvig's own contribution.

***

I pointed out recently that even with the announcement of *Basic Christian Teachings*[246] a little Church history ought be related to inform young people that although we are a long way from the Apostles in time and distance we are spiritually speaking housed in the same building with them. All more or less informed Christians and in particular all Christian pastors without doubt agree with me on this. But when the next question is: How this can be? The most serious of them will probably find it difficult to explain, for no one has given us a clear conception of the transmission of Apostolic Christianity over the seventeen to eighteen centuries that separate us from the Apostles. The answer ought to be made manifest to us, if it is not to remain in Egyptian darkness[247] for our children.

We must summon up the courage to see this matter in the light of our Lord rather than ask what the men of learning and the scribes understand by a 'church' and how they make a distinction between the 'visible' and the 'invisible'. We must ask only how the good news of salvation from sin, death, and the kingdom of Satan, together

---

246. *Basic Christian Teachings* was first announced in 1847, then published as an article series between 1855-61, and as a book in 1868. See Section II of this book.

247. Ex 10:21-29. 'Darkness' was one of the plagues of Egypt in Moses' liberation struggle.

with Baptism and Holy Communion, came from Jerusalem to the ends of the earth to bring salvation to all those who 'believed and were baptised'. If we see it thus, then the Spirit reminds us of the words of the Lord, "You know where I am going and you know the way."[248]

The Acts of the Apostles presents itself to us as the incomparable beginning to the story that we have requested; for here we learn how through faith and Baptism the Gospel came bodily to Samaria, to Antioch, the birthplace of the name 'Christian', and thence with the Apostle Paul to our part of the world and all the way to Rome, where the Apostle even met Christians outside the gate![249]

In fact the story is only really a matter of tracing the same good news on its path from Rome to us; and our Lord has ensured that this is a minor matter. When we come to think about it, we all know that 600 years after the birth of Christ, precisely when the false prophet Muhammed arose and brought sad times to a long-established Christendom, the Lord began to create the New Christendom to which we more or less belong. For the Gospel was then transmitted from Rome to England, a century later to Germany, and another century later from there to Denmark and Sweden. All this happened in a proper 'apostolic' way, so to speak, in that it was the true Apostolic faith and Baptism that came to us, and it was through friendly persuasion alone that Christianity was transmitted. Indeed, especially in the case of Ansgar – who has been called 'the apostle of the North' because he was the first to bring the Gospel to Denmark and Sweden[250] – we can see that he was a truly pious and diligent evangelist who trusted in the Lord alone and was willing to give his life for His name's sake. However, he found in our part of the world far more indifference than opposition and after forty years of untiring labour ended his days in peace.

Not long before the time of Ansgar, Emperor Charlemagne[251] had already begun to make the Turks Christian – with a sword over their heads. This method spread, and already on the introduction of Christianity into Norway (in 1000) King Olav Tryggesen and King Olav the Holy[252] employed the sword – not as their only weapon but nevertheless one that was all too visible; and from then on it became a sitting right to wage war on unbelievers until they got themselves baptised. By this most unchristian

248. Jn 14:4.
249. Acts 28:15.
250. The Benedictine monk Ansgar (801-65) is credited with bringing Christianity from Bremen to both Sweden and Denmark and is therefore known as 'the apostle of the North'. He is also credited with building the first Danish church in Hedeby.
251. Charlemagne (c.742-814) united most of Western Europe and from 800 became the first Holy Roman Emperor since the fall of Rome's western empire three centuries earlier.
252. Olav Tryggesen (Olaf I Tryggvason) reigned 995-1000; King Olav the Holy (Olaf II Haraldsson, aka St. Olaf) reigned 1015-28.

method faith and Baptism came to Pomerania and Prussia[253] (in 1200) and to America (in 1500), but by then it seemed that the Christian faith was dead and buried both in the Old and the New Christendom. Simultaneously, all manner of papistry, including the invocation of saints, the worship of images, and the sale of indulgences, paved the way for a new idol worship even worse than the old heathen one.

It now transpired that it was indeed the true Christian faith that we had gained from Rome and that the Spirit which *animates* it had also *accompanied* it. For when Martin Luther emerged (in 1517) to turn the Christian faith against all papistry, the word of the Lord was recalled, "The girl is not dead; she is asleep."[254] Then it was seen that the faith was alive, and just as our forefathers followed Luther according to the Word of the Lord and were given something "to eat", so we dare to hope that the faith will be strong and live on until the Lord comes again to judge the living and the dead.

This is the first giant stride to becoming truly Christian in what is customarily the terribly confused and turbulent history of the Church, but the Lord has made it easy for us, for all we need is the courage that faith always gives. The second step is not quite so easy, but fortunately there is also a Word of the Lord here: "One thing is necessary."[255] So when we ask how we have acquired the Christian enlightenment that we now possess, with the opportunity to grow constantly in the grace and knowledge of our Lord Jesus Christ, then our supporters both young and old need not be ashamed to answer that it has come of its own accord – when the faith came alive, when the Word in preaching, prayer, and song became available to the common people, and when the Bible story became known in general. An even clearer historical answer is not nearly as difficult as it has been made out to be, and in our enlightened times it should therefore in no way lack children of the light.

In a sense, what has happened to the Christian Church is the same as has happened to all great and famous people in this world who, without a general education from the start, only at best *end up* with such a one, thanks to the art of book-printing. It is only because people could not see or were unwilling to believe that Christ's Congregation – this unrivalled selection of all manner of folk – is just as real as He himself was a real person, that the unreasonable demand has been made of Christ's people that they should be equally enlightened from birth to death and should therefore have had no human *passage* whatsoever. Christian people only exceed all the other major peoples of the earth in that, like their Lord and King, they were filled from the womb with the Holy Spirit. Even in their tender childhood they were strong in the faith and full of wisdom, with the grace of God over them, so that like Jesus at the age of twelve they

---

253. Pomerania is a former name of a region on the south coast of the Baltic Sea, now divided between Germany and Poland. By 1871 Prussia was the leading state of the German empire.
254. Mt 9:24; Mk 5:39; Lk 8:52.
255. Lk 10:42.

surprised all the scholars with their questions and responses. Lastly, it is because, as with the Lord, after an intervening period of obscurity there suddenly arose a matchless light in the dense darkness, so that Martin Luther's countrymen must have said of him – as the people of Nazareth said of our Lord: "From where has he acquired all that wisdom? We *know* his father and mother and his brothers and sisters!"[256]

Thus, with the few words we have concerning the Lord's childhood, we can give a simple and popular outline of the story of Christ's Congregation from the days of the Apostles to Martin Luther. We can then fill it out with a few or many details depending on the circumstances; for we know it is always true of the enlightenment of believers that, as Scripture says: "The one who gathered much did not have too much, and the one who gathered little did not have too little."[257]

The crucial point is whether we ourselves have gained a clear conception of the miracle that Christian people and their story constitute in the history of the world. In this regard we must primarily focus on what was long overlooked: the essential difference between the Old and the New Christendom. For it is not as if there were an old and a new *Christianity*, since according to both Scripture and the testimony of history there has not only been one faith and one Baptism but also one Lord and one Spirit; it is because the Spirit had to create for itself a *new* body among the peoples, for the old one was out-of-date and almost useless.

As soon as we focus on this divine masterpiece, all our astonishment at the unworthy figure of Christianity in the Middle Ages ceases to be, as it does at the outdated Greeks and Romans, who were clearly in their dotage, and at the new-born English, German, and Nordic Christians who could not be other than childlike. The only real reason for this astonishment, explicable solely through the divine nature of the Lord and then the Spirit, is that the children became much wiser than their parents with regard to Christianity, and the disciples surpassed their teachers by far! The historical fact that Martin Luther was a German and that in the midst of the new Christendom there arose a truly Christian enlightened reformer who both saw and showed how the Christian Congregation could and should be renewed in the Spirit of Christ – this is striking proof that Martin Luther was right to impress upon us that in the Church of the Lord enlightenment is the work of the Holy Spirit.

If we now gather Luther's Christian enlightenment into its sum total, the core teaching is that only the Holy Spirit – and no human being or human class – is the Lord's vice-regent on earth, and that the Lord's own institutions, Baptism and Holy Communion, are the only means of salvation among His people. They accomplish

256. Job 28:20; Lk 2:41-52.

257. Ex 16:18 (on manna). Drawing on this same verse, Grundtvig had written his famous lines about the Danish national character in 1820: "In this lies our wealth, on this tenet we draw:/that few are too rich, and still fewer too poor." See *Living Wellsprings* (2015) p. 191.

both what they can and what they must accomplish when the Word on God's side and faith on our side meet in truth, and, with the power of the Spirit, fuse together in the heart. But for this to happen, the Gospel must be preached spiritedly and freely to all people in the language they are born into; the Holy Scripture *in the native language* must be available to all; and believers must address each other in hymns and songs of praise and spiritual songs, also in their mother-tongue, so that they can "play beautifully for the Lord" in their hearts.[258]

After three hundred years of testing Luther's enlightenment and seeing its effects in the wider world on friends and enemies, and on both the Christian Church and the peoples of the world, we can boldly state that the foundational Lutheran doctrines comprise: Christian enlightenment – the Spirit, the Word, and the faith as the powers; Baptism and Holy Communion – preaching, singing, and Bible-reading as the means; and freedom for the Gospel and the use of the mother-tongue as the conditions.

These foundational doctrines stand and fall with the Christian Church, meaning with its King and its Spirit – so they will prove immutable. But we are still far from a living and consistent *implementation* of them, for we have made no progress in real life since the days of Luther but have merely gone sideways like a crab. So we must comfort ourselves with the thought that this was in order to take a run-up to the huge jump which cannot surpass or obscure Luther's giant stride but is an essential *continuation of it* in order to approach our goal, which is the full-grown Christ.

We know that with all real giant strides it is the energy and the urge, the power and the hope that alone determine the outcome, but in the Age of Enlightenment all giant strides must happen in the *light*, just as when the Lord entered public life by taking a giant stride out of the River Jordan before the eyes of all the people. It is therefore fitting that we let the light shine on the Christian people's path further on than *we* have come, so that the Church can see where it is heading and can do what the Lord provided for in giving us the Spirit which proclaims what is to come. For when we observe the Old and the New Christendom side by side, we can clearly see that the Old went downhill and the New came up again, and that whatever the reason is for this, it must be a sign and a pledge to the Church that the Lord who loves His own until the end will give to the last the same as the first. It is thus of vital importance that we remain convinced of the full correctness of this fact. Fortunately, this is not so difficult, for it is clear that not even the Church in Ephesus under Polycarp,[259] let alone the Church in Rome under Gregory the Great, can bear comparison with the Apostolic Church in Jerusalem. In the first six centuries, from every spiritual view, the

---

258. Ps 33:3.

259. Together with Clement of Rome and Ignatius of Antioch, Polycarp of Smyrna (69-155) is regarded as one of the three chief Apostolic Fathers. He is said to have known John the Apostle and to have been a devout Christian. In his mid80s he was martyred in Smyrna (now Izmir, Turkey).

Christian people fell from an unparalleled height almost to the level of the peoples of the world, so that under Gregory the Great there seemed to be no more than a monk's cloak that separated them. On the other hand, even though we allow for the success of the English Church in the time of Bede,[260] it is outshone by the German Church in the days of Martin Luther, who threw away his monk's cloak and pilgrim's staff in order, if possible, to reach the Apostles.[261] Thus, however far back we go, we can see that Christ's Church in the New Christendom has never sunk back, but on the contrary has *risen*, and as far as possible raised the peoples of the world with it. If we wish to know how high up the Church raised itself in the Christian sense, all we need to do is ask which of the Church Fathers Luther dwelt on, namely Ambrose[262] and Augustine,[263] who 200 years before Gregory the Great were also one-third closer to the Apostles. This realisation must give us the courage with our Lutheran enlightenment to trace more closely the reasons for both the Church's old debasement and its new elevation.

The interaction between Christian life and native language – in the living speech, song, and Bible-reading that Luther and the three centuries since have shed light on – teaches us forthwith that from the beginning there must have been a great difference between the Church in Jerusalem and those in Ephesus and Rome, partly because there was such a contrast between Hebrew, Greek, and Latin, and partly because the first two were the original languages of the Bible. For just as the Spirit had naturally chosen for optimum effect the languages that were best suited for the expression of spiritual matters, so must that choice facilitate and enhance incalculably the use of Scripture and reading among the corresponding peoples.

For the New Christendom this in turn prompted the huge task not only of creating new written languages where there were none before, but also of developing languages in a Christian and biblical direction that were completely foreign to it, and finally of taking possession of the original languages of the Bible and in the new written languages competing with them, so to speak, in praising the Spirit. The first giant stride was taken by the brave English, whose creation of a written language set an example for both the Germans and the Nordic people which was soon followed. If one knows the English translations of the Bible, their sermons, and their Christian

---

260. The 'Venerable' Bede, as he is known (c.672-735), was a monk at the monastery of Monkwearmouth and Jarrow, in what is now Sunderland, England. He is called the 'Father of English history' on account of his major work, *Historia ecclesiastica gentis Anglorum* (*The Ecclesiastical History of the English People*).

261. Following his frightening experience in a thunderstorm in 1505 Luther entered the Monastery of St. Augustine at Erfurt. He left it for a professorship in Wittenberg in 1511.

262. The four "Fathers of the Church" are Pope Gregory the Great (c.540-604), St. Augustine of Hippo (now Annaba, Algeria, 354-430), St. Jerome (347-420), and St. Ambrose (340-97). Ambrose became Bishop of Milan, and is credited with introducing the antiphonal chant.

263. Augustine is seen by many Protestants as the Father of the Reformation for his belief in redemption from original sin and his blueprint for the 'City of God' in a book with that title.

poetry, one can only be astonished at this giant stride, and yet since then the English Church has not come much further in a Christian direction. The other giant stride was taken at the Reformation by the Germans, who successfully competed with the old Latin Church in speech, song, and writing to express the Christian Spirit and imitate the biblical language. Yet not only has the German Church made no progress since, it has actually sunk much further from that level, especially with the decidedly Latin direction it gave to its education whereby both spiritually and biblically it ceased to be a *rival* of the Latin Church and sank into being its *imitator*. The turn has now come for the Nordic peoples to take their giant stride in a Christian direction, and if this is successful, it must make the Nordic Church the rival of the Greek in every respect. This claim may seem somewhat bold, for Greek is the original language of the New Testament, but it could be so much more successful than the German contest with Latin to the extent that Greek can now be learned much better than Latin could in the time of Luther. It depends simply on the foundational Lutheran doctrines – on the Spirit, the Word, and the faith, on the Lord's own institutions, on freedom for the Gospel and the people's mother-tongue. These need to be taken more urgently and applied root-and-branch to the whole of human life; towards this goal Christ's Spirit, when we have Him,[264] will propel, illuminate, and strengthen us.

The Greeks have begun to awaken from the spiritual lethargy and torpor in which they have lain for who knows how long; this is not only a good omen but a benefit for the Nordic giant stride which must be seen as inestimable. If the Nordic stride succeeds to the same degree as the German three hundred years ago, then only one thing remains to reach and rival the Hebrew Church. At first sight this might seem to be an audacious thought, as though it might develop into a contest with the Apostles themselves, but the idea is all the same fundamentally Christian, for the Spirit that has omnipotence can do no other than complete the good deed He has begun to the day of our Lord Jesus Christ. Moreover, it is foolish to speak of preaching the living message of the Gospel to all people without counting on the Apostolic ability to *help*, which can be found among others in the glowing tongues that can speak of God's great work for all people under Heaven in their own language.

To be sure, how this will come about is a mystery to us, especially since in the New Christendom we do not see any such people who in all probability can take that giant stride or understand how the deadest of all written languages, Hebrew, can be revived; yet we know that such difficulties can neither deter nor hinder God's Spirit from its great work, which is so vitally necessary if the prophecies of the Old Testament are to be fulfilled and illuminated. To this belongs in every sense the spiritual resurrection of the Jews "from death to life", as Paul rightly calls it; and when the Jews arise in the

---

264. Grundtvig uses the masculine pronoun, *ham*, here.

Spirit of Christ, then their rivalry with the Apostles is just as natural a consequence as the illumination of the prophets and the fulfilment of the work of the mission.

Very likely it will also be the Hindus[265] who in the New Christendom will take this last giant stride whereby the choice of the heathens comes to touch the hem of the Apostles' raiment, or as the ancient prophet Zechariah says, "… take hold of the skirt of him that is a Jew, saying, We will go with you: for we have heard that God is with you!"[266] We are led by this conjecture to consider the ancient written language of the Hindus, Sanskrit, which is evidence that they belong to the major cultures in which each has its historical commission in the world, and then to see how the English, German, and Nordic Churches have together worked to christianise East India.[267] This has not so far been successful, but it will be so as soon as we let ourselves be taught by the Holy Spirit to take the offensive spiritually.

What sets the crown on this wonderful history of the Church of the Christian people is the special letters to the seven Angels of the Church in Revelation;[268] for just as the Spirit has always testified that the seven churches, pictured as lamp-stands in the midst of which the Lord Himself walked, must constitute the entire Christian people, like seven tribes or seven main branches, so is it impossible to see the Hebrew, Greek, Latin, English, German, and Nordic Churches succeed one another, each with its own form, without thinking that this must be the six asking for the seventh! The closer we compare the letters with the corresponding churches, the clearer it becomes that the one is not in need of the other, for the mouth of the Lord has spoken it[269] and His Spirit has gathered it.

The first letter, to the Angel of the Church in Ephesus[270] (where also the last Apostle ended his days[271]), is clearly addressed to an Apostolic Church which is drawing to its close, whereas the second letter to the Angel of the Church in Smyrna (where the Apostle-apprentice Polycarp lived) fits well with the Greek Church, which has long

---

265. As early as 1810 Grundtvig was redefining the letters to the seven churches in the Book of Revelation as a prediction of the seven great churches in the historical advance of Christianity. In 1860 the idea found poetic form in *The Seven Stars of Christendom*. Grundtvig believed the sixth church to be the Nordic – and the seventh, not yet materialized, to be the Indian church.

266. Zech 8:23.

267. In the case of Denmark an appeal by Frederick IV led to the establishment of a mission for the natives living in the Danish East India Company colony of Tranquebar in 1706 by two German missionaries from Halle, Bartholomaeus Ziegenbalg and Heinrich Plütschau. The mission printed and published the Bible in the Tamil language and is active to this day. On its 300th anniversary in 2006 its history was published in *It began in Copenhagen. Junctions in 300 years of Indian-Danish Relations in Christian Mission* (eds. H.R. Iversen & G. Oommen) (New Delhi, ISPCK 2005).

268. Rev 2-3.

269. Isa 40:5.

270. The seven churches are all in ancient Asia Minor, now on or near the west coast of Turkey. They are Ephesus, Smyrna, Pergamum, Sardis, Thyatira, Philadelphia, and Laodicea.

271. i.e. John of Patmos.

suffered at the hands of false Jews (Muhammedans with circumcision[272]) but dares to show that it has survived, while the letter to the Angel of the Church in Pergamum, where Satan has his throne, is self-evidently directed to the imperial, papal Rome.

These then represent the Old Christendom, and the fact that the Angel of the Church in Thyatira must belong to the first Church of the New Christendom can be seen from the 'morning-star'[273] which will identify it, as it is clearly identified among the English in both Bede and Wycliffe.[274] The rest is best left to the future, not because the German Church is recognisable in the letter to the Angel of the Church in Sardis, but because this did not become clear until the Nordic Church had gained its form and has been identified immediately in the letter to the Angel of the Church in Philadelphia. However, as regards the seventh and final letter to the Angel of the Church in Laodicea we can speak much more freely, since none of us yet knows to whom it is addressed. It can only be the *last* Church, for it has the Lord with it as its 'Amen'; it will hold 'Holy Communion' with Him; and it will share His 'seat of honour'. For just as everything in the fifth letter was concerned with Scripture, everything in the sixth has to do with Baptism, and in the seventh with Holy Communion – whereby the Consummation follows. In passing, when we hear the last Church castigated for being lukewarm and full of conceit, of which it is then cured, our thoughts go naturally to a Church with learned Brahmins[275] at its head, for such a Church would necessarily face this temptation and overcome this danger in order to survive.

Lastly, it should also be noted that the Pauline Apostolic Letters are addressed to seven Churches, which from a spiritual point of view coincide with the seven Churches in Revelation; for while the letters to the Romans and the Corinthians obviously manifest *themselves*, as do the letters to the Latin and the Greek Church, so has the German Church held its own as the letter to the Galatians. We can see that the letter to the Ephesians can only be taken up spiritually by a Hebrew Church, just as the letters to the Thessalonians can only be taken up by the Church that experiences the Day of the Lord; so the letters to the Philippians and Colossians, even though they are not so clearly recognisable, must belong with the fifth and sixth, or the English and the Nordic Church.

From this we can see that it is the fault not of our Lord or the Holy Spirit but of ourselves that the Christian Congregation, as the people of Christ, still needs a written history that is as matchless as that of the Hebrews, and so much the more gloriously as the New Covenant outshines the Old!

---

272. This definition is not atypical of Christian thought in Grundtvig's time.

273. Rev 2:28; 22:16.

274. John Wycliffe (1330-84), theologian and lay preacher, wrote an English translation of the Bible and is regarded by many as a precursor of the Reformation.

275. The Brahmin caste in Hinduism are priests and teachers of sacred learning and religious ritual.

9. A People's Identity in Relation to Christianity (1847)

Introduction by Ole Vind

In *A People's Identity in Relation to Christianity*, published in *Danish Church Times* on 17th October 1847, Grundtvig was responding to an article in the daily newspaper *Berling's Times* which accused him of confusing Danishness and Christianity. The charge was understandable in a sense, since the two are closely linked in Grundtvig's theology. He therefore sought to defend himself by explaining this link.

Now aged 64, he admits that in his youth he had indeed confused Danishness and Christianity, alluding not least to his *World Chronicle* from 1812, which preached penance and conversion for Denmark's salvation. The book created a storm of protest for its vehement attack on highly-respected contemporary theologians and philosophers. But after *The Church's Retort* in 1825 and the lost libel action that followed, Grundtvig realised that true Christianity is not a religion of laws and rules to dominate people's lives but an offer of salvation through free belief in the Gospel of Christ. Along with Grundtvig's view of history in *Nordic Mythology* from 1832 came an understanding of the relationship between humanity and Christianity: "Human comes first, and Christian next,/ for that is life's true order".[276] As described in *Genesis* all the peoples of the world are divinely created after the fall of the Tower of Babel and thus play a role in world history, which is governed by Providence – also before and outside Christianity. Grundtvig did not share Luther's view of the Fall of Man whereby humanity inherited complete sinfulness and was dependent solely on Christ's redemptive mercy; according to Grundtvig, the divine image had *survived* in humankind both through the Word and through Christ.

It was thus possible for Providence to select certain peoples to work *with* the Word *and* the Spirit in the evolution of world history towards a new paradise on earth. This optimistic view contradicted Luther and the Lutheran orthodoxy in the Danish State Church. Despite its condemnation of the Roman Catholic Church,[277] the Lutheran Church had maintained a form of spiritual compulsion among its own, but to *compel* faith was anathema to Grundtvig, for it was both inhuman and unchristian. He also

---

276. From the eponymous poem, see no. 123 in *Living Wellsprings* (Aarhus University Press, 2015).
277. Grundtvig shared this view most powerfully in his poem 'A Roman Song', see p. 166 in *The School for Life* (Aarhus University Press, 2011).

railed against the pietism and godly assemblies of the time – the "dead saints" who would make Christianity a religion of rules.

For Grundtvig, all the peoples of the earth had their place in a divinely-created world order. The burgeoning awareness of 'Danishness' to which he contributed to such a high degree called for a *sense of community* with both predecessors and successors as a prerequisite for all spiritual life, including the Christian. If true Christianity was to survive, it was crucial that it did not make itself master over the newly-awakened life of the people but simply offered them the Gospel as a spiritual gift to believe and follow.

Translator's note. The Danish title of this essay is *Folkelighed og Christendom*. The former word is notoriously difficult to translate; indeed whole books have been written about its meaning. The above translation, "A people's identity" is therefore an approximation of the concept: "that which makes a people a people".

∗∗∗

"Following their master's example the Grundtvigians confuse Danishness, Nordic-ness, and Scandinavianism with Christianity and often work with what pertains to the people and the nation which, when transferred to the religious sphere, looks very suspicious."[278]

To judge by its name, this droll news from *Berling's Times* is about a sect that I am the leader of! I would have only smiled at this, if I did not know that there are many more people than the humble country pastor sitting in the judgement-seat over bishops and professors as well as over the Vartov pastor,[279] and all of them are very uneasy about my so-called 'confusion' of Danishness with Christianity. However, since I know this to be so and that people in any case need further enlightenment on both subjects, the article reminded me that I who am best placed to supply the requisite information have perhaps neglected to do so as plainly and clearly as I could. I deliberately mention only Danishness and Christianity here, knowing that I have never mentioned 'Nordicness', let alone mesopotamian[280] 'Scandinavianism', in such a connection with Christianity. Even the most purblind country pastor cannot believe that I have confused these words. And as for what the so-called 'Grundtvigians' may have done – that concerns me even less, inasmuch as they are totally unknown to me!

278. *Berling's Times*, 5th October 1847. Founded by Ernst Berling in 1749, this daily newspaper, now known as *Berlingske*, is amongst the oldest newspapers in the world.
279. i.e. Grundtvig himself.
280. Lit. 'between two seas', in this case the Skaggerak/Kattegat and the Baltic Sea. 'Scandinavia' comprises Denmark, Norway, and Sweden.

I have never been any good at founding a 'party', but then I have never tried. History taught me early on that what happens to parties is the same as with Epictetus' lettuce;[281] whoever does not wish to pay what it costs must do without it. So if, like me, one wishes to make the effort to look a little more closely at the subject, one will soon discover the following about the so-called 'Grundtvigians'. The one will praise my sermon or church singing[282] but censure my mythologising, my historicity, and my pure Danishness, or at the least my blindness to the excellence of the 'godly assemblies'[283] and the missionary societies; while the other will do the opposite! So even if I had two half-parties, there would never be a whole one! Even when individual people praise both my Danishness and my Christianity, the end result is most often a reservation that my Danishness must of course be 'christianised' before it is worth mentioning – and that is far from my thoughts.

I endeavour ever more clearly to keep Danishness and Christianity apart, not as being incompatible but as being so very different that the one is only valid in a corner of the North, the other over the whole world, the one for a time, the other for time and eternity.

Despite this, I cannot deny that in my youth I mentioned Danishness and Christianity in one breath so often and in such a vague connection that people might easily think that in some way or other I was confusing them. So I am the one who is best situated to explaining a relationship that has been obscure not only for me but for the whole of Christendom, namely the proper relation between a people's life, culture, and identity – and Christianity.

With regard to the original relation we all know that Christianity – even in the land of the Jews where it arose, not to mention the heathen countries to which it spread – related to every people's character like a heavenly guest in an earthly home; it came not to be served but to serve. Although all traces of this were extinguished as far as possible in the days of the priestly hierocracy, the original relation nevertheless remains the only right and natural one.

If, like all of us nowadays, we have got on the wrong and unnatural side of the world

---

281. In the *Enchiridon* (Teaching Manual) of Epictetus (55-135 CE) the Greek philosopher writes: "What is the price of a lettuce? An obol perhaps. If then a man pays his obol and gets his lettuces, yet you do *not* pay and do *not* get them, do not think you have been defrauded!"

282. Since by his own admission Grundtvig was 'very unmusical', this must refer to his hymn composition – and perhaps to the fact that hymns in his church were sung louder and faster than in most other churches, though to this day still by a *sitting* congregation.

283. The 'godly assemblies' comprised gatherings of revivalist Christians, especially among the common people, from c.1790-1840. They were highly critical of the established Lutheran church and held their own religious services, often with itinerant preachers. They were part of the popular movement that led to the end of the Absolute Monarchy in 1848. Their influence also led to the breaking of the parish-tie in 1855 and to the law of 1868 allowing for the establishment of Free Churches with or without affiliation to the established Church. These latter developments were both strongly supported by Grundtvig. See Text 2.

of ideas, then it is proper and natural that the last thing we 'discover' proves to be right! So in the circumstances it is reasonable enough that in my youth I made mistakes and in my old age I am innocently censured. However, since for all nations and for Christianity itself this matter is of the greatest importance, I must not lose any opportunity to make it clear to my countrymen and especially Danish *Christians* that the original relationship between the people and their religion is the only proper one. The more it has been dislocated, the more we must work together to renew it for the benefit of all.

For if we consider how Christianity first came to Denmark, we know that it was not as an assailant whose place is justice in the shaft of a spear and a threat to put the people under the yoke. On the contrary, Christianity came in the form of a mild, defenceless monk who asked permission from the King of Denmark to preach the good news of the Saviour born in Bethlehem, and to christen and baptise those who were persuaded to believe in Jesus Christ. We know that the King of Denmark granted this permission, not because he himself was a Christian or had decided to become one, but because he found the evangelist Ansgar to be a tender-hearted, honest, upright, faithful man and he drew conclusions about the master from the disciple and about the gospel from the evangelist.[284]

Thus the position of Christianity in Denmark originally depended on the influence that the Word itself could acquire among the Danish people. Had the intention been for it to sneak into the kingdom and, when it had gained a number of supporters, to place the King and the people under its yoke, that would have amounted to insidious treason. It would have been like the bitch in the fable that begged for a doghouse in which to whelp and when the pups were fully-grown defied the owner by saying, "Take the house from me and my pups, if you dare!"[285]

If *this* had been the spirit of Christianity, then it would have been a bad spirit rather than a good one. It would have been like the Roman spirit, hostile to the spirit of all other peoples, i.e. the human spirit in any other form and in particular the spirit of truth, which is naturally God's own spirit. The Roman spirit was a mean falsehood from first to last, like an assailant who under the mask of peace and friendship steals into the land he wishes to subdue. Indeed, it was a double falsehood, in that if our relation to the divine is not one of the heart, then it is not a true relationship at all but a false one.

---

284. Grundtvig's own footnote: "The Life of Ansgar and his Disciple Rimbert, translated into Danish by Ley." Ansgar (801-65), the 'apostle of the North', is credited with bringing Christianity to Denmark from Germany and building the first Danish church in Hedeby in 848.

285. Among the fables of Aesop (620-560 BCE) is one about a bitch, ready to whelp, who begs a shepherd for a place where she might litter. Her request is granted and she gives birth to her pups. She next asks permission to rear them in the same spot, and the shepherd again consents. The pups grow up and become her bodyguard, whereupon she asserts her right to the place and scares away the shepherd.

Even its opponents have usually admitted that neither violence nor falsehood is in the spirit of Christianity, and they have never assumed otherwise, even in their *abuse* of Christians. But if the opposite is 'love and truth in the spirit of Christianity', it follows that this can never annihilate or oppress any people's life and nature in its name, as the papists undoubtedly have done.

In this context the final point we must note is that from the beginning we Protestants have declared the common procedure of the papists in the Middle Ages to christen people and kingdoms as being absolutely *unchristian*. But so far we have made believe that, wherever it happened by such stealth and violence, a people was forced to pretend they had been completely overwhelmed by Christianity, and that it was not only permissible but even necessary *forcibly* to maintain the prescribed or induced Christian *appearance*. Not until we realise that this Christian appearance benefits neither the people nor Christianity but is to the great detriment of both can we renew our efforts to set Christianity and the people in a free relationship with one another. This was originally the case in our own country, and we must admit that it should be the case wherever Christianity is found. The easiest way to reach this insight is to focus specifically on Christianity and come to the realisation that it is not a new law of God (as the papists believe) which seeks to rule the world as the Law of Moses ruled the land of the Jews. It is a heavenly *gospel*, a proposition without equal, which serves the good of all believers who receive it in good faith! This is the shortest way to believing that any use of force or other temporal means in the Christian cause is harmful to both sides. Non-believers naturally derive no benefit from the gospel and can only be strengthened in their suspicion and resentment of it the more they are coerced or compelled to believe it to be a great treasure and glory.

Here too, however, 'a short cut is often a false path', as the proverb runs. For we can both see and admit that of course Christianity as a gospel benefits only those who receive it in good faith. It may for its own sake wish all coercion to be removed, yet one can still labour under the delusion that Christianity bears within it a law of God that seeks to keep in check all non-believers who *reject* the gospel.

It can also be shown that this excuse, with which Protestants have sought to gloss over the spiritual slavery they themselves condemned yet lauded, was only empty evasion, since it was indeed faith in Jesus Christ and His gospel that they wished to force upon people. It was precisely a confession of the faith they did *not* have that was forced upon non-believers. However, this has no bearing on our loathing of the so-called 'ruling church' until we realise that whether it be law or gospel that manifests itself as divine revelation, its truth and benefit depend on it taking up a *free relationship* with the children of humankind. Any other faith relationship is completely false, abominable to the true God, and unbearable for the truthful person.

This and this alone hits the nail on the head, for only thus can all possible escape routes be blocked. If people wish to defend or excuse spiritual slavery through misusing either the story of the revelation or the fancied benefits of spiritual slavery under certain circumstances, there is no need to begin an endless dispute with us. We only need to show that if any so-called divine revelation has set itself in a tyrant-and-slave relation with mankind, it has proved its falseness in the very process! However much of worldly benefit one can derive from lying and falsehood over the question of salvation, it is still certain that people can gain the whole world yet lose themselves in the bottomless abyss of lying and falsehood.

We know that there are those who will not heed this evidence because in spiritual matters they unfortunately do not *care* to hear the truth – like Pilate. The main point here is that all Christians, and most of all Danish Christians, should come to the insight that on the question of salvation, spiritual slavery under all circumstances is as unchristian and ungodly as it is inhuman. If only Christians everywhere would join together with the children of natural humankind[286] on this point, Christianity and the people's life and culture everywhere, and soonest of all in Denmark, would again return to their original, free relationship, which is the only right and natural one.

For it is not merely a thing of the past but has been demonstrated so clearly in the present that we only make fools of ourselves by denying that the life, culture, and identity of all peoples is actually awakening everywhere in Christendom in our day! With more or less light and power it is endeavouring to make its presence felt against all things foreign which either already rule over it or threaten to do so. Among such peoples Christianity is clearly in danger of losing its influence. However, far from desiring any form of spiritual slavery whatsoever, Christianity by its very nature loathes and fights fiercely against it; and far from wishing to suppress a people's culture, Christianity has itself awakened it to life and will nourish it into growth. When this is realised, such peoples would be mad to reject an ally against all foreign dominance, an ally whose matchless power is proven down the ages! They would be mad to envy the gentle angel-voice that only seeks to make good whatever influence people voluntarily grant it. At least where Denmark is concerned, I am sure that by advancing religious freedom and the life, culture, and identity of any people by all means possible Christianity will win more respect and influence than it has ever enjoyed before. This will not happen merely because it thereby acquires any great merit in the eyes of those whose identity in so many ways is being suppressed, tormented, and almost killed off. It will happen because religious freedom and a people's identity are what Christianity, in order to work in the spirit, must either find, or must create, if it is missing!

This is what the reformers of the 16th century glimpsed when they helped their

---

286. Grundtvig's word here, *Naturmennesket*, denotes the human being from nature, i.e. not yet reborn in the Spirit.

peoples to cast off the foreign yoke that the Pope and his clerisy had imposed upon them in the name of 'Christianity' but under the *false* name of 'Christ's vice-regents on earth'. The reformers also introduced vernacular language into the Church as a condition for the living influence of true Christianity. That is why these reformers are still praised as folk-heroes and demi-gods even by those who neither care for, nor will ever adopt, their Christianity. The reformers in the growing enlightenment of the 19th century needed only to tread in their predecessors' footsteps to be sure of opening Christianity to a far more fruitful sphere of activity and making itself most beneficial to the people whether or not they wished to *become* Christian. For that choice can only be left to the heart of each individual, and only decided when human nature and Christianity meet in free and living interaction.

I am well aware that many state church orthodoxies regard religious freedom as something that Christianity ought to fight *against* – just as many so-called 'holy' people think the same about human nature. This can only come about because they are ignorant of *living* Christianity and the spirit that quickens, and because they have a dull and unnatural concept of both of these. Otherwise they would know what every living person otherwise knows, that faith is far freer than thought. Whoever does not naturally believe in God and has no desire for eternal life has no eye either for the gospel of the Son of God with the eternal Word of Life. So if Christianity is to have a beneficial effect, it must, as we said, either find religious freedom and a people's culture or it must call them forth.

There are those who will admit that both religious freedom and humaneness should exist wherever Christianity is to be of benefit, and yet they deny this to be true of a people's life, culture, and identity. This comes from them imagining humaneness to exist in heaven, or somewhere in the air but not on earth, for on earth one can never find humaneness without culture, whether the latter embraces the former or, as in the case of Jesus Christ, the former embraces the latter.

If we look at the life and culture of the Hebrews and the Israelites – which are much clearer to us than our own because our pastors have *preached* about them and our best children's books have *described* them – then we note that everything in the land of the Jews was organised to maintain and *strengthen* their life, their culture, and their identity. Even when it had sunk into the valley of death, it was wonderfully awakened by John the Baptist before Christ came. For he turned "the children's hearts to their parents and the parents' hearts to their children" in order to prepare the way of the Lord and present him with a "well-prepared people".[287]

Let us now turn to the identity of the *Danish* people. This may well seem somewhat hazy to us, since no one has taken care of it for centuries, but Danish life and culture

---

287. Mal 4:6.

are what we know best because by nature we have them within us. We cannot then help but see a prevailing indifference to *spiritual* matters – our blindness to the world of the spirit and our deafness to all the trumpets that shake it. Not only our zealous pastors but also our brightest brains bemoan these facts. Such indifference finds its explanation in the lack of a living *spiritual* culture. As a people we are spiritually dead. What remains alive of Danishness resembles a hair on the inconsolable widow at the gate into Nain as she follows her only son to the grave.[288]

Of course in such circumstances it is no use talking to the Danish people about a 'life in Christ', which is inevitably the only *living* Christianity. When we nevertheless do so, we can feel that it is as if our Master were doing what He never actually *did*, namely speaking to the dead young man on the bier about the path to eternal life. So if we can and will do something in the name of the Lord, we must, like Him, first have *compassion* over the tragic death, tell the widow not to weep, and say to the young man, "Get up!" For wherever this temporal life is missing or is only a burden of deep-felt grief, any talk of eternal life is, if not a mockery, then at least quite useless. Even if we cannot understand *why* this is the case, it is nevertheless how it continues to be, so that the death of Danish life and culture is our people's *spiritual* death, and this can only be cured by raising it up. This must happen before we can talk meaningfully to the people about *Christianity*.

That is all there is to say, I argue, and I have most certainly not confused Danishness and Christianity for many a year. On the other hand I will not answer on behalf of my younger days, for then it is true that I dreamed that one must be a living Christian and then a Dane into the bargain! Yet even nature in me overcame discipline, so I spent a good number of my pastoral years turning the old chronicles and *Beowulf* into Danish.[289] Although they clearly sought to do so, these books could not waken our people's culture from the dead – and even less could they make people *Christian*! The reason why a people must become self-aware before any other spirit than their own can speak to them, is the same one that demands that an individual becomes self-aware before one can speak to them about what they possess or lack as a person, what dangers they can run into, and what means of rescue exist for them. For we all know that what raises human life above animal life is the Word by which the world's spirit unfolds itself to us and by which the present becomes merely a transition from the past – without the day to the future beginning, and without the year ending. We live in an eternity that *includes* us – and is therefore of necessity incomprehensible to us! Just as for us the Word of the Invisible finds life and power only in our mother-

---

288. Lk 7:11.

289. Grundtvig was a leading scholar of Old English and in 1820 he published the first modern translation of *Beowulf* (in Danish).

tongue, so does our living relation to the past and the future depend on our feeling an inner connection to our parents and our descendants. So if the Word of God is to find a well-prepared people in Denmark and everywhere else, as it did in the land of the Jews, then plain words in the mother-tongue must first have turned the children's hearts to their parents and the parents' hearts to their children. Then they will feel that death in all its guises is indeed theirs, that death is our arch-enemy, and that Christ is the only true saviour who can and will grant us eternal life.

I realise that for many a country pastor and even many a bishop all this may seem rather serious, since even for myself it is a very serious matter as to what extent any of us will be found gifted enough in the name of the Lord to raise the dead. But, as I said, even the most purblind country pastor should be able to see that I am not confusing Danishness and Christianity but am distinguishing more sharply between them than any pen has done to this day! And the reason I wish the People's High School[290] to be exclusively Danish is not that I believe Danish can make us either omniscient or blessed but that we must first *be* Danish, just as everyone must first be alive before there is any point in talking to them about temporal and eternal life. Whoever wishes to speak to the dead will not be the object of my envy, either in the enjoyment they thereby derive or the honour they thereby gain. I repeat merely what I have said before: that I would rather speak to living thieves than dead saints, for the former may well come to their senses and change their ways, whereas the latter can do nothing whatsoever!

290. After spending 3 summers in a row in England in 1829-31 Grundtvig began to formulate his ideas for a 'people's high school'. See further in *The School for Life* (2011).

10. The People, the People's Church, and Popular Belief in Denmark (1851)

Introduction by Ole Vind

The background to this article, published in Grundtvig's own periodical *The Dane* in 1851, was a government bill from 1850 introduced at the first-ever democratic Parliament, of which Grundtvig was an independent member. The 1849 Constitution had renamed the State Church the "People's Church"; it stated that there was complete freedom of religion and that civil and political rights were not conditional on religious affiliation. It further affirmed that the Constitution of the Danish Lutheran Church was to be grounded in future legislation.

However, while expressly permitting freedom of conscience the Constitution stood firm on the State Church's demand that people worship only in their own parish – the so-called 'parish-tie'. This limited them to Baptism, confirmation, marriage, and burial *only* in their own parish, while allowing for the occasional Holy Communion to be taken elsewhere. Conversely, the parish pastor was duty-bound to follow the authorised rituals and the Confessional books of the Danish Lutheran Church.[291] This was the background for the demand by one of Grundtvig's warmest supporters, N.M. Spandet, to remove the compulsion for Baptism and confirmation only within the parish and to allow for civil marriages.

The proposal triggered intense debate and was attacked in the press as a threat to both the Church and Christianity. Grundtvig gave it his Parliamentary support, arguing that freedom of worship may have been set down on paper, but was still not a reality. He labelled the Church's attitude ridiculous, contradictory, and unchristian, setting his criticism in a historical perspective of 800 years of an unchristian display of force by the Church in Denmark: by the Catholic Church, the Lutheran State Church, and now the so-called 'Danish People's Church', one after the other.

It was not enough for Grundtvig that he and like-minded citizens should be allowed to leave the Danish Church and form their own church community; the Church itself needed reforming. Its pastors and theologians were in such complete internal confusion and disagreement on faith, doctrine, and ritual that Grundtvig could not clearly distinguish either a joint creed or a joint teaching. And yet the cohesion of the Church depended on both popular and civil agreement.

---

291. For the Confessional Books of the Evangelical Lutheran Church in Denmark, see note 62.

Grundtvig feared both that the Church would dissolve into numerous smaller churches independent of the state, as had been the case in the USA, and that a return to the regimented State Church under the name of 'the People's Church' might well lead to a *synod*, which would legislate for the Church – as anticipated by the Constitution. This would be dominated by the clergy and could easily become an empty shell, as the diversity of popular beliefs regarding all things between Heaven and earth would lead to numerous sects being founded *outside* the Church.

Instead Grundtvig proposed 'a free People's Church', a completely new form of 'church' in the history of Christianity. Its pastors should continue to be state civil servants but would be allowed to discharge their office and interpret the Bible according to their own faith and conscience. Freedom of conscience within the congregation was to be guaranteed by allowing parishioners to *choose* their pastor and to attend a church *outside* their parish if they so wished. This was known as 'breaking the parish-tie', and thanks largely to Grundtvig, it passed into law in 1855. Despite pastoral *freedom* never being accepted, Grundtvig's promotion of freedom as a core value has exercised a huge influence over the Danish People's Church, which is known for its 'roominess'. As he writes early on in the article, "the Church was made for the people, not the people for the Church".

Consequently, the legislation foreseen in 1849 has never been passed – the latest attempt failed as recently as 2014. Thus the decentralised Danish People's Church has neither constitution nor synod, and nobody can claim to speak on its behalf: a great strength and a great weakness simultaneously.

***

I

I do not need to tell readers of *The Dane*,[292] male and female alike, that it is the Parliamentary bill on civil freedom of religion that with some force leads my thoughts towards the Danish people's position on the Church. Not only the pastors and professors are preaching about it, but so are all the newspapers! *Berling's Times*[293] in particular is remarkable for its edifying sermons, primarily about my learned friend, Councillor

---

292. Between 1848-51 Grundtvig wrote and published a weekly paper, *The Dane*, in which he covered political subjects in Denmark, especially the conflict in Schleswig-Holstein.

293. Founded by Ernst Berling in 1749, this daily newspaper, now known as *Berlingske*, is amongst the oldest newspapers in the world.

of State Spandet,[294] who has put forward this terrible proposal, but also about the publisher of *The Dane*, who from the outset has supported it.[295] What is required in the context is to regard this vital matter of national importance with a certain calmness and a certain depth, since most of what we hear and read about is clearly most 'disquieting' in both the Danish and the Swedish sense.[296] Nor can I find any sign of depth in the episcopal book on the Provisions of the Constitution[297] or in the much more 'clerical' than 'spiritual' letter to the Danish Parliament. So it is a good deed I am attempting when I endeavour to set about a calm, in-depth reflection on the question of the Church. Whether or not it is successful must be put to the test.

Since I like to begin all questions on Church relations with the one whom I in earnest call 'Our Lord', I shall also begin here with His well-known words: "The Sabbath was made for man, not man for the Sabbath."[298] If He is right in saying this, then I am also clearly right in saying that the Church was made for the people, not the people for the Church, and that what calls itself 'the People's Church'(*Folkekirken*)[299] can never without obvious contradiction claim even the smallest civil right either over the people or across from them. However, something that once called itself 'the Church' on quite different principles than those of Our Lord demanded a right of *coercion* over the people of Denmark, and for a period of no less than 800 years our kings, from Knud the Holy to Christian VIII,[300] have to a greater or lesser degree allowed the Church this right of coercion over the people of Denmark – first the so-called 'Catholic' Church and then the so-called 'Lutheran' Church. None could become husband and wife without the Church giving its permission. No child could be born into the world without it being taken to Church before it knew the difference between left and right, there to be baptised into a specific faith. Finally, no person could come of age outside prison unless they had been to lessons with the pastor, had been examined by him in the teachings

---

294. Niels Møller Spandet (1788-1858) was a judge, a politician, and Deputy Speaker of the new democratic Parliament in 1849. In 1811 Spandet and Grundtvig had lived together in a student hostel in Copenhagen. Spandet worked tirelessly for freedom, especially in church and social matters. In 1850 he created a national controversy when he presented Parliament with a bill advocating civil marriage and freedom from compulsory Baptism. Tens of thousands signed a protest that he was destroying Christianity and the Church, but he enjoyed Grundtvig's full support.

295. i.e. Grundtvig himself.

296. The Swedish sense of Grundtvig's Danish word *urolig* is 'unamusing'.

297. *The Constitution Provisions on Church Relations in Denmark* (1850) by Dr J.P. Mynster, Bishop of Zealand.

298. Mk 2:27.

299. The word '*Folkekirken*' was first used in 1841 by Peter Kierkegaard, Søren Kierkegaard's elder brother. It was incorporated into the democratic constitution of 1849, which stipulated that "The Evangelical Lutheran Church is the Danish People's Church and as such is supported by the State."

300. Knud IV (the Holy) reigned from 1080-86. He was murdered in Albani Church in Odense during a popular rebellion and became the only Danish king to be canonised by the Pope – as early as 1101. His remains are exhibited in the crypt of Odense Cathedral. Christian VIII reigned from 1839-48.

of the Church, and had solemnly assured him – whether or not they had much or little faith – that they believed everything that the pastor required them to say 'yes' to.

The right of coercion that this Church holds over the Danish people has always been an unchristian and inhuman injustice. It is expressly abolished in the Danish Constitution of last year in the provision (§ 84) that no one can be refused access to the full enjoyment of civil and political rights on the basis of their religious confession. If for no *other* reason, the Danish people should be very grateful to King Frederik VII and the Constitutional Assembly, since through this provision no one is denied – and all are granted – the freedom to decide their church relations as a matter between themselves and God. This is not the business of the temporal authority or any of their fellow-citizens, since in this context we as fellow human beings only have the right and duty to advise, inform, and comfort one another if we can.

However, this civil liberty to lie to ourselves and our Lord, to speak our mind about God and eternity – whom no human beings have seen or can conceive, and by the constitutional law of Truth cannot say other than what they believe in their hearts – this civil liberty exists only on paper in the Constitution; we do not have it in our day-to-day life. For our pastors continue to *report* on those parishioners who refuse to marry, or baptise their children, or turn 18 without being confirmed. This is surely a mistake. Since all civil servants must uphold the Constitution, all the old statutes about keeping civil reports on people must be regarded as *abolished*, including registration of their faith and their church habits. It is clearly preferable to allow church relations to work themselves out in this somewhat disorderly way than to pass new laws that renew all the quarrels and strife which after hundreds of years of spiritual slavery can only accompany a sudden transformation of the relationship between civil society and the Church. Nevertheless, it is not Parliament or any of its members but the clergy and the government ministers who have prevented matters from quietly working themselves out as far as possible. It is our *clergy* who have argued that the old statutes and right of coercion remained in force until they were specifically abolished, and in many ways our ministers have upheld this contention. It is as if the so-called People's Church or State Church had inherited a particular right of coercion over the Danish people which through an amicable agreement must be replaced, though without compensation.

This agreement includes licences to enter into mixed marriages[301] and the ministry's bill to this end, as well as the demand for a so-called 'synod' or 'church council'. This is scheduled to have an undefined but essential influence on the attitude of the Danish people towards their pastors and what is called 'the Church'. Solely to put an end to

---

301. The 'mixed marriages' were between members of different faith communities, typically a member of the 'People's Church' and a Jew or a Roman Catholic.

all this nonsense and with a clear case for the people's rights and the Constitution, our legal experts, being as much of the Church as of the people, have put forward a bill for the Act on Civil Religious Freedom which is now being proclaimed as an attack on the People's Church and all that is sacred and honourable to the people of Denmark.

However serious this matter is in itself, the way in which it has been approached by both the clergy and many others has been so utterly ridiculous that one would think the interested parties felt it themselves! For while they claim that it is the civil religious freedom guaranteed by the Constitution that they cannot be reconciled to, they nonetheless appeal with the straightest of faces precisely *to* the Constitution against the terrible attempt to implement it! They even claim this through the right, supposedly granted by the Constitution, to the title of 'Evangelical-Lutheran People's Church', despite the fact the Constitution has expressly abolished all privileges that relate to rank and title.

They argue thus: The People's Church is a church to which all the people belong, with the exception of those who have clearly turned their backs on it. This People's Church is to be what we call 'Evangelical-Lutheran', which means allowing people to be married by a pastor, to have their children baptised by a pastor when their wife has given birth, and to confirm their Baptismal Covenant once they reach fourteen, or at the latest eighteen. They continue their complaint: This generally disquieting religious freedom that the Constitution allows citizens in no way relates to the Danish people who belong to the People's Church but is only for the few outside it. And even then it is worth noting that although according to the Constitution they may hold whatever faith they wish, they must *have* a faith, whether they like it or not.

This quite peculiar way of thinking, which is found in both the 'open letter' from the Copenhagen pastors and professors to the Danish Parliament and in the Bishop of Zealand's[302] understanding of the Constitution's clauses on religious freedom, is based on many misapprehensions about Christianity and the Church as regards both our people and our civic life. They are so plentiful that I shall not attempt to enumerate them, let alone repudiate them one by one, but only seek as best I can to illuminate the question from all sides. Once it is sufficiently explained, the misapprehensions must lapse of their own accord.

Let us take our long-lived Lutheran State Church first. We all know that although the entire Danish people are reckoned to belong to it, this is not because they all freely subscribe to Luther's *Catechism* or what the Altar Book or Augsburg Confession say. On the contrary, even pastors and their teachers have openly declared themselves against these books as guidelines for the Church's teaching or ceremonial functions. One only needed to wander round the churches in the capital to be convinced that

---

302. Bishop of Zealand, Jacob Mynster (1775-1854).

the old Lutheran State Church had from one side – i.e. the pastors' side – been completely dissolved. One could receive Communion and have one's children confirmed by whichever pastor one wished, so, also from the congregations' side the State Church was dissolved, inasmuch as churchgoers associated themselves with the various pastors in their teaching and church duties. Admittedly, in the capital both Baptism and marriage were still compulsory church matters, since only by special licence could one purchase the freedom to be married or baptised by whichever pastor one chose. *Outside* the capital the compulsion on the congregations' side was total. Anyone without a special licence had to settle for the ceremonies, teachings, and confirmations as performed by their parish pastor. If the parish pastor changed, one often acquired a new scholar whose teaching and administration of the church ceremonies was more or less the exact *opposite* of the previous one. So it is as clear as sunlight that the demand on parishioners was either to be indifferent to the Word and Sacraments of the Church or to change their faith and doctrine like the serfs changed squires and settled for what they got. Since this latter is impossible, there naturally ensued a dreadful disdain or an apathetic unconcern for all Church matters, and whoever actively resisted was fined or imprisoned – with no regard for the faith that they wished to retain and spread or for whether or not the way they wished the Church ceremonies to be performed was set down in the Law and in the Altar Book.

Clearly this Church edifice, half dissolved and half petrified, was now a graveyard for all true faith and piety, but since the government would allow none of us to withdraw from it to look after our *own* edification, I exerted my inventive powers to make the continued stay within it *tolerable* for living people. I discovered that this was possible in Denmark if we abolished *compulsory* church for both clergy and congregation. Thus with regard to Church teachings and duties every pastor could freely follow his understanding of Christianity and the Bible, and all the inhabitants of our land could freely avail themselves of the pastor of their choice, provided they announced their Church activities to the parish pastor for proper registration in the parish register.[303]

This was the purpose behind the abolition of the parish-tie, which almost succeeded until the Bishop of Zealand and the Copenhagen clergy prevented it. When some of us then endeavoured to have it written into the Constitution, the attempt also came to nothing in the face of similar opposition, even though the rumour in Parliament was that the abolition would follow of its own accord and need not therefore even be mentioned in the Constitution.

We must also take note that the abolition of the parish-tie will do no more than exchange the ruling State Church with a serving People's Church unless the pastors

---

303. This included church attendance, Holy Communion attendance, and the registration of birth, baptism, confirmation, marriage, and death.

retain their self-assumed freedom to say and act in church more or less as they please. Then all differences and contrasts among the people would also find their expression among the pastors. But it was precisely the opposite of this that the Bishop of Zealand had in mind when he drew up a new Altar Book which the pastors were to follow to the letter in all Church ceremonies, whether or not they were in accord or in conflict with their own convictions. A similar intention lies behind the current demand for a 'Church council' (or synod), by which according to a majority of votes 'Church uniformity for all' is adopted.

Thus the so-called 'Evangelical-Lutheran People's Church' is in utter confusion without anyone being able to define the faith it confesses, the doctrine it pursues, or the degree of participation it requires of all its members. For we all know that its pastors are at loggerheads over faith and doctrine and are themselves in total disagreement as to how Baptism and Holy Communion should be administered. So even though the Constitution did not allow all our demands for civil freedom from all Church coercion, nevertheless all those who have a genuine faith and are considered to be members of the so-called People's Church, which has no faith, were clearly in great need of civil religious freedom. Yet Parliament has heard that only those with no faith strove to attain this, and in nearly all the papers we can read that it is a great insult to offer this to members of the People's Church.

It is said that those who are dissatisfied with the faith and worship of the People's Church can simply leave it and either move to another faith community or start a new one!

Not really, I must answer, for if we wish to abide by the Constitution in one respect until a proper new law is passed, and if we do not want such a law on universal religious freedom, then nor will we who have so far been counted members of the People's Church be allowed to leave it until such a proper new law is passed! And this will not happen until a Church synod has been consulted which perhaps will only let us leave under such difficult and ignominious conditions that for the sake of our Danish citizenship and civilian honour we could not countenance them.

Moreover, even if there is an honest intention for us freely to leave the so-called 'People's Church' whenever we like, and even if we can use the religious freedom guaranteed by the Constitution without all the fuss about civil and political rights, we are still confronted by the great obstacle that the People's Church has no common faith which a genuine Church community would acknowledge and around which all its worship could be gathered. We have only a thousand parish pastors, yet they are in total disagreement on faith and doctrine and differ completely in their conduct of public worship. Yet all so-called members of the People's Church through Baptism – and outside Copenhagen also through confirmation and attendance at Holy Communion – are still bound to their parish pastor, and in the case of marriage to the bride's parish pastor. They in turn may preach first this faith, then the other; today they baptise, confirm, and marry in one way, tomorrow in another, as the personalities change. And now comes the big question: Who could and who should leave the Church? Should it be all those who today have a pastor whose preaching and conduct of divine service they cannot agree or be satisfied with? And where should they then go, so that they can be seen to be *outside* the People's Church?

Like myself, the majority of those who may or will leave because they do not find themselves free in the so-called People's Church have nothing against Luther's *Catechism*, or the Altar Book and the Augsburg Confession, except that these have been forced upon the people of Denmark and are now being so badly mismanaged or appear so dead that whoever has Martin Luther's faith in no way deserves such pastors or their teaching or their conduct of divine service.

Then again, if we are to *leave* the People's Church, where are we to go? We cannot go to the Catholics or the Calvinists, and if we wish to establish our own faith community, we shall be told – for as long as Luther's *Catechism*, the Altar Book, and the Augsburg Confession are not done away with – that we are not an 'independent' faith community that can be recognised, but are within the scope of the so-called 'Evangelical-Lutheran People's Church' and must act according to the decisions of its synod!

Imagine, however, that we were not rebuked in this way and that there was no synodal decision to introduce a new uniformity into the People's Church, so we old-fashioned Lutherans were even easier to recognise than in Prussia and could be easily distinguished from the newly-fashioned Evangelical-Lutheran Church. How should this People's Church relate to Parliament and civil society when it stands outside a large number of our people, very likely outside all those who set any great store by faith and divine worship? In this 'Evangelical-Lutheran People's Church' will infant Baptism still be compulsory, even though according to both the Gospel and Luther's teaching this must be a free choice? Will Holy Communion still be compulsory, even though – if the Apostle Paul was evangelical and Martin Luther was Lutheran – the Church must sternly threaten the unworthy guests with the judgement of God? Will confirmation still be compulsory, even though this was not the case until Christian VI[304] and is based neither on the Gospel nor on Lutheranism? Finally, will all members of the People's Church still be forced to marry in church – something that the Gospel is unaware of and Martin Luther clearly rejected in that he himself was married in a civil ceremony which not only took place outside the Church but, being between a monk

---

304. Christian VI (reigned 1730-46) introduced compulsory confirmation in 1736. This was made a condition for marriage and for leasing a farm.

and a nun, was also in conflict with all the concepts of his time for Church weddings.[305] If, moreover, marriages contracted in the People's Church are to be annulled by the jurists for not being civilly recognised – and yet the parties involved are not excluded from the People's Church and do not lose their right to a church wedding – is it not clear that if all this is to be the case, the 'People's Church' is exposed to universal scorn and derision? Or do we trust its ability to defy § 8 of the Press Act which forbids the mockery of the doctrine and worship of any existing faith community? And do we then apply § 3 of the Constitution stating that 'the Evangelical-Lutheran People's Church' is 'supported by the State' without asking about its relation to the people or whether it works to the benefit or detriment of faith, piety, and morality?

If all this is required, then I fail to see the purpose. I do understand that it opposes extending the civil right of religious freedom to the People's Church. But if we want a true 'church of the people' in which the people find themselves well served and are not tempted to leave or be driven to abolish it, then we must somehow make participation in the People's Church a *free* issue that is not taken into consideration when discussing civil and political rights.

The conclusions are as follows. First, the Constitution is clearly being violated if a new law is passed by which civil religious freedom or civil independence from our Church creed, as guaranteed to all in the Constitution, is limited to the few who have not been coerced *into* the State Church – on the pretext that almost the entire population belongs to the People's Church.

Second: the people of Denmark are being openly deceived into the delusion that the abolition of Church coercion amounts to a complete or even a partial end to Baptism, confirmation, a wedding, or any other Church ceremony. Their repeal cannot diminish people in the eyes of any, nor can it disgrace the Church that requires these things of its members. On the contrary, the fundamental law of the Christian Church is that it is *voluntary*, as it must be for every honest Church community. And even the most godly institutions must lose reverence in their own eyes and all their blessings on those who are coerced or compelled by temporal or civil powers. 'Do not force the good into the bad' runs the saying, and whoever is therefore coerced by so-called 'church benefits' has every reason to conclude that the coercer does not see them as a benefit!

Third: Baptism, confirmation, and the wedding ceremony must be a matter of free choice, even for members of all Christian churches, so in a Christian respect it is perverse to make them a compulsory *civil* matter. If we are not to mock the so-called People's Church, then in a civil respect they must stop dissolving marriage-ties at the

---

305. In 1525 Luther married Katharina von Bora, a nun who was 16 years his junior and had fled from a convent in Nimbschen to Wittenberg. Their household eventually included their four surviving children, one of Katharina's relatives, and after 1529 six of Luther's sister's children, as well as student lodgers to help the family's finances.

town hall which have been bound by obligation to the Church; otherwise people will say that what God has joined together the magistrate shall put asunder!

||

When the talk turns to 'the people's beliefs' in Denmark, I like to tell the story of what happened to me some 20 years ago. A peasant farmer from Zealand came up to me to ask for Saxo's *Chronicles of Denmark* in the new version that I had produced.[306] He had the book under his arm and his hand on the door-handle when he turned round, looked me up and down a little, and said, "Is it all here, because I have read the old translation, and you like to keep what you have got." I assured him that this was indeed the case, since I had not to the best of my knowledge omitted a single word. But I could not hold back a little momentary smile over his amusing remark. In this case it was quite groundless, but it was at a time when there *were* grounds for suspicion of the modern bookworms who gnawed away at all the old books. My smile made him all the more suspicious, and he felt he had to unburden his heart despite it being something one should not speak about. He was actually referring to 'that stuff about the trolls'. Also in this respect I assured him with a clean conscience, and when I also confided that I thought quite differently about these old stories than did educated people of the day, we parted the best of friends.

I have noted that my self-assumed father confessor in *Berling's Times* seeks to impute that whenever I say something amusing that has happened to me, even in Parliament, I have concocted the story for the occasion. But I have never practised such 'imaginative flights', which are the easiest, but also the worst, kind of all – namely to fabricate 'facts' that one can later 'appeal to'. So I know that my story of the Zealander and myself is a true one; indeed I have often thought of him since, and of 'that stuff about the trolls' which he could not let go of. It is sad, I thought, that whereas from time immemorial our people's beliefs in Denmark and the North have been so rich and beautiful, all we have left now are ghosts, witches, gnomes, and trolls. All the giant gods and goddesses, the sylphs and the valkyries have disappeared. But then I thought: that is the fault of the monks, who condemned all those natural and popular beliefs as 'heathen'. They impressed a great deal upon our people in the name of Christianity; if it was not to be mere dalliance, all the witches must go, along with much that made the troll-horde far more frightening than before. No wonder that only the worst of the people's beliefs that were given a Christian appearance survived the Middle Ages.

306. Saxo (c.1160-post 1208) worked as a scribe for the great Bishop Absalon (1128-1201). Saxo's *Gesta Danorum* (Deeds of the Danes) was handwritten in elegant Latin in 16 volumes. The early volumes contain mainly legendary material, but references to documented events become more and more common in later volumes. *Gesta Danorum* was first published in 1514. Grundtvig's Danish translation was published in three volumes in 1818-22.

Admittedly in the 18th and 19th centuries our Protestant clerics in alliance with the ransackers of this world, the natural scientists, endeavoured to eliminate popular beliefs for good. They called them all 'superstition', so no one should even be *allowed* to believe that the sun rose and set! But 'such strict masters no longer govern', as the saying goes, and a faith, when it is genuine, rarely lets itself be overcome unless it be by another faith that is either more true or more agreeable. In our case it was simply pure *unbelief* with which they wished to replace popular *belief*, but they only succeeded to a minor extent, perhaps because there are so many women and children in the world who cannot live without faith and who will always be the kindest creatures on earth.

Let us turn now to the people's beliefs in Denmark as they actually are, unconverted by the medieval monks, scorned by scholars and scribes, and for a long time left to themselves as old wives' tales, heartlessly mocked and opposed. What we see now of course is a half-dead jumble of the most fantastic and often absurd fancies, partly of heathen, partly of papist, and partly of scientific origin. Thus the People's Church, which should be able to incorporate and animate the whole population, cannot help but consist of many dissimilar and quarrelsome parts, while the name 'People's Church' is the emptiest of titles when the Church cannot address the whole population and satisfy the hearts of the *people*.

If anything sensible is to be done from the Church's point of view, then it must 'throw in the towel' and make the civil arrangements completely independent of the individual citizen's relationship to the Church, which then becomes everybody's *own* business, as in North America. Alternatively, we must find a new arrangement for the Church that allows such freedom to each person's faith and thought concerning 'the divine', and in general on the relation between Heaven and earth, time and eternity, the visible and invisible, that we can hope the entire population will thereby feel themselves fulfilled, more or less. On the other hand we can choose a middle way: we can retain or re-erect a state church with stiff uniformity and specific duties for the temporal authority which in turn are to be paid for through certain civil advantage. Meanwhile outside this state church the people's beliefs are left to themselves and to native and foreign speculators. This, I think, would be a great mistake! The consequence would be that the stone-dead State Church here as in China is only recognisable by its many precious graves and tombs, and even as a spiritual grave is twice as ridiculous with its title of 'People's Church'. Meanwhile popular beliefs divide up into a number of sects, all of whom are envious of the State Church, peevish about the temporal authority which maintains its useless burden on them at public expense, and incapable of the living interaction with the People's School which is a condition for popular education.

I am fairly sure that this 'Church council', whenever it takes place, will with a majority that always echoes our clergy declare itself in favour of the lamentable middle way, and it is reasonable to assume that this will also be the preference of the Sovereign in

Council in Parliament. Yet I must forcefully argue against it and seek to put forward my own solution, which is for a *free* People's Church. Even if it is an innovation in Christianity, it is in no way impossible or unheard of.

Far too many years ago I suggested that we loosened the ties on our pastors' lives so that they could move freely about the Church within the boundaries set by the people's beliefs, general enlightenment, and the Bible, even when liberally interpreted. At the same time I argued that we should break the tie that binds individuals to their parish pastor. I have also proposed that we established nurseries (seminaries) for incoming pastors where the sole criteria would be innate ability and the acquired skill to understand and address the people about matters of the spirit and the heart. If we did this, I believe, very few of them would make use of the freedom to set up and pay for a *separate* church community. The advantages are obvious, since the government would retain practically all the clergy in a lightly dependent but amicable relationship, would control their training, and would be able to supervise their activity on a regular basis. These three things constitute the entire benefit of a State Church without causing any of the irreparable damage that always comes when the temporal authority attempts to control the people's beliefs and the pastors' teaching. Matters of the spirit and the heart cannot be commanded by temporal means, any more than hands can take hold of the living word that issues from our mouths. Consequently, the only matters of faith and doctrine that can be controlled by the temporal power are always only empty shadows of the spirit and the heart that either mock all living people or must be vainly protected by the temporal power from a violence against all things living that reveals the emptiness of the shadows. Moreover, since our pastors in the State Church have arrogated to themselves a freedom that can never be removed without scaring off all freeborn, active souls from a pastoral calling, the only new measure would be the breaking of the parish-tie, which clerical freedom also clearly necessitates. Otherwise we shall drive out of the so-called 'People's Church' all those who actually *have* a faith and who are naturally unwilling to live and die under their parish pastor or exchange him for another. There will always be some inconvenience for the individual in having to find another pastor when their own parish pastor fails to address or satisfy them, but in the vast majority of cases this inconvenience will be much less than it would cost to find a separate church community which one could agree with, or to establish a new one.

Thus, if every parish pastor continued as now to be a civil servant in a temporal sense, but was limited in a church sense to the churchgoers inside and outside his parish who freely embraced him, there would be religious *freedom* in the People's Church. There would be as much order as freedom can bear and allow, given the free nature of Church relations, with the life and pleasantness that people need and every wise government desires. This free relation between the pastor and his congregation is also far from unknown to us; indeed in Copenhagen it is quite well-established, not only in that it partially exists in every parish but in that it has, everywhere and always, been the case with the *German* churches among us. The pastors at St Peter's[307] and Frederik's Church[308] have never had 'parishioners', only a free congregation, which rose and fell in numbers depending on the members' appreciation of this or that pastor. The only drawback which has been noted was of a temporal rather than a spiritual kind: churchgoers there have to *pay* their pastor, whereas in the People's Church all pastors are paid out of the public purse.

If we had taken this path at the turn of the tide in 1848, or even at the same time as the Constitution was introduced,[309] the present awkward position over religious freedom would have been avoided, for we would all have felt that we *had* religious freedom, even if in a somewhat disguised form. It would not have troubled anyone very much to have a Baptismal, confirmation, or wedding certificate, if pastors were free to baptise, confirm, and marry more or less as they wished. Conversely, all would have been free to seek Baptism, confirmation, and marriage with any of the appointed pastors they wished. Now that things are on the move in this area, it will be necessary to abolish completely the Church's influence on the *civil* position. If this is done cautiously, so that marriage is declared to be civilly valid from the day it is officially inscribed in the parish register, the Baptismal certificate civilly valid when it confirms the birthdate inscription in the register, and civil confirmation validly conducted with the transcription of the school register, the rest will sort itself out once the People's Church is freed from restrictions. Experience will soon show what an incalculable gain it will be for popular and civil unity to have preserved a spiritually *liberated* people in a People's Church where the pastors of their own accord, despite differences of faith and doctrinal disputes, endeavour to keep the people *together* and improve their lot though unifying forces.

Admittedly, very little attention is paid to the words 'of the people',[310] meaning in our case the Danish and Norwegian people. And there is so little understanding of their great importance in every sense that most readers barely know what I mean by them. But in a free People's Church the words 'of the people' will form their own link

---

307. St Peter's Church in Copenhagen has a German-speaking congregation within the Danish State Church. It is the oldest preserved church in Copenhagen, having been given to the Germans in 1585 by King Frederik II. Today it has some 900 members and together with a German school it forms the German cultural centre in Copenhagen.

308. Frederik's Church (the Marble Church) was planned in the 1740s but not finally consecrated until 1894. Built mainly of Norwegian marble (hence the vernacular name), the church received the backing of Grundtvig and eventually the financial support of the wealthy businessman C.F. Tietgen. Among the statues surrounding the church are effigies of Ansgar, Kingo, Brorson, Kierkegaard, and Grundtvig.

309. On 5th June 1849.

310. 'Of the people' (*folkelig*) is a core phrase in Grundtvig's thinking and the title of one of his most famous songs. See no. 82 in *Living Wellsprings* (2015).

between conflicting parties and among them find support and development through competition. This is not difficult to understand. What is 'of the people' cannot be other than linked to the fatherland; it finds its only living expression in the mother-tongue; and it can only thrive among old friends from time immemorial. We read that although the ancient Egyptians had very different beliefs and forms of worship, they nevertheless venerated the original divine couple 'of the people' and the country: Isis and Osiris (the people's heart and the people's spirit). In like manner, we would share the same view in Denmark. Once civil religious freedom cures us of the madness of wishing to employ temporal and heavy-handed means to make our faith and spiritual outlook dominant in a larger or smaller circle, we shall not lose the desire to make our presence felt in as large a circle as possible. One puts a finger in the earth and smells the way to where one is! Then one endeavours to get to know the race of people whose heart and spirit one wishes to influence, to acquire the people's language as the great driving force, and finally to enlighten the people about themselves and all that is theirs, since it is only thus that one can convince the people and be sure that they are under one's influence.

Once our pastors can be described as 'of the people', it follows not only that the people, if they have any faith, will again become churchgoers, but also that in Denmark and throughout the North we can predict that the People's Church will in a sense become 'Evangelical-Lutheran'. Not in the sense in which *some* would take the name, since that would only be appropriate where pastors had sworn themselves to the Augsburg Confession[311] and the whole congregation to Luther's *Catechism*. But it will be 'Evangelical-Lutheran' insofar as it is understood in our Constitution, where it is not linked to any book or creed but refers to the fundamental doctrine that Luther shared with the good news that is known to the people under the name '*Christi Evangelium*' (Lat., 'Christ's gospel'). This shared Church principle states that our own conceptions and handiwork are of no consequence for our salvation, which is dependent solely on the Word of God and our heart's faith in it. This Evangelical-Lutheran principle will become dominant in our free People's Church through its own dynamic, a claim I make on the basis not only of Reformation history in the 16th century but also of the Nordic way of thinking in general. However great the difference will always be between the principle and its implementation in our Church, its living application in the People's School will lead to beneficial and shining enlightenment. For it will assert the Word and the Heart in the same place as the Way of Thinking that they have in the true *human* life, which in all our educational institutions is either overseen

---

311. The Augsburg Confession is the primary confession of faith in the Lutheran Church. It was agreed at the Diet (Council) of Augsburg on 25 June 1530 by Lutheran princes and representatives of 'free cities', and comprised 21 Chief Articles of faith and 7 statements concerning abuses of the Christian faith in the Roman Catholic Church.

from a great airy height or is darkened instead of being enlightened and transformed. This is because they either place the visible and tangible at the top of everything or they begin with reflections on life instead of life itself. I am speaking here of life as it finds expression *in the Word* and makes an impression *on the Heart*, corresponding to power in the one and pliancy in the other, so that our entire *Way of Thinking* develops naturally through a spiritual birth and growth.

In closing, I must ask readers of *The Dane* again on this occasion to consider seriously with me whether all the talk about people growing up as 'heathens' and regressing to 'heathenism' has any currency.

With regard to these words we must first note that they are quite innocent, since heathenism only means what has been part of the people from time immemorial and 'heathen' everywhere denotes the old, natural, pre-Christian human being. So it is in a sense quite correct to talk about all our infant children before they are baptised as 'the little heathens'. But if they are born Christian, there is also Christian blood running in their veins, and if we believe that everything they have of heathenism blows away at Baptism – where we no longer blow on them and exorcise the devil as the papacy does – then it is obviously an empty fancy. For believing in such a transformation in a human child from heathen (innate, old, and natural) to Christian (new and supernatural) merely by tangible means and relevant readings would be a sorcery from which Christianity would incur inextinguishable shame if it promised it. Our daily experience teaches us that nothing like this happens at Baptism, nor has Christianity ever promised it. On the contrary, it has made a specific faith and an open confession of this faith the condition for the *divine* effect of Baptism and has also described the change of the old to the new human life as a progressive *renewal* and *transfiguration* of Christ's human nature among his faithful as effected by the Spirit through love. This may seem to many as unbelievable as the old heathen life becoming new and Christian as if by magic, but it is clearly something quite different. For here the means employed are appropriate to the purpose, and experience provides a favourable testimony of a quite different kind from the transformation of heathenism to Christianity or the change and ennoblement of the old human life alone through Baptism as an act by a church civil servant.

The second thing I would ask my readers to note is that there is a popular belief in the effects of Baptism, Holy Communion, and even of the pastors' self-assumed marriage of human spirits and hearts, weal and woe, here and hereafter without regard for the faith or lack of faith of the bridal couple. This belief of the people, which I permit myself to call a grievous superstition and 'papist leaven', exists in an inseparable relationship with the fundamental papist superstition that their consecrated bishops and priests are Christ's temporal vice-regents and heaven's doorkeepers who command all human souls and salvation. So we are only making ourselves look ridiculous, if we are scandalised by the Pope and the priestly hierarchy yet attribute to priestly hands and priestly mouths the power, with no regard for our faith or our heart's nature, to make all our marriages and our lives 'unchristian' simply by denying us the ceremonies of Baptism, Holy Communion, and marriage.

11. On a Christian Separation from the People's Church (1855)

Introduction by Ole Vind

The direct occasion of this article, published in *Danish Church Times* on 2nd December 1855, was a piece in the same periodical by the writer K.C. Knudsen, a supporter of Grundtvig's belief in freedom within the Church. Knudsen had not only sharply criticised the Danish Church as a self-contradictory and fundamentally unchristian State Church, but had gone one step further than Grundtvig in demanding that all true Christians should immediately turn their backs on it.

Grundtvig, now aged 72, had long held this possibility open, but now he counselled against a too-hasty decision in the hope that his own demand for Church freedom would soon be realised. Parliament had just agreed to his demand for 'breaking the parish-tie' and would soon, he hoped, allow pastors the freedom to preach the Gospel and administer the Sacraments according to their own faith and conscience.

There was another and deeper reason for the article, however; namely Søren Kierkegaard, "the late storm-rouser", who had died on 11th November. Grundtvig criticises Kierkegaard's 'storm' against 'official Christianity', which he had begun in December 1854 with "burning arrows" aimed at "all the pastors who without exception undertake to serve Christianity in the pay of the said temporal authority". Kierkegaard's ideal Christianity – which would not concede that there was any true Christian alive, let alone a pastor – was in Grundtvig's view totally *unchristian*, and committed the gravest of sins in making Christianity *inhuman*. This was tantamount to blasphemy, and perhaps even a forerunner for the Antichrist who would herald Judgement Day and who could be expected to appear as the Devil in a Christian disguise.

According to Grundtvig, Christianity on earth, like Christ himself, had been born in the form of a child. Over the years the child had grown in maturity and enlightenment, but it was still far from being perfect. Grundtvig's belief that the people and their history were its vehicle ran counter to Kierkegaard's claim that only the individual and the moment mattered. Kierkegaard had no time for the collective – for the 'people' or the 'congregation'; for as a mass or a multitude they represented only a *lack* of Spirit and Truth. Grundtvig therefore regarded Kierkegaard as a particularly dangerous man, since many of the Church's enemies would take up and exploit his attack on the Church and its clergy. The ignorance of the times, and those who only recognised scientific truths, would gladly accept Kierkegaard's exposure of the hypocrisy and lies under the surface of Christianity.

Grundtvig viewed Kierkegaard as more than just a gifted writer, for he expressed the ahistorical and anti-Christian spirit of the times and its battle against Christianity. Grundtvig now preferred to remain *within* the Danish People's Church in order to work for greater popular enlightenment from that position, but only on condition that the next step be taken to secure full freedom for the clergy; otherwise he really *would* leave the Church and would counsel others to do so. Written immediately after Kierkegaard's death, the article argues that this pastoral freedom should be so all-embracing that even Søren Kierkegaard could have been a pastor! Nowhere else does Grundtvig state his case for Church freedom so strongly, nor his belief that only *with* such freedom can the Christian faith win through.

***

It has become a matter of great importance for me to read the monthly periodical which has started publication under the name 'Our Promoters of the Organisation of Religious Relations in the kingdom' and to comment on it in *Church Times*.[312] Although I am growing tired of repeating what I have written so often before, I must not hesitate yet again in stating clearly my unreserved opinion about the imminent separation from the People's Church, which the periodical, or actually its publisher, seems pregnant with.

I need not repeat here what I have so often said: that I fully agree with Martin Luther and all those who on behalf of Christ and His Church request only one thing from the temporal authorities at the church door: namely, what Diogenes in his barrel requested of Alexander the Great: Would they mind moving a little out of the way so that our Lord's sun can shine on us?[313] Then the whole world can see the people who wish to live and die as Christians and can use the occasion to heap free abuse on them as much as it likes.

I also assume that this prayer to the temporal authority will not be taken as a nasty remark or a shield against the burning arrows that have recently been fired at 'official Christianity' and all the pastors who without exception undertake to serve Christianity in the pay of the said temporal authority. This is my earnest and sincere prayer – for the sake of my own Christian work, the Christian faith, and the Christian Church. It is accompanied by the open declaration that somehow or other the Christian

312. Founded in 1845, *Danish Church Times* is a monthly journal on church politics of Grundtvigian observation.
313. In this famous anecdote (according to legend and later to Plutarch), Alexander the Great visited the Greek philosopher Diogenes of Sinope at Corinth, stood over him, and asked him what he desired. Diogenes replied "Get out of my light."

faith, Christian preaching, and the entire worship of God must *very soon* be given its freedom, for that is the only element in which it can thrive, flourish, and bear mature fruit. If the temporal authority will not introduce a great degree of genuine freedom into the People's Church, then all genuine and enlightened Christians will feel forced to withdraw from it. I need to underline the words 'very soon' twice in this context, since I see that round and about people are beginning to say of me what they said of one of the ancient prophets: what he was speaking about would not come about 'for many days'. So they think that I mean so 'few days' that I myself will resign tomorrow if I have to give up the hope that the temporal authority, either in the few days left to me, or immediately after, will give the clergy in the People's Church the same freedom that they have now finally given churchgoers with the breaking of the parish-tie.[314]

However, what I must try to clarify and enjoin here is that enlightened Christians should not *leave* the People's Church while they still have the hope that within it they can very soon gain what is still missing as regards the freedom that is essential to the growth of Christian life. Nor do I find in the present circumstances the slightest reason to surrender that hope. So whether it is called tepidity, cowardice, or solicitude for my livelihood, I can and will not endorse or advise any effort to cause or prepare any immediate withdrawal.

Our Lord has arranged it thus that for over a generation I have demonstrably not lacked the courage to bear the scorn of those who mock old-fashioned Christianity, nor have I considered my 'living' to be any great sacrifice if it stood in the way of my pastoral work. Being used to the blows that the world gives and the fact that I do not have many days left to worry about my livelihood, I am hardly likely at my advanced age to be either more cowardly or greedy towards the world. I have the right to demand of all my fellow Danish Christians that they believe it is for quite different reasons that I oppose an immediate withdrawal from the People's Church as long as it is not only possible that during the confusion Christian life can be maintained and transmitted but it is also quite reasonable that at an opportune time Christian life can be given the essential freedom to move, develop, and purify itself!

To what extent I am right in believing that Christian life in our People's Church can and will acquire the not insignificant degree of freedom that it lacks is a quite different question, and one on which my fellow-Christians may well have another opinion. I will nevertheless ask them not to come to a hasty judgement, for it is not yet proven that they are either more zealous for the house of the Lord than I am, or that they have deeper insight into the Lord's domestic situation and a better understanding of the signs of the times. My way of thinking about these matters was already

---

314. The parish-tie as set down in the Danish Law of 1683 limited parishioners' worship to their parish church. Grundtvig fought long and hard to break this tie, and was finally successful through a Parliamentary Law in 1855.

formed many years ago and under far more desperate circumstances, when for seven years I was forced to hold free services without the Sacraments.[315] Even so, I gave up the idea of an immediate withdrawal for the sake of my underage and unenlightened fellow-Christians, and for the sake of the life of the Danish people and civil society. For Christian love demands that we remain within the People's Church for as long as we dare, meaning for as long as we believe we can defend them both for Christ and His Church. For their sake too we must wish to become much closer in the Spirit, much stronger in the Lord, and much wiser about the Christian life than we are at present. If we withdraw, we must fear that we are stepping backwards rather than forwards and are shaming our Lord rather than honouring Him!

If our withdrawal is to do honour to the Lord, we must be mature enough in every sense for Him to "live in us and walk in us",[316] so that He is unmistakably our God and we are unmistakably His people. We must be mature enough either already to be, like the Church of the Apostles in Jerusalem, "one heart and one soul" in the Lord, or be capable of becoming so with one giant step. From what I know of myself and my fellow-Christians, we have in no way reached that point, and in our present position our Lord will only help us do so if we seriously aspire to it, pray to Him for it, and wait upon Him and His hour. Admittedly the state of spiritual slavery into which we are born can please the Lord far less than it pleases us, but all the same it must be His acceptable will that we do not withdraw from it before we can use our freedom for His honour and our own true benefit. In this regard, all the withdrawals from the State Churches that have so far taken place are cautionary examples, for none of them has brought about anything that resembles the Church of the Apostles, whereas the separations – the less necessary and the more voluntary they have been – have borne worse fruit.

It is true that we who have found the words from the mouth of the Lord at Baptism to be the rock that defies the gates of Hell can withdraw, if necessary, and work towards the restoration of the Lord's tumbledown house with a different kind of certainty than all others. But by the same token we can also, far better than previous Christian generations, bear the yoke, bide our time, and even in very pressing circumstances build up another temple whose glory, despite its poor appearance, will be greater than that of the first temple. We must be thus enlightened, or one day become so, that we realise there are far greater hindrances to the full effect of the Lord's Holy Communion than all those that temporal authority has placed in our path. So here too we must begin the purification process from within, if the external purification is not to be a botched

---

315. Between 1832 and 1838, while Grundtvig was still under censorship, he was allowed to hold evening prayers at Christianskirke in Copenhagen. Here he could preach but he was not allowed to administer the Sacraments.

316. Gal 5:25. "Since we live by the Spirit, let us walk with the Spirit."

job. Despite all the temptations and dangers of withdrawal we must of course choose this path if there is no prospect of the People's Church acquiring the liberation that the development of life must require, this being that the pastors are released from their parish-tie. They will then be neither duty-bound to administer the Sacraments to their parishioners, nor will the parishioners any longer be duty-bound to receive them. And the so-called 'parish-pastors', with their voluntary churchgoers and their invited communicants, will then constitute larger or smaller congregations which in a Christian way can organise themselves as they wish, under the supervision of the State.

Since this is neither more nor less than a breaking of the parish-tie on both sides, the temporal authority should be easily persuaded, provided there are no vociferous objections from the more or less indifferent parishioners who will make up the majority almost everywhere, and especially through Parliament argue their old claims on the parish pastor. It is reasonable to assume that either this hindrance will lapse of its own accord, or the temporal authority will find it necessary not only to grant the parish pastors this freedom but grant them even more than many of them would wish for. This in my view would be the effect of the Church storm we have recently witnessed, one that will not die down together with the man who raised it.[317] This is because in all of his dreams independence was only an instrument for the spirit of the times that is sick and tired of the many dramas of the past. In particular it is sick and tired of the most tedious and protracted of all spiritless dramas: namely, the *Divina Comoedia* which since the Middle Ages has been played all the way through to our 'New Year Time'.[318] It has caused as much annoyance to the world as it has done almost irreparable damage to Christianity.

At the moment we might imagine that it was the unparalleled will-power, thinking ability, and writing art of the counteracted late storm-rouser,[319] who conjured up an artificial tempest over the State Church with its 'official Christianity' and its dearly-bought martyrs. The storm will die down of its own accord as soon as he is gone, they argue, and the world will return to the view of Church relations that was so clearly apparent throughout my struggles against the false, useless, and unchristian web

---

317. The man in question, Niels Møller Spandet (1788-1858), was a judge, a politician, and Deputy Speaker of the new democratic Parliament in 1849. In 1811 Spandet and Grundtvig had lived together in a student hostel in Copenhagen. Spandet worked tirelessly for freedom, especially in church and social matters. In 1850 he created a national storm when he presented Parliament with a bill advocating civil marriage and freedom from compulsory Baptism. Tens of thousands signed a protest that he was destroying Christianity and the Church, but he enjoyed Grundtvig's full support.

318. Grundtvig believed that human nature was developing in the course of history towards a complete clarity about itself – from the Age of the Imagination (classical times) through the Age of Feeling (medieval times) to the approaching Age of Reflection – the 'New Year Time' mentioned here.

319. The 'late storm-rouser' is Søren Kierkegaard, who had died on 11 November 1855, three weeks before this article was published.

of lies about all Christian people and states that raised a storm from below against Spandet's proposal. But we would be wrong to imagine this. We must not think that what has so far failed to penetrate has therefore had no effect, and in particular we must not overlook the enormous difference it makes to the world whether, while the name of 'Christian' is still a civil title of honour, we ask people for honesty's sake to limit its name only to those who have a valid claim to it and intend to live up to it, or we surprise the world with a brand-new discovery: namely that not only is the 'church drama' the most tedious and scandalous of all but that the name of 'Christian' in our day is so far from being a title of honour as to be a badge of shame! We had much better leave it to the thousand pastors who receive money for displaying it and who insinuate it into people not just by the thousands but by the millions. With the greatest pleasure the unbelieving world allows the little falsehood to pass in the claim that no one answers to the name of 'Christian' any more. It is as though this was a logical consequence of the admitted truth that the vast majority of pastors and laymen in state churches neither could nor would do so. In all its merciless and indefensible severity the world also finds the claim so probable that it must be taken as the plain and simple truth and therefore can be applied to life at least in order to avoid like the plague all churches that call themselves 'Christian' and to proclaim aloud what the world has always whispered to itself. For it says of all priests who pass themselves off as 'Christian' and who have the means to 'christen' both large and small that the more informed they are and the greater the appearance of Christianity that they can assume and propagate, the fouler they are as hypocrites!

Over time this new discovery, together with the old discovery of the Bible's incompatibility with the innately infallible natural sciences, will most likely lead everywhere to a serious persecution of Christians verbally and physically. It will take the form of a massive effort to erase the name of 'Christian' as the crudest lie on earth. Especially in good-natured Denmark this will take a long, long time, so I imagine that our temporal authority will as usual seek to calm the world down by purifying the People's Church of what seems most scandalous and intolerable about it to the present world. This is no longer what it once was: the old Hymnal or the old Altar Book. It is now the entire compulsory organisation which makes the so-called Christian pastoral care and public worship a shameful and scandalous *theatrical* production. Here there are a thousand actors playing chained freethinkers and paid martyrs, at one and the same time the absurdest and saddest figures imaginable. Once the Danish authorities realise that this scandal can be abolished by a much simpler and milder means than dismissing all the pastors in one fell swoop with or without their pensions and demolishing their corresponding churches, then if I am not very much mistaken they will employ, even eagerly, this means as their only expedient, however strange and intolerable it may sound in civil service style.

There are only two ways in which the authorities can disarm the irrefutable objections that the world, in this case the reading-world, holds against 'official Christianity'. They can either demolish the State Church that was the workplace of official Christianity (the new worlds call it its 'den of thieves') or it can give our State Church so free an organisation that it can no longer be called 'official'. This will come about when the law no longer cares whether we have few or many 'Confessional Books' or 'Authorised Altar Books', and when the State puts its pastors on oath only as regards their faith and conviction regarding 'New Testament Christianity'. Then even Søren Kierkegaard could become a pastor in 'the People's Church' without being committed to any other version, practice, or exercise of Christianity than what he found himself inwardly called and driven to, according to the free relation in which he had placed himself with regard to our Lord and the New Testament!

I know that many among us still think and say that, rather than completely let go of the reins and allow the pastors in the State Church to run as wild as they like, our temporal authority, the State, ought to abolish and demolish its State Church. I have even less wish to quarrel with anyone over this, least of all those who will find the freedom of their Christian Church even more unrestricted. But as I say, I doubt that the Danish government would ever prefer this solution, which would prove hardest in emotion and most hazardous in contemplation, and I can add that a truly wise, meaning worldly-wise, government could never do such a thing. For experience has taught us that the hold which the temporal authority must always wish to exert over the religious element among the people – an element which is absolutely essential but no less dangerous and frighteningly strong – is best seen in a People's Church where the religious element is kept alive and in a steady state through its freedom, while the temporal authority looks after its teachers' training, appointment, and remuneration, and supervises their conduct. Experience has also taught that, by way of contrast, none of this ensures that the temporal authority maintains a hold on the religious element when the relation between pastor and church is *fettered*, either to both sides or to one of them. For in that case the powerful religious element is either strangled or bursts out of prison, because what this element represents is precisely the freedom of the human spirit and the human heart!

I have also heard that a number of more or less Christian pastors have hinted that their consciences would never allow them to be pastors in a People's Church where they were at least legally obliged and placed on oath to be presenters and administrators of the Christian Sacraments according to what we Christians call 'the Lord's own institution'. The only response to this is that pastors would then be free to *leave* the

People's Church and establish Independent Congregations,[320] which naturally would have the civil right to join whatever contractual relation with their pastors they wished. Yet it is rather strange that the same pastors' consciences have allowed them to remain *within* a State Church where not only Baptism and Holy Communion are administered in very different ways, but where in Schleswig the pastors' relation to administering the Sacrament is as free as one can imagine.[321]

The peculiar misinterpretation of 'pastoral freedom' in the temporal organisation that is known as the State Church or the People's Church actually comes from the quite baseless assumption that such a temporal organisation could also be a *Christian* one – that it could be the third sacrament that had the other two in its safe-keeping, in other words, a form of gross papistry! So we might at least expect that pastors who willingly accept that a society bound by temporal beliefs and teachings is in no way the community and church of Jesus Christ, would not then claim that this temporal society can or should, rightly and usefully, impose on its civil servants the same duties that we believe Jesus Christ imposed on His civil servants in a totally different and entirely spiritual community. This futile confusion among Christian pastors is so much the more unreasonable in that it is as clear as sunlight that since all the pastors in the People's Church are allowed to present and administer the Sacraments according to their faith and conviction, Christian pastors in the People's Church should also be allowed to present and administer the Sacraments according to *their* faith and conviction. It is equally clear that when we demand of the temporal authority a law on the administration of the Sacraments in the People's Church, we are immediately allowing it by the same right to pass such a law according to its *own* faith and conviction, whether or not these confirm or contradict *our* faith and conviction! So if we are not to follow the papist idea that an ordained clergy constitutes an infallible Christian Church which in all Church matters heeds and uses only the temporal authority as its temporal arm, it all turns into the clearest contradiction in terms that one can deliberately become involved in!

---

320. In 1855 an Act of Parliament, for which Grundtvig was a prime mover, allowed parishioners to worship outside their parish church and thus 'to break the parish-tie'. In 1865 Pastor Vilhelm Birkedal of Ryslinge on Funen, an opposition member of Parliament, was dismissed from Parliament and his pastorate for inflammatory speech. In the crisis year of 1864 he had prayed publicly: "God grant the King a Danish heart, if that is possible!" But Birkedal refused to leave Parliament or the pulpit and with the support of his congregation he set up an alternative church, first in a barn and then in a custom-built church financed by friends. Under the Independent Congregations Act of 15 May 1868 Parliament recognised his Ryslinge church as an independent congregation under the People's Church (and the Bishop's supervision). Following this, a number of such congregations appeared across the land; at the time of the present publication there are 29 of these. They are not to be confused with the Free Churches, which are outside the People's Church altogether.

321. Administratively, Denmark consisted of the kingdom of Denmark and the three duchies of Schleswig, Holstein, and Lauenborg to the south. The 1849 Constitution was only valid within the kingdom and not in the duchies; the subsequent problems of this division later led to war and defeat by Germany in 1864.

The end of all this, like the beginning, is that I confess to the unswerving conviction that unless Christian pastors in the People's Church can very soon expect to be exempted from performing in the long-running church comedy and be released from their civil office, they must leave the People's Church with as many or as few who care to follow them. Outside the People's Church they must build as best they can on the unshakable rock that is God's Word of Truth in all its power. However, since they rightly expect that the People's Church will very soon grant them the indispensable freedom that comes with the complete breaking of the parish-tie, then rather than pulling out they should strongly advise against all such withdrawal on Christian grounds, since within the People's Church they will be able to build on the same unshakable rock with less danger, a more acceptable responsibility, and greater success, than outside it.

I not only confess, as before, this hope of a total breaking of the parish-tie but I also guarantee that after even a *partial* break of the tie and under the raging attack on our so-called 'official' Christianity, this conviction has become so firm and intense in me that I have no fear whatsoever that it can be put to shame.

For this hope to be fulfilled and for this newly-won freedom to be fruitful for Christian life, it is both desirable and necessary that all of us who appreciate the freedom of the Church should diligently seek to spread the word of its vital necessity and to awaken an appreciation of its great value. It will then be universally seen and felt that even though it is wrong to say that there can be no true Christianity or genuine witness to the truth in a state church, thank God, it is nevertheless very true that all state churches, including the papal church-state, under which faith and doctrine are temporally *bound and prescribed* are as inhuman as they are unchristian and as damaging as they are dishonest. So when they boast of their Christians by the million, all honest and reasonably enlightened people, not to mention all honest and informed Christians, both laugh and cry over them as being the most ridiculous buffoonery and the saddest disappointment under the sun!

12. My Relation to the People's Church (1856)

Introduction by Ole Vind

During a pastoral convention in 1856 Grundtvig's wide-ranging demand for Church freedom was criticised as being destructive of the Church. He responded with this article, published in *Danish Church Times* on 2nd March 1856. It explains his lifelong conflict-ridden relation to the Danish State Church, renamed 'the Danish People's Church' in the 1849 Constitution which introduced democracy to Denmark.

In his youth Grundtvig had attacked the Church for bending to the rationalism and the new historical-critical exegesis of the Bible,[322] against which he had defended his belief in 'old-fashioned' Lutheran Christianity. In open conflict with the Church authorities in Copenhagen, he turned for a number of years to philological and historical studies before he was called to the pastorate in Præstø in 1821 and then the curacy of the Church of Our Saviour in Copenhagen in 1822.

His conflict with the Church authorities culminated with *The Church's Retort* in 1825 (see Texts 1 and 4), which ended with him losing a libel case and being placed under censorship. In the same year, Grundtvig made his 'matchless discovery' that the foundation of Christianity is not the Bible (as it was for Luther) but the oral Confession of faith by the Church which dates back to its earliest days – even before the Bible was written. His renewed criticism of rationalism was now tinged with the optimistic colours of his more positive major works of the 1830s on the basis of freedom, enlightenment, and education for all. To this we can date his key demand for complete spiritual freedom for 'Church, State, and School' (i.e. University), which included an ongoing criticism of the Church's narrow-minded limits on the freedom of churchgoers and pastors alike.

Freedom of faith and worship was guaranteed in the 1849 Constitution, but despite Grundtvig's repeated attempts it was not until 1855 that his demand for 'breaking the parish-tie' passed into law, allowing worshippers the freedom to choose which church they attended. Pastoral freedom was still a long way off, however. Until that came about, Grundtvig maintained the right to leave the Church and establish his own faith community. The demand for pastoral freedom is reiterated here, this time

---

322. The historical-critical method had become a powerful biblical tool by Grundtvig's time. Its aim was to look behind the text to examine its time, its place, its context, and its sources to shed fresh light on its message – but it thereby also threatened to relativise alleged absolute truths.

citing "Søren Kierkegaard's whip", i.e. his attack on the Church in 1855. The powers-that-be should have learned that any *compulsion* in preaching or administering the Sacraments would strengthen Kierkegaard's criticism of the pastors as 'actors' who performed their enforced roles for payment only. Only total freedom would guarantee the honest pastor's validity.

In 1853 a commission was set up to discuss the governance of the Danish Church as envisaged in the 1849 Constitution. One possibility was to establish a synod, which Grundtvig strongly opposed, fearing that it would be dominated by the Church authorities. In 1856 he still had very little trust in them.

***

Readers of *Church Times*[323] have seen that the Copenhagen Clerical Conference,[324] of which I myself am a member, has accused me of working for the destruction of the Danish People's Church! The charge is both so undeserved and so droll that I am tempted to respond with only a smile and a gibe, for the Clerical Conference in our capital city can hardly be so ignorant of the state of affairs in the Danish Church at the beginning of this century or of my own work. Even if the clergy are unwilling to thank me for what I have contributed to the building of the Church in Denmark, it should at least not charge me with seeking to demolish it!

I confronted the charge personally at the Conference with a cool and calm presentation of my relation to the Danish State Church and the People's Church (*Folkekirken*) from 1806 to 1856, and I shall do the same here with my pen and then allow present and future readers to judge between us.

The fact is, I found the Danish State Church completely broken internally and, as everyone could see, dilapidated externally; yet neither the government nor the clergy seemed to be especially concerned. In the thinking of the day, the clergy, the bishops, and the entire official church were a mockery, a burden, and an expense; it was from the scholars and teachers that all education, happiness, and blessing were expected to flow. This was in sharp contrast to what the Bible and the Confessional Books[325] said, and, following Christian V's ritual,[326] what was sung and ministered in the Dan-

---

323. Founded in 1845, *Danish Church Times* is a monthly journal on church politics of Grundtvigian observation.
324. The Copenhagen Clerical Conference (the association of pastors in the diocese of Copenhagen) was founded in 1843.
325. For the Confessional Books of the Evangelical Lutheran Church in Denmark, see note 62.
326. 'Christian V's Ritual' (388 pages) was introduced in 1685 in an attempt to make church practice uniform throughout the kingdom of Denmark and Norway. The Bishop of Funen and hymn-writer, Thomas Kingo (1634-1703), was instrumental in promoting music and hymn-singing in the ritual, which, despite the conflicts over liturgy in the 19th century, remained in force until 1912.

ish State Church. In 1806 the so-called Danish Chancellery,[327] which had almost un-limited powers over the State Church, divided up the country into county deaneries with the intention not only of taking education out of the power of the Church but also of placing the Church under the guardianship of the educational authorities. It was only Frederik VI's personal respect for Bishop Balle[328] that prevented all the bishoprics from being immediately abolished. The same Chancellery in the same year published and recommended a brand-new liturgy which made it quite clear that public worship was generally regarded as a church-drama to be directed according to the taste of the moment and in particular the distaste for all old-fashioned Christianity.

At this point, former Bishop Mynster[329] and I were the only members of the younger generation who defended the old-fashioned Christian and Lutheran form of worship. It became clear from public negotiations on the matter that the clergy in the Danish State Church preached, confirmed, and administered the Sacraments in all sorts of ways, each according to his own head and ideas. One of our renowned professors also took the opportunity to declare publicly that whatever might now be introduced, he would nevertheless continue as before to confirm in the name of "God, Providence, and Immortality".

In my dimissory sermon[330] I declared myself for *old-fashioned* Christianity and com-plained that "the word of the Lord had disappeared from His house". It turned out (only two years after Bishop Balle had retired) that although old-fashioned Christianity still had the letter of the law completely behind it, in the view of the Copenhagen clergy it could not be tolerated in the Danish State Church. It was therefore only through the intervention of Bishop Balle that I was permitted to stand on its threshold as a personal chaplain even though for a long time the highly-esteemed clergy of our capital city could not bear my dimissory sermon – not even in prison![331]

Meanwhile, although the old Church Laws were being openly trampled into the ground, everyone who was born within the preserves of the Danish State Church remained bound by their parish-tie,[332] and could not break it without being exiled or imprisoned. With my old-fashioned Christianity it was immediately clear that I was

---

327. The Royal Danish Chancellery was the central governing organ in Denmark from the 12th century until 1848.

328. Bishop of Zealand, Nicolai Balle (1744-1816).

329. Bishop of Zealand, Jacob Mynster (1775-1854).

330. To qualify for holy orders pastors-in-waiting had to give a dimissory (probational) sermon, after which the Bishop could 'dismiss' them as being fully qualified. Grundtvig entitled his dimissory sermon: 'Why has the Word of the Lord Disappeared from His House?' Although he passed the exam with honours he caused a controversy with the sermon's provocative content.

331. The reference is Grundtvig's repeated but vain applications for a pastorate in 1819. He had applied to, among others, the Citadel Church (*Kastelskirken*) in Copenhagen, a church for soldiers manning the citadel, which had acquired a prison extension in 1754, whereby inmates could listen to the church services through sound channels.

332. The parish-tie as set down in the Danish Law of 1683 limited parishioners' worship to their parish church. Grundtvig fought long and hard to break this tie, and was finally successful through a Parliamentary Law in 1855.

in a very dubious position, so no one will be surprised when I say that it was only due to a coincidence of events that I did not break away, as Norway did from Denmark, to a position as perpetual curate in Akershus.[333] What was only discovered a little later, and what did not seem to shake me at the time was the desperate plight to which the Lutheran and Christian element had been consigned, especially among the common people. With regard to Baptism, confirmation, and Holy Communion they were chained to their parish pastor, however self-willed and unchristian the way in which he administered the Sacraments, and however heathen the manner in which he taught and confirmed his candidates.

My lack of concern for these children who believed in the Lord and the powerful idea that anyway there was a 'God's Hour' in the offing that should be patiently awaited were the only factors that explain my silence year after year, during which I was busy with other matters. In 1822, through the special favour of Frederik VI,[334] I eventually became perpetual curate at the Church of Our Saviour in Copenhagen. But even then I was clearly thinking more about the treatment of Christianity at the university and among the reading public than the poor Christian parents and children in all the parishes where they today had, or tomorrow would have, a parish pastor who far from preaching the gospel of Christ or administering the Sacraments according to His Words of Institution sought to sweep aside all speech and song to this end as superstition and papist leaven.

It was during the battle with the Faculty of Theology in the person of Professor Clausen[335] that I had to give up all hope that old-fashioned Christianity would be either a little or even quite dominant in the Danish State Church, and I immediately resigned my office.[336] Only at this point did I realise that the Christian goal meant neither a little nor a lot of *civil* supremacy but only the freedom to preach, confess, and follow the gospel of Christ. I was more than willing to leave to my opponents the entire State Church and all its 'livings' as well as the so-called 'great custodians' on which Christianity had spun no silk, provided I and my like-minded were allowed to turn our backs on the State Church and take care of our own salvation. When this too

333. Denmark-Norway was one kingdom until 1814. Early in 1814 Grundtvig applied for a pastorate at Akershus, Oslo, but was not called.

334. Frederik VI (1768-1839).

335. Following a vitriolic attack on Professor Henrik Clausen's rationalist theology, Grundtvig was found guilty of libel in 1826 and sentenced to life censorship, meaning that he could publish nothing without the consent of the authorities. After 11 years the ban was lifted by the King on 24 December 1837.

336. Grundtvig resigned his position at the Church of Our Saviour, Copenhagen in May 1826, a week before Pentecost and the celebration of 1,000 years of Christianity in Denmark. He had written some new hymns for the occasion, including 'We welcome with joy this blessed day' (no. 53 in *Living Wellsprings* (2015), but he was refused permission to sing them. Perhaps this is just as well, for by his own admission he was 'very unmusical' (ibid. p. 28), while Vilhelm Andersen wrote of him: "Grundtvig did not hum his hymns to a lute like Brorson, but hummed them according to their rhythm" (quoted in GS 1952 p. 14).

was denied us, I am sure that at least posterity will admit that as a pastor and scholar in the Christian faith and enlightenment I had only two paths of action to choose between. I could rebel against the State Church, establish in defiance what would be called a 'sect', and administer the Sacraments without regard to church buildings and parish boundaries – like the reformers in the 16th century. Alternatively, I could attempt something that had never happened in Denmark before and set free the Christian element from the centre of the State Church. It is quite possible that posterity would say that since I was coming up for fifty years of age and had *been* a pastor in the State Church, I ought immediately to have chosen the first solution as the only possibility; it must have been my lack of courage and energy that prevented me from doing so.

I have no wish to quarrel with anyone about this, but the fact is that I did *not* do so, preferring the peaceful, and, as at it turned out, unproductive path for all of seven years (1832-39). I settled for what was a very poor kind of freedom: to preach as I wished at Evensong in Frederik's Church in Christianshavn,[337] provided that I did not confirm or administer the Sacraments, and to stick to the so-called *Evangelical-Christian Hymn-book*.[338] By 1839 I could no longer postpone my own sons' confirmation,[339] nor refuse to confirm my friends' children and give them the bread and wine. In vain had I begged the King and the Bishop for the little more freedom that I badly needed, and even then I followed the King's hint and returned to the service of the State Church.[340] For 17 years now I have settled for the modest freedom that the pastorate at Vartov offers, and I must appear to have closed my eyes to the yoke under which all other Christian pastors in the country have doubtless sighed to a greater or lesser degree. I have put up with all this simply because I hoped that eventually the temporal authority would agree to convert the dominant State Church into a *People's* Church. I had proposed this in 1834 in my study on the Danish State Church,[341] and my closest Christian friends both inside and outside the Provincial Assemblies[342] endeavoured to prove its necessity and benefit, but no significant step was taken before the breaking of the parish-tie last year. I therefore need to draw on all my knowledge of history in order to defend myself against the claim that as soon as the Democratic Constitution of 1849 allowed us religious freedom, I would employ it to break away from the so-called State Church, which does not really mean anything other than the Faculty of Theology and the officially appointed clergy.

337. Christianshavn is an area in central Copenhagen.
338. *Evangelical-Christian Hymnbook for Use in Church and Home* was published by Ove Høegh-Guldberg in 1798. Grundtvig disliked the Enlightenment ideas he believed it contained.
339. Johan (b. 1822) and Svend (b. 1824).
340. In 1839 Grundtvig became pastor of Vartov Hospital Church, a post he retained until his death in 1872.
341. *An Impartial View of the Danish State Church*, see ch. 5 above.
342. In 1831 the government of Frederik VI introduced Provincial Advisory Assemblies in Holstein, Schleswig, Jutland, and the islands (Zealand, Funen etc.) to discuss a new form of government. As a result the first democratic constitution was approved by law in 1849.

Following the breaking of the parish-tie I am even more minded to wait for the *clerical* freedom which we still lack, so I am not at all surprised that my opponents call it an empty threat when I continue to speak of my resignation as something that will take place the moment I surrender the hope of an adequate freedom within the People's Church, nor that they comfort themselves with the thought that the withdrawal which I would spearhead would in any case hardly be on a large scale. However, I must note that they may very easily be wrong in both of these assumptions!

When I speak of a possible 'resignation', it is in no sense as a threat to the dominant church order or disorder in Denmark, but can at most be called a threat to those among my clerical friends who will not make common cause with me in my demand for the freedom of the clergy. Of course it is true that I would just as little take 'two or three' with me as I would open my mouth to call on numerous people of all kinds to follow me. But regarded from the other side, my withdrawal would be on quite a large scale because I would place the structure of our Church on a firmer and broader foundation than the master builders of the last fifteen centuries have dared to avail themselves of, and this might also have quite wide-ranging consequences outside Denmark. Nor are my friends in any doubt that I will carry out my intention to resign if I should see the day of implementation of Ørsted's Church Commission,[343] which would establish a 'church council'[344] that in all church matters should inherit the influence of Parliament on legislation. For whether it consisted solely of bishops or comprised an equal number of clerical and temporal members, scholar and lay, I could be sure that such a council would never give its permission for the freedom of the clergy. Whether it enjoined the old Church Laws or introduced brand-new ones, or sought a mixture of the two, I would have to advise all old-fashioned Christians and their pastors sooner or later to set themselves free.

Whether it be for the sake of my own calmness and livelihood or, as I believe, for the sake of the Christian Church, the Danish people, and my younger clerical friends that I wish such a withdrawal to happen as late as possible, I would nevertheless like to convince both the Copenhagen Convention and the Roskilde Convention, and in particular Professor Clausen, that the 'freedom' I propose would best serve not only the

---

343. Anders Ørsted (1778-1860) was Denmark's third Prime Minister after the introduction of the democratic constitution in 1849. During his brief period of government (Apr. 1853-Dec. 1854) he established a Church Commission to look into the question of whether the Church should be governed by itself as a Synod, or by Parliament as the Constitution laid down. Agreement could not be reached either in 1853 or at the second commission in 1868. Thus legislation for the politics of the Church remains in the hands of Parliament, with the Church (which has no synod) being an advisory body. In 2012 it was Parliament that passed a law allowing gay couples to marry in Church and it was thereafter the role of the 10 bishops to draw up the appropriate liturgical ceremony.

344. Grundtvig opposed the concept of a church synod. As recently as 2014 the Danish Lutheran Church as a body *continued* to do so. Consequently, no one speaks 'on behalf of' the church in Denmark, and the church as such has no opinion about anything. Affairs of the Church are governed by Parliament (on the advice of church leaders).

government and the people but also every able bishop, pastor, and theological professor. All that would remain would be the poor wretches of all schools and confessions who would find the hunt for a 'living' in the precincts of the Church basically destroyed.

I am well aware that among my clerical friends there are those who say that when I include all those who are best served by the freedom of the clergy in its broadest sense, I am forgetting Christianity and the 'Holy Catholic Church'.[345] But as surely as our Lord Jesus Christ is Truth itself, so surely does He refuse to be preached or confessed for money or temporal laws. He, His Spirit, and His Church must be left out of the equation when the question of the freedom of the clergy in a People's Church is under discussion. It is also as clear as sunlight that just as no pastor in the People's Church can be bought or forced to be the Holy Spirit's instrument in the conduct of his office, nor can any Christian seeking out a Christian pastor be fobbed off with someone who for the sake of the law and his livelihood *mimics* a Christian pastor. So there is a strange confusion when one assumes that a Christian pastor must invariably administer the Sacraments yet concludes from this that all pastors in a State Church or a People's Church, be they Christian or not, must abide by the law at the risk of their livelihood, and therefore be forced literally to follow a specific, designated Altar Book, even though we all know that those who allow themselves to be threatened and forced to do so are simply playing fast and loose with the Lord's institutions and are shaming themselves in the sight of God and man.

So here we stand with the 'religious drama', which might lead one to think that, if nothing else, Søren Kierkegaard's whip had driven all the pastors away from the Danish People's Church. It had thus become their unanimous, solemn request to the authorities that they be so disestablished as to be able in all fairness to demand of their adherents the following: that they must not regard their pastors as *actors* or *bribed witnesses* to the truth but as honest, serious men who speak according to their convictions and offer the best illumination which they can on the course of life and the question of salvation. If, in our People's Church, laws about doctrine or liturgy are to be made and obeyed, then whatever we may imagine, they will still be a yoke for our pastors to which they must submit if they are to keep their livelihoods; and we are still making their witness as dubious and unfruitful as possible.

As Bishop Mynster has admitted, doctrine in the State Church must be free, but liturgy compulsory. It cannot upset a pastor to read aloud from the Altar Book what everyone knows is a guide for which he has no responsibility; this would only be right if Baptism and Holy Communion were regarded by all concerned as mere church customs which, like heathen and Jewish ceremonies only have a figurative meaning and are therefore merely stages in a 'religious drama' where the pastors play their roles well or

345. Always in this Article of Faith the word 'Catholic' means 'universal'.

badly but always innocently provided the law is obeyed. On the other hand if Baptism and Holy Communion are only 'Christian' in the Word that is *spoken*, whether or not it is written, and if this Word is both a witness to the faith of the Church and a power from God in the question of salvation, then it is easy to see that the pastor who takes these words into his mouth and spits them out again with his teachings is in obvious contradiction of himself and must be scorned in the eyes of both himself and his serious listeners. No one wants such a pastoral living to be created by our Church Laws.

'Perhaps not', some of my clergy friends will say, but since we have freedom of religion we can in all fairness demand that no one applies for a pastoral living in our Evangelical-Christian Church unless he can and will administer the Sacraments according to the Lord's institution without denying himself!

I have already given the right answer to this question: namely, that even we who speak the Word of God's mercy from the pulpit and at the Sacraments because we believe it, become *dubious witnesses* if we have committed to speaking it and receiving our livelihood only on that condition. So we must never demand a civil commitment from others that is intolerable for ourselves. Imagine, however, that this was not the case. Imagine that everything was in order, provided no one applied for a pastorate except those who at least without self-contradiction, were willing to follow the Church prescripts as to what should be confessed and testified at the Sacraments in the name of the Lord and His Church. Is it then likely that all those who cannot honestly take the words of our Altar Book into their mouths would resign and leave their pastorates and their livelihoods in the People's Church? Is it not much more likely, according to all experience, that even if the best, most honest, and most serious of our opponents would do this, the worst, the rash, the indifferent, and the false would definitely not? The consequence would be that we had the worst rather than the best opponents as our fellow-servants in the People's Church.

I believe that this consideration concerning the pastoral office and livelihood in the People's Church – which will always be most attractive for the incompetent, the lazy, and the indifferent – must lead to the conviction among the serious, the honest, and the competent men of all schools and parties concerned, that either we must abolish the People's Church or we must make the pastoral office within it so free that it may be attractive for the most serious, the most capable, and the most determined men and speakers of all confessions. They will then keep each other awake, have a productive influence on the people, and fulfil the demands of all, so that few if any will be tempted to resign; they will thus take up a less oppositional attitude to the People's Church and to the power that supports it. I am well aware that it is difficult for both governments and parties to reach this apparent self-denial, and it goes without saying that just as a number of my friends take comfort in the hope that the old Church

Laws which they like will be put into effect, so do a number of Professor Clausen's[346] friends comfort themselves with the thought that once we have a legislating 'church council' in which the theologians are allowed to dominate, they will have Church Laws drawn up that serve their own purposes and make the opposite party withdraw or see how it can give in to them. Nonetheless, I do not give up the hope that what has not happened anywhere else can succeed in our extremely peaceful Denmark, where for over half a century now we have seen that an almost unlimited freedom for our pastors will, after the breaking of the parish-tie, be much more tolerable and serve to arouse and maintain our religious life. When this freedom, which has so far been both ungoverned by law and partly illegal, becomes lawful and cheerfully applied by our best men, do we not believe that it would be far less damaging and far more beneficial in every respect than has so far been the case?

---

346. For Professor Clausen see pp. 57-58.

II

BASIC CHRISTIAN TEACHINGS

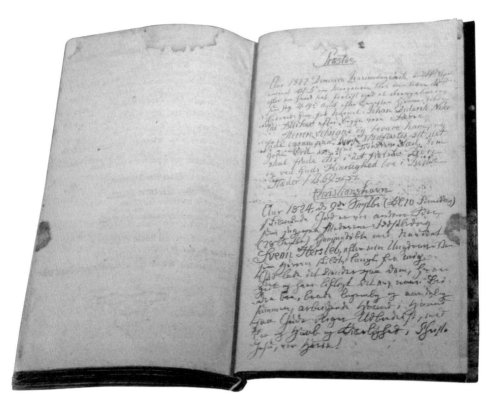

6. Grundtvig's bible

In his preserved bible in the Grundtvig Memorial Museum at Udby Grundtvig has written that it is a present from Constance Leth, dated 17th April 1807. At the time (1805-08) Grundtvig was staying in the manor home of Carl and Constance Leth, tutoring their son and infatuated with Constance. The translation is known as *Christian VII's Bible* from 1787. On the inner end-paper Grundtvig has noted certain important events in his life: births, confirmations, and deaths. He notes under 'Præstoe', the town where he was pastor at the time: "In the year 1822... on 14th April around 5 am, my dear wife was delivered of a boy child..." Under 'Christianshavn' he writes: "In the year 1824 on 9th Sept. (10 am) God granted us a second son." And then: "1851 Jan. 14 my beloved wife *Elisabeth Christine Margrethe Blicher* passed away, my faithful spouse for a whole lifetime ..."

Introduction by Hans Raun Iversen

Like his contemporary Søren Kierkegaard, Grundtvig was quick to send his writings to print. Thus the chapters in *Basic Christian Teachings* were published continuously by Christian Kragballe[347] as they were received (1855-61) and were not collected in book form until 1868. The book contains 21 chapters in all, the first 15 of which are translated below.

They were written as a counterpart to Martin Luther's *Small Catechism*; their Danish title, *Den Christelige Børnelærdom*, translates literally as 'Christian *childhood* teachings'. However, they are far from being directed at children. It is perhaps best to regard *Basic Christian Teachings* as Grundtvig's version of Luther's *Large Catechism*. If Grundtvig has a 'Little Catechism' it is to be found in his much-loved hymns, which form a vital part of the Danish musical canon. Just as *Nordic Mythology* (1832) was the teachers' book of the Danish People's High School, so was *Basic Christian Teachings* the teachers' book for the Danish People's Church.

Basic Christian Teachings is arranged so that chapters 1-8 (Texts 13-20) contain an account of Grundtvig's view of the Church in the form of a detailed exposition of the Apostolic Creed, the Lord's Prayer, and the two sacraments of Baptism and Holy Communion. Programmatically, ch. 2 (Text 14) treats the fundamental covenant between God and humanity, which is established through Baptism, where the Apostolic Creed is confessed for the first time by a believer (or in the case of infant Baptism on behalf of the baby). It is notable that ch. 3 (Text 15) immediately afterwards deals with the Renunciation of the Devil, for this reflects Grundtvig's dualistic view of life and his belief in the 'principle of contradiction' that God's offer cannot be accepted until the Devil has been rejected. At the same time *Basic Christian Teachings* is characteristic of its times in its occasional polemical partiality; for instance, in ch. 7 (Text 19) Grundtvig takes a swipe at Søren Kierkegaard's so-called 'Christianity of the New Testament',[348] which the latter claims is missing from the Danish Church, while in ch. 8 (Text 20), the same is true of Grundtvig's position on the Roman Catholic doctrine of *seven* sacraments. Chs 9-15 (Texts 21-27) contain thematic treatments of the link between the old, created, human life and the new, reborn life of Baptism – and thus between the human and the Christian life, which is the fulcrum of Grundtvig's theology.

---

347. Christian Kragballe (1824-97), theologian, teacher, pastor, and poet, published the periodical *Church Collector* (*Kirkelige Samler*) from 1855-62. This regularly included new hymns by Grundtvig, as well as the articles that eventually made up *Basic Christian Teachings*. Kragballe also translated books into Danish, e.g. John Bunyan's *The Pilgrim's Progress*, and published many of Grundtvig's hymns in Swedish translations.

348. See note 419.

The remaining 6 chapters of *Basic Christian Teachings*, omitted here, add to the theological substance of chs 1-15 but lie outside normal catechism material. Thus chs 16-18 contain practical theological instruction and topical church politics; chs 19-20 recapitulate Grundtvig's view of history; and ch. 21 seeks to glean the meaning of "The Eternal Word of Life from Our Lord to His Church". This is the key to Grundtvig's view of Christianity and is widely explored elsewhere in this volume.

This introduction cannot examine all the challenges presented in the work but must concentrate on mediating a deeper understanding of the structure behind *Basic Christian Teachings* and thus the main theological substance of its first 15 chapters.

The first thing we note is that Grundtvig omits The Ten Commandments, which Luther expounds in the first part of *his* Catechism. For Grundtvig they represent the general pre-Christian people of the Old Testament, and as such they are of vital significance for his view of history and humanity. But the crucial point in the new *Christian* covenant is what the living God is saying to us *here and now* as the cornerstone of its foundation. This does not happen in the Bible, though it is an excellent book of historical enlightenment; rather, it happens in the Church's *worship*. Grundtvig first proclaimed this in *The Church's Retort* in 1825; later it became one of his briefest but pithiest formulations in his view of the Church and Christianity:

> Only at the font and table
> do we hear God's Word to us. (1863)

This does not mean that the sermon from the pulpit beside the baptismal font and the altar table is *actually* God's Word, as dialectical theology has been preaching for 100 years. The theology of preaching in the 20th century has not offered lay people the possibility of understanding in any other way Grundtvig's use of the Danish word *ord* as meaning both the 'Word' in the singular and 'words' in the plural. This is central to most of his hymns but goes over the heads of most people. Almost every time Grundtvig uses *ord* after 1825 he is not referring solely to verbal expression or to the Word in Jn 1, but to the specific words from Jesus' own mouth, the Lord's Prayer, the Words of Institution at Holy Communion, and to the Apostolic Creed, whose content was present long before it was formulated into a formal Confession of faith. This is a radical departure from Lutheran orthodoxy, and a return to the roots of the living Word/words which, through the Holy Spirit, have founded the Church:

> God's Church is built of living stones,
> here in the North they are sited;
> stones which empowered by God's Word
> faith and the font have united.

[234]

Church is by Spirit best sustained,
neither by king nor priest constrained:,
only His Word makes Church holy. (1836)[349]

How can Christ possibly be present in the gathering which His presence transforms into a Christian congregation? He is so in that He speaks here and now *to* that congregation. His words sound, *ergo* He is present! If we close our eyes, can we hear who is speaking? If we can *hear* the speaker, we can have no doubt that He is present. In Grundtvig's day there was no way of recording the Word, so the witness of experience was enough to convince him. Since it is Jesus' own words that sound, He is present. Neither king nor priest is required, if only His very own words sound. If we can hear those words, then He is present, says Grundtvig, for, as he famously states of the kingdom of our Lord on earth: "Its riddle is a Word of God/creating just by naming" (1853).[350] The gathering becomes Christ's Congregation solely because He is present and borrows its voice to speak His words.

Together with the focus of Lutheran theology on the Living Word, the theology of the Early Church also contributed to Grundtvig's discovery of the power of the *spoken* word. All that he discovered he had in fact already read in Irenaeus, who speaks about "a rule of faith" for true Christianity. When Grundtvig spent the long late hours 'talking' to Irenaeus about true Christianity and Christianity's truth, he could hear the Lord's own words, for Irenaeus had known Polycarp, who had known John, the beloved disciple, who had spoken intimately with the Lord Himself.

"Only in the Spirit is God with us and only through the Spirit does God work in us, from the Day of Ascension to the Day of Judgement," writes Grundtvig at the end of 'On our Third Article of Faith' (Text 17).[351] Spirit is life-force: it can only work in freedom, it can best express itself in speech, and it prefers to link itself to fixed forms. Just as we are only truly 'present' when we are *spiritually* present, so can God only be present today in the *force* of the Spirit. It blows where it will,[352] but first and last it blows out from God's mouth, just as it breathes out through our throats. Here – in the throat and the mouth – breath and spirit take the form of words which continue to have the creative power that is peculiar to the Holy Spirit. Similarly, the *human* spirit, which remained with us as God's imprint when He blew His Spirit into our nostrils, gives our small words a creative effect when, for instance, the speaker can make an audience of one mind – as we hear in the song, 'What a great wonder is human life':

---

349. See no. 329 in *The Danish Hymnbook* (Det Kgl. Vajsenhus 2003). Editor's translation.
350. See no. 39 in *Living Wellsprings* (2015).
351. See p. 271ff.
352. Jn 3:8.

Thousandfold bodies and souls in one
the great human spirit can gather,
pierce them with words as with lightning-shafts,
and all in a single thought tether.[353]

Here is the anthropological-theological constant which has kept oral speech alive in the Church. Our innate, spirit-born ability to use small words to express God's great ones has helped them to be passed from mouth to mouth and church to church since Apostolic times. As Grundtvig writes in the first chapter of *Basic Christian Teachings*, his sole purpose is to enlighten us concerning the faith that is communicated through Baptism as it has enlivened each new generation. Everything comes into focus here:

> The audible testimony of the Church of Christ at Baptism – on the nature of Baptism, its conditions and its fruits – must be accepted and trusted as His Apostles' and His own testimony. It has been transmitted from mouth to mouth and from generation to generation as the Word from His own mouth which must never leave the mouth of His Church and from which His Spirit shall never depart …[354]

Those who are created by God's Word through God's Spirit bear them onward from one generation to the next through Baptism and Holy Communion – ever since the days of the Apostles. In Grundtvig's understanding the two Sacraments are always celebrated with the same core liturgy in the Apostolic Creed, the Lord's Prayer, and the Words of Institution, whose power derives from their being God's words in Spirit and Jesus' words on earth. Both the Bible and Church history testify to this.

Thus the free and sovereign God's Word is present in the Church and is audible from His Son's own mouth. It speaks a promise and seeks a response, as Grundtvig writes in a poem entitled 'The Eternal Word of Life' from 1855-56:

If you trust what you have heard,
add your Yes, and Amen too,
then with water and the Word
my right hand baptises you;
you are thereby born anew,
so will matchless joy ensue.[355]

---

353. See no. 85 in *Living Wellsprings* (2015).
354. See p. 242.
355. Editor's translation.

In the chapter on 'The Divine Trinity' (Text 27) towards the end of *Basic Christian Teachings* Grundtvig writes:

> Thus, although with the Christian enlightenment that we have gained we must have been cured of the delusion that we can clarify and describe what we have neither experienced nor can experience in this life, we can nevertheless *glimpse* what a Christian doctrinal structure would look like as a design for the new Jerusalem.[356]

Although any doctrinal *structure* from Grundtvig appears to be a contradiction in terms, and although he himself never drew up such a structure, it is possible to produce such a chart without losing sight of his insistence that Christianity was *life* and not *dogma*.

Grundtvig's Christian structure

Oral Word of Life	The Apostolic Creed	The Lord's Prayer	The Words of Institution
Life Expressions	Faith	Hope	Love
Life Signs/Church Characteristics	Confession of Faith	Preaching the Word	Song of Praise
The Trinity	The Holy Spirit	The Son	The Father
The Kingdom of God	Justice	Peace	Joy
Eschatology	The Forgiveness of Sin	The Resurrection of the Body	Everlasting Life
Man	Spirit	Soul	Body
Outward Man	Hand	Mouth	Heart
Inward Man	Life-force	Truth	Love

The Oral Words of Life from the Lord's own Mouth create the Life Expressions of Faith, Hope, and Love, which are immediately transmitted through the Life Signs: the Confession of Faith, the Preaching of the Word, and Songs of Praise, which again mediate the Oral Words of Life. The Church sustains 'God's Word to us' through listening, through being inspired, and through transmitting that Oral Word. The chart corresponds to the three persons in the Trinity – and with the dimensions in

---

356. See p. 370.

the Kingdom of God, in Eschatology, and in Man. If God is Three in One, all that is created in His image is naturally also threefold.

Can we take over Grundtvig's 'matchless discovery' of the Oral Words of Life at Baptism and Holy Communion and yet settle merely for referring to them? Can we even in general approve of Theology as being founded on the Oral Words of Life? My answer is that we can indeed maintain Grundtvig's prime goal in his view of the Church and his theology of the Oral Words of Life. Otherwise we would be forced to discard at least half of his hymns from *The Danish Hymnbook*, for that is their subject! Grundtvig's theory that Jesus Himself dictated the Creed in the 40 days between the Resurrection and the Ascension has been set aside as unhistorical. Nevertheless, like the Lord's Prayer and the Words of Institution, the beliefs that constituted the later Creed were undoubtedly held in a continuous line dating back to Jesus' own words and deeds. We must dismiss the fundamentalism that colours Grundtvig's exposition of the Creed, when he cherishes the 'original' texts and their literal use in worship, but otherwise there is good reason to celebrate the Word in Church in the belief in God's presence which is closely linked to the words spoken by Jesus Himself and taken into the mouths of the congregation. With an echo of Acts 17:28 and Rom 10:6-10, Grundtvig encapsulates the theology that is central to the Church's view of itself, where Christ Himself is the living Word:

> We are, with thanksgiving,
> both touched and are living
> in Christ, in the Word that God gives.
> When that Word is spoken
> and love is its token,
> then truly that name in You lives.[357]

---

357. See no. 397 in *The Danish Hymnbook* (Det Kgl. Vajsenhus 2003). Editor's translation.

13. Basic Christian Teachings

Preface

This material on the relation between basic Christian teachings and the Christian life was first printed in Kragballe's *Church Collector*. It is collected and published here at the request of friends whom I trust will welcome it, whereas it will naturally offend those who think that the Christian life in no way depends on basic Christian teachings but on the teaching profession, the rigidity of parish boundaries, and the entire contrivance of the People's Church (*Folkekirken*).[358]

Without wishing to enter into the great dispute about Independent Congregations, I cannot help expressing my utmost astonishment that such a conflict could be waged in Denmark, where for centuries we have been considering free Independent Congregations.[359] They were to have neither Ordination, Altar Book,[360] Hymnbook, or Catechism in common with the Danish People's Church, and yet they could exist under its supervision and enjoy the same civic rights without the slightest danger or damage.

It is well-known that this too has been the arrangement not only with the German-Lutheran churches in the capital[361] where the parish-tie was broken, but also throughout Schleswig until 1864.[362] So when 6 of our bishops and hundreds of pastors claim that Independent Congregations outside the parish-tie, despite having Ordination, the Altar Book, the Hymnbook, and the Catechism in common with the Danish People's Church are undermining and dividing it, it is hard to know where their memory or their intelligence has gone to. Since our present Minister of the Church has been a

---

358. The word '*Folkekirken*' was first used in 1841 by Peter Kierkegaard, Søren Kierkegaard's elder brother. It was incorporated into the democratic constitution of 1849.

359. In 1855 an Act of Parliament, for which Grundtvig was a prime mover, allowed parishioners to worship outside their parish church and thus 'to break the parish-tie'. In 1865 Pastor Vilhelm Birkedal of Ryslinge on Funen, an opposition member of Parliament, was dismissed from Parliament and his pastorate for inflammatory speech. In the crisis year of 1864 he had prayed publicly: "God grant the King a Danish heart, if that is possible!" But Birkedal refused to leave Parliament or the pulpit and with the support of his congregation he set up an alternative church, first in a barn and then in a custom-built church financed by friends. By the Independent Congregations Act of 15 May 1868 Parliament recognised his Ryslinge church as an independent congregation under the People's Church (and the Bishop's supervision). Following this, a number of such congregations appeared across the country; at the time of publication there were 29 of these. They are not to be confused with the Free Churches, which are outside the People's Church altogether.

360. i.e. Liturgy.

361. i.e. Copenhagen.

362. In the disastrous war of 1864 Denmark lost the duchies of both Schleswig and Holstein to Germany under Bismarck.

pastor in Schleswig,[363] the question presumably only has to be raised for it to find a satisfactory answer.

September 1868

Nik. Fred. Sev. Grundtvig.

***

Together with Martin Luther we have parted company with the Pope in Rome and abolished all that we regarded as papistry, so when we hear the words 'basic Christian teaching', we envisage one of two things: either the lessons which the pastors whom we consider 'Christian' teach our children – and what we demand of them at the public examination that takes place in our churches before the children are admitted to Holy Communion – either that, or the teachings that constitute the five sections of Martin Luther's children's book, which we call his *Small Catechism*.[364]

In the first case our idea of 'basic Christian teaching' is diffuse and imprecise, and in the last case we take it as a foregone conclusion that 'Lutheran' means in every sense the same as 'Christian' and that one is brought up as a Christian by reading a book and learning it by heart. But neither of these suppositions holds true, for it goes without saying that 'basic Christian teaching' must embrace all the foundational Christian doctrine that our Lord Jesus Christ and His Apostles, who had His unlimited authority, have laid as the foundation of the Church. As the Apostle Paul writes: "For no one can lay any foundation other than the one already laid, which is Jesus Christ."[365] So we

---

363. From March 1868 to September 1869 the Minister of Culture (under which the Church belonged) was Aleth Hansen.

364. The five sections of Luther's *Small Catechism* (1529) are: 1. The Ten Commandments 2. The Apostles' Creed 3. The Lord's Prayer 4. The Sacrament of Baptism 5. The Sacrament of Holy Communion. In the Preface to his book Luther wrote: "Therefore dear brothers, for God's sake I beg all of you who are pastors and preachers to devote yourselves sincerely to the duties of your office, that you feel compassion for the people entrusted to your care, and that you help us accordingly to inculcate this catechism in the people, especially the young. If you cannot do more, at least take the tables and charts for catechism instruction and drill the people in them word for word." The *Small Catechism* was not in fact a "children's book" as such, but was soon employed as the basis for confirmation, a ceremony which to this day is widely popular in Denmark among 14-year-olds (70% nationally), performed after 6 months of preparation and in conjunction with the local schools. Confirmation was introduced by Christian VI in 1736, and marked the end of 6 years' schooling (8-14). From day one children had learned the catechism and various hymn verses by heart, and before leaving school they were publicly examined before their parents and the congregation by their pastor. To fail the exam brought shame, for they could not then acquire the character reference to enable them to work outside their home. Their parents had to pay the pastor again for a new course, and if the children had not passed the exam by the time they were 19, they could be sent to prison. In general, however, it was in everyone's interest that they passed, including the pastor's, so his questions could occasionally be tailored to the individual candidate. The examination was officially abolished in 1909. Although confirmation is still widely considered to refer to the youngsters' *Christian faith* – to which candidates have to assent – Grundtvig's emphasis was much more on *God's* confirmation of *His* Baptism – an emphasis which is shared by many pastors today.

365. 1 Cor 3:11.

must not blindly assume that what Martin Luther or any other teacher in the Church many hundreds of years after the time of the Apostles calls 'basic Christian teaching' really *is* that. Instead we must ask the Church what is the *nature* of this foundation that the Apostles have laid on behalf of the Lord, not in a book but in *the Church itself* as a gathering of Christian people.

On the other hand, what we must more or less take completely for granted is that Christ *has* a Church on earth – and that we can *find* it. We already presuppose this in the very question of 'basic Christian teaching', for where there are no parents, there are no children! So if there were no longer any Christian parents on earth, there would be no Christian children either, and if there were no Church of Christ on earth, there would be no Christian *people*, young or old, and no basic human teaching which could justifiably be called 'Christian'. When we therefore ask in earnest about 'basic *Christian* teaching', the presupposition is that either we ourselves are members of Christ's Church or are considering becoming so as soon as we have learned what the foundational Christian teaching is and can agree with ourselves on accepting it. I am therefore assuming here that the so-called 'Lutheran' Church into which I was incorporated through Baptism was and is a branch of the Church of Christ which the Apostles established according to Christ's own institution and on His behalf – and that it will continue to the end of the world. Far from setting up a brand-new Church, Martin Luther, both before and after he broke away from the Pope in Rome, was a member and faithful servant of the *Church of our Lord Jesus Christ*.

In this Church of Christ we must all know that Baptism in the name of the Father, the Son, and the Holy Spirit is the only form of admission, with the testimony that this Baptism is not just with water but with 'water and Spirit'.[366] It is therefore not just a *ceremony*; it is the heavenly water of rebirth whereby the Holy Spirit in the name of our Lord Jesus Christ grants us forgiveness of sins and the child's right to Heaven with the hope of eternal life. This is spoken and witnessed expressly at every Baptism in the Church of Christ which Martin Luther was a member of and teacher in, as I am myself. So this is undeniably a substantial part of the Church's witness to basic Christian teaching, for it is an irrefutable part of foundational Christian doctrine in which way and with what means one *becomes* a Christian, and what a person gains and fundamentally becomes by *being* a Christian, that is, by being truly incorporated into the Church of Christ.

Baptism by water in the name of the Father, the Son, and the Holy Spirit teaches us in which way and with what means a person is incorporated into the Church of Christ and becomes a Christian; as with the Lord's blessing at Baptism – "Peace be with you" – it teaches that by becoming a Christian, one gains peace with God and the

---

366. Jn 3:5.

forgiveness of sins. It is similar with the Lord's Prayer, which at Baptism is placed in the mouth of every individual Christian, and teaches us that by becoming Christian, each person becomes a child of God. The Baptismal Covenant also teaches us what kind of father, what kind of son, and what kind of holy spirit it is in whose name a person is baptised a Christian, and what is required of each person who through Baptism according to the Lord's institution wishes to be incorporated into Christ's Church. This comprises the renunciation of the Devil and all his deeds and all his nature; faith in God the Father who is the one true God and maker of the earth; faith in God the Father's only-begotten Son, who is the Son of Man, Jesus Christ; and faith in the Holy Spirit through whom the Virgin Mary conceived and gave birth to Jesus, and who is Himself the divine soul in the entire Church of Christ and in the communion of saints of our Lord Jesus Christ. In Him is the forgiveness of sins, the resurrection of the body, and the life everlasting, as the Apostles' Creed at Baptism states.

The audible testimony of the Church of Christ at Baptism – on the nature of Baptism, its conditions and its fruits – must be accepted and trusted as His Apostles' and His own testimony. It has been transmitted from mouth to mouth and from generation to generation as the Word from His *own* mouth which must never leave the mouth of His Church and from which His Spirit shall never depart but always accompany and seal that testimony. This then, in its truest, strictest, and most blessed sense is the 'basic Christian teaching', which not only will enlighten all who have ears to hear[367] concerning their rebirth as children of God through faith in the Gospel of Christ, but which will revive the spiritually half-dead person too. So this 'basic Christian teaching' contains and imparts the saving power of the Gospel of Christ in the Holy Spirit to all the human hearts that believe the testimony of the Lord and His Church.

This testimony and this basic Christian teaching also correspond wonderfully well with what Scripture calls "the teaching of Christ",[368] whereby He Himself becomes the mentor of His entire church and of what Scripture describes as God's testimony to His only-begotten Son and the eternal life in Him. This is imparted to all those who faithfully embrace the testimony, eternal life, and what Scripture points to as the Word of faith, which is to be the soul of our entire Christian preaching and is to bring Christ so close to the Church as the Word in its mouth and its heart. The Church therefore never asks who will rush up to Heaven to fetch Christ down or who will rush down to the abyss to fetch Him up from the dead, but with the confession of this Word in its mouth and with faith in this in its heart it feels the assuredness of salvation.

---

367. Mk 4:9 et al.
368. e.g. 1 Tim 6:3; Heb 6:1; 2 Jn 1:92.

If with this Christian awareness we now return from the Church to Luther's *Small Catechism*[369] as the book that has long borne the name of *being* our basic Christian teaching, we find that of all the books we have read not one has a greater claim to bear this name, insofar as any one book can do so. This is because throughout it reminds us of the basic Christian teaching that we have found through our Baptism into the Church of Christ. However, we also realise that, as with any other book by a single Christian author, even by an Apostle, Luther's *Catechism* bears no comparison whatsoever with the testimony and the basic Christian teaching in the mouth of the Church with its living voice.

It is with something of a heavy heart that I pursue this further. Firstly Luther's *Catechism* truly marks a giant stride in Christian awareness; for three centuries it has contributed more than any other book to fixing our gaze on our faith and Baptism. Secondly, this little book is very close to my heart, from both my childhood days and my first years as a pastor. However, now that there are those who are appealing to the *book* rather than to the mouth of the Church and the Lord, it is essential to demonstrate that even as a description of basic Christian teaching – which could never take the place of the sole, living valid testimony of the Church – the little book contains major errors and deficiencies! For it contains both too much and too little, and describes only fragments of our 'basic Christian teaching' without pointing to their Christian consequences and context. Finally, it confuses the Church's testimony with the individual's opinion of it and the enlightenment which that brings.

There is simply too *much* in Luther's *Catechism* as a description of our basic Christian teaching. Indeed, its first part with the Ten Commandments does not even belong to *Christian* teachings, as Luther himself realised, stated, and impressed on his readers in no uncertain terms, so the only question is why it is included. It is quite another question whether or not Christian parents and teachers do well or ill, act wisely or unwisely, in impressing on their charges the Ten Commandments from the Law of Moses to illuminate the *divine* Law which the Gospel of Christ has in no way come to abolish but to confirm and, with the removal of the curse of the Law, to fulfil in love.

For one thing is what is peculiar to Christ and His Gospel, what constitutes foundational Christianity altogether, and what must also constitute basic Christian teachings to the exclusion of all else. Another thing is what and how much Christ's Gospel presupposes among the children of humankind who are to be found willing and amenable to *believing* the Gospel and being saved by the grace of God. For since the Gospel as the *offer* of God's love presupposes the Law as the *command* of God's love, so is the Gospel itself not a law and cannot include either a little or a lot of the Law of Moses.

---

369. Luther's *Small Catechism* was published in 1529.

Nevertheless, just as Luther's *Catechism*, when regarded as a description of our basic Christian teaching, contains too much by including the Ten Commandments from the Law of Moses, so does it also contain too *little* when it omits the renunciation of the Devil and all his works and all his ways, which clearly is part of our foundational Christianity since it is an inseparable part of the Baptismal Covenant of the Christian Church – in other words one of the conditions for incorporation into the Christian Congregation. Only on this condition is the Christian Baptismal Covenant in Spirit and truth justifiable as the sole condition for entry into the kingdom of God.

Lastly, in Luther's *Catechism* the faith of the Christian Church, the Lord's Prayer, and the Lord's only institutions, Baptism and Holy Communion, are treated solely *outside* their Christian context, as though they each had their own specific authority and importance. This is so despite the fact that the Three Articles of Faith only have their rightful authority and importance as inseparable parts of the Christian Church's unchangeable Confession of faith at Baptism, and that this confession only has validity as the condition of Baptism in combination with the renunciation of the Devil. It is equally certain that the Lord's Prayer is only the expression and sealing of the hope of the *whole* Church as the hope of the children of God, for at Baptism according to the Lord's institution the prayer is placed in the mouth of the *whole* Christian Congregation. Baptism is quite simply the water of rebirth and renewal in an insoluble union with the Baptismal Covenant, just as Holy Communion is quite simply the fellowship of Christ's body and blood on the presumption of faith and Baptism.

From this it is as clear as sunlight that even allowing for the claim that any book has the least right to bear the name 'Basic Christian Teachings', we nevertheless require a much better book than Martin Luther's as a description of the Lord's own institutions of Holy Baptism and Holy Communion – with all that originally and essentially belongs to them, and nothing more besides. For on the one hand we must assume that the Lord's own institutions contain all that is needed to become a child of God with a child's right to inherit eternal life; and on the other hand the Lord's own institutions are the only thing that can surely and clearly be traced *back* to the Lord, without whom we can do nothing. They can be distinguished from the words and deeds of all other individuals, and they distinguish *His* Spirit from all other spirits.

Such a book of basic Christian teachings – which also points out that the Word of Holy Communion does not belong among them in the true sense but is only the *explanation* of the basic teaching for adults granting them the first-fruits of God's kingdom – such a book may be considered invaluable nowadays and can clearly be of great use if used properly. But obviously it can do just as much damage if misused; and although it will share something in common with every visible or invisible life and light, with all that truly enlivens and enlightens, and first and foremost with the

Gospel of Christ, we should nevertheless in creating and recommending such a book make every possible effort to ensure that its proper use is so distinguishable from its misuse that as far as possible all uninformed misuse is thereby prevented.

To this end it will by no means be enough for us to swear most solemnly that we would never allow such a book to take the place of, or even be placed alongside, the one, audible, enlivening, enlightening testimony of our Lord and His Church at Baptism and Holy Communion. But we must also show as clearly as possible that all the lustre of the Christian life and light that such a book can have is borrowed from the *real* life and light in the Lord's own institutions. Such a book borrows its divine lustre from the life of God's children, which the Lord with His audible Word of God creates and grants in the water of rebirth and renewal, and in particular in the audible Word of God which nourishes and strengthens, encourages and satisfies in the fellowship of His body and blood. It borrows its lustre of Christian enlightenment from the light of life that the Lord Himself has lit and placed not under a bushel but on a lampstand in the Word of the Baptismal Covenant to shine for all those who are in the house. In addition we must show as clearly as possible through the whole history of the Church from the actual days of the Apostles until our own that whenever the right relationship between the Voice of the Lord and the *description* of it was forgotten in the Church, then a so-called orthodoxy, however biblical, became no more than an appearance without substance. It could not disseminate, defend, or prove itself, indeed it did not even know that true Christianity can and must do so, and it neither can nor will be disseminated, defended, or proved with worldly means, be they worldly power, worldly wisdom, or worldly attraction.

Since many both say and *would* say that this Christianity is not 'the Christianity of the New Testament', then in a sense they have appearances on their side; for if by the 'New Testament' we only mean the book which we ourselves have called the 'New Testament' and not the 'New Covenant', i.e. the Baptismal Covenant, then we ourselves are confessing that our Christianity is not the Christianity of any *book* but the Christianity of Christ and His Church. But in our mouths that is the same as saying that our Christianity is not a dead but a living Christianity, not a shadow but a reality, and those who invoke 'New Testament Christianity' will not admit that they thereby mean something that is not living, real, and active, but only a lifeless appearance and an impotent shadow!

If on the other hand we believe that the Christianity which we trace back to the one, audible, enlivening, enlightening testimony of our Lord and His Church at Baptism and Holy Communion according to our Lord Jesus Christ's own institution is *not* in agreement with the Apostolic Writings that we call 'the New Testament', then we must wait until the Day of Judgement for the evidence. For we dare to claim that not only is our Christianity in agreement with the part of the 'New Testament' that either announces itself as an Apostolic Writing or can reasonably be considered as such, but that it is also the *only* Christianity that is in agreement with it.

For the Apostolic Writings do not *call* themselves the 'New Testament' any more than they anywhere pretend to be other than the Christian foundation and basic teaching or the rule of faith, or the voice of the Lord, or the source of life, or the body of Christ. So if we pretend that it is only a *share*, large or small, of all that is found according to the Apostolic Writings in true Christianity, we are in open contradiction with those writings, which throughout refer to an audible, enlivening, almighty Word of God to us all. It is both 'spirit and life', the heavenly Father's own Spirit and our Lord Jesus Christ's own life; so no Christianity that lacks this Spirit and this life can in any way be in agreement with the Apostolic Writings.

Just as Christianity according to the Apostolic Writings is truly a power from God for salvation, so will this power from God, according to the same Writings, reveal and prove itself in its effect among all believers and baptised who make up the people and Church of Christ on earth. In the footsteps of the Son of Man this Church will grow with a divine growth from Christian childhood to Christian manhood, indeed until it measures up to the Lord Himself, not as His rival but as His bride and spouse. And we shall find that all those who have laid another Christian foundation than the one that is set in and through Baptism and Holy Communion according to the Lord's own institution will either never experience a new human life in the Lord's Spirit unique to Christ's Church but regard it as pure mystical nonsense and idle fantasy – or they will clearly show that they know nothing about it, since they pretend that something is spiritual life and Christian growth and perfection which neither resembles the Lord's human life nor is in agreement with the Apostolic Writings.

Lastly, it is clear that according to the Apostolic Writings true Christianity as the revelation of the heavenly Father's matchless love will be most attractive in every way for 'the little ones' – those not yet come of age, the simple, and the humble. Experience will show that the true Church comprises especially those who have no standing at all in this world, whether through high birth, wealth, power, scholarship, or learning. So it is clearly quite impossible that such a Christianity which is derived from, and rests on, books, and especially on an ancient book, should be in agreement with the Apostolic Writings. The origins of the New Testament are obscure, its authenticity can be rendered doubtful at any moment, its basic language can only be known to a few and even by them imperfectly understood, and its proper interpretation can only be a matter of dispute between believers and unbelievers, genuine and bogus scholars, until the end of the world. It is impossible that such a Christianity or such a Church in which the learned and intelligent of this world made up the soul and the core should according to the Apostolic Writings be 'apostolic'.

One may of course, without contradicting oneself, argue that our Christianity –
which we trace back to and build on the one, audible and enlivening testimony of
Christ and His Church in and through Baptism and Holy Communion according to
the Lord's own Words of Institution – corresponds with the Apostolic description.
Nor can we claim that it has the same Spirit and life in it that the Apostolic Writings
presuppose and which must be found in the Gospel of Christ that is truly to be a
power from God for salvation for all believers. But since this Christianity is clearly
the only one that can possibly correspond to the Apostolic description, in defending
it we have two major advantages over all our opponents: one is that we can point to
the future as being what alone will decide the dispute, the other is that we can show
that our Christianity stands and falls with Jesus Christ and His Church on earth.

As regards the first, it is obvious that only the future can show whether our Christianity corresponds to the Apostolic description or not; for whether our Christianity
is a power from God can only be seen in its effect on humanity after it has begun to
operate, in other words after a congregation, large or small, has freely embraced it in the
Christianity demonstrated through and in Baptism and has gained a position in which
it is recognisable to every other so-called Christian church. So long as we are mixed
with a whole host which for temporal reasons apparently have the Creed, Baptism,
and Holy Communion in common with us, the effect of God's power, which can only
operate among the fewest, must of necessity remain in the shade, where it can easily
be overlooked. Moreover it goes without saying that according to both the Apostolic
Writings and the laws of human life, the life of the Church can only reach its goal at
the end of its path, so that while it is growing it cannot possibly be considered fully
grown. It cannot therefore perfectly correspond to the description that the Spirit has
so far given of what He who searches all things knows beforehand.[370] And so to the
second point: it also goes without saying that we trace our Christianity back to, and
build on, one, audible, enlivening, enlightening testimony of our Lord and His Church
at Baptism and Holy Communion according to the Lord's own institution. For we
cannot point to any other Church with any other Baptism and Holy Communion that
can possibly be built on Christ's own institution. So if ours was not that either, then
Christ would have no Church and would have had none on earth for many a century;
nor could He be God's only-begotten Son with all power in Heaven and on earth and
be with His Church to the very end of the age.[371]

We can smile at all possible objections to the authenticity of this Christianity –
which we trace back to, and build on, one, audible, enlivening, enlightening testimony
of our Lord and His Church at Baptism and Holy Communion according to our Lord

---

370. Ps 139:1; Jer 17:10; Rom 8:27. "And he who searches our hearts knows the mind of the Spirit."
371. Mt 28:20.

Jesus Christ's own institution. And we shall see these objections be blown away like chaff to the wind so long as we stand firm in the faith in Jesus Christ and the Holy Spirit which is the Spirit both of the Father and of the Son, the Spirit of both truth and love, the divine vice-regent in the kingdom of God while it is still only spiritually present. But this faith, both according to the Apostolic Writings and all Christian experience, is always on earth surrounded by doubt and exposed to danger, since, being far more precious than gold in the eyes of God, it must also pass through the ordeal by fire. It is nevertheless a great comfort that where, as in our case, childlike faith does not *carry* the basic teaching but is carried *by* it as the Lord's own teaching, there the tempter of childlike faith must at once come into conflict with Him who has proved that He is "the seed of woman" that crushes the serpent's head,[372] and who will always show that He is the good shepherd from whose hand no wolf can tear the lamb.[373] For this Lord's basic teaching is the shield of faith with which we can extinguish all the Devil's burning arrows. And since our path between Baptism and Holy Communion is the living path between faith and love, then our Christian hope grows with every step as the hope of glory for the child of God, and with its wondrous power it will wage war on all fear. This power is known to us as 'Christ within us', in whom we are capable of everything when we believe and feel that without Him we can do nothing.

372. Gen 3:15.
373. Jn 10:11.

14. The Christian Baptismal Covenant

It was thirty years ago, in 1825,[374] that I first began to insist on the right of the Apostles' Creed to count as the rule of faith[375] for the entire Church and as the rock on which is built the everlasting spiritual house of God, made of living stones and where it must forever stand. I was very much aware of the position that the Creed held in the life of the Church in relation to Baptism and as part of the New Covenant instituted by our Lord and established with all those who wish through Baptism to be admitted into the fellowship of the Church of our Lord Jesus Christ. But in the spiritual world we had become so used to mistaking the written word for the spoken, and death for life, that it was a long time before I could make our scribes and scholars even *sense* what I meant. So there may still be some who think that this is what Lessing[376] once argued, as does Delbrück[377] in our own time: that all Christians should direct their faith according to what can be read in the writings of the Church Fathers about the Apostles' Creed as the rule of faith for the believing community.

Most people have by now realised that I am referring to the Creed in the Baptismal Covenant. This must not be sought in any written document but must be heard at Baptism, where it sounds as the *condition* for Baptism and as the expression of the Christian faith into which we are baptised in the name of the Father, Son, and Holy Spirit. We must assume that it has been spoken in the same way in the Church from the moment Baptism was instituted by the Lord Himself. It is just as much heresy to baptise in the name of the Lord on any other terms than those He Himself has laid down as it is to baptise on His behalf with another Baptism than the one He Himself instituted.

The Creed at Baptism must be regarded as unalterable, and cannot derive from the writings of the Apostles since Baptism is older than Scripture and the Apostles wrote only for the believers and the baptised. Nevertheless, quite a number of our 'scribes' stubbornly continue to claim that we must *not* call the Creed or the Baptismal Covenant as such 'a Word from the Lord's own mouth', belonging to His own fundamental teaching on which they must base all their learning. However, if we alter the Creed, we are insulting both Scripture and the scholars, and are moving closer to the Pope and papistry again! It is all such patent nonsense that it is barely worth a response. For either these good people do not know what they are saying, or they are willing

---

374. For a summary of the Clausen libel case, see note 241.
375. The concept of 'rule of faith' was introduced by Irenaeus; see note 30.
376. Gotthold Lessing (1729-81) was a German writer and philosopher of the Enlightenment.
377. Johann Delbrück (1772-1848) was a German philologist and philosopher.

on behalf of Scripture and the scholars to insult outrageously the entire Christian Church – as if the Church based its faith on something that fell from the sky yet could not explain where it came from! It is as if they accept that it has not come from the mouth of the Lord! But that is precisely where the Word of faith must have its home if He who lives within it is to be the rock and foundation that the Church itself has claimed He must be – though always according to Scripture. One cannot insult the entire Christian Church without thereby insulting the Lord Himself. If the Church's faith were based on something other than the Word of faith from the Lord's own mouth, then the Lord was either so careless as to demand a faith from His Church as the condition of salvation without even saying *which* faith, or He was too impotent to gather a Church to Himself that would base its faith on His Word.

If, as some have asserted, we are indeed moving closer to the Pope and what has been called 'papistry' by claiming the Apostles' Creed and the entire Baptismal Covenant to be words from the Lord's own mouth and the indisputable, but also sole, condition for the water of rebirth and renewal according to the Lord's own institution, it would still not matter one way or the other. Luther insisted on the Three Articles of Faith, the entire Baptismal Covenant, and Baptism in the name of the Father, Son, and Holy Spirit, even though he was well aware that he shared these with the Pope in Rome who had mixed a good deal of papistry together with it. Similarly, we must also assert the only Christian view of the Baptismal Covenant and the indissoluble link between 'faith and Baptism' whether or not we share this view with the Pope and any papistry. Indeed, all this talk about the connection of the Pope and papistry with the Baptismal Covenant as the Word from the Lord's own mouth and the only condition for salvation is nonsense! The Pope rightly says that we must separate the Baptismal Covenant and what we generally call the Sacramental Word from everything else that goes under the name of the Lord's own spoken words (*Traditio Dominica*). But the Pope does not do so himself! So in that regard he clearly belongs with the scribes of whom our Lord says, 'Do what they say, but not what they do'.[378] For among all our magisterial scholars there is clearly not one who does less than follow the Pope in being best served by following his good advice that the Baptismal Covenant is the Word from the Lord's own mouth and the only condition of salvation.

This has nothing whatsoever to do with all superstitious belief in the Pope as the vicar of God on earth and his papistry as the condition for salvation. First and foremost he rightly declares: 'Whoever has ears, let them hear! This is the Word from the Lord's own mouth that whoever rejects the Devil and all his works and all his being, and believes in God the Father, Jesus Christ, His only-begotten Son, and the Holy Spirit as our Apostles' Creed says, and is baptised in the name of the Father, Son, and Holy

---

378. Mt 23:2.

Spirit ... whoever does this finds through the Holy Spirit his peace with God in the forgiveness of sins and is reborn to eternal life and will then be renewed by the Holy Spirit.' But then the Pope takes us by the arm and says, 'That was the Word and institution of the Lord, listen now to what I say as St. Peter's successor, the doorkeeper of Heaven and the vicar of Christ: If you want to be saved and do not want to be excluded from the Holy Church, handed over to Satan, and burnt in Purgatory, then you must do whatever I have a mind to order and command!' Surely then, everyone of sound common sense can grasp that the Pope in Rome is the greatest windbag under the sun!

The reason why our 'erudite' people, chock-full of learning, seem unable to grasp so obvious a truth is simply because they have the unpleasant feeling that fundamentally they take the same view about the Baptismal Covenant as the Pope! So they too are talking unacceptable nonsense when they establish the Baptismal Covenant among us and baptise us for the Lord's sake with the assurance that we thereby gain forgiveness of sins and rebirth in the Spirit to eternal life, but then go on to tell us that if we wish to be saved, there is much else we must believe and do on the strength of their word as scholarly pastoral guides. Otherwise – despite the Baptismal Covenant with our faith and Baptism according to the Lord's institution with "His peace" and "everlasting blessing in the waters of heaven" – we shall miss out on eternal salvation!

In order for us to be unshakeable in Christ and 'Christ's teaching' we must set aside all nonsense from the Pope and from papists and Protestants alike on the question of salvation. We can then defend our Christian view of the Baptismal Covenant as the Word from the Lord's own mouth and the only condition for salvation, notwithstanding that we confess our faith in Scripture and our need for Holy Communion.

In recent times this has been boldly denied, so even if both papists and Protestants were talking nonsense, so were the Grundtvigians,[379] and they might as well admit that their opponents could be right, despite their nonsense!

Far be it from me to deny the possibility that either my friends or I can talk nonsense – and have probably done so once in a while – but I nevertheless claim and can prove that in regard to Baptism and the Baptismal Covenant I have not talked nonsense since my eyes were opened to the following crystal clear truth: Just as spiritual rebirth is the only genuine and perceptible beginning of eternal life in the Spirit, so is the only condition for Baptism the same as that for salvation. For according to the Lord's institution, Baptism imparts the waters of rebirth and renewal in the Holy Spirit.[380] This truth is in no way contradicted, but is presumed and strengthened, by the

---

379. 'Grundtvigianism' denotes the movement that built on Grundtvig's view of life as a gift from God for which we should be actively grateful and glad. The movement led to the building of parish halls for lectures and meetings, to the innovative people's high schools and free schools, to the establishment of free churches within the national church, and to the co-operative movement within agriculture.

380. Grundtvig believed that the ritual of baptism actually *conferred* a rebirth in the Holy Spirit.

illuminating writing of the Apostle[381] that presumes precisely this faith and Baptism and precisely on these terms presumes salvation. In many ways it serves to clarify and expound the Baptismal Covenant, the Word concerning Baptism and the new life that we are born into, not of corruptible but of incorruptible seed – the living Word of God that lasts for ever. With this comes the knowledge that in Baptism we have not only an institution of the Lord for the beginning of salvation, but in Holy Communion we have a *further* institution of the Lord for the promotion and consummation of it! The new human life in the Lord's Spirit is, at its birth in Baptism, little and weak – like all human life, including that of our Lord in His birth from His mother's womb. In the words of renunciation, faith, and prayer at Baptism, as the Apostle writes,[382] this life finds the mother's milk which like new-born children we crave; and in the so-called 'hard' words on eating the Son of Man's flesh and drinking His blood at the table of the Lord this life finds the solid food that nourishes and strengthens it to achieve its full growth and win its crown.

Imagine someone saying to us: "In our hearts we believe everything that Baptism has taught us, and we have faith that the Lord's Baptism is truly the water of rebirth and renewal in the Holy Spirit, but for that very reason we believe this is enough for salvation. We will have nothing to do with the so-called Apostolic Writings, nor will we receive their enlightenment regarding creation or the Lord's birth, suffering, death, resurrection and ascension, nor will we accept Holy Communion – what you call sharing the Lord's body and blood!" Would we respond by muttering: "Then you are not Christians, your faith is in vain, your Baptism invalid, and your hope of salvation forfeited"? Would we not rather say: "Be careful that you do not lie to the Church of our Lord in this matter, for then you are lying to the Holy Spirit. We cannot believe that what you say is true, that you believe everything you have confessed about Baptism's power of rebirth and renewal in the Holy Spirit, and yet you *dismiss* not only the witness of the Christian teachers to the Scriptures but also the entire witness of the Church to Holy Communion! However, it is your own choice as to whether you exclude yourselves from the illumination of the Scriptures and the blessing of Holy Communion. If you can nevertheless stand firm in the faith and take comfort from Baptism – which we do not believe you can – we do not doubt that the Spirit of Truth will impel you towards both Holy Communion as the table in the kingdom of Heaven, and to the illumination of the Scriptures which is indispensable to the education of God's people."

If we return now to the Baptismal Covenant, we are likely to meet far more objections from our scholars than we can answer or predict concerning its adequacy as the

---

381. 1 Pet 1:22; 1 Cor 15:54.
382. Heb 5:12; 1 Cor 3:2.

only Christian condition for salvation. But since it is equally certain that the Baptismal Covenant is *indeed* the sole condition for Baptism at the Lord's institution, all such objections can only be objections to the spiritual rebirth and renewal that Baptism *grants*, or to the Lord's own *wisdom* in setting only this condition for Baptism! Such obviously unchristian objections are simply laughable when they do not admit to their own unchristian nature but seek to base themselves on the Christians' own Holy Scripture or on Holy Communion, which is precisely a means to salvation for believers and baptised in this covenant.

Our scholars make such a fuss over telling us that our Baptismal Covenant lacks a commitment to holiness – which both Scripture and Reason demand for those who would be saved – or a commitment to Love – which is required by Scripture and presumed by Holy Communion – and that the entire covenant contains not a single word regarding Redemption and Reconciliation through the Blood of Christ – which is expressly underlined at Holy Communion and emphasised by Paul the Apostle as the prime doctrine of Christianity. But if this should be true and if these inadequacies were to make the Baptismal Covenant unsuited to being the sole condition for salvation, then we can only blame the one who *instituted* Baptism and *established* the Covenant. He would stand uncorrected and unreliable, however much we might try to make good His faults and thereby deny the faith in Jesus that we confess. For no disciple is greater than his master,[383] but the trained disciple should be *like* his master.

Although we are unwilling and unable to take responsibility for defending our Lord's wisdom against all idiotic objections, for His and the Church's sake we must publicise the stupidity of the conceited when we see it. The reason why all manner of commitments are missing from the Baptismal Covenant is because they take for a law what is in fact a gospel. The gospel is not a *command* about what we should do in order to be saved but an offer to *make* us saved if we honestly accept the Lord's conditions: 'If you renounce and believe, says the Lord, I will baptise you with the Holy Spirit.' If there are to be any objections to this, they can only be that our Lord does not have the *power* to baptise with the Holy Spirit, or that He has no *right* to baptise in these circumstances. All other objections are utterly unfounded, for salvation comes not from deeds but is granted undeservedly by God's mercy. If the Lord can defend his core teaching – the kingdom of God is close at hand, repent and believe the gospel! – then He can also defend His Baptismal Covenant, which at the door to the kingdom of God expressly states what He *means* by repenting and believing the gospel. And we dare to maintain: If our Lord cannot save those who honestly answer yes to the questions asked of them at Baptism, then He cannot possibly save sinners for whom He came down to earth according to Scripture, which is what we poor sinners need

---

383. Mt 10:24; Lk 6:40.

Him to do! Whoever is already holy and spotless needs no purification, and whoever already loves God with all his heart and his neighbour as himself needs no Saviour from perdition but is as sure of everlasting life as he who is already living it, according to the Word of the Lord to the scribes: "Do this, and you will live!"[384]

In passing, it is strange that we lack an express *definition* of 'holiness', which would include our confessing faith in the Holy Spirit, praying for enrolment in the Holy Church, and hoping for all things in the communion of saints. Similarly we lack a deference to 'love'; the entire Christian faith has its source in faith in God's paternal love, the everlasting source of love, where all comfort takes its rise in our faith in the communion of saints which without reciprocal love is quite impossible.

It is different with the Baptismal Covenant's silence concerning the forgiveness of sins and eternal life as the effect of the Lord's suffering, death, and resurrection. At first glance this omission must always seem surprising and cause momentary concern to a Christian familiar with Scripture. But it comes about because we who are versed in the Scriptures – even when we have sought and found true life – are nevertheless continually tempted more or less to forget this in our study of books! For as soon as we place ourselves in the relationship we were in at the very start and use that as our viewpoint, all anxiety and astonishment fall away and allow room for our admiration of the Lord's wisdom.

In the early days no one was baptised without first having heard the preaching of the good news about the Son of God who became man, suffered, died, and rose for us. All those who sought Baptism did so solely to share in the salvation that the life and death of Jesus Christ had granted them – this was a matter of course. But because the Lord could not and would not demand any more of a person at Baptism than was possible for the old Adam to grasp, trust, and affirm, He did not insist on a Confession of faith in the communion between the Lord and His Church whereby everything that is His becomes ours. That is only what the *new* Adam grows up to understand, and only then what the Word of the Lord in Holy Communion expressly testifies to.

Finally, let me tell my fellow-Christians why I have responded so briefly in writing to so much that has been written disputing the Creed in the Baptismal Covenant as the divine rule of faith and the living Word of God from the Lord's own mouth.

The reason lies partly in the nature of the dispute, since the mouth cannot possibly claim advantage over the pen in a written polemic, except by carrying out what the pen clearly cannot do: namely, express and convey the spirit and the life that the pen can only describe and point to. But I also have another reason that stems from the nature of the matter and the question before us.

---

384. Lk 10:28.

I know from personal experience that even as a scholarly priest of the school of Martin Luther I felt a deep need for a recognisable Word from the Lord's *own mouth* that could serve as a golden rule for both the shared faith of the Church and for Christian learning and scriptural interpretation, and equally as a divine means of expression for the spirit and the life which our preaching cannot match and our writing even less so. This deep need, which I am sure is shared by all those versed in the Scriptures and all relatively informed Christians, is what I found fulfilled daily and ever more joyfully in the whole sacramental Word that the Apostles have imparted to us as they received it from the Lord. Both first and last with the Creed in the Baptismal Covenant it is the rock upon which the faith of the Church must rest and from which living waters flow, becoming among believers a fountain of eternal life.

So, that is why I know that the Christian question in this matter is not whether we can think up objections in order to wriggle away from the Word from the Lord's own mouth. The Christian question is solely whether for the sake of the Lord and all truth we dare to believe that in the Lord's own Words of Institution we find this divine Word of faith, hope, and love from His own mouth in their full vitality. We all feel the need for them – which the Lord somehow or other must and will supply. We cannot *prevent* anyone wriggling away from the faith and the Lord; but whoever does not wish to do so will never wriggle away from the *Word of the Lord Himself* at Baptism and Holy Communion, or wriggle away from their Baptismal Covenant in which alone we can find our communion with the Father, Son, and Holy Spirit in whose name we are baptised.

15. Renunciation in the Baptismal Covenant

When we think seriously about it, we all know that our Baptismal Covenant consists of two parts: the renunciation and the confession. It goes without saying that these two are inseparable. Just as taken together they constitute the Baptismal Covenant, so when separated each acquires its true meaning and clarification seen in their internal relation. Whilst in the Gospel of Mark we find the Lord's teaching described in a few lines: "The kingdom of God has come near. Repent and believe the good news!"[385] so do we see in Baptism, the water of renewal, precisely that the kingdom of God has come near. To this Baptismal Covenant belong these two conditions upon which the Lord, with His Baptism of water and Spirit, will lead us into the kingdom. The renunciation therefore tells us what the Lord means by repentance, and the confession tells us what the Lord means by faith in the Gospel.

Not until we regard the renunciation from its proper side as the Christian expression of repentance, and in its proper place as the condition of our entry into the kingdom of God, do we see the *importance* of the renunciation and understand its necessity without heeding what the grouchers say: that it seems as though belief in the Devil also belongs in the Apostles' Creed![386]

It would clearly be a flagrant fraudster who promised salvation to a sinner *without* repentance. It would be like promising someone on the wrong path that, without turning round, he would reach the destination he was turning his back on! Similarly, it would be a flagrant fraud against the grace of Baptism into rebirth and a new life, if, as one of its conditions, the Baptismal Covenant did not express the *rejection* of all lies and wickedness. If one is turned towards the grace and truth that the Apostles' Creed gives expression to, without this rejection of the Devil it could not be honestly *meant*. This is the first point we need to note. The second point is very much the same: that we must place neither more nor less in the renunciation than an honest turning away from, and rejection of, all lies and wickedness. We must not allow ourselves to be swayed to right or left by all that has been said or can be said about the *purpose* of the word 'repentance' or 'change of heart' (*metanoia*) as it is used in the book of the New Covenant.

---

385. Mk 1:12-15.

386. The renunciation of the Devil precedes the confirmation of the Trinity, an example of Grundtvig's use of the 'principle of contradiction': one cannot say yes without first having said no. The Danish Lutheran Church is one of the few Lutheran Churches to have retained the renunciation.

What we can and must say 'yes' to with our renunciation at Baptism must be no more than what we can, with God's help, honestly and sincerely say yes to before the rebirth and renewal that has its source in Baptism. It is not that we have already *overcome* the evil spirit, or that we feel upright and strong enough to *withstand* all his attacks, only that we rescind all allegiance and loyalty to him and, with God's help, will never join forces like traitors with this spiteful enemy of our Lord and our own salvation. This is how the omniscient and merciful Saviour has determined renunciation, and this is how we should regard it *as* determined by Him, when we examine what the word 'renounce' must mean in our Baptismal Covenant.[387]

The word *forsage* is not one that is in common use nowadays. We may have a word that sounds that way but it is like the Germen *verzagen*, meaning 'to be dispirited', which is quite different from its meaning here. We therefore need the information that *forsage* in our Baptismal Covenant has the same meaning as 'forsake' in English, meaning 'to turn one's back on and let go of', while the corresponding word in the Latin Baptismal Covenant is *renunciare*, meaning to 'decline' or 'reject'. This is exactly what the Apostle Paul means when he writes (2 Cor 4): "we have renounced secret and shameful ways"; and again (2 Tim. 2): "God's solid foundation stands firm, sealed with this inscription: 'Everyone who confesses the name of the Lord must turn away from wickedness'."

In this renunciation, the seal of truth is clearly inscribed on the Christian Baptismal Covenant; for with it the Lord is demanding from all his followers a *hostile divorce* from the Devil, who according to his own statement is "the father of lies".[388] In not demanding a divorce from anyone else, or from anything else that smacks of 'devilry', the Lord is ensuring the divorce which truth *must* make and which cannot have anything other than the lie in opposition to it.

In so doing, our Lord acknowledges that the real Devil exists, or to put it more clearly: that the lie really does have a father, who knows this to be so of his own accord and is conscious of himself as the archetypal Liar, the implacable enemy of eternal Truth. However, just because this is a pre-condition it does not make it in any way a Christian *doctrine*. It must only be defended as a human *conception* from time immemorial which, on the Word of the Lord, Christians have a right to declare valid for as long as no one can disprove its truth. At the beginning of this century nearly all our scholars were comfortable with this, but experience has already made them so wise that they must admit it can no longer hold good. Doubtless they will soon come to the perception that the existence of a spiritual 'father of lies' can just as easily be

---

387. The Danish word that Grundtvig uses for 'renounce' is *forsage*, much like the English 'forsake', which is the point of his explanation.

388. Jn 8:44.

denied, without self-contradiction, as can the existence of lying and falsehood. In other words, one can no more imagine a 'no' without a 'no-er' than one can imagine a 'yes' without a 'yes-er'!

The idea of an archetypal 'Liar' who is also the great Tempter is not something new which Christianity brought into the world but an ancient conception *presupposed* by Christianity and presupposed for ever, like sin and death; it is something that everyone knows, and for all friends of the truth this is completely indisputable. Such knowledge would not be required if, instead of retaining the Graeco-Latin word for 'devil' (*Diabolos*) in our Baptismal Covenant, we had replaced it with the corresponding Danish-Norwegian word *Fanden*.[389] However, since the word *Fanden* means 'the Tempter' but the word *Djævel* means 'the Slanderer' we come a little closer to the basic meaning of the ugly, impure spirit which is, as we have seen, 'the Liar'. We would do well to impress this upon ourselves, not only because this is the Lord's express testimony but especially because 'the Truth' is the only concept that clearly includes all that is good, just as 'the Lie' is the only concept that includes all that is evil. We can thus prove, by renouncing the archetypal 'Liar' with 'all his deeds and all his being', that we are forsaking all spiritual evil that can be named.

If we now assume the renunciation of the Devil at Baptism to be a turning away from the father of lies and all his offspring, and the Christian expression for 'repentance', then it is clear that although the Law must not be incorporated into our 'basic Christian teachings', its entire content is presupposed. It is therefore only in the form of order and prohibition, threat and curse, that Christians have nothing to do with the Law, whereas they must constantly look at themselves in the mirror to know what it is that the Saviour will break down and what He will build up in His Church and in all His believers.

The Baptismal Covenant presupposes God's Law not only in the renunciation of the Devil but just as completely and even more clearly in the Confession of the Holy Spirit, with the Holy Church, the communion of saints, and the forgiveness of sins. Similarly the renunciation of the Devil stretches beyond sin to everything that the evil spirit works in the soul. This includes the spiritual darkness and spiritual death which are also the Devil's works, since the father of lies is also the prince of darkness and the great killjoy with the murdering power of death.

This is a very important point which has so far been overlooked but certainly needs to be emphasised. It is not just because Christian enlightenment and enlivenment cannot succeed unless we turn our backs on darkness and death; it is especially in order to

---

389. To this day *Fanden* and *Satan* are the Danish words for 'the Devil'. As intensifiers both are in much wider use than the equivalents in English-speaking countries. Thus as a mild expletive of surprise or shock *Hvad fanden?* is better translated as 'What the hell?' rather than 'What the Devil?'

see the renunciation of the Devil in its proper light – as being no less evangelical than it is lawful! For the purpose of our renunciation is that whatever we thereby separate ourselves from will be spiritually destroyed *for* us and *in* us by the Lord, in whom we place our heartfelt trust in our Confession of faith. So it is good news indeed that we shall be free not only of the Lie, the root of sin, but also of darkness and death. For the darkness of error and ignorance are simultaneously the Liar's own fabrication and his own *chain*, and the deadly coldness and hardening of the heart are just as much the punishment for sin as for its very pleasure.

This is also the deep reason for the possibility of repentance as expressed in the renunciation of the Devil at Baptism. For since the Lie is the root of all sin, sinners are of necessity themselves ensnared in the Lie's meshes, and until their honest and sincere *rebirth* they cannot say 'yes' to renouncing or to genuinely breaking with all falsehood and sin in themselves. On the other hand sinners can honestly and sincerely say that they renounce the same Devil with all his deeds who has been the murderer of humankind from the beginning as well as the father of lies, and who is just as much the spiteful enemy of human beings as of truth. The sinners' relation to spiritual truth is like their relation to spiritual light: the Lie must create darkness to hide behind, since it cannot *bear* the light, and sinners have therefore placed the chains of darkness around themselves – and there they now lie, unable to break them. However, it is otherwise with spiritual life; for spiritual death, which is cold and unfeeling in the heart, is just as much the Devil's own choice as it is his punishment. This does not need to be the case with human sinners, for like Eve in Paradise, they are tempted and seduced by the Liar, who with a snake's guile dupes them into believing that, far from costing them their lives, sin will lead them to the divine life that their Creator begrudged them! So when human beings conceive a faith in God's only-begotten Son as the Prince of Life who can and will save them from death, they gain the desire and the power both to hate and to break sincerely with the man-murderer from the beginning. They break with all the falsehood with which the Devil seduced the naïve, inexperienced human child out of Paradise and its Tree of Life and into the desert, there to sit inconsolably in the shadow of death. When we believe in the forgiveness of sins in the Church of Christ, the sinner's essential fear of the divine light disappears and our natural love of the divine life awakens – the life that the Tempter falsely promised us but which the Saviour has *within* Him and is willing to share with all His believers.

When we thus regard the renunciation in its insoluble connection with the Confession of faith in the Baptismal Covenant, then and only then do we see why it is always the Devil's work to separate what the Lord has joined together in the Baptismal Covenant. For neither repentance nor faith, as the Lord has illuminated them and joined them together in the Baptismal Covenant, can be true and genuine without this connection, this spiritual marriage. How can a sinful person honestly renounce the Devil, the father of lies, the prince of darkness, and standard-bearer of death, without believing in God's only-begotten Son as the Truth, the Light, and the Life? Nor can we turn to truth, light, and life without turning *away from* lying, darkness, and death; so whoever nevertheless says they do what they clearly *cannot* do is lying against the truth; they are denying the obvious truth, truly contradicting, and thereby condemning, themselves.

Here we can see the eternal, divine seal of truth clearly stamped on God's firm foundation in the Christian Baptismal Covenant, which therefore, also among the ancients, especially Irenaeus,[390] and even in the Apostolic Writings, is specifically called the Truth (*aletheia* and *veritas*). For the Christian Baptismal Covenant is the living expression of what the academics, in a poor *ad hoc* phrase, call 'the principle of opposites', but which Christians would call 'the fundamental law of truth': that what cannot be argued with self-contradiction cannot be conceived in truth or justified without falsehood, and is therefore a tangible lie. On the other hand, what cannot be denied *without* self-contradiction cannot either be suspected without falsehood or disputed without lying, so it is truth as clear as sunlight! Everyone who wishes to be Christian and be baptised must accept this principle of truth in the renunciation and Confession of faith in the Baptismal Covenant; they cannot deny it without thereby relinquishing his Baptismal Covenant and setting aside all claim to Baptismal grace and the name of 'Christian', which is only granted on both conditions for Baptism by Him who not for nothing has said, "Whoever is not with me is against me, and whoever is not against me is with me."[391] No one can be both for and against the eternal truth. Only the principled Liar, in true self-contradiction, can falsely say he both is and is not!

Opponents will doubtless argue that they cannot possibly let this clarification of renunciation in the Baptismal Covenant stand unchallenged; but it is not for our opponents but for our *fellow-Christians* that we explain and illuminate our Christian Baptismal Covenant. Our opponents do not allow the Baptismal Covenant or Baptism to hold good for what Christians believe about them, so nor should Christians let go of their faith and their Baptism. Thus, when we illuminate and endeavour to explain the Christian foundation and the basic Christian teachings in the spirit of truth, it is enough for us that those who have honestly entered into the Baptismal Covenant and who have either found, or expect to find, rebirth in Baptism can find themselves enlightened and edified thereby. In particular they can find themselves strengthened against the many foolish objections under the appearance of wisdom which have recently been piled up *against* the renunciation of the Devil. Many Christians are tempted

---

390. Irenaeus (c.130-c.200). Born in Smyrna (now Izmir, Turkey), he is one of the first great Christian theologians. His book *Against Heresies* (c.180) in defence of the Church is a detailed attack on Gnosticism. He became Bishop of Lugdunum (now Lyon, France), where he died.
391. Mt 12:30; Lk 11:23.

to let them go, along with the *conjuration* of the Devil (exorcism). Our opponents have made every effort to confuse renunciation with conjuration – despite there clearly being the same difference between them as there is between the sinfulness that we all have in common and the Devil's actual possession of the *body*, which in most cases will be found doubtful and in every case belongs to the rare exception.

It is doubtless the case with all Christian enlightenment that in the *half*-light many have been unaware of their lack of faith. But they also come to see what Christianity gives expression to and what it presupposes, and they realise that the offer of this unrivalled purchase of all the treasures of Heaven nevertheless has its own specific price, for which it allows no power of bargain whatsoever. This is solely because at heart they have actually never believed in Jesus Christ made flesh; for as the Lord has said, "Whoever lives by the truth comes into the light, so that it may be seen plainly that what they have done has been done in the sight of God."[392]

Thus there were many who under the darkness of the papacy fancied that they believed in everything which we confess concerning both our Lord Jesus Christ and the Holy Spirit; but as the light of the Reformation revealed, this was far from being the case. The same thing will happen with the many who fancy that they believe 'Scripture' but who, when they see what Scripture means and assumes, will also see that this was far from being so. As regards renunciation of the Devil at Baptism, Christian enlightenment will doubtless satisfy a number who have been offended by it. This is either because they misunderstood it, or they could see neither its essential connection to the Creed, nor how indispensable it was for the testimony that no one has the right to name Jesus' name or take comfort in the grace of God and the forgiveness of sins in the name of the Saviour unless he first abandons all injustice! For just as everyone must know that truth and justice are inseparable, so only he who follows the truth does right. In like fashion, falsehood and injustice are inseparably linked, so it is impossible to hate a lie and love injustice, or excuse or justify injustice with anything other than a lie!

On the other hand, it is true that both this knowledge and the knowledge of everything that must be reckoned to the Devil's deeds and being – or rather, his odious practices (*pompa*), which are just as much those of the prince of darkness and spirit of death as they are of the father of lies – must make all true Christians much more vigilant and much more particular with themselves than they have been. Especially it must make them the best friends of all spiritual knowledge and freedom and the declared enemies of spiritual fraudsters, killjoys, and hypocrites. This cannot but be rewarded with such growing life-power, increased Christian enlightenment, and consolidation of peace and joy in the truth, that they will bless the day when the light dawns for them

---

392. Jn 3:21.

as regards renunciation and thereby sheds its heavenly radiance on the Saviour's face. His glory as the only-begotten of the Father is 'grace and truth', His Word is both life and light, His breath is peace, and His gaze brings joy to all His believers.

In our day, the renunciation of the Devil in the Baptismal Covenant has been the great stumbling-block with which scholarly opponents of the faith have had the power to torment Christians for as long as they were committed to tracing their Baptismal Covenant back to Scripture. But it is as clear as sunlight that the renunciation is the precious gemstone and immovable foundation stone in the building of eternal Truth, provided it is allowed to stand on its own ground, borne by the Word of His mouth which bears all things and is spirit and life, as He Himself has told us. This experience will not only calm our fears over every obscurity in living Christianity that our opponents refer to when they call us the 'children of darkness'; it will do much more by becoming the experience that we *are* and *shall be* the Spirit of Truth to which the unbelieving world is unreceptive. We become receptive to this Spirit through our renunciation of the father of lies and the spirit of lies; we shall lack neither the life nor the light that belong to fighting the good fight, completing the race, and keeping the faith. This will make us joyful in the Lord for ever, for we shall feel the power of God within us which will overcome the world, banish all darkness from our gaze, and destroy death completely for us. We may be sinful but we are pardoned, fallen but raised, darkened but re-enlightened; we are gloriously transfigured Christians!

16. The Apostles' Creed in the Christian Baptismal Covenant

All of thirty years have passed since it dawned on me that no writing of any kind or from any time gives *full* expression to the unchangeable Christian faith. Only 'the Word of faith in our mouths' does this – the oral, audible, public Confession of faith at Baptism according to our Lord Jesus Christ's own institution. This public confession has expressed the faith from the beginning and will express it until the end of the world as the shared faith of all Christians in which we are baptised in the name of the Father, Son, and Holy Spirit. The light that shone for me is like any real light, be it sun or moon. Once they have risen, they continue to shine for their allotted time, doing their duty without caring the slightest that all those who are blind and all those who deliberately shut their eyes *have* the right and indeed *are* right to say what is a fact: that they cannot *see* the light! Of course we must never forget that all spiritual light in this world, even the clearest, compares only with the sun and moon behind a cloud; for spiritual light always has many hindrances to break through – like the clouds.

This breakthrough of the Word of Truth which is spiritual light cannot happen with the pen. It is also equally as clear as sunlight that it is impossible to use writing to demonstrate that the Word of the heart in the mouth is quite different from, and far superior to, the Word in the pen on paper, so the most that any writing can demonstrate in this context is its own spiritual impotence. It follows inevitably that if the spiritual Word has performed any great spiritual *work*, it has not been from being on paper but from being ardently passed from mouth to mouth. So if we are to cherish any well-founded hope that the spiritual Word now and hereafter will perform any great spiritual work on earth, we must behave just as we read how the Apostles did on the great Day of Pentecost and thereafter for as long as they could preach the Word. We must open our mouths and tell what we ourselves believe and what we have felt by way of its power and effect, with the hope that this Word of faith in our mouths and hearts goes through the ears and makes its way into the hearts of our audience. There, we must hope, it will find the same faith as it has found in *our* hearts, and bring forth the same confession from their lips as it has from ours. If we are successful, we can copy the Apostles as far as we are endowed, and either write down what happened in the fullness of time or write letters to those who have heard and believed the Word. For those believers who have learned to read and have actually read it, such a letter can always offer some illumination and confirmation, some edification and comfort. We must also remember that it is not the unbelievers that we are writing for and to, so we must assume neither the air of preaching on paper nor the air of repelling opponents of the Word with our pens; otherwise we are only wearying the believers and laying burdens on them that the majority cannot bear.

So I am also writing here only for and to Christian readers who *themselves* are baptised in the faith that we all confess at Baptism and who find it proven that the faith that we who have hitherto been christened and baptised into, according to the Lord's own institution, is also the only shared, universal unchangeable Christian faith. Together with the corresponding Creed, this is the divine Word of faith, stating that faith is and must be the only unshakeable foundation for our living Christianity and that of the whole Church.

In so doing, I take for granted that it is a settled matter between my Christian readers and myself that our Creed at Baptism as recited throughout Christendom – wherever it has not been demonstrably changed – is what it *calls* itself: the genuine *Apostles'* Creed, as ancient as the faith, as Baptism, and as the Church. Among all Christians this Creed must remain as unchangeable as the faith itself, Baptism, the Church, the Lord, and the Spirit.

Among us then, the question is only what *kind* of faith our Creed expresses and what this Confession of faith at Baptism, in its insoluble connection with the renunciation, brings with it and accomplishes within us. I shall endeavour with my pen to point as clearly as possible to this, while leaving it to the Spirit, the human mouth, and the Church to make this knowledge living and fruitful.

Our Creed is not like a piece of alphabetic writing on paper! As a truthful Word in the believers' mouth it is the living expression of the entire Gospel of Christ which is a power of God for the salvation of all those who believe what we confess at Baptism. For it goes without saying that no other faith is needed for the forgiveness of sins and rebirth than the faith in which we are baptised with the forgiveness of sins and rebirth. Whoever demands of us a different foundation for faith is also preaching a different gospel – which is his own or the Devil's, but not the Gospel of our Lord Jesus Christ.

We cannot therefore possibly admit that in our Creed at Baptism anything small or large is missing as regards what a person must believe in order to become a true Christian and, in Baptism with the forgiveness of sins, be reborn by the Spirit to the life of the new person and of our Lord Jesus Christ. On the other hand there may well be something that the person who is *not* reborn cannot believe and which therefore our Creed at Baptism does not express, but which all believing and baptised, pardoned and reborn people will *come* to believe. This is clearly the case with the Lord's Word to us at His table with Holy Communion, which is a sense of the flesh so intolerable that only those reborn in the Spirit can truly say they believe it.

This is a fundamental truth of Christianity: that our Apostles' Creed at Baptism expresses what we all *must* believe in order to be true Christians, and that no new faith must be demanded of true Christians except the faith in the Words of Institution at Baptism that all worthy guests at the Lord's table must possess. This foundational Christian truth in no way ignores the fact that the Christian Church has a *holy book* which is very credible and which can make Christian readers who have the Holy Spirit firmer in their faith, surer in their hope, and wiser to God's counsel and God's ways. However, the foundational Christian truth of the Creed at Baptism excludes *of necessity* not only all papist articles of faith, but equally all literary and learned biblical and scholarly objections to the universal validity and the entirety of the Creed.

No scribe nor priest, no bishop nor pope, no apostle nor angel from Heaven must demand any other faith or Creed from the Church or exclude any person from the Church unless they are proved to have *denied* or defiantly *opposed* the Creed, or the plain words of the Baptismal Covenant. Any deviation from this makes the Church's faith unsound, turns Church teachers into faith masters, and entangles the Church in all the unavoidable disputes of the scribes concerning the origin, authenticity, extent, content, and interpretation of Holy Scripture. These are genuinely complicated matters about which few Christians can have any well-founded conviction and to which no true Christian scribe in the course of time can claim to have given an infallible testimony or a crystal clear account.

When we look more closely at our Creed at Baptism as the brief but complete foundational principle of the Christian faith we immediately realise that just as it teaches us what *kind* of a 'Father', 'Son', and 'Holy Spirit' He is in whose name we are baptised with the Baptism of our Lord Jesus Christ, so does the Creed reveal to us the distinguishing *mark* of the Christian faith: namely, that the one true God, the Creator of Heaven and earth who rules over all things, is a real father who has a real son and is so wonderfully loving a father of humankind that He allowed His only-begotten Son to become a real human child with the name of Jesus (the Saviour) Christ (the anointed). He allowed Him to suffer torture and death on the cross, but raised Him again from the dead, took Him up into heaven, set Him at His right hand, and will let Him judge the living and the dead; and finally, God the Father grants that His Holy Spirit at all times and in all places creates, nourishes, and sanctifies a Christian Church which in holy fellowship has the forgiveness of sins, the resurrection of the flesh, and the life everlasting.

This is the same way in which we Christian scribes have always endeavoured to interpret the well-known scripture: "God so loved the world that He gave His only-begotten son that whosoever believes in Him should not perish but have everlasting life."[393] Yet we owed the Church proof firstly that this scripture was a genuine recording of words from our Lord's own mouth and secondly that what we read into them

---

393. Jn 3:16.

came not from ourselves but was received from the Lord. However, we could not prove the former to those in the Church who had the greatest urge and need for it, the under-aged and the ignorant; the latter could only be proved by assuming and demonstrating the Creed at Baptism. This cannot possibly be proved or interpreted by written language; instead it proves and interprets that writing by saying the same thing in justified and clarified words. So we hear *why* God so loved the world, *who* was His only-begotten Son in whom we should believe, *what* is meant by believing in God's only-begotten Son for our salvation, and *how* through faith in God's only-begotten Son we have everlasting life.

[394]Wherever this is preached and interpreted with spirit, it is so self-evident that no one who wishes to be, or wishes to call himself 'Christian' would dare contradict it; but just as on our Christian preserves we allow no objection whatsoever against the fundamental Christianity of our Apostles' Creed, nor can we in the bosom of the Church allow any objection whatsoever against the purity and absolute truth of the Creed, so if there are any who call the conception of Jesus Christ by the Holy Spirit remiss or insignificant – or His birth by the Virgin Mary, His crucifixion and death under Pontius Pilate, or His descent into Hell, the kingdom of the dead, or His actual ascension, or His seat at the right hand of the Father and His second coming at the Day of Judgement, or any other element of the Creed – then we must maintain our unshakeable claim that the Word of faith in all its statements as well as in its entirety is a pure speech, like silver refined seven times,[395] and no one gains the Christian hope of salvation without building on the faith, complete and utter, which is expressed in the Christian Creed, whether or not he can explain to himself or others the reason for each statement in that pure speech.

This is one side of the question; on the other side we who call ourselves messengers of Christ and who are to inform the Church of the faith that the Spirit has granted us through Scripture or other means must take good care not to turn this information into 'articles of faith', either in the Creed in general or in its individual statements. Clearly, when we are firmly convinced that the illumination we offer is not our own but the Holy Spirit's, then we can manage with the certainty that the Holy Spirit, which is not just for us but for the faith and the Church as a whole, will confirm and testify to its illuminating powers among all our faithful audience.

For the free use of those who believe what we all confess, we can therefore state specifically that God the Father is called expressly "Creator of Heaven and earth" because human beings must not believe in any other God than their own and the whole

---

394. This paragraph follows Grundtvig's original syntax precisely and gives a flavour of the complexity of his writing. In the Danish it amounts to 207 words.

395. Ps 12:6.

world's Creator; so it must be obvious to everyone that the God to whose fatherly feeling we as Christians attach supreme importance is no other than the one true God and Creator. If we are nevertheless to be accused of idolatry because we worship the Son *and* the Holy Spirit as well as the Father, and because the preachers of the Gospel and our holy writers have always called both the Son and the Spirit 'God', the Creed still remains impeccable. The Church only has to answer for the worship that flows from the divine communion between the Father, Son, and Holy Spirit which the Word of Baptism makes real. In the meantime it is a matter for the Christian scribes alone to defend their use of the name of 'God', which is in any case easily justified, inasmuch as we – better than whoever wrote the Athanasian Creed[396] – have still kept the golden example of the Apostles in view: namely that although we may speak of God both in Heaven and on earth as though there were many gods and many lords, we nevertheless have only one God the Father, from whom all things *are*, and one Lord Jesus Christ, in whom all things *are*. This example will henceforward become clearer to us and make its presence much more keenly felt when we realise that the word 'Almighty' in our reference to the Father in the Danish Creed,[397] just like *omnipotens* in the Latin Creed, is only a makeshift word for want of a noun corresponding to the Greek *Pantocrator*, meaning He who has all things in His power – which in the context of the Creed is best translated as 'overlord'.[398] We are also fortunate that the Danish word 'three-in-oneness'[399] is a far better translation of the Latin *trinitatis* and the Greek *trias* to express the divine three-person consciousness which, with a foreign and ambiguous artificial phrase, we call 'the three persons of the Godhead'.[400]

This is the first and great statement we can make about the Creed and its proper use to draw the line between the Lord's *own* teaching, which is the foundation of the faith, and our *Christian* teaching which, even when it coincides completely with the Apostles' teaching, is not the actual foundation of the faith but its confirmation of the Holy Spirit on an unshakeable foundation: for the Apostles write that Jesus Christ is Himself the only justified foundation on which we can build either with gold and silver and precious gems (as the Apostles built) or (as the popes and our scribes have built) with wood, reeds, and straw, to be consumed in purgatory. We must not be surprised or shocked that this understanding will take time to be absorbed, since the difference between the Lord's and the Apostles' teaching has recently been misused to

396. Athanasius (c.297-373) was the 20th Bishop of Alexandria, whose episcopate lasted 45 years. He is credited with writing the first creed that included the three persons, but it is seldom used mainly because it ends with condemnation of those who do not believe: "And they that have done good shall go into life everlasting; and they that have done evil, into everlasting fire. This is the catholic faith; which except a man believe truly and firmly, he cannot be saved."

397. Grundtvig uses the Danish superlative *almægtigst* here.

398. Grundtvig uses the Danish noun *Over-Herren* here.

399. Grundtvig uses the Danish noun *Tre-Enighed* here.

400. Grundtvig uses the Danish phrase *de tre Personer i Guddommen* here.

obscure everything, as though Christianity at heart was not Christian at all, not the *actual teaching* of our Lord Jesus Christ. We would doubtless never have come into the light ourselves if the Spirit had not made us take it to heart that, like the Apostles, we must all hear the Word from the Lord's own mouth, by which we can recognise His Spirit from our own and from all the spirits of delusion.

The second major statement we can make about the Creed and its Christian use is that the name of God's only-begotten Son, 'Jesus Christ', even though it is unchangeable in every language, must still fuse together with the words in our own mother-tongues that dynamically express the concept of 'Saviour' and 'the Anointed One'; for only then can we have the feeling that Jesus Christ answers to His *name* and is truly what His name is meant to express. Through this we make clear that our salvation finds its living expression in the 'Jesus' of the Creed, so that it was as the Saviour that God's Son was born, died, and rose again, and that the name 'Christ' (Messiah) in the Creed is the living bond between the Old and the New Covenant. It goes without saying that the Spirit's scholarly instruments offer much information about the *nature* of salvation, redemption, and the riches that lie in the name of Christ and the anointment by God which Christ shares with all true Christians. Nevertheless, they cannot make *new* articles of faith out of such statements but must let the Church understand them as best it can and take what it can bear.

The third major statement about the Creed and its Christian use is that the Holy Spirit in whom we confess our faith, and in whose name together with the Father's and the Son's we are baptised, is the same Holy Spirit through whom God's only-begotten Son was conceived and born of the Virgin Mary as 'Jesus Christ'. What is added to His name in the Creed are His deeds and the effect by which He is known, just as the Father is known by the creation of the world and the Son by His earthly life. So our concept of the Christian Church and Christian Church life only comes alive through faith in the Holy Spirit as the self-aware Spirit of the Father and the Son and the life-force of the Church. To this belong all the other statements about the creation of the Church through faith and Baptism, about the formation of our holy fellowship through prayer and Holy Communion, and lastly about the spirit and the flesh, sin and grace, life and death, and time and eternity. In these cases again, such statements must not be turned into articles of faith for the Church but be left to the free use of the Spirit and the Church.

The fourth major statement on the Creed and its Christian application is that together with the renunciation it must be taken and trusted *in its entirety* as the Word of our Lord's own human mouth, since otherwise Baptism could not be an institution of the Lord Himself. Essential and equal to this belong both the *condition* for Baptism which He commended to the Apostles and the *words* for Baptism. These cannot be known as 'Christian' without being in an indissoluble link with the Word of faith which teaches us the name of *which* Father, Son, and Holy Spirit into whom we are baptised. To this major statement we must add all the statements we can make about the relation between the Lord and the Spirit, about the relation between these two and the Apostles (the servants of the Word), and the Church, and through them with the Father who is to be worshipped 'in spirit and in truth', meaning *alive* in the Son and the Spirit. However, we must not confuse these statements – which in the course of time may come across as more or less unclear – with the *main* statements, which are clear to all and absolutely essential if they are to adopt the faith with Baptism and understand the hope of life in our Lord Jesus' Christ's name.

The same is naturally true of the statements we can make about those individual elements of the Creed which experience has taught us from within and without are the most exposed to misunderstanding, doubt, and objection. Here too we must distinguish as sharply as possible between the universally valid main statement – which proceeds from the Word of faith itself – and the statements which proceed from elsewhere; such elements include the Lord's 'descent into Hell', His 'sitting at the right hand of God', and 'the resurrection of the flesh'.

The main statement about these elements is that they must be taken and believed in the meaning that the words give, so the Church must not allow any objection against them from its scholars, for these elements belong to the Creed and to the entire Church. Indeed they must have belonged from the very beginning, whether or not they were written down and whether or not, early or late, here or there, others have dared to exclude them or to change any of them.

As for the 'other' statements concerning firstly 'descended into Hell' and 'sitting at the right hand of the Father', it is the nature of the case that we cannot clearly imagine either Heaven or Hell but only the earth and what happens on it, so we should not try to give the Church a clear idea of 'the descent' and 'the right hand', much less demand it of them. We can only state that with regard to the descent into Hell – according to the word *inferi* which is used in the Latin Creed and *hades* which is used in the Greek – we are to think of 'the kingdom of the dead' in general, of what is called 'the resting-place' and 'the place of torment'. We must also remember that everything which is stated in the Creed about our Lord Jesus Christ is stated about Him as the *Saviour*. Thus we must accept that the Saviour came spiritually to the souls of the dead and preached not the Law but the Gospel to them. As experience proves, at present this statement is running into much opposition; but that must not keep us from reiterating it, any more than it should tempt us to make an article of faith out of it. It must only urge us to be even more attentive to every word we say about it, and to make it obvious to the Church that either we must assume the Gospel is preached to the dead who have not heard it in life, or we must deprive them of all hope of salvation – which God's love never allows. For to guess at a salvation outside the Gospel of Christ and a faith within it is, for Christians, so clear a contradiction in terms that even with a minimum of enlightenment we cannot fall into such an error.

As regards the seat of our ascended Saviour at the right hand of the Father, we cannot really make any other statement than the one our Lord Himself made in emphasising the Song of David: "The Lord said to my Lord: 'Sit at my right hand until I put your enemies under your feet.'"[401] For it goes without saying that the phrase 'right hand' should be taken metaphorically, since the reference here is not to an earthly but to a heavenly right hand in which the Father holds His power, meaning the Holy Spirit, which is the power from on high that gives the Son of Man, Christ, the Spirit at His service, also in his capacity as the Son of Man.

With regard to 'the resurrection of the flesh' we can see in the Apostolic Letters that this statement in the Creed was previously rejected or at least doubted and disputed;[402] the Church was both tempted and shocked. However, the Apostles set the same store by it as they did by the statement on the resurrection of the Saviour, so the two elements must stand and fall with each other. This is the major statement we can make for the Church on this subject, with the solemn warning never hereafter to allow the replacement of 'the resurrection of the flesh' with 'the resurrection of the body', which unfortunately has long been the case. Probably nothing bad was intended by this, but we know that ignorance has sought, and will continue to seek, a hiding-place behind the indefinite word 'body' – as though the body in question was not one of flesh and bone. We must hold firmly to the phrase, 'the resurrection of the flesh', for the sake of the Lord and the Church, which would otherwise be cheated of the hope of everlasting life in all its spiritual and physical fullness. To this we must add all the illumination we have regarding the spirit and flesh of humankind, made in the image of God, and clearly revealed to us in the Son of Man whom we worship, our Lord Jesus Christ. This will be shown even more clearly to the latter-day Christians, who will see the Lord's return to His Church, when, without any intervening death, they shall be physically renewed and transfigured, so their flesh is forever a pleasant dwelling, a perfect instrument, and a sunlit mirror for the Spirit of God. All this increasing enlightenment must be left for free appropriation, which we are sure cannot fail to be the case wherever the Spirit rules, as it issues from the Father to glorify the Son on earth.

---

401. Ps 110:1; Mt 22:44.

402. 2 Tim 2:18, "Hymenaeus and Philetus … have departed from the truth. They say that the resurrection has already taken place, and they destroy the faith of some"; 1 Cor 15:12ff, "But if it is preached that Christ has been raised from the dead, how can some of you say that there is no resurrection of the dead? If there is no resurrection of the dead, then not even Christ has been raised."

17. On our Third Article of Faith

Christianity in its genuine, original form is something new on earth. No one knows this unless they have heard and believe God's Word about it, as Scripture states: "How should they call upon the Lord without believing in Him, and how should they believe without having heard?"[403] Faith comes from hearing God's Word. That is why the Apostles of our Lord Jesus Christ wrote down their Christian knowledge only for and to Christians who had heard and believed and were baptised with Christian Baptism. This has only rarely been noted or imitated by the bishops and priests who were supposed to be the Apostles' successors, and it is a major cause of the great tangle we have got into over the proper meaning of the Apostolic Writings and all Christian matters. In vain and to our detriment have we both verbally and in writing quarrelled and haggled about them with ignorant Bible readers rather than share this enlightenment with believing Christians. If we wish to enlighten and benefit the Church with our Christian writings we must turn back to the Apostolic custom of focusing solely on believers and addressing them alone – with the specific addition that we know that when ignorant readers are presented with our writing they cannot but misunderstand our purpose.

So what I write here about our Third Article of Faith is written only for those who know how the Creed sounds at the Baptism with which we are baptised and whose content we believe. The reason I am publishing this article is only because it is the best way to reach the eyes of my fellow-believers in the Danish language and because the whole world is welcome to see what I as a believing Christian and servant of the Word am writing to my fellow-Christians about our common faith.

I would therefore like you all to note first that, since Martin Luther's little children's book,[404] what we are used to calling 'the Three Articles of Faith' are only a tri-partition of the Word of faith that is always recited at Christian Baptism; it is on this Word that we are baptised, once it is wholly confessed with an audible 'yes' to the Baptismal questions.

I then ask you to take to heart that this Word of faith at Baptism has been known to the Church from time immemorial as the sole element in our Baptismal Covenant.

---

403. Rom 10:14. Behind this chapter lies Grundtvig's belief that through the power of the Holy Spirit we meet the living Christ in the living Church, particularly in His Words of Institution at Baptism and Communion. Christianity is therefore not a 'school matter' but a Church matter – see ch. 4 in *The School for Life* (2011): 'Is Faith Truly a School Matter?'

404. Luther's *Small Catechism* was published in 1529.

This is the agreement we are to make on behalf of our Lord with all those who through Baptism in the Lord – in the name of the Father, Son, and Holy Spirit – wish to be received into the Church of our Lord Jesus Christ and thus share in the forgiveness of sins and the sure hope of salvation that He has promised to grant to all those who believe and are baptised. So it follows logically that whoever either *pretends* to say 'yes' to this Covenant and agreement or later *departs* from his word, has no benefit from his Baptism nor any share or part in what the Lord has promised those who truly believe His word and remain faithful until death.

Finally I assume here that you, my readers, have grasped this Word of faith to some extent through what it relates about God the Father, our Creator, and about God's Son, our Lord Jesus Christ and Redeemer. However, most of you are in great need of further enlightenment about the Holy Spirit and the role of the Word of faith at Baptism which expresses His work for our salvation.

Thus, for a number of years now I have observed that many who were well aware of what we confess at Baptism concerning the Father and the Son were very much in doubt as to what it actually is that we confess concerning the *Holy Spirit*. Since the reason for this must lie in the obscurity of the words by which the translators have rendered the Third Article into our mother-tongue, as well as the unacceptable changes they have made as they please, followed by their attempt to introduce them into our Lord's unchangeable Baptism, I shall now endeavour to shed light on both of these for my fellow-Christians.

We Christian scribes know the Word of faith in Greek and Latin from those who passed down Baptism and Christianity to us. We are better informed about the Christian sequence for salvation through knowing the Apostolic Writings[405] in their original Greek. Consequently we all know that the First Article of Faith expresses the reason why God has shown us such loving care and will forgive us all despite our having sinned. For He is the Father from whom all fatherliness takes its name both in Heaven and on earth, and He is our Creator, who would not have created all humankind in His own image *in vain*. Similarly, the Second Article of Faith expresses the *means* whereby God has revealed His gracious, fatherly character to us by giving us His only-begotten Son, the judge of the living and the dead, as our Saviour and Redeemer. Lastly, our Third Article of Faith expresses the fruits for us both of God's grace and of His only-begotten Son's incarnation as the means whereby His grace in Christ is shared *with* us and bears the fruit of salvation *among* us. Again and again the Spirit of God the Father and our Lord Jesus Christ, the Spirit of Grace and Truth with God's audible Word, calls and gathers believers and the baptised to His Holy Communion, where all worthy guests share the Lord's body and blood and their love

---

405. The 'Apostolic Writings' comprise the whole of the New Testament.

of God and their neighbour, and where they gain the living fellowship of eternal life with the soul and the body.

Our Creed at Baptism is thus a concise summary not of any Scripture but of God's evangelical counsel for our salvation. It is the Word of faith that our Lord Himself has placed on the lips of the Apostles and the entire Church to distinguish His people and His kingdom from all the peoples and kingdoms of this world and to give His entire Church a Word of God to which it can safely attach its faith and by which it can distinguish His Spirit from all the spirits of the world and all the spirits of error. Unfortunately, from early on this basic Christian enlightenment was overshadowed when those who should have been officers of Christ and servants of the Church made themselves *masters* of the Church and its faith, against the Lord's strict prohibition. It was as if they were what only the Lord's Spirit can be: the principal vice-regent in our ascended King's kingdom on earth; or as if it were only bishops and priests and not the entire believing and baptised Congregation of the Church that our Lord Jesus Christ will accompany, enlighten, strengthen, guide, and sanctify with His Father's Spirit.

Martin Luther realised this basic papist error and rightly castigated the self-exaltation with which the Roman Pope and his so-called clergy had set themselves in the Holy Spirit's place, or had led people to believe that the clergy alone had the Holy Spirit and were the spiritual leaders whom the rest of the Church should blindly trust and follow in the matter of salvation. It was a giant stride of Luther to separate our Three Articles of Faith in our Baptismal Covenant from all the self-made articles outside it, and a giant stride to take and understand our Third Article of Faith properly by following the only Spirit that calls, gathers, enlightens, and sanctifies the entire Church, which has begun its good work, and will complete it for the Day of our Lord Jesus Christ. But that was not enough for our scribes,[406] for they took the place of the Pope and his clergy, claiming that our Three Articles of Faith were a summary of Scripture which they alone understood how to interpret! This was how our scribes exalted themselves to becoming lords of the Church and the faith, yet they contradicted themselves when they admitted that the entire believing and baptised Church indeed *had* the Holy Spirit but that only the few who had searched the Scriptures could be *enlightened* about faith and salvation.

Even if our scribes had kept strictly to the Creed at Baptism and given it unanimous testimony, it would still have been their fault – in claiming the necessity of *scholarship* for the certitude of faith and salvation – that the Church sank as deep into scepticism as it had once before into superstition; now it doubted in particular who actually *possessed* the Holy Spirit and what could the entire Church expect of such people?

---

406. i.e. Lutheran scholars.

Moreover, doing as they pleased and acting on their own, our scribes made the Third Article of Faith, which was already very obscure in our language, even darker by writing and saying '*Christian* Church' instead of '*catholic* Church', 'resurrection of the *body*' instead of 'resurrection of the *flesh*', and finally by inserting an addition of their own making, 'after death', between 'resurrection' and 'everlasting life'. I would like to have informed the Church as to what can serve as an excuse for both the old and the new errors, which were in no way intended to distort the Creed. However, that would involve too much detail here and perhaps even be difficult for most readers to understand. More importantly I must beg the Church to take note that however valid His servants may think it, our Lord cannot accept any excuse whatsoever if they distort His words, knowingly or unknowingly, for the consequences are always the same for His Church. If it does not accept God's Word pure and simple, it cannot understand or enjoy the full blessings of that Word.

I say that our Third Article of Faith was already more obscure in our mother-tongue than it should have been, both in its use of the foreign, homespun word 'Church' instead of 'Congregation' or 'Gathering of the People' (in Greek and Latin *ekklesia*), and in its use of the indefinite 'society' instead of 'community'. Things took a further turn for the worse when 'Christian' – a word which the learned can quarrel over until Judgement Day – replaced 'universal' – which everyone could see expressed what everywhere and at all times was identical. When they replaced 'resurrection of the flesh' with 'resurrection of the body', the Congregation was tempted to dream of another *kind* of body than the one of flesh and bone, which could only lead the Congregation to think that it was not until *after* death that Our Lord would grant us a share of eternal life, even though He had promised all his faithful that He would open a life-source in them with His Spirit that would be a wellspring to an everlasting life.

[407]It is thus our primary concern as Christian scribes to inform the Church that our Third Article of Faith should express in Danish neither more nor less than our faith in the Holy Spirit's presence in the entire holy Church as being the holy catholic gathering of the people, and in the communion of the saints with the forgiveness of sins, the resurrection of the flesh, and the life everlasting. If the Church already knows this, then it hardly needs our enlightenment in order to see that the word 'Church' and every other obscure word that has been used instead of Christian 'Congregation'

---

407. In the following paragraph Grundtvig's original Danish words, followed by the English translation, are as follows: *kirke*=Church; *Menighed*=Congregation; *Folke-Samling*=Gathering of People; *Samfund*=Community; *Fællesskab*=Communion; *christelig*=Christian; *almindelig*=catholic/universal; *legeme*=body; *kjød og ben*=flesh and bone; *de hellige*=the saints. The matter is complicated further by the fact that Grundtvig uses two words that are normally best translated as 'Church': *Menighed*, meaning the Church as people, and *Kirke*, meaning the Church as institution. It is impossible to retain this distinction throughout in English, where the word 'congregation' is more closely linked to the individual church, so I have added the word 'Christian' before 'Congregation' to underline the distinction.

or 'Gathering of People' has proved very damaging, both as an eclipse of the Church's relation to the Spirit and as a loophole for the Pope and all those who as 'Lords of the faith and the Church' wished to set themselves up in place of the Holy Spirit, or at least be assumed to have the Holy Spirit all to themselves and thus be the sole medium between the Spirit and the Church.

Similarly, we believe the Church will be open to the further enlightenment which, in accordance with the other Words of Institution both at Baptism and Holy Communion and with the Apostolic Writings, we must provide concerning the work of the Holy Spirit. As Luther remarked in his explication of our Third Article of Faith, this begins with the preaching of the Gospel and does not end until the entire Church has been glorified, including *bodily* glorified, in the everlasting life.

The first point to notice here is that the Holy Spirit which accomplishes the entire work of the Godhead in the Church and in whose name we are baptised equally with 'the Father' and 'the Son', must not be assumed to be a mere power or a kind of angel; it is what we have called 'a divine person', meaning the power of God on high, which is self-aware and shares itself wherever it wishes, for in a divine sense it is independent and free.

What is true of all spirits, including spiritual weaklings like us, is that they are invisible and can only reveal themselves in the invisible word through the power they place in it and the effect they thereby produce in circles of the spirit and heart, large or small. This is also true of the Spirit of the Lord and His Church, which is the Holy Spirit issuing from the Father. In order to distinguish the Holy Spirit and His work from all erroneous and inferior spirits it is vital to know the Word through which He *works and reveals* His spiritual power, just as we reveal our spiritual power or impotence in our words, and just as every people's spirit reveals its power in that people's mother-tongue. This Word of power of the Holy Spirit in which He reveals Himself and with which He accomplishes all His divine work in us, is the Gospel or Christmas message of Christ. It is vitally expressed in the Word of our Lord Jesus Christ through His divine institutions, Holy Baptism and Holy Communion, and primarily in the Word of faith which everyone at Baptism must confess and must believe in order to be received by the Lord into His Church.

Only where this Word of faith, Baptism, and Holy Communion is spoken purely in its proper place and in its proper order do we find the Spirit of our Lord Jesus Christ; only in those who in their hearts *believe* this Word does He accomplish His work; only those preachers of the Gospel in whose preaching this Word of the Lord is the *soul* are impelled by the Holy Spirit; and only they and they alone are His instruments for carrying out His work in the Lord's Church.

Naturally, this world in which we live never *can* nor *will* believe in our Lord Jesus Christ. The Spirit of our Lord Jesus Christ does not speak of His own accord but only of what He hears, and He gives us a divine testimony to the Word of the Lord by making it spirit and life for us. But *this* world will never admit that He is what we call Him with the Word of the Lord at Baptism: 'the Holy Spirit', the Spirit of holiness or of purity of heart and truth. Nor is it worth arguing with the world about this, since in the course of time it can only be proved in and for believers through the working of that Holy Spirit on their hearts. What the Spirit of our Lord Jesus Christ can prove, has proved, and proves each day to the world is only that He is the Spirit above *all* spirits. The Lord's Spirit proved this with His first revelation at the great Pentecost, when he endowed the Apostles with the ability to speak the Gospel of Christ with life and power to all peoples *in their own language*. The Spirit of the Lord has continued to prove this over the course of time and proves it far more completely as the days pass. Wherever Christ's true Gospel is preached and heard – with Baptism and Holy Communion according to the Lord's own institution – it takes possession of every people's language. Then His 'instruments' can speak with far *more* life and power about Jesus Christ and all that is His than the instruments of the *people's* spirits have been able to about a people and their heroes and demi-gods and their own version of faith, hope, and love. However, this divine continuation and verification of the miracle of Pentecost with the glowing tongues has remained obscure to most Christians because their natural way of thinking has been infected by the inanity of the world. For it goes without saying that if one has no feeling for the spirit and language of one's *own* people as being the life-power in word and thought of the invisible things inside and above us, the divine and the human matters, then one cannot make any comparison between this spirit and that of our Lord Jesus Christ and His Church.

There is therefore not much point in writing to the Church about what it means to be gathered and born into a new Israel by the Lord's Spirit at Baptism and Holy Communion, into a spiritual people of God raised above all the peoples of the world as the Lord is raised above all lords and His Spirit above all spirits. Nor is there much point in writing about 'the communion of saints' whom the Lord's Spirit cherishes with the Lord's Prayer and the Lord's Table and which also surpasses the most living fellowship between earthly parents and children, brothers and sisters, friends and married couples as much as the love of God and our Lord Jesus Christ surpasses all natural human love. For to be able to appreciate this, we must first know the natural life and culture of our own people from its best side. Although carnality continues to be dominant, in our *best* side there is so much spirituality and cordiality that we can gain from it the living measure which can teach us to appreciate the unparalleled power and love in the spirit of God's people and the heart of the Christian brotherhood.

It is doubtless possible to write better than I can about the gifts of the Holy Spirit in the name of our Lord Jesus Christ to the whole Church and to the Christian Community, since each of us who feels they are a sinner also feels that they are in dire need of forgiveness. We experience how it is found nowhere but in the Church of our Lord Jesus Christ and how each of us who feels our mortality also knows something of the bitterness of death and knows that, in contrast, no plant grows except in God's Paradise and there is no comfort except the hope of the soul and the body for eternal life. However, for as long as we have no living sense of our acceptance as God's people and of our incorporation into the community of saints, we cannot have the full and satisfying assuredness of the forgiveness of sins, the resurrection of the flesh, and the life everlasting that the Holy Spirit grants. For He is not sent to any individual but to the entire Church; He does not grant forgiveness and eternal life to us individually but only to all and everyone in the entire Church that He is gathering and in the Congregation that He is creating.

On the other hand, using both the mouth and the pen we must impress upon believers that a major obstacle to their Church awareness and to their feeling any 'heart-fellowship' can only be swept away by making the Creed, Baptism, and Holy Communion according to the Lord's institution a completely free matter, in both a temporal and a civic regard. Far from luring or threatening anyone to a confession of their faith and to rebirth in the Lord's Baptism and brotherhood at His table, Christians must counsel all people and beseech them never to lie to God by confessing a faith they do not have, or by deriding the Lord's means of salvation. This they do when, without any faith in the Father, Son, or Holy Spirit, they have themselves baptised in the name of the Trinity and, without any request for a 'heart-fellowship' with our Lord Jesus Christ and all His friends, are unworthy to eat His flesh and drink His blood. For only then will it be revealed that in those who believe and are baptised the Lord has bought Himself a 'peculiar people'[408] and that at His table all His friends learn to love one another as He has loved His own.

It is therefore very sad that also among us there are many believers who shun freedom and in so doing turn away the Lord's Spirit which calls us all *into* freedom and can only be revealed *in* freedom, since all spiritual slavery can only darken and conceal His work. For when we hear millions confessing the Word of faith and being baptised and fed with the Word of Grace and everlasting life without it being *seen* on them, then their unhappy and ungodly slavery to sin and death is unmistakeable. It is impossible to place one's faith in the Word, with God's Spirit inside one, and to keep that faith, unless we see through this indefensible copycat game being played with the Word of faith and the means of grace. It is in an attempt to force or contrive any one of God's gifts, but these are offered solely from His own free grace and can only be received from the hand of the Lord *with free faith and gratitude*.

---

408. 1 Pet 2:9.

Only when we deeply lament, instead of defending, the disorder that worldly Christianity and Church discipline[409] have created, can we in the midst of such disorder begin to glimpse God's path on earth and His order of salvation for all peoples. Among all those, be they few or many, who truthfully say 'yes' to the Baptismal Covenant and seek rebirth in Baptism He begins His good work with the forgiveness of sin. Without this, no rebirth to everlasting life is possible, since the wages of sin is death, but *from* this, rebirth inevitably follows. For when our Creator forgives us all our sins He takes us into His grace, as a father can forgive his naughty but repentant child. God's grace must be the source of eternal life, as it is written: "For the wages of sin is death, but the gift of God is eternal life in Christ Jesus our Lord."[410]

However, just as it is in the name of our Lord Jesus Christ as much as for His sake and through the words from His mouth alone that we can gain forgiveness of sin, resurrection of the flesh, and everlasting life, so is it first at the Lord's Table through the words from His mouth that we are made sharers in the body He sacrificed for us and the blood he shed for our forgiveness. Through these the Lord's Spirit – in our loving communion (in Greek *koinonia*, in Latin *communio*) with Him and with one another – helps us to feel the blessed assuredness that all our sins were wiped clean when the handwriting that condemned us was nailed to the cross with our Lord Jesus Christ. In His love we have crossed over from death to life, so that the death of the body, though we must suffer it, will not damage us but will be gloriously defeated by our resurrection in 'flesh and bone' – in the name of our crucified Lord who to this end rose from the grave for us.

Only when we truly connect our faith and confession to Baptism and Holy Communion as the Lord's means of grace in His great work of redemption and salvation do we feel that the Lord's Spirit, the eternal life-force, becomes active in us, so that we can grow in the grace and knowledge of our Lord Jesus Christ.

The good news that out of His great love God has sacrificed His only-begotten Son so that all who believe in Him should not perish but have everlasting life only sheds its light on us when we learn through the Word of faith at Baptism what kind of *God* it is who loves us so much, *who* is His only-begotten Son sacrificed for us, *what* it means to believe in Him, *by what means* we are saved from perdition, and *how* we thus gain everlasting life.[411] Similarly, this good news only becomes spirit and life for us when it

---

409. 'Church discipline' (1 Cor 5 et al.) is the practice of censuring church members to elicit repentance and reconciliation through a progressively administered procedure of 1) admonition, 2) suspension from Holy Communion, and ultimately 3) excommunication. In Denmark in the late Middle Ages miscreants, whose sin was often of a sexual nature, could be publicly named in church and shamed outside it with the iron collar attached to the church wall; such a collar can still be seen in the bell tower at Varnaes Church in South Jutland.

410. Rom 6:23.

411. As one of only a handful of western theologians Grundtvig did not accept that the Holy Spirit also issues from the Son (*filioque*).

comes as warm, living words from our Lord's own mouth. The written word can never do this; it can only be derived from the spoken word and can only point to that. Our Third Article of Faith – or our Confession of faith in the Holy Spirit and His work in which life has come to us – is again revealed; for only in the Spirit is God *with* us and only through the Spirit does God work *in* us, from the Day of Ascension to the Day of Judgement. Therefore, however much we believe in the Father and the Son, as the Creed runs, it can only be a dead faith if we do not also believe in the *Holy Spirit*. For it is only the Spirit that quickens and accomplishes all things which the Father has promised us and which the only-begotten Son has earned and bought for us. So just as the new life in Christ Jesus has always grown weaker and darker as faith in the Holy Spirit faltered and the Third Article of Faith became obscured, so will the future always prove that the new life in Christ becomes stronger and lighter to the degree that faith in the Holy Spirit is strengthened and our Third Article of Faith is illuminated for us.

18. The Lord's Prayer

Our Lord Jesus Christ's own prayer, 'Our Father', was created to teach His disciples how to pray. It is so much part of our Basic Christian Teachings that we barely need to mention it, let alone be told to take it deeply to heart, to discuss it, and to illuminate it. Taking this matter so lightly has caused great damage, for not one of us can have a well-founded assurance of being 'God's child' without having sought that assurance precisely in the Lord's Prayer.

For far too long we have laboured under the delusion that like everything else we can only read about the Lord's Prayer in the Apostolic Writings, but as all experience teaches, it does not help much to *read* the prayer. As Martin Luther has enjoined, to *pray* the Lord's Prayer requires more than just having learned it by heart. With us, as with the Lord's first disciples, this means that we have received it *from the mouth of the Lord Himself* and have been given the power to be God's child through faith in His name. This can only be the case if the Lord's Prayer belongs to Baptism, not just as it belongs anywhere in the Christian service but specifically and inseparably to Baptism according to the Lord's own institution. Here the Lord Himself teaches all His disciples to pray and gives them the same power to be God's children as well as to pray as such, which basically amounts to the same thing; one can no more be God's child and pray to the heavenly Father who has made the dumb speak than one can truly be God's child without actually being so!

Consequently, the Lord's Prayer comes to us all at Baptism primarily as the assurance from the mouth of the Lord Himself that when we believe in our hearts what we confess with our mouths at Baptism – words upon which we are baptised in the name of the Father, Son, and Holy Spirit – then we are truly "children of God". As Scripture says: "In Christ Jesus you are all children of God through faith, for all of you who were baptised into Christ have clothed yourselves with Christ."[412] In response to those high-flown people who look down on all the Basic Christian Teachings, Martin Luther spoke a great truth when he made a point of saying that if he could only *speak the first words* of the Lord's Prayer properly, he would be very happy! For we can be quite sure that none of us can call the maker of Heaven and earth 'Our Father' with the heart's trust and confidence unless we feel sure that we *are* His children. This is why the Apostle Paul expressly states that it is only with the Spirit of the chosen Son

---

412. Gal 3:26.

that we can shout "Abba, Father!",[413] in that *His* Spirit testifies with *our* spirit that we are God's children. He Himself placed His prayer on our lips at Baptism to be our daily prayer and His divine pledge of our rebirth in Baptism as God's children. As a prayer therefore it is only spoken appropriately by God's children, in whose mouths and hearts it can alone be Truth. Through this prayer a beautiful, shining light rises over two great mysteries that had previously been obscure to us all. First, where were we to find the external divine assurance that in Baptism according to the Lord's own institution we are reborn as 'children of God'? And second, how with our own spirit should we recognise the internal witness of God's Spirit that we *are* God's children? Now, however, we see that the same Lord's Prayer which we received at Baptism from the Lord's own mouth is the external *divine assurance* of our child's right to Heaven, and when we feel able to pray the prayer from the bottom of our heart, it is powerful proof that we *are* God's children, that with our spirit of the divine *Father's* Spirit we *are* the testimony. So we cannot possibly pray the Lord's Prayer as God's children unless we truly *are* God's children.

It is not until we regard the Lord's Prayer in its living Christian context, both in our rebirth at Baptism and with the testimony of the Holy Spirit in the believing heart, that we see from where we have *received* this prayer, namely from the mouth of the Lord Himself, and for what *purpose* we have received it, namely as an external and internal pledge of our right to be called, and our power actually to be, truly, God's children. Once we have realised this, we see the reason why the Lord's Prayer is and must be the unceasing prayer of all Christians both in private and in public, the prayer of each individual and of the entire Church, since it is the only prayer that God's children have for themselves. They can trust that it contains and expresses everything that God's children on earth have in order to pray to their heavenly Father and be sure that He hears, grants, and always fulfils their prayer, for it is the prayer of His only-begotten Son.

On Sundays therefore, when our old pastors, having prayed for the Church, the royal family, and for all the sick and the sorrowful, far or near, used to say: "Everything else that we wish to pray for we shall include in our Lord Jesus' own, consummate prayer, the Lord's Prayer", it could be both well-intentioned and in a way edifying. Yet it also testified to a lack of Christian enlightenment; for as Christian people and God's children all that we have to pray about to our heavenly Father is already divinely included and expressed in the Lord's own consummate prayer, and indeed must be so, for otherwise it would not be the consummate prayer of either the only-begotten Son, our Lord, or of God's consummate children.

---

413. Mk 14:36; Rom 8:15; Gal 4:6.

We must not conclude from this that every other prayer than the Lord's Prayer is forbidden for Christians or unworthy of God's children on earth: the Gospel is not a law, so it forbids nothing. As the Apostle writes, "Everything is permissible for me, but not everything is beneficial."[414] So if another prayer than the Lord's Prayer can be beneficial on earth, whether for God's child himself or for other people, then it is not only permissible but is also God's own Spirit stepping forward for us with an ineffable sigh and impelling us to pray it. This is just as we see it in the Gospels, where God's only-begotten Son, our Lord Jesus Christ, prayed here on earth both for Himself and for others, also with more and different words than those which in the Lord's Prayer He had laid on the lips of His first disciples and at Baptism on His entire Church. We can only conclude that the Lord's Prayer contains and expresses everything that God's children need for all time and in all places in order to pray with full assurance that their requests will be granted. Every other prayer that we pray, either out of our frailness or on particular occasions or in particular circumstances, is only 'Christian' insofar as it is Christians who pray it and wait for it to be granted and insofar as it can fuse together with the Lord's Prayer or at least be linked to it. Thus, Jesus prayed to His heavenly Father for the restoration of life to Lazarus, for the preservation of Simon Peter's faith in the midst of his denial, and for Himself to be spared the bitter chalice – though only insofar as the work of redemption could remain undamaged and only on the premise that the will of God the Father could be done in Heaven as it is on earth.

We believers must also assume that such a consummate prayer for all God's children on earth is as certain as the divinity of our Lord Jesus Christ; but we also realise this more clearly the longer and better we pray this prayer in our Lord Jesus' name. For the brighter its content shines, the greater its expression of life for us, so that all the prayers we or others have put together, and have for a while believed to be clearer or richer in content, pale in the face of the Lord's Prayer as sun and moon pale against the radiance of God's glory.

As with the Three Articles of Faith, so with the seven prayers in the Lord's Prayer: just as the three are one so are the seven one. Thus we cannot pray just one of the seven prayers in the Lord's Prayer without actually praying them *all* – and thus the whole Prayer. So we cannot really affirm one of the Three Articles without affirming them all, and all the statements within them. It is thus as clear as sunlight that no one can from the bottom of his heart call the true God his 'Father' without genuinely *feeling* that he is God's child, for God's fatherly spirit hovers over the whole prayer. So not until we *believe* the prayer do we understand it, and not until we place a corresponding childlikeness into the whole prayer can we pray it from the bottom of our hearts and in the name of the only-begotten Son, our Lord Jesus Christ.

414. Paul in 1 Cor 10:23.

Ever since the days of Martin Luther, this has been taken very lightly. No one has noticed that the name that God's children pray to should be 'hallowed', the kingdom that they pray to will indeed 'come' and the will that they pray to shall indeed 'be done on earth as it is in heaven', for this is the name, kingdom, and will of our heavenly Father! Even less has it been emphasised that prayer in our Lord Jesus' name, which not even the Lord's Apostles had command over when He went to the cross, amounts to far more than just placing the name of Jesus on one's lips; even unbelievers can do that whenever they like, and have indeed done so countless times. Yet both points are of such importance that whoever does not feel this cannot possibly call "Abba, Father!" to the true God or pray a single word of the Lord's and all God's children's prayer in our Lord Jesus' name.

Thus, so long as we do not feel that it is specifically the name, kingdom, and will of our heavenly Father we are speaking and praying to in the Lord's Prayer we can neither have a proper feeling that the prayer is an *evangelical* one, which is as far distant from all prayers under the Law as the Gospel of Christ is from the Law of Moses, nor can we move any more than our lips, in other words, move our hearts to begin with the name, kingdom, and will of God instead of with our daily bread and the forgiveness of sins.

It follows from this that as the first Tablet of the Law has to do with what we owe God and the second with what we owe our neighbour, a true prayer according to the Law should first be directed to God's *honour* and only then to the raising and saving of the fallen. However, we cannot find it in the *Law* as it is in the *Gospel*, with joy and mercy, for in these we find God's love as revealed in the Gospel. This tells us that although we did not love God as we should according to the Law, God nevertheless loved *us* and sent His Son to redeem our sins. God is well aware that only His undeserved mercy and fatherly love can move our hearts to love Him again as He has first loved us, so neither in word nor deed will He make good His *legal* demand on us. Only now can we see that God has never done so, even though the Lord's Prayer begins with what belongs to God when His fatherly care spreads its wings over us and our prayer; for then His name, kingdom, and will as Father fuse together with ours as His children. Whatever is to the honour of our heavenly Father, to the glory of His kingdom, and to the fulfilment of His will is also to the everlasting honour, peace, and joy of His children. It follows from this that as God's children we pray from our hearts first for what is the ground of our salvation and only then for what we need for today and tomorrow while the hourglass runs.

Thus we come via the path of the Gospel to what we could never come to via the path of the Law: to seek first the kingdom of God and His justice, being certain that everything follows in its wake when our heavenly Father, who knows what we need, grants us everything. Then what is written confirms itself: that the rights of the Law are fulfilled in those of us who seek not the flesh but the Spirit, for the love that is the fulfilling of the Law[415] is poured into our hearts through God's fatherly care in the granting of the Holy Spirit so that our hope of salvation is not put to shame.[416]

However, just as it is only God's fatherly care that can give us the will to pray the Lord's Prayer properly, so is it only in our Lord Jesus' name that we can be given the *power* to do so – and in general to be God's children. The deepest reason for this is that our Lord Jesus Christ is God the Father's only-begotten *Son*, which at first glance would seem to exclude *us* from the child's right in the house of the heavenly Father, but on closer scrutiny shows only the *need to believe* in the name of God's only-begotten Son and to pray the Lord's Prayer in His name in order truly to be God's children and pray this prayer. Since God is all that He is for ever and ever, everything that He *is* for Him to be Father is also for ever, and those who in the course of time shall be God's children can only be so through faith in God's only-begotten Son for ever. This is also why in calling us God's chosen children, Scripture sets a justifiable line between ourselves and God the Father's only-begotten Son. However, since God's choice must be a true lineage and adoption which truly gives us both a child's right and an eternal right of inheritance to the kingdom of God, not only must we from the beginning be in such a relationship to God the Father's only-begotten Son – through whom all things have been – that we can have complete spiritual and cordial communion with Him; it must also be the faith's *secret* that this communion commences through faith! So we come to the feeling and the joy that everything belonging to the only-begotten Son is *ours*, just as everything of ours is His; in other words we come to the same unity with the Son as the perfect love that has for ever existed between the Father and the Son.

To pray the Lord's Prayer in Jesus' name is therefore not just to pray it as *His* prayer, nor is it enough that we only expect it to be granted for *His* sake; we must pray it on His *behalf*, just as He prays it on ours, that is, in the feeling of unity with Him, through faith and in the Holy Spirit. This is why it was impossible for the Apostles to pray in the name of our Lord Jesus *before* they had received the Spirit of God the Father in common with Him, and it is impossible for us too without the same Spirit. This helps us to feel communion with the Lord and attests our divine child's right in the only-begotten Son by giving us the power to pray the Lord's Prayer in our Lord Jesus' name.

Consequently, all the so-called 'interpretations' of the Lord's Prayer that are given without this light are made haphazardly in the dark, and give the 'consummate' Prayer the appearance of dark poverty rather than revealing its riches. Even Martin Luther's interpretation, although one of the very best, has the major flaw that it sets forth the hallowing of God's name, the coming of God's kingdom, and the fulfilment of God's will as feeble repetitions of one and the same thing, and with

---

415. Rom 13:10.
416. Rom 5:5.

a focus on God's name, God's kingdom, and God's will in general rather than God the Father's in particular.

For when it is made vividly clear to us that it is the *Father*-name of God that must be 'hallowed' from all defilement and abuse; that it is the kingdom of God the *Father* that will come with the love that is all in all; and that it is the will of God the *Father* that will be done as fully, exclusively, and perceptibly on earth as in Heaven, then we immediately see that we are hereby praying for the very best, for 'the consummate' in every way. This has by no means been achieved, however cleanly and purely God's Word is learned, however perceptibly God's kingdom is among us, and however wisely God prevents evil counsels and ungodly works. To the same degree that our longing increases for what we are praying, the Spirit gives us a foretaste of the powers of the coming world; for in every believing heart where the Spirit issuing from the Father is allowed freedom of action, the Father-name of God is *hallowed* in secret, the kingdom of God *comes* in secret, and the will of God the Father is *done* in secret on earth as it is in Heaven.

However much there is to say about each step on the heavenly ladder that the Lord's Prayer truly becomes when it is received from His mouth and is enlivened and enlightened by His Spirit, we must never forget that we cannot with the pen express a single word out of our own spirit and life-force, let alone out of God's; we can only point with our pen to the mouth from which God's Word issues and to the heart where through faith it enters and makes its dwelling. This pointer is for the enlightenment of those alone who have their eyes open to the great light that arose over us, as we sat in darkness and in the land of the shadow of death. For them this pointer will be clear enough, so they will see how divinely well-founded is all the love they have felt for the Lord's Prayer as the prayer above all others, and all the trust they have placed in the Lord's Prayer as the only-begotten Son's own prayer, which is always assured of being granted by the heavenly Father. They will see furthermore that in a Christian sense much is required of anyone who 'wishes to know more than their Lord's Prayer', whereas what has previously been accorded great praise goes for very little: that is, to know one's Lord's Prayer no better than the majority of both scholars and laymen these days.

In my own case it took quite a long time before I realised how considerate the Lord was in teaching us at Baptism to *pray*, just as He teaches us thereby to *believe*. In Baptism He also grants us the child's right and with His blessing of peace the forgiveness of sins. Despite my pointer I must not be surprised if the same experience befalls many other disciples, so they find it hard to believe their eyes and ears and learn to live with the divine wealth of riches that the Lord has deliberately placed in His divine Basic Christian Teaching. And although I must sincerely congratulate all my fellow-Christians on these many blessings, yet forecast for them that we shall in fact receive none of them unless in faith we take possession of all that has been granted to us collectively, I shall nevertheless with God's help not forget that it is He alone who has begun and can complete His good work in us, and that the Spirit which issues from the Father has all the virtues of the heavenly Father and quite clearly His fatherly patience.

19. Christianity in the New Testament

We all know that in everyday speech the words 'New Testament' mean neither more nor less than the Christians' own Holy Scripture – in contrast to the Holy Scripture that belongs to the Jews, to which the Christians gave the name 'Old Testament'. But 'testament' is a foreign word for us; it comes to us from Roman law as a legal term to denote the last, witnessed will of the deceased. Very few people know what the book title that we have given to the Christians' holy writing actually *means*. This might also be immaterial if the same designation were limited to the book. But it is the same with the designation 'New Testament' as it is with the 'Church': that out of weakness or for other poor reasons, we have used the same designation for two fundamentally different things. This always causes confusion, and when ignorant or wily people hold forth, it is the cause of *endless* confusion. By employing a foreign word to designate the entire Christian Congregation as well as our Sunday-house and its housekeepers with the word 'Church', we have obscured the most honest and reasonable talk about things which are worlds apart. And when wily priests and popes set themselves up in place of the Lord and put the external before the internal, they see the most desirable opportunity in this vagueness of speech and half-light of thought.

It was just like the scholars giving the same designation to the whole of Christianity and to our Sunday book. In so doing they obscured even the most honest and reasonable talk about things which are worlds apart. So when vain and ambitious schoolmasters and scholars set themselves to replace our reading in faith and spirit, they found the most advantageous opportunity in the ambiguity of the language and the uncertainty of the congregation. The fact is that the Greek word *diatheke*, which in Latin is translated as *testamentum*, means both what we call a 'covenant' and a 'testament', so that 'Christianity' in Greek can be called *kaine diatheke*, a new covenant, but not in Latin *novum Testamentum*, nor in half-Danish, half-Latin *'det ny testamente'*. Despite this, both in our biblical translation and in the Lord's address to us at Holy Communion we use the designation 'new testament' to cover Christianity in general, just as we use it for the Apostolic Writings. Thus, ignorant and wily people can very well mix the two up by saying that the 'new testament' *is* Christianity, with the result that the chalice of the 'new testament' becomes the chalice *to the letter* and the ministers of the 'new testament' become ministers *to the letter*, even though the Apostle specifically wrote that he did not mean this literally but rather meant the exact opposite: they are to be ministers to the *Spirit*![417]

While it might be a matter of indifference whether we call the Apostolic Writings 'the New Testament' or 'the new book' or 'the new covenant book', it has given rise to a dangerous confusion that we gave the book the same designation as Christianity – with all its spirit and life. For by a concealed word-play we have put the letter in place of the spirit and a written testament in place of the living covenant and pact. So when we come to unravelling this terribly complicated relation, we must begin by saying openly: The new covenant between our Lord and us is the Baptismal Covenant, which is established between all those who according to our Lord's own institution wish to be baptised in the name of the Father, Son, and Holy Spirit, to whom, through reciting the Creed at Baptism, they link themselves indissolubly without reference to the book that we call the 'New Testament'.

There is not the slightest reason to call this claim an insult to the Apostolic Writings. For not only is it a fact that the New Covenant at Baptism was established from the very first with no regard to the Apostolic Writings. It is equally obvious that when our Lord and His Apostles ordained Baptism and established the New Covenant they could not possibly have taken into consideration writings that did not exist! So nor should we – unless of our own free will we are willing to deviate from our Lord and His Apostles and thereby misappropriate His Covenant and its institution. Finally, far from presenting themselves as the 'New Covenant' or the 'Christian Foundation', the Apostolic Writings constantly refer to an *oral* Word of God, to a covenant of the *heart*, and to a *living* foundation.

Conversely, if anyone claims that the Baptismal Covenant, the very expression of Christianity with regard to its authenticity, is actually *independent* of the Apostolic Writings and that therefore these have nothing to do with it, whether it be as confirmation, illumination, or explanation, then they are pursuing their own claim and calling it mine! For I have assiduously attempted to show that the Apostolic Writings throughout *presuppose* this Baptismal Covenant and Creed of ours and thereby testify to their Apostolic authenticity, just as the same Apostolic Writings contribute to such a great understanding of the Baptismal Covenant and true Christian enlightenment that we must consider them indispensable.

Finally it has recently been said that if this is so, then there are no grounds for dispute but only for agreement between all those who acknowledge the Baptismal Covenant and the Apostolic Writings as foundational Christianity. They can always be understood better, but they can never be changed. This has been precisely my con-

417. 2 Cor 3:6. "He has made us competent as ministers of a new Covenant – not of the letter but of the Spirit; for the letter kills, but the Spirit gives life."

viction and claim from the outset, though no one would accept it. They cannot take it from me, but on the contrary are driving me further towards providing them with all the information I can about the true and proper relation between the Baptismal Covenant and the Apostolic Writings. This relation had become so disturbed that they not only called the book what the *Covenant* is, they even made the book that presupposes the Covenant the actual *source* of that Covenant, and turned the book that is the work of the Apostles and the property of the Church into the Apostles' deed of institution and the statute book of the Church!

That is why I have always declared those people to be my fellow-Christians who of their own free will enter into the same Baptismal Covenant as I, and who baptise with the same Baptism, keep the Covenant, and treasure Baptism as the water of rebirth in the Lord's Spirit. I declare all of them to be my fellow-Christians, however unreasonable their thoughts about the origin of the Covenant or the institution of the rite, or the age, authenticity, power, clarity, and definition of the Apostolic Writings. However, for the Lord's and the Church's sake I must not keep silent when faced with an upside-down idea of the New Covenant, of Christianity, and of the 'life lived in Christ'. Such an idea is not only indefensible and would make faith and the Church dead and defenceless, but also, to the extent that it controls us, it makes our faith and hope dead and powerless, so we would lack the clean conscience and hope of God's glory which is the evangelical submission of Christianity and which will, after the new Covenant, be the fruits of Baptism for all believers.

I have diligently attempted to demonstrate my prime claim that with an upside-down view of the Covenant and the Bible our faith and our Church would be totally indefensible and defenceless. I have not wished to attack the faith and the Church but on the contrary have defended both, since the majority have little *feel* for spiritual weapons and therefore no *fear* of them. Moreover, our scholars have been so careful as to leave to worldly authorities the defence of the faith and the Church against both the Pope and the Turk.[418] With this in mind it is only recently that we have been able to sense the indefensibility of this upside-down way of thinking. In such a spiritless time as that which either still runs parallel to ours or lies very close behind us, only a minority know anything about spiritual temptation and its contingent misgivings within ourselves. So everything that the multitude is mindful of within must find verbal expression without. On the one hand our temporal laws strictly forbid papists, Baptists, and all foreign 'faith communities' from making proselytes or acquiring adherents in the kingdom; yet on the other hand the innate opponents of the faith will not turn their weapons away from this upside-down way of thinking but employ them to fight it as though it were an ancient and indefensible superstition in our enlightened times.

---

418. 'Turk' here is synonymous with Muslim.

This is why confusion is increasing by the day, and the majority who still keep the Christian faith, not knowing which way to turn, surrender all their spiritual defences, suspect all enlightenment, and settle for believing that basically they are in the right!

With the coming of religious freedom papists, Baptists, atheists, and Mormons have acquired a quite different boldness and scope. Meanwhile an excellent hairsplitter,[419] who presumes the possible truth of Christianity, even in its most unreasonable form, is raising the banner for what he calls 'New Testament Christianity', understood solely as the Apostolic Writings and literal Christianity. So it is only now that there is a burgeoning rebellion in the camp as all those who have any kind of Christian faith feel the need to defend it against those who boldly claim that we have *no* Christianity, nor ever can have! Those who so far have precipitately mixed up or confused the book called the 'New Testament' with the New Covenant between our Lord and ourselves concerning a clean conscience and a blessed eternity are forced to admit that their way of thinking has been if not extremely upside-down then at least rather distorted and no longer defensible.

For the hairsplitter tells them: "You and I agree that New Testament Christianity is the only proper sort, and you claim that all the Christianity which you preach in the churches on Sunday is 'New Testament Christianity'! This is the same Christianity which leaves an impression on your confirmation candidates, which comforts your churchgoers and penitents, which is described in your books and which you allow to be maintained by its worldly arm. It is the Christianity which you are paid to bear witness to and are happy to live side by side with, titles, orders and all. But either you know nothing about the New Testament and are blind guides, or you must know that this is damn well not the Christianity of the New Testament![420] It is as clear as sunlight that it is the exact opposite, so in Christian terms you are rogues!"

The hairsplitter pretends that he has no knowledge of the Baptismal Covenant or the Christian means of grace: Baptism and Holy Communion. Or he pretends that they are only minor details of no regard. He argues that the subject is only 'New Testament Christianity', so in order to make the whole of Christendom believe the *opposite* of New Testament Christianity he uses all manner of schoolboy tricks and sleight of hand. It is as if true Christianity cannot possibly be found, witnessed, and transmitted in a so-called 'state church' because in its entirety it is an unchristian hotchpotch – as though everything that can be attacked through written language was thereby made unchristian for all time, and that is a quite separate matter. In this respect he stands his upside-down way of thinking on end and carries it into effect

---

419. 'hairsplitter' is Grundtvig's designation for Søren Kierkegaard.

420. A rare case of a curse from Grundtvig's side, put into Kierkegaard's mouth: the Danish word is *pokker*, from the German word for 'pox' (small pox, syphilis etc.), cf. English 'poxy'. Alternatively, *pokker* is a mild term for the Devil, which is what the present translation attempts to render.

with unyielding rigour. Day by day it becomes clearer that if one does not wish to be forced into agreement with the hairsplitter, one must let go of the upside-down idea that the book called the 'New Testament' is the real source, foundation, or rule of faith for true Christianity. The hairsplitter will then stand or fall as a Christianity expert and persecutor of priests and must either refute himself or be seen as the open enemy and denier of Christianity.

I am in no doubt that all those of us who are willing to speak out as Christians not least on behalf of light in the Church consider it both good and highly necessary that we gained this illumination. It is good that through talking and wrangling about our Christianity, we do not allow ourselves to be fooled into believing how Christianity never did and never could begin: namely, with the book that was first written and then read in the Christian Church. We must always begin *the way Christianity did itself*, and stand by that, for the Apostolic Writings not only presuppose *oral* preaching, confession, and sealing of the Christian faith, they actually testify to it! So there is no dispute between Christians and the world, or between believers and unbelievers. The dispute is only between Christian scholars among themselves or between them and unchristian scholars. The question is firstly whether the Apostolic Writings are genuine, then their extent and present form, and finally their proper interpretation and their relation to the New Covenant and the Christian Church. These are learnèd and to some degree very debatable questions which upside-down thinking has burdened the Church with. Instead of using Scripture to illuminate and confirm the faith, they have aroused and nourished all kinds of doubt among those who did not dare to trust a single scholar or any worldly authority who dictated 'true Christianity' and the 'correct interpretation of Scripture'.

However, I have a second and far more important reason for shedding light on and opposing the upside-down idea of the so-called Christianity of 'the New Testament': namely that it is *the basis of life*. It cannot be made as clear as the aforementioned basis of *light*, which we have to place first because we can live tolerably well in the twilight but we die as soon as it is day or night, light or darkness. I have always insisted that the new life means participation in the righteous, true, holy, and eternally joyous human life of God's only-begotten Son. This can only be communicated to us through the Word from the mouth of God. So it is mere infatuation to fancy that we have received a new Christian life from the air that the wind blows or through the strokes of a pen and letters in a book, or through a Word of God that is not addressed to us, or through the words of the priest, the Pope, or the scholar, however true they may be or however well-versed they make us. When Jesus sets out to save us from death and grant us eternal life, He leaves behind on earth in His Words of Institution the Word from the mouth of God that is 'spirit and life'. It can save us, it can make us blessed, and it can show us our salvation and His deeds. It is neither the Pope's doing nor our own, for the spirit and the life we receive from and through His mouth is clearly *His* Spirit and Life and not our own or anyone else's.

This way of thinking about the Words of Institution at Baptism and Holy Communion as giving us life – just as the Baptismal Covenant that is inseparable from them creates light and imparts the Spirit to us – doubtless still seems strange to the majority of believers. It also follows from my claiming all strokes of the pen and written letters to be dead and impotent that I cannot believe my own pen and letters can make any living impression on my readers. But when the Spirit helps us to become scholars, He teaches us what writing can and cannot do. And since it is useful for pointing to all truth, I shall use it to point to the truth of the Word from the mouth of the Lord which alone guides the Christian spirit, the Christian light, and the Christian life.

Let me first remark on the dilatoriness of believers in acquiring the truth from the mouth of the Lord at Baptism and Holy Communion as their source of life, from which source flows all living relation to our Lord Jesus Christ and in Him to our heavenly Father. This dilatoriness has its origin first in the papist confusion of the words of human beings with the Word of God, and next in the Protestant muddling of mouth and pen, speech and writing with regard to both the divine and the human. It is a miracle of God when such a deeply ingrown prejudice is pulled up by the roots, but it is no miracle that we can say it and write it a hundred times without anyone actually taking note of what we mean, or understanding that we are fighting against both the papist and the Protestant fallacy. We may be able to make it much clearer that the Word of God by which Heaven and earth were created – the Word that in the beginning was with God and was God – could not possibly be derived from a written letter. But we cannot make this truth plainer: that no one except the man Jesus Christ, the only-begotten Son, the Word of the Lord in person, can speak 'the Word of God' in all its power and with a human tongue.

In contrast, it will certainly promote the understanding among all truth-loving and believing Christians that, mystery or not, it is a fact that in the Lord's Church the quickening spirit and new life are only imparted through the Word from the mouth of the Lord to us at Baptism and Holy Communion. To this end we must endeavour in all our speech and writing about the kingdom of God to arouse and sharpen attention to the fruits of the Spirit and the effects of Christianity. These alone can prove that the particular spirit and new life that the Lord has promised His believers and that we are proud to possess is not illusion and idle fancy. All truth-loving and believing people know in their hearts, and discover as soon as they repent, that they have become and will continue to be Christians solely because they believe that our Lord Jesus Christ can and will grant them and all His believers a truly clean conscience and a sure and living hope of salvation. So they can be well satisfied that, true or not, in order to have spirit and life together with Him we must believe in the Baptismal Covenant and the other Words of Institution at Baptism and Holy Communion as the Word of God from the Lord's own mouth. Sinners that we are, unless we can acquire a truly clean conscience, and, doomed to death as we all are, unless we have a sure and living hope of salvation, then we cannot have spirit and life with the Saviour. If we cannot have such a clean conscience and such a hope of salvation without faith in the Word from His mouth to us, then it is no use making even the strongest protests against the defensibility of this faith, or inventing other possible ways through which we find it more reasonable to receive eternal blessing. For then we would miss out completely on the truly clean conscience and the sure hope of salvation that we seek in our Lord Jesus Christ and dare not expect to find in anyone else, since we believe that only He has the eternal word of life.

This is an important contest: Is it through what is known as 'New Testament Christianity' or through what I call 'Christianity from the mouth of the Lord Himself' that we acquire a truly clean conscience and a sure and living hope of salvation in the name of our Lord Jesus Christ?[421] Towards this end and with these lines I urge all my Christian readers – for I am certain that if they have not known it before, that they will hereby realise that I am not inventing anything new! It is the salvation sequence and the institution of our Lord Jesus Christ Himself that I point to, and it is these which, with my mouth turned to the grace of God granted through His Holy Spirit, I am endeavouring to put into effect and make fruitful for the interests of the kingdom of God, which are righteousness, peace, and joy in the Holy Spirit.

---

421. The clean conscience comes from being redeemed from sin, as the baptismal ritual puts it. The same thought is expressed in Grundtvig's hymn 'Spirit of all truth and love' in a line that translates literally as: "With a clean conscience You descend to the little ones."

20. The Seven Sacraments

The so-called 'seven sacraments'[422] belong to papistry, which we would rather do without. But since the papists tenaciously claim that all seven belong to our Basic Christian Teachings, and since they include both Holy Baptism and Holy Communion in their seven sacraments, two of which they say we have stolen, the entire Church should be made aware of the true context of the matter. This is even more so when we clearly see from the disputes concerning Holy Orders, Matrimony, and Penance that the papist leaven is still far from being completely removed for us to celebrate Easter with unleavened bread. This is always what happens with 'official' or 'legal' and 'duty-bound' matters in a Christianity that is heavily protected by all manner of carnal and worldly weapons. As a result, far fewer questions are asked as to what is demonstrably *true* Christianity, what need we *have* of it, and what benefit human life can *derive* from it. Instead there are more questions about what the Pope and his priests, or what the worldly authority and the clerical officials and the university teachers who create Doctors of Theology, want 'the one true Christianity' to be *called*. So those who dare to open their mouths or scratch their pens against this, whatever their grounds and their proof, must either be burned alive or put in the clink or exiled abroad or at the least wear a muzzle and face severe censorship all their days! In such circumstances it is an old rule that among the papists there are seven sacraments and among the Protestants there are only two – and, for safety's sake, among the High Churchmen only one, namely Holy Communion; so they are nasty heretics who say there are either more or fewer.

As we know, in such church-states and state-churches there is no point in talking about 'greater enlightenment'. Nor do those who are unwilling to test 'the joys of heresy' have any interest in other 'church candles' than those which the so-called church-owners, using the income from church tithes, permit to be lit or snuffed out at random, or as the relevant parties are pleased to decide.

However, as a special exception, we who live in little Denmark, even in the midst of our State Church chaos, have each been allowed to light a candle to see better with it! And now that our strict Lutheran State Church has transformed itself into a free

---

422. The Seven Sacraments in Roman Catholicism are: Baptism, Confirmation, and Holy Communion (the sacraments of initiation into the Church and the body of Christ); Penance and Anointing of the Sick (the sacraments of healing); and Holy Orders and Matrimony (the sacraments of service). Throughout this chapter I retain the capital letter for all seven sacraments.

Evangelical-Lutheran People's Church,[423] it must be our official duty to let our light shine as brightly as possible for all those who live in our country. And since the Catholic Church in Bredgade[424] is also letting its light shine on its pleasantly broad road to Heaven, it will be doubly necessary to use Christianity's own light to illuminate more clearly the most attractive nature of all the broad roads.

Despite the fact that some would say I am more of a papist than a Lutheran, I am nevertheless certain that every pope would rather be spared such papists as me, and that Martin Luther would have nothing whatsoever against such successors as myself. Under the Pope's nose I further argue from the strictly Lutheran basic principle of all Christian enlightenment that the Holy Spirit is the *only* vice-regent of Christ on earth and that this vice-regent of Christ, as the divine life-force, is only active through the Word and the faith. This is *God's* Word and *human* faith, so these must be in a vital, loving activity wherever we can speak in a Christian sense of creating or sustaining, developing or enhancing a Christian human life.

In accordance with this Evangelical-Lutheran basic principle for Christian enlightenment which I call unshakeable and which is not only irreconcilable but also incompatible with all papacy, I have for many years informed my readers of what I knew about the seven sacraments. However, in this case I am not only in debt to all Christian readers but am also aware that the message I have passed on has had great deficiencies which I shall now endeavour to remedy.

From this Evangelical-Lutheran standpoint we must first and foremost ask what the word 'sacrament' means in a Christian sense; if we do not know this, it is ridiculous to quarrel about either two or seven or fourteen Christian sacraments! When we realise that 'sacrament' is not only quite strange among us but that the Latinists, to whose language it belongs, know as little as we do about the Christian thought which this academic word expresses, then it is as clear as sunlight that all dispute about the *number* of sacraments has been conducted in the dark and cannot be continued a moment longer until some light is shed.

In short we are saying: we will not argue about the number of sacraments, since there is no corresponding word from the mouth of the Lord concerning His own institutions and nothing in the Apostolic Writings. Thus the word 'sacrament' cannot be used to illuminate but only to darken the Gospel of Christ. Let us instead hear what it is that the papists wish to include under the name of 'sacrament' in the same main category as Holy Baptism and Holy Communion, which have been instituted by

---

423. i.e. in the new democratic constitution of 1849.

424. Bredgade is a main street in Copenhagen. St. Ansgar's Church was dedicated in 1842; it is the parish church for local Catholics and the cathedral for all Catholics in Denmark. Statistics for 2016 state that out of a population of roughly 5.5 million there were 44,644 Roman Catholics in Denmark. The number is gradually increasing due to immigration.

our Lord Himself. He did so while He was visibly present, and they carry the matchless testimony of the Spirit and the Church that Baptism is the water of rebirth and
renewal in the Holy Spirit, and Communion is the communion and fellowship of the
body and blood of Christ!

Next, we hear from Peter Lombard,[425] the famous 12th-century academic and Bishop
of Paris, and from all the papists after him, that the so-called seven sacraments are: Baptism, Confirmation, Communion, Penance, the Last Rites, Ordination, and Marriage.

When this papist academic tells us that he calls these 'the seven sacraments' because
both he and even St. Augustine[426] have judged that the word 'sacrament' can and must
mean a 'holy sign' and a 'signified sacredness', we decline to follow him down this
unnecessary detour. For we do not have the power to know how he has reached his
unjustifiable conclusion or how he can excuse the fact that he and the papists have
thrown the corn (God's word) into the hob of chaff (God's message to man), there to
be overlooked, forgotten, and if possible disappear completely. We should therefore
not even have referred to his academic style about the holy *sign* and the holy *thing*
that is supposed to constitute the sacrament if the Protestant and papist theologians
alike had not 'ploughed with his heifer'.[427] This among other things is what the whole
academic dispute is about between Lutherans and Calvinists as regards both Baptism
and Communion, in particular the latter.

Abandoning all this *papist* talk of 'sacrament' we follow the Spirit of truth and Martin Luther in immediately distinguishing Baptism and Holy Communion from their
forced and altogether unworthy company, since from the very first and to the very last
they are without parallel in God's house. They are the only recognisable institutions
of our Lord Jesus Christ Himself and the only life necessities for the people who are
created by the Spirit through Word and faith to praise the Lord. For it is in Baptism
according to the Lord's own institution that believers are born to be God's children
in and with the Lord, and it is in Holy Communion according to the same institution
that believers and baptised are nourished under divine growth in and with the Lord
until as full adults they can be measured alongside Him.[428]

The fact that Baptism and Holy Communion have both a visible and an invisible
character is not their hallmark; if it were, they could be bracketed with everything else
which is partly visible and partly invisible or which is partly a visible 'sign' and partly

---

425. Peter (the) Lombard (c.1096-1160) was Bishop of Paris and author of the standard theology textbook, *Four Books of
Sentences* (c.1150), in which he compiled and commented on the authoritative statements in biblical passages (Lat.
sententiae).

426. St. Augustine (354-430), born in Thagaste (Algeria), became a Christian in 387 and wrote about his conversion in
Confessions (401); he was a highly influential theologian who helped formulate the concepts of original sin, saving
grace, and the just war. He was Bishop of Hippo (Algeria) from 396-430.

427. Judg 14:18.

428. Eph 4:13.

an invisible, merely designated, 'thing'. The Lord's institutions for the raising up of the fallen have both visible and invisible elements solely in order to comprehend the *whole* human being, who is a union of the visible with the invisible. Thus the visible elements in Baptism and Holy Communion are not signs of the invisible elements in them but belong just as really to the thing itself: to the divine remedy in its entirety, as the body belongs to humanity. Whether or not we can guess *why* for His Spirit's use with His Word in Baptism Our Lord has taken up water, and in Holy Communion taken up bread and wine, is no more the question here than whether or not we can guess the reason why our own human body, in order to be enlivened by God's Spirit, needs precisely the component parts it possesses. Among all the visible things that the Lord had command over He chose for His Baptism the unrivalled means of bodily cleansing that is *water*, and for His Holy Communion the finest bodily food for human life that are *bread and wine*. From this we can see that by the Lord's *own institution* the visible things are images of the Spirit-forces that are at work in them, as well as being seeds of the new, the pure, and the cleansed corporality which the Lord wishes to grant all His own, so that also *bodily* they are glorious among His saints and admirable to all His believers. Since, according to both the Creation account and the worldly wisdom that only reluctantly allows for a Creator and a Creation, 'water' is the mysterious womb of development for the human body – over which God's Spirit hovers during all Creation – Christians are no more tempted to the papistry of reading an incantation over the waters of Baptism to consecrate the power of its Word than they are tempted to the papistry of bewitching the bread and wine of Holy Communion into something that can only be done on earth by God's Word become flesh.

As the water of true rebirth and renewal in the Holy Spirit for both soul and body, Baptism according to the Lord's institution is in harmony with all our so-called natural, i.e. corporal, and temporal birth in that we thereby come visibly into the world but also invisibly and physically *into the light*, meaning that we come into ourselves and become conscious of ourselves in this world.

Holy Communion according to the Lord's institution – as the communion in His body and blood both for the soul and for the body – is in harmony with all our so-called natural, i.e corporal, and temporal life-nourishment. We visibly eat and drink, and our soul, invisibly but also physically and temporally, is fed and nourished in desire, word, and thought to take *in* and as far as possible take *possession of* all this world and its splendour. Once we realise this, we are not tempted by the papistry of jumbling together Baptism and Holy Communion with something else, let alone with all that one imagines must taste good to all Christians, or what can give even Turks[429] and

---

429. i.e. Muslims.

heathens a certain Christian sheen, which the self-appointed Christian vice-regent[430] says he will surely persuade our Lord to settle for.

One is more likely to be tempted by one's *vexation* with all papistry to throw overboard all the so-called Christian elements such as the Spirit, the Word, and the faith, as indeed the Calvinists[431] have attempted to do. But that should be an example to warn us, for they took the life out of both Baptism and Holy Communion, so the Quakers[432] found in them only shadows of the Lord's institutions to reject.

Martin Luther, who honestly endeavoured to set Baptism and Holy Communion in their proper, living, divine light, also endeavoured to regard in the same light both what he retained and what he rejected. Although for his part he did not place much emphasis on any of the self-made rituals, he allowed the question to remain open as to how many of the old Church rituals could be considered edifying and biblically justified, once the papists' sacramental veil had been stripped away.

As regards us Danes, our scribes endorsed this element in the foundational Lutheran principles; but they also accepted quite tamely that just as Baptism was a citizen's duty for all who were born, and Holy Communion a duty for all lawful witnesses, so was Penance a citizen's duty for all those who wished to take Communion. Similarly, a Wedding Ceremony was the duty of those who wished to marry, Ordination a duty for those who would be priests, and finally Confirmation a duty for all those who did not wish to be sent to prison![433] From this the common people could not possibly learn that there was a significant difference between Our Lord's own institutions and other Church rituals that the Pope, or Luther, or Christian VI[434] had introduced.

This is how it still stands, or rather lies, with us; and it is hardly in order to add a Christian ritual to this confusion when the people are calling so strongly for a 'Church constitution'. So much the more energy must we put into *enlightening* the so-called 'Church', including as regards the question that if we want greater emphasis on other areas than preaching the Gospel, Baptism, and Holy Communion, for them to be genuine and fruitful they must be *free*, since it is otherwise against Luther and not a good move. Yet it is not a papist move, for the Church rituals that people are most

---

430. i.e. the Pope.

431. Calvinists are followers of John Calvin of Geneva (1509-64), whose overall Protestant theology is contained in the *Institutes of the Christian Religion* (1559). His doctrine of salvation was affirmed by the Synod of Dordt (1618-19) as the basis of Reformed Theology. Its main tenet is that God alone decides who receives His grace and who does not.

432. Quakers are members of the Religious Society of Friends, founded in the 17th century. Believing in the 'inner light' to all, they assert the priesthood of all believers and have no formal system of belief nor formal ceremonies; they are strongly opposed to violence and war. The obscure origin of their name probably has to do with 'quaking before the Lord' (Isa 64:2; Nah 1:5).

433. Church discipline of the time allowed for the imprisonment of youngsters who turned 21 without being confirmed.

434. Christian VI (1699-1746) was famous for introducing a law in 1733 that forced young men to remain in their local area and be subject to the local nobility; it was abolished in 1788.

attentive to are not the old ones which one could make-believe were 'Apostolic' but the truly self-made ones, so it is impossible that either our Lord or the Apostles could have set great store by them or given their blessing to them.

Confirmation among the papists is an ancient Church ritual in which the bishop, who alone is called to perform it, makes the sign of the cross over the brow and then anoints it with oil in the name of the Trinity. This is performed not as a salvation ritual for all those who are baptised but only for those who request it, and particularly those who are thinking of becoming priests, since Confirmation always comes before Ordination. It does not therefore appear to be a life necessity but only a spiritual confirmation and corroboration for those who wish to be ordained to preach the Gospel, defend the faith, and serve the Church.

It is debatable whether Martin Luther was right to discard this ancient Christian ritual. I myself conclude that this came about only because Luther rightly rejected the tangible anointing with oil at Confirmation and Baptism and because Confirmation, being firmly nailed to the episcopal seat, more or less[435] forced his hand. For he not only retained the sign of the cross at Baptism but would have approved of our practice of signing the cross over both the brow *and* the breast, whereas the papists only do this over the breast at Baptism and over the brow at Confirmation. Like everything that seeks to separate what God has joined together as 'head and heart', this separation in practice is only papal leaven, so we can both defend our practice at Baptism and also justify that we call the public presentation in Church of privately baptised children as being 'Confirmation of Baptism'. But we cannot then later condone under the name of Confirmation a self-made Church ritual that should be the sole condition for taking Holy Communion yet also be conditional on a certain proficiency in reading, writing, and arithmetic as well as a valid vaccination certificate against smallpox! This is worldly papistry that is not only as ridiculous and inexcusable as any other clerical error but is absolutely unacceptable from a Christian viewpoint, since it raises a totally heathen toll-bar before the Lord's table and even demands a toll-fee that believers and baptised perhaps cannot pay.

On the other hand and under whatever name, we ought to make it an invariable custom that before they are presented at the Lord's table all those who were baptised at so young an age that on the establishment of their Baptismal Covenant they could not answer for themselves, should publicly acknowledge and confirm that Covenant and then with the laying-on of hands be assured of the spiritual and Christian validity of their Baptism. I would defend this as a necessary consequence of infant Baptism, and I dare to believe that this resembles far more than the papist Confirmation the Apostolic ritual that the papists appeal to.

---

435. Luther wanted *any* priest, not just the bishop, to have the right to confirm.

With regard to Confirmation as to so much else, it is not just that the papists, as the Protestant theologians predicted, have either disdained the written evidence or have been ignorant of the content of Scripture. They claim Acts 8 for the Apostolicity of Confirmation and for the bishops' exclusive right to impart this;[436] and there is indeed an account of the Apostles Peter and John going down to Samaria, where the preacher Philip (the deacon) had baptised many 'in our Lord Jesus' name' without them receiving the Holy Spirit, which they only received when the Apostles laid their hands on them and prayed for them. It is doubtless true that this account points to an Apostolic practice that seems to be assumed in "the second gift of grace" (2 Cor 1)[437] and in the expression "confirm or strengthen" (*episterizein*), which is used more commonly of the Apostle Paul's second visit to the churches he had founded. There can be no objection to Latin Christians calling this Apostolic custom 'Confirmation' in their language, but when the papists claim that the 'Apostolic' Confirmation was just like theirs and that their bishops had the authority and exclusive right to impart this Apostolic Confirmation, then as usual they owe us the evidence for both, and simultaneously incur a debt to the history of the Church which they cannot possibly pay.

This is the fundamental error of the papists and the source of all papistry: that without any proof and despite the clearest refutation the Pope in Rome sets himself up to be 'Apostolic' and thus the principal heir of the Apostles as well as Christ's viceregent and second self. In the very strictest sense what the Lord according to Scripture told His Apostles holds good: "Whoever listens to you listens to me; whoever rejects you rejects me; but whoever rejects me rejects him who sent me",[438] and "whatever you bind on earth will be bound in heaven, and whatever you loose on earth will be loosed in heaven".[439] What the Pope does not pay attention to in this so-called scriptural 'proof' – just as little as the Protestant theologians have in their scriptural 'proof' in the case of pastors – is not only the unverifiable claim that either the Pope or some so-called 'official' of Christ has 'Apostolic authority' but also the ridiculous notion of assuming to themselves such an authority that they clearly cannot match and so demonstrably cannot possess either.

It is equally certain that according to Scripture our Lord told His Apostles: "It is not you who speak but my Father's Spirit which speaks through you",[440] just as He said, "Whoever listens to you listens to me."[441] So the one cannot do without the other,

---

436. Acts 8:16-17 (on new believers): "the Holy Spirit had not yet come on any of them; they had simply been baptised in the name of the Lord Jesus. Then Peter and John placed their hands on them, and they received the Holy Spirit."
437. Gr. δευτεραν χαριν (2 Cor 1:16). Paul's return is seen as a second divine bestowal of grace.
438. Lk 10:16.
439. Mt 18:18.
440. Mt 10:20.
441. Lk 10:16.

just as the spiritual nature of the address to the Apostles must be the very reason for the unity of the Apostolic Word with the Lord's Word and its corresponding authority. Protestant theologians have completely overlooked this, while the Pope has paid partial attention to it by declaring his Apostolic Word to be 'infallible'.[442] This claim is ridiculous, since no one can keep his tongue so firmly in his mouth and his pen under such control that he never speaks or writes a word about the kingdom of God that is incompatible with the Word of the Lord. Nor would a so-called 'Apostolic Word in the name of the Lord' ever have the same power and effect as the words of the Lord Himself and His Apostles in His name. So whether one calls oneself 'Apostolic' or 'Peter's successor' or 'vice-regent of Christ' or one dubs oneself a 'biblical Christologist and Theologian with Apostolic authority', that person is only put to shame when he cannot in reality speak with the tongues of the Apostles and perform the Apostles' deeds. Without this, he is only making a laughing-stock of himself by imparting to others this 'Apostolic substitution', be it at Confirmation or Ordination, for which he clearly has no authority. He lacks the power to do so, and in contrast to Baptism and Holy Communion – where he can impart a Word from the Lord's own mouth and a deed of His own to point to and trust – he must himself give proof of his power and glory that it is not merely a human word he is speaking but truly a Word of God that has a corresponding power among believers.

Martin Luther was absolutely right to reject the Apostolicity of all the self-made sacraments, whether they were claimed to be essential for Christian life or achieved the same effect under every bishop as they could under an Apostle's laying-on of hands. It would be best to keep both the Confirmation of Baptism and the Ordination of Priests as edifying Church rituals which will always be a blessing to the same degree that the Church and its teachers are 'Apostolic', for the Lord's Spirit will always be consistently strong over the Church and thereby take effect accordingly through Word and faith. Thus, if our Church were only granted civil freedom – so that its free will in the Spirit and its free sustenance in the Lord were recognised – we would doubtless soon be proved to have chosen 'the good part' by waiting for salvation solely from the Lord's own institutions and to be laying only a certain *indefinite* emphasis on Confirmation and Ordination as well, or as moderately as we can execute them under supplication to the Holy Spirit.

We can smile cheerfully at the Pope's anathema and at what even more laughably amounts to the same thing: the so-called sympathetic shrug from the episcopal High Church at us wretched Lutherans who, because we have no unbroken Apostolic

---

442. Although the doctrine of papal infallibility existed in the Middle Ages and was the majority opinion by the time of the Counter-Reformation, it did not actually become a dogma until the First Vatican Council of 1869-70 – after Grundtvig wrote these words.

Ordination of bishops, naturally also lack Ordination and Confirmation and do not even have the slightest authority to the Lord's own institutions, Baptism and Holy Communion; without both covenants, the old and the new, we must surrender to God's universal mercy for all heathens!

I shall not lecture the haughty episcopal Church with its black spiritual poverty here, but I will inform my readers of what I have discovered to my great surprise: namely, that the so-called Apostolic Consecration of Bishops in unbroken succession, which the High Church prides itself on and ascribes its matchless splendour to, is the emptiest of all its conceits. In Christian antiquity there was never any Consecration and thus even less an unbroken Apostolic succession. Even Peter the Lombard finds it necessary to confess that although in his words a bishop has the sole right both to ordain and confirm, his episcopal status is not a higher rank of consecration (*ordo*), but only a rank and an office (*dignitas* and *officium*), since the Church has never had any higher rank of ordination than the deacon's (preacher's), through the handing down of the Gospel, and the presbyter's (priest's), through the handing down of the chalice. This must be proof enough that not even in the darkness of the papacy has there been any episcopal consecration that either pretended to be Apostolic or ascribed to the bishop any greater spiritual gifts and Christian authority of office. So whether or not the English bishops or other bishops wish to have a formula for imparting authority to each other through consecration, they do so at their own peril and on their own account, in truth reckoning without their host. It is true that the English bishops' lawyer (Bingham[443]) appealed to an African synod as proof that the Consecration of Bishops was an early Christian practice, but as ill luck again would have it, even after this synod the Consecration consisted solely of the laying-on of hands and the holding of the Bible over the bishop's head, which would suggest rather the bishop's *sub*ordination than his *super*ordination and could not possibly be 'Apostolic'.

Our Ordination of Pastors to preach the Gospel freely as it is, and to officiate at Baptism and Holy Communion according to the Lord's own institution, is all the Christian consecration there has ever been in the Church for 'pastors and teachers' since the days of the Apostles, so it is doubtful whether we have been right or wrong to consecrate at one and the same time preachers and priests (deacons and presbyters). The fact that we consecrate with the laying-on of hands under the invocation of the Holy Spirit without any tangible tradition either from the Bible or from the chalice is in every sense a Christian step forward, since we must not give the Church's common property into the individual's hand or attempt to conceal that it is solely the gifts of

---

443. Rev. Joseph Bingham (1668-1723) wrote ten volumes (1708-22) on *Origines Ecclesiasticae, or Antiquities of the Christian Church*. He reaffirmed the decisions on clerical succession made in 393 at the Synod of Hippo (now Annaba, Algeria – the 'African synod' mentioned below).

grace from the Holy Spirit that can create for the Lord and the Church capable and cultured church officers. Scripture states (Acts 20) that it is the Holy Spirit that sets the pastor over the Lord's flock. We cannot defend the requirement of a certain linguistic skill and an academic training as the condition of Ordination as a rule without exception; but when we have emphasised the importance of learning the original language of the New Testament and of undergoing academic training in the mother-tongue, at the same time as we abolish the entire clerical guild system with its monopoly on enlightening and edifying the Lord's free Church, that rule will nonetheless be a very Christian one.

Turning to the Wedding Ceremony, we immediately see that the papists confuse the days of the New Covenant with those of the Old and the institution of marriage with the so-called 'Christian wedding'. As to why we have also done so, we can only say that we should simply stop doing this and instead diligently inform the Church that marriage is in no way a Christian institution but a human and civil one which has no other promise of Christian blessing than everything else that believing Christians do in the name of our Lord Jesus Christ.

On the other hand we would do well to note that even at their wedding ceremonies the papists do not raise any questions of conscience as we do, but merely ask whether the person in question is willing to enter into lawful marriage according to the Church's ritual; and that is how it should be.

Incidentally, the only thing that makes the Wedding Ceremony a sacrament for papists is the wedding ring, over which the priest gives a blessing and sprinkles holy water. Apart from the holy water there is nothing in particular to criticise here, so long as no spiritual power is ascribed to the ceremony. For the wedding-ring is the most beautiful sign of fidelity, and the unbreakable fidelity between Christian married couples should indubitably prove that Christians have their own blessing in all their human relationships.

However, as long as the Wedding Ceremony here in Denmark is still a civil duty for pastors to conduct at random and a civil duty for all customers of the People's Church to undertake, it will naturally continue as before to create far more damage and indignation than benefit and edification. Not until a civil wedding becomes a purely civil matter and a Christian wedding the Christians' own concern can we speak of how a Christian marriage can best be consecrated.

We saw recently and all too clearly[444] how far even most Christians among us remain outside this Christian enlightenment on the question of marriage, when nearly everybody agrees that however faithless and unchristian the majority of our Church

---

444. Under the Parliamentary debate on freedom of belief in 1850 Niels Møller Spandet argued for compulsory civil marriage. See note 294.

members are, they should all have a Christian wedding! I have heard the peculiar utterance, not as a joke but in earnest, that the poor young Christian girls who had faithless fiancés would seldom if ever hold a Christian wedding unless it was a *compulsory* matter. When we consider how little such 'Christian' weddings have long meant here in Denmark, we can barely stop a smile spreading at such comforting words! In all seriousness, however, we must say that the Christian girl who can marry an openly faithless man should be no more discriminating over a wedding than she is over a bridegroom. Unfortunately, it remains true that we still hold firm to the papist leaven and still disappoint one another and indeed ourselves with a Christian pretence, even when we know it to be the emptiest pretence under the sun.

We come now to what we call in brief, if not with precision, 'Confession' – but what the papists call Penance (*penitentia*). Although our Confession has not played so obvious a role for us as Penance has played a major role for the papists, here again from both sides – both that of the so-called 'Father Confessor' and that of the so-called 'penitents' – much store has been set by this Church ritual. It is a ritual that cannot be defended – and even worse, we little people of the North, all of our own free will, have made Confession an exclusive condition for Holy Communion! This is so much the more peculiar in that we have otherwise been among Luther's most obedient disciples and must know that Confession and Absolution, regarded as a matter of salvation, were and are the foundation of all papistry and priestly hierocracy and undermine the entire process of Christian salvation – as Martin Luther revealed in a masterly way during his battle against indulgences and all other papistry.

However, this irrationality of ours, together with the fact that the self-made sacrament of Penance has managed to obscure the Lord's own institutions so terribly, ought to make us cautious about condemning Confession and Absolution in themselves as Christian rituals without a demand to be more than just that. Since both here and in Norway the question of Confession has been raised recently, I think it essential that it should be treated separately, so here I shall settle for noting that the forgiveness of sins indiscriminately, on behalf of one's pastoral office, with or without Confession, is the cornerstone of all state churches that wish to give millions of people a Christian appearance and to give that appearance a claim to reality.

As the seventh and last of the papists' sacraments I shall merely touch on the 'Last Rites', which are naturally consecrated with an episcopal reading and involve an anointing of the dying person's eyes, ears, nose, mouth, and hands, occasionally also the feet (and with males the loins) as the words are murmured, "With this holy anointing may God forgive you all the sins you have sinned with your sight, hearing, smell, taste, and touch etc." There is a very good Christian justification for why all the Protestant state churches have followed this ancient ritual, but it is in no way biblical; despite Luther's advice, the testimony of history, and all common sense, they have taken the clearly spurious Epistle of James[445] for gospel truth, for we cannot deny that as help for both health and forgiveness of sins the papist Last Rites are both mentioned and recommended in the Epistle of James.[446]

Incidentally, this anointing, which we cannot deny is an ancient ritual in Christianity, probably had its source in the Jewish rite of embalming, which our Lord, far from disdaining, warmly embraced; the Last Rites have therefore doubtless been as edifying in their Christian form as they have been scandalous in their papist form.

Since we have replaced the Last Rites with the sprinkling of earth on the coffin, and the requiem with the funeral sermon, it all seems innocent enough. But the funeral sermon has often been even more indefensible than the requiem, and when the burial in so-called 'consecrated ground' with words of commitment from the pastor was given the slightest value as regards salvation, or was passed off as being indispensable for a Christian burial, then we were also dabbling our way towards creating a *new* sacrament that was so much more ridiculous in not being performed over the dying body rather than the dead corpse, and being literally assumed with soil to be helping people to heaven.

---

445. Luther denied that the Epistle of James was authentic and called it an "epistle of straw".
446. Jas 5:14.

7. Manuscript of hymn, 'Christ's Church as a rock among us'

No. 343 in the current *Danish Hymnbook* (2003) 'Christ's Church as a rock among us' (*Tusind aar stod Kristi kirke*) was written to celebrate the 1000th anniversary of the conversion of the Danes by St. Ansgar in 826. It was first published in *Danish Festival Hymns for the Millennium Festival*, 1826.

21. The Christian Signs of Life

For as long as Christianity has existed in the world every serious-minded person who has felt attracted to it as being the divine truth has also felt that the question of salvation cannot possibly be an integral part of *eternal* life without having an appreciable influence on the *temporal* life of man. Whoever actually denies this and expects from Christianity only a 'blessed death' reveals their own spiritual death and exposes Christianity to the bitter and obviously well-deserved scorn of the unbelieving world. If Christ's gospel were no more than a so-called 'Word of eternal life' that made temporal human life even deader than it was before, then no truth-loving person could or would need to believe in such a gospel. For whatever is without spirit or is spiritually dead and powerless in *time* cannot possibly be full of spirit or spiritually all-powerful in *eternity*. To this end our Lord Jesus Christ Himself has borne witness that we must be spiritually *reborn* in the course of our temporal life in order to have a share in eternal life, and that this is a truth about life on earth that must be believed before we can believe the truth about life in Heaven.

Thus, although the papists' concept of Christianity was as spiritually dead and powerless as could be, short of being totally self-contradictory, even the papists themselves sternly insisted on a so-called 'Christian way of life', meaning the monastic life, which was to be regarded as the property of the whole Church. Every member could have a share in this so-called godly and Christian monastic life by believing in it and by contributing each according to his ability to its maintenance, welfare, and glorification. However, from a spiritual and Christian point of view this so-called godly and Christian monastic life was no more than an *appearance* which revealed the spiritual death that it sought to hide; this has been so clearly exposed that it requires no further evidence, at least not amongst Martin Luther's disciples.

As regards these disciples of Martin Luther, the so-called 'Lutherans', there is no denying that they erred badly in what they said and wrote when they argued as though they really believed that the temporal life of man, being ungodly and irredeemable, must be cancelled out in the name of salvation, and that we must think only about a 'blessed death', because as the Ecclesiast says, "the day of death is better than the day of birth."[447] Like their Calvinist counterparts the Lutheran doctrinal systems were based on the dead letter and the concept of 'Scripture', while the academic life of our scribes

---

447. Eccl 4:2. Grundtvig paraphrases; the actual words are: "the dead who had already died are happier than the living who are still alive."

was obviously even less godly than that of the monks. This being so, the papists could with some justification accuse us of having an even deader concept of Christianity than they had themselves! Nevertheless, the Lutherans still made the better choice in lining up on the side of life, for they left the spiritually dead life of appearances to the papists and took comfort in the Spirit which, despite their apparent death, could and would make them alive with Christ.

In the midst of their unjustifiable condemnation of the entire natural life of human-kind and their eulogies over the 'blessed death' and the 'blessed corpses', the Lutherans nevertheless demanded in earnest a *living* faith for true Christianity, a faith that should demonstrate its spiritual power and its reality in a spoken Creed, in preaching the Gospel, and in songs of praise in the mother-tongue. We make bold to declare that with these words we have named the proper *Christian signs of life*, which must never be entirely absent wherever there is true Christianity, nor can ever be found together except where the quickening Spirit of the Lord is the Church's divine advocate, its comforter, and companion guide to all truth.

What nevertheless gave even the sincere Lutherans the appearance of death in their daily life and stunted the growth of their Christian life was their confused and self-contradictory way of thinking about evangelical freedom under State Church enslavement, about rebirth in Baptism together with faith and life according only to Scripture, and finally about the Christian renewal of human life without a previous human life to be renewed. So that once with God's help we see light in the light of the Lord, our Confession of faith will be much firmer and fuller, our Gospel preaching much plainer and more powerful, and our songs of praise much clearer and more beautiful, revitalising the whole of our temporal human life in heart and Spirit. Though unprovable, the Christian quality of this form is certain enough, for this noble, heartfelt form of life will only be found where the Christian Creed, preaching the Gospel, and the song of praise flourish. Admittedly we have recently seen that this enlightenment is still a rarity among us, for when Søren Kierkegaard not long ago tried to frighten the life out of us with his charcoal drawing of 'The Begging Monk'[448] as the only true disciple of Christ, who literally carried his cross on his back and followed him, then he was met as usual with crass ignorance about the Christian life. Yet, fortunately, he found in the corners the *morning light*, which will lend glory to life and which was urged on by the black rain-cloud to vigorous strides forward on its heroic path.

On this particular occasion it became quite clear that all disputes and discussions about the Christian life are just so much talk if we do not presuppose and maintain that the Christian Church, created by Baptism according to the Lord's own institution,

---

448. The reference is to Kierkegaard's attack on the Church in *Practice in Christianity* (Indøvelse i Kristendom, 1850) and *The Instant* (Øjeblikket, 1855).

has its own peculiar life-spring in this alone, and that the Church's Creed at Baptism is therefore the only Christian confession and, as the living expression of the Christian faith, is both the first and the last sign of Christian life. On the other hand, given this fundamental knowledge about Christian life as a life of faith and the Confession of faith in Church being the essential true sign of life, we can clearly see that it is only in a living preaching of the Gospel and in songs of praise in accordance with our Creed that the Christian life can and must continually show itself more powerfully and more openly. Simultaneously, the whole course of the Christian Church must demonstrate whether the new Christian life is more or less human than the old one, either as it was led before Christ came or as it is lived without the Baptismal faith in Christ or the rebirth to His own human life in Baptism according to His own institution.

We might now make bold to assert that our Basic Christian Teachings actually conflict with Scripture, because the debate about the true meaning of the words of men who are now dead is endless. Moreover, book-knowledge and Scripture-knowledge are and must be so vastly different from one another that even if all Christians were clever readers only very few of them would have a solidly based conviction either about the biblical character of Christianity or about the Christian character of the Bible. Nevertheless we Christian scribes triumphantly defend the claim that far from denying our Basic Christian Teachings about 'faith and Baptism' our Holy Scripture is in fact in total agreement with them, and offers in particular the Creed as the primary Christian sign of life, a glorious witness, in the words of the Lord: "Whoever publicly acknowledges me before others, the Son of Man will also acknowledge before the angels of God."[449]

Of necessity we must first and last give the same weight to the Creed outwardly as we give to faith inwardly, since the Confession of faith in the new life corresponds to breathing in the old life. Yet it is far from our purpose thereby to exclude either the preaching of the Gospel or the songs of praise, which are also signs of life that can as little be excluded where the Christian life is to grow and prosper as the life that is born of faith can thrive and mature without the corresponding hope and love. This hope and this love have the same relationship to the living preaching of the Gospel as faith has to the living Confession of faith. So that where the Creed is the only sign of life, there the life of faith will always be found to be weak and sickly and in every trial fighting for its life. This is further explained by the fact that not only did the Christian faith first enter this world through the preaching of Him who came from above and in truth spoke the 'Word of God' but also, according to the Apostle's express testimony, this faith is transmitted only through the living profession of the Word of faith. So the Apostle asks not only, "How then shall they call upon him without

---

449. Lk 12:8.

believing in Him?" but also and equally importantly, "How shall they hear without someone preaching?"[450]

So despite the fact that the Christian Creed can be found alive, and still *is* alive even where in general the preaching of the Gospel in the Church may be said to be extinct, the Creed will either soon die out and take faith to the grave with it, or it will gain such power as to bear again the *living* preaching of the Gospel, as it undoubtedly did in and through Martin Luther.

For what actually was the case with us at the beginning of the 19th century was apparently the case throughout most of the Christian world at the beginning of the 16th century: the living preaching of the Word of faith was to human eyes either totally extinct, or was so obviously moribund that for it to continue to transmit the faith from generation to generation it had to be miraculously reborn. And clearly reborn it was in and through Martin Luther! Again with spirit and life he preached the ancient Word of faith in the mother-tongue of his people, and thus revived the preaching of the Gospel not only among the kindred tribes in England and the three Nordic kingdoms but even to a certain degree among the Latin nations, as can be seen everywhere, but most obviously with the Calvinists.

What was proved by this miraculous event was not so much 'the universal priesthood' (as the Calvinists thought, since Martin Luther was himself ordained); rather the rebirth of the preaching of the Gospel in him proved that the Christian priesthood has just as little exclusive authority or sole right to that preaching as it has any spiritual control over the Lord's institutions.

Far from attributing the slightest part of his calling to his ordination or his ability to preach the Gospel, Martin Luther rejected any claim that ordination be regarded as a sacrament to believers. Obviously it could not be an inherent part of his own ordination that the living preaching of the Gospel should be reborn through him, for this rebirth is a far greater, recognisable miracle of God than the regular preaching of the Gospel can ever be.

Although Ordination may therefore be what I truly believe it to be in spite of Luther's denial – namely the Spirit's sacrament for the Christian scribes who believe in it – it cannot give the slightest lustre to any papistry or hierarchy of priests, whatever the Lutheran evidence. Here it is a question of understanding the Apostle correctly when, in speaking of the preaching of the Word, he asks: "How shall they preach except they be sent?"[451] On the one hand this leads us almost to think of an outward, visible commission, like Ordination with its laying-on of hands; on the other hand the Apostle Paul cannot have been thinking exclusively of this, since he himself was

---

450. Rom 10:14.
451. Rom 10:15.

an exception. Indeed he often asserts his exceptional position in being sent out in a manner known only to himself by the ascended Lord to preach the Gospel with His Spirit. Since, as we know, Martin Luther generally had a very Pauline idea of the Christian life, it is understandable that in front of the Pope and his miscreant priests he supported the Pauline commissioning with a certain one-sidedness. Of course we cannot condone this indefensible one-sidedness by which an exception is turned into a rule, and in fact on behalf of the Apostle Paul we must make the objection against Martin Luther that not only did the Apostle allow himself to be ordained as a missionary with the laying-on of hands, but he also expressly attributes a priestly gift of the Spirit to this laying-on of hands by the Elders; and finally he admits there is a special commissioning to baptise which he did not have. But even taking all this into account the fact still remains that the ascended Lord has reserved the right without any human mediation to commission preachers with the Spirit. When they themselves have been baptised they have the right to baptise whoever they will, so that no priesthood, however genuinely Apostolic it may be, can have a Christian basis for claiming a monopoly either to preach the Gospel or to baptise.[452] In other words they cannot demand a Christian right to spiritual control over either the Christian light or the Christian life. An awareness of this may, indeed must, under certain circumstances produce what is known amongst us as 'revivals' and 'godly assemblies', the quality of whose Christianity must therefore in no way be denied on behalf of the priesthood as being an unacceptable lay activity. It must be judged, like the priest's office, by the relationship to the Christian Confession of faith and song of praise in an indissoluble union first with Holy Baptism, which through rebirth opens the Christian life-springs, and then with Holy Communion, which in communion with the Word itself creates and sustains the Christian stream of life.

For just as the Church's Creed at Baptism is the undeviating rule for all Christian confession and must be the core of all Christian preaching of the Gospel, so must all Christian life be derived exclusively from the Lord's own deeds with the words of His mouth at Baptism and Holy Communion. Only by elevating Christian life does the Church's song of praise become Christian. Thus, it is just as sure a sign of spiritual *death* among the papists that the song of praise in the mother-tongue has been dropped, as the Lutheran song of praise in the mother-tongue is a clear sign of *life* and a valid witness to the Christian character of Lutheran preaching. For the song of praise will always correspond to the preaching because it is with the hymn of praise that the congregation responds to the address. That is why Calvinist preaching in the mother-tongue *also* gave birth to a corresponding song of praise, but only in a Jewish,

---

452. The Conventicle Decree of 1741 in Denmark-Norway prohibited any religious meetings not authorised by the state church and held under the supervision of a state-approved pastor.

not in a Christian form. This denied any Christian life to Calvinist teaching, and on account of its superior attitude to the life-spring in Baptism and the life-stream in Holy Communion, it did not have the best claim to that life. So long as Baptism and Holy Communion are regarded only as shadowy images either of circumcision and the paschal lamb or of spiritual rebirth and the staff of life, they stop themselves from crossing the Red Sea dryshod, and going straight into the Promised Land!

Admittedly, the Lutheran preaching and song of praise had their flaws and their deficiencies, for they did not relate 'faith' to the Word of faith clearly or vividly enough, and they could not therefore clearly and vividly enough help Christian life at its well-spring and in its outflow of the Lord's own words and actions at Baptism and Holy Communion. But because, however dimly, the Lutheran preaching and song of praise presupposed and actively asserted the real presence and life-giving power of God's Word through the Lord's own institutions, Christian life still revealed itself more powerfully and more clearly through them than had been the case for many centuries. Since the faults in the Lutheran preaching of the Gospel and the song of praise have now 'corrected' themselves, so to speak, or rather have allowed themselves to be corrected by the Spirit in the Church's Confession of faith and the life within the Lord's Words of Institution, we have the right to claim that these faults had their root in the lack of light and power that the infant is not accountable for, since it goes without saying that the new-born Christian preaching and the Church's song of praise in the days of Martin Luther and on his lips were only in their infancy.

This perhaps illustrates best how obstructive and inappropriate are any other doctrinal ordinances outside Holy Scripture, be they orthodox altar books or hymnbooks. It cannot be otherwise for the living development of the Lutheran preaching and song of praise in a Christian direction, because even in its most tolerable forms they can only be called a meagrely apportioned and monotonous fare. Such 'food' may be considered necessary in old age, it may prevent feverish illnesses, and it may even delay death for a while; but in childhood it will be far more likely to weaken vitality, prevent physical development, and stunt the child's growth. If, therefore, those two wonderful children of Luther – reborn Christian preaching and the song of praise in each nation's own mother-tongue – are to grow to maturity in the power of the Spirit and, to their glory, become immortal on earth, as we hope and pray they will, then we must disregard all the sulks and frowns of the dullards and give free rein to the preaching of the Gospel and the song of praise in accordance with the Spirit's impulse within the boundaries of the Creed. For this is true 'evangelical freedom', the freedom in Paradise to eat from all of the trees in the garden except the Tree of Death, which is the sort of academic knowledge and theology that puts itself in our Lord's place in order to judge His words and deeds: His Word *to* us and what He works *within* us. We must not give up building on, and resting in, the witness of the Spirit and the Church to the Christian faith and Creed, and to the Lord's institutions as His own deeds, together with the Word of God which He Himself actually is and which He alone has within His power. We must not call into question this foundation of the faith and the very source of the Church's life (the rock with its spring). Nor must we make proud, under whatever name we choose in the seat of judgement, to decide for *ourselves* whether we really do have a living Word of God among us, whether that Word of God is true and good in every way, and whether it really can accomplish great things such as purifying the soul and making life out of death. For then we are standing like Eve beside the forbidden tree, holding court with the serpent on which fruits are pleasant and good in order to acquire a knowledge of good and evil: just as Scripture says, "But I am afraid that just as Eve was deceived by the snake's cunning, your minds may somehow be led astray from your sincere and pure devotion to Christ."[453]

If from this angle and on this path we now approach the question of the individual's Christian certainty of their salvation, which has recently been dragged into the quarrel on the Christian validity of Baptism administered according to the ritual of the Altar Book,[454] then the same thing happens as with all questions of Christian enlightenment; namely, that although we do not find it adequately answered in *any* doctrinal system, we nevertheless find here the great Lutheran principle for Christian enlightenment (these principles of the Word and the faith) to be as fruitful as it is unshakable. Admittedly the papists are right to claim that every individual must build their guarantee of salvation on their participation in the faith, hope, and love of the whole Christian Church, so that it was Martin Luther's great venture to direct every soul in particular to the inner witness of the Holy Spirit as the only token of God's grace and everlasting life. On the other hand, this venture had been made necessary by the deadness with which the priestly hierarchy and compulsory Baptism had smitten the very *concept* of 'the Church'. For just as God is not the God of the dead but the God of the living, so is the Holy Spirit not the spirit of the dead Church, but the spirit of the living Church alone. Thus it is a totally false and pernicious conviction of salvation that people draw from their certainty of having membership of a spiritually dead Church, in which the Christian means to salvation and the Christian necessities of life (Baptism and Holy Communion) are either corrupted or are at any rate not alive and working. For a dead Church such as this is only a self-made spiritual fire insurance society which, in return for a formal payment and an annual subscription undertakes to guarantee its members against all spiritual fire damage both in purgatory and in Hell!

---

453. 2 Cor 11:3.

454. Grundtvig refers to his argument with Bishop of Zealand, Jakob Peter Mynster (1775-1854), whose proposal for a new Altar Book included a change in the wording of the Baptism ritual which Grundtvig strongly opposed.

Martin Luther was right when he said that all the guarantees which such a spiritual fire office could give either to avoid Hell or to enter into Heaven are nothing but fraud and murder of the spirit. And when Luther constantly referred to that external and clear Word of God through which we can and must get to know and understand the Holy Spirit, then his mistake lay, as it did throughout his evangelical work, only in the fact that he confused all his biblical preaching with the Creed and the Words of Institution, as if all of it was an altogether clear Word of God which enabled us to get to know and understand the Holy Spirit.

Thus, as soon as we learn to separate what only we and not our Lord have joined together, so that the Church's Confession of faith at Baptism according to the Lord's institution becomes the clear hallmark both of the Church and its Spirit, then it will become obvious that as members of this Church, as the Christian and spiritual people of God, we can receive the same assurance on the question of our salvation as the Church has through its awareness of the Christian signs of life in the Confession of faith, the preaching of the Gospel, and the song of praise. It is equally obvious that these signs of life will grow stronger and stronger, both in general and in detail, the freer the Confession of faith, the preaching of the gospel, and the song of praise are, whilst every external constraint against the Spirit's preserves both weakens the manifestations of life and conceals the signs of life. For just as no one can be completely sure of the sincerity and stability of their Christian Creed when this confession is a civic decree and its opposite a civic offence, so the Christian preaching of the gospel and the Church's song of praise can never become the strong and clear manifestations and signs of life that give a spiritual guarantee of strength and growth unless they are completely free of external constraint. So whoever sets himself against the freedom of the clergy and the freedom of the hymnbook sets himself, wittingly or unwittingly, just as much against every certain assurance of salvation as against that Spirit which only works with *freedom in freedom* and for the glorious freedom in every way of God's children. Conversely, wherever all things spiritual are free, there we can boldly say to every believer who questions us about the validity of his Baptism: "Why ask me? Ask the Holy Spirit! He who is the Spirit of both faith and Baptism will at once tell you if you were born of water and Spirit to enter into the kingdom of Heaven, and if you are not, He will both urge you and show you the way to be so."

22. Christian, Spiritual, and Eternal Life

Nowadays, when one writes about *real* life as it is lived before our very eyes and from day to day in Denmark, it is actually difficult to be understood! Indeed, everyone who does so actually expects to be grossly *misunderstood* by most readers. So, if we are not believed when we write about earthly things, how can we be believed when we write about heavenly things? It is therefore a divine wonder that some people still speak and write about Christian, spiritual, and eternal life – which apparently no one practises! From the creation of the world until now only one person has actually practised it on earth, namely, the only-begotten in every sense and matchless Jesus Christ, who was crucified in the Holy Land under Pontius Pilate and is now seated in Heaven at the right hand of God, from where He shall come to judge the living and the dead at the Last Day.

This being so, it was no trick when Søren Kierkegaard, to the great applause of the world, described our so-called Christian preaching, Bible-reading, Church worship, infant Baptism, and Holy Communion as an immense tomfoolery and a merry farce! It turned into tragi-comedy, then into deep tragedy, and even into profanity, as many people came to fancy that we so-called pastors, we 'black-gowns',[455] were deceiving them. We were telling them that if they would just listen to us with approval, have their infants baptised, and go to Holy Communion occasionally, then they were participating in a secret life that was for us incomprehensible, yet in a real sense, a Christian, spiritual, and eternal one, just as our Lord Jesus Christ had lived it on earth and promised it eternally to his faithful followers.

No, this was no trick, and Søren Kierkegaard[456] was careful not to write that through his own insight or from the New Testament he had acquired a light and a power to live a real Christian, spiritual, and eternal life which he could transmit to others. Instead he wrote that from his own experience and from the New Testament he had learned and could clearly demonstrate that everything which pretends to be a Christian, spiritual, and eternal life as described in the New Testament – the true and infallible account of the life and teachings of Jesus Christ – is a gross falsehood, a monstrous delusion, and even a great profanity! In this way he clearly pledged both his own honour and the New Testament to the Danish reading public with the contention that no Christian, spiritual, or eternal life exists on earth. So it is up to us and the same Jesus Christ whom

---

455. Danish clergy wear a black cassock and a white ruff collar when on official duty.
456. Søren Kierkegaard (1813-55) was no longer alive when *Basic Christian Teachings* was published in its full version in 1868.

we confess together with the guiding and comforting Spirit to show the world that such a life does exist, even though it has long been hidden and is hard to recognise.

It is more than evident that the solution to this unparalleled task can be achieved only to a small degree by the pen. For we cannot with our pens *create* such a Christian life, when even the Lord's Apostles could not transmit or communicate it with their pens despite their hands presumably being guided by Christ's own spirit. It is also as clear as sunlight that since we do not even *claim* that the Apostolic Writings themselves possess, or lead, a Christian, spiritual, and eternal life, we cannot then, without facing contradiction, ascribe to these writings the ability to transmit or communicate the Christian life which they themselves neither possess nor lead. Nor, without risking blasphemy or ridiculous pride, can we ascribe to our own writings the divine life-force and life-transmission which we deny to the Apostolic Writings!

However, the *same* Apostolic Writings are a true description of the life of Jesus Christ and of Christian life as it was found by those who wrote and those who lived it in the Christian Church. They are also a prophecy of the growth of Christian life in the Church until it reaches the goal and pattern set by Jesus' own life. As such they can be useful and illuminating for those who believe in Jesus Christ and participate in the Christian life. In the same manner our writings too can be useful and illuminating for living Christians, in part when they give a truthful description of the ways and means whereby the present weak, vague, and obscure Christian life has been transmitted to us, and in part when they are a prophecy of how Christian life will grow in the history of the Church until it reaches the fullness, power, and glory of the Lord.

To this end I have devoted a lifetime of writing as best I could and with considerable diligence to making people aware that it is through the Word of the Lord's own mouth spoken at Baptism and Holy Communion and through nothing else that His Spirit and his life-force are communicated. Whenever we rejected or falsified this Word from the mouth of the Lord Himself, His spiritual life disappeared; and when we retained the Word unaltered but only half believed it and expected Spirit, life, and growth to come from other channels, we lost trace of *Christian* life.

From the perplexity in the days of Søren Kierkegaard as well as the confusion during the recent controversy about 'Altar-Book Baptism'[457] it is clear that the usefulness of my writings has not been nearly as great as I wished. But then I had not expected much else for as long as our Christian life – which has neither its source nor its growth in words on a page – could through 'the Word and the faith' at Baptism and Communion be neither more widespread nor more clearly developed than all the signs indicate. I hope, however, that my brief description of 'The Christian Signs of

---

457. In 1838 Bishop Mynster proposed that the direct question regarding renunciation of the Devil should precede only adult and not infant baptism, a proposal that Grundtvig vehemently opposed and one that was ultimately rejected.

Life' may have paved the way for growing enlightenment on the question of living a Christian life, which we have lacked up to now.

It is a Christian insight into life – which enlightens without completely clarifying – that we can summarise these Christian signs into Confession of the faith, preaching the Gospel, and singing God's praises in the language of the people. I have strongly felt the absence of these when I searched for the Christian life in myself and the Church, and when I had to defend our Lord Jesus Christ against the disrespectful accusation that He had permitted his life to die in the Church or had been unable, with the exception of a brief Apostolic period, to bring it out of its swaddling-clothes or nurture it to youthful flowering, let alone to adult maturity.

Following the Apostolic Writings we take for granted that 'faith, hope, and love' are the spiritual and everlasting content of Christian life, but as long as we cannot adequately distinguish between these three in heathen, Jewish, or Christian speech, nor between them in our everyday and our Sunday speech, we cannot demonstrate any clear expressions or signs of life that are *peculiar* to Christianity. All claims to leading a *Christian* life therefore seem to be arbitrary and to involve us in a confusing controversy about the distinction between 'spiritual' and 'physical' in human life and in Christianity's relationship to what our human spirit calls 'spiritual' on the testimony of experience.

We must first discover the Christian expressions of life in the Confession of faith at Baptism, in the Christian hope as we have it in the Lord's Prayer at Baptism and Holy Communion, and in the Christian expression of love in Christ's words of devotion to His believers, or in His declaration of love to his bride, the Church, in Holy Communion. Only then can we show in our Church life the Christian confession, a Gospel proclamation, and a song of praise which are the peculiar and unmistakable signs of Christian faith, Christian hope, and Christian love – what we call among ourselves 'faith, hope, and love'; and only then can we speak clearly and judge thoroughly.

The Christian life in itself will undoubtedly continue to be a profound mystery to us, but the same is true of our entire human life, which is separate from that of the animals; no one can make the Christian life known except through comparable spiritual manifestations of life. If anyone objects that the Christian signs of life, Confession, preaching the Gospel, and the song of praise, are only words and not action, then we rightly answer that the invisible Spirit of humankind as well as of God can demonstrate its life only through the invisible Word which can be heard by the ear and felt in the heart. Every action, by the hand and by all visible things, is loosely related to the invisible Spirit, but we can only glimpse the relationship through a Word of enlightenment and even then we shall only see obscurely in a vague and ambiguous way. Thus, although Christian love, when perfected, will also seek to express itself in a matchless generosity and bodily sacrifice, not only do the Apostolic Writings testify that we can give all we own to the poor and we can give our body to be burned and still not have Christian love, but it is also evident that many people have done both these things without calling themselves 'Christian' or desiring even to be so. Thus, even the most dedicated works of love can only be signs of *Christian* love when they are clearly related to the Christian confession and the Christian song of praise.

This is the outward significance of enlightenment as to 'the Christian signs of life'. The significance inward and upward is even more important for all of us. For while we seek in vain to probe the mysteries of the Christian life, whether it be the mystery of the call to preach the Gospel (the plea of the Christmas message), or the mystery of nurture through Holy Communion, the Christian life-path becomes brighter and easier for us when we see how and in whose company we can seek and expect Christian faith, Christian hope, and Christian love, strengthening the faith, extending the hope, and increasing the love. Moreover, we are comforted by this enlightenment as regards the gap between Christian life among us and the Church today and the description of the Church by the Apostles, partly among themselves and the first fruits of the Church but especially in the figure of Jesus Christ with all its fullness and purity. We are reassured, not like those bookworms who believe in the perfection of an alien life and gnaw away at describing it, but like the bright boy who is reassured by the distance between himself and his adult brother or his aging father. For when we are turned in the right direction concerning our vital consideration of Christian life as a spiritual *human* life – which is just as real and far more human than our *physical* life – then Christian life begins with a real conception according to the will of the Spirit, and, as the Lord says, with a real birth by water and the Spirit. It then continues, as did the Lord himself, to grow in age and wisdom and favour with God and humankind. When this happens, then like the Apostle Paul we are not anxious about our distance from the goal, but strive to forget what is behind us in favour of what is ahead, and in living progress to stretch towards the wreath and the crown.

It is true that when we observe Christian life as well as human life on their path through this world, the mind tells us that there is light behind us but darkness ahead; for we can never understand more of life than what we have experienced. However, on the *Christian* path there is an extraordinary, even a superhuman light, and the Lord has said that whoever follows Him shall never walk in darkness, for He Himself is the true light of the world.[458] What lightens like a lantern our path through the darkness is, as the Apostle writes, a true prophetic Word,[459] which is recognised by its correspondence with the rule of faith[460] and the sure foundation of human life.

458. Jn 8:12.
459. 2 Pet 1:19.
460. The concept of 'rule of faith' was introduced by Irenaeus, see the references in ch. 3.

Thus it is an essential consequence of the Baptismal Covenant that the spiritual life to which we are born in Baptism can in no sense be devilry but in every sense be divine, for Christianity quite clearly presumes that human life in the image of God can only be reborn and renewed by a miraculous separation from devilry. How much of us as we are now born should be considered devilry and how much during our lifetime we have to participate in both our release from devilry and in our growth in all divinity is a puzzle for the healthy human mind that can be solved only by experience. No wonder that independent efforts to analyse and decide the matter have led only to confusion! The more we listen to the description by the scribes of what is called the 'order of salvation' or what Scripture calls putting off the old self and putting on the new,[461] the less we understand the matter; for they create only a boundless confusion in which it seems as if all human life must be eradicated as devilry, or that there is *no* devilry, and human beings should either direct their new Christian life themselves or stand beside it as idle observers.

When one is a living Christian oneself, even if one has not come of age, one realises that neither of these alternatives is true. If there were no Devil, no Satan, no father of lies, no man of darkness, no murdering angel, or if he had no power over man, then there would be no Word of Truth in the Gospel of Christ: not the slightest truth in the message about the Son of God as the Saviour of the world from the power of sin, darkness, and death, which can only exist and be active in an unclean spirit of this world. If, on the other hand, all human nature had become devilish at the Fall, the Son of God could no more have become a real human being than He could have become a devil. Then the *new* being could not have been made in God's image through a rebirth and a renewal of the *old* being but only through a brand-new creation entirely independent of the old being. How the very complex question of sanctification and salvation could take place in fallen and sinful humanity, corporately as well as individually, is hidden from our eyes, just as the Son of God becomes human in all respects yet without sin. Our life as humans cannot show us the new being, who grows up and is liberated from sin and Satan by being cleansed from what "contaminates body and spirit".[462] If we are to know this, the Spirit of truth as the Spirit of our Lord Jesus Christ must reveal it to us. However, since during the growth of the new being we cannot dispense with our tentative knowledge of life's development, the Lord's Spirit will also inform us about this when we pray as it is written: "He will tell you what is yet to come".[463] When this still does not happen, it must be because the Church's faith in the Holy Spirit is either so shaky or so vague that He either cannot be called upon or He can-

---

461. Eph 4:24.
462. 2 Cor 7:1.
463. Jn 16:13.

not be distinguished from the spirits of *delusion*. Only recently, by placing our trust in the Confession of faith at Baptism as a Word to us from the mouth of the Lord Himself, have we gained a sure and definite belief in the Holy Spirit as a divine part of the Trinity and thereby discovered the nature of the 'confession' of the incarnate Jesus Christ upon which the spirit of truth can and shall be distinguished from the spirit of delusion. So it is not until now that we have received 'the revelation of the Spirit' concerning the usefulness for the whole Church and for all of us of keeping the faith and of fighting and winning the crown.[464]

Just as God's Spirit has had the good law from time immemorial that His guidance is 'down-to-earth', so is His revelation about the growth and progress of Christian life so down-to-earth that it offends all those self-opinionated people who want grandiloquent ideas alone to be seen as 'spiritual'. Equally it is so 'human' that we will take it to be a revelation of our own spirit unless we note how strange it seems to us from the start, and how hard it is to find ourselves in it.

To implement the commandment to *love* in the Christian Church and for Christian *life* to be everlasting, it must of course be a consummate *life of love*, yet we know that in this world from beginning to end it can only make itself known as a life of *faith*. This is so 'down-to-earth' and so 'human' that we might think no revelation of it would be necessary; similarly the Apostle Paul writes expressly to the Corinthians, "For we live not by faith, but by sight,"[465] and to the Galatians, "The life I now live in the body, I live by faith in the Son of God,"[466] which is a rule of faith that permeates all the Apostolic Writings. Yet despite this, the entire history of Christian life and all knowledge of Scripture teach us that such 'plain' enlightenment was very rare, and even where it did exist, for example in Martin Luther, it was far too dull to shed light on life in general as a true life of faith – what the world calls with a shrug 'a mere poetic life of the imagination'. Nevertheless, that does not make it any the less true and real, for divine poetry (*poiesis*) is a *real* creation, and the divine imagination is the Spirit that enlivens and demonstrates its power to make even our body spiritually alive by taking our physical tongue into its service so that it expresses not what we ourselves think but what God thinks both of Himself and of us.

Perhaps even more down-to-earth and human is the realisation that Christian life in the Church and among all of us follows the same seasons of the year as our former *human* life; it grows only gradually from spring to harvest, or from the dim life of the child to the powerful, clear-sighted life of the adult. Thus was our Lord born and grew up on earth like any other son of humankind, and thus must human life,

---

464. Rev 2:10.
465. 2 Cor 5:7.
466. Gal 2:20.

whether old or new, be a true and genuine *human* life and always resemble *itself*, if it is to live up to its name. Nevertheless, as we know, the Apostle Paul is probably the last of the biblical writers to have been, in Christian terms, an infant before he became a man. Since then the Church has never used the old life as a mirror for the new, and in consequence it has grown far more strongly downwards than upwards, believing in the end that one might just as well begin the Christian life from the top as from the bottom; one might just as well begin with the Lord's Table as the Baptism of renewal or with the hymn to love as with the Confession of faith.[467]

Furthermore, it is of course a very down-to-earth and human fact that it is the same human life that is fallen which is to be raised, the same prodigal son that was lost who was found, the same one that was dead who became alive, the same lost and exhausted sheep that was carried home on the shepherd's shoulders.[468] In the same manner the new being is, strictly speaking, no other than the old being, but simply another person in the same figurative sense that Saul became another person when he was anointed and the Spirit came upon him.[469] It is quite clear that God's Son belonged to the old being when he came to earth as the offspring of a woman, of Abraham's and David's seed.

Even the new human body of the resurrection was basically the same as the body that was nailed to the cross. Nonetheless, all the scholars who have emphasised that Christian life was the life of our Lord Jesus Christ and no one else have more or less cut off the 'new human life' in Christ and His Church from the old human life, as if the latter were a physical life of sin which had to be destroyed and pulled up by the roots for the new and entirely different human life to succeed it. This basic error led not only to all those monastic rules but also to all our so-called orthodox dogmatics in which our fundamental corruptibility and spiritual inability to do good was made the foundation for the work of reconciliation, even though it was evident that all human life in need of salvation, reconciliation, rebirth and renewal in the image of the Creator would be destroyed. The natural consequence was that it became clearer day by day that the old human life, now abandoned, went to blazes, while that which called itself 'the new life' was no life at all, had no power whatsoever, and did nothing but at most write dogmatic works and learn them by heart. Or the new spiritual life became inhuman, a life of the Devil, battling against humanity and under all sorts of false names raising to the skies the wilfulness and self-righteousness that have always been characteristic of Satan, the murderer of human life.

467. i.e. 1 Cor 13 and the Apostles' Creed.
468. Respectively, the Prodigal Son, Lk 15:11-32; the Widow's Son, Lk 7:11-17 et al.; and the Lost Sheep, Lk 15:1-7.
469. Grundtvig follows the common belief that Saul changed his name to Paul as a result of his Damascus conversion. In fact Paul is another name for Saul, as can be seen in Acts 13:9, which describes him as "Saul, who was also called Paul".

That is why both Anders Larsen[470] and Andreas Rudelbach[471] can still agree to condemn me for this down-to-earth realisation: that according to His own words the Son of Man, who came not to destroy but to save human life, conducts Himself in Denmark as He did in the Holy Land. He does not kill His Danish disciples but forgives them their sins and opens a wellspring in them which flows into an everlasting life; they therefore give Him hearty thanks on behalf of the old man, the old Adam, who also had his sins forgiven and rose from the dead to the new life in the image of God that had become so outworn and corrupted that it would have been forever lost without this powerful and loving renewal.

Finally, it is a quite down-to-earth human truth and even an evangelical truth that God the Father and His Spirit treat us the same way as they want us to treat our neighbour. They overcome evil with good, which according to all human experience is the only way evil can be thoroughly conquered, driven out, and replaced. Even God's own law, which can crush the proudest human heart with thunder and lightning, cannot eradicate the slightest evil desire or lust, which yield only to the good and loving desire and demand – of which evil desire is a distorted image. Similarly, pride cannot be driven out by the heart and in the heart except through humility; so too, sensuality, which is impure love, can only be driven out by pure love; and covetousness for the glories of this world can only be driven out by a sincere desire for the glories of God's kingdom. Yet I know of no Christian moralist since the days of the Apostles who has ever described sanctification in this Spirit or in this light. Like the mystics,[472] such moralists began with the heart, and thus began in the darkness of the old being who was to be reborn and nurture himself with his own love (love of himself) of God and his neighbour. From first to last this was a false, artificial Christianity. Or they began with the Law, not as a mirror but as a living force and power which was to demolish the temple of idols and out of its ruins erect the temple of the Holy Spirit. This was attempted despite the Lord's testimony that when sanctification begins from the *outside* one can build only graves full of impurities and dead bones, and despite all human experience that when sanctification begins from the *inside* we can put on the whole armour of the Law and fight even the slightest evil desire until Doomsday without moving it a hairsbreadth. Since Christian life in the world will always continue to be a life of faith, and thus spiritual and invisible,

---

470. The lay preacher Anders Larsen Gamborg had attacked Grundtvig in a 32-page pamphlet entitled *On the Battle for the Church in Denmark*.

471. Andreas Rudelbach had been Grundtvig's friend and co-publisher of the anti-rationalist *Theological Monthly* (1825-28) but they had quarrelled over Grundtvig's view of the Creed.

472. The Christian 'mystics' flourished in the High Middle Ages in Europe (1100-1450) proposing new models and guidelines for Christian communities. Among them are Bernard of Clairvaux, Francis of Assisi, Thomas Aquinas, and two women: Hildegard of Bingen, and Julian of Norwich.

while we nevertheless lead a physical life of the body, the Christian Church and all its members must, as the Apostle writes, use the force of law,[473] be it the Mosaic or the Danish Law, to regulate their outward conduct. If we wish to live and grow as Christians, we must guard against giving our legal conduct a Christian appearance, and even more against changing the Gospel of Christ into a so-called new 'Christian law', aimed at forcing our souls into a Christian way of thinking and our hearts into a Christian life of love. Attempting this, we either know nothing about Christian living or we are squandering it, for we can be neither saved nor sanctified by the Law without falling from grace.

We can already see this tangled knot in Christian life as being a life of *faith* from all the letters of Paul the Apostle. If this knot has not choked Christian life among non-Jewish Christians from the very beginning then it has certainly stunted its growth, causing a malady that has been obvious since the days of the Apostles. Since it can only be loosened by the resurrection of the body from the dead at the Last Day or by a transformation of the flesh among those who wait for the visible return of the Lord, it is important not to try to cut the knot but to live with it in faith as a thorn in the flesh and to be content with the grace of God whose "power is made perfect in weakness".[474]

Even when we hold firm to the faith that the Christian spiritual life into which we are reborn in Baptism and in which we are nurtured by Holy Communion is truly an everlasting life, we must nevertheless give up the idea that we can gain a clear insight in this world into the *eternity* of Christian life. This is because it is only in perfect unity with the Lord and His Church that this clear insight can come about, and because this insight is impossible except when the inward becomes outward. All our senses and bodily functions then become as spiritual as the Word of faith, hope, and love is spiritual on our lips and in our hearts. Our whole body then becomes an eternally pleasing habitation, a perfect instrument, and a clear, unblemished mirror of the Spirit, the divine power which has issued from the Father in order to begin and complete the good works throughout our Lord's Church. This work will only be completed on the Day of our Lord Jesus Christ, and it will work in us toward this end only when we truly deny ourselves, give up all spiritual independence, and willingly let the Holy Spirit as a divine person guide our heart and our tongue as the renewed, divine life-force which alone can create, maintain, and nurture our new human life in the image of God in Jesus Christ.

---

473. Num 27:11; 35:29. Rom 10:4. For Paul, God's justice lies beyond human law; no law can bring about salvation.

474. 2 Cor 12:7. In this verse Paul speaks of his own "thorn in the flesh", which has occasioned much debate – was it a physical ailment, an emotional affliction, a constant temptation of some kind, or something else? However, he describes the benefit of the thorn as being "to keep me from becoming conceited", and in v.9 God tells him, "My power is made perfect in weakness."

23. Inborn and Reborn Human Life

A monkey only needs to stand on its hind legs, wear clothes, and imitate our way of eating and a little of our tailoring for it to be justifiably considered in our eyes a human being like other simple folk. As long as this is so, there is no point in talking or writing about *actual* human life, be it the inborn child-life with which we emerge from our mother's womb or the reborn child's human life into which we are born through the Lord's Baptism in water and Spirit. Moreover, even though we have the gift of speech – the written and spoken word, which genuinely and recognisably separate us from the speechless animals – human life remains in pitch darkness if our speech is but idle talk, lost in its own sounds. For then human language is not so different in kind from all the braying and barking, let alone its imitation, which starlings, magpies, and especially parrots can be trained to perform.

In human language and human speech there must be something amazing and unparalleled which neither bird nor beast can be trained to copy, in short something creative and divine. We must call it so because in our experience we have it in common only with one another, and consequently with our common, invisible God and Creator. It is only when we have realised this that we are qualified to reflect on the various stages of human life and the various forms in which this life has been or can be revealed to us. We are soon aware that human language and speech have three purposes peculiar to this world, three characteristics that distinguish them from all that we call drivel and parroting. Although there may be considerable differences in the extent to which power, truth, and love can be vividly expressed in human speech, something of all three of them is found in all human speech worthy of that name. So when we come across speech that has no power in it, we call it dead and empty; if it is without truth, we call it false and counterfeit; and if it is without love, we call it inhuman and heartless.

Human life finds its sole power of expression, its certain purpose, and its clear mirror in our human conversation with a higher, invisible power, possessing inner truth, and sincere love. If this is an unshakeable fact, then we have a standpoint from which life can be viewed, from which we can see ever more clearly that between our inborn and our reborn human lives there is a world of difference. They differ in quality, breadth, and degree with regard to their vitality. They differ in the truthfulness, love, and goodness with which human life expresses itself in human speech. And yet it is the very same human life that we are speaking of, with the same laws and original characteristics, and the same energies and hallmarks. Thus in its darkest, poorest, and murkiest form it is nevertheless of the same basic nature as in its richest, purest, and clearest form. To put it in a nutshell, the thief on the cross who shared the same human life as God's only Son, our Lord Jesus Christ, and to whom he cried, "Remember me, when You come into Your kingdom", received the truthful, uniquely powerful and loving answer, "Truly I tell you, today you shall be with me in Paradise."[475]

If this were not so, God's only Son could just as little have willed Himself to be and become a real human child born of a woman as any woman-born *human* child would or could have been a real divine child, born of water and spirit. For then divinity would have excluded humanity, and humanity in turn divinity, and there would no longer be any spiritual or heartfelt reciprocal feeling, no inclination, no interaction. It is therefore completely out of order when Muhammedan[476] theologians under all manner of names have agreed with Muhammed and the Koran in declaring divine and human nature so different in kind that no living contact between them was conceivable. They deny the possibility of the incarnation of God's Son and the fusion of divine and human nature in the personality of our Lord Jesus Christ, and consequently they deny the possibility of the entire concept of redemption. Finally they deny the possibility of any divine revelation to mankind and the divine granting of our prayer requests. They believe that the former, which is a fundamental falsehood, causes all the other greater or smaller falsehoods, and that since humans were not created in the image of God, they have no need to 'fall' or be 'reborn', or in general have any concept of a true living God, His Spirit, His Word, and His kingdom.

By way of contrast, it is obviously contradictory, nonsensical, and utterly tedious when theologians – be they Catholic, Protestant, Evangelical-Lutheran or Biblical – admit and argue for our creation in the image of God and that image as being re-stored through faith in the Son of God and the Son of Man, our Lord Jesus Christ, yet simultaneously claim that the Fall, which happened between the Creation and the restoration – and which makes rebirth and restoration indispensable to salvation – should have deformed or rather totally destroyed mankind and all human life in God's image. According to them, there is not an atom or seed left of the inborn glory and the God-created relationship with us, so everything that the Muhammedan theologians claim about humankind in general is true of the fallen being. The whole history of revelation and the whole work of redemption is thus a series of impossibilities that can only be overcome by a dead and impotent written word that what is impossible for human beings is possible for God.

---

475. Lk 23:42.

476. As was common in his day Grundtvig uses the designation 'Muhammedan' to mean Muslim; this usage is now unacceptable to most Muslims (cf. Martin Luther King's common use of 'negro'). Similarly, Grundtvig often uses 'Turk' as a synonym for Muslim, since Turkey was the land closest to Denmark where Islam flourished.

I call this written language 'dead and impotent' because in its dead and impotent literalness it can appear to be useful in overcoming all kinds of impossibilities. For as soon as the Word of the Lord becomes spirit and life for us, we realise that what is true about this Word and what it can and will destroy are only the real impossibilities which are impossible where omnipotence is lacking. This in no way applies to, nor can or will destroy, the figurative impossibilities that we should rather call 'undoabilities' or 'unsayabilities'. I refer here to the things that neither God nor human beings can do without being in open conflict with themselves, or say without openly contradicting themselves. To claim in this connection that everything we find impossible is possible for God would be a mockery of God and a denial of the truth. Against this the voice of God within us and our awareness of truth, our 'conscience', revolts when the Word in our mouth and heart is openly denied all opportunity to express any spiritual or eternal truth unless it were the only truth available to humans – in other words, that there was *no* spiritual and eternal truth, or that it was not the truth which was true, but that *lying* was the truth.

For most people this must sound like hair-splitting or very 'dark speech',[477] but this is not so for Christians, who believe that the Saviour of the world, God's only Son, our Lord Jesus Christ, is both eternal truth and the Divine Word itself in His own divine person. From this it follows that what conflicts with eternal truth is 'undoable', i.e. impossible for God, and that any such word that was true would extinguish and destroy the light of the Word itself. This is impossible for the Word that is God and became flesh, in the sense that it would be impossible for God, for He neither can nor will deny Himself, because denial of the truth is confirmation of the lie and equivalent to a real 'un-word', the first-born son of the un-Spirit, the Liar, the Devil.

It also follows from this that all the scholars who strictly adhere to the dogma that through the Fall human beings became so alien to God and all things divine as never to have been created in God's image in the first place – but were either animals or non-persons – also claim, quite rightly, that all sinful people are children of the Devil who nevertheless, through faith in Him who came to destroy the works of the Devil, shall be re-created as children of God! Nevertheless, they believe that this will happen in a manner quite incomprehensible to us and quite impossible for the true God and the everlasting Word of Truth!

This is undoubtedly in direct conflict with what we know of the Lord's teaching and with the Apostles' written testimony. Yet these theologians argue from the outset that it is a characteristic of God that everything that is impossible for human beings is very possible for God – including the ability to destroy with the one hand what He has built up with the other, and even raise a proud building that can defy Time and

---

477. Num 12:8.

the portals of Hell! I imagine that these theologians must think it to be a part of our basic Christian teachings that what is possible even for uneducated folk and what the Devil can do as easily as anything – namely contradict himself with every breath – would be wrong to assert as being impossible for God. Although this is madness, I have no other explanation as to how theologians who not only swear that God's revealed Word is to be found in the Bible alone but also maintain the so-called 'inspiration' of every jot of Scripture, nevertheless have no qualms about arguing to be God's Word the exact *opposite* of what Scripture says. This requires a secret initiation by the Spirit into a soaring fantasy that mocks all borders, including those between light and darkness, between truth and untruth, and between wisdom and madness!

The Lord says: "The reason I was born and came into the world is to testify to the truth. Everyone on the side of truth listens to me.[478] It is not the healthy who need a doctor, but those who are sick. I came not to call the righteous, but sinners to repentance.[479] Whoever belongs to God hears what God says, but[480] you belong to your father, the devil, and you seek to carry out your father's desires who was a liar from the beginning. When he lies, he speaks his native language." When the Lord says all this, He testifies that no one comes to Him without being drawn by the heavenly Father and being taught by God,[481] and all His teaching is in keeping with this. If this were not so, He must surely be studiously contradicting Himself if it was also His genuine opinion that all humankind except Himself – and this includes His mother Mary, His father Abraham, and the disciple He loved – were just as much children of the Devil as Cain and Judas Iscariot! The only difference would be that some believed that as God's only Son He could and would in some impossible way turn the Devil's young into children of God and that through this faith they truly *became* children of God, whereas those who could not and would not believe in this impossibility remained for ever the Devil's young!

The pen does not care what is written by it, nor does the paper blush, but every Christian surely feels that he could never allow such blasphemous words to cross his lips. He would turn away in disgust from any who in the name of the gospel of Christ spoke such profanity in direct conflict with the word and teaching of the Lord as well as all conscience and sound common sense.

Moreover, as a story of divine revelation among human children, the so-called Bible Story can only be true on the condition that human life, before and after the Fall and before and after the Rebirth, is extremely homogeneous and basically the same. If Adam's human life in the image of God had been entirely *destroyed* by the

478. Jn 18:37.
479. Lk 5:31-32.
480. Jn 8:47.
481. Jn 14:6.

Fall, then God could not even *speak* to the fallen Adam, nor could Adam answer Him. Even less could Adam's child Abraham be called the friend of God,[482] or God speak to Adam's child Moses as man to fellow-man, or God's spirit rest upon Adam's children, Samuel and David, and upon all the prophets and John the Baptist. God would have been unable to use human tongues in His speech or touch human hearts with His voice; Adam's kin would have been put under a spell and bewitched into a species of animal or a devil's brood, or into a monster with bestiality and devilishness shackled unnaturally together, having nothing to be saved from or to. If this had been the case, what the Devil's children have always thought and said would make sense: that our so-called 'human existence' was no more than part of the fallen angels' punishment in Hell and imprisonment in the chains of darkness – something to which the Egyptians gave good expression when they said that the 'gods of the fear of hurricane and lightning' had hidden among the animals.[483]

Our Holy Scripture and our born-of-a-woman Jesus Christ tell us that despite the Fall and all its fearsome consequences Adam and Eve's human life in God's image has been transmitted unbroken to our Saviour as the 'seed of woman'.[484] In Him, the second Adam, all humankind is purified, reconciled with God, and raised to a new life in the righteousness of truth. If we accept this, we must necessarily also see the new Christian life in the Lord's Church as being the very same life that originated with Adam, was transmitted through Eve, was fallen, despoiled, abused, and corrupted by the evil in us all. It was then *raised* from the Fall, was redeemed, healed, and divinely endowed in Christ. Through Baptism, human life was perpetually reborn in the Christian Church, and for ever and for all people this Christian rebirth and restoration presupposes – and through the Holy Spirit springs from – the original life of humanity, which like Eve is the only human mother of life on earth. She can never sink so deep or be so impoverished or corrupted that she cannot seek and find mercy in God and bear children for the All-Highest, for as the prophet says: "Should I who let others give birth have my womb closed up?"[485]

Over this necessarily obscure housekeeping of God's mercy the light now rises when we regard the Word with God and human beings not merely as the only medium of revelation, but in consequence as the light of life of which Scripture says that everything being revealed is light,[486] and that the Word is the light of life which gives light to everyone coming into the world.[487] We should also regard it as the sole expression

---

482. Isa 41:8; Jas 2:23.
483. A possible reference to among others Set (or Seth), the ancient Egyptian god of storms and chaos.
484. Gen 3:15. At least as far back as Irenaeus (2nd cent.), Christ has been identified as the 'seed of woman'.
485. Isa 66:9: "'Do I close up the womb when I bring to delivery?,' says your God."
486. Eph 5:13.
487. Jn 1:9.

of *spiritual* light, so that the Word among us is both the divine image of life and the image of light in which God created humankind.

Accordingly, in the *Word* to humankind concerning invisible, spiritual, and eternal things we can follow the complexity and development of human life. We can trace the Fall with all its grievous and corrupting consequences as well as our rehabilitation with all its blessed and joyful fruits. While we cannot be tempted to *disregard* the destruction of human life in sin and its loss in death, we cannot equally fail to appreciate life as the uniform nature and unbroken context of the Word. And in this we also see the light rising over the relation of all peoples and tongues to the new Christian life and the new tongues, as of fire, which rest over each of them finding expression as the Spirit moves and speaking of the same great work of God's mercy in all peoples' own language.

This illumination of human life and human language by a living voice is an inseparable and essential condition for all sound speech concerning the Word of God entering into and engaging with human life, i.e. in all human speech on divine revelation and its impression on human hearts and its expression through human tongues. We can claim that this illumination is more simply human than it is actually Christian, for it has to do with both the relation between God and human beings and between spirit and dust in general, and consequently it can also be imagined to have existed *before* the coming of Christianity. The Christian revelation is also literally the incarnation of the Word, its 'taking flesh', and Christian worship of God in spirit and truth is the reception of the Word of the body and the outpouring of that Word (the Word heard and the Word confessed). Essentially, the illumination of the Word has its source in Christian life, and is utterly indispensable for the full development, growth, and enlightenment of human life. It is an obscure and complex question as to how this illumination of the Word in the conditions of human life fermented and spread abroad as a doctrine of Logos or 'Christologies'[488] in the ancient Greek Church. We still find it hard to clarify this, and thus there is no illumination available here. By contrast it will be an incalculable contribution to our understanding if we look at the life of the Word and the Tongue in the history of God's peoples and our own particular people, so to this end I shall endeavour to direct the attention of all enlightened Christians.

It would be a digression to introduce the reader to this observation of the Hebrew and the Danish language and to compare their ability to express spiritual matters with spiritual words, so I shall leave that for another time. In closing, let me therefore attempt in general to cast light on the terribly misunderstood link between what is of 'the people' and what is properly "Christian". I shall do so by drawing attention to

---

488. Grundtvig's own footnote: "One needs to know that 'Logos' in Greek corresponds to 'Ordet' in Danish" (i.e. 'the Word' in English, ed.).

the indissoluble link of every language to the heart, thought, and development of the people for whom it is their mother-tongue.

Wherever the Spirit of Christ and the Gospel arrive, they do not bring with them the Hebrew, the Greek, or any other language, and they are not bound *by* them when addressing believers. Under every sky they borrow the *language of the people* as a means of expression and action. Two things follow from this: that from the outset Christianity must settle for the degree of convenience that the local language offers to carry and express spiritual light and life; and further, that with all the power and right that God's Spirit has to bend and employ all languages to its will, to the demands of truth, and the need for love, it must, in order to reach its goal of animating and enlightening people, move *in the direction of the people* in the spirit of their mother-tongue.

If a heathen language – let us say, Chinese, though I know not with how much or little right – did not have the words and expressions for the invisible yet living God as the Lord of all things visible, then the Spirit of Christ could not possibly reveal either itself or the Word of God's mercy in that language. To reveal oneself and divine truth to someone can only happen through words that are known and can be appropriated, making that person aware of God and the divine, the invisible, and the eternal – which is what these things are in truth.

That bending and development which the Spirit of God must exert on every heathen language to make it suitable for expressing the revelation of both the Old and the New Covenant is of great magnitude, and yet it is the necessary basis for the spirit and origin of the mother-tongue. A heathen language may often lack words for 'godly' and 'godliness', for 'spiritual' and 'spirituality', but if it is to receive these and numerous other developments and directions of God's Spirit, it must not at the outset lack words such as 'God' and 'spirit', or basic spiritual words such as 'truth', 'conscience', 'freedom', and 'love', which are essential to divine revelation if it is to embark on its living work. Moreover, we know that experience teaches us that the living development of every language in a spiritual direction only takes place alongside a corresponding development of the life of the people in general. This being so, we are compelled to regard the life of the people in any one place as the basis and precondition for the new Christian life, since it is only in the life of the various peoples that human life is truly present, just as it only through the peoples' own languages that human words are actively at work.

Just as it would be inane to seek to ban and as far as possible eradicate the ancient, primordial life of humanity in order to make room and scope for the new Christian human life, it would be equally wrong-headed and an inane attempt to anathematise and as far as possible uproot the life of the people to replace it with *Christian* life. For if we say to the spirit of the people, "Away with you, unclean spirit, and make room for the Holy Spirit!" we may get rid of the people's spirit but we are so far from replacing it with the Holy Spirit that we risk closing off ourselves and the people from all spirits, from all spiritual influence and inspiration, and from *all* understanding and enlightenment of the spirit and the heart.

24. Word and Faith According to Christ's own Teaching

'The Word and the faith' was the general watchword at the great turn of the tide, the so-called Reformation of the 16th century, and no other reformer set such heartfelt spiritual store by these fundamental forces of the working of God's grace as Martin Luther. Nor is any Christian reformation, i.e. 'renewal', imaginable without those fundamental forces being regarded in the Lord's and their own light, interacting vitally and constantly. For just as it is written that everything came into being through God's Word, and nothing without it, so is that Word the only living, recognisable expression of the Spirit in both Heaven and earth. Similarly, just as the Lord testifies that with faith everything is possible, so does experience testify that for lack of faith everything spiritual is *impossible*.

With 'the Word and the faith' we have actually formulated the foundational doctrine for all true enlightenment, not only for Christianity but for all the divine and human workings of spirit and heart. Yet this in itself is far from being a renewal in general of Christianity between God and human beings or in particular of Christian life from the days of the Apostles – meaning life through faith in the Son of God. Indeed, this renewal, this actual reformation, which was Martin Luther's wish and which his life and career demonstrate, seems all the more to have been almost strangled at birth and either way only now appears to be crawling out of its swaddling-clothes.

To be sure, the reasons for this disfavour and slow progress are many, and are best gathered in the fact that what was sought and achieved was a state church which resembled the church-state! For when a state church is most tolerant of the Word and the faith, it is nonetheless always a swaddling-cloth of steel wire or a corset that life in its childhood form can barely tolerate. However free the external movement had become, we would never have progressed without enlightenment concerning the Word and the faith, which was reserved for the *present*. So we no longer speak separately about 'the Word and the faith' or 'the Word and the sacraments' as being two equally divine fundamental forces which should only work together towards Christian rebirth and renewal because that is what God wants, since they could each *separately* accomplish everything. Instead we say that it is only 'the Word of faith' and 'faith in the Word' that we are speaking of and that their joint action and interaction, as much from our side as from God's, is the necessary assumption and condition of the Christian's human life.

It is fair to say that all this was Martin Luther's opinion when he spoke about the Word and the faith or the Word and the Sacraments; for he rejected any elevation of the wild faith that commits to something other than an outwardly recognisable Word of God; and he was equally strongly against the papistry of taking the so-called 'sacraments' as being the means of grace unless it was with God's Word. He may have passionately asserted that without this the water of Baptism was no more than plain water, yet he retained the dangerous combination of 'the Word and the Sacraments' as though separately they could offer either complete or partial salvation. He may have understood and enjoined that when Scripture gets bogged down in history and scholarship, it is no longer vitally committed to the grace of God and the Word of everlasting life, yet he offered no other outwardly recognisable Word of God than the *written* word, to which faith must adhere in order to be Christian, to be considered active, and to overcome the world.

It is therefore far from our intention to boast of our enlightenment regarding the Word and the faith as being brand-new, since we gladly admit that it is the same ancient Christian enlightenment which our Lord Himself provided by lighting His candle to shine for all those in His house, the candle by which Martin Luther found his way out of the darkness of the papacy. So for the sake of Truth and the Church we must not only admit but actually remind ourselves that even for Luther much remained obscure as to how the Word and the faith and the Word and the Sacraments related to each other and were combined in the great work of rebirth and renewal in Christ's Church. Day by day the thought and the speech of the Lutheran scribes on this vital subject became duller and more confused, so that nowadays, even when we use the plainest words and clearest thought about ancient Christian enlightenment, we still have trouble making ourselves understood. This foundational doctrine about the Word and the faith – the Christian Word of God and the corresponding faith of the Church as the two inseparable fundamental forces in the order of salvation – was hidden during the papacy, but re-discovered by Luther.

Fortunately, however, women and children, or even people in general, are not, and never have been, like the scribes and scholars who so often have no faith at all in everlasting life, or are so stubborn in their delusion that by ransacking some written word or other they have either found or will find one of the *days* of everlasting life, and that if the unlettered and uneducated are to have a share in it, then it is only through their believing the scribes and learning their writings and their way of thinking by heart!

It is the testimony of Scripture that when the Word became flesh and dwelt among the children of humankind with the glory of the only-begotten Son, the Jewish *scribes* would not come to Him who alone had the Word of everlasting life, in order to gain life from His grace. No more can we expect our contemporary scribes, although they call themselves 'Christian' and labour under that delusion, to stand in line to grant any power to the fundamental Christian enlightenment to which the Apostolic Writings are testimony, namely, that we have *among* us the Word of everlasting life, full of grace and truth in the Word of faith, hope, and love from the very mouth of our Lord Jesus Christ, with His own voice speaking to all of us through His own institutions of Holy Baptism and Holy Communion. This Word of God's grace is assuredly the same as that which the Apostolic Writings describe and testify to, but of course it cannot be found alive and dynamic in dead and silent written words where it has neither spirit nor life. It is only to be found in the believing, immortal mouth of the Church as the audible confession of Christ's gospel, its loud proclamation, and its joyful song of praise, which are its living, universally valid, unshakable testimony.

Let us consider what it means that 'The Word became flesh' in order to dwell among us – when the heavenly Father's only-begotten Son most clearly revealed His glory in human form with divine words and deeds. In all four gospels we find plenty of scribes among His audience tempting Him and seeking His life, but only one of them actually coming up to Him to *find* everlasting life. And even he, Nicodemus by name, whom we meet in a friendly conversation with the Lord, dared not come in the daytime, and was shaken in His faith in the divine teacher as soon as He showed him to the waters of rebirth and the steam-carriage of the Spirit.[489] This only needs to be *heard* for one to find everlasting life. Nicodemus never came back to the Lord before He died, so it is still a question whether his faith ever truly came alive!

Let us further reflect that the Lord's twelve Apostles were unlettered men, and that the thirteenth, His only scholarly Apostle, Paul, belonged first to His most spiteful enemies and had to be driven by the ascended Saviour, with violence and force as it were, to conversion and faith! Let us then be amazed that there are still certain scribes among us who allow themselves to be empowered by the Word from the Lord's mouth and seek within it everlasting life, rather than wonder that there are not more of them!

This is not the place for a deeper study as to why it is hardest for scribes to come to the Word of the Lord's mouth and gain life from it when, as Scripture says, the Lord Himself has testified that human beings live by the Word that issues from God's mouth,[490] and the Apostolic Writings testify throughout that He places this Word in the mouth of His Church! Only in passing will we mention that although the written

---

489. Here Grundtvig really does use the steam-carriage as an image of the Spirit (*Aandens dampvogn*). The first steam carriage was built in 1769 by Nicholas Cugnot. By 1843 there were commercial steam carriages at work in London, most of them on rails. In 1843 together with his 18-year-old son Svend (b. 1824) Grundtvig had actually travelled in a steam *train* on a railroad/railway (the words are recorded in Broseley, Shropshire as being synonymous in the early days). In a letter to Lise dated 25th June 1843 he wrote, "I have spent the week since Monday with Mr Wade here in Oxford. We travelled most of the way by railroad, which was not at all pleasant for me (*som slet ikke behagede mig*)." In a further letter to Lise dated 15th August 1843 he wrote "We took the railroad from Darlington to Leeds... and then rolled along above and below earth to London."

490. Mt 4:4.

word is not even a shadow-image of the spoken word, in no way resembles it, and is no more than an arbitrary sign for it, nevertheless the meaning follows the word in all languages, so, for the unenlightened, the mixing and confusing of speech and writing are not only tempting but almost unavoidable. Women feel that there is a similar difference between the same loving words flowing from warm lips compared with those from a cold pen as there is between the kiss of those same warms lips compared with the kiss of cold letters – yet even they dare not believe their hearts more than the pens of the scribes! When the Spirit is truly speaking to the Church and demonstrating with fire and power that He is present in the mouth's words about matters of the spirit, of the heart, of eternity – which He neither can nor will be in the *written* word or any other work of human hand – only then does the human heart in us all, and particularly in the woman, feel that it both dares to and, for the sake of conscience and truth, is driven to lay its faith in the Spirit's testimony with no heed for any objection from all manner of scholarship or worldly wisdom.

When we therefore write about these things, we must seriously recall that according to the foundational enlightenment of the Word from the Lord's own mouth and the faith in it which we endeavour to maintain, our *writing* cannot possibly give birth to any living conviction among our readers that human beings live only through the Word as warmly as it issues from God's *mouth*. We must either assume this living conviction already exists among our readers, or we must write to them thus: 'If you wish to understand us, go and listen to what the Spirit says orally and audibly to the Church! All that we can otherwise do with the pen for our readers' spiritual benefit is to make signs that can only be understood and applied by those who have heard God's Spirit and are more than open to the Word from the glowing tongues that prove themselves to the burning hearts!'

We can no more transmit spiritual life with our fingers and pens than we can light a spiritual candle with them; we can only point to both of these in the spoken Word of the Spirit, which no earthly eye can see and which no one knows unless they have heard its voice and felt its power. For it is only through the power of its living Word that the Spirit can prove its spiritual, invisible, and intangible truth and reality. Nonetheless, as testimony the Apostolic Writings are absolutely indispensable to the Church, and even our own Christian writings are neither ineffective nor superfluous for Christian readers in our time, but are essential for those who feel the need to account for their faith and their hope, both for themselves and each other.

Thus we hear and receive in faith the testimony of the Spirit concerning God's Word to us from the Lord's own mouth at Holy Baptism and Holy Communion; we hear the testimony of faith in this Word of God as being one in spirit with both the Lord Himself and God's Word concerning eternity, which is divinely aware of itself; we hear that in the course of time it became flesh, became like one of us in every way except without sin; and we hear that in Spirit He is with all His people, that He is truly alive as a spiritual body and presence until the end of the world. When as a result of this we feel ourselves reborn through Baptism into the kingdom of God and incorporated through Holy Communion into the Lord's spiritual body, which is His community, we all more or less feel the need to make something clear to ourselves and others: namely, that despite it sounding in the ears of worldly wisdom every bit as secretive and fanciful as the spirit which the wildest, darkest fanatics usually call 'God's Holy Spirit' and have often called 'Christ's Spirit', our faith and confession is both recognisable and completely different from everything else. Moreover, it has within it the clearest co-inherence and the plainest comprehensibility for all real people who believe themselves to be created in the true image of God to participate in His everlasting life.

Worldly wisdom claims that this presumption of man's true creation in God's image for everlasting life is an irrational fancy which builds solely on Genesis and stands or falls with the ancient book, whose divine infallibility we shall not seek to prove. In claiming this, the world forgets two incontestable things. If human beings are not created in the image of God as truly as any child can bear their parents' image, it would be impossible for us to have any true, living idea of God or His attributes – which we are capable of when there is something in us that is also in God. Secondly, if the world recklessly wishes to deny humankind all capability of knowing God, it will find itself refuted by the incontrovertible fact that through the Word of Spirit in his mouth human beings are not only recognisably separated from all other dumb creatures, but are spiritually raised above all the visible and invisible world into an invisible, spiritual world which in the Word of the mouth has its own sun with the light and warmth of life. So either the word of humankind is itself the invisible creator of human beings or, since that is an obvious self-contradiction, the invisible human word must be a uniform, living image of the creative Word of God.

Scripture tells us that after the Fall Adam begot a son in his own image,[491] who in his invisible word for a living expression for matters of the spirit and heart carried his 'patent of nobility' in his heart and on his tongue. Similarly, if human beings truly are creatures in God's image and thus the spiritual children of God, begotten in God's image, it follows that out of God's omniscience and goodness He anticipated the Fall and knew how to restore humankind, since He could not possibly allow His work to be destroyed or His child to perish. This is where in the fullness of time redemption is linked inextricably to creation from the beginning of time, so that in the world of thought and word they logically presuppose each other. Redemption is admittedly a deep secret, but no deeper than creation in the image of God! Moreover, since in spite

---

491. Gen 5:3. "When Adam had lived 130 years, he had a son in his own likeness, in his own image; and he named him Seth."

of the Fall human beings retained a significant *likeness* to God, which lies in the Word, then not only was a lasting divine revelation made possible for humankind, but so too could God's only-begotten Son become a real human being, born of a woman, without being any the less God's Son. For the Word of God and the word of humankind, which were originally one and the same, needed only to fuse together for the Son of God to become the Son of Man, and the Son of Man to become the Son of God. All that was required was that when God's Son became flesh, it came about not through the will of the flesh but through the will of the Spirit whom we confess: that our Saviour may have been born of a woman but it was of the 'Virgin Mary', conceived by the Holy Spirit. So, being born of a woman, God's Son was a real person, the brother of all mankind via His mother, yet with nothing of the infection[492] that is transmitted by sexual intercourse. For just as the word of humankind has flowed out of the Word of God, so is the human being who is created in the image of God created in the only-begotten Son, who is the image of God from eternity; humans were therefore only children of God at second hand, as it were – in the only-begotten. The Fall was a fall away from God's only-begotten Son, which had to be redeemed if the only-begotten Son who was innocent of it would be willing to abase Himself to become a human child, take upon Himself all guilt, and suffer the spiritual and physical death penalty which is the wages of sin. Whether this redemption would truly and for ever benefit sinful humankind depended on whether sinful people could and would let themselves again be accepted into the innocent Son of Man who had borne all human sins and suffered death for them, but who as God's only-begotten Son had taken His sacrificed, but never forfeited, human life back from death, for death only has the right to, and power over, *sinful* flesh.

To be sure, this re-admittance of the human into the new innocent human being, and thus into God's only-begotten Son who is both God and human, is another deep secret, yet it is no deeper than our original relation to God's only-begotten Son. For human beings come back not to something foreign but to their own God's Son in humankind, which God's Word in the human word suffers for and takes up into Himself. This restitution is no more mysterious and unintelligible than the Fall itself, so the one must be equally as possible as the other.

After these considerations we return to the foundational doctrine of Christian enlightenment in the Word and the faith – on the precondition of our true and loving creation in God's own image and our well-founded child's relationship with our

---

492. Grundtvig uses the Danish word *smitte* here, which is commonly used about infectious diseases. The equation of sexual intercourse with the transmission of sin is traditionally attributed to Augustine (354-430), whose *Confessions* describe desire as being mud (2.2, 3.1), a whirlpool (2.2), chains (2.2, 3.1), thorns (2.3), a seething cauldron (3.1), and an open sore that must be scratched (3.1). The Danish word for this concept of original sin translates literally as 'inherited sin' (*arvesynd*).

heavenly Father, of which we cannot be deprived. The wonderful redemption comes through God's only-begotten Son, who did not regard His divinity as stolen plunder but as a blessing with which His love for humanity did not allow Him to be alone. This redemption becomes not only a probability but also a logical consequence. And yet, it was only made possible through the matchless work of love in the only-begotten Son's incarnation, childlike humiliation, meek self-sacrifice, and patient torture and death, as bitter as it was innocent. Finally, we realise that the Word of Truth about the act of love by God's only-begotten Son, our Lord Jesus Christ, must be the Word of God to which the heartfelt faith and trust of fallen humankind must attach itself. It will thereby be raised with the crucified and risen Son of Man and through His power lead a new human life in God's image. It will be transfigured in Heaven with the ascended Saviour as assuredly as the old life of the human in God's image, in thrall to sin and death, was dissolved on earth.

We could not possibly fathom how this good news, this Christmas message, this Gospel of Christ as the Word of God's grace and everlasting life, would reach our ears, nor how it would be believed in our hearts in order to redeem, save, and sanctify us. Worldly wisdom will always consider this revelation to be foolish, as Scripture predicted, so we cannot believe in the crucified Saviour without being the greatest fools in the eyes of the world. However, as the Apostle Paul enjoined, this cannot possibly prevent God's so-called foolishness from being the highest wisdom.[493] So when human life with faith in God's Son approaches the age of maturity, the believer will also begin to see the Lord's light and in part discover the divine wisdom under the fool's coat.

We thus know, and have seen it confirmed by centuries of experience, that God's Word concerning His only-begotten Son's incarnation, torture and death, His descent into hell and ascent into heaven, had to empty and humble itself in order to give birth to, and find, the genuine, heartfelt, saving faith just as completely as when the only-begotten Son allowed Himself to be born of the Virgin Mary. For a long time this abased God's Word had to bear its divinity on earth just as secretly as our Lord Jesus Christ bore His when He was growing up in Nazareth and submitting to His earthly parents. We have been made fully conscious of this and therefore attach our Christian faith boldly and exclusively to the Word of faith at Baptism as the Word of God that our Lord Jesus Christ Himself, while speaking divinely on earth with a human voice, has laid in the mouth of the whole Church in His Creed. He has also made this a condition for the life-force of rebirth, nurturing, and saving which He has concealed in the common so-called 'Words of Institution' at both so-called 'sacraments'. But we call them for what they are: the works of the Lord Himself with the words of His mouth to us who believe what the entire Church confesses. So with the power of the

493. 1 Cor 1:25.

Holy Spirit Baptism becomes the water of renewal and Holy Communion becomes an everlasting nourishment for the human being, who was created in God's image, suffered a deep fall, but was raised just as high again. With this knowledge, we can see the light rising over the great secret of piety which is the life of God's Church in this world, dearly-bought not with silver and gold but with the innocent blood of God's Son. This purifies us all of sin and imparts itself to us as the divine heart's blood in jars of clay[494] with divine power in the midst of our frailness.

It was not through the Fall that the Word and the faith became the basic forces through which human life on earth can and will gain immortality and heavenly transfiguration; from the very beginning they were the same as they are now for us as human beings. It was alone through faith in the revealed God's Word that humankind, created from dust in the image of his Creator God, could and would be developed into divine consciousness, clarity, and glory. For from the very beginning the mystery of human life was that the dust-body should become spiritual and the human soul should learn from experience to understand God's Spirit and become divinely conscious in the embrace of the only-begotten Son as His bride. The Word of God's mouth is the only recognisable life-expression of the Spirit on earth by which, through our hearing it, the forces of the invisible world make their physical presence felt in the visible and tangible world. It can therefore only be the power of God's Word that drives our whole development, transformation, and transfiguration in a spiritual direction with an immortal end. Since faith is the human heart's assurance of what is hidden from our sight and withdrawn from even the most sensitive touch, the entire work of God's love among us depends on faith, which, like the heart's hand, willingly grasps and closes around God's Word. Thus it was doubt – as much inside Paradise as outside it – which brought down humankind, caused the heart to fall, deprived it of the Spirit as the life-force of God's Word, and made it the slave of sin and the plunder of death.

If human beings had *kept* their faith, held *firm* to God's Word, and thereby *retained* God's Spirit, then the so-called poetic view – the figurative self-observation for which we were created and are wondrously suited – would have day by day confirmed itself and held its own until the body had become the Spirit's acceptable dwelling, its perfect instrument, and its clear mirror. Similarly, the human word would immediately have developed into a true and clear expression of God's Word's impression on the human heart. But through doubting the truth and the lovable nature of God's Word and through the chaff that flew as a result, human beings were spiritually and physically driven out of Paradise and were left in a painful and desperate relation to God's Word from the beginning, which was originally a prophecy of our development towards divinity proving and fulfilling itself in a faithful humankind. It was once a declaration

---

494. 2 Cor 4:7.

of love, a gospel, glad tidings of great joy, but it now became a commandment to love which fallen, sinful humankind could neither embrace nor obey, yet for the sake of our conscience and the truth we had to believe and submit to it. Both heathenism, with its false or at least distorted and confused God's Word, and Judaism, with its perpetual rebellion against the Law, are intelligible enough. For unless we see signs and miracles we naturally do not believe in God's Word which judges us, and since we can always doubt *bygone* signs and miracles, the cold faith that they command is lost almost as soon as the miracle is over!

From this viewpoint let us now regard God's Word of grace, that Word of redemption which like the Word of creation lovingly addresses the human heart, demands nothing of it but faith, and promises it life and salvation undeserved. This Word can be loved by fallen man, meaning it can be ardently believed; and although it is *hard* to believe, since the world and all worldly-mindedness oppose it, in order for it to have its wonderful effect it must be embraced by a firm, living faith that does not demand signs and miracles but in its hope of overcoming the world feels the courage to defy it. Nevertheless, this hope will find itself disappointed and will disappear along with all cheerfulness unless the Lord has already granted us in secret the new life with its ever-increasing love that is itself the assurance of victory and immortality. So God's Word – which among believers is to accomplish its great work of love in the salvation of sinners – might just as well be a Word of rebirth and loving fellowship as one of absolution and redemption, a Word of faith with the Holy Spirit. This is why the Lord says, "Blessed are those who have not seen and yet have believed!"[495] For God's Word to be able to do its saving work on the human heart, it must not only be believed as pure, divine Truth but must also be believed as divine Spirit and Life. This heartfelt, trusting faith cannot be found where we only believe because we have seen with our own eyes, or where we meditate and build our faith on something other than God's Word itself and its divine impression. This blind-born faith – which we who defy the world's scorn must call it – seems even more difficult to preserve for fallen rather than unfallen man, both because the Word of redemption seems more unreasonable than the Word of creation and because God's Word of grace only works in secret. That is why the 'eyes of the heart' cannot be opened so soon nor enlightened so clearly as they would have been in Paradise if human beings had preserved their original faith. On the other hand, the Word of redemption is a much clearer revelation of God's fatherly love than the Word of creation, so the heart comes to love it far more easily; and love, which makes all things easy, most likely and most certainly makes faith in love *easy*. Moreover, in His loving wisdom the Lord has ensured that faith in the Word of redemption has two immovable pillars: one is in the audible Confession of faith at

495. Jn 20:29.

Baptism which is the surest of all outward testimonies; the other, and the surest of all inward testimonies, is the united affirmation of God's Spirit and our conscience in the absolution which God's Word of grace immediately grants the believer. Thus, in the Church's testimony we shall always find reason enough to believe, and in the feeling of God's Peace which "God's Peace be with you!" grants us, we shall be able to say to the Church as the men said to the Samaritan woman, "We no longer believe just because of what you said; now we have heard for ourselves, and we know that this man really is the Saviour of the world.'[496]

This would also be completely unintelligible if it were not that all people, as soon as they hear the Word of faith, would much rather receive and preserve it in their hearts had the Lord not taught us in the renunciation of the Devil that we must first be converted before we can believe the Gospel, whereas all experience teaches us that conversion is so difficult for all sinners that it seems impossible, and that all faith in God's grace in Christ received without conversion is stillborn.

However, this does not come about through the difficulty of Christian conversion in itself. If Christian conversion only consists of the sincere wish to be free of the one who, as the great man-murderer, is the most spiteful enemy of the human heart, the prince of darkness, the father of lies, and the most vicious enemy of the divine light and the true God, then basically no one found it more difficult to convert to the divine Saviour than the Prodigal Son in the parable when, starving to death as a swineherd, he comes to his senses and wishes he were back home in his loving father's house.[497]

A true conversion is as impossible for all his children as it is for the father of lies himself. To the extent that we have allowed ourselves to be persuaded by the sweet, insinuating words of the tempter to take him to us in place of the Father, to the same extent is conversion to our heavenly Father and His only-begotten Son naturally difficult. For it presupposes that during our defection and under the rule of sin we have nevertheless actually, like a mustard seed, retained our faith in our heavenly Father's love which we have dreadfully failed to appreciate and have repaid with dark ingratitude. Christian conversion, which the Christian faith clearly assumes, also presupposes – however vague, yet definite and real – faith in God's fatherly love, in whose image humankind is created. This is what gives the Christian order of salvation the appearance of folly, which is the cross that all the Lord's disciples must carry after Him. However, it does not any the less verify the great foundational doctrine of enlightenment which does honour to God's wisdom: namely, that from first to last it is the Word and the faith, God's Word and the human heart's faith

---

496. Jn 4:42. This formulation is a good example of Grundtvig's strongly Johannine theology.
497. Lk 15:11-32.

in it, whereby all God's work on earth is accomplished, as the Lord has said, "The work of God is this: to believe in His Son, for the Son and the Word are for ever one and the same."[498]

498. Jn 6:29 for the first half of this sentence, Grundtvig for the rest.

25. Christian Marriage

Marriage is the focus of human life as well as the cradle of civic life. This has not escaped the attention of our bishops, pastors, and scholars, old and new, so they have always endeavoured somehow to take control of marriage, to call it Christian, and then to sanctify it. But since they had not worked out the proper relationship between Christianity and human life in general and were unwilling merely to christen the marriages of true Christians, every attempt to do so not only failed but complicated and confused the relationship between marriage and Christianity.

On the one hand the papists made the marriage ceremony a so-called 'sacrament' in order to christen and sanctify marriage without any regard for the married couple's own faith and thought. On the other hand, they not only pronounced the life of the hermit the holiest of all, but by forbidding marriage to their priests they also declared marriage to be so unchristian that not even through the sacrament of the marriage ceremony could it be christened and sanctified; among temporal people and for temporal reasons it could only constitute a kind of indulgence.

Such open defiance of the divine institution of marriage in Paradise, both for the propagation of human life and for the accomplishment of our human goal, was in every way so inhuman and ungodly that the so-called 'spirituality' (the clerisy) that derived from it and was hardened in the process could not but become the plague of human life; it turned out to be the devilry with which the marriage ban has been stamped for many a long year.

Also in this regard the Lutheran Reformation was a giant stride in the rescue of human life and the renewal of Christian enlightenment; for Martin Luther boldly asserted the honour of marriage as a divinely-ordained institution by defying the Pope and taking a wife to live with in the most Christian household that had been seen for hundreds of years. It is hard to imagine a more powerful retort to the papal ban than this monk's marriage to a nun![499] However, marriage could not tread the path of enlightenment in its proper relation to Christianity before the original (natural) life of humankind in general was placed in its proper light. This was so far from being the case in Luther's day that never before in Christianity had humankind's original life in

---

499. On June 13th 1525 Martin Luther (1483-1546) married Katharina von Bora (1499-1552), a nun 16 years his junior who had fled from her convent and taken refuge in Wittenberg. Katharina took over the Luther household and with their four surviving children (plus six of Luther's sister's) she helped to define Protestant family life and set the tone for married clergy.

its fallen state been so densely darkened as it was under the lectures of the Protestant scribes in the churches and the universities.

It is a fundamental misunderstanding of the Spirit and of Scripture to believe that the profound Apostolic words "In myself, in the independence of my flesh, there is nothing good"[500] mean that there is nothing good in fallen humankind and therefore no remnant at all of what God had created in it; for what God created was all good! This maltreated passage was then made a rule of faith, according to which the same Apostle's true and pitiful depiction of the position of sinful yet pious person under the Law, with an impotent desire for the good, was considered to be a description of the believing, reborn being under God's grace! When this happened, the Christian Gospel was belied, however unintentionally; for it is beyond question that it promises its believers the power to be God's children and to behave accordingly. So both the old and the new human life were enveloped in a pitch darkness that concealed the enormous difference between God's great wonder in linking rebirth to creation and an Arabian Nights tale[501] that rushes in leaps and bounds from Heaven to Hell and back again.

For there is no wilder tale imaginable than the one in which God creates human beings out of the dust of the earth in His own image and likeness, and then these human beings fall from grace in Paradise and lose their image of God and their likeness to God, so there is no longer a single good sinew in their lives! Nevertheless God continued to love the thoroughly bad human beings as a father loves his mischievous but basically good-hearted child; indeed, He loved them so much that in order to save His first child He sacrificed His own legitimate child, His everlasting only-begotten Son, so that through faith in Him the changeling, the devil-child in human skin, could be saved from damnation and as God's elected child inherit everlasting life! The tale also relates that this changeling, in whom there was nothing good at all but only pure evil, nonetheless repented its sins, changed its ways, and believed in the Saviour! With this faith the human being was then made righteous by God's grace, filled with the Holy Spirit, reborn in Baptism with water and Spirit, and nourished at Holy Communion with food and drink to an everlasting life. And it was believed that all this happened without it making any recognisable difference to our real human life and life-path until, through a blessed death, we passed into the other world and entered eternity! This is an obvious self-contradiction and self-refutation, in truth an impossibility, equally impossible for the true God and truthful human, a contradiction that in vain seeks to conceal its mendacity under the pretext of it being impossible for humankind

---

500. Rom 7:18.

501. *One Thousand and One Nights* (aka *Arabian Nights*) is a medieval collection of folk-tales in Arabic from the Middle East and South Asia.

but not for God, for whom all things are possible! This runs on into the blasphemy that a lie which was too gross and too tangible should pass for the truth with God!

In this pitch-dark presumption of the possibility of what is unthinkable, unspeakable, and unfeasible, no jumble of ideas seems too great concerning the relationship of human marriage to Christianity. Yet it has nevertheless been so fearfully great that the thought arose that it was possible to acquire at one and the same time a Paradise blessing on one's marriage, a curse under the Law, and a promise of the Gospel in a wedding ceremony that was not even a sacrament and was the same for all members of the State Church, be they voluntary or compulsory.

However, we have now acquired the intelligence to see that it is the perpetual and unchangeable *Confession of faith*, and nothing else of any other conceivable name, that can and will determine what is 'Christian' and 'unchristian'. Similarly, it is altogether on the words from the mouth of the Lord Himself concerning His own institutions that we must base all our Christian expectations if we are to have a Christian pledge of their fulfilment. In addition to this we must definitively assume the absolute reliability of our Holy Scripture as the story of the divine revelation and the kingdom of God. When we take all this into consideration, we ask neither how the scribes at various times have read and interpreted the prophetic and theological runes and riddles (hieroglyphs), or what more or less unreasoned ideas they may have had concerning human life in either its original, fallen, obsolete form and state or in its reborn and renewed ones. We ask only what mode of thought *must* be, or as far as we know, *can* be the right one concerning human life with its great, mysterious vicissitudes; and we do so in the justifiable context of the Christian faith and in general with the Word to us from the Lord's own mouth. This is both the only distinctive sign we have of the Lord's Spirit and the Lord's Church, and the only Word in which the Lord can be recognisably present and active among His own while he remains hidden to the eyes of the world.

Once the Spirit of faith and the Creed rests upon us, what strikes us like lightning is that in order for our Lord Jesus Christ, whom we believe and confess, to be God's only-begotten Son born of the Virgin Mary, not only must humans have been created in God's image, as Scripture states, but we must also have been created in such a way that divine nature could unite with human nature and through the human body be able to reveal the Godhead's glory! Moreover, however much this living image-likeness must have suffered through the Fall, it could not possibly have been erased completely if the human life of God's Son was to be created in Mother Mary's womb so that He was flesh of her flesh and bone of her bone, just as Eve was of Adam's.

On the other hand the good news (the Gospel) of the Saviour (Jesus) in general, and of the forgiveness of sins prior to everlasting life in particular, presupposes that human life in God's image suffered a fundamental breach at the Fall and that the

Son of Man, who was to heal that breach, would Himself have to be *free* of sin. We believe that this is achieved by God's Son having only a human mother and no human father, since the Holy Spirit took the man's place in the conception. Thus we see, in the God-man, a human being like one of us in every way, yet without sin.

We cannot possibly determine of our own accord the extent to which this fundamental breach that constitutes sinfulness extends to all of us who are born of a man and a woman through carnal knowledge, because sinfulness is a fundamental defect that must have as much damaging influence on our way of seeing and thinking as on our life-force. Since the defect in the eyes of Christians must be so great that it could only be healed by the humbling and sacrifice of God's Son, and even then only healed by a true rebirth and re-creation, we might easily think that the defect could never be great enough and that the greater one imagined it to be, the better it was, for then the necessity of rebirth and the glory of grace in atonement and redemption, in absolution and rebirth, became ever more self-evident. Here again, however, the saying is true that 'enough is as good as a feast' and that whether one shoots over or under the target, either way one misses it.

The Apostle Paul and our Lord Himself have already enjoined, and experience has made it thoroughly clear, that in sinfulness and delinquency there is a limit beyond which we cannot step without paying the cost, and that this limit must not be overstepped when we decide to sin to the utmost so that God's grace can be all the greater when we genuinely despise and disown it. Yet it must also be sheer madness to imagine that sinfulness could be so boundless in the entire fallen human race that it could either disown grace or deliberately sin against it, as the Devil and his offspring have always done and will continue to do. For it truly is sheer madness to claim that fallen human nature is fundamentally *corrupted*, so that even when fallen human beings appear at their very best there is still nothing good about them! In that case there would be nothing left of the human being on which God could take pity or have mercy, nor anything in its fundamentally bad nature that could be touched by repentance and conversion, or persuaded to faith in God's grace and truth, or be reborn as God's child and renewed in God's image in which they were originally created. Conversion, faith, and devotion are completely unthinkable and self-contradictory without goodwill.

Such goodwill, which the Lord has placed before us in the Parable of the Prodigal Son, must always be presupposed and actually discovered in fallen man, in the image of the fallen Adam, just as according to the testimony of Scripture it was found in Abel, Seth, Enoch, Noah, Abraham, Isaac, and Jacob, David, Zechariah and Elizabeth,[502] John

---

502. Zechariah and Elizabeth were the parents of John the Baptist.

the Baptist, the Virgin Mary and Joseph, her betrothed, and Simeon and Anna.[503] So they were all presumably degenerate children of God, yet His real children nevertheless, who remembered their heavenly Father and fundamentally were minded to obey and resemble Him, even though they had wasted His first love; in doing so they lost the power to do His will and forfeited communion and fellowship with Him.

Only thus can we gain an idea of fallen, sinful, lost man, and of human life outside Paradise in the wilderness. It fits well with the Prodigal Son in a country far away from his father's house, who sank so low that he was willing to eat pig-food, but was nevertheless a worthy object of his father's pity, mercy, forgiveness, and full re-establishment of all his childhood rights. This happened because he felt and confessed that he was guilty of his own misfortune and intended to change his ways; he would rather be his father's hired servant than the servant of sin under the false, empty title of being 'his own master'.

As we can see, in this depiction of fallen man's relation to God and the image of God, all idea of 'merit', of self-righteousness, or of the power to help or save oneself, disappears, while the opportunity to be comforted, pardoned, reborn, and renewed is preserved.

Thus, our heavenly Father has a lost child on earth to find and a dead child to bring alive. But since the heavenly father-love of God is pure and rich, unselfish and generous, He can without any self-contradiction conceal the multitude of sins in the penitent person and make amends for all their loss. The penitent is guilty to death and wretched, yet humble and trusting, good-willed and grateful; and as the Lord demonstrates in the Parable of the Prodigal Son, and Himself testifies to in pure words, there will be more rejoicing in Heaven over one sinner who repents than over ninety-nine righteous people who do not need to.[504]

Nevertheless, there are those who, appealing to Holy Scripture, have claimed that in the old being God's image is completely erased and everything well and truly eradicated, and only the *appearance* of piety with dazzling vices is possible. If this were the case, it would have been impossible – without belying the Holy Story – to exercise this condemnatory judgement on Abraham, the father of all believers, on Moses, the faithful servant in God's house, on David, the man after God's heart, on the prophets, and on Him whom the Lord Himself called more than a prophet, called Him 'the angel

---

503. Lk 2:25-38. Simeon was a pious Jewish elder who was present at the dedication of the baby Jesus in the temple. The Holy Spirit had prophesied that he would see the Messiah before he died, and when this happened Simeon himself prophesied to Mary and Joseph that Jesus "is destined to cause the falling and rising of many in Israel, and to be a sign that will be spoken against, so that the thoughts of many hearts will be revealed. And a sword will pierce your own soul too." Simeon gave thanks for the revelation in the words that are known in Latin as the Nunc Dimittis, which contain the first prophecy of Jesus' mission to the Gentiles as well as to the Jews. Also present was an elderly widow, Anna, who lived at the temple, praying and fasting for the redemption of the Jews.

504. Lk 15:7.

of His presence'.[505] What they have completely overlooked is that it is impossible to make an exception for a single one of Adam's natural children from the judgement called down upon him and all his kin, in other words upon the fallen nature of man. We can just as little put the birth of the new being *before* the child born in Bethlehem without turning the entire Gospel of Christ into falsehood and fable. By nonetheless pursuing this path – what Bishop Eusebius in his Church history[506] called "making Abraham and all Christ's forefathers in the flesh Christians *before* Christ's coming, and God's reborn children *before* their rebirth in water and Spirit" – they have blinded themselves to the obvious truth that if rebirth is to be possible, imaginable, and truly practicable, there must still be preserved in fallen human beings traces and remains of an *original* goodness and glory, as creatures in God's image who know about God and themselves. As surely as faith, hope, and love express the entire inner human image-likeness to God, so surely must there be a real remnant of the faith, hope, and love in the fallen human who is to be raised, in the lost human who is to be saved, and in the degenerate human who is to be reborn, who originally through the Word constituted human life in God's image.

If with the Book of Creation before us we now consider original human life, or Paradise life, in the light of the Lord, we can clearly see that faith in the power of God's Word, Life, and Truth, and the hope of immortality in Paradise, were the faith and the hope of our first parents with which they stood and fell before God's countenance. It seems doubtful, however, whether they lost or retained their *mutual* love, which for them meant loving their neighbour as themselves; *within* their love God's love grew in heart and soul and strength, and *from* their love it was meant to flourish and flower as the Paradise rose.[507] It follows from their living link that our first parents must have fallen as deeply from their mutual love as they did from their faith and hope; indeed, we can hear Adam's words with which he actually separates himself from his wife as his own flesh, blood, and bone when he tells the Creator, "The woman you gave me seduced me."[508]

However, we can no more think that the mutual love between our first parents and thus between man and woman was completely eradicated and ceased with the Fall than we can imagine this happening with faith in God's Word or with the hope of immortality. Instead we must imagine that just as in the Word humans retained their recognisable likeness to God, so did a remnant of faith, hope, and love accompany

---

505. Isa 63:9. Probably a reference to the pre-incarnate Jesus.

506. Bishop Eusebius of Caesarea, Israel (c.260-c.340) is known as the 'Father of Church History' for writing a pioneering chronological account of early Christianity from the 1st to the 4th century.

507. St. Ambrose (340-97) relates how the rose of Paradise had no thorns on its stem. After the Fall it grew thorns to remind human beings of their sins, yet its perfect flower still remained.

508. Gen 3:12.

them out of Paradise and into the wilderness. It stood to reason that, helpless and mortally wounded by the wages of sin, all three would soon die out, but perhaps they could be saved and strengthened by the wonder of God's grace and in the fullness of time; by the same God's grace and in the revelation of all His riches they could be reborn and renewed in His image which created us.

The Apostle Paul has written in capital letters of how the remnant of our Paradise-faith, Paradise-hope, and Paradise-love was sustained in the wilderness, and this is no less a wonder than the children of Israel being sustained by manna in the desert.[509] This is the teaching of God's Word and the history of God's kingdom from the time of Adam to the time of Christ, and never more clearly than in our contemplation of the hero of faith, Abraham, the angel of hope, John the Baptist, and the queen of hearts, the Virgin Mary. They were all made of the old leaven, the fallen creature, but they were strong in faith in the new Heaven and the new earth, joyful in the hope of its coming, and sincere in their love. So we cannot possibly follow the old being and trace the Paradise life on heathen islands rather than on Israel's mainland, nor can we assume that God's grace would show itself so richly anywhere else but where faith in God's Word was preserved so that in a human way the 'Word' could become 'flesh' and reveal its glory; or where the hope of everlasting life could be so maintained as to be fulfilled with His coming, which is eternal life and light; or where love could be so wondrously nurtured that God's Son could find a mother on earth and truly become the seed of woman. Thus, wherever Christ's Gospel has found a hearing and a heart, a remnant of the *old* human being's faith, hope, and love must have been preserved so that the first Adam could be awakened to listen, enlivened to understand, persuaded to believe, and touched to love the message of joy of the *new* being, the second Adam, who is the Lord from heaven. We can see that this has happened to an astonishing degree among heathens in their own lands, such as the centurion in Capernaum, to whose faith in God's Word the Lord Himself testified, "I tell you, I have not found such great faith even in Israel."[510] The same thing happened with the Canaanite woman whose hope,[511] and the woman with an issue of blood whose love,[512] although they had grown wild like trees in a forest, bore comparison with the best that was to be found in Israel.

It is true that from the Latinists[513] as well as from many other false ideas we have learned that the Jews were strong in faith; but with the Master as witness we learn something quite different: "Unless you people see signs and wonders, you will never

509. Ex 16:31.
510. Mt 8:10; Lk 7:9.
511. Mt 15:22-28; Mk 7:24-29.
512. Mt 9:20-22; Mk 5:25-34; Lk 8:43-48.
513. i.e. Roman Catholics.

believe."[514] The entire history of the Jews, from the exodus out of Egypt[515] to the destruction of Jerusalem[516] confirms this. The Jews were not the most loving of people either, as we can see from all their love-relationships – between parents and children, between good friends and especially brothers and sisters, and between married couples – which is why the Lord also testifies that it was because of their hard-heartedness that Moses gave them the Law concerning divorce. However, Israel had its strength in its hope, and indeed still has this hope in its high age and in the midst of its diaspora,[517] and this was the reason why Yahweh gave them as little as possible to believe under the Law. He also more or less cast a veil over their lack of mutual love with his basic law that they should honour their father and mother, refrain from murder and adultery, and not demand their neighbour's property. But He gave them all something to hope for, from His promise to Abraham – "through your offspring all nations on earth will be blessed"[518] – to the clearest of prophecies about "Israel's hope"[519] as God's anointed, the Christ, the Messiah. In contrast, among all the heathens the Romans were the people with the strongest faith, which is why the Apostolic Letter to them deals almost exclusively with 'the faith'. We should all keep fresh in our minds the fact that it was just as much the Romans who preserved the Christian faith in the Middle Ages as it was from Rome that all superstition emanated.

If finally we look at heathen life in our far North we note that next after Israel no people has been so animated by such a strong hope of immortality! Whereas here in the North there was precious little 'hope', we can trace in a song like 'Denmark, loveliest field and meadow'[520] an unrivalled love between parents and children and between man and woman. Since these are just as much love's fundamental relations in Christian or 'the new being's love' as they are in heathen or 'the old being's love', it is reasonable to conclude that once we Danes were christened[521] it would most likely be among us that the light should dawn on the inner link between marriage and Christianity.

However long it has been overlooked and however boldly it is often denied, it remains as clear as it is certain that the faith, hope, and love of the old being must be uniform with that of the new being. Otherwise it would be impossible for the old

---

514. Jn 4:48.

515. Ex 14.

516. Mt 24:1ff; Mk 13:1ff; Lk 21:5ff.

517. The diaspora of the Jews began with the Romans' destruction of Jerusalem in 70 CE and is considered to have ended with the establishment of the new state of Israel in 1947.

518. Gen 22:18.

519. Jer 17:13 et al.

520. This song was written c.1685 by Laurids Kok (1634-91), and a tune was added by Poul Rasmussen in 1811. As Denmark's first 'fatherland song' it has remained popular to this day.

521. This process begins with the arrival of Ansgar (801-65), the 'apostle of the North', from Germany and the building of the first Danish church in Hedeby in 848.

being to acquire from any kind of revelation whatsoever a real idea of the new being's faith, hope, and love, which it must have had in order to desire them and recognise them in itself. Thus the love between parents and children and the love within marriage between a man and a woman in the old life, insofar as it existed and insofar as it stretched, must have been altogether uniform with the love between the heavenly Father and His earthly children and with the love in the marriage between Christ and His Church in the new being's life. And just as the Lord Himself has told us that we must become like *human* children before we can be reborn as *God's* children, so will the Spirit say that we must become like human partners in marriage before we can be incorporated into the great community with the Lord, like a bride with His bridegroom and a wife with her husband. Paul has impressed upon the Church that there is a living interplay between Christ's own marriage to His Church and Christian marriage as such.[522] Paul expressly states that Christian husbands should love their wives as Christ loves His Church, and the Christian wives must submit to their husbands as the Church submits to its head and Lord, Christ. It follows that not only the Lord's marriage to His Church presupposes the married love of the old being, but that the new being's married relationship also becomes a pattern and preparation for the Lord's everlasting marriage.

It would be inexplicable how this could have escaped the attention of our scribes for so long – despite they themselves at every wedding following the Altar Book to impress upon us what St. Paul writes about Christian marriage in the fifth chapter to the Ephesians – if we did not realise that with dead eyes one can either see no life at all, or one always overlooks it in the description! Now, however, it cannot surprise us that the same scribes who were completely blind to real life in the Spirit also passed lightly over the Letter to the Ephesians, so that even at a wedding, when they specifically appealed to the letter's great words about the mysterious link in marriage between Christ and His Church, it never struck them that it was a 'profound mystery' in Christian life but simply that it was just one more mystery in Holy Scripture.

If we open our eyes and endeavour to act better in future, we must draw two important conclusions from this illumination of the marriage relationship in the life of the new being. The first conclusion is that all talk of *Christian* marriage between other than true Christian married couples is nonsense, since for marriage to be 'Christian' it must be what the Apostle calls a marriage "in the Lord".[523] Christians' irresponsibility on this point would be reason enough for Christian life to have failed to see much growth through marriage. On the other hand the care shown by Christian pastors in choosing Christian wives has borne such blessed fruit in the Lutheran parish that

522. Eph 5:22-32.
523. 1 Cor 7:39.

it gives grounds for great hope, if only the Church from now on "consults with God and its own good heart"[524] on the question of marriage and also makes clear where the blessing for a Christian marriage can be found and where it must be sought – and nowhere else.

This is the second important conclusion to be drawn from the illumination concerning the relationship between marriage and Christianity. For if Christian marriage is to be a pattern and preparation for the Lord's marriage with His Church, it must expect to gain its divine blessing from the Christian means of salvation. This expresses and creates the mysterious love-relationship and boundless fellowship between Christ and His Church, that is, from Holy Communion, and not from any self-made marriage sacrament or merely a wedding according to the Altar Book. We must all be aware that only by eating the flesh of the Son of Man and drinking His blood can the faithful Church become flesh of His flesh and bone of His bone, so the two become one flesh. In this way the origin of human marriage and its original purpose is subsumed into the Christian community, and the heart's enlightened eyes will indeed discover this. Although this will only happen gradually, the same eyes must soon be clarified to realise that from the very beginning the marriage relationship was a cradle of human love and this must be equally so in the reborn human life; for love of one's neighbour can only begin with love of one's nearest and dearest, which one's partner undoubtedly is in Christian marriage as much as it was in Adam and Eve's. Only through Christian marriage can the love that is the fulfilment of the Law pervade and permeate Christ's community so that it wears its best clothes for Him as a bride for her bridegroom.

If one asks for the origin of the belief over many centuries that the Church was of the firm conviction that the unmarried state, where it was truly Christian and godly, was the state that was holiest and most pleasing to God, and that even the Apostle Paul in one of his letters appears to claim this,[525] then I must first invalidate this objection – and all objections to the Christian way of thinking based on *Scripture*. I note that the full agreement between Scripture and Christ's teaching is doubtless an essential presupposition among Church scribes, but this cannot be used to prove anything, since it constantly needs proving itself! Next I urge our scribes to remark that what is found in only one Apostle's writing, and only in one of his many letters at that, can never be related to the entire Church community and its life. Finally I dare to believe that what the Apostle Paul wrote to the Corinthians about marriage was regarded by himself as his own view and good advice with regard to a particular time and circumstance.

It is obvious that if every Christian had kept *out* of marriage, Christianity would

524. Quoted from the old Danish church ritual.
525. I Cor 7:8.

have died out many centuries ago, and if all enlightened Christians today wished to remain *unmarried*, then posterity would be both less Christian and less enlightened than the present generation. It is equally obvious that the Christian generation which will experience the Day of Judgement will not marry, because it neither can nor shall have need of any Christian posterity. It will have reached its maturity, its growth will have reached its goal, Christ's goal, and its enlightenment will have reached its zenith, which is crystal clarity in the Spirit. When the Apostolic Church, which is the bride's motherly example, had a strong presumption that the Lord was soon coming again in judgement, and was experiencing a living foretaste of the consummation, its reservation concerning marriage was perfectly understandable, even had it been much greater and more general than was the case. And since experience taught the Christians in the Roman Empire that neither Christian life nor Christian light was increasing, but was indeed declining horribly from generation to generation, it was quite natural that they expected nothing good from the future before the Day of Judgement, which they thought was coming very soon if it was to find 'faith on earth'.[526]

In the new Christendom outside the Roman Empire, and above all among us after the Reformation, and with the renewal of clerical marriage through Martin Luther, we are constantly in wait and, spiritually speaking, we expect of the future what the past has lost – and what the present is missing and longing for. Since we cannot expect the Lord to come in clouds[527] before the Spirit and the bride have shouted, "Come, Lord Jesus,"[528] we must become so much the wiser day by day as regards Christian marriage. We must appreciate it all the more as the only living nursery for those in the future who, in spiritual and Christian terms, will stand on our shoulders and see the work finished. They will tread in our footsteps until, in the Lord's own footsteps, they pass us and come so close to Him that in a way they can measure themselves *with* Him. Only then, in the last but one Christian generation, born of woman in the fashion of the old being, will we come to stand so close to the new being as the son of the priest Zechariah and Elizabeth of the daughters of Aaron did to Jesus of Nazareth, who was "conceived by the Holy Spirit and born of the Virgin Mary". This penultimate generation will baptise the last Christians with something like the same feeling that John had when he baptised Jesus to fulfil all righteousness[529] and to be in *this* world, just as the Lord was in this world, to wait for the revelation of His glory. Moreover, at the same time and according to the Lord's prophecy, this world will suffer what it did in the days of Noah, when people married and were married until the Flood came and took them all away; for thus will be the arrival of the Son of Man when He

---

526. Lk 18:8.
527. Mt 26:63-64; Mk 13:26; Lk 21:27; Rev 1:7.
528. Rev 22:17.
529. Mt 3:15.

comes again to bring home His bride to His Father's house, where the bridal wreath is the crown of life.

The ending will reveal that the 'holy kiss', which like a kiss of love will seal the communion of saints in the seventh and last Church,[530] can only be born, raised, in-structed, enlightened, and transfigured in a Christian marriage that is not created by any self-made wedding but solely by the Holy Spirit among living Christians at Holy Communion in the name of our Lord Jesus Christ.

530. Rev 2-3.

26. Faith, Hope, and Love

"I do not write to you because you do not *know* the truth, but because you *know* it and know that no lie comes from the truth."[531]

Thus our Lord's friend, the Apostle and Evangelist John, teaches us to understand the Apostolic Writing: not as a letter from Heaven to the Jews and heathens through which they can get to know Christianity or become Christian, but as a letter from a friend to fellow-Christians to enlighten, confirm, and fortify them in their knowledge of Christian truth. So it is not the Apostles' fault that our scribes have abused, and in general continue to abuse, the Apostolic Writings as a source of Christianity and a rule of faith, despite the Apostles' protest in their own handwriting. The pen is least of all equipped to uphold the Word from the Lord's own mouth in its proper place in Christian thought against those who are not already *living* Christians and cannot therefore possess, understand, or pursue any Christian thought for the present. We must therefore leave the blind *guides* of the blind to their blindness and to the mercy of God, who seeks to move us all out of darkness and into the kingdom of His beloved son. We must also remind the Christian reader that it is not just the question of the Christian basis of faith and source of life that makes all the difference – like night and day – between thinking something to be true and Christian because it is written in *the Book*, or thinking it is written in Christian Scripture because it *is* true and Christian; for this overriding difference is apparent in every question concerning Christian education.

So when we read in the Apostle Paul about 'faith, hope, and love' as a Christian trinity, we can see that it is crucial to ask whether the Apostle wrote this because it already *was* a basic Christian teaching that faith, hope, and love are the living content of Christianity in sum, or that they are a basic Christian teaching *because* they are to be found in Paul's First Letter to the Corinthians chapter 13. In other words, does the Christian truth and importance of this basic teaching rest on Paul being a genuine apostle and in particular on chapter 13 and every word in verse 13, chapter 13 being genuine? And does it also rest on the degree to which our scribes could combine this notable word of Scripture with all the other genuine words of Scripture that had the same right as shared scriptures to determine both what was genuinely Christian and what belonged to the basic teachings of Christianity?

531. 1 Jn 2:21.

Even when the scribes did not follow the Protestants in searching for the idea of Christianity in Scripture, they nevertheless sought it like the papists, where it is equally unlikely to be or be found, namely in a self-appointed spiritual or priestly caste. Unlike the Protestants who looked for the idea of 'Christianity' in the Scriptures, our scribes, like the papists, searched for it where it could not possibly be found, namely in a spirituality of their own making, i.e. in the clerisy. So it is understandable that although all of them were aware of the Apostolic words concerning faith, hope, and love, they in no way allowed themselves to be directed and counselled by them as a basic Christian teaching. This was so whether it was a matter of defending or purging so-called Christian communities or establishing and evaluating so-called doctrinal systems.

In contrast, we do not ask either the dead letters or the mortal clergy about the conception of Christianity, which must be both living and spiritual. We receive the conception where it is given and addressed to us in the institutions of our Lord Jesus Christ, Baptism and Holy Communion, in the Word to us from the Lord's own mouth. When we read in the Apostle about what 'remains' in the Church – faith, hope, and love, of which the greatest is love – then the Holy Spirit as the spirit of Christ immediately acknowledges this saying as an expression not open to improvement for the beginning, middle, and end of the Christian life, that is, the authentic, active, and full life lived in Christ that links and unites all true Christians in the communion of saints.

However, because the Holy Spirit as the Spirit of Christ never speaks of its own accord but draws on what is recognisably the Lord's, it assiduously infers the concept of 'life lived in Christ'[532] in the 'faith, hope, and love' from the conception of Christianity in the Creed, together with the Word of Baptism and Holy Communion. From this alone we can learn to recognise the Christian scheme of salvation and what kind of a faith, a hope, and a love make up the whole inner workings of a 'life lived in Christ', which is as far as possible to reveal and imprint itself in true Christianity in a corresponding confession, preaching, and hymn of praise.

I have previously shown[533] that far from being an innovation that came about through Christianity, 'faith, hope, and love' are actually as old as the human race. This is true however limited their extent and however contaminated they must have been, for they must be presupposed and really present wherever the gospel of Christ is to be heard, understood, and received. Yet the 'faith' must be distinctive; it must be *Christian* faith; the hope must be *Christian* hope; and the specific love *Christian* love. These three constitute a Christian trinity, so that if the concept of 'life lived in Christ' is to be a living and defensible reality, then it must equally well be the case that this

---

532. 'O life lived in Christ' ('*O kristelighed*') is one of the greatest of Grundtvig's 1,500 hymns. It is translated as no. 41 in *Living Wellsprings* (2015).

533. Grundtvig's own footnote: "Most recently in my article about Christian marriage."

concept is given to us through the Lord's own words and institutions. If it were different, and we had a free hand in choosing what kind of faith, hope, and love should constitute the concept of a life lived in Christ and how far the scheme and sequence in which they are mentioned were the correct ones, then we would never reach any valid decision on the questions which demand a satisfactory answer before any Christian teaching can be given. Martin Luther felt this acutely, and enjoined it triumphantly: that there must be an external Word of God to certify all Christian teaching and expose all the infatuations that have embellished themselves with that name, appealing to an internal Word of God as the direct revelation of the Spirit. However, when he vainly tried to wrench such an external Word of God out of the literal words of the Bible and thus placed sheer Bible-reading before the wisdom of the self-willed scholars and over unbridled conceits as touchstone and judge, the attempt of course failed completely. Dead letters cannot carry, communicate with, or guide life-spirits; it is always a death sentence on life to make death its schoolmaster.

It is a quite different matter with the living, audible Word of the Lord at Baptism and Holy Communion. For here it can carry, communicate, and guide the Spirit that will not speak of its own accord but takes from what belongs to the Lord and proclaims it to us. There must be such an external Word of God in the Church so that we can recognise what belongs only to our Lord Jesus Christ in the world of Spirit and Word. Similarly, the Spirit is swift to teach us that just as the Church's Creed from the Lord's mouth is the immutable expression of the Christian faith with no room for improvement, so the Lord's Prayer, which He places in the mouth of His church at Baptism – the 'Our Father' that is the children's prayer in God's house – clearly expresses all that the reborn person of God requires and expects of their heavenly Father through Baptism, for it expresses the Christian 'hope'. Correspondingly, the Lord's words at the table, which in the bread and the chalice at Holy Communion He Himself in reality places in the mouths of His church, are truly the living expression of Christian love, just as love in its fullness is the full devotion of the heart.

The reason why this salvation sequence consisting of faith, hope, and love and instituted by the Lord Himself has been overlooked is that on the one hand the Lord's Words of Institution were not taken seriously enough by His Church as the sole means of salvation, and on the other, people were deluded into thinking that faith, hope, and love in a *divine* sense could mean something else than faith, hope, and love in a *human* sense, even though it is clear as sunlight that if this were the case human beings could not possibly recognise or comprehend what it was that the Spirit of God called 'faith, hope, and love'.

We earnestly regard the Lord's own Words of Institution at Baptism and Holy Communion as 'the works of the Lord', only recognisable through the Word to us from the Lord's own mouth and only communicated through the breath of His mouth. At the same time we boldly make the assumption that 'faith, hope, and love' in relation to our Lord Jesus Christ and to other people are the sincere guarantee of the truth of what He tells us; that 'hope', be it firm or vague, be it linked to temporal or eternal matters, is a comforting expectation of a coming good; and that 'love' between Christ and us, like all love between people, is an inclination of the heart that can only be consummated in a total fellowship. We see a great light arising over the life of the Christian Church in which, as far as it has come, it clearly recognises itself, and through which it can predict in the Spirit both the goal and the way that leads to it. What deeply troubled our best Lutheran forefathers and made them afraid of continuing among themselves to regard the Christian life of faith, hope, and love as the only authentic life lived in Christ was the vague, dim, and incomplete state in which they found life, and especially love, at their best. However, this no longer confuses and scares us, for on the one hand in the Word from the Lord's own mouth we have an unfailing touchstone for the Christian validity of faith, hope, and love, and on the other hand we are taught by the Holy Spirit as the Spirit from the Lord's own mouth concerning the full humanity of the life lived in Christ. This life has its secret gestation in our well-disposed hearing of the Gospel in which God's Spirit speaks; it has its birth in the water and Spirit of Baptism according to the Lord's institution; and it has its growth into perfection at the Lord's table. For the *expression* of faith, hope, and love makes a similar living *impression*, so that for us the Christian life begins with faith, grows with hope, and is perfected by and in love.

The Spirit that searches all things, even the depths of God,[534] brings the teaching that faith, hope, and love, precisely as it is written, constitute the whole life lived in Christ, or Christianity of the heart. In addition the Spirit teaches us that a brief description of the kingdom of God answers precisely to one of righteousness, peace, and joy, insofar as the kingdom of God can be revealed on earth in days of faith and hope, i.e. in the Spirit. Thus righteousness corresponds to faith, peace to hope, and joy to love as the righteousness of faith, the peace of hope, and the joy of love.

Although this teaching is so great and gives us the true concept of Christianity and of the kingdom of God, it is nevertheless so down-to-earth! It simply shows the internal connection between the Christian life and the Christian condition, which no one has doubted. In fact this teaching is so reasonable and joyful that when the Church opens its eyes wide, it will give it its full power without any opposition. The Spirit verifies this completely through the Lord's own words to us in what we call the Third Article of the Creed, where forgiveness of sins, resurrection of the body, and everlasting life clearly make up the common ballast of the Church that we must take possession of in faith, hope, and love in order to harvest its fruits in righteousness, peace, and joy.

---

534. I Cor 2:10.

Nevertheless the Church, even in the Lutheran parish, will have much to struggle with before it enters into the basic Christian way of thinking, meaning that if one has come into Christianity 'the wrong way round', it is painful to be turned the right way round! If there is anything that for centuries the Church has become thoroughly used to searching for in the dark instead of the light, it is the kingdom of God in this world with our Lord Jesus Christ as its spiritual king and with the Holy Spirit as His true, authorised viceroy or His 'other self'. Among papists and Protestants, the Christian maxim about the kingdom of God as righteousness, peace, and joy in the Holy Spirit has among the former become even more grossly abused and among the latter more loosely translated than the maxim about faith, hope, and love. The latter, with their ecclesiastical kingdom (church-bound kingdom) would foist onto Christ a kingdom of this world, while in our state churches (kingdom-bound churches) Christ was denied by all real kingdoms in this world and referred to another world that would first dawn beyond the grave.

Therefore, just as we must turn our backs on the scribes if we wish to see the 'life lived in Christ' or the Christian life in the Lord's light, so must we turn away from all popes and archbishops in order to see the 'kingdom of God' in the same light that in reality is the 'light of truth' according to the Lord's words to Pilate: "My kingdom is not of this world. If it were, my servants would have fought to prevent my falling into the hands of the Jews ... Even so I am, as you say, a king. In fact, the reason I was born and came into the world is to testify to the truth. Everyone who is of the truth listens to my voice."[535]

In our thinking we can either follow those who wish to be believed as representing the spiritual itself (the estate spiritual and the papist clergy) and who make out that whatever crosses their minds is Christian truth; or we can follow those for whom spirituality, airiness, or their own rationality are synonymous words, declaring both divine and Christian truth to be 'dark speeches'[536] whose meaning we can only guess at until the Day of Judgement. So long as we follow either of these, neither the fact that Christ said His kingdom is the kingdom of truth, nor that the Apostle Paul has written that the kingdom of God is in the Holy Spirit, i.e. a spiritual kingdom,[537] will help us in the least towards a living and defensible concept of the Christian kingdom of God. Only by taking – like the apostles and their foster-children – the word of faith at Baptism as the foundational idea of Christian truth and – with the same standard-bearers – by believing in the Holy Spirit as the Spirit of Truth and the consciously divine power of God in God's word to us, only then do we become ready to receive

---

535. Jn 18:36-37.
536. Num 12:8.
537. Rom 14:17. "For the kingdom of God is not a matter of eating and drinking, but of righteousness, peace and joy in the Holy Spirit."

and act upon the teaching concerning the kingdom of God as exclusively spiritual yet nonetheless true and real, every bit as real as the fact that true justice, peace, and joy are to be found in this world.

The belief that righteousness, peace, and joy can be found in this world does not become real for us until, like the Apostles and their foster-children, we embrace the Word of faith at Baptism as the basic concept of Christian truth, and believe, with the same standard-bearers in faith, in the Holy Spirit as the Spirit of truth and the consciously divine power of God in His Word to us. The Christian kingdom of God together with righteousness, peace, and joy are like the divine Christian gifts of faith, hope, and love. If there were nothing human in which the kingdom of God could mirror itself, that kingdom would be incomprehensible to all humanity. But since we all have the possibility of knowing that in the kingdoms of this world with civil associations there is already righteousness, peace, and joy – for they are what the people demand of their kings as the only way in which their realms can flourish – so too can we all grasp that when our Lord Jesus Christ grants to His Church as His spiritual people the righteousness, peace, and joy that are truly spiritual and in spirit and heart are truly real, then He is showing Himself to be a king above all kings who makes His kingdom flourish above all the kingdoms of this world.

With this in mind let us look at what in general, and especially in Denmark, calls itself 'Christianity', a 'life lived in Christ', and 'Christendom'. Not only do we immediately note an unbounded confusion of concepts, we find the situation so intolerable that unless we dare to hope for improvement, then, like those born blind but given sight by the Lord, we should today rather than tomorrow turn our backs on both the State Church and the Church State and save ourselves from the tangle by using the Word of faith that is always uniformly and freely preached and received, and by using the Lord's institutions. These are the means of salvation for believers only, but they are freely available, so that hope and love can come to answer to faith, and so that the spiritual people of God can truly take possession of the spiritual kingdom of God which is righteousness, peace, and joy in the Holy Spirit. Provided that we dare to hope for considerable improvement in our situation, we must hold on in the tied and bound position to which the Lord has called us. The Christian enlightenment which we have achieved under very unfavourable circumstances must teach us that with a grain of civil freedom in regard to the spirit and the heart, our situation will be so much improved that both enjoyment of God's grace in Christ and the purification that must always begin from within if it is to be genuine can take giant strides! Indeed they will have to do so before the Church is qualified to be the "city on the hill"[538] to bear all the enmity of the world – which it must do in the end, as it did in the beginning.

---

538. Ps 87:1. "He has founded his city on the holy mountain." Mt 5:14: "A city that is set on a hill cannot be hid."

That is why both before and after the introduction of religious freedom,[539] I have hoped for a breaking of the parish-tie[540] and welcomed it as a halfway house to the freedom that the Spirit of Christ, as the Spirit of Truth, must demand if it is to remain active among us. Therefore I am constantly hoping that our pastors can be freed from their oath of office[541] insofar as it imposes on them temporal ties in their spiritual calling to preach the gospel and be housekeepers for the secrets of God. Once this tongue-tie is loosened, I shall bid welcome to the other half of the freedom that the Spirit of Christ and Truth demands in order to look after its divine errand among us. This errand is in spirit and heart to separate all things human from the temporal and sinful, just as they were in the incarnation of God's Word in Jesus Christ, Mary's son, and to cherish the Church as being humanly in the image of God just as He (the Holy Spirit) cherished Jesus on earth as the beloved Son in whom the heavenly Father both is and reveals that He is well pleased.[542] Since the Spirit of Christ, being the divine Spirit of Truth, has all human tongues in His power and will show this even more clearly at the Last Day of Pentecost than at the First, so with Him as our true guide there is no difficulty learning to understand His 'message to the Church' and learning to believe Him at His Word until, by a corresponding Christian life-experience, it proves and accounts for itself.

For the Christian life is like human life in all its forms. All sound common sense about life develops only slowly under our self-observation of it in the light of truth. Or, as we often say, just as life to some degree explains itself, so is it only through leading a Christian life in faith, hope, and love that the Church and we within it can come to an understanding and illumination of the relation in which Christian faith, Christian hope, and Christian love harmonise with each other, with their source in the Lord's own mouth at Baptism and Holy Communion, with their fruits in the spiritual kingdom of God on earth, and finally with the three divine witnesses in heaven. For it follows as a matter of course that our threefold human life in the image of God must find its explanation in the threefold life of the Godhead, or as we are say, the divine Trinity. Only to the degree that we reach this clarity will it be both timely and beneficial to work on a Christian doctrinal structure. We are beginning to see light in the Lord's light shed on Christianity, on life lived in Christ, and on Christendom, in the sequence of salvation, in the life of God's people and in the domain of the kingdom

---

539. Freedom of religion in faith and practice was confirmed in the first democratic constitution of 1849.

540. The parish-tie as set down in the Danish Law of 1683 limited parishioners' worship to their parish church. Grundtvig fought long and hard to break this tie, and was finally successful through a Parliamentary Law in 1855.

541. In the Danish Lutheran Church the pastoral vow is taken by new priests who have been 'called' (i.e. already appointed) by a specific congregation. It is spoken and signed after the so-called 'Bishop's exam' (an episcopal interview) but before actual ordination. With minor modifications the present pastoral vow dates from 1870, when it replaced the Latin oath of 1685.

542. Mt 3:16-17.

of God. So it is only now that we can draft a basic sketch on paper which with all its faults and incompleteness nevertheless aims at the right goal.

For as long as we fail to recognise the difference between faith and teaching, or life and a way of life, or life and death in the spiritual world, let alone between the spiritual life-forces and their effects … in fact as long as we do not even know what Christianity, life lived in Christ, and Christendom *mean* in the mouth of God and in the language of the Spirit but only what we ourselves call them in the language of the world, nothing more ridiculous can be imagined than raising a Christian doctrinal *structure*. And yet we have actually outdone ourselves in foolishness in wishing to set up *two* doctrinal structures: a dogmatic and a moral one, or a rule of faith and a rule for life, each on its own premises, and this necessarily leads only to death for the one and unbelief for the other.

The Church is in the greatest need in every sense of all the Christian teaching that we can give as regards faith in God the Father, in Jesus Christ His only-begotten Son, and in the Holy Spirit – as this belief is confessed at Baptism and sealed there. This is little known in our Church because both opponents and defenders of the doctrine of the Trinity are competing to obscure and confuse it. Above all it is a matter of life and death for the Church that faith in the divine self-awareness of the Holy Spirit again becomes living and fruitful. So I shall contribute with my pen as best I can to an article on the Trinity. There it will be seen what has become clear to me and what still remains obscure to me in the relationship between the Christian concepts of God and of humankind and in the fellowship between God and human beings in Jesus Christ which I see as a fellowship around the kingdom of God that is one of righteousness, peace, and joy in the Holy Spirit. In other words I shall set out my relation to a Christian doctrinal structure whose outline I can glimpse but am unable to link together so this relationship and fellowship can be seen in their clear coinherence.

27. The Divine Trinity

"There are three that testify in heaven, the Father, the Word, and the Holy Spirit; and these three are one."[543]

Our Lutheran scribes have been so careless as to place this very doubtful and debatable wording at the head of all Christian testimony concerning the divine Trinity, not only in their artificial theoretical systems but also in their basic Christian teachings. They have thus generated the opinion in the world of learning and in the Church that with the authenticity of this wording stands or falls the Christian faith in the Father, the Son, and the Holy Spirit. In so doing, the scribes placed in the hands of opponents of the faith the sharpest of weapons, which they employed so mercilessly in the 18th century that by the end of it hardly any scribe dared to subscribe to faith in the true Trinity, while the Church hardly knew *what* to believe. It is said without warrant in our refurbished New Testament of 1817[544] that this wording concerning the three heavenly witnesses is in fact missing in all manuscripts and early translations, so such an assurance can only make lay readers in Denmark afraid. It is not controversial to say that the authenticity of this debatable wording is more doubtful than most other so-called quotations that are cited as being 'authoritative' (*loca probantia*) and flaunted as such. If the Christian faith really is to be derived and demonstrated from the *Bible*, then the scribes' blunders have become completely unverifiable for us; for when they proclaim that the particular Scripture from which we have derived, and on which we have built, the Christian faith must be abandoned as spurious, then it is no use offering us twenty other biblical passages instead, for the Church has once and for all lost its faith in the infallibility of its scribes upon whom its faith in the book stands or falls.

Since it is impossible under all circumstances of our own accord to prove either a little or a lot of the authenticity of the Apostolic Writings without the presupposition of the Christian faith and Church, we must acknowledge that our Lord must have had a hand in the monstrous errors of our scribes which, early or late, our ingrown prejudice will never be free of: namely, that the written word is the foundation of faith and the prime source of knowledge for the Church. Or rather it would be, if our scribes in the 17th century – when they passed off every syllable in Scripture as

---

543. 1 Jn 5:7.

544. Grundtvig's dating of 1817 must refer to what is known as 'Frederik VI's New Testament', actually published two years later in 1819. This revision was based on 'the Resen-Svane' translation of 1647, a precise but heavy version, barely intelligible in places.

'inspired' – had not declared a patchwork bookseller's item whose inauthenticity was as plain as a pikestaff[545] to be the genuine ur-text, before they went and built the foundational doctrine of Christianity on one of the most baseless written words, so the Church either had to give up its Christian faith or find another firm foundation and valid authority for it. In comparison with this it appears merely insignificant that the only manuscript which we can say has carried the doubtful passage about the three heavenly witnesses, the one from which the New Testament was printed in Alcala (the Complutense Bible),[546] does not have the language that they quote. Nor could the language, even were its authenticity to be as certain as it was doubtful, in any way justify our faith in the Father, the Son, and the Holy Spirit, since here the second person to whom we testify in the Creed and the Baptismal Word is not called 'the Son' but 'the Word', and the language allowed for, but did not confess to, Jesus being God's Son, which according to John's letter[547] and all experience is the foundational doctrine of Christianity by which it stands or falls. It is plain to see that even half of this would be more than enough to prove the folly of the scribes in question, who boasted that they could prove the whole of Christianity from Scripture and yet took for granted as so-called 'proof' all that they themselves actually needed to prove!

We have at last discovered what has been overlooked for so long because it was before our very eyes: namely, that just as the Christian Church with its own life must prove its existence, so must it also presuppose and maintain that the faith which it confesses at Baptism – and no other – is the true Christian faith by which all books and all so-called Christians' Christianity must be judged. It may of course be a matter of complete indifference to the Church whether or not the Bible is the genuine word of the Apostles, whether there are three heavenly witnesses called the Father, the Word, and the Holy Spirit, and whether these three are one. We can let those who are not versed in Scripture on God's kingdom but only in Scripture alone dispute among themselves; we shall limit ourselves to the claim that if the language concerning the three heavenly witnesses is to be genuinely Apostolic and Christian, then 'the Word' must mean 'the Son', our Lord Jesus Christ. In that case the phrase concerning the unity of the three expresses no more than what can be verified in the Creed and the

---

545. The reference is to the so-called Elzevir edition of the Greek New Testament first published in Leyden, Holland in 1624 with a relatively reliable Greek text.

546. The Complutensian Polyglot Bible was the first printed multi-language edition of the entire Bible, produced and sanctioned by the Catholic Church. The translators first met in the city of Alcalá de Henares (in Latin, *Complutum*) in Spain, hence the name. The project was supervised by Cardinal Francisco Ximenes de Cisneros (1436-1517), under whom scholars produced accurate printed texts of the Old Testament in Hebrew, Greek, and Latin, and the New Testament in Greek and Latin as well as the Aramaic Targum of the Pentateuch and an interlinear Latin translation of the Greek Old Testament. The Bible was published in 600 six-volume sets, of which 123 are known to have survived.

547. I Jn 1:1-4.

Baptismal Word; if it is to contain more than this, that is no business of the Christian Church. The scribes have often spoken and written about the unity of the three heavenly witnesses in such a way that their opponents, with more or less justification, have found a clear self-contradiction in their thinking. Whether they were right or wrong, the Church's view of the Trinity's reality was thereby obscured and confused rather than clarified. We must therefore set their mind at rest with the clarification that if the passages in Scripture which the scribes have appealed to really did assume the same confusion, they could not possibly be genuinely Apostolic! The same is true of the made-up word 'Trinity' (Greek *trias* and Latin *trinitas*); if there is anything in it that cannot be justified, that is a matter for the scribes alone and not the Church, whose only task is to acknowledge and defend what it confesses in its entirety at Baptism and on which it baptises accordingly.

Only insofar as the 'Trinity' or unity of the three witnesses does not contradict or invalidate the real three-in-one of the Church may we on behalf of the Church acknowledge and defend this made-up word. It is the name of the everlasting communion in which the Father, Son, and Holy Spirit enjoy and employ the one true divinity in the order and relationship which their proper names, 'Father', 'Son', and 'Holy Spirit' express. Even then the enemies of the Lord and the Church will claim that either we are worshipping three gods or we are guilty of a clear contradiction in terms. However, with the assurance that we indeed have with us the Lord who is Truth we can listen calmly to the unprovable charges of idolatry or gross mendacity and say with the Apostle Paul, "There is but one God."[548] For however many are called gods in Heaven or on earth – as though there were many gods and many lords, we have nevertheless only one God the Father "from whom all things came and for whom we live; and there is but one Lord, Jesus Christ, through whom all things came and through whom we live."[549] This superior position of the Father, for which we have the scriptural testimony of both Paul and our Lord, may appear to demand a correspondingly inferior position of the Son – which the so-called 'orthodox' scribes have either made a heresy or have protected themselves from taking with the sign of the cross. But the positioning is nonetheless necessary, for two parallel bearers of the Godhead as two separate entities is a clear contradiction. The Son's subordination, which lies in the very word 'son' if it is taken literally, must be limited specifically to what lies in the quality of being 'a son' – as Scripture says. For although "the Son can do nothing by Himself", He has been given the power to have life in Himself, and yet "whatever the Father does the Son also does", "so all may honour the Son as they honour the Father, for just as the Father raises the dead and gives them life, even so the Son gives life to whom He is

---

548. 1 Cor 8:6.
549. Ibid.

pleased to give it".[550] As a consequence of this subordination – which lies in both the name of 'son' and the indivisibility of divine sovereignty – heretics old and new have attempted to make the Son less than God. However, as it is written, in so doing they have denied both the Father *and* the Son; for God could not be the eternal Father if He did not have an eternal Son, and yet He must be the eternal everything – which He is!

The Christian Trinity is thus a divine Father and a divine Son and a divine Fellow-Spirit, which in that order and sequence is with eternal self-awareness equally good concerning all things divine except as regards 'independence'; for God the Father with the divine Father-name has reserved this for Himself alone.

By deriving the idea of the Christian Trinity solely from the shared Creed and the Baptismal Word we avoid all self-contradiction and all heresy; we also avoid the fundamental error of thinking that there should not really *be* a 'Holy Spirit' but only a kind of 'holy' spirit as unaware of itself as our own spirit. For in the Baptismal Word the name of the Holy Spirit must be uniform with the name of the Father and the Son, expressing self-awareness or spiritual personality according to the Lord's own word, which is why Scripture often speaks of Him as if He were a spiritual 'Person' who does not speak of His own accord. We also read that "He searches all things, even the deep things of God"[551] and that "He dispenses His divine powers to whosoever He will."[552]

This then is how we should understand and describe the Christian belief in the Trinity. When we then come from a Christian viewpoint to regard the attempts to explain and illuminate the divine Trinity, neither the Greeks in antiquity, nor the Latinists in the Middle Ages, nor the Germans in modern times must tempt us to imitation, for they either began with a lack of faith or they led towards it. However, with the light that is now burning we can not only see that the misfortune was a necessary consequence of those blunders, we also realise that there is an illumination of the Trinity's divine relationship which faith and Spirit not only tolerate but demand, so that the Word of everlasting life in good soil can bear fully ripe fruit.

It follows logically that what is divine – which in itself exceeds human conception – cannot possibly be made clear to us except through our participation in the divine life which illuminates itself. When therefore, with our self-opinionated knowledge, we fancy that we can test the Trinity and expound the Godhead, then it is because we do not believe in the living, self-aware God but construct a pantheism that is the worst form of idol worship, since humankind thereby actually deifies itself, as though it were in itself that the idea of the Godhead first began to come to consciousness. This is clearly as unchristian as it is ungodly, for such self-deification sits well only

---

550. Jn 5:19-23.
551. 1 Cor 2:10.
552. 1 Cor 12:11.

with the Anti-Christ, who *poses* as the one God. As the Lord said, "I have come in my Father's name, and you do not accept me; but if someone else comes in his own name, you will accept him!"[553]

However, this so-called 'interpretation', which is no more than a warping of the concept of the divine Trinity, can only take place and gain access because human beings, created in God's image, must possess, and must be able to find, an image-likeness and a shadow-image in themselves of the divine Trinity. This image-likeness is in the threefold life of the heart, the mouth, and the hand, and the shadow-image is found of the corresponding three concepts of the soul: love, truth, and the life-force. In our interpretation of the divine Trinity we must also take note of both of these, as Scripture constantly reminds us, by figuratively ascribing to God a heart, a mouth, and a hand, and by emphatically calling God (the Father) 'love', the Son 'truth', and the Holy Spirit 'the life-force'. But just as it is only through the Creed and the Baptismal Word that we learn the proper order and sequence in the Trinity, so is it also only from the life of Christ, the true Christianity, that we can be enlightened about the revelation of the divine Trinity through its living and personal activity. If humankind had not fallen, we would have to assume that under God's control we could have gained, through development and self-observation, a vivid idea of the divine Trinity and a realisation of the activity of its persons. But after the Fall, when humankind in every way needed an extraordinary revelation in order to gain true knowledge and worship of God, it is not until the Christian revelation that we acquire knowledge of God's threefold personality, and only through the human life of the new Christian that we trace God's activity in His person.

On the other hand, once our proclamation of the Spirit and the Baptismal Word in an indivisible relation has helped us to gain faith in God the Father as our absolute Lord (*pantokrator*) and Creator, in God the Father's only-begotten Son who came in the flesh as Jesus Christ, Saviour and Judge, and in the Holy Spirit as the everlasting life-force of the Christian Congregation, then we realise that the divine Trinity in its living revelation truly does correspond in person to the Trinitarian concept of love, truth, and shared life-force, and that the manhood of the Son, our Lord Jesus Christ, in the heart, the mouth, and the hand is a living expression of divine love, truth, and power. Moreover, we can conclude that the life of the Church Congregation in Christ must contain recognisable traces of the personal activity of the divine Trinity.

However, before we can draw the least conclusion from this, we must have discovered the Christian signs of life in the living Confession of the Church, in the Spirit's preaching of the corresponding Gospel, and in the Church's song of praise from that wellspring. When these come alive, they undeniably express a distinctive Christian life,

---

553. Jn 5:43.

since their living expression always proves a corresponding living impression. Even if we also reflect that these Christian signs of life presuppose a threefold Christ-life of faith, hope, and love in which we must be able to trace the personal working of the Trinity, we immediately confront an insurmountable obstacle to our clear perception of the Trinity (contemplation face to face) in the corresponding threefold nature of God's kingdom as the kingdom of the Spirit, of the Son, and of the Father. Since the life of the Church is only spiritual until the Lord comes visibly again, our life-experience is limited to God's kingdom in the Spirit, for it is only through the person of the Holy Spirit that the person of the Son and the Father work in the Church. From this angle we have the best view of what is otherwise clear from all sides: that all living Christianity stands or falls with faith in the person of the Holy Spirit; for only in the Spirit is God truly alive and making *us* alive. That is why faith, which the Holy Spirit in person animates, is the foundation of the entire life lived in Christ under the Lord's apparent absence, as we read in the words: "For we live by faith, not by sight"[554] and "what we live is lived in faith in God's Son".[555]

It will be a different matter when our Lord Jesus Christ comes in glory and personally sits on the throne, as is written: "Dear friends, now we are children of God, and what we will be has not yet been made known. But we know that when Christ appears, we shall be like Him, for we shall see Him as He is."[556] And again, "your life is now hidden with Christ in God. When Christ, who is your life, appears, then you also will appear with Him in glory."[557] This is a question not of the scribes' wisdom but of the Church's life, and we must not allow ourselves to lose our way or be confused by the dispute over the Book of Revelation and the so-called 'Millennium', but must just remind ourselves of what all living Christians can understand: that the kingship of our Lord Jesus Christ as well as His kingdom on earth is only real in the Spirit, and that one day it will be just as real in every sense as He is a real person with body and soul. Furthermore, it is as clear as sunlight that the kingdom of the Son and of truth on earth is just as concealed and just as much a matter of faith as is Christ's kingdom, and that one day it will inevitably be revealed in glory so that the world is judged with justice and the peoples judged with truth, while all the deceiving mouths will be blocked.[558] The same justice, peace, and joy which now constitute God's kingdom in Spirit will also do so then, but both in the Spirit and for the hand, so that the inside becomes the outside, as the Lord has said it would: "He who made the inside made the outside also."[559]

---

554. 2 Cor 5:7.
555. Eph 4:13.
556. 1 Jn 3:2.
557. Col 3:3-4.
558. 1 Kg 22:23.
559. Lk 11:40.

Finally, we can glimpse in the distance and beneath the surface the Father's kingdom whose coming we pray for every day in the Lord's Prayer and in which the Father's personal life and activity will reveal itself, as we read concerning Christ's Second Coming:[560] "Then the end will come, when He hands over the kingdom to God the Father ... for the Son shall reign until the Father has put all the Son's enemies under His feet, and death is the last enemy to be destroyed. For He 'has put everything under His feet.'[561] When the Spirit says that 'everything' has been put under the Son it is with the exception of the Father, who put everything under Christ ... so that God may be all in all."

To be sure, the so-called 'orthodox' scribes have claimed that this passage could and should be understood to refer to the Son only as 'the Son of Man', but we need not argue the point here, since we shall not attempt with Scripture to prove anything about the Son's and the Father's kingdom. We use it only because in our view it denotes better than anything what Christ's Spirit has also revealed to us about the Father's kingdom as being the kingdom of Love of His person. This will not be revealed until the good fight is finished which Truth in person has fought with Falsehood in person over time,[562] and when all that is personal is subjected to the Truth; only then can the Love that cannot love anything other than the Truth prove to be all in all. But this must be so, for Love alone is the bond of perfection which bestows all that it embraces, everlasting life and perpetual joy. This is in conception clear enough, but how the conception will be truly fulfilled through the Father's revelation in person we will not be able to imagine until we come into the Son's kingdom.

However, once we have used this enlightenment to trace the activity of the Trinity's person on Christ's life in the Spirit, we immediately discover that just as faith reveals the effect of the Holy Spirit's person, so must the hope of God's glory be ascribed to the activity of the Son's person, as we read: "I hope in the Lord Jesus Christ",[563] and again, "the hope of glory, which is Christ in you",[564] while the love that is the fulfilment of the Law, must be ascribed to the activity of the Father's person, for only He is love, and it is love's matchless merit that it comes of its own accord.

Since it is the Word of faith at Baptism through which the Holy Spirit works as the divine spokesman and advocate who in person realises the corresponding Christian faith, it must be the Son, concealed in the Spirit, who in person realises hope through the Baptismal Word and His own 'Lord's Prayer' in the mouth of the Church. Similarly, it must be the Father, concealed with the Son in the Spirit, who through the Word

---

560. In the following Grundtvig paraphrases 1 Cor 15:24-28.

561. Ps 8:6.

562. 2 Tim 4:7.

563. Phil 2:19.

564. Col 1.

of Holy Communion contributes in person to the rise and growth of divine love, as it is written: "He who loves me keeps my commandments, and the Father will love him and we shall both come to him and build and dwell with him."[565] And again: "For this reason I kneel before the Father, from whom every family in Heaven and on earth derives its name. I pray that out of his glorious riches He may strengthen you with power through His Spirit in your inner being, so that Christ may dwell in your hearts through faith. And I pray that you, being rooted and established in love, may have power, together with all the Lord's holy people, to grasp how wide and long and high and deep is the love of Christ, and to know this love that surpasses knowledge – that you may be filled to the measure of all the fullness of God."[566]

Thus, although with the Christian enlightenment that we have gained we must have been cured of the delusion that we can clarify and describe what we have neither experienced nor can experience in this life, we can nevertheless *glimpse* what a Christian doctrinal structure would look like as a design for the new Jerusalem. Since life in the faith and God's kingdom in the Spirit are not only a true pattern, but also a real foretaste of what will be gained in the Son's and the Father's kingdom through the complete revelation of love and hope, a new light truly shines like a seven-branched candlestick over the path of life that our Lord Jesus Christ has laid for us and accompanied us along; indeed He Himself *is* that path and has acknowledged Himself to be so in the words: "I am the way and the truth and the life. No one comes to the Father except through me."[567] We feel assured that with every step we take along this path, the more clearly shall we know the righteousness, peace, and joy which is God's kingdom in the Spirit, in the Son, and in the Father, until we reach the glory which the Son had with His father before the world's foundations were laid and in which He knows the Father as the Father knows Him.

---

565. A paraphrase of Jn 14:15-17.
566. Eph 3.
567. Jn 14:6.

Chriſtelige

Prædikener

eller

Söndags-Bog

af

Nik. Fred. Sev. Grundtvig

Ordets Tjener.

Förſte Bind.

KLÖBENHAVN 1827.

Paa den Wáhlſke Boghandlings Forlag .

Trykt hos C. Græbe .

8. *Christian Sermons or The Sunday Book*

The title-page of the book (*Christelige Prædikener eller Søndags-bog*) vol. I from 1827 depicts the Church of Our

Saviour (*Vor Frelsers Kirke*) in Christianshavn, Copenhagen, with its characteristic outside spiral staircase. King

Frederik VI not only gave Grundtvig an annual grant of 600 Rigsdaler, but personally called him to serve first at

Præstø (1821) and then, despite massive protests from the senior Copenhagen clergy, at the Church of Our Saviour.

It was here that Grundtvig preached his Pentecost sermon in 1824 (no. 37 in this book) and here in 1825 that he

made his 'matchless discovery', which ever after inspired him: that the oral confession of faith and the Sacraments

of Baptism and Holy Communion practised in the earliest church actually precede the writing of the Bible. During

this period Grundtvig lived just opposite his church, in Prinsessegade 52, where he wrote his famous hymns 'We

greet you again, God's angels bright' (no. 8 in *Living Wellsprings*) and 'We welcome with joy this blessed day' (no. 53

ibid). When this latter hymn was rejected for the millennial celebration of the coming of Christianity to Denmark,

and in addition he lost the libel case against him (1826), Grundtvig resigned his pastorate in dismay and defiance.

III

SERMONS FOR THE CHURCH YEAR

Introduction by Michael Schelde and Edward Broadbridge

N.F.S. Grundtvig was first and foremost a Lutheran pastor. The sermon is therefore a dominant genre in his writings and he preached over 3,000 of them in his lifetime, A few collections were published after his death, but the major work was led by Christian Thodberg and his successors, who from 1980 onwards published 12 volumes of Grundtvig's sermons from 1822-39 and 4 volumes of his Vartov sermons from 1839-42.

16 of Grundtvig's sermons are translated here. The first 12 follow the Church Year from Advent to the 27th Sunday in Trinity, to which are added his sermon at the opening of Parliament in 1865, and 3 brief sermons given on the Sundays preceding his death. Grundtvig preached his last sermon in Vartov Church on 1st September 1872, the day before he died peacefully in his home. For a chronology of his life as a pastor see the Timeline on pp. 19-20.

Grundtvig's Preaching Career

Grundtvig's very first sermon, from 17th March 1810, was entitled 'Why has the Word of the Lord Disappeared from His House?' It was a dimissory sermon and the final step in the theological exam that would allow him to become a pastor and serve as curate in his father's parish at Udby, a reluctant move but one of obedience to his aging father. The examiners awarded Grundtvig a distinction, and although he had previously stated that he would never preach such a sermon outside the exam situation – in other words, to an ordinary congregation – when he proudly published it later that year, many clergy took offence at the following words:

> The holy men of the past believed in the teachings they were appointed to preach, but is that true of pastors today? No indeed, and that is why the Word of God has disappeared from his house!

Grundtvig was therefore already something of a controversial figure when he was installed as curate for his father in Udby-Ørslev parish on the 1st Sunday After Trinity 1811. Nevertheless, he buckled down in the country parish and by all accounts served faithfully, if pietistically, until his father's death. He preached his last sermon there on the 9th Sunday After Trinity 1813, before returning to Copenhagen, where he had no pastorate but was an itinerant preacher until Christmas 1815. He then earned a scanty living as a writer until King Frederik VI awarded him an annual grant in 1818. Early in 1821 and without applying for the post Grundtvig was called to the parish of Præstø-Skibbinge, 95 km south-west of Copenhagen. Here he preached from Palm

Sunday 1821 until the 25th Sunday After Trinity 1822. He returned to Copenhagen as curate at the prestigious Church of Our Saviour from the 1st Sunday in Advent 1822 until his resignation from the post on the 6th Sunday After Easter 1826.

For six years Grundtvig remained without a pastorate, but in 1832 he resumed his preaching ministry, mainly at evening worship at Frederik's Church in Christianshavn, Copenhagen. In contrast to these various comings and goings, his final appointment at Vartov Church lasted 33 years, from 1839 until his death in 1872.

Grundtvig's Preaching Style

Sermons are meant to be heard, so when we read Grundtvig's sermons today outside the context in which they were delivered, our first response is that they are of their time – which was a very different time from ours. First of all, their syntax is bewildering to a modern listener. By and large we can manage only two minor clauses and one major clause per sentence before the meaning is obscured or lost – whereas Grundtvig regularly employs five or six clauses. His sermon on Christmas Day 1843 (Text 29) opens with a Danish sentence of 207 words, including 10 minor clauses and 5 major clauses – and this could go on for a whole hour.[568]

The later Vartov sermons are marked by the views that Grundtvig adopted following his 'matchless discovery' in 1825 and which were now reaching maturity. Sin, the Devil, evil, and death are a reality, but despite the Fall humanity still retains a remnant of the image of God, and history has a momentum that reveals the overwhelming power of the words from Christ's own mouth. The Lord's Prayer, the Words of Institution for Baptism and Holy Communion, and the Apostolic Creed passed on by oral tradition from the earliest days constitute "true Christianity". Grundtvig's sermons are full of rhetorical devices, biblical quotations, and appositional phrases, delivered with great power and intensity. They develop over time partly in interaction with their historical context and partly as a result of his own theological understanding. His youthful anger and condemnation of the contemporary Church never leave him, but they are gradually combined with a more measured awareness of human frailty and a deep gratitude to God – always Grundtvig offers an insight and an exhortation. This is best illustrated by his sermon before the opening of Parliament 1856 (Text 40). Grundtvig himself sat in Parliament for a number of years, so he knows the ropes as both pastor and politician, and he lets fly at a favourite target:

---

568. Since Grundtvig's language, especially his syntax, is difficult for modern Danes to follow, in 2013 a study group at the Grundtvig Academy rewrote this sermon in modern Danish and published it online.

For every so-called 'state church', in which an entire people is civilly bound and forced to confess the same faith whether they share it or not, shows not only a dreadful indifference to the truth and an equally dreadful favour for hypocrisy in the highest and holiest concern known to man, it is also, like a prodigiously large stone church, the heaviest stone that can be rolled onto a people's heart, a burden under which Denmark's tender people's heart has sighed for far too long.

So it is a great achievement of Parliament to agree to break the parish-tie and grant churchgoers the freedom to worship *outside* their parish. Grundtvig is optimistic:

Now that everyone in the country can choose their own spiritual adviser according to their heart's desire, and the prospect has been opened for every congregation to sing the hymns it likes best, the Danish People's Church can become a matchless wonder to the gratification, comfort, and joy of the whole people

Two contemporary accounts of Grundtvig's preaching have survived. Bishop of Viborg Otto Laub (1805-82) writes:

Grundtvig begins in a faint, monotonous, drowsy tone – but one does not fall asleep. Nor is it long before he is speaking in a different tongue, though with the *same* tongue. He carries his listeners forward with him; they could not predict where he was going, so they did not fall into their own thoughts along the way. Without any order but not without continuity, without any notable pauses his speech passes through all the regions, the high, the low, and the flat, through fire and water. One also tarries in lovely paradises, with the pure air of the mountains and the mild winds of the motherly valleys, with Easter morning on the horizon.[569]

The more critical Bishop of Zealand, Hans Martensen (1808-84), writes that there were often exalted prophetic visions in Grundtvig's preaching, but:

On the other hand, what I did not experience was the deepest religious layer which one is most in need of, that which speaks to our own inner being, that which nurses and guides our souls, that which enters on the inner paths and the inner states ... The

569. Quoted in F. Abrahamovitz, *Grundtvig – Danmark til lykke* (Grundtvig – To Denmark's Joy) (Høst & Søn, Copenhagen 2000) p.208.

psychological and ethical elements are the weakest in him, the historical and the prophetic the strongest.[570]

The Child in Grundtvig's Preaching

Grundtvig is full of enthusiasm over the birth of Christ, for Christmas is a "children's festival" and what is impossible for human beings is "child's play" for God.
Very occasionally he would use the pulpit to present a new hymn he had written for
the congregation, often for a church festival. On 23rd December 1820 he published
the 10 verses of 'A child is born in Bethlehem' and in his sermon two days later he
told the congregation that it was as though they had been present in spiritual form,
participating in the events in Bethlehem that night. In the Church of Our Saviour
in 1825 he ended his Christmas sermon by reciting 'We greet you again, God's angels
bright',[571] now a beloved Christmas hymn known to all Danes, in which the angels
are pictured running up and down the ladder between Heaven and Earth – another
of his memorable images.

In another sermon about the child Jesus (Text 31), Grundtvig praises Joseph and
Mary for not allowing their 12-year-old son to stay and be educated by the rabbis
in the temple, as they would undoubtedly have held on to the boy genius had they
been allowed to do so. But Joseph and Mary wanted him home again, for they
"regarded Jesus as a treasure entrusted to them by God whom they would not hand
over to strange hands at any price". Both Grundtvig himself and his own children
were home-educated.

The Priority of the Feminine

In the selection of poetry texts for the previous volume in this series, *Living Wellsprings*,
a whole section was devoted to women who had inspired Grundtvig, and a number of
hymns about women in the Bible were also included. This feminine side to Grundtvig
receives further illumination in our choice of sermon texts. Thus in a Lent sermon in
1837 on "Woman, how great is thy faith!" (Text 32), Grundtvig turns to the power of
the feminine vis-à-vis the masculine with the following powerful claim:

> If we consider what the Spirit testifies – that faith, hope and love are the three things
> that contain all that is genuinely Christian – we shall soon realise that two-thirds of
> Christianity, namely faith and love, are 'feminine'. Since faith is the first and love the

---

570. Ibid. p.209.
571. See no. 8 in *Living Wellsprings* (2015).

greatest, hope, which is the masculine element in between, can be no more than an empty spiritual death and impotent fantasy if its feminine elements are missing.

Grundtvig ends this sermon with the extraordinary exhortation, "Long live all women believers!" To modern readers this may sound patronising, but it was certainly not his intention. We recall his support for the author of the first feminist novel in Denmark, Mathilde Fibiger, evidence of which will appear in the next volume in this series, *The Common Good. N.F.S. Grundtvig as Politician and Contemporary Historian*.

By 1848 Grundtvig had already been preaching to his predominantly female congregation in Vartov for nine years and he does not hesitate to tell them that:

> the Lord could not be the perfect human being without in fact being man *and* woman. Only the perfect human being is created in God's image and according to His likeness; only in the perfect humanity, both male *and* female, can God's power be revealed and perfected. (Text 33)

In particular Grundtvig cherishes Jesus' mother – for the simple reason that so did God! And this despite the Lutheran disdain for Mariolatry. In his 1837 sermon on the Annunciation (Text 34) Grundtvig adopts an essay style rather than his usual sermon style to praise his biblical heroine:

> Wherever the Christian faith is found, the failure to appreciate the Virgin Mary and the ancient Church language rests fundamentally on the failure to appreciate the human *heart*, a failure to which an inordinately mistaken belief and a tendency to arrogance, especially among us men, may give rise, but which is as indefensible as it is damaging. For by disdaining the *human* heart we cannot gain *God's* heart, which honoured the Virgin Mary.

The Holy Spirit Taken Literally

Grundtvig is a keen champion of the Holy Spirit and its literal *activity* on earth, as in his famous hymn, 'Spirit of all truth and love':

> Spirit of all truth and love,
> bond of earth to heav'n above
> which alone You tighten;

grant new tongues to strong and weak,
hearts infused the truth to speak,
as Your flames enlighten![572]

In sermons given in our secular times God the Holy Spirit comes a poor third in the
Trinity, a point that Hans Raun Iversen underlines in his introduction to *Basic Christian Teachings*: the Word/words in our mouth are reiterated in sermon after sermon
by Grundtvig as being the motive power of the Church, here in his sermon for Palm
Sunday 1855 (Text 35): "He has set His Spirit in us and placed His Word in our mouths,
and it shall not retreat from our mouths or the mouths of our offspring through all
eternity." His Pentecost sermon in 1824 begins with the words: "There is no Church
festival that is so poorly attended as Pentecost, at least in Denmark", and in the following he beautifully encapsulates the Trinity festivals thus:

> Christmas is the festival of faith, Easter the festival of hope, and Pentecost the festival
> of love! Then we are not surprised that Pentecost comes last in our Christian life rather
> than *between* our Church festivals. For when the Tree of Life from the Word's root grows
> in the Church garden, then faith is its trunk, hope its blossom, and love its fruit!

The Vartov Sunday Morning Service

Grundtvig's enthusiasm was infectious and uplifting, and his Vartov congregation
grew steadily in number. Originally the church served the sick and elderly of Vartov
hospital, but he was so successful in attracting a wider audience, including the dowager
Queen Caroline Amalie, that his congregation eventually had its own hymnbook. The
10 o'clock morning service[573] attracted his 'friends' and sympathisers and was well attended every Sunday, not least for the 'songs of praise' that he so championed. Hymns
and sermons come together in Grundtvig, and although he admitted that he himself
was "very unmusical" and could not sing in tune, he remains the greatest hymn *writer*
in the language. His hymns were sung more slowly than nowadays, but faster than
before, so he was actually accused of 'galloping the hymns' at Vartov!

In *Two Visits to Denmark 1872-74* we have an account of a Sunday service at Vartov
from the English writer, Edmund William Gosse (1849-1928), who was present at one
of Grundtvig's last services in Vartov Church: "For a man of ninety, he could not be
called infirm; his gestures were rapid and his step steady. But the attention was riveted

---

572. See no. 37 in *Living Wellsprings* (2015).

573. The 10 o'clock morning service is still conducted in every parish throughout the country except when a pastor is
serving two parishes.

on his appearance of excessive age. He looked like a troll from some cave in Norway; he might have been centuries old."[574]

The primary purpose of Grundtvig's sermons – and most other sermons of the time – was elucidation of the text in relation to the faith, with an exhortation to the congregation to seek and do God's will. Where many a sermon used to end with a rhetorical and personal question to believers in the pews, Grundtvig generally ends in gratitude and with all praise to God. He can condemn contemporary trends, but it is always in order to urge the congregation to keep on following Jesus, "for the Lord's disciples never leave Him, however far behind they are in His footprints" (Text 35).

The Sunday morning service at Vartov can best be described as a service of hymns and prayers, with the living sacraments of Baptism and Holy Communion at its heart. The sermon is merely one element, and in a sense subordinate to the hymn-singing, which testifies to the life in the congregation, living as it is in the 'New Year of the Lord' yet close to Jesus and the first Apostles through the Living Word. This is expressed programmatically in his hymn 'All who are given wings to fly':

> To ev'ry bird that would inspire,
> to each and ev'ry angel choir,
> whose song you shall inherit,
> say you are willing to compete
> in praising God with singing sweet
> for voice and wings and spirit![575]

The most tangible link between hymn and sermon is to be found in Grundtvig's preparation for publication of his monumental *Song-Work for the Danish Church* (1837), where the still unpublished hymns are included in the sermon, which is often a commentary on their content. His later editions of *Festival Hymns* for use in Vartov Church, first published in book form in 1850, began life as loose sheets handed out to worshippers as they arrived. Grundtvig was nothing if not inspired by the Sunday service and the opportunity to communicate the thoughts in his head and the poetry in his heart with an oral power issuing loudly and forthrightly from his mouth. Just as Grundtvig's final poem speaks of death as a homecoming,[576] so does his very last sermon (Text 41) refer to "the kingdom of God's beloved Son, where home-coming sons and daughters for ever compete to give thanks in the name of our Lord Jesus Christ".

---

574. For the full description see *Living Wellsprings*, p. 29.
575. See no. 3 in *Living Wellsprings* (2015).
576. Ibid. no. 162.

28. 3rd Sunday in Advent

7 December 1843 (Matthew 11:2-10)

Holy God, our Father! – Your Word is Truth! Your Word to us is Spirit and Life! – The Word of faith which must be heard! Heavenly Father! Let Your prophetic Word always be a voice in the wilderness: Prepare the way for the Lord,[577] and like an angel walk before the face of the Lord and prepare the way for Him to our hearts, the way to our tongues, and the way through the times to the Day of Judgement, all through Your Holy Spirit, in the name of our Lord Jesus Christ! You who are in heaven.

"What did you go out into the wilderness to see? A reed swayed by the wind?"[578] This is the question our Lord asks as He speaks to the people about John the Baptist. It is the same question that our pastors of old asked in the Lord's name after the Gospel had been read, when they spoke of church attendance. And it is the same question that our young pastors must ask in the same Lord's name and after the same Gospel reading for as long as the Lord is alive and the Gospel is preached, for as long as the Lord lives in hiding and the Gospel is openly preached on earth until the end of the world. For as long as the world stands, the Lord calls pastors where and as He likes, anoints them with His Spirit and sends them out to preach the Gospel. This is not a new Gospel, but the old one that we have heard from the beginning: "If any preach a different gospel from the one we heard from the beginning – even an angel from Heaven– may he be cursed," says the Apostle Paul and the Holy Spirit with him.[579] Everywhere that the old Gospel is heard in the power of the Spirit, it sounds like a voice from Heaven calling in the wilderness: "Prepare the way of the Lord!"[580]

Thus sounds the Gospel in all hearts that are open to truth and have a desire for life; for they are all in their *natural* state, like the wilderness. This is the very wilderness into which our first parents were driven from Paradise; the wilderness in which we all awake one sad morning and call in vain for our Paradise dreams, for our childhood playmates that flee from us as soon as we eat of the Tree of Knowledge of Good and Evil; the world's wilderness, where the heart finds neither path nor rest but only a constant *longing* for them, a longing to hear an angel's voice and to have him as company. So in this wilderness it is never futile to shout, "Prepare the way of the Lord!" Prepare the way for Him who travels with peace and guides souls to rest, who has

---

577. Isa 40:3; Mt 3:3; Mk 1:3; Lk 3:4; Jn 1:23.
578. Mt 11:7-8. Lk 7:24.
579. Gal 1:8.
580. Mk 1:3.

the Word of everlasting life and gives it, unmerited and without payment, to all who believe in Him. So then, prepare the way for the Lord Jesus Christ, whose name will travel with the sun and eclipse its radiance, whose name shall be established on earth as the house on the rock that defies all storms, all floods, and the portals of Hell, whose name shall for ever be praised in Heaven as the sole name in which tired souls found rest, fallen souls found restitution, and sinners found salvation. For these are granted by the Lamb who bore the sins of the world, who sacrificed Himself and with His holy, precious blood redeemed all the peoples and heathens, tribes and languages that wished to belong to Him and exchange their flesh and their spirit, infected and consecrated to corruption, for His Spirit and His flesh, which is pure and holy and sealed to everlasting life!

Always thus sounds the Gospel of Christ like a voice in the wilderness, and the world hears its *echo* as a *voice*; for all those for whom the world is a wilderness are *themselves* a wilderness to the world, a circle whom the world's people shun, except when an echo is heard that is strangely haunting, that promises Heaven unmerited, and pours out streams from the hidden wellspring that bring joy to all children of humankind. This is what happened in the wilderness by the River Jordan when John the Baptist preached God's kingdom with many a word of comfort and joy to the people; and this is what happened at every river and in every garden wherever the Spirit brought the Word of the Lord's coming and the Lord's ways; and thus will it continue until the end of our days. Then the Lord's messenger will ask, always in His name as He Himself once asked, "What did you go out into the wilderness to see?" Why did you insist on leaving the path of light, the state of growth, and the enjoyment of life here, where the Gospel is preached only to the poor – a light for those who sit in darkness, life for those who fear death, Paradise for those who feel that the world with all its glory is only a wilderness for them? "What did you go out into the wilderness to see? A reed swayed by the wind?" A tongue swayed by the Spirit as if it were no more than a theatre play for the ear and the eye? For the inner eye that always opens when the light that burns for all eternity shines down from on high? For the eye that opens itself and sees glimpse upon glimpse of the lost Paradise with the Tree of Life and the River of Life, and glimpse upon glimpse of angel-wings soaring up and down over the name of Christ?

If there is nothing else you want, you might as well save yourself the trouble! For you will pay for your moment's desire with many hours of pain over what you before called 'heavenly' and 'divine' and with many a pang from the Word that seeks to be believed and never allows to go unpunished any regard of it as empty talk, as a resounding gong or a clanging cymbal,[581] as worldly glibness born only to flatter the ear, then disappear.

---

581. 1 Cor 13:1.

So, "What did you go out into the wilderness to see? A man in soft clothing?" An evangelist with hats for all the heads and cushions for all the arms that cry out for peace where there *is* no peace? Who preach grace, mercy, and peace, life and salvation not only unmerited but unconditional, or at least without the conditions the Lord has laid down, without the serious warning against taking God's grace in vain and with an unrepentant heart cultivating anger for the Day of Wrath and the revelation of God's righteous judgement? If that is what you wish to see, then you are in error – like those who beside the River Jordan not only saw the man in the garment of rough camel's hair and a leather belt[582] but heard the rough words: "You brood of vipers! Who warned you to flee from the judgement of Hell? Produce fruit in keeping with repentance. For the axe has been laid to the root of the trees, and every tree that does not produce good fruit will be cut down and thrown into the fire."[583] They always make a mistake, those who look for soft preachers in the wilderness, for look, "they are in the King's Guard!" They have been brought to the palace with pomp like Balaam,[584] for there are pearls in the world's eyes that can hardly be bought too dearly!

So, "What did you go out into the wilderness to see?" A prophet? A man who is driven by the Spirit of God and Truth? A man in whose mouth the Most High has laid His words, and whose eyes the Spirit opened to see the world and humankind as they are, the concealed ways where they walk and the fixed places where they end up, the bottomless abyss in the uttermost darkness, and the eternal heights with the wondrous light where the Most High dwells? Indeed, said the Lord. "This is more than a prophet!"[585] This is the one about whom it is written: "I will send my angel before your face who will prepare your way before you!"[586] And the Lord's messenger says the same every day: "Well may they say that you are looking for a true prophet who sees the ways of both life and death from beginning to end and tells what he sees, there you made no mistake, there you will find more than you sought, 'for you are not far from God's kingdom',[587] for here is more than a prophet, here is a messenger from the Lord who tells all His servants, 'Go before my face and prepare the way for me and whoever hears you hears me!'"[588] So, however insignificant we are in the eyes of the world, and however poor we may be in our station, if we will please Him who sent us saying, "Whoever wishes to be the greatest must be the servant of all!"[589] – and however sparingly we are equipped with spiritual gifts compared to Israel's prophets

---

582. Mt 3:4.
583. Mt 3:7-10.
584. Num 24:17.
585. Mt 11:9.
586. Mt 11:10.
587. Mk 12:34.
588. Lk 10:16.
589. Mt 20:26; Mk 10:43.

and apostles, there is nevertheless more than a prophet and more than an angel wher-ever we preach the Gospel. For the only-begotten Son who will be with His Church for ever is *with* us and sends us out as *angels* to prepare the way for Him. He follows behind us, even though He was far ahead of us, and He comes to all those who hear us and believe in Him whom we *proclaim*, calling Him by His name, calling 'our Lord Jesus Christ'; to them He comes with His Word of everlasting life, teaching them that He *Himself* is the way, so they need not search and ask the *way* to God's kingdom, for the way is *with* them and the kingdom is coming *to* them, God's kingdom, which is righteousness, peace, and joy in the Holy Spirit!

So, my friends, this is the new housekeeping which God established in the fullness of time when He sent His Son, born of a woman, the child of Bethlehem, to the great gladness of the shepherds and all peoples, widely dispersed as they are. Under all the skies of Heaven they find themselves to be a scattered herd without a shepherd, who get lost in the wilderness as childlike souls, lost in the wilderness but with a vague memory of the lost Paradise. It is a housekeeping in the house of our Lord Jesus Christ, in the holy, universal Church, where prophets are constantly being roused who are *more* than prophets, because He has *come*, the long-awaited hope of Israel and the desire of all Gentiles! He stands in the midst of those who ask after Him, even though they do not know Him, just as he does there at the River Jordan. That is why the prophets who proclaim Him, and preach the forgiveness of sins and an everlasting life in His name, are *also* angels, the Church's angels who prepare His way by calling aloud in the wilderness, "Prepare the way for Him who walks on straight paths, who from eternity has made the clouds His chariot and who rides on the wings of the wind."[590] Now he has abased Himself to live life on earth, to live with the tongues of our dust for His chariot and to ride on the wings of our breath. Yet He is equally the living, almighty God's Word, who in the beginning was *with* God and *was* God but became flesh in order to dwell amongst us with a glory as the only-begotten of the Father, full of grace and truth;[591] for the Law was given by Moses; grace and truth came to the world through Jesus Christ![592]

Yes indeed, it always sounds like a fairy-tale to the world, this message of Christmas and the good news. With this we are sent to prepare the way of the Lord who was ahead of us yet follows after us in the Word that *was* from the beginning. This is the Word of faith to which we testify with our preaching, even though it has a far greater witness than ours in the deeds it has performed from generation to generation, and shall continue to do so wherever it is received. The Lord uses our testimony so that

590. Ps 104:3.
591. Jn 1:14.
592. Jn 1:17.

you shall come to the faith and experience the power of His deeds. You shall experience that it is neither dream nor fairy-tale but God's deed and truth, so you can say to each one of us, "Now we no longer believe because of your words alone, for we ourselves have *known* that this Jesus is the Christ, the Saviour of the World, and that those who receive Him gain life in His name."[593] So you can say of us all, "For a little while they were a burning, shining light, but they were not the light itself which enlightens all people who come into the world, they were only sent out to testify to Him, the true light, and prepare the way for Him as the morning-star and the reddening dawn that will arise in our hearts, the everlasting morning-sun which He will be for all believing generations, until He comes visibly in the radiance of the midday sun to reveal all His Father's glory and to transfigure us all in its light!"

That is why all the years of the Lord, the lesser and the greater, begin with a time of Advent. Here, the words 'The Lord is coming, prepare the way for Him' are the watchword on every lip, the Gospel of the day in every place. Also among us, also in these short winter days, God makes this time of Advent fruitful and blessed, so that many small wildernesses may be glad and lay down a way for Him who can and will transform the dry place into a wellspring and make the wilderness bloom like the rose.[594] Many voices will issue from us to cry aloud in the world's wilderness from generation to generation and prepare the way for Him who wishes to celebrate Christmas and Easter and Pentecost with us all, to be born and grow up among us, to die and rise for us, and to create a Heaven for us where the Spirit speaks of God's great and wonderful things with *our* glowing tongues!

So, that is how He comes to us and our children, the same Jesus Christ, God's only-begotten Son, born in Bethlehem of the Virgin Mary. The same Jesus Christ to whom John testified and who gave John the testimony in today's Gospel, and will give the same to all His messengers – Jesus Christ, who sits at the right hand of Almighty God our Father yet also stands among all those disciples who come together in His name. May He thus come to us and dwell with us! May He thus come to all who await redemption, to all who dwell in the wilderness, whose souls thirst for God, the living God and the wellspring of life! May He come with His Father's Spirit, the Holy Spirit that opens wellsprings in the wilderness, calls forth waterfalls from rocks, and makes rivers flow out into the valleys and over the hills! Amen! In our Lord Jesus' name, Amen!

---

593. Jn 4:42.
594. Isa 35:1.

29. Christmas Day

25 December 1843 (Luke 2:1-14)

All praise and honour be to You, our God and Father, for the joyful tidings! Indeed, all praise, honour, and thanks be to You for ever for the Christmas tidings to Your house on high, to more than angel-joy and gladness, to everlasting communion with Your only-begotten Son, the Beloved, in whom You find favour! All praise, honour, and thanks be to You from the heart's core for sending us the joyful tidings with the angel-host that sees Your face, hears with amazement Your magisterial voice, and accomplishes Your commission with joy! And for confirming Your Christmas tidings through Your only-begotten Son, who is in Your embrace, is God with You for ever, but became human like us, born of a woman! And for sealing this in Our Lord Jesus' name in the hearts of all believers through Your Holy Spirit, which searches Your depths, works through Your omnipotence, comforts with Your love, accompanies us with Your light through the world's confusion and death's wilderness to the land of the living, to the home of peace, to the everlasting dwellings of gladness, Your house, our Father! You who are in heaven!

"And you will sing as on the night you celebrate a holy festival; your hearts will rejoice."[595] This is one of the many prophecies in Isaiah which received visible, heavenly fulfilment when God's Son became human. According to the Gospel of the Day, it was fulfilled literally for the shepherds on the night God's Son was born in Bethlehem of the Virgin Mary. When they heard the multitude of the heavenly host singing "Glory be to God on high, and peace on earth, good will to all men", the shepherds actually heard a night-song to inaugurate a feast-day whereby a new festival was introduced to the world, the Christmas festival for the child born in Bethlehem. This news spread so far and wide to all four corners of the world and became so ancient throughout Christendom that for this reason alone it is called the most joyful of all festivals on earth. Indeed this has been so in every sense from the morning-hour when the shepherds returned from Bethlehem with praise and honour for all that they had heard and seen – right up to this very Christmas morning. For we all know that, despite the unbelief which is the besetting sin of our time, and despite the coldness of heart which like death is the wages of sin, untold numbers awoke with joy today because it is Christmas, the festival of joy, which Christmas brings to great and small, and especially to children – incomparably!

Already, as we have heard, the ancient prophecy of the night-song for a feast creating glad hearts, or for the inauguration of a joyful festival, was fulfilled not only for

---

595. Isa 30:29.

Bethlehem's shepherds but wherever people believed in the Christmas tidings and held a feast for the Son of the Virgin Mary, to whom she gave birth in Bethlehem, in a stable, and whom she laid in a manger. This prophecy will continue to be fulfilled for as long as there is Christendom on earth, for that is how long the Christmas festival will last and how long it will be the incomparable, joyful festival, if not for others then at least for those who best know how to enjoy themselves, and to enjoy themselves in the purest sense of the word, namely our children.

So we have already learned that Christmas is a children's festival with angel-songs and glad hearts! But in saying this we feel that in these few words there is such a wealth of riches enclosed and 'captured', so to speak, that we wish they would open up before our very eyes so that the child and the angel-song and the glad heart were brought into the light. This would actually happen if the Christmas preaching and the Christmas hymn were what they *should* be, what they obviously *can* be since the Christmas message is true, and what they cannot *help* but be if the child in Bethlehem is to be the living reason for our faith, and if His Spirit, that of our Lord Jesus Christ, were over His entire Church, and if Christmas joy were shared in the hearts of all. Then our Christmas preaching and our Christmas hymn in the plainest of words would reveal both the highest and the deepest and the indescribably loveliest feature of childlikeness, of angel-song and the heart's joy!

We must take this to heart, my friends, so as not to put the blame on God or the world for what our preaching or our hymns or our hearts lack. For it is part of our childhood teachings in the Lord's house that all that is good is God's *gift*, the gift of grace, and if we lack this, then the blame is our own. For God the Father who gave us His beloved Son wishes to give us everything *with* Him, and gives richly to those who *call* upon Him. If on the other hand we wish to cling to our confession of our guilty sin and merely hug ourselves and each other, then we shall never gain what we lack, and we shall have forgotten completely that Christianity is not a new Law but a Gospel, a joyful message from heaven. And this joyful message is that because we are wretched sinners and because the Law cannot quicken us and our righteousness cannot save us, a Saviour is born who is Christ the Lord in the city of David, the Child of Bethlehem, the Prince of Christmas! He brings forgiveness of sins, God's peace, and heavenly joy to all those who believe in His name, the name of Jesus. To this name all knees shall bow[596] in Heaven and earth, and *beneath* the earth, and all tongues confess[597] that Jesus Christ is Lord, to the honour of God the Father!

We must remember this with feeling, and have the *heart* to believe the glad tidings – to believe in this Son of God and of the Virgin Mary, who was wrapped in cloth

---

596. Phil 2:10.
597. Rom 14:11.

and laid in a manger – and then again was wrapped in cloth and laid in the grave. But He rose in triumph from the dead and sits in glory at the right hand of God the Father Almighty, and He will come in His Father's glory to gather all His people to His Father's house. If we have the *heart* to believe this, then we shall also learn that Christmas is *still* a children's festival with angel-song and glad hearts, and that this is so for us to a much greater degree than for our *forefathers*; indeed it can be so for us almost to the same degree as for the shepherds in *Bethlehem*!

My friends, I am well aware that this sounds almost unbelievable to most people. And I am too old to take any pleasure in melodious words with no power or truth. But I know it is *true* and that God has the overflowing power to prove that what is impossible for humankind is possible, indeed is *child's play*, for Him! So I purposely say that precisely here and now our Christmas joy can and will be so great among us as it has never been here or anywhere else since the days of the Lord Himself and His Apostles!

This comes about because only now can the great light that was lit in the evening-hour, the light of Christmas Eve, truly illuminate our hearts and eyes so that we see what we actually need, and what God has given us in His only-begotten Son. He not only suffered and died and rose for us but can and will truly dwell and grow, walk and work, and be glorified and reign, in all His believers! Yes indeed, only now, and with God's help and through the Holy Spirit, can this great secret of God's devotion, God's revelation in the flesh, in the incarnation of the Son and the Word in the power of the Spirit, be revealed to us, to us and to our believing children. And it can grow all the more, so that our heavenly childlikeness will develop as the angel-song echoes for us and the glad heart is reborn within us!

Yes indeed, my friends, even as from experience we get to know the child's faith and the child's hope, the child's eyes and the child's heart in ourselves and others, so must we feel and confess that if childlikeness were free of *childishness* and could be united with youthful courage, adult power, and elderly wisdom, it would be a joy to live, and the glad heart would follow of its own accord. Nowhere else on earth has this feeling been deeper than in *our* part of the world, so it must still be found far more potently at the bottom of *our* hearts than anywhere else. This wonder, the union of childlikeness with all things human, which is good and great and to-be-wished-for, this is the very core of the gospel of Christ and the work of the Holy Spirit. Although it is still far from everything that has been granted us in God's only-begotten Son – for we shall one day become as He is so as to see Him as He *truly* is – this is the very first step. It is already so great and glad a step as is possible for God Almighty and only achievable through His heavenly Father-love which in His Holy Spirit He instils into our hearts.

So, the child of Bethlehem was both God and human. And although it sounds like a fairy-tale, He can and will make all believers both God and human too! Jesus Christ was clearly a human being whose like had never been seen before, and God will make such people of *all* His believers first and foremost, such people whose childlikeness, separated from all things childish, will live in loving communion with youthful courage, adult power, and elderly wisdom. For so it lived in Him to the very last moment, when on the cross He prayed for His enemies, comforted His mother, and bowed His head with the child's words, "Father, into Your hands I commend my Spirit!"[598] Doubtless our Lord had no wish to demonstrate His youthful courage like a daredevil and tempt God by throwing Himself off the top of the Temple, but He showed it far more clearly in His meeting with the Tempter in the wilderness, in following the Devil through the air, in defying all the glory of the world and in believing in the true nourishment of God's Word for the life of man!

The Lord refused to use His adult power as a king at the head of His people to crush His enemies and throw off the heathen yoke. He showed it far more gloriously by bearing poverty, scorn, and slander, by bearing His cross, struggling, suffering, and dying, and by showing His wisdom, radiating through all His words and putting to shame the old, the learned, and the scribes. Amen!

30. New Year's Day

1 January 1838 (Galatians 3:23-29)

In the name of our blessed Lord Jesus: Holy Father! – Your Word is Truth! Your Word is Life and Spirit! – The Word of faith which must be heard! Heavenly Father, send Your Spirit and create us and renew the earth's form in Your image and in Your likeness. Our Father! You who are in heaven!

"There is neither Jew nor Greek,[599] neither slave nor free, neither man nor woman, for you are all one in Christ Jesus."[600]

This is how the Apostle Paul describes the situation in the great New Year that was created on earth when in the fullness of time God established His new household. In this, everything was to be united in His only-begotten Son, our Lord Jesus Christ. Christ's Church has stood for so long on earth as a house of God that we can see the absolute truth of what the Apostle said: that whoever willingly enters this house of prayer for all people[601] in a sense forgets their *own* people and their *own* father's house.

598. Lk 23:46.
599. i.e. Gentile.
600. Gal 3:28.
601. Isa 56:7.

For they are transformed into new people who take no pride in being Jews or Greeks, kings or queens, but only in being Christians. So, my Christian friends, when we look back at bygone days, it is truly a great and matchless wonder how they have flocked from east and west and south and north to sit at the table with Abraham, Isaac, and Jacob for the great banquet of all peoples. Through the prophets of Israel God had proclaimed this, and through Jesus Christ His only-begotten Son He has served this feast on earth, with His heralds proclaiming over all the world: "Come hither, you that thirst, come hither you who have no money, and purchase here – without money or its value – both wine and fattening food! Hear me! Eat and regale your souls that they may live well!"[602] Yes indeed, this is the Lord's doing, for it is strange for our eyes to see peoples and tribes by the hundreds withdraw from being themselves and appear to dissolve into Christendom, where the great gap between freeman and slave, and man and woman, is fundamentally abolished.

However, when we look again at our own times with wide-open eyes, we cannot hide the fact that this Christian era seems largely to have disappeared, and a new era to have begun in which not just Jews and Greeks but also all the peoples of the world *remember* their names and strive to break free of all that restrains their natural state. As was to be expected this has given rise to much dissension, disagreement, and dispute. It has become the major quarrel in every country as to whether this 'New Year of the people' should be regarded as a happy golden year or a dreadfully poor year. To judge by appearances, all Christians must assume the latter, since it is clear that through such dispute Christendom must lose the *Christian* appearance which gave it its name, and must dissolve into the heathen elements from which it was long ago compounded. Yet our Master says, "Judge not by mere appearances",[603] and it has quite rightly become a universal proverb that 'appearances deceive'. So when Christians answer to their name as "Disciples of Christ and Children of the Light and the Day",[604] they must regard both what is past and what is to come with eyes that differ from any of the parties that follow their *own* heads. We can no more vote with those who think that the world becomes happier when all people are allowed to show who they truly are than we can regard it as a misfortune that they are *allowed* to do so! For it is clearly God's governance which ensures that everything that is hidden in the dark will be brought into the light and the counsels of the heart shall be revealed. We therefore emphatically declare: This year will be like last year, in the future as in the past, that in truth no one on earth is free and happy who has not seen the heavens open and found a path to them! And no one does so without believing that Jesus Christ came in the flesh, the child born in Bethle-

---

602. Isa 55:1-3.
603. Jn 7:24.
604. I Thess 5:5.

hem and raised to Prince and Saviour at God's right hand. And we emphatically add: Hereafter it will be in no way harder but in fact easier to *find* that path to Heaven and to be a Christian in the true sense of the word, for all things, including the changing of the times, "serve those who love God".[605] When everything is allowed to show itself for what it truly is, Christianity will do the same, and after this it will be clearer than ever that the Gospel is God's power for salvation for everyone who believes – and clearer than ever that in an acknowledgement of the secret of God, both Father and Son, lies all the hidden property of knowledge and wisdom – for the Son who as eternal truth contains all truth and reality, and for the Father who as eternal love is the wellspring of all the life that lives and all the power that is at work.

Indeed, my friends, as enlightened Christians we have every good reason to rejoice at the New Year, when again there are Jews and Greeks in the world, for then there are also clearly Christians! Doubtless they are fewer in number than they would wish to appear, yet in fact they are far more and far better. So from now on it will be clearer than ever that in the Lord's house there is neither Jew nor Greek, nor slave, nor man or woman, for all are one in Christ Jesus. This can only truly come about when the children of humankind are allowed to reveal themselves spiritually as they *are* and to follow the inclination of their hearts, so that those who are Turks[606] or heathens at heart are also known as such, and only they confess their Christianity whose hearts enjoin them to kneel in Jesus' name and place on their tongues the glad confession that Jesus Christ is Lord, to the honour of God the Father. At this point there will doubtless be a number of trials that Christians will go through, since their way is so different from that of all other peoples, and since as Christians they have no land of their fathers on earth, only in heaven. But all things will nevertheless be easy for them, since they all feel that they are one in Christ Jesus and can manage all things in Him who strengthens them. Until Christians have gained this blessed feeling that shows them the heavens opened, our civil freedom in all spiritual matters that the New Year brings will grant all true, enlightened Christians the calmest and most successful of days that ever existed on earth. For they clearly show that neither is it in their spirit to seek to force consciences and torment hearts, nor did they cease to be human beings and citizens when they became Christians. On the contrary they became *both*, in a better, transfigured form, according to the pattern of Him who was in every way a natural human being, only without sin and permeated by divine nature. This form takes pleasure in mirroring itself in human beings, because humans were originally created in God's image and according to His likeness![607]

---

605. Rom 8:28.
606. i.e. Muslims.
607. Gen 1.26-27.

So, my friends, whether I regard the New Year from the position and viewpoint of natural or Christian man, it comes shining before my eyes as a golden year for all things human! A year which like everything under the sun will have its great blemishes and yet will come to an end! It will be replaced – as Palm Sunday is replaced – by a quiet week, but it will be merry, fruitful, blessed, and memorable for the human heart! Although it is hard to see what we can only dimly glimpse in the lap of the future, it is clear that in a time of enlightenment and spiritual freedom Christianity will find itself more in its element than ever before, for its founder is the Light of the World and its spirit is truly the spirit of freedom. He can truly do all that He wishes, but He will not be flattered by *any*, for truth is above everything for Him. So, such a light-body – animated by the spirit of freedom as the Lord's people, the Christian community in origin and in fact for ever – cannot but outshine and eclipse all else on earth in the days of enlightenment and freedom. Moreover, the heart of God the Father, the heart of everlasting love, is quickened and animated by the Spirit of truth, so Christian enlightenment is not cold like the world's enlightenment, but glowing and fruitful like the sun's. And Christian freedom is not like the world's freedom, rebellious and selfish, but like free breath, enlivening and beneficial. This being so, Christianity in the New Year must gain a form so radiant, so lovely, and so blessed that wherever there is a glimmer of Spirit, it can only be admired! And wherever a human heart still beats, it can only be found lovingly kind, so that as with the Lord's arrival in Jerusalem great crowds will shout, "Blessed is He that comes in the name of the Lord!"[608]

Therefore, Christians, I wish you a blessed New Year, with the inner assurance that it will come not only in the *golden year of eternity*,[609] which alone satisfies the longing for the glorious freedom of God's children from all sin, sorrow, and death, and alone fulfils the hope of God's glory implanted in us at Baptism to grow with a divine growth. It will also come in the *temporal* year, with a spiritual victory over sin and death, with light in the Lord's light over all things human on earth, with cheerfulness under all its transformations, and with power as the desire to work diligently while it is day and to show the world many of our Father's good deeds! Here and now I proclaim to all that is human a blessed New Year, for when Christians have eyes to see and the power and the right to show what they are in Christ Jesus, then they do see and they show that the new being in Him is in no way *un*-natural. For the only thing that is unnatural for the Word is what is brutish and devilish. The new being in Christ Jesus has gathered

---

608. Ps 118:26; Mt 23:39.

609. The 'golden year' is a favourite phrase of Grundtvig's, found in a number of his best-known hymns. It may refer to Jesus' life on earth, as in *Blomstre som en rosengård* (Then the wilderness shall bloom), to man's Christian life, as in *Øjne I var lykkelige* (Blessed were you the eyes that saw Him), or to eternity, as in *Vidunderligst af alt på jord* (The kingdom of our Lord on earth). With thanks to Jørgen Bækgaard for this information.

all of the old being[610] into itself, not in their fallen, sinful state, but in their duty, their loveliness, and their suitability to reveal God's goodness and wisdom as it came from the Creator's hand, as the great, divine work of art in time, to be crowned in eternity. Therefore we shall see what the world neither believes nor can understand and yet will be astonished and refreshed by: that although in Christ Jesus there is neither Jew nor Greek, neither slave nor free, neither man nor woman, sharply divided, for all are one in Him, yet the entire human multitude is *surrounded* by Him, the great man who is also the Lord from heaven. He *manifests* Himself in His Church, so that Christians have both the light and the power to acquire all that is good among Jews or Greeks or any other people on the earth's sphere, be they slave or free, man or woman. Then they can be everything to all people, and, like the Apostle, they can wish to be so in order to gain some for Christ.[611]

A joyful new year is hereby proclaimed especially to our earthly fatherland and our kinsmen in the flesh,[612] a Danish and Nordic golden year that will radiate through history as one of the most prosperous and envious periods of the human race on earth. For like the long summer day in the North there will be *enlightenment* in these regions, and when the tribes have received light and been allowed to show what they are, it will be seen that a nobler human heart never beat in any heathen breast! And nowhere else was the world so willing to let Christianity show what it is, and do what it can, indeed nowhere on earth was there less of that pride which stands on its rights and disdains God's gifts of grace and repays good deeds with stone-throwing, than where we rightly celebrate the "loveliest field and meadow, ringed by waves of blue".[613]

So, Christian friends, even though in God's house, when it gains its true form, there will be neither Dane nor Norwegian, Jew nor Greek, we must thank God twice over, and twice over greet with joy this blessed New Year, which Christianity will experience on earth as an image and pledge of the New Year in *Heaven*, for "the lines have fallen for us and our children in pleasant places."[614] Here it will befall all people of God to grow most steadily, and here it will be granted to all people of God to develop and use all His beneficial powers and to spread abroad all the blessing that exists in the fullness of Christ's Gospel; here ingratitude and defiance, although they cannot be absent, will come late, and be bearable, and will last as briefly as possible.

And now, just as it is in Jesus' name that the happy New Year is proclaimed and in the same blessed name that we receive all that in time and eternity can rightly be

610. i.e. Adam and humanity.
611. Paul, see 1 Cor 9:22.
612. 1 Cor 10:18.
613. The lines are the first two of a poem written c.1685 by Laurids Kok (1634-91), to which a tune was added by Poul Rasmussen in 1811. As Denmark's first 'fatherland song' it has remained popular to this day.
614. Ps 16:6.

called good and joyful, let us all thank God and the Father in our Lord Jesus' name. And let us pray in the same name that His Holy Spirit may constantly enliven and enlighten, touch and lead, strengthen and guide us, so we may honour Him as Creator and Sustainer, our Father and Redeemer in life and death, in our body and our spirit, which both belong to Him, Amen! In the blessed name of Jesus, Amen!

31. 1st Sunday after Epiphany

10 January 1841 (Luke 2:41-52)

Holy God, our Father! – Your Word is Truth! Your Word is Spirit and Life! – The Word of faith which must be heard! Heavenly Father! Let the life of Your Son, our Lord Jesus Christ, reveal itself ever more purely and clearly in us, who believe in His name, and let Your Holy Spirit accompany us and our children to salvation and an awareness of the truth, in the name of our Lord Jesus Christ! You who are in heaven.

Christian friends! We hear in the Collect of the Day that the Gospel of the 12-year-old Jesus in the temple has directed the thoughts of our good fathers to their own children and the entire younger generation of those who spiritually are children of the older generation. We hear the latter praying that the good seed of the Word may also bear good fruit with the former, so they offend no one but live to the glory and honour of God as shining examples. We would not be Christians if our thoughts did not go the same way and place the same prayer in our own mouths. For as Christians that is what we are called to do, to be in this world as Christ was, and above all to share His loving embrace of children. This comes quite naturally to the human heart and inevitably prompts all those who believe in Jesus Christ to wish and pray sincerely that our children, like Him, will grow in wisdom, stature, and grace in God and among humankind! If this wish and prayer are to be more than empty air, are to be our heartfelt *request*, then we also feel that as Christians we are all called, in larger or smaller circles and with the power that God gives and the light and opportunity He offers us, to be His *fellow-workers*, to labour assiduously to make His name hallowed, His kingdom come, and His will be done on earth as it is in heaven. If we are to work to please God and benefit His kingdom, we must work in the Lord's Spirit and in *His* fashion. Otherwise our work is wasted, as the Apostle writes of those who may well build on the right foundation but build only with wood, hay, and straw, which cannot withstand the trial when all our deeds are tested in the fire.[615]

---

615. 1 Cor 3:12-13.

My friends, here a concern is raised that is certainly distressing, and yet, God be praised, it is also comforting. I refer not to our concern that many so-called Christians do not *wish* to grow in the grace and knowledge of our Lord Jesus Christ but would rather hinder than promote the Christian growth of our children. Nor do I refer to those who are only 'Christian' in name, for it goes without saying that whoever does not wish to believe in Jesus Christ and place their hope in Him would not help *others* to do so! It is simply a *mistake* that they are called 'Christians' and a great error for us to regard them as what they neither *are* nor *seek* to be. It is sad enough that so many people do not wish to know what would bring them peace,[616] but it is much sadder if, out of our wasted zeal for their enlightenment and repentance, we forgot to care for those who wish to *be* Christians and are in need of all the enlightenment and edification that with God's help we can *give* them. No, the sad but comforting concern I refer to is the concern for the real Christians' work to help our children grow up in the grace and knowledge of our Lord Jesus Christ, a task which over many generations we must say has failed almost everywhere. The younger generations in general have gone backwards rather than forwards, so that youngsters who recently grew up in the Church are so much further from being 'like Christ' than those who grew up three hundred years ago in the days of Martin Luther. We can all see that this concern is a sad one, since the entire Church as well as every Christian should grow according to God's will and progress, from glory to glory, as Scripture says,[617] and as a matter of course. That there is a comforting element in this reflection is not so easy to set eyes on, and it is therefore what, with God's help, I wish to shed light on today, to the honour of God and the encouragement of His Church.

On the one hand it has been shown that never since the time of Martin Luther has there been such diligent work for the young in Christendom to surpass the old in Christian enlightenment, knowledge, and wisdom. And it is equally certain that these efforts have failed. The more that schools were established for children's Christian education and the more strictly the children were kept at school, the less Christianity, the even less biblical knowledge, and the less grasp the coming generation had of the Gospel teachings. Indeed, the latest generation was so ignorant that it did not even *know* who Jesus Christ was or that one must believe in Him to be a Christian! Both of these are actual facts and both are lamentable omissions, to be sure. However, if we do not dwell on this but instead examine the reason why *all* efforts failed and the hopes of many Christian generations were frustrated, comfort comes from where it is least expected – like water from a rock, or a wellspring in the wilderness.

616. Lk 19:42.
617. 2 Cor 3:18.

Many possible reasons can be imagined as to why the task failed of helping children to grow in the grace and knowledge of our Lord Jesus Christ, but only one is of comfort, and it is the one that we would least expect. This is not because it is unpleasant for all flesh and blood to hear it – like every discovery that "honour belongs to God and shame has covered our faces".[618] For it is part of our original sin that when something well-intentioned is unsuccessful we blame God as far as possible, or – which amounts to the same thing – we blame 'circumstances' or 'other people'. Only when *these* fail to satisfy do we turn to ourselves, even when it is most obvious that it is us who are at fault!

The failure of this work in the service of our Lord was in no way due to our God in Heaven lacking the power or the will to bless it; nor was it that we lacked the true Gospel and genuine means of grace of our Lord Jesus Christ and therefore built on a false foundation. The young had no less desire to hear God's Word nor less need for the Saviour than the old. The work failed because the older generation mistakenly built with their *own* materials, which could not pass the test; or they built backwards and began with the roof, which naturally fell down of its own accord and hid the foundations. This is in every way a sad truth, but the fact that we have reached this conclusion shows that the work was not completely wasted. If we pursue the information that we have gained, then our work in the Lord, far from being in vain, will be crowned with a successful outcome. There is no need to slight our good fathers or rebuke them for a zeal that lacked insight, for it is only to the glory of God and the expansion of His kingdom, for the advance of the coming generations in wisdom and grace with God and man, that we must make known the realisation that our fathers made a mistake. We must attempt to show where the fault lay, so that we and our children can avoid it. Their mistake was, we dare to say, that however highly they honoured and however diligently they read the Holy Scriptures, they did not truly respect what was written in the Gospel of the Day or elsewhere concerning Jesus Christ and the *growth* of all God's children. This was due to the prevalent misunderstanding that unconsciously followed them in their reading of Scripture and blinded their eyes to everything that had to do with raising children in the training and instruction of Christ.[619]

The prevalent misunderstanding, which we still encounter, was that scholars and scribes were better equipped than the most devout parents to give children a Christian teaching and upbringing, and that such learned and scholarly people could take children much further in Christian knowledge and wisdom than one would imagine their tender age and inexperience would allow.

618. Jer 51:51.
619. Eph 6:4.

The error was twofold: the teachers and scribes were considered far better guides for children on the path of salvation than the Christian parents to whom God had entrusted them, and to whom the Apostle Paul always turned when he spoke about children. And the discipline of these teachers and scribes exceeded nature in every way, so they could conjure knowledge and wisdom out of the children far beyond their years and experience. This twofold error blinded the eyes of our forefathers, so they were unable to see what was obvious to everyone in today's Gospel. There sits Jesus aged twelve in the Temple among the teachers, the best teachers and scribes in the land. He listens to their wisdom and asks them questions, and all those who are present are full of astonishment at His intellect and answers!

What would have happened if it had been one of our *own* parents who had found one of *us* aged twelve sitting in school among the cleverest and wisest teachers, like a wonder-child whose questions and answers revealed an intellect and a thoughtfulness that astonished all the audience? Truly, our parents would be delighted at the sight! They would sigh deeply and wonder whether they should take us home to their remote little village where there seemed to be no opportunity to make great strides in the knowledge and insight to which God had given us such wonderful dispositions. If the teachers had then asked whether they could *keep* this hopeful son, and surely and swiftly make of him the great and radiant light to which God and nature had so clearly designated him, the parents would have been unable to find an expression for their gratitude to God and humankind! And however much these parents loved their son and however deeply they would miss him, they would see the separation as a sacrifice that they should make for their God, for their Church, and for their dear son, whose advance in wisdom and all that was good *depended* on this. That such a mentality was not foreign to Israel we can see among others in Saul, later Paul, who was a similarly precocious wonder of knowledge and wisdom and was brought up at the feet of Gamaliel,[620] one of the most famous and devout leaders of Israel.

But Joseph and Mary thought differently, as we can hear from the appalled Mary's reproach, "Son, why have you treated us like this? How could you have the heart?" and as we can see from the fact that they took Him home again to Nazareth! We cannot doubt for a moment that the teachers wished to hold on to such a disciple, for He would have done them greater honour for every day He spent listening to their speeches and astonishing the audience with His questions and answers. Dear Christian parents, did these teachers perhaps think that they were *more* devout and *more* familiar with God's counsel than Joseph and Mary? No, that was far from being so. But their eyes were stiff, so they did not realise that Joseph and Mary regarded Jesus as a treasure,

---

620. Acts 5:34-39. Gamaliel (died c.54) was among the leading rabbis of his day, "a teacher of the law, who was honoured by all the people".

entrusted to them by God, whom they would not hand over to strange hands at any price. So they kept Him faithfully until He reached the age of discretion and could choose His path on His own responsibility.

Nor would they therefore see the hint that came from God's Spirit in the following words, "And Jesus grew in wisdom, stature, and grace with God and humankind." They would not see the heavenly testimony that Joseph and Mary were *right* to take Jesus out of the teachers' midst, a step that did not hinder but *encouraged* His development towards His matchless calling. Nor could they see the enlightenment that the *Spirit* gives: that true wisdom comes with age and goes hand in hand with the heart extending its kindness in the eyes of God and humankind.

Let us not dwell a moment longer than necessary on our forefathers' blindness, for they nevertheless had a heart that believed God and sought everlasting life in the name above all names, and they found it in their childlike trust of His words: "Seek and you will find; knock and the door will be opened to you!"[621] Let us not exalt our own perspicacity and give it thanks for the light that has arisen; let us rather thank God and our devout parents! For assuredly they played a part in this, and their belief that Christian teaching was a task for scholars was never so erroneous as to deny that they themselves were also driven by a higher spirit and deeper feeling, now with Luther's *Small Catechism*,[622] now with a verse from a hymn that had comforted them in adversity and fear, and now with a heart-wrenching word in Jesus' name, sealed with a burning tear from the depths if they had not thereby laid the foundations and built just a little, according to their children's age, but better than all the scholars and scribes. Let us remember this and walk in the light that God has lit for us. Let us work to help our children advance with the Lord in wisdom, age and grace. And let us rest assured that our deeds in the Lord, however foolish they may seem to the world, shall not be in vain! In the Christian teaching and upbringing of the children that God has entrusted or will entrust to us let us not ask how the *world* judges and what the *world* offers, demands, or threatens. For their sake and ours let us first seek the kingdom of God and His righteousness and be assured that all else which is needed He will add![623] And let us never again forget that wisdom, stature, and grace will accompany us, and that our advance in each of these is God's work, which we must not seek to master or improve. Let us never forget that just as God in the beginning gives the child life before He gives light, so must the spiritual life go before the light. It is not for nothing that the Lord's Spirit names 'grace' first when He says, "Grow in grace and knowledge of our Lord Jesus Christ."[624] These are words of deep wisdom, that whoever

---

621. Mt 7:7.

622. Luther's *Small Catechism* was published in 1529.

623. Mt 6:33.

624. 2 Pet 3:18.

does not love God does not know Him,[625] so it is folly to think that our knowledge of God can go before or go beyond our love of Him who is Love itself! Indeed, let our Lord Jesus Christ first and last stand before our eyes as He wanders from the school at the Temple with Joseph and Mary back home to Nazareth, where He is obedient to them and advances in wisdom, stature, and grace in God and humankind! Here we see the pattern that we can confidently follow in the Christian upbringing of our children. Indeed, here we see the light of the world in whose footsteps none stumble or fall, and here we shall have God's blessing on our work. Then the children who are born will be formed into a people who praise the Lord better than we do, and see far more clearly into the blessed depths of His knowledge and wisdom. Amen. In the name of our Lord Jesus, Amen!

32. 2nd Sunday in Lent

6 March 1837 (Matthew 15:21-28)

In our Lord Jesus' name! Holy Father! – Your Word is Truth! Your Word is Life and Spirit – The Word of faith which must be heard! Heavenly Father, we pray to You in the name of our Lord Jesus Christ for Your Holy Spirit, which quickens and sanctifies, that He may be with us as He always is with the Word from Your Mouth, Your Spirit is good; may He lead us on a straight path to the everlasting heights! Our Father! You who are in heaven!

"Woman, how great is your faith! Your request is granted!"[626] Praising women is far from being either new or uncommon in this world. On the contrary, from time immemorial we have been far too inclined to deify and *worship* women. Even in the midst of Christ's Church and Congregation the entire worship of God was once close to disappearing in a self-made, unhealthy, and ever more empty 'Mariolatry'. Yet it is necessary in our day to remind ourselves regularly how priceless and precious true womanhood is in the eyes of the Lord.[627] This is clearly the case in the Gospel of the Day where the Lord pretends to be hard-hearted in order to give the depth of the woman's heart the chance to open itself and be gladdened by the wealth of His blessing, clearly heard in the words "Woman, how great is your faith! Your request is granted!"

---

625. The reverse of 1 Jn 4:8, "Whoever does not love, does not know God."

626. Mt 15:28. The episode is also commemorated in Grundtvig's hymn, 'Woman, how great is your faith', no. 18 in *Living Wellsprings* (2015).

627. Translator's note: Grundtvig uses the singular 'woman' (*kvinden*) throughout, where I vary usage in the translation. He also uses the word *kvindelighed*, which translates literally as 'womanliness'; again the translation varies.

We all very much need to remember these words, for according to 'Natural Man'[628] we live in an age of the intellect and are continually tempted to disdain the deepest and best feelings of the heart. This is partly because they are vague, but even more because they are humiliating, as they were for the woman in today's Gospel who says, "Even the dogs eat the crumbs that fall from their master's table." Nowadays self-conceit and arrogance are the governing vices in the world. Everything that is naturally to find favour in our eyes must be as clear as sunlight to us, and must set our own precious person in a favourable light. So while recent generations of men have constantly become more 'womanly', in the sense of more pusillanimous, disloyal, improvident, and adulatory, these men have constantly conceived an increasing contempt for what is noble, deep, and, even in God's eyes, inwardly beautiful and charming in women, meaning their willingness to believe, their humility, and their unselfish love, which we all know comes so naturally to women that where it is completely missing, it is an abomination to us all.

Christian friends, we must be on vigilant guard against the ingratiating behaviour and effeminacy of the age, which even among staunch heathens laughably seeks to assert its right to its own powers and enlightened intellect. And while we are on guard, we must make every effort to work towards awakening a deep respect for the female in her genuinely human and Christian form, for that is not just proper and fair, it is absolutely essential for growth in the grace and knowledge of our Lord Jesus Christ.

If we consider what the Spirit testifies – that faith, hope, and love are the three things that contain all that is genuinely Christian – we shall soon realise that two-thirds of Christianity, namely faith and love, are 'feminine'. Since faith is the first and love the greatest, hope, which is the masculine element in between, can be no more than an empty spiritual death and impotent fantasy if its feminine elements are missing. In contrast, the feminine elements, faith and love, without the help of any man, will conceive and give birth to a living hope, just as the Virgin Mary conceived and gave birth to Him who would be the hope of glory in all of us. Christian friends, this is the deep reason why Christ's Community on earth is called His 'bride', and the Church our 'mother'; for as with faith, 'womanliness' has a motherly relationship to us, and as with love it has a marital relationship to our Lord. The Apostle Paul reminds us that this is a great mystery,[629] and experience teaches us that it can be distorted and misused, but can nonetheless continue to be a divine truth from which our Christian life springs and by which it is nourished and grows.

'She-priests' is the world's common term of abuse for those of us who constantly preach faith and love of our Lord Jesus Christ with the regular chorus that "knowledge

---

628. Grundtvig's word here, *Naturmennesket*, denotes the human being from nature, i.e. not yet reborn in the Spirit.
629. Eph 5:32.

puffs up, while love builds up".[630] Moreover, those pastors who are truly driven by the Holy Spirit will always be the ones who least deserve reproach for either ignorance or effeminacy. Yet despite both these facts, we immediately feel that we would far rather be called 'she-priests' and lead both men and women into the kingdom of God than be called 'strong spirits' and yet be blind guides leading them with us into the grave! Little by little we come to appreciate the name, since if we subtract the rudeness, it expresses precisely what we must constantly strive to be better at. If faith is 'feminine', the Church must be also; and indeed she is indubitably an elderly lady who must always live with being called an 'old woman' by mischievous boys; indeed, she is even called so out of love by her adult sons! If experience has taught that not only are love and faith feminine by nature but that women also have most heart for our Lord Jesus Christ and His Gospel, then 'woman-like' priests or, if you wish, 'she-priests' must be the best name that we can ask of the world, while 'servants of the Word and Church' is our proper name, and one which divinely expresses all that we should be. Like our Lord, we came into the world to serve, not in order to *be* served,[631] not even to save our lives in completing the work with which we are entrusted.

Here we come back to the living, divine Word – our Lord Jesus Christ's view of women and womanhood, which is the prime consideration here. Whatever we may think of these matters on the basis of our experience and reflection, it would not be a subject that we had to point out and impress upon the Church if we did not know in truth that not only do we think like that, but so does our Lord! So just as we began with the Word of the Lord in the Gospel of the Day, "Woman, how great is your faith! Your request is granted!", so will we end with a consideration of the Lord's relationship to 'the woman' in particular and then to 'women' in general in those days when He was like us in all things, except in His sinlessness.

What must strike us immediately, and in fact determines everything, is that just as Jesus is not called "the seed of man" but "the seed of woman" in the first prophecy,[632] so did He find no father on earth, but only a mother, as God's son born of a woman. From this we can see as clear as sunlight that on the one hand only on our mother's side are we *related* to the Saviour – and we can hardly benefit from this relation if we show contempt for the woman, our mother – and that on the other hand this proves that He who searches all hearts found in women an ease of communion with God's Spirit which men lacked and which must be attributed to women's willingness to believe, their humility, and their love. This has its true seat in women, and it gave birth to the great promise of marriage on the lips of the Virgin Mary, "I am the Lord's servant,

---

630. 1 Cor 8:1.
631. Mt 29:28.
632. Gen 3:15.

may Your word to me be fulfilled!"[633] Here lies the faith in God's Word contained as something that is a matter of course, while the heart in deepest humility expresses its full devotion, indeed its *surrender*, to God and thus reveals what the Spirit calls 'the inner self'[634] in the woman's heart which is so precious to God. So, my friends, the believing woman's heart takes all the Lord's words for gospel truth, as the woman in today's Gospel takes upon herself the name of dog and says, "May Your word to me be fulfilled, let me be a mere dog", as she answers, "so long as You will be a good master to men and think of me the little that I need". That is why the Lord answers the woman's heart in a way that He would never answer the man's, "Your request is granted!" In fact even though as a man on earth He was sinless, He goes so far as to find it necessary to pray in Gethsemane, "Yet not as I will, but as You will."[635] For a man can suffer, but has no desire to do so, whereas a woman has a desire to suffer for the one she loves!

If we then let our eye follow the Lord on His matchless priestly path, we not only find women constantly in His company, we find it expressly stated that it was women from Galilee who served Him with their stores and met His needs,[636] something that most men, even among His most ardent listeners, doubtless only seldom if ever considered because they lacked a woman's love. If we then ask who was His best audience, we would probably name the disciple whom the Lord loved most,[637] but it was only a single listener, Martha and Lazarus's sister, Mary, whom we read sat at the Lord's feet and chose the good part, which she would never lose.[638] If we take a step further, to the cross and the grave, we find not only under the cross His mother beside the disciple whom He loved, but beside one of the men a whole gathering of Galilean women.[639] They not only remained with Him until they saw Him give up the spirit and His body laid in the grave but continued to think solely of Him, so that even though they knew He had been anointed by Joseph and Nicodemus, only the Sabbath prevented them from immediately giving Him their ointment in the grave, and on Sunday morning while it was still dark they made haste to show Him the last honour. Indeed, one of them, Mary Magdalene, could not even calm herself down at the song of the angel, "He is risen", but anointed the empty grave with her tears when she did not find His body. This is why it was the women who saw the angels at the grave, where even Peter and John only saw earthly clothing, and why Mary Magdalene was the first to see the

633. Lk 1:38.
634. 1 Pet 3:5.
635. Mt 26:39; Mk 14:36; Lk 22:42.
636. Mk 15:41.
637. Jn 20:2.
638. Lk 10:39.
639. Mt 28:55; Mk 15:40-41.

risen Christ. Thus, just as the Lord was born of a woman, so was it a woman's lips that gave birth to the great good news of the crucified but risen Christ, while the Apostles were still in doubt. Long live all women believers! Amen! In Jesus' name, Amen!

33. 2nd Wednesday in Lent (Ash Wednesday)

22 March 1848 (1 Corinthians 1:25)

Christian friends! When the Apostle Paul and we who follow in his footsteps call the Word of Christ's cross 'the foolishness of God',[640] whereby it pleased Him to save all believing souls in order to put the world's wisdom to shame, it was clearly far from being either his thought or ours to argue the case for foolishness, ignorance, and stupidity, as if they were more pleasing to the true God, the maker of Heaven and earth, than enlightenment, knowledge, and learning! They must indeed be very *far* from our own thoughts if we are truly to follow the Apostle, who was admired among wise and unwise alike and who expressly testifies that in this acknowledgement of our Father and the Lord Jesus Christ lie hidden all the properties of knowledge and learning. We must focus on Him, the Son of Man who from childhood was full of wisdom and treated the wisest people He met as we treat self-opinionated children, and with our far more developed intellect and experience we must oblige them to realise that they are fools in comparison with us! The truth is plain and simple that our Lord's wisdom is so much deeper than the world's wisdom as the heavens are higher than the earth, and as the eye that searches the heart[641] is so much deeper than the eye that only sees the outermost and roughest surface of all things, meaning only what is tangible.

So, my friends, this world which only loves its own only *knows* its own, and knows only about its own matters! It cannot therefore comprehend what belongs to God's Spirit, but calls it sheer 'foolishness'. It has equally little understanding of what belongs to the human heart, but despises it as vagueness and weakness. This is why God's wisdom is always taken for foolishness in this world, and in the darkened state of our souls is believed by us to *be* foolishness, even though it is the very deepest and only true wisdom. We may in part[642] realise this when God who bade the light shine in the darkness makes the same light, His living Word, shine in our hearts and like a reddening sky in the morning makes it drive away the dark shadows of the night.

---

640. 1 Cor 1:25.
641. 1 Sam 16:7.
642. 1 Cor 13:12.

[643]Of this manifold wisdom of God, revealed by His Spirit to those whom He loves through their faith in the love with which He loved us, and to which He devoted His only-begotten Son so that through faith in Him we might escape perdition and gain everlasting life ...of this manifold wisdom of God there is nothing that lies closer to us – and yet nothing that from the beginning seems more unnatural and bears the appearance of foolishness – than the Word of the cross, that is, the passion of Christ as an article of faith and a shining example for all God's children on earth; for it is not the shame and ignominy of the cross and in no way merely the deep mystery that Christ's suffering can be of benefit to all who believe in Him, it is not just this which offends the self-conceited world and the carnal reason and intellect both inside and outside us, but most of all it is the weak, the powerless, and the helpless, in a single word the 'womanly' element in the entire story of the Passion, that is a 'foolishness' for all the wisdom of this world.

So, my friends, it is God's wisdom that His power on earth is consummated in His fragility. His only-begotten Son shivered and trembled in Gethsemane when His soul was "overwhelmed with sorrow to the point of death".[644] He not only fell on His knees, He fell on His face to the earth, He sweated blood and went to the cross as a lamb to the slaughter.[645] He did not utter a reproach when He was cursed and did not threaten when He suffered. But precisely here He was developing the divine power which saves us from sin and death, precisely here He was performing His matchless heroic deed to the admiration of angels and the salvation of all believers. This is *God's* mysterious wisdom, which has always outraged and always will outrage the *world's* wisdom, the massive self-conceit which can see power and superiority only in headstrong words and outward grandeur, and which always overlooks and disdains the hidden inner self which is so precious to God.

Nevertheless, Christian friends, we have allowed ourselves to believe what the Apostle calls 'the foolishness of our preaching',[646] whereby it pleased God to have salvation proclaimed, since the world in its wisdom did not know God in His wisdom. This we have heard, and, in our sense of God's peace which passes all understanding and keeps hearts and minds in Christ Jesus[647] we have learned to love the so-called 'foolishness of God'. Then we also swiftly learn that what the Apostle writes is far wiser than men; in other words, appearances are *against* God's wisdom only because

---

643. To give readers a sense of Grundtvig's prose style, even when delivering a sermon, I have retained his original syntax in the following sentence, which runs to 164 words in Danish and 196 in English. English is always longer in translation since it separates the definite article from its noun, whereas Danish merely adds a suffix. Thus Danish *Aanden* (one word) becomes English 'the Spirit' (two words).
644. Mt 26:38; Mk 14:34; Lk 22:38.
645. Isa 53:7; Jer 11:19.
646. 1 Cor 1:21.
647. Phil 4:7.

it reaches down to the source of riches of *all* wisdom and knowledge, in the deepest love in which both light and life, both knowledge and clarity lie hidden, until they are one day revealed in the Father's kingdom when God will all be all things in everything.

My friends, Scripture says that the Lord is neither man without woman nor woman without man,[648] and this is a dark tale for the wisdom of this world, only foolishness in its eyes. But it is a morning-star for the believing heart, and wisdom for the opened eyes of the heart, for the Lord could not be the perfect human being without in fact being man *and* woman. Only the perfect human being is created in God's image and according to His likeness; only in the perfect humanity, both male *and* female, can God's power be revealed and perfected. What is *man's* name in the inner human being without Spirit? And what is *woman's* name without Heart? The Spirit is the revealed God-man, and the Heart is the hidden God-woman. The strident word with signs and wonderful deeds is the Spirit's work, and the quiet suffering is the great work of the Heart. The Spirit's work is life and light, while the Heart's work is love and clarity. So as assuredly as all temporal life has its source in everlasting love and all temporal light has its source in everlasting clarity, just as assuredly must God's power on earth also be perfected in human frailness. Thus our Saviour, after having worked as Spirit and man, had to suffer and die as the heart and the woman in the God-human, just as we all, when we have understood the power of His resurrection will in the end understand the communion and fellowship of His suffering.

That is why on the night when He was betrayed the Lord said to His disciples, "You will be scattered, each to your own home. You will leave me all alone. Yet I am not alone, for my Father is with me."[649] Indeed, the Spirit, God's Spirit with the revealed life-force, abandoned our Saviour when His soul was struggling with death; but the Heart, God's Heart with its everlasting love, the hidden source of all life and power, never abandoned Him. In this way God's power was consummated, and, through His divine suffering and death as the most loving sacrifice, He bought and saved us for eternal salvation, and prepared for us His heavenly clarity and glory. Amen!

34. The Annunciation

12 March 1837 (Luke 1:26-38)

In our Lord Jesus' name! Holy Father! – Your Word is Truth! Your Word is Life and Spirit – The Word of faith which must be heard! Heavenly Father, let Your Word in

---

648. 1 Cor 11:11.
649. Jn 16:32.

the Holy Spirit come over us and Your power overshadow us, so Your Son may be spiritually reborn in us as the living hope of Your kingdom and glory and grow in us to our Lord Jesus Christ's full stature and everlasting joy in Your blessed communion. Our Father! You who are in heaven!

"Greetings, you who are highly favoured! The Lord be with you. Blessed are you among women."[650]

Christian friends! If we believe that Gabriel, an angel of God who stands eternally before His countenance, has truly brought this greeting from the heavenly throne to a virgin on earth, then we must indeed celebrate her, even if we did not know the consequence of her honoured favour from God on High. For life, everlasting life, is God's pleasure and there is much joy before His face, so no person can have been born on earth whose eternal joy and bliss should be more certain in our eyes than that of the Virgin Mary, who without flattery or falsehood must be called 'the blessed'. If we also believe that the Holy Spirit came over this young woman of the House of David and overshadowed her so that she truly became the mother of the Saviour of the world, God's only-begotten Son, the eternal King of the House of David, then, as we hear in her hymn of praise, it is as clear as sunlight that all Christian generations must celebrate her. For we cannot imagine that any believer or thanks-giver can linger on the remembrance of God's Son, born of a woman, without extolling with great wonder the life that bore Him and the breasts that He happily sucked. This is all the more certain, in that none of us can recall our Baptismal Covenant and our shared Christian faith without the Virgin Mary immediately standing before us as the one who brought God's only-begotten Son into the world, for we all confess our faith in Jesus Christ, the only-begotten Son of God the Father, "born of the Virgin Mary".

In these circumstances it might seem much more pardonable that our forefathers deified the Virgin Mary[651] than that we almost forgot to celebrate her, just as it is undeniable for all human children with a loving mother to think too much of her rather than too little.

Nonetheless, Christian friends, experience has taught us that in the last few centuries there has been incomparably more true, *living* Christianity – despite the Lord's

---

650. According to Lk 1:28 and Lk 1:42 the first two sentences are spoken by Gabriel, but the third by Elizabeth, mother of John the Baptist.

651. In 553 the Council of Constantinople declared Mary perpetually a virgin and sinless. Finding no biblical support for the Catholics' worship of Mary as 'mediatrix', Luther developed a theology in which Mary received God's love and favour but, as with the saints, her merits could not be added to those of Jesus Christ to save humanity: "They put that noble child, the mother Mary, right into the place of Christ." In the Protestant Church, Mary is revered but not venerated.

mother being almost completely forgotten rather than deified. So although we cannot possibly attempt to think and speak about everything as it deserves without also thinking more highly of the Saviour's mother than we usually do, we must nevertheless declare her deification and adoration to be idol worship which in no way can be combined with Christian enlightenment. On the other hand our failure to appreciate her and our oversight of her, albeit indefensible, at a certain level of enlightenment must be considered almost unavoidable. For as soon as we have the slightest healthy reflection in our Christian thinking, we must immediately realise what Scripture constantly impresses upon us: that beside the Trinitarian God we must not worship *any* creature, nor trust that creature on the question of salvation, not even an archangel, let alone a daughter of Eve who, however devout and pleasing to God she may have been and into however great a state of bliss she has entered, like Abraham knows nothing about us and cannot help us.

Moreover, if she heard herself being deified and worshipped, she would take no pleasure from it but would be inwardly indignant and distressed, for what made her pleasing to God was precisely her own faith and hope in Him alone and the deep, humble feeling of her own humble self, in fact her own nothingness compared to the Most High. It is in this alone that the heart, and in particular the devout woman's heart, is pleasing to God. We show extreme ignorance about both divine and human matters if we are fooled into thinking that the unchangeable God should at any time take pleasure in anything other than what pleases Him now and for ever. He would find no pleasure in a vain, puffed-up woman, nor choose her as His Son's mother, any more than He would have done so in the days of the Virgin Mary. On the contrary, just as in the past the devout, humble, believing, and loving woman's heart could so reconcile what was holy with our fallen earth that He selected and blessed it as a mother's heart for His only-begotten Son, the Saviour of the world, so to the same degree that He finds this kind heart, will He always marvellously visit it, bless it, comfort it, and gladden it.

When they saw that it was gross idolatry to worship even the most devout woman of the fallen sex, the papists took refuge in the fairy-tale that Mary was 'sinless', which in no way excuses their worship of her but only hinders our salvation. So we must remind ourselves that her mystery is nothing other than the wondrous depths of the human heart so heavenly that they can even be found on this fallen earth. What made the Virgin Mary pleasing in God's sight and enabled her to become the mother of the Son of the Most High was solely the goodness of her hidden heart, which the Holy Spirit testifies is found in all devout, believing women and is exceedingly precious to God! This does not make the great mystery of devoutness that God is revealed in the flesh and that His only-begotten Son born of a woman understandable to us; but it does teach us that therein lies no *unnatural* secret. It has its grounds in the deep and mysterious connection that must of necessity exist between the Creator and the created "in His image and according to His likeness",[652] a connection we must obviously be God Himself to comprehend.

This reassurance of the mystery of the Saviour's conception and birth is the first thing we gain with the knowledge that the Virgin Mary was only pleasing to God and became His Son's mother because she had the humblest, godliest, most devout and loving woman's heart that ever beat on earth. But this is not our *only* gain and not even our *greatest*, for there is already one that is *greater*: that we now can cherish the incomparable heavenly quality of the Virgin Mary without ever being tempted to idol worship. And the *greatest* gain still remains: namely, that we learn far better to know and follow God's way on earth and His order of salvation among all people; and that we again learn to cherish the heart, and especially the heart of the devout woman according to its worth, which alone enables Christ truly to acquire His form among us. For despite the fact that He will be with us to the very end of the age and will be reborn in every believer who is baptised, it will only ever be to the degree that our mothers and the entire Church have their heart in common with the Virgin Mary. This is simply the same as when with plain words we say that the Christian hope, the hope of God's glory, which is Christ in us, will always be found dead or alive, weaker or stronger, depending on whether our faith is greater or smaller, heartfelt and childlike, humble and loving. Christian friends, the fact that we can never express in living words the kind heart that must rule in Christ's Church for Him to be born and grow there spiritually – apart from saying that the Church must be a Virgin Mary! – could not but make the papists believe that they found their idolatry of Mary upheld by the Apostolic Fathers. This makes it easier for *us* to be accused of papistry when we speak with propriety about the Lord's mother and with spirit about the new Jerusalem which, as the Holy Spirit testifies, is the mother of us all. But Irenaeus[653] and the other bishops of old who had had the Apostles as their friends and mentors in the art of preaching for edification were completely innocent of the gross *abuse* of their words. We too are similarly innocent of the indignation that any may conceive of *our* words when they are weighed on the golden scales of truth. We must make every effort nowadays to remember that the worse the allegations are against us for our Christianity, the happier we shall be if we know that they are lies.

We might then rightly ask: If it is truly so that as the Lord's mother the Virgin Mary may be perpetually blessed and celebrated in the Lord's Church, and the Church may see in her the pattern it must follow in order to imitate God and her Son, how

---

652. Gen 1:26-27.

653. Irenaeus (c.130-c.200). Born in Smyrna (now Izmir, Turkey), he was one of the first great Christian theologians. His book *Against Heresies* (c.180) in defence of the Church is a detailed attack on Gnosticism. He became Bishop of Lugdunum (now Lyon, France), where he died.

could our Lutheran fathers, who were not lacking in humility, faith, or love, be blind to this? To which the answer is simple: they were *not* blind, nor any the less unfeeling on this question, as we can see from the Lutheran hymn, 'A virgin pure is Mary mild' and especially from the wealth of hymns in praise of her, such as the recent one by Thomas Kingo for the Day of the Annunciation, 'The message came from angel choirs'.[654] This is enough to show how familiar our Lutheran fathers were with the belief that the Virgin Mary was the Lord's mother with the same heart's feeling that must be found in us, if the Lord is to be spiritually born and grow in us. The Virgin Mary disappeared from our preaching and hymn-singing immediately for the same reason as did all talk in the Church of a living community, of the Church as the Daughter of Zion, of the Lord as our brother, and of us as limbs of the Lord's body. It happened only to the degree and for the same reason that the living speech about Christ *within* us and the Holy Spirit *with* us fell silent and died out, namely to the same degree as the childlike faith and heartfelt faith in God's Word passed away. It follows as a matter of course that to the degree that this faith is reviving and growing among us, so must we equally in speech and song give expression to the way of thinking and feeling that characterised Christians of old.

We cannot *remain* at the Reformation, which is in no sense the birth of faith or the creation of the Church but only the first step after centuries of mistaken belief on the home path to the Apostolic Church. In this Church the Holy Spirit is in truth the shepherd, and Jesus Christ the bishop. He is not far away but close to all who call on Him, the Lord in whom as Christians we "live, move and have our being".[655] Wherever the Christian faith is found, the failure to appreciate the Virgin Mary and the ancient Church language rests fundamentally on the failure to appreciate the human *heart*, a failure to which an inordinately mistaken belief and a tendency to arrogance, especially among us men, may give rise, but which is as indefensible as it is damaging. For by disdaining the *human* heart we cannot gain *God's* heart, which honoured the Virgin Mary. We, over whom Heaven also says "The Holy Spirit shall be upon you", then become more and more heartless and proud of our intellect and knowledge instead of thinking and responding together with Mary for our heart's sake, "I am the Lord's servant, May Your Word to me be fulfilled!"[656] For in so doing we place our hearts in God's hand, He who knows how to cleanse us of all defilement of the flesh and spirit so that we can perfect our holiness in our devoutness towards God. Amen! In the name of our Lord Jesus, Amen!

---

654. The first hymn, no. 72 in the current *Danish Hymnbook* (2002), was written by Hans Thomissøn in 1569 and edited by Grundtvig in 1837. The second hymn, no. 71 in the current *Danish Hymnbook*, was written by Thomas Kingo in 1689, and edited by Grundtvig in 1837.
655. Acts 17:28.
656. Lk 1:38.

35. Palm Sunday

1 April 1855 (John 12:12-19)

Our Lord Jesus Christ and our Father! Maker of Heaven and Earth! Your Word is Truth! – To us through Your only-begotten Son come Spirit and life! – The Word of faith, hope, and love, which must be heard, believed, and confessed, so that Your good work through Your Holy Spirit may be fulfilled in us until the day of our Lord Jesus Christ. Our Father! You who are in heaven!

"So the Pharisees said to one another, 'Look how the whole world has gone after him!'"

These are strange words that we read in the Gospel of John on the occasion of the Lord's entry into Jerusalem after the raising of Lazarus. People in their thousands have come out to meet Him, spread their clothes on the way, wave palm-branches for Him, and sing with His disciples: "'Hosanna to the Son of David!' 'Blessed is He who comes in the name of the Lord!' 'Hosanna in the highest heaven!'"[657] These are strange words, which sit well in the mouths of the Pharisees! For those who only saw the exterior and settled in every way for appearances could not but see the homage of the multitude as a great event, even though we know it was no more than hot air and a fiction. The same crowd of people who on Sunday shouted "Blessed is He who comes in the name of the Lord!" shouted much louder the following Friday, "Away with Him! Crucify Him! His blood be upon us and our children!"[658]

These are strange words, because they continue to return many hundreds of years after the Lord is dead, arisen, and ascended. They come again every time the crowd for a moment voluntarily joins in the Christian song of praise and yet always comes closest in the end to rejecting and banning the Christian faith. The mockers had no need whatsoever to shout so loudly in our ears, for we servants of the Lord are well aware of this; we have always known it and never set any great store by the world's so-called 'Christianity of the moment', the millions of 'Christians', the so-called 'Christian' states and all that belongs to them. Indeed we know even more than this; we know that when the Lord's Spirit has made His last sign on earth – corresponding to the last sign in the days of His flesh when He raised Lazarus who had lain four days in the grave and was already stinking – on the great yardstick of things the whole world

---

657. Mt 21:9.

658. Mt 27:23, 25. The widespread belief that those who shouted Hosanna! are the same who shout Crucify! a few days later after a secret trial has no basis either in Scripture or human psychology. It is far more likely that we are dealing with two different groups of people: friends and enemies of Jesus respectively.

will first go after Him and almost immediately it will turn out that the world will no longer even allow the Lord's Spirit and the Lord's name in its midst!

My friends, the world is no different now, and will be no different in the future. So when the mockers shout that if we want permission to call ourselves 'Christ's disciples' we must leave this world or otherwise whip ourselves through it and whip the world to declare open war on our Lord Jesus Christ's name, faith, and community, we must leave that to the mockers themselves. For that is not how we have *got to know* Christ, nor is it how we have been *brought up by* Him, our only mentor. He would never ask His or our heavenly Father to take us *out of* the world, but only to deliver us from evil, just as neither the Lord nor His disciples forbade the crowd to shout "Hosanna to the Son of David" on His entry into Jerusalem or exhorted them, to be honest, to shout soon afterwards, "Crucify Him, Crucify Him!"

In our day and age there is not the slightest temptation for the Lord's servants to be carried away into believing that the world is 'going after' the Lord! The world is well aware of its own *disbelief,* so it claims that its desire to call itself 'Christian' nevertheless is neither to give itself the appearance of faith in Jesus Christ or because it expects forgiveness of its sins and salvation in His name and for His sake. It is merely a badge of honour which it claims the right to wear, because it is neither Jewish nor Turkish,[659] but seeks to be virtuous according to Christ's exhortation and example and regards Him as a teacher come from God. As the Lord's servants in our day and age the only thing we ask of the world is that it should let those of us who believe in the Lord Jesus Christ, the only-begotten Son of the Father, conceived as human by the Holy Spirit, retain our Baptism in the name of the Father, Son, and Holy Spirit for ourselves. It should similarly allow those of us who believe in the real presence of Christ's body and flesh at the Lord's Holy Communion to retain this Sacrament for ourselves. We have asked the world to do this, and will continue to do so, just as we diligently seek to inform the world that if it wishes to keep peace with our Lord Jesus Christ and to enjoy the temporal benefit of the presence of His Spirit and Gospel, which following His example they wish to share with the whole world, then the best path to follow is to let His institutions[660] – unabused and undisputed but otherwise whenever it wishes – adore and praise His matchless love of humanity, His beatific Word, and His mighty deeds, which are the virtues that called us from darkness into His singular light!

So my friends, this is our true attitude as Christ's disciples to a world that reckons itself part of 'Christendom' and calls itself 'Christian' without having Christ as its

---

659. i.e. Muslim.

660. In Lutheran Christianity the only two Sacraments are those instituted by Jesus Himself: Baptism and Holy Communion.

master, or in the faith, hope, and love from our Lord Jesus Christ being willing to seek His righteousness, peace, and joy. And when the mockers shout that just as long as we are at a standstill with the world – and even allow ourselves to be maintained by the world while we preach the Gospel of Christ – just as long are we distancing ourselves from our Lord Jesus Christ and the Christianity of the New Testament. For this surely demands a wretched poverty, a battle with the world to the death, and a hatred of our own lives of all those who wish to be Christ's true disciples by taking up their cross and following Him! To these people we say: their mockery is as old as the New Covenant itself and even older than what we call the 'New Testament'. For they said of our Lord Jesus Christ Himself, "He is a wastrel and a wine-bibber!" They thought the precious spikenard oil wasted on His body and could have been sold for three hundred pence and given to the poor![661] And yet they found appropriate all that was done by the rich men of the world, Joseph of Arimathea and Nicodemus, to ensure the Crucified an expensive burial as the culmination of a true witness to the truth who was counted among malefactors. All such mockery is very old and may be even older, and yet not a single one of the servants of our Lord Jesus Christ has for this reason committed suicide or run away with the world from his Lord, or sold Him to the world for thirty pieces of silver or a barrel of gold, or for all the kingdoms of this world with their magnificence. Nor for this reason has our Lord Jesus Christ discarded a single one of His servants, either in their youth or in their old age, or failed to acknowledge him, be he in wealth or want, with good or bad reputation, in days of armistice or strife, in life or in death.

It is equally assured that just as the world never 'goes after' the Lord, even when it appears to do so, as with the entry into Jerusalem, so do the Lord's disciples never leave Him, however far behind they are in His footprints; for the Lord never leaves them, even if it seems so. This was the case with His ascension as well as in the spirit-less time which His Church has recently lived through and been sullied by. He has set His Spirit in us and placed His Word in our mouths, and it shall not retreat from our mouths or those of our offspring through all eternity. It must be brought home to the world – the more the better – that not only is His Word to us spirit and life but that His entire Community will experience this with ever greater blessing, ever more deeply and highly, with or without the will of the world. His Congregation will continue to sing Hosanna to the Son of David and praise the Spirit that issues from His Father and comes to us all in the name of the Lord, our Lord Jesus Christ, with His righteousness, His peace, and His joy, which lasts forever! Amen.

---

661. Jn 12:5.

36. Easter Sunday

26 March 1837 (Mark 16:1-8)

In our Lord Jesus' name! Holy Father! – Your Word is Truth! Your Word is Life and Spirit – The Word of faith which must be heard! Heavenly Father, glorify even now Your only-begotten Son, our Lord Jesus Christ, on earth, so that His Word may always rise like a lion and ascend like the eagle, as a testimony to all people that the name of the crucified and risen Lord Jesus Christ is the only one under Heaven in which the fallen can be raised up, the sick healed, and sinners saved and brought to salvation by Your Holy Spirit, which in Jesus' name You have granted us as our Comforter and Advocate for ever, Our Father! You who are in heaven!

> Today Hell is sighing and chiding,
> the kinfolk of Adam have won;
> defiant in crowds they are striding,
> redeemed by the hidden God's Son!
> "The ranks of the dead I had swollen,
> yet all of them now He has stolen!"
> Alone on the Crucified's Word
> to Heaven from Hell they are spurred!
> The God-Man released them from prison!
> The crucified Lord is arisen![662]

Christian friends, this is the hymn of the Church to us on this happy morning from those far-distant times. But it is truly sad that these triumphant notes died out on the lips that gave birth to them. Nowhere in Christendom is faith in the risen Lord more moribund than among the Greeks, where nowadays tender hearts must sigh deeply over the old Easter hymns whose words they barely understand any longer and whose joy they cannot share at all. This is truly sad, and yet there is overwhelming joy that the Church's ancient hymns and songs of praise can still find a living resonance in our hearts and on our lips, so we feel and show that the Portal to Hell has not gained power over the House on the Rock. Nor has Time which destroys all things been able to damage the living monument that our Lord Jesus Christ left behind here on earth, consecrated by His blessing and animated by His Father's Spirit which quickens all things!

---

662. This is the fourth verse of an otherwise untranslated Easter hymn, *I dag sukker Helved og klager* ('Today Hell is sighing and chiding') from Grundtvig's *Song-Work for the Danish Church* (1837).

9. Hymnsinging in Vartov Church

This painting by Christen Dalsgaard from 1868 (in the Royal Library, Copenhagen) shows Grundtvig sitting by the doorway of the Vartov sacristy beside his son Frederik, with a lady and two children preparing for hymnsinging at the church. Now aged 85 he carries a magnifying glass in his hands. Characteristic of the Vartov congregation was their faster hymn tempos (though nevertheless slower than by modern standards). This was known wittily as 'the Vartov gallop'! Then as now the congregation was seated for the hymnsinging. Grundtvig wrote a number of hymns which were given their first airing by his congregation and were later collected in the *Vartov Hymnbook*. He handed out the very first of his hymnsheets at Christmas 1845, and the hymns soon became as popular as the four that he already had printed in the authorised *Danish Hymnbook* of the time.

So, my Christian friends, at this glorious festival of the Resurrection we who feel the Lord's presence with zeal and joy rightly recall to His honour that the life of His Church and Congregation on earth and the constancy of the people who worship Jesus Christ the Crucified are not only what is called a 'testimony' to His resurrection and ascension; they are a constant repetition of His triumphant struggle with Death and manifest proof that Jesus Christ has the power to lose His life and to take it back again. How many generations have not succeeded one another in the eighteen centuries since the Angel of Light sat on a stone in a grave and cried to the weeping, astonished women, "He is arisen and you shall see him" ... since He Himself for the first time came in to His disciples through closed doors[663] and announced His divine presence with the great words, "The peace of God!" – words which surpass all understanding? How many generations did not sink into the grave without there being a generation that bowed its knee in His name, as the victor over Death, without there being a generation that dared to celebrate Easter in His honour, and in His name defy the great enemy before which all flesh quivers? So sing joyfully:

> Despite your sting, O death,
> aborted is your cause!
> Despite your grip, O Hell,
> and Satan's evil jaws,
> you lost in all disgrace!
> God's name be ever praised![664]

There is something that is even more honourable for the Crucified, something quite matchless in the world and manifest proof of His power to awaken the dead and bring alive any whom He wishes. It is this: Not only did the generations change, so did peoples, tribes, and languages; and although the gifts varied, the Spirit as well as faith and hope remained the same. And now we see the great miracle: the whole of Christendom – all the peoples, tribes, and languages that in the days of the Apostles received the Gospel of the risen Lord – are dead and buried, yet a *new* Christendom has arisen in the wilderness, among Scythians and Barbarians,[665] no less firm in the faith in the God-Man, and no less joyful in the hope of the everlasting light and God's glory!

For this promise of the Father that His Son would shine as bright as sunlight over all the earth with a glory as of the only-begotten of the Father, full of grace and

---

663. Jn 20:19.

664. This is the sixth verse of an otherwise untranslated Easter hymn, *Op, Sjæl, bryd Søvnen af* ('Up, soul, and break your sleep') from Grundtvig's *Song-Work for the Danish Church* (1837).

665. Col 3:11. The Scythians lived north of the Black Sea and were considered wild and ungovernable; Barbaria in the NT means non-Greek, and therefore uneducated.

truth, the Almighty permitted what our forefathers and we did not understand until we entered into the sanctuary and saw this light in the *Lord's* light. The Father of our Lord Jesus Christ permitted the great eclipse of the sun, which has recently ended,[666] to conceal Heaven both for believers and for non-believers. And He permitted that the name to which all knees in and on earth shall bow should be nailed to a cross between malefactors with a royal title only of scorn and derision. Dead and powerless, He was handed over to His few despondent friends. They laid the embalmed body in the grave, in the depth of a cavern with a stone that was very large for the entrance, as well as for the lips that would with songs of praise forever confess Jesus Christ as their Lord to the honour of God the Father. Clearly, God did all this in order to manifest and glorify His Son on earth, and to show this to the last people who joined the Church the same as the first, so that this name is above all names both in time and in eternity. Death has lost its sting not only for Jesus Christ Himself but also for everything that belongs to Him!

So, Christian friends, this means that not only should we celebrate the Easter festival with joy, but that all the days we live in our passage through life have been changed into one great Easter festival, a feast for our Lord Jesus Christ's name, for His Word, His Church, and all that He would call His own on earth. Already the world is beginning to see with astonishment how the light is rising over the Lord's grave, and hearing with shock something that sounds like angel-songs ascending from the place where He lay! The guard that should have prevented Him from rising is clearly dead to the world, so we cannot praise the Lord enough with great words and bold speeches for what God has done and for what He makes ever clearer day by day – to the honour of the Crucified and to the quickening, the encouragement, the gathering, and the strengthening of His dejected, scattered, and powerless people! The world still seeks to fool itself that this is only a mirage, that Jesus Christ did not rise from the dead but was stolen away by the disciples, or that He sneaked out of the grave only *apparently* dead while the guard slept. Nor have His name and Word and divine honour been *truly* resurrected by the Father's Spirit to a new and powerful life-path to the end of the world. Only stupid people like us believe this, stupid but cunning, impotent but daring followers of an ancient superstition who are trying to make the last seduction worse than the first! In every possible way we are seeking to spread the rumour that *life* has come, divine life in His Word, and that His name has arisen before our eyes with a radiant wreath so matchless and so enlivened with His blessing that with a great Alleluia we must testify for great and small alike. The God who bade the light shine in the darkness[667] has radiated our hearts, so that we

---

666. There was a partical eclipse of the sun in Denmark on 24th March 1837.
667. Isa 9:2; Jn 1:5; 2 Cor 4:6 et al.

see His glory in the face of our Lord Jesus Christ! Yes indeed, the world gives us all the blame, and builds upon this the hope that, if not before, then one day when we bow our heads and surrender the spirit, it is all over with this *appearance* of ghosts in the churchyard that we conjure up with the evil arts to dupe simple people into believing in a glorious resurrection from the dead, a resurrection to everlasting life.

It is absolutely certain that if we had done what we are accused of, the world would have every justification in nourishing that hope; for as Gamaliel said, "If the work is of human origin, it will fail."[668] What can be more certain than that if a dead person of his own accord proclaimed both victory over death and a resurrection to an everlasting life, not all the world's power and wisdom, even in alliance with all the arts of Hell, could save him from very soon being deeply disgraced. It would be like someone wanting to help others but being unable to help himself! Like wanting to grant everlasting life to others while being unable to save his own soul from death. But it is for this very reason that we know we are free! For this very reason we know that the life that has come into our dead faith and our buried hope, the life-force that animates our speech and breaks out in our songs of praise in honour of the Crucified, is not *ours*; it is the Holy Spirit's life-force, which the Father gave His only-begotten people as Comforter and Advocate for ever. This is why the world has never been so disappointed in its expectations as it one day will be, never since the day when the High Priests and Pharisees gave silver coins at random to His enemies, and did not haggle with them as they did with Judas; in fact they gave with *both* hands.[669] For they had to hush up the fearsome rumour about the angel who struck like lightning, knocked the stone from the grave, and sat on it, and the rumour that the Lord had awakened like a sleeper, risen up like a hero, and had shaken off His earthly raiment, arising like the golden sun emerging from the coal-black sky!

Indeed, never before has the world been so openly disappointed in its expectations and wise calculations as it will be soon, and indeed in our eyes already *is*! It is over three hundred years since the decisive battle was fought in the quite remarkable war that Martin Luther so cheerfully praised, in which life brought an end to death. But as soon as the first thunderstorm had passed, the world felt relieved and discovered that it was not nearly as dangerous as it appeared, for no *final* resurrection actually took place! Christ's body, which is His Church, did *not* arise, but only received a *pledge* of resurrection through the Holy Spirit, as Scripture says: "For Christ also suffered once for sins, the righteous for the unrighteous, to bring you to God. He was put to death in the body but made alive in the Spirit. After being made alive, he went and made proclamation to the imprisoned spirits."[670] So Christ has led only a concealed life on

---

668. Acts 5:38-39. Gamaliel (died c.54) was among the leading rabbis of his day, "a teacher of the law, who was honoured by all the people".

669. Mt 27:3-8.

670. Isa 53:8; 2 Cor 13:4; 1 Pet 3:18-19 (quoted here).

earth, unappreciated and at times defiantly denied and contemptuously forgotten, but now He is taking on His victorious body again and revealing His glory, as He did after His resurrection and ascension in His old Congregation.

1. Come, let us drink of that water again,[671]
not from the spring that was struck from the mountain,[672]
but from the source that in death is a fountain,
wellspring of blessedness, gushing like rain:
Jesus, our life-force, our hearts You empower.

2. Light penetrates over all like the sun,
Heaven and earth, even Hell, now are brightened[673]
as the foundation of all is enlightened.
Easter the whole of creation has won,
feels in the Word's resurrection its power!
Amen in our Lord Jesus' name, Amen!

37. Pentecost

6 June 1824 (Acts 2:1-11)

There is no Church festival that is so poorly attended as Pentecost, at least in Denmark. If we did not already know this, we could draw that conclusion from the fact that there is so little Christianity in Christendom, and that the Christianity that remains is more dead than alive. It is as clear as sunlight that there is no other of our festivals for which the ringing of church bells should so deeply and sweetly move all Christians with a living faith and a joyful hope. There is no other festival of ours at which Christians should feel such a vibrant need to gather in the holy name of the ascended Christ and listen to the Word that has travelled with the sun, creating light and life on earth. Still it travels, on the wings of our breathing, high over the heads of mortal men, yet ready to dive into the depths of the heart of all believers and there reignite the glowing tongues that speak of the wonders of God in words taught not by human knowledge but by the Holy Spirit. Those words never travel in vain, but like the snow and the rain they achieve all that they were *sent* to achieve!

---

671. This hymn in its full translation is no. 29 in *Living Wellsprings* (2015).
672. Ex 17:6.
673. Lk 8:17; 12:2-3.

My friends, in the strictest and deepest sense Pentecost is a *Church* festival, the Christians' celebration of the *Church*. This is so obvious that even those who ignore it nevertheless vaguely *sense* it, so we should not be surprised that only a few actually *celebrate* it! For we are all well aware that in our time the Church Congregation – a truly sincere, vibrant community in faith, hope, and love – belongs with the Christian *antiquities*, which only seem to have existed in order to be described and disputed by scholars! This is because in our society the concepts of 'soul' and 'Holy Spirit' are now erroneous, even among the Lord's disciples, or simply dead and empty! It is as if people only knew John the Baptist rather than Him who came in the name of the Father, Son, and Holy Spirit! So when the Lord announces to His disciples on the hill of the Ascension[674] that John baptised with water but in a few days they will be baptised with the Holy Spirit and fire, and when we read that "He came and rested on each of them like tongues of fire",[675] then for most people this is almost like 'dark speech'. They can let it stand on its merits, or they can exercise their keenness of judgement on it without it making much difference, and why should anyone who thinks either of these things go to church at Pentecost anyway? "To church", I say, by which I mean of course not just any house built in the shape of a cross for people in their Sunday best, but the house that is still being moved by the 'rushing mighty wind' from Heaven which filled the room where the Apostles were sitting: the house that still resonates with the voice that gathered the multitudes from all the regions of Heaven to hear Him walking on the wings of the air and bringing good tidings from Heaven to earth; the house where the glowing tongues that blazed there still gleam and glimmer so that in astonishment we hear God's miracle permeate our mother-tongue and speak in our own language!

It must therefore never surprise but in a way *gladden* us that we are few who go to Church at this festival of divine consecration, since we are clearly only few who have faith in this consecration, few who have faith in the Holy Spirit, and inevitably therefore few who have faith in the Church in which He both rings and chimes, preaches and sings, enlightens and enlivens, and indeed is all in all! May God grant that we who have gathered here are among those who have *received* the Father's promise, or who wait in faith for it, just as the disciples were once gathered in unity. This they could not have done with faith in the Lord's Word without recalling what is written in Exodus 19 about the thunder and lightning over Sinai[676] and the divine Word from the resounding voice, or without recalling the Feast of Pentecost and the Apostles' expectation of 'even greater things than these'.[677] If the making of the Law once shone with heavenly radiance in written words on tablets of stone, then that radiance must

---

674. The Mount of Olives, Acts 1:5ff.
675. Acts 2:3.
676. Ex 19:18.
677. Jn 14:12.

inevitably be even greater over the proclamation of the *Gospel*, with its fiery characters being written on the temple-walls of the heart! Indeed, when the Lord promised to be present wherever two or three were gathered in His name,[678] He was comforting not only every individual who felt themselves to be an outcast from society, but was also making it known to them that He would be powerfully close at hand when called upon. The supplicants would be the few who felt most deeply the emptiness of the world for those who ask for the abundance of the Spirit and long most intensely for His Community, whose power is perfected in frailty!

So, my friends, let us rejoice at this festival, and, as God may give it grace, sanctify it by impressing upon ourselves the truth, half-forgotten in the Christian Congregation, that however little our worship bears comparison with what we read in the Gospel of the Day, it is still only here in our solemn assembly with the preaching of the Word and the resounding song of praise that we can see an image of the glorious consecration of Christ's Church. Only here can we recall in Spirit what it was that began, and what it is that will perfect, the good and wondrous deed that our Congregation is!

It may be so with Christianity in general that it only works with its full power and is only revealed in all its radiance where the Church and the Christian Congregation stand as the house on the rock and the city on the hill, where Christ's Word has a royal throne on His servants' lips and a shining palace in the bosom of the Christian Congregation, where the miracle that eternity will explain all things in the course of time astonishes the world – the miracle being that we are all one Body and one Spirit in Christ Jesus. Yet the divine consecration of the Church is the only event in the holy history that finds reproduction solely in our solemn gathering on the Lord's Day, just as it is here especially that living faith in the Holy Spirit develops and illuminates itself. I cannot better express this truth than by saying: We celebrate Christmas at the cradle, and Easter in the garden, but Pentecost only in the Lord's Church!

We celebrate Christmas at the cradle because with each smiling child comes a living image of God's only-begotten Son who "thought it not robbery to be equal with God but humbled Himself and took upon Himself the nature of a servant".[679] Since the glad tidings of the child born in Bethlehem are for the light and life and joy of young and old alike, who like children wish to be borne and led by Him into God's Paradise, and since the Christmas message finds only a friendly cradle on the lips of its mother, it assuredly finds an open embrace in the child's heart! The angel proclaims to the children of dust the glad tidings that our Father in Heaven has sent His Son to earth as a little child, with divine power to make good all our affliction and adversity and with a brother's heart to quench all our sorrow and dry all our tears. What pushes the angel away is

---

678. Mt 18:20.
679. Phil 2:6-7.

only the foolish pride that does not hold our humanity to be a gift from God but a 'robbery' from the Creator. This pride does not exist in children, who, far better and greater and more humanly than we adults, never consider their advantage but are subservient to us and accept with gratitude the least or greatest proof of our goodness and love!

So, Christian mothers, few though you be, you are like the hidden heart's goodness, precious to God and, says the Apostle, influential in making people Christian, also *without* words![680] You know best how happy is the Christmas that is played beside the cradle when with the bells ringing at the break of day your subdued sigh at the gathering of God's children is soon comforted by the echo of the Christmas hymn beneath the surface and the smile of the little infant reminding you of the child in the manger and seeming to whisper, "My angel also sees our Father's face in heaven!"

This then is Christmas, which the shepherds celebrated at the manger and which undoubtedly is always celebrated most touchingly and blessedly beside the cradle, by mothers and children in the domestic, pastoral circle where the angel's smile and the child's happiness proclaim far more than spoken words that unto us a child is born,[681] who brings us God's goodwill and thus Heaven as a Christmas present.

And so to Easter! Who has better kept Easter sacred than Mary Magdalene, who stood alone in the garden[682] weeping by the grave until she heard her own name from the Saviour's lips and stammered out, "Master!" She ran to tell the disciples that she had seen the Lord and had heard Him say that He was ascending to His Father and our Father! Has this perhaps no meaning? Is Easter perhaps not celebrated with the same deepest feeling in the heart's solitary state with the Lord among the graves? Did we never stand one Easter morning as the sun was rising and the churchyard raised up above the meadow surrounded by the monuments of winter and even more closely by the graves and the deep furrows that Death ploughs to sowing with tears and reaping with songs of praise? Did we never stand there as the bells rang for worship and the sun rose higher and the lark was singing and our eyes rested on the garden where winter had visibly ceded its place to spring and realise that even in our solitary state we lacked neither for company nor anything on the outside? Did we not then with deep emotion quietly sing the old Easter hymn:

> Christ is risen from the dead,[683]
> and saved us all from outcome dread;
> so joyfully we therefore stand

680. 1 Pet 3:1.

681. Isa 9:6.

682. Jn 20:11-18.

683. These two verses are from a different version of Grundtvig's hymn 'Christ is risen from the dead', no. 22 in *Living Wellsprings* (2015).

to sing His praise throughout the land!
Kyrie eleison!

If He did not rise that day,
then all the world had passed away;
but since again He did appear,
we praise our God and Lord most dear!
Kyrie eleison!

No indeed, even in our solitary state we lack for nothing, provided we have the belief that death is the wages of sin but that everlasting life is God's gift of grace in Christ Jesus our Lord. I venture to believe that the Lord's resurrection offers no greater radiance for the human eye than for that of young people for whom the thought of death arouses sweet dreams of the glory of this earthly life or whose hearts groan at the feeling of the emptiness of worldly life when in quiet moments they see the hero returning triumphant from the kingdom of death leading Death and Hell in chains and stretching out His friendly hand with the bread of life and the chalice of salvation to the kinsfolk of dust in the valley of tears! Truly He celebrates Easter in every garden where life, in reality or figuratively, arises from death as flowers grow on graves, and He celebrates it with the book before Him. This book is the Holy Scripture which may be compared to the garden of the Lord's grave, from which He again rises spiritually in the Word, puts to shame the world's wisdom, strikes to earth its champions, comforts His grieving disciples, and teaches them to understand the Scriptures. Then they realise that according to the prophets' words Christ had to suffer before He entered into His glory!

And so to the pouring out of the Pentecost Spirit over the servants of the New Covenant. They are to be servants of the Spirit, not of the written word! The Pentecost Spirit comes as divine words on human lips, with heavenly fire and quickening powers, as the consecration of the great House of Prayer for all people, where the currents that the Lord divided at Babel[684] should again meet in Jerusalem. This is a miracle that crowns all the Lord's previous ones, indeed sets upon them the crown of life! Where else does life have its image and likeness except where it is still lived, albeit weaker today but stronger tomorrow, yet always alive? Where else except in the gathering of Christians who address each other with songs of praise over the Word that is mighty in the saving of souls?

It is true, to be sure, that we can see a shadow-image of the spiritual life in the Christian Congregation that God's Word creates, sustains, develops, and illuminates.

---

684. Gen 11:1-9.

[423]

We can see it in the summer-life that is developed by hidden powers and permeates and gladdens the whole of creation, bursting into leaf in the lilies of the field and arching itself into the bowers of the forest, lauded by the birds of Heaven with the blush of dawn for its prophecy and the blush of twilight for the name it left behind. But it is also true that our earthly nature in its summer splendour and fullness attracts the flesh more than the Spirit, and cultivates among those who delight in the flesh no living concept of the Spirit of pure truth and love that expresses spiritual matters in spiritual words. Instead it cultivates an unclean spirit of the world that steals the fire and radiance from the sun in order to inflame the desires of the flesh and set flashing colours on poisonous flowers! This is a truth, and moreover what else resembles God's Word so much as the Word on the human tongue created in His image and likeness? Where else under Heaven are the invisible ways, untraceable by man, upon which spirits and hearts actively meet for embrace and sword-play except in the invisible yet real world which the Word marvellously creates whenever it spreads its wings and rushes through the air, so that not only the ear but the spirits must listen and not only stones but also hearts resonate?

So my friends, if we are to have a different living concept of the Feast of the Consecration of the Church in Jerusalem than a dim rumble of thunder in the distance, of which only a confused echo remains in popular tradition, then we must go to church, where God's Word is proclaimed not as an epitaph found in a disused church on a tombstone to Simon Peter and his fellow-Apostles – of whose importance we are unaware since no one knows any longer what it means to be baptised with the Holy Spirit and fire! No indeed, wherever God's Word is proclaimed as something that never dies and is never weakened, it is as life and Spirit no less now than when Simon Peter stepped forward, raised his voice, and said with the prophet Joel, "And afterward, I will pour out my Spirit on all people. Your sons and daughters will prophesy, your young men will see visions, your old men will dream dreams!"[685] Jesus Christ the Crucified, who broke the chains of death because they could not possibly hold Him and whose witnesses to the resurrection we are, as He sits at God's right hand, He it was who poured out the Holy Spirit upon us according to His Father's promise! Only in such a gathering where God's Word truly dwells and is proclaimed and acts in power to show that "there are different gifts but the same Spirit".[686] Only where the Spirit by confessing Jesus Christ who came in the flesh and by adopting the prophetic Apostolic Word vitally and unconditionally as it is described as revealing itself to be the Spirit that came over the Apostles to be the everlasting Advocate and Comforter in the Lord's Church, only in such a gathering can we exuberantly recall the Day of

685. Joel 2:28.
686. 1 Cor 12:4.

Pentecost when the Lord's messenger was clothed in power from on high, when the house which that great Son of David, the heavenly Solomon, built for his Father was filled with His glory, and three thousand souls sacrificed themselves as a first fruit to the eternal priest of the Order of Melchisedek![687]

So let the world smile in scorn at this comparison between the Apostles' Pentecost and ours; it shall not touch us! For we believe what we read about Christ's temple that was filled not with cloud but with a current of light and warmth from the source of life. We believe this at the deepest level, however little our congregation corresponds to its high origin and to the great promises that ring out over it from heaven; and precisely therefore we know that the way to imitate the Apostolic Church is not to leave it nor to regard it as irrelevant for us. The more clearly we realise that just as the Lord and the Spirit, faith and Baptism, and the heavenly Father with His wondrous love are always the same, so is the Church also always the same one that the Lord built on a rock to defy the Portals of Hell and the same one that the Spirit inaugurated as the forecourt to Heaven. The more clearly then do we see and the more deeply feel that the mockery of the Church and the impotence and confusion into which the Christian Congregation sank is not the Lord's nor the times' doing, but only our own! And when this feeling becomes all-powerful in our souls, so that we long for the Lord who is close by when called upon, and we sigh for the Spirit that enlivens and builds all believers together in the course of time into a divine temple of living stones, then our hearts begin to burn, our tongues to blaze, and the Word of faith to penetrate us as rivulets of life's flood that delight the City of God, the dwellings of the Most High!

So, my friends, when we begin to experience what it means to have *living communion* in the Spirit with the Lord and all His Christian Congregation – the communion of saints into which we are consecrated through Baptism – then we clearly see that Christmas is the festival of faith, Easter the festival of hope, and Pentecost the festival of love! Then we are not surprised that Pentecost comes last in our Christian life rather than *between* our Church festivals. For when the Tree of Life from the Word's root grows in the Church garden, then faith is its trunk, hope its blossom, and love its fruit! Then we are not tempted to doubt the slightest word of what we have read about that first Pentecost on Zion, where the lightning over Sinai became a tongue of fire with the Lord of Love; for the fire of the Law is devouring zeal, but the fire of the Gospel is a melting love! If the mouth speaks naturally from the heart's superfluity, then the tongues must inevitably unite in Jerusalem, where hearts melted together

---

687. Gen 14:18-19: "Then Melchizedek king of Salem brought out bread and wine. He was priest of God Most High, and he blessed Abram." Cf. Heb 5:10: "You are a priest for ever in the order of Melchizedek." And Heb 7, according to which Jesus is made King of Righteousness and King of Peace after His death. Luther taught that Melchizedek was a historical figure who was an archetype of Christ.

in the Father's love, just as they were separated at Babel when the heathens departed from the face of the living God to wander each into the erroneous path of his heart. If, alone by the power of His Word, the Lord's people, thinly sown and broadly scattered in a hostile world, are to be gathered, bound, and united in faith, hope, and love, then this Word must not only be more than written letters on stone tablets or linen pages; it must be even more than what we with our tongues of dust call 'living'; it must be a Word which makes itself actively known and, as the Lord says of His Word, be life and Spirit in truth, as the Word is only on the divine tongue!

However, dear friends, if we have ever for a moment sat on the threshold of the house of God in which the Apostles proclaim His miracle with glowing tongues – which we in wonder must call our own since the Word upon them is no stranger to us but addresses us as sweetly and vibrantly as our mother-tongue – or if we have ever stood listening at the partly-open door and felt with sighing and exultation that whoever is inside cannot possibly have any doubt, but must fall on their faces and confess that God is truly in these speakers and interpreters of His, then let us never forget that such moments are a mysterious glimpse of the only-begotten Son's glory on earth which the Holy Spirit entrusts us with, so that we can rejoice in our festival and be proud of the Church that the world scorns. Tomorrow these glimpses will be no more than a dream if we build on and trust in *them* rather than building on and trusting in the simple testimony of the Lord's resurrection and of the Church of the Holy Spirit with the communion of saints, the resurrection of the flesh, and the everlasting life. For this testimony from the Apostles with the Gospel is actively transferred to us through the Christian Congregation and ratified by the God of Heaven through the power and blessing He has sent to accompany the simple faith in our Creator, Redeemer, and Consecrator. These three testify in Heaven but are one, and make up one on earth, so that the Father draws us to the Son and the Son unfolds to us the Father's house, where the Spirit makes us inhabitants to the everlasting song of praise! Let us daily impress upon ourselves ever more deeply David's song of yearning, "One thing I ask from the Lord, this only do I seek: that I may dwell in the house of the Lord all the days of my life, to gaze on the beauty of the Lord and to seek Him in his temple."[688]

And let us impress upon ourselves even more deeply that nothing shall befall him who believes in this Holy Spirit as God's wisdom and goodness in His own divine person. Whoever honestly believes in Him as the Advocate and Comforter whom the Lord has sent us from the Father with the glowing tongues shall never find himself fatherless or homeless on earth. For even when the sanctuary that the Spirit so evidently consecrated seems to have sunk into the dust or been taken up into Heaven or built

---

688. Ps 27:4.

on a rock that is too high for us, even then the Spirit guards our entry and exit to the house, built without hands. It may be concealed from the believer's sight, but with the Word of faith that we proclaim the house is always close to him in mouth and heart! Indeed, there are not many of us who are aware of God's great miracle, which inevitably happened with our mother-tongue and with the tongue of all heathens in the wilderness to make them qualified to be a living instrument for the Spirit driving the prophets and Apostles. When Christians come to realise that they are *all* Galileans who expressed what no eye saw and no ear heard – namely, God's mysterious counsel for the forgiveness of sinners and the glory of His dwelling which the Spirit builds – and when they realise how they not only wrote books imagining what the speeches meant but also how they spoke out in their own mother-tongue with which they were born far away from Zion and Tabor,[689] then they must all kneel in wonder at the Lord's work and feel that only on tongues glowing with fire on the altar of God that is divine love, only on such tongues could the hard, cold, rugged giant-language of the North be warmed, melted, and forged into a living expression of the great Gospel of peace, the Word of God's love, and into Zion's melting song of praise to the beloved and welcoming dwellings of the Lord of Sabaoth![690] To prove that this has happened, let it be not just a sign but a living, joyful pledge that it truly is in the wondrous house of the glowing tongues, in the Apostolic Church where our forefathers celebrated the festivals and listened so faithfully to the distant but glowing words on the Apostles' lips, that the tongue may exclaim:

> Almighty flame, come from above,
> and light in me the fire of love![691]

Then to be sure the prayers on our tongues shall be granted! And if we keep the simple faith of our fathers and wait with them upon all things from the Father who has given us His beloved Son and all things from the Spirit that came over the Apostles and works all things in the Lord's Congregation,[692] then every day of the Lord, and most of all every Pentecost Sunday, our gathering shall be a finer, clearer image of that gathering on Zion. It shall be a more recognisable and more worthy continuation of the heroic deeds of the Spirit and the Word to the honour of Him who sits at God's

---

689. Mt. Zion was the site of David's palace and Solomon's Temple in Jerusalem; Mt. Tabor in Galilee is often identified with the Transfiguration of Jesus.

690. 'Sabaoth' (Gk) means 'armies' or 'hosts', and is used as such in Rom 9:29 in Jas 5:4, as well as in the Sanctus of the Te Deum.

691. The lines are from a hymn by Kingo, slighrly reworked by Grundtvig in no. 387 of *Song-work for the Danish Church* (vol.1, 1837).

692. Rom 8:28.

right hand and of the Church that He built, the brotherhood which He founded to everlasting radiance and glory! Amen! In Jesus' name, Amen!

38. 10th Sunday after Trinity

12 August 1855 (Luke 19:41-48)

Our Lord Jesus Christ and our Father! Your will be done! Your Word is Truth! – To us through Your only-begotten Son come Spirit and life! – The Word of faith, hope, and love, which must be heard, believed, and confessed, so that Your good work through the Holy Spirit may be fulfilled in us until the day of our Lord Jesus Christ! Our Father! You who are in heaven!

"If you had only known on this day what would bring you peace."[693]

These were the words of our Lord to Jerusalem, the city of David, as He came down from the Mount of Olives and for the last time fixed His gaze on the Jewish capital where He was to suffer and die as an innocent man, with the blinded multitude soon screaming, "His blood is on us and on our children!"[694] Like all Christians we believe that with the blood of His cross our Saviour made peace between God and man, and that He makes daily peace between all human children who believe in Him. If we realise this, then we can see how stone-blind the inhabitants of Jerusalem were to what would bring them peace, for as enemies of Christ's cross they bade defiance to the Saviour, and made a witness against themselves the blood that will speak up for them and for all sinners to everlasting peace.

Christian friends! The concern of today's Gospel reading is, as we heard, peace, and the right way to peace. When the Lord weeps over Jerusalem and says, "If you had only known on this day what would bring you peace, but now it is hidden from your eyes", He is assuming that peace was what all the people greatly needed and wished for! But He lamented deeply that the inhabitants of Jerusalem, far from seeking peace on the right path, were, on the contrary, stone-blind to it and took no care of what would *bring* them peace!

The first question serious people must ask of this Gospel text is undoubtedly: Was our Lord right? Is peace really such a great and indisputable benefit for man? And

---

693. Lk 19:42.
694. Mt 27:25.

the second question is: Do we know better than the inhabitants of Jerusalem what will bring us peace?

Every serious person must answer the first question with a 'yes'; and the minor nations to whom we, the most peaceful of all peoples, naturally belong will find that there is no question to answer here. But we also note that the minor nations take the second question far too lightly as to what will *bring* us peace so that we seek it on the right path.

Peace is like freedom in this world; there is an external peace and an internal peace which must work together if peace is to be absolute. Yet far too rarely and far too briefly do they work together. External peace cannot benefit or gladden people if they do not also have internal peace, whereas internal peace can comfort us in all external strife, so it is clearly not external but internal peace we must have if we are to know what *brings* us peace.

On the other hand freedom is like everything else in this world in that it can be either true or false, and it is far harder in the internal than the external to separate the artificial from the genuine or the false from the true. We can be desirous of peace, both the internal and the external, and still not know what will *bring* us peace – the genuine, true peace that gives rest to the soul and will last for ever.

All human experience has therefore taught us, as it did in Jerusalem, that no one quite knows what brings them peace except for those who have heard the Christian Gospel and believe it in their hearts. For the Saviour, our Lord Jesus Christ, is, as He Himself says, the only one who can bring rest to the soul and who will also give His disciples His peace. This is God's peace, which takes the heart into its keeping so that it does not fear and is not frightened, but comforts itself with the thought that all the strife of this world will end in a victory for God's people and an everlasting peace, the great, blessed eternal rest that God has prepared for His people.

But look, my friends, with every step we take in this world, be it outward or inward, we meet the artificial alongside the genuine and the false alongside the true; and we often find that the artificial shines brightest! Since it is always the 'best buy', we are tempted to choose it! So there also exists a false, artificial, so-called 'Christian' peace, with which many have comforted themselves, for the time being. Yet at the same time they miss out on the true, *genuine* peace, for that is what happens when they fool themselves into believing that they have the peace of God and our Lord Jesus Christ simply by confessing their faith in Him, the Prince of Peace, without having any faith in their *hearts*. They endeavour in every possible way to elicit or compel this empty air all around them and they boast of having taught whole cities, peoples, and kingdoms what will bring them peace, so the Lord does not need to cry over them as over Jerusalem: He can just bless them every Sunday with His great "Peace be with you!" and God has prepared His great eternal rest for them all!

Truth-loving people can well understand that this is foolishness – and they see it being confirmed on a daily basis. But when the enemy of all true peace boasts, "I told you so! All this peace proclaimed in the name of Jesus Christ is mere vanity! It is not peace with God but peace with the world, in other words the same false and artificial peace that the peoples of the world seek, praise, and go to Hell with!" then we must turn our ears away from this false world. For it falsifies all that it can get its hands on, and turns it in the direction of the little flock who believe what they confess and confess freely what they believe about Jesus Christ – without regard for the world's contradiction, scorn, and mockery. And as surely as we ourselves belong to this little flock, so shall we surely see that this faith and confession carries with it the genuine, true peace of God, for our hearts cheerfully acquire at Baptism and Holy Communion their "Peace be with you!" In this they find a peace that the world can neither give nor take, a peace that lasts under all the struggles of this world, and a pledge of the great eternal rest that God has prepared for His people when this world's form perishes, together with all this world's strife and toil. Amen!

39. 27th Sunday After Trinity

26 November 1837 (Matthew 17:1-12)[695]

In the blessed name of our Lord Jesus Christ: Holy Father! – Your Word is Truth! Your Word is Life and Spirit! The Word of faith which must be heard! Heavenly Father! You who glorified Your Son, our Lord Jesus Christ, before the eyes of three disciples on the Mount of the Transfiguration, glorify Him also for the sake of our eyes in the Holy Spirit, in that we hear Your voice from Your majestic glory. "This is my beloved Son, in whom I am well-pleased!" Our Father, You who are in heaven!

> "There he was transfigured before them. His face shone like the sun, and his clothes became as white as the light."[696]

In the Church tradition of our forefathers this Gospel text about the Lord's transfiguration on the mountain is so seldom read and expounded that for believers among both the clergy and the people it was something of a feast day every time it came round! And although in this, as in all our feast days, there is something that smacks

---

695. A 27th Sunday in Trinity is a rarity. In Grundtvig's lifetime it only came around 8 times, in 1788, 1799, 1815, 1818, 1826, 1837, 1845, and 1856.
696. Mt 17:2; Lk 9:29. The setting in Mt is 'a high mountain'.

more of the Old Testament than the New, this is still how I view the matter. I believe, and indeed I know, and I therefore thank God, that in New Testament days joy in the Lord was not limited to a few feast days in the year, for new life in the Lord is a constant feast day and a daily banquet! The only day which we as Christians rightly separate from the others as a special feast day is the Lord's Day, when He gathers us in His house and at His table to speak in inner unity about the things that belong to God's kingdom. Praise be to God that this feast day is not a rarity but comes round every week, like the ancient Sabbath, for as long as the year lasts. This brings joy to all true and faithful Christians, and we would do well to keep this in mind, so that we learn how to associate with each other in God's house and make our joy complete.

On the other hand there is no point in trying to make ourselves more 'Christian' or more 'happy' on the Lord's day than we actually are; on the contrary, that is merely a game of shadows which eats away at life and the love of truth. So I must confess that for me there is no small difference between weekdays and the Lord's day, and that the Gospel text of the transfiguration on the mountain – although it is equally close, equally true, and equally joyful on any other day – is nevertheless doubly cherished, luminous, and exhilarating when in the course of the years it meets us as one of our Sunday Gospel readings. Extraordinary events in my clerical life have also contributed to this. Firstly there were many years when I never preached on this Gospel text, and then finally it was my first text after years of silence![697] When it came around a second time, it was the same thing,[698] so today is the first time this Gospel text meets me in the order of the day. Even today it has something new to offer as the text for the last day of the Lord in the Church year; for I am reminded vitally and joyfully that the great Church year on earth will also end with a transfiguration on the mountain in the Spirit, most clearly and gladly corresponding to what we hear in today's Gospel.

So, Christian friends, let us take this to heart and for ever thank our heavenly Father that Christianity is far more and much happier than the matchlessly great and true story of God's wondrous deeds among human children in days gone by, far more than a uniquely exalted and true contemplation and perception of the relation between Heaven and earth, God and man, the past, the present, and the future, time and eternity. Christianity is indeed all this, and it is so for all people, even in the forecourt of the heathens, but in the Lord's house and, for His own chosen people who believe and are baptised, Christianity is so much more, so much deeper, and so much happier. For us it is life and spirit: the divine human life on earth of our Lord Jesus Christ, which through the power of the Holy Spirit in the

697. In 1818.
698. In 1826.

[431]

living, spoken Word of God repeats itself in secret in each of us and in public in the entire Christian Community.

For every elderly, experienced Christian who is moving towards the end of his days, there comes a holy day when the Lord in Spirit takes him up to the holy mountain. There like Moses not only can he look out at his leisure over the Promised Land from the river to the sea,[699] but with the three disciples he finds himself together with Jesus, Moses, and Elijah and sees the Saviour's face like the sun in all its power and his clothing, white as light. Then he shall hear our heavenly Father's voice from the majestic choir on high saying, "This is my Son, whom I love; with Him I am well pleased. Listen to Him!"[700] So too shall it manifestly be with the Lord's Church: towards the end of its days it shall be like Moses in his old age when "its eyes were not weak and its strength was not gone".[701] It will faithfully have followed the Lord on its humble path and not been offended by His 'hard words' that we are to eat the flesh of the Son of Man and drink His blood in order to live through Him as He lives through the Father. Then He will manifestly take His Church up to the mountain-top, where there is not only an unimpeded view of times gone by, of the ways of God on earth, and of His order of salvation among all peoples, but also an open, smiling view of the Land of the Living[702] and its permanent, everlasting dwellings. And at the mountain-top Jesus is transfigured before them and is talking to His prophets and saints about God's mysterious counsels, so that His face is shining like the sun in spring and His clothing is as white as light. His effect on His believers is like the sun's on the earth, His human nature with divine perfection is as clear and transparent as light, and His Gospel is confirmed by His Father's voice testifying eternal blessedness for the faithful heart that loves His beloved Son in whom He alone is well-pleased!

Such a day shall assuredly arise over the house of the Lord, such a time shall come to transfigure the Son as He has transfigured the Father, to prove that as the Father lives in the light, the Son also puts on light as His clothing and proves that Christ's Congregation lives not by bread alone but by the Word of God's mouth.[703] This time shall come and indeed is visibly approaching, it is coming soon, when the Spirit and the Bride say, "Come!"[704] Come indeed, Lord Jesus! It is coming into sight, guided by His Spirit on the plain and simple path. For in the middle of the plain we see the mountain rising where the Lord will go up with His closest disciples and be changed,

---

699. Deut 34.

700. Mt 17:5.

701. A paraphrase of Deut 34:7.

702. 'The Land of the Living' is the title of one of Grundtvig's greatest hymns, written in 1824. Under the title 'I know of a land' it is no. 65 in *Living Wellsprings* (2105).

703. Deut 8:3; Mt 4:4; Lk 4:4.

704. Rev 22:17.

be transfigured before them. In plain words we shall see a Christian enlightenment beginning which as surely as the Lord lives will lead to a transfiguration of Himself and His Gospel. We shall begin to listen to a living Word of God which as surely as Jesus Christ is God's beloved, only-begotten Son, must confirm itself through the Father's testimony from His majestic glory that He has given us everlasting life and that this life is in His Son.

However, just because the time of transfiguration is approaching, we do not have to believe that it has already arrived, or that it can come in a few hours or days or years of our time. It can come in a few hours of God's time, when a single day is a thousand years for us, or in three or four years of the Lord's time, which in our time has increased to eighteen centuries. So, my friends, it is fitting that we should be speaking freely about these things, for the living enlightenment of the Lord's life and way begins here and now. Thus in His great Church life He is meeting right now with John the Baptist before starting out on His teaching task. Soon there will be an increasing age of enlightenment corresponding to the three to three and a half years when He openly went around proclaiming the Gospel and showing the children of humankind so many of His Father's good deeds – an age of enlightenment as in those days, just as the previous age of Christianity has corresponded to the 30 years from the Lord's birth to His Baptism in the River Jordan, and the age of increasing enlightenment to our ascent in the Spirit of the Mount of Transfiguration. If it has taken eighteen centuries to get to the foot of the mountain, it may easily take a couple more before we reach the top in the clear air, where we shall see Moses and Elijah. For although it will go much faster than usual from now on, there is a true saying that 'All things take time', and how much more so when they are 'great things' such as the transfiguration of the Christian Congregation in the Lord. According to His word this is among the 'even greater' things than are seen on earth,[705] when He manifestly "revealed His glory as the only-begotten of the Father full of grace and truth!"[706] If we are looking for a specific notion of what must happen before this great Day of the Lord can come and this transfiguration take place, then we only have to turn to Holy Scripture in the belief that there lie hidden all the properties of knowledge and wisdom to be revealed in due course by the Spirit to whoever loves the Lord. We do so in the knowledge that this book of the Lord was written in ancient, long-dead, or dormant languages, and has come to us via such dim-lit paths that there are thousands of questions as to its actual scope, its original audience, the meaning of its words, and the coherence of its thought. Few of these can we answer with assurance and any clarity so that they can be understood by every Christian! Yet answered they must be – with assurance and clarity, so that the entire Christian Congregation sees

---

705. Jn 14:12.
706. Jn 1:14.

light in the Lord's light before the mountain is climbed and the great, uniquely festive, and joyful hour of the Transfiguration strikes!

Should we then lament this wait, or be impatient? Not at all! That would be folly and show a great ingratitude to our heavenly Father, who has so much goodness left for us, which previous generations had to do without, that we must not begrudge our children their new opportunity to praise Him who alone is good and whose loving-kindness is everlasting. We must appreciate that our eyes see and our ears hear what many prophets and righteous people have longed to see and hear, but never experienced: to see the Mount of the Transfiguration move beneath our feet, to see the wondrous path by which it shall be climbed at leisure, and hear the indistinct but deep and quickening voice from on high which we know will reveal itself to be the Father's resounding voice over His beloved Son.

Our forefathers sat sighing over the great, divine book of enlightenment and thought that the book itself would inform them about all God's ways and the transparency of the Godhead in our Lord Jesus Christ, the countenance of God's image. They thought that it must be the fault of their own sins that the book would not reveal this, so they never got further than they were at their beginning. We on the other hand, who come to the book from the right side and with powerful aids such as God's living Word and His enlivening Spirit, can see in the light of time a thousand passages where before they saw only darkness, and we do not fear the dimly-lit places, but notice them and smile at them, for from them – with a sign from the Spirit – shall issue a new light that will illumine the face of our Lord! Amen, in Jesus' name, Amen!

40. Sermon Before Parliament

4 October 1856 in Christiansborg Palace Church (Proverbs 4:23)

In bidding members of the Danish Parliament welcome and asking for Heaven's blessing on their daily work, may I seek to impress upon them an important, and in our day widely unappreciated, truth, expressed in the proverb of wise King Solomon: "Above all else, guard your heart, for everything you do flows from it."

What better words to impress upon the representatives of the Danish people in the spirit of true human freedom and civil freedom? As surely as God sees into the heart, so must warmth of heart, as the heart's guard, be the condition for heaven's blessing. And as surely as no people would bless other laws and arrangements than those that please their hearts, so can I only underline what alone brings with it the blessings of Heaven and earth and the importance of which all lawmakers should therefore understand. All the legislative assemblies of our day, large or small, royal or popular by name, either forget completely or pay far too little attention, and then only loose attention, to one thing above all: the desire and right of the human heart to *freedom* in its affairs. Failure to appreciate this desire and right has consequences, which are either death and apathy, or rage and violence, because whatever we do comes solely from the *heart*, from which human life issues.

To be sure, we who are here know this, as does everybody when they have a quiet moment to reflect that the mysterious depth in us that we call our 'heart' and which none of us can measure is the cradle of both our joys and our sorrows, our fears and our hopes, our desires and our loathings, in other words of our happiness and unhappiness. So the same heart must inevitably be the matrix for all our life-force, whether it be expressed in words or deeds, or whether it be the life-force we each more or less call our own, or the life-force we share with all our people or the entire human race which we call 'the Spirit'. If we wish to be happy and to contribute what we can to making our *people* happy, we must never forget that human happiness is a matter of the heart, and that the human heart has its own laws. Together with the life-force which derives from it the human heart invariably follows these, and no other law or legislative assembly can change or prevent this.

Thus, wherever civil laws are passed concerning the heart – for what it should believe or what is supposed to make it happy or unhappy – only violence is done to that heart, which is powerless to change the law. All that happens is that the heart is wounded and people are made unhappy. If this is the case wherever people live and build, then above all it is true of our own little Denmark, which is inhabited by the most hearty people under the sun! Whether or not one believes this, it has been the case with the Danish people in general as far back in time as we can go, just as it will always and everywhere be the case with a woman; for as we all know, every possible argument from reason is completely lost on her when we want her to count herself lucky over what has wounded or crushed her heart.

Today we are meeting in the Danish People's Church, which like the Danish people in general, receives its laws from the King and Parliament alone. On this occasion there is challenge enough to apply the valid proverb about heart and life to our 'People's Church', which, for it to answer to its name and because it is sustained financially by all our people as such,[707] must as far as possible be ordered manifestly according to the people's heart. We have organised our Church like this and consolidated it in the Constitution as best we could as a shared expense, an arrangement that we could never defend if we had not immediately made the question of faith, which all know to be a matter of the heart, a free choice with no influence on civil relations and rights. For

---

707. Paragraph 4 of the Danish constitution of 1849 is unchanged: "The Evangelical Lutheran Church is the Danish People's Church and as such is supported by the State."

every so-called 'state church' – in which an entire people is civilly bound and forced to confess the same faith whether they share it or not – shows not only a dreadful indifference to the truth and an equally dreadful favour for hypocrisy in the highest and holiest concern known to man; it is also, like a prodigiously large stone church, the heaviest stone that can be rolled onto a people's heart, a burden under which Denmark's tender people's heart has sighed for far too long.

However, if there is to be any fairness in maintaining such a 'people's church' at the people's and the country's expense, it is not enough for the people to be allowed to be outside our People's Church, we must ensure as far as possible that they can be *inside* it, can derive benefit and gladness from it, meaning that they find within it the fortification and the solace, the enlightenment and the edification, which their hearts need and demand. If to find this a large number of people actually *leave* the People's Church, at a new expense and sacrifice, then the People's Church will of course be a thorn in their side and such a heavier burden in that it will always brand them as sects and heretics.

To prevent this great drawback, which is also a great civil misfortune, we have recently taken a giant stride by passing the bill to loosen the parish-tie.[708] This has also had the effect of overthrowing the little parish papacies that have been as intolerable for the human heart as the great papacy itself, which seeks to extend itself to the whole of Christendom. Now that everyone in the country can choose their own spiritual adviser according to their heart's desire, and the prospect has been opened for every congregation to sing the hymns it likes best, the Danish People's Church can become a matchless wonder to the gratification, comfort, and joy of the whole people. We only need to pass a similar bill to loosen the tongues of the pastors in our People's Church so they may speak freely *from* the heart and *to* the heart as they themselves believe Christianity and understand the Holy Scriptures. And we only need to impress upon the government that this freedom should be subject to neither hindrance nor appeal, a right which our pastors and bishops as well as the teachers of our pastors have assumed to themselves and enjoyed for over half a century now.

For this to come about, and for the heart in this its highest concern to be assured of retaining its freedom, legislation for our People's Church must, according to the Constitution, be in the hands of the King and Parliament, since all experience shows that where the so-called clergy are in control of Church Law, whether wholly or partially, it becomes callous to a great degree. For a dominant clergy has never had the slightest sympathy for 'the people's heart' and has never cared about the spiritual death that is the inevitable consequence of all theocracies. Life issues from the heart,

---

708. The parish-tie, as set down in the Danish Law of 1683, limited parishioners' worship to their parish church. Grundtvig fought long and hard to break this tie, and was finally successful in 1855.

but that has always walled itself in and fortified itself in the stone church so that it stands or falls with it.

I say this in particular with the greatest earnestness, and I dare to hope that it will not be spoken in vain. For half a century now I have been known in Denmark and throughout the North as the one who has fought most ardently for this faith and this teaching, which for three hundred years has done what it could to be a civil compulsion and threat to our people and pastors. I champion the cause of pastoral freedom in every way, since it is clear that I must see all compulsion against conscience and all clerical governance as being not only in conflict with the Spirit of Christianity and its needs but also intolerable and demoralising for civil society, whose cornerstones, honesty and veracity, can never have more dangerous enemies.

May Denmark's Parliament therefore continue to stand firm on its constitutional right concerning the People's Church, and stand firm on the side of freedom, which the heart from which it issues cannot do without! Then I can promise that the free People's Church of Denmark will be a blessed and fruitful mother of life in the spirit of freedom and the power of truth in every direction, while spiritual death and serfdom can only prevail where the hand is used to achieve what can only be achieved by the Spirit, destroying assiduously the heart from which both popular and civil life should issue. For it is an immutable fact that human life comes from the heart, in word and deed, and in both its temporal and eternal relations!

41. Three Last Sermons 1872

12th Sunday After Trinity
18 August 1872 (Mark 7:31-37)

According to the Gospel reading of the day the multitude were "overwhelmed with amazement" at the great sign of love with which our Lord Jesus Christ healed the deaf and mute man. Quite rightly they shouted, "He has done everything well. He even makes the deaf hear and the mute speak!" We too may be just as overwhelmed by, and admire, the praise that God's Spirit laid on the tongues of the people; for it goes far deeper than they imagined. Our Lord Jesus Christ does indeed do everything well among His believers by making the deaf hear and the mute speak, so that we can both *receive* the Word of God's grace with the faith of our hearts and then *serve* that faith, to our salvation. But we must be just as overwhelmed with amazement at what we read: that it was with no more than a deep sigh that our Lord Jesus Christ healed the deaf and mute man. For it is in no way with a sigh but with joy that He does everything well for the fallen souls who will believe in Him, so His sigh here must come from Him seeing that the deaf and mute man would not be using his hearing and his speech to God's honour and his own salvation but would misuse all God's gifts so that in him they bore not life but death as their fruit.

So, Christian friends, here it was with the Lord Himself as it would be for every servant of His Word when people come to him with a little child and ask him to lay his hands on it and give the Lord's blessing,[709] while he anticipates in the Spirit that the child will derive no benefit from this but only a harder judgement because the child took God's grace in vain; for such a servant of the Lord dare not refuse what the Lord has promised to grant to all those who ask for it. Yet he can only do so with a deep sigh, like the Lord when He placed His fingers in the ears of the deaf man, touched his tongue, and spoke the divine *effata*: Be opened! A deaf person could hear and a mute person could speak, but only in the flesh, not in the heart and the spirit. For as with all the Lord's good words to us – as He expressly said of the Peace blessing in His name: "If there is no child of peace in the house, the peace returns to the Lord and His messenger."[710] So just as the Lord forbade those who were witnesses to the healing of the deaf and mute man to speak about it, so must we wish that the godparents would keep silent about each Baptism that we know was in vain; and yet we must expect that they will talk all the more about it, like the witnesses to the great sign of love He showed to the deaf and mute man.

In contrast, since we do not know for whom Baptism will be in vain, God be praised, we enjoin the witnesses quite rightly to testify with gratitude to the good deed of God, whereby He who is rich towards all those who call upon His name grants them in Baptism all they need for salvation: ears to hear and tongues to serve the Word of faith and life.

13th Sunday After Trinity
25 August 1872 (Luke 10:25-37)

Christian friends! According to the Gospel text of the day a man went from Jerusalem (the city of peace) to Jericho (the city of palms) but fell into the clutches of thieves, was disrobed, plundered, and misused, so he lay helpless and half-dead. This man manifestly corresponds to the Paradise-man in the first Adam, while the priest and the Levite who carefully observed him but passed him coolly by correspond to the law-abiders who doubtless knew what was written in the Law-book about love of God and one's neighbour[711] but appeared not to know where to find him! In contrast, as soon as the Good Samaritan sees the helpless man, he takes pity on him, hastens im-

---

709. The reference here is primarily to the pastor's role at Baptism.
710. Lk 10:6.
711. Deut 6:5; Lev 19:18.

10. Grundtvig's 50th anniversary commemorative coin, 1861

To commemorate Grundtvig's 50th anniversary as a pastor, Harald Conradsen designed a medal to be minted in silver and bronze and bearing a contemporary portrait of Grundtvig, now aged 77. On the flipside stands a child carrying a cross, beside a baptismal font, above which hovers a dove. Around the edge of the 43 mm coin are the words: OVER DAABENS PAGT MED TROENS ORD HELLIGAANDEN SPREDTE LYS I NORD (lit. Over baptism's covenant with the Word of faith the Holy Spirit spread light in the North) and the dates "29th May 1811-1861." A single *gold* medal was minted and given to Grundtvig himself.

On the day in question his third wife Asta surprised him in the morning, first with a series of embroideries from a circle of women admirers, and then with a visit from the schoolchildren of the Queen's Charity School, for the opening of which in 1841 Grundtvig had written the song 'Where Spirit has a mouth and voice' (no. 137 in *Living Wellsprings*, 2015). The young children carried a large 'Dannebrog' flag which they themselves had sewn and which they now raised on Grundtvig's new flagpole as they sang, 'We welcome with joy this blessed day' (no. 53 ibid). Grundtvig held a service in a packed Vartov Church, after which he received a new armchair. In the afternoon the dowager Queen Caroline Amalie and friends from Denmark, Norway, and Sweden brought him a seven-branched candlestick (now in the Marble Church in Copenhagen). King Christian VIII appointed him an honorary bishop (i.e. without a diocese). In the evening, after dinner in a huge tent at his home, 'Gladhjem', a large number of youngsters gathered to sing for the assembled guests, after which his admirers donated to Grundtvig a considerable sum for him to publish 5 volumes of his collected works.

mediately to his rescue, risks his life for him, and does not let go of him until he is healed; the Good Samaritan corresponds to the God-man, our Lord Jesus Christ, who abased Himself for fallen man, and suffered death on the cross for our sake. When He returned to His Father's house, with His Spirit set as His agent in His house,[712] to this house He gave two gold coins, Holy Baptism and Holy Communion, for healing and everlasting life, so that like Him we shall through the Father's glory rise from the dead and lead a new life in His footsteps – which means to remain in our Father's love and to keep His commandments.

The Gospel text of the day is thus a small yet clear church-mirror in which we see the life of humankind with Adam and Christ coming from and to the Father's house on high, with the life of everlasting love in *miniature* in each of us and in *full* in the entire believing Christian Congregation. For what happened to the man who fell among robbers also happened to all the heathen peoples on earth and to the Law of Israel; but the Word of God's grace awakened them through faith and Baptism to become a newborn people of God who take up their inheritance with the only-begotten Son as their neighbour.

So, Christian friends, let us as His neighbour, we who fell into the hands of robbers but were wrenched away and received the brotherly love of God's only-begotten Son, according to the law of God's grace copy Him in mercy and love to His honour, who seeks not His own honour but that of Him who sent Him! Then we shall swiftly feel the heavenly powers of everlasting life moving in our hearts and singing with the Christmas angels, "Glory be to God on high! And to the earth be peace, goodwill in the children of humankind!" Amen!

14th Sunday After Trinity
1 September 1872 (Luke 17:15-17)

When according to the Gospel text we hear our Lord Jesus Christ saying to the grateful Samaritan who worshipped Him, "Your faith has saved you!", we may easily be surprised. It is not that it was a miracle that the man in question had such faith to prompt this when a word of Jesus could cleanse one or ten lepers, but because elsewhere we read about the Lord in the New Testament that He could not reveal His glory in Galilee because of the people's lack of faith. It would seem to follow from this that without faith He could help no one. But it must be understood to mean that also with the laying-on of hands He could physically heal the sick yet not thereby reveal the divine origin of His Word, either to those He healed or to the witnesses of the healing.

Moreover, the riddle is solved with the Lord's words, "Were not the ten cleansed?

---

712. i.e. in the Church.

But where are the nine?"[713] Were there none to be found who turned round to give God the glory except this foreigner? If we think sensibly about this, we soon discover that one may have a supernatural belief in a doctor yet not have faith that his words are more powerful than our own, or that he is closer to God either in family or goodness than one of us.

Such a belief must also arise in us if our faith is to save us from sin and death. We see this in the Samaritan from the Gospel of the day, when he felt himself cleansed from the outer leprosy which like the inner one seemed incurable, except by God alone. That is why he turned round to Him whose words had shown such a wondrous power, and worshipped Him, then thanked Him.

Although the nine had perhaps convinced themselves that they were following Jesus' words more strictly by going to the priest as He commanded, the Lord nevertheless made it known that it was the Samaritan, who had neither rights nor duties according to the Law of Moses, who followed the only right path and turned back to give God the glory.

Only this faith in God's fatherly loving-kindness can give birth to the heartfelt gratitude from which the true word of thanks issues to express our reciprocated love for our fatherly God. He opens our hearts to offer the reciprocated love of His children which makes it possible that our divine Father's love can save us wretched sinners from the power of all falsehood, darkness, and death and transfer us from Satan's power to the kingdom of God's beloved Son, where home-coming sons and daughters for ever compete to give thanks in the name of our Lord Jesus Christ. Amen!

---

713. Lk 17:17.

IV

LETTERS AND SPEECHES

Introduction by Michael Schelde and Edward Broadbridge

During his long life Grundtvig wrote thousands of letters in a total production roughly calculated at 80,000 pages. 500 or so of these letters are preserved, as well as 1,500 or so letters written *to* him. We include below a small selection which offers a more personal side of his theology compared to the previous sections. Alongside these central thoughts on theology and faith are four speeches given at important moments in his life, relating even more closely to his personal faith.

Letter to a Bishop (1822, Text 42) is thought to have been drafted while Grundtvig was pastor in Præstø (1821-22) and is directed to Bishop Münter of Zealand (in office 1808-30). Grundtvig asks for advice regarding the re-marriage of divorcees, since the wedding ritual is no longer viable in their case. The prohibition on divorce ended with the Reformation in 1536, and by 1800 around 100 couples a year were being legally divorced. By 1810 Bishop Münter was so concerned about the increasing numbers that he wrote to the King complaining that divorce undermined marriage, decreased the birth rate, and led to unstable upbringing and a lack of patriotism. The King declined to become involved. We do not know whether Grundtvig ever posted this letter, or if he did, how it was received. What is of most interest here is to see Pastor Grundtvig grappling with a practical pastoral matter and humbly pleading for guidance from his bishop. Should he change the liturgy, as many a priest did, or should he avoid the couple altogether?

Letter to Christen Olsen (1826, Text 43) was written to Grundtvig's friend in his youth, Christen Olsen (1785-1833), who at the time was pastor in Lynge-Broby parish on Zealand. The parish lay close to that of another friend and fellow hymn-writer, Pastor Bernhard Ingemann, to whom Grundtvig sends his greetings. The background for the letter was Grundtvig's book *The Church's Retort* (1825, Texts 1 and 4) and the subsequent debate which ended with Grundtvig resigning his pastorate on 8th May 1826. He was already aware that he might be placed under censorship – "a Christian writer who will perhaps soon lose his freedom of speech" – and indeed on 30th October 1826 that is what happened. He contemplated leaving the country for Norway or England, and was more than prepared for the latter option. Yet despite the seriousness of his situation he writes with a light heart: "seriousness and merriment can get on well together". This is because, following his 'matchless discovery' in 1825 that the *original faith* is to be found in the Creed and in the institution of the sacraments of Baptism and Holy Communion, his "struggle between the chaotic and the organising principle has ceased and has been replaced by an inner harmony". He now feels a sense of being 'liberated', with his head ruling his heart and with a firm intention to wait upon the Lord.

Inspired by his three trips to England in 1829-31 Grundtvig sent a **Letter to the King 1831** (Text 44) stating that he was again ready to serve the church as a pastor. Now aged 47 he asks for permission to return to the Church, and supports his application by referring to his 20 years of service and by accompanying it with a copy of *On the Clausen Libel Case* (Text 4). This, he hopes, will explain his theological position and help the King to look favourably upon his request to set up a Danish-German congregation *outside* the State Church "for the sustenance of the old-fashioned Christian faith". At the same time he promises to respect whatever "the maintenance of good social order and custom may require". Despite their cordial relations, acting on advice Frederik VI rejected Grundtvig's proposal.

In another **Letter to the King 1833** (Text 45) Grundtvig thanks His Majesty for permission to preach at the Evening Service in Frederik's Church but seeks permission also to administer Baptism and Holy Communion. Again he presents himself as a champion of the 'old-fashioned' Christians who no longer have any "guarantee that our children are baptised and confirmed in our Baptismal Covenant" by the so-called modern parish pastors who are no longer following either the Confessional Books or Altar Book liturgy. He pursues his argument further by requesting that the King as head of the Danish State Church should allow worshippers to 'break the parish-tie' and attend services where the pastor's words and deeds are closer to their own beliefs. But again the King turned down Grundtvig's request.

Much as Grundtvig admired the spirit of freedom and industry in England, he regarded the people in general as materialist and the Church of England as dysfunctional. His trips in 1829-31 had proved a great source of inspiration for his Old Nordic studies, his new versions of old hymns, and his thoughts on the relationship between freedom and collectivity in the society taking shape in the first half of the century. Before he left for his fourth trip, together with his son Svend, he wrote to his friend Gunni Busck: "I shall doubtless clash with half-blood or full-blood papists in Oxford, and it is no use hiding the fact that there are stiff necks and uncircumcised hearts over there, so trouble is certain and the effect of my activities very doubtful." And that was indeed the case. In the first of **Two Letters from the England Trip 1843** (Text 46), he meets a Mr Palmer, who speaks as if the Church "only consisted of bishops and whoever else they were willing to allow inside. In contrast I know that with or without bishops the Church consists of all those who 'believe and are baptised' …It is a great shame that so many talented and courageous young men should be trapped in the old papist or hierarchical snare." In the second letter his criticism of the 'deadness' of the Anglican Church is confirmed when he and Svend arrive late for Matins at St. Paul's Cathedral and are told by a young policeman on guard that they are "too late" and are sent away again! Grundtvig cannot believe his ears, for wherever the Word is still being proclaimed it is never *too* late. Aware that he has left Lise alone on their Silver Wedding Day he not only adds affectionate words to her but also hopes that, as he approaches 60, his two sons will one day "stand on his shoulders". Even before

II. Grundtvig's grave and coffin

Grundtvig is buried beside his second wife, Maria, in a vault in 'Clara's Graveyard' on Køge Ridge, 45 km south of Copenhagen. His coffin can be glimpsed to the right under the vault. The graveyard is named after Clara Sophie Carlsen, who was married to the manor owner, Hans Carlsen, but lived only to the age of 30. Her dying wish was to be buried on Køge Ridge. Grundtvig's grave and coffin are accessible only on Clara's birthday (15th May) and Grundtvig's birthday (8th September). The apple and sunflower on the coffin are gifts from admirers, photographed by the editor in 2015. Grundtvig's third wife, Asta (Clara's niece), is buried nearby. For details of Grundtvig's death and funeral see p. 450.

they were born, his wish for his children was "that the spirit of their fathers might be over them and the kingdom of God their goal!"

Near the end of his stay he wrote to the dowager queen, Caroline Amalie, who had granted him funding for the trip. He said he was leaving an England "that has had a decisive influence not only on my little life but on the life of the whole human race ... My spiritual relation to England is assuredly more poetic than historical, but that is precisely why my visits have a poetic reality if not for others then for myself." Grundtvig feels ten years younger now, for old memories and new hopes have been quickened in him.

Elise Stamp (1824-83) was the daughter of Henrik and Christine Stampe, who owned the manor farm of Nysø near Præstø. They had met when Grundtvig was pastor of Præstø in 1821, and since 1829 he had been corresponding with Elise, whose daughter he had baptised in 1841. The many letters between them testify to a long friendship based not least on her letters requesting his theological views, which Grundtvig took great pains to answer. In **Letter to Elise Stampe 1857** (Text 47) he makes a subtle distinction between 'the community of saints' and 'the communion of saints' and emphasises that all fellowship in the Church and Congregation depends on the words of the Creed in the mother-tongue. All power and honour belong to God and we are saved by His grace alone, but we must not be idle: "as Christians we have the same relationship to our Saviour as He has to His Father, so we must show the world His good works as He showed His *Father's* good works". Salvation is freely offered, but it must also be received, for it is "the living God's Word with the Spirit and the living faith in our hearts that brings it about".

In the course of his long life Grundtvig experienced the death of two wives, Lise (1787-1851) and Marie (1813-54). Although Grundtvig first took a fancy to Lise's elder sister, he fell deeply in love with Lise herself and once sent her four letters in the course of a week! Their marriage, after seven impecunious years of engagement, lasted over 32 years, from 12th August 1818 until 14th January 1851, and produced 3 children: Johan (1822-1907), Svend (1824-83), and Meta (1827-87). Lise was a strong supporter of her husband, but over the years he spent an increasing amount of time in his study. Surrounded by books and manuscripts, and filling his room with acrid pipe-smoke and left-over food and drink, Grundtvig became absorbed in his work, while Lise looked after the home and the children. She was economical with their limited income but was gradually reduced to the role of housekeeper rather than housewife. After a long depression she died and was buried by Grundtvig himself on 21st January 1851 in the churchyard of Our Saviour's Church (**Beside my Lise's Coffin 1851**, Text 48).

Grundtvig cast aside the traditional year of mourning, for he already had a close relationship with Marie Toft, herself widowed in 1841 and 30 years Grundtvig's junior.

For their engagement on 4th August 1851 he wrote the famous love poem, 'What is it, my Marie?'[714] All agreed that Grundtvig was a rejuvenated man and that Marie was an ideal partner. Their shared happiness, spiritual, intellectual, and physical, culminated in the birth of Grundtvig's third son, Frederik, on 15th May 1854. Unfortunately, Marie did not survive the ordeal, and died on 9th July. Grundtvig himself conducted her funeral at Vartov Church on 17th July and again gave the oration: **Beside my Marie's Coffin 1854** (Text 49). The comparison between this passionate eulogy for Marie and the more reserved tones he employs for Lise is significant. Marie was buried in a vault at Køge Ridge, where Grundtvig lies beside her.

On 16th April 1858 Grundtvig married for the third time. Lady Asta Reedtz (1826-90) had been Marie's friend, was a wealthy widow with four children, and Grundtvig's junior this time by 40 years. Asta greatly admired him both as a seer and as a powerful presence, and their marriage was blessed with a daughter born on 10th February 1860, by which time he was 76 and she 36. Grundtvig named her after his three wives: Asta, Marie, Elisabeth. With her accommodating nature Asta Grundtvig set her stamp on the household by inviting numerous guests to 'Gladhjem' (Happy Home) and then 'Store Tuborg' (Great Tuborg). In 1861 she was there when Grundtvig's 50th anniversary as a pastor was celebrated at Vartov, when he was awarded the honorary title of Bishop of Zealand. He was by now such a national institution that a medal was minted in his name!

It was Asta who inaugurated the Friends' Meetings around Grundtvig's birthday, which brought joy and inspiration to him. The first was held in 1863 for friends who supported his view of the Church. 11 laymen and 11 clergy invited Grundtvig to a meeting at Casino Theatre in Copenhagen on 9th-10th September, immediately after Grundtvig's 80th birthday celebrations on 8th September. Asta played a central role in these birthday meetings by opening their home to a large group of people in 1865, 1866, 1869, and finally at Pentecost 1871, when Grundtvig celebrated his 60th year as pastor. At each of these meetings Grundtvig gave an address, and in the **Speech at the Friends' Meeting 1863** (Text 50) he looks back over the years and comments on the phenomenon of 'Grundtvigianism'. By 1863 this was becoming a movement, but Grundtvig prefers the phrase "Lutheran Christian enlightenment" and reiterates his closeness to Luther. Again he speaks of leaving the Church to start his own congregation (aged 80), but he rejects the move "only because I still have left a morsel of Abraham's hope" that pastoral freedom *within* the Church is not far off.

A new meeting was planned for September 1872 but following his death on the 2nd, his funeral three days later took the form of a memorial ceremony.

---

714. 'To Marie, My Fiancee', no. 157 in *Living Wellsprings* (2015).

Grundtvig's Death and Funeral

Dr H.P. Barfod relates what happened while Grundtvig's wife and children were at Copenhagen Zoo and his son Frederik, aged 18, was reading to him in their home, 'Great Tuborg', on the afternoon of Monday 2nd September 1872:[715]

During the reading he saw that his father had fallen asleep. He did not set any great store by this, since it happened now and then, so he went out into the garden for a while and waited until his father had rested.

When Asta arrived home around 4 pm, she went straight in to her husband. She saw that he was ill, as he sat in the armchair in front of his writing-table. He tried to speak to his wife, but he could not manage any meaningful words. He held out the pipe in his hand, but then collapsed, and Asta thought he was dead. Meanwhile a message had been taken to Professor Engelsted, who lived across the road from Great Tuborg. He came rushing in and found that there was still life in the old man, so he tried to give Grundtvig a stimulant, but to no effect. Grundtvig took his last breath peacefully a few minutes later.

By then, Niels Lindberg, who lived in the house at the entrance to the driveway had arrived, and he and Frederik carried Grundtvig into the bedroom and laid him on the bed. Asta was overcome by remorse and reproached herself for having left him that day, "Oh, if only I had had a last word from him and a goodbye from his lips!" she lamented, but she thanked God for hearing His servant's prayer that he be spared a lengthy sick bed.

On Thursday evening 5th September, several hundred men and women gathered round Grundtvig's coffin at Great Tuborg. Speeches were made by Pastor P.A. Fenger and Pastor Peter Rørdam, and among the hymns sung were Grundtvig's own 'To bid this world farewell aright' and 'Peace, to soothe our bitter woes'.[716] The coffin was then carried to the Church of Our Saviour in Christianshavn, where the funeral took place on 11th September. Among the huge following were some three hundred pastors in their vestments as well as other pastors in ordinary clothes. The King, the Dowager Queen, and the Crown Prince sent representatives, and Grundtvig's opponents of old, Bishop Martensen and Professor H.N. Clausen, were present, together with a number of government ministers. At the church, speeches were made by Pastor Frits Boisen, Pastor Peter Rørdam, and Pastor P.A. Fenger, who administered the sprinkling of the earth on the coffin.

---

715. Translated from *Minder fra gamle Grundtvigske Hjem* (*Memories from old Grundtvigian homes*) vol.3 62ff.

716. 'To bid this world farewell aright' (*At byde verden ret farvel*) is no. 64 in *Living Wellsprings* (2015). 'Peace, to soothe our bitter woes' (*Fred til bod for bitter savn*) has been translated as no. 203 in *Grant me, God, the Gift of Singing* (2nd ed., Vancouver: The Danish Lutheran Church of Vancouver, B.C.), which contains 81 Grundtvig hymns listed under Index 7 in *Living Wellsprings* (2015).

The funeral procession was led by a large number of students followed by the pastors and many others in one of the largest corteges the capital has ever seen, including people from throughout the country, and many also from Norway. The procession passed along Frederiksholm's Canal and then turned into Løngangsstræde to continue along Vester Voldgade to the railway station. In the canals all the boats flew their flags at half-mast, as did many houses, while all the windows along the route were packed and the streets full of people.

The hearse and cortege stopped outside Grundtvig's Church at Vartov. The door was open, the lights on, and the tones of the organ streamed out of the church. The hymn was 'Christ is risen from the dead',[717] which was sung by the thousands of voices outside, the like of which had never been heard before.

At the station, the cortege broke up, but between six and seven hundred people followed in a special train carrying Grundtvig's body to Køge, where it arrived at 4.30 pm. The church bells were tolling, numberless flags were flying at half-mast, and brothers-in-arms and the local trade guild accompanied the coffin through the town with banners decorated with flowers.

At Køge Ridge outside the town Grundtvig was laid to rest beside his second wife, Marie, in the open grave vault of the Carlsen Family. Here there were speeches by Professor Hammerich and Pastor Sveistrup from Vejen. The service closed with the Confession and the Lord's Prayer, and after the singing of 'The peace of God defends the heart',[718] the cortege dispersed. Grundtvig lies in a lead coffin inside a heavy coffin made of light oak.

***

42. Letter to a Bishop (1822?)[719]

In Jesus' name.
Dear Right Reverend!

Until now I have had the good fortune to avoid officiation at the marriage of divorced spouses; however, in my present office this cannot continue. I see the first marriage of this kind drawing near and can no longer hesitate to request my bishop's advice

---

717. 'Christ is risen from the dead' (*Krist stod op af døde*) is no. 22 in *Living Wellsprings* (2015).
718. (*Guds fred er mer end englevagt*) translated in full as no. 254 in *Grant me, God, the Gift og Singing* – see note 716.
719. Nicolai Edinger Balle (1744-1816) was Bishop of Zealand from 1783-1808.

on a matter that I find the gravest in the entire discharge of a pastor's duties. If the Right Reverend Bishop could effect a change here, he would earn the warmest thanks not only from me but from everyone who endeavours conscientiously to tend his holy calling as the servant of God's Word.

Since the matter is of such great and far-reaching importance, I request the Right Reverend's permission to present it in more detail than the individual case might seem to necessitate. Marriage in itself is indubitably not an originally *Christian* arrangement, for it is both older than the Christian Church and a relation grounded in human nature, with such a significant influence on all social life that no legislation has been able to lose sight of it. This being so, the civil validity of marriage depends in no way on the Church ceremony or blessing but on its accordance with the civil laws that uphold legal relationships. A wedding is only the seal that the Christian Church sets on a marriage as being 'Christian', as being in accordance with the precepts of Christianity on marriage among its adherents, thus declaring it to be indissoluble except in case of the one part clearly showing himself or herself to be a despiser of Christianity.

It is natural that the State, where it professes Christianity, should wish to link the wedding ceremony to every marriage between its subjects, since it must exert all its strength to sanctify a relationship from which its own life and power issue, the contempt of which must bring about its downfall. If it is the will of the State that marriage should be universal, it must of necessity also declare Christian marriage to be the only *valid* form. For on the one hand the servants of Christianity cannot administer any *other* kind of marriage, and on the other hand it is in the State's greatest interest that what is supposed to consolidate and sanctify the marriage relationship should not be profaned and made ineffectual. However, since it allows Jews within it,[720] it is immediately forced to make an exception, and since experience testifies much too loudly that all those who call themselves Christians are far from being so, the State is faced with the unpleasant inevitability of extending the exception in general. If the number of married couples living in conflict and disagreement becomes many, then out of concern for domestic peace and child-raising the State must consider it necessary to allow *divorce*, even in cases where Christianity disapproves of it. Once such a divorce is permitted, the State is forced, by the resulting moral laxity and the number of illegitimate, helpless children, to permit a *new* marriage between divorcees, even though Christianity forbids this.[721] It cannot of course ignore the truth of experience that the more easily divorce is made obtainable and new marriages contracted, the more divorces will continue to occur if no inner improvement takes place among the people in general. The State cannot therefore watch without concern a bond being

---

720. i.e. within the State.
721. The biblical basis for this is Mt 19:1-11.

thus loosened that is fundamentally its own; in all moral relations the State is bound, and like Solon,[722] must settle for giving the best its people can receive.

This is the situation at present: our wedding rituals are naturally intended for marriages that are, or appear to be, Christian; in other words they do not clearly contradict its precepts. A wedding continues to be essential to a legal marriage, but there have been legal marriages which contradict the precepts of Christianity and to which our wedding rituals are inapplicable. All the same, a number of pastors are using them, perhaps thoughtlessly, while others attempt to modify them as best they can according to circumstances, and thus the wedding ritual as such can only be diminished in the eyes of the people into an insignificant ceremony.

Even worse, we are led to believe that we can consecrate an *un*christian marriage by lying and somehow stealing the blessing. For when as servants of the Word we ask the bridal couple whether they have taken counsel with God we are in fact asking whether they are contracting a marriage in agreement with His Word, even when we know that they cannot truly answer 'yes'. When we ask whether they are free of the vows made in *other* marriages, we know that they cannot answer 'yes' without lying, and yet it is solely by virtue of taking this 'yes' to be true that we can declare their marriage 'Christian', pronounce them 'man and wife' before God, and as such give them the blessing. No conscientious pastor can do this after mature consideration, for that would be playing with God's Word and blessing; yet the question remains, What is he to do? Should he refuse the wedding ceremony or change the ritual of his own accord? The first is without doubt the more proper, but since we cannot expect that many pastors would be willing to expose themselves to the unpleasant consequences this could have, the majority will naturally choose to change the ceremony, particularly in a time when the State is silent on the matter, provided that no one actually complains.

However, such a change is not only difficult, it does not even serve its purpose without soon leading to complaint; for if the bridal couple do not notice that the ritual has been changed, they are all the same led to believe that their marriage has been declared 'Christian'; and if they do notice, their lethargy must be boundless if no one complains. Once the complaint is lodged, the pastor would be culpable, not because he had omitted what God's Word, that is, his calling and most solemn oath,[723] bade him do, but because he had changed what he had pledged to follow. The problem should therefore certainly be submitted to the close attention of the government, if

722. Solon (c.638–c.558) was an Athenian statesman who, on second-hand evidence, seems to have legislated for political, economic, and *moral* improvement.

723. In the Danish Lutheran Church the pastoral vow is taken by new priests who have been 'called' (i.e. already selected) by a specific congregation. It is spoken and signed after the so-called 'Bishop's exam' (an episcopal interview) but before actual ordination. With minor modifications the present pastoral vow dates from 1870, when it replaced the Latin oath of 1685.

only out of regard for our pastors, for even if they were willing to expose themselves to the unpleasant consequences of a breach of the law, it must be a matter of great urgency for the State that those public servants who are actually appointed as the spokesmen of conscience should not in their administration of the law be tempted to act against their conscience. Nevertheless, I believe that also from another side the State must realise that it is in its own interest that a change should take place, for if it is essential that its wishes – [*breaks off here*]

43. Letter to Christen Olsen (1826)[724]

8th July 1826, Christianshavn

Dear Friend!

Although there is hardly a Zealander between Kullen and Kulsbjærg[725] with more courage and daring to trust his own eyes than myself, I would never have ventured to believe my own eyes when I saw your handwriting on a letter, if it had not been accompanied by credible proof, worth waiting for, that after a lengthy time for reflection you would be considerate enough to anticipate the need for a *hallmark*, if the letter were to be credibly written by you yourself. To prove that I regard the letter as genuine I can do no better than answer it, for although you might require a little oral testimony from me confirming the authenticity of your missive, I must ask you for the present to believe your own eyes, since I cannot myself accompany it and have, as you know, no parish clerk to send as my substitute. From this you can gather that I am still of the belief, thank God, that seriousness and merriment can get on well together, provided that, as the saying goes,[726] merriment joins forces with seriousness and one does not forget that the weft goes over the warp.[727]

I do not need to tell you that over the past year my faith has been subjected to greater temptation than one might imagine from my published writings and in particular my review of the *Rhymed Chronicle*.[728] For you doubtless know that this year has been fundamentally one of deep seriousness in which it was a great achievement to be able

---

724. Christen Olsen (1785-1833) was a friend of Grundtvig's youth and later the pastor of Lynge and Broby parish, near Sorø on Zealand.

725. Kullen is a range of hills in south-west Sweden; Kulsbjærg is a range of hills in south Zealand, Denmark.

726. 'Seriousness and merriment always go well together': in Danish, *Alvor og gammen, altid godt sammen*.

727. i.e. when weaving.

728. In an edition of *New Evening News* (*Nyt Aftenblad*) in 1826, Grundtvig had reviewed a new edition of the *Rhymed Chronicle* (1825) by the Danish historian Christian Molbech (1783-1857). The *Rhymed Chronicle* (1495) was the first printed book in Danish.

to bring *any* merriment to the weft, and yet I would not exchange it for the merriest of years, even in our language the purest merriment I have experienced. Be its effect in the world great or small, now or in the future, this year has marked an *epoch* in my inner path which I can only call 'great', for the struggle between the chaotic and the organising principle has ceased and has been replaced by an inner harmony. What the Lord has created in me was not actually chaotic but only seemed so until the principle of order clearly rose above the living focal point around which all things Christian, not immediately but soon, will organise themselves, as though of their own volition. This focal point is the Lord who is the Spirit. You have doubtless noted that it is the second part of our *Small Catechism*[729] I am speaking of, in particular as the most especial part, and as the 'head' that orders all our Christian ideas and controls our feelings as the living expression of the Christian Spirit. In ruling over me the Spirit has replaced the matchlessly united, but obscure and therefore perpetually misunderstood, *duumvirate* of Spirit and Letter. You may well have heard that I have become 'catholic'[730] in the head – and indeed I have; but I venture to claim that this does not mean I am any the less Lutheran in the heart. For Luther was 'Lutheran' and the Augsburg Confession is a solemn confession of the faith of the holy catholic Church with its serious protest against the Pope in Rome and against all the abuses which with him and through him had crept into the Church. It is nonetheless the seemliest path to develop my Lutheran catholicity from a free position, not as a dismissed Lutheran pastor but as one who is liberated![731] I thus find rich occasion on a daily basis to thank the God whose thoughts and ways are so raised above the best of our own as Heaven is raised above earth, and who therefore has compelled me to do what with calm consideration I thought best, though without having had the courage to do it unguided.

I am now working on a reflection on the truth of Christianity[732] in which I shall show, as clearly as God grants me the light and the grace, the ostensibly indefensible and the materially irredeemable factors in our Church attitude. The importance of this question, especially for a Christian writer who will perhaps soon lose his freedom of speech, is not primarily because I have any plans to move to another country, however

---

729. The five sections of Luther's *Small Catechism* (1529) are: 1. The Ten Commandments 2. The Apostles' Creed 3. The Lord's Prayer 4. The Sacrament of Baptism 5. The Sacrament of Holy Communion.

730. 'Catholic' in the sense of 'universal'.

731. Grundtvig's point is that he was not 'dismissed' but resigned voluntarily and felt a sense of release in consequence.

732. The completed work, *The Truth of Christianity*, was first published in 1827 in *Theological Monthly*.

much I might wish to do so for the sake of myself and my nearest and dearest.[733] I have not given up my hope of a smooth field[734] and cannot do so without thinking that the Lord created not only me but many human children and servants of the Son of Man for nothing. But God alone knows how smoothly it will turn out and how hilly the road may be, and if I have ever thought, even unconsciously, that from His revealed judgements I could infer His inscrutable ways,[735] and on the beaten paths find the untraceable path, I am no longer deluded but will, like a watchman on the wall, wait for His intimations and with His assistance pursue them. So although I secretly nourish the hope of remaining in our country, of behaving myself and working freely with voice and pen for the coming of the kingdom of God among us, I am nevertheless packing a bag and will if necessary endeavour to subdue a deep sigh with the promise of joy, like the woman who has brought a human being – a child of God – into the world. If I am to leave Denmark, it must be for either Norway or England, and although the former seems the most reasonable to us, my eyes are turned more to 'over there', so I am attempting to master the English tongue, which can only succeed at my age with God's singular assistance.

Best wishes to your brothers and sisters and dear Ingemann[736] from Lise and

Your friend
Grundtvig

---

733. By the date of this letter, 8 July 1826, Grundtvig had been charged with libel by Professor H.N. Clausen and risked being placed under censorship; in frustration he had resigned his living at the Church of Our Saviour in May 1826. The final judgment against him came on 30 October 1826, when he was fined and placed under lifelong censorship. Through a change in the law allowing for limited rather than permanent censorship, Grundtvig's own censorship was revoked in 1837. Meanwhile, in 1829 he did in fact move to London for three months, and in 1831 after two more summer visits he wrote home to his wife, Lise: "This foreigner, truly to his own surprise, finds himself so much at home in London as he would anywhere in Denmark apart from his home and his family life. The lack of these cannot be replaced of course, but if I had you here with my offspring and you were as accustomed to the country and language as I am, I would not mind much living here for a few years in the hope of better times to come for my activities back home" (Letter to Lise, 18 July 1831).

734. i.e. for his free activity.

735. Rom 11:33.

736. Bernhard Severin Ingemann (1789-1862) is the fourth great Danish hymn-writer along with Kingo, Brorson, and Grundtvig. He produced over 50 works, including plays, poems, and historical romances. Although they were never close friends, he and Grundtvig exchanged no fewer than 146 letters over 40 years until they fell out over the 'resurrection of the flesh', for which Ingemann had a distaste.

44. Letter to the King (1831-32)

(Concept.)[737]

Most Gracious Majesty![738]

In hereby declaring myself willing to be a pastor for my fellow-believers – the old-fashioned Lutheran Christians, whom His most gracious subject had asked His Majesty for permission to constitute a free Danish and German Church without expense or inconvenience to the State – I further declare my most humble willingness to submit to all the regulations that His Majesty's wisdom may consider necessary for an orderly keeping of the parish registers and all that the maintenance of good social order and custom may require.

I therefore request most humbly His Majesty's most gracious attention as to what my conscience as a pastor and teacher in the Christian Church, as a faithful Danish subject and as an author of note – who throughout a long public career dares to hope has gained a reputation for truthfulness and love of the fatherland – requires me to declare and testify.

I declare and testify that with 25 years' experience of writing and 20 years of service behind me, and with the degree of Christian enlightenment I have acquired and many times set forth in public writing, irrefutably and unchallenged, that a *separation* from the Church between the old-fashioned Lutheran Christians and the modern Christians is inevitably necessary, and that for the sake as much of civil unity and free scholarship as for the freedom of Christian conscience and human honesty, and for His Majesty's closer illumination in this regard, I allow myself the most humble freedom to enclose a brief piece, *On the Clausen Libel Case*,[739] in which I most recently and most briefly have endeavoured to explain this distressing relationship.

However, most gracious Majesty, if it is now inevitably necessary that the fundamentally opposing parties in the State Church on the question of faith and salvation in some way or other must be separated *within* the Church, I judge on my honour and conscience and to the best of my knowledge that the separation would be undertaken in the gentlest and most beneficial manner, if His Majesty would most graciously

---

737. i.e. Draft.

738. Frederik VI (1768-1839) reigned from 1808-39. He was favourably disposed towards Grundtvig and had helped to finance Grundtvig's England trips in 1829, 1830, and 1831.

739. Following a vicious pamphlet attack on Professor of Theology H.N. Clausen, Grundtvig was found guilty of libel and placed under publishing censorship from 1826-37. In protest he resigned his pastorate in 1826. He was allowed to hold evensong sermons at Christianskirken but forbidden to administer Baptism and Holy Communion. For the full text of this work see ch. 4 above.

permit the pastors whose conscience no longer allows them to fulfil their offices in the State Church to leave it, together with their audience,[740] be they many or few, and in a church sense shift for themselves.

Moreover, most gracious father of the country, I and my audience, whom conscience impels to break the ice and make a beginning with this humblest, amicable, and pious prayer for such a permission, belong – as His Majesty, the whole country, and indeed the entire Nordic reading-public, know – not to those who are disaffected with the internal and external condition of the Danish State Church as laid down by the constitution, the law of the land, and church ritual, but on the contrary to those who are sincerely pleased with all this. In my own personal case, everyone is well aware that for over 20 years I have worked with voice and pen to bring the State Church back to its lost equality with the statutory requirements and the clear content of our Confessional Books.[741] Nonetheless, since circumstances have become so strangely embroiled that we must now request the humblest permission to *leave* the State Church, it is clear that on the one hand the State risks nothing whatsoever by allowing such a reasonable request, and on the other hand a rejection could only place the government in the unpleasant position of employing some severity against those in the State Church who undeniably have the law and the laudable testimony of history on their side.

Truly, under such circumstances I would hope that such a request would be most graciously granted also in any other land than here, where no heart of the father of *any* land beats so loud and has beaten for so long as under the monarchy of Denmark. I therefore feel most certain that this request will be granted, once the circumstances are made as clear to His Majesty and His confidential servants as they are for me. However, since in the nature of the case it is well-nigh impossible – and I as a historian cannot be unaware that most of our statesmen, not to mention those who hold high office in the State Churches, regard the matter from a quite different viewpoint – it is thus my sole hope that the God who has kings' hearts in His hand and light for His raiment, and before whose countenance I testify that I have presented the case impartially in its true and real context, will do far more than we can ask or understand in the promotion of the honesty and truthfulness in the cause of salvation that our conscience tells us He wishes should reign among us all – and for the sustenance of the old-fashioned Christian faith which, it is clear, only became so old because God's Providence was watching over it and was wondrously prolonging its days.

---

740. i.e. congregation.

741. For the Confessional Books of the Evangelical Lutheran Church in Denmark, see note 62.

With this joyful conviction of having done my best for mercy and truth to meet, and for justice and peace to embrace in the dear land of their fathers, with unswerving loyalty and devotion, I remain

Most humbly,
Nik. Fred. Sev. Grundtvig.

45. Letter to the King (1833)

Your Majesty[742] has most graciously permitted me from 3rd March this year until further notice to celebrate Evensong in Frederik's Church[743] according to the ritual, and I therefore wish to convey my deep-seated thanks; but the prayers of many faithful subjects unite with mine to ask Your Majesty as the gentle father of our land and the head of the Danish State Church that permission also be most graciously granted me until further notice to administer Baptism and Holy Communion in the same church as well as Confirmation according to the Altar Book of 1812[744] for whomever may so wish it!

This sincere and most humble request arises for me and doubtless for many others solely out of a care for the old-fashioned Christian faith and for our children, which is just as essential as it is natural, and which I most graciously ask permission to set forth freely and openly.

It is a fact that towards the end of the previous century a modern Christianity developed that in many ways contradicts the old one. Because this modern Christianity found many supporters among the clergy in Denmark as well as in Germany whence it came, a heavy and distressing disparity unavoidably arose between many parish pastors and those of their parishioners who held firm to the old faith and naturally desired their children to be brought up in it. The law of the land gave them the fullest rights to do this, despite neither they nor even the government being able to prevent those

---

742. Frederik VI (1768-1839) reigned from 1808-39. He was favourably disposed towards Grundtvig and had helped to finance Grundtvig's first England trip in 1829 to study the Old English manuscripts at the British Museum.

743. Frederik's Church, aka the Marble Church, was named after Frederik V (1723-66), who reigned from 1746-66. He laid the cornerstone in 1749, but the church was not finally consecrated until 1894.

744. The first Altar Book (or Liturgy Book) in Denmark was compiled and published in 1556 by Bishop Peder Palladius (1503-60). Born in Ribe, Palladius was a student of Luther and Melancthon in Wittenberg and later became the first Lutheran bishop of Zealand as well as Professor of Theology at Copenhagen University. He is best known for promoting Luther's teaching in Denmark, not least through his visitations to all 390 parishes in his diocese between 1538-43, reflections on which are collected in his *Visitation Book*.

pastors who had the spirit of the times with them pursuing that spirit and teaching the children as they pleased, in deep disdain for the faith of their fathers. In their sermons and their confirmation classes these so-called 'modern' pastors consider themselves no more bound by the Confessional Books of our State Church[745] or Balle's *Textbook*[746] than by the Altar Book, which they claimed to be full of outdated forms which only gave offence instead of edification. By confusing both what was insignificant with what was essential and important, and what were a few outdated and inappropriate expressions with what was inseparable from the old Christianity, they found it easy to give their vociferous claims the appearance of truth. In order to remedy this intolerable lawlessness in the Church, the government already in 1806 set up a commission to try out proposals for changes in the liturgy and to submit a report to his most gracious Majesty, but it soon transpired that it was in particular the unchangeable expressions of the old Christianity that they sought to abolish, and moreover everyone wished to be allowed to follow his own thinking, so the whole case collapsed of its own accord.

However, in the course of the present century the indifference from the previous one to all religion appeared to be waning and the complaints from the old-fashioned Christians over the intolerable behaviour of many pastors both inside and outside the Church were becoming audible. In consequence the Royal Danish Chancellery[747] enjoined all pastors to follow the Altar Book to the letter. But, as is the nature of the case, this did not have the desired effect, since many thought they possessed a kind of prescriptive right to the changes they had permitted themselves to make. This was very much the case with one of the most authoritative clergymen, Archdeacon Clausen,[748] who, when one of his parishioners complained recently that at Baptism he had high-handedly omitted an important part of the Christians' unchangeable Baptismal Covenant, not only referred publicly to his practice over 43 years but also induced the Ministry in Copenhagen to join him in issuing a complaint over the presumed errors in the Altar Book that perforce required correction.

Although I am unaware of either the changes that have been applied for or what the government's wisdom will determine, it has hereby become obvious that in the regulations of the Altar Book we old-fashioned Christians have no guarantee that our children are baptised and confirmed in our Baptismal Covenant from which we cannot possibly withdraw. It is therefore a logical consequence that Archdeacon Clausen

---

745. For the Confessional Books of the Evangelical Lutheran Church in Denmark, see note 62.

746. In 1791 Bishop of Zealand Nicolai Balle (1744-1816) published the influential *Textbook for the Evangelical Religion* for use in schools.

747. The Royal Danish Chancellery was the central governing organ in Denmark from the 12th century until 1848.

748. Archdeacon H.G. Clausen (father of Professor H.N. Clausen, see Texts 1 and 4 above) was himself a highly respected university professor whom Grundtvig mistakenly accused of being a 'rationalist'. On his European travels Clausen had encountered in Berlin the works of Friedrich Schleiermacher, and a new concept of faith based on feeling which he sought to introduce to replace the strict rationalism of the 18th century.

must be applying to change this very same Baptismal Covenant, the one that he has altered of his own volition. So whatever the government determines in this regard, a heavy yoke is placed upon the consciences of the old-fashioned Christians who have so-called 'modern' parish pastors.

If it be permitted for a humble cleric – yet one who over many years has earnestly endeavoured to get to know the true needs and state of the Church – to express his conviction in general, then it is this: if the present tension, based on the nature of the case and increasing daily, between the old and the new is not to bring about much unpleasantness and eventually a veritable schism, then the Altar Book must contain two forms between which pastors are allowed to choose, while their parishioners are again allowed at the Sacraments[749] and confirmation to make use of whichever pastor in the State Church they desire.

Once the parish-tie is thus broken[750] and those pastors who wish to leave things as they are receive permission to do so, then I am sure that as their numbers increase on a daily basis the matter will sort itself out. Whether or not His Majesty's trusted men find this wise and simple to propose, I know that in the present circumstances it will serve the cause of peace and call forth many good wishes for the King and the country if until further notice I am most graciously permitted to administer the Sacraments and confirmation in the old manner for whoever wishes it. For in the nature and circumstances of the case the tension at present is greatest in the capital, and here, where the parish-tie has long been broken without the slightest inconvenience, except for Baptism, such permission for an aging pastor can barely raise a stir. It is therefore my duty to beseech and entreat His Majesty most humbly and sincerely for this permission, which I do with a double trust in that I am glad to believe I am known from His side as being driven neither by personal advantage nor any other ignoble purpose but solely by my care for the inalienable freedom of conscience. This I willingly grant my opponents and am sure that His Majesty will never deny it to the old-fashioned Christians to whom I confess I belong with life and soul, so that only death can part us.

Most humbly
His Majesty's faithful subject

N.F.S. Grundtvig
Pastor.

---

749. i.e. Baptism and Holy Communion.

750. The parish-tie, as set down in the Danish Law of 1683, limited parishioners' worship to their parish church. Grundtvig fought long and hard to break this tie, and was finally successful in 1855.

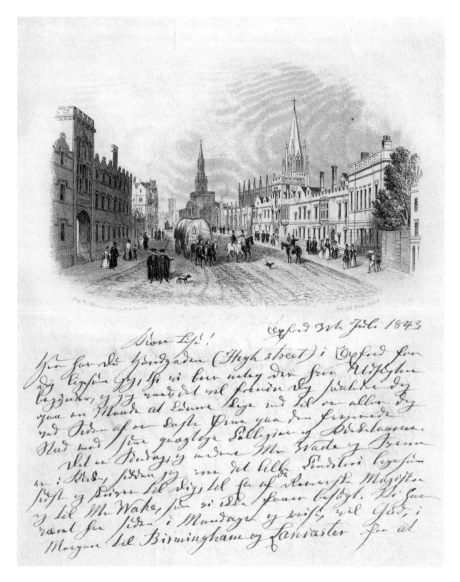

12. Letter to Lise from Oxford, 30th July 1843

During his four lengthy trips to England in 1829, 1830, 1831, and 1843 (over a year in all) Grundtvig was inspired by many people and experiences – but never by the Church of England, which he found conservative, hierarchical, and stuffy. He gained far more from his stay at Cambridge University in 1831, where his idea for a People's High School began to take shape.

    The letter begins: "Dear Lise! Here you can see the High Street in Oxford just like me, for we are staying exactly where the view begins, and I know it will please you to be able in a way to look in on us, or at least alongside us, to cast your eye over the foreign city with its magnificent colleges and church towers." Further on he complains of the Church of England hierarchy: "It is a great shame that so many talented and courageous young men should be trapped in the old papist or hierarchical snare." For the full letter see Text 46 apposite.

46. Two Letters from the England Trip 1843

1) 30th July 1843, Oxford

Dear Lise!

Here you can see the High Street in Oxford just like me,[751] for we are staying exactly where the view begins, and I know it will please you to be able in a way to look in on us, or at least alongside us, to cast your eye over the foreign city with its magnificent colleges and church towers.

It is Sunday, and while Mr. Wade[752] and Svenn[753] are in Church, I am sitting over the little confectioner's shop like last time and writing to you, to one of the Roman masters,[754] and to Mr. Wake,[755] whom we shall not be visiting. We have been here since Monday and, God willing, shall leave tomorrow for Birmingham and Lancaster to see the famous lakes of Cumberland[756] and our good friend Mr. Barrow,[757] who lives there. Our stay in Oxford this time has been much quieter than the last one,[758] since I have seen neither Pusey[759] nor Newman,[760] and most of the fellows[761] are away, but we have nevertheless been rather busy with lunches and dinners at All Souls College with Mr Waldegrave,[762] as well as at Magdalen College, which lies close by and is where Mr. Wade and I shall have dinner today with President Dr Routh,[763] an old man of 88 who is still

---

751. The letter was accompanied by a picture of Oxford High Street. See illustration opposite.

752. Rev. Nugent Wade (1809-93) was chaplain to the English consul in Elsinore (1833-39) before returning to England. In his diaries he gives an account of his meetings with Grundtvig in 1834 and thereafter. Although they disagreed on a number of theological issues, Wade was much impressed by Grundtvig and entertained him on his visit to England in 1843.

753. Svend (Svenn) Grundtvig (1824-83) was Grundtvig's second son by his first wife, Lise. On this his fourth trip to England he took Svend with him. The three-month trip took them from London to Oxford, Bristol, then Birmingham to Manchester by steam train, Edinburgh, York, and Cambridge.

754. Probably Mr. William Palmer (1811-79), a Fellow of Magdalen College, Oxford.

755. Sir Charles D. Wake (1791-1864) had published a popular commentary on the New Testament, and had twice written to Grundtvig in the hope of meeting him, but it was not to be.

756. Part of the Lake District was in the former county of Cumberland.

757. John Barrow (1810-81) was a tutor and librarian at The Queen's College, Oxford.

758. i.e. in 1831.

759. Edward Pusey (1800-82) was Professor of Hebrew at Christ Church College, Oxford, and one of the leaders of the Oxford Movement, whose members moved theologically from the Church of England towards Anglo-Catholicism.

760. Cardinal Henry Newman (1801-90) was a leader of the Oxford Movement, whose move from the Church of England led him finally to becoming a Roman Catholic cardinal.

761. 'Fellows' are the college's senior members, who together with the principal constitute the governing body. They may also include visiting professors, post-doctoral researchers etc.

762. Samuel Waldegrave (1817-69) was a Fellow of All Souls College, Oxford from 1839-45, and Bishop of Carlisle from 1860 until his death.

763. Rev. Dr Martin Routh (1755-1854) was a classical scholar and from 1791 President of Magdalen College.

both agile and lively. Svenn has frequently visited the Bodleian Library,[764] aided not a little by the librarian Dr Bandinel[765] immediately taking a paternal interest in him, giving him a small room to work in, and treating him in general like a little prince on whom everything must dance attendance, so he has had good fortune beside him just as when he went to Roskilde.[766] Yesterday afternoon he and I walked to the nearest forest in order to have been in an English forest, and when we stopped for a couple of minutes we agreed that from all we could see it was so 'homely' that we might just as well have been on Zealand as between Oxford and London. Yesterday we also saw two colleges that we had never seen before, namely Trinity and Merton. In the first we found nothing to admire unless it was the silverware, but in Merton, which is the oldest of the colleges (from the 13th century) we found a kind of chapel porch that in Denmark could pass for a proper church! Inside was a beautiful church with painted windows, and we found a library so rough and ready that some old folios were still hanging in great iron chains from the shelves.

The people I have spoken to most this time are the young masters, who are nearly all papists, including a Mr. Palmer[767] who recently returned from Sweden and had heard from the Swedish pastors that he entertained 'Grundtvigian' ideas so often that he was pleased to find me here. Of course we could not agree, since *we* speak about *equality* in the Church, whereas *he* speaks as if it only consisted of bishops and whoever else they were willing to allow inside. In contrast I know that with or without bishops the Church consists of all those who 'believe and are baptised' – believe what at Baptism we all confess and are baptised into in fellowship with the Father, the Son, and the Holy Spirit. It is a great shame that so many talented and courageous young men should be trapped in the old papist or hierarchical snare, but it is nevertheless a good thing that here too the question of the Church is being seriously discussed, and with God's help I hope to accomplish so much here that at least the young men will learn that one can believe in a holy, catholic Church without having anything at all to do with the Pope or his saints or his purgatory or his rosaries.

As for books, I find so many here both old and new which I would love to see and use in Copenhagen that if I had room and the money, I would come home with a whole library!

I have really no idea about the coming trip to Scotland, so I actually wish that it had already been undertaken, but then again it may be so fruitful that afterwards I

---

764. With its beginnings in the 14th century the Bodleian Library was re-opened by Sir Thomas Bodley in 1602 as the main research library of the University of Oxford with over 12 million items, the second largest in the country after the British Library.

765. Rev. Dr Bulkeley Bandinel (1781-1861) was the chief librarian at the Bodleian Library from 1813 until his death.

766. Most likely a reference to Svend's walking-trip to Roskilde in 1842.

767. See note 754.

would simply not have done without it, and my next letter will very likely be dated from Glasgow or Edinburgh. Since, contrary to expectation, we received no letter last week, we have no idea at all where you are, but today I assume you are in Lyngby[768] with dear Busck,[769] and I hope you may have such beautiful sunshine as I can see there is in Oxford from my half-open window. Be sure to write once a week so that there is no longer than necessary between the news of our loved ones. Greet them all from us whenever possible, and especially Johan and Meta,[770] whom I always imagine by their mother's side and would be uneasy to imagine them elsewhere. At the moment I am living so much with Svenn that I really long also to live more with his brother and sister than hitherto, for my children are at heart, I trust, all equally close, and it would trouble me deeply to think otherwise!

My silk handkerchief has been returned and I found my lost slippers in Oxford, so by Svenn's calculation all is well on board!

Stay well, dear wife, and think of God's angels surrounding and guiding us on both sides, for that is what in truth they do, and that is a lovely thing to remember!

Your
Frederik

2) 20th August 1843 (Sunday), London

Dear Lise!

Svenn and I wanted to go to Matins[771] at St. Paul's[772] today but we arrived a few minutes after the service had begun and were turned away by a young policeman with the message that we were "too late". Yet again the deadness of the High Church is revealed, for where there is the slightest life in the feeling that the Church exists for the sake of humankind – and indeed for the sake of human salvation – then it should be possible to call any church worship as well as any conversion 'late', but wherever the Word is still being proclaimed, never '*too* late', for we must hope for the best and know that the last word often achieves more than the first.

Thank you for your letter of the 12th and 13th, from which I see that we both

---

768. Lyngby is a suburb north of Copenhagen.
769. Pastor Gunni Busck (1798-1869) was a close friend of Grundtvig.
770. Grundtvig's other two children.
771. Lat., Morning Service.
772. St. Paul's Cathedral in London was founded in the 7th century. The third (wooden) cathedral on the site burned down in the Great Fire of London (1666). It was rebuilt under the architect Sir Christopher Wren (1632-1723) and reopened in 1710.

received letters on our wedding day![773] Even though they were both a bit old, they resembled even more the married couple themselves and reminded us that there will never be any point in calling back the years that have passed or forcing the feelings that have burned out. We are in every way and at all times far below what we should be, and just as our youthful feelings were far from being as pure as they should have been, so was it also foolishness to expect that those on the edge of old age should have preserved all the freshness and fullness that we might wish for. In this, as with all wealth and poverty, the latter seems more wretched than the former, even though the faults and dangers of wealth are the greater. But when God has preserved our hearts so that they beat fondly for one another and seek to share everything, then we must thank Him for a joy that is not an everyday one and we must much prefer the truthful if impoverished expressions to those that are sparkling but empty; nor must we envy the world for the *appearance* of wealth which it endeavours to give itself when it has less than nothing to offer! If it had been God's will that our Silver Wedding had dawned in some friendly part of the land of our fathers, with our children around us, and more or less alone, then I am sure that it would have been one of the happiest days of our lives, but it has turned out differently, with me spending it on an English stagecoach and an English railway[774] alone with Svenn, while you are in Pedersborg[775] presumably alone with Meta since you make no mention of Johan. It is therefore no surprise that the day was marked for the most part with a little heaviness of heart, and that it must be a comfort to us that God's blessing and the heart's joy are bound to neither years nor days, so that when we gather again, our Lord will doubtless give us what we can bear. This is even more surely so, the more we have guarded against making ourselves or each other believe that despite all separation and unfavourable circumstances our feelings were still as vigorous and united as we could wish and as they would have been 25 years ago, if we had found ourselves in the same external situation.

I am of course pleased to hear about Johan's deliberation; may God make it a firm and fruitful one, for after sixty years what I daily wish for more and more, and almost impatiently, is that my sons may join me in my work, according to their aptitudes and powers, both to ease me towards its end and to train themselves to a spirited continuation of it. For if they only can and will understand this, they will find that no father would less desire his sons to be his shadows and his echo than myself. I truly wish that, as our mother-tongue so gloriously puts it, they 'stand on my shoulders' to see further, and that when I sink down they will have the courage and strength to continue

773. Frederik and Lise were married on 12 August 1818.
774. Grundtvig and Svend travelled by stagecoach and railway up the west coast of Britain and eventually to Edinburgh.
775. Pedersborg is a parish in the diocese of Roskilde, west of Copenhagen.

to work in the same spirit with all the differences that powers and talents, time and circumstance set as the conditions for all that is living, natural, and opportune, and which alone make our activity gratifying and fruitful. Such a joy is assuredly far more than I am worth, and nowadays a great rarity, since youth usually makes believe that only in what is brand-new and totally independent can it find room for a free and enjoyable life-path. But since that is spiritless folly, I have always hoped, and continue very much to hope, that God will grant me the happiness which He knows conditioned my wish for children before they were born: that the spirit of their fathers might be over them and the kingdom of God their goal![776]

To judge from your letter, you have not gone to Rørdam,[777] so we could meet in South Zealand, though your next letter may show a change of plan. If my money holds out, I think it most reasonable that this should be in September, when as far as I am able I should like to visit our friends in Zealand whom I otherwise find it more difficult to get to.

Since we arrived in London the days have been somewhat dull, but as I still have plenty to see and do, I cannot easily turn my nose homeward for the next fortnight.

Now, dear Lise, stay well wherever you are and greet those around you! I hope that Johan has returned from Falster,[778] even though I am somewhat uneasy that according to your letter he had not arrived by the 12th, as Meta said he would, and which seemed reasonable.

I am thinking of writing a few lines to Meta[779] and in any case you must greet her from us and say that of course we not only often think about her but also talk about her and all our nearest and dearest!

Most lovingly
Your Frederik

---

776. Neither Johan (b.1822) nor Svend (b.1824) became a pastor. Frederik (1854-1903), born to Grundtvig's second wife, Marie, studied Political Science at Copenhagen University, but after his father's death in 1872 he eventually took holy orders and emigrated to the USA in 1881, where he served as pastor in Clinton, Iowa until his return to Denmark in 1900.

777. Thomas Skat Rørdam (1832-1909) was the first 'Grundtvigian' to become a bishop, serving as Bishop of Zealand from 1895 until his death.

778. Falster is an island in south-east Denmark.

779. Meta (1827-87) was Grundtvig's first daughter. His second, Asta (1860-1939), was born to his third wife, also Asta (1826-90).

47. Letter to Elise Stampe (1857)

My dear friend!

Please do say the 'communion' (*fællesskab*) of saints,[780] since you both[781] believe this to be the only proper Danish word that corresponds to the Greek 'communion', and you also feel the blessing in the word!

When we baptise children we must occasionally have reservations about exchanging the not entirely false yet awkward and half-dead 'community' (*samfund*) with the straightforward and vibrant 'communion'. But just as that is how it is written on the tablet of the heart – though not in ink but with the living God's 'breath' – so is the same word written on the Congregation's tongue, and we must in no way prevent it from sounding thus for God and for all His angels, for our own heart and for each other. For this reason you have doubtless noticed that in my prayer after the sermon I always say community (*samfund*) and communion (*fællesskab*) just as much as I say Church (*kirke*) and Congregation (*menighed*). Please do remember that God's Congregation is far from being limited to those who are now scattered in heathenism and the flesh, mostly with tongues tied and many chains round their limbs; they are all "the believers and the baptised" present and absent from the day our Lord was taken up into the cloud to the day He is revealed in it again. We only have communion with God's Congregation to the extent that we actively adopt and express this Word of God in our mother-tongue. Experience will also assuredly teach us that it is only when we say 'Congregation' or 'people's gathering' instead of 'Church' – and 'communion' instead of 'community' – that we feel the grace of Baptism and Holy Communion from and with the Holy Spirit. This grace is prophetically and vibrantly expressed in these two articles of our Creed, as our spiritual link and union of hearts in the same Spirit with the Lord, with all His people and with His Congregation of friends.

I forgot last time your question about "is shed" or "was shed" in the prayer for Holy Communion,[782] for the word in both versions expresses one and the same for believers. For us, Christ is the same yesterday as today. It is of no use to us that the Lord once actually shed His blood for us if He does not do the same today in the Spirit; and equally, His blood cannot now be shed for us in Spirit and truth, if it has not also been actually shed for us previously.

---

780. For Lutherans the word 'saints' in the Apostles' Creed denotes all true Christians throughout time and eternity. The Danish phrase is *de hellige* (lit. 'the holy people').
781. Grundtvig includes Elise's mother, Christine Stampe (1797-1868).
782. KJV has 'shed'; NIV has 'poured out'.

What you are really asking this time, and where it seems to me you have involved yourself rather incautiously, is in fact the old dispute about our participation in God's deed and the work of salvation. This is so delicate a question and so ticklish a subject that I barely dare to hope that I can speak both soundly and more or less lucidly about it, and to do so in writing about both subjects is a somewhat hopeless matter. I must give up on lucidity, and say that it is characteristic of sound teaching in the matter of salvation that the power and the glory are our Creator's and Redeemer's alone, without any separation between them. So imagining that we ourselves in spirit or heart can *do* anything is both laughable and lamentable. However, imagining that we could become and remain participants in everlasting life without taking an active part in it and without being concerned about God's kingdom and His righteousness, that is *truly* lamentable, for it leads to a sinful certainty under the appellation 'the Peace of God' which is the most dangerous of all. This is clearly the narrow gate that the Lord mentions, which many seek, but which only few find because it is only to be found in "serious effort" in the midst of apparent futility, just as the Son says of Himself that the works that He does are actually not His own; He lets the Father do them, in Him and through Him.[783] For according to the Lord's own words, as Christians we have the same relationship to our Saviour as He has to His Father, so we must show the world His good works as He showed His *Father's* good works. Just as without Him we cannot do anything, so are we capable of everything *in* Him, living not our own lives but *His* life, He who is dead and risen *in* us as well as *for* us. This is the mystery that I will not strive in vain to elucidate, since it can only become transparent in the loving embrace of 'God's Word' and our 'faith in love', which is the Bride.[784]

However, this leads us to the clearest thing we can say on the question of salvation: that from first to last it is the living God's Word with the Spirit and the living faith in our hearts that brings it about. As in a fellowship, it is as unfathomable as love; it works and accomplishes in us the forgiveness of sins, the resurrection of the flesh, and the life everlasting! Let us rest in that faith! Then the soul finds rest, and we continue to work, just as the Father and the Son work "until this very day"[785] and until all things are accomplished.

It pleases me to hear that you have the prospect of coming in now and again this winter,[786] and I see no reason why this should be so rare, since your mother is clear-eyed enough to see that you derive no benefit from being constantly occupied with your own soul and left to your own thoughts. Letters can be of some help, but, let

783. Jn 14:12.

784. Rev 21:2. In Eph 5:22-32 Christ and His Church are compared to the union of husband and wife.

785. Jn 5:17.

786. Grundtvig was living in central Copenhagen at this point, while Elise Stampe lived in Præstø, some 70 km outside the city.

us agree between us, they do not actually cause our thoughts to dwell affectionately with the letter-writer. So I wish that also with *this* letter your thoughts may dwell affectionately with your friend,

N.F.S. Grundtvig.

48. Beside my Lise's Coffin (1851)

21st January 1851, the Church of Our Saviour

Not earth only heaven, not time only eternity, can heal the wounds that death inflicts. I stand here today, an old man, taking a perceptible step towards his own grave, burying his children's mother, the bride of his youth, who for forty years, including seven years before her promise at the altar, lovingly shared prosperity and adversity, but mostly the latter.

I myself am at a loss, and have nothing to say to those who have lost a tender mother, a dear sister, a precious female friend. I have nothing except what the Creator has given us all with our human hearts: tears to shed for ourselves and our loved ones, for our human life in death's dark vale, which like the flower of the field is resplendent and fragrant today but withers and dies tomorrow, so none knows its whereabouts. But, praise be to God, I also stand here today beside myself and in the midst of a gathering as minister to the Word, God's Word, the great Gospel. As such I have comfort to bring to myself and to all who mourn beside this or any other bier, or any corner of the bier that this earth comprises for human children on the edge of the insatiable grave, devouring us from generation to generation. Being minister not of the letter that kills but of the Spirit that quickens[787] I have comfort for all who hear the gospel and believe: for it is beside the bier and at the grave that the Spirit tells us: "You shall not mourn like the others who have no hope!"[788] These are words of comfort, my friends! For this 'shall' is not a statute that condemns our honest and bitter sorrow at the grave of our family and loved ones. "You shall not mourn like the others who have no hope" is a message of joy from on high which comes to quell and end our sorrow.[789] It announces that we must not be consumed by, or subside into, mourning, but must be strong enough to lift ourselves above it, because we have a hope that the others lack.

787. 2 Cor 3:6.
788. 1 Thess 4:13.
789. Cf. Grundtvig's hymn, 'Easter dawning ends all mourning', no. 24 in *Living Wellsprings* (2015).

Hope, the hope of eternal life! We can all feel it. The Spirit chose the right word, the only word in which we can find comfort in the face of death. If we find no comfort in the hope that we as Christians have ahead of all the others, it is only because we do not keep this hope alive and beating in our breasts, but have only heard in passing: 'There is *supposed* to be just such a hope, it is called the hope of God's glory.' For if we actually *have* this hope of a blessed abundance, the Spirit only needs to remind us that it is here we find the comfort with which we must end our sorrow; it is here that we also find the rich comfort reaching out to us all. With this hope, our sorrow at the grave of our loved ones and on the edge of our own loses all its bitterness and is transformed into a gentle, sad longing to live where *none* die, where we are gathered with our loved ones, where we shall never again be parted but see both them and ourselves in the radiance and glory that should not be compared to the flower of the field but to the stars of the heavens and the rays of the sun.

My friends, we all know that such a source of comfort, such a blessed abundance of the glory can only be found in the hope of eternal life and God's glory when it truly lies in the human breast, because, as Scripture writes and the Spirit speaks, this hope embraces all of humanity in soul and body, so not a hair is lost. All this is ennobled, transfigured, matured in the abundance of life, strength, and beauty with the stamp of eternity, the garland of immortality. "It is sown perishable, raised imperishable; sown in dishonour, raised in glory; sown in weakness, raised in power; sown a natural body, raised a spiritual body."[790]

That is indeed the hope that others do not have, yet is the only thing that can quell the sorrow at the grave of our loved ones and ourselves; for the invisible in us, which knows itself to be our soul, feels so fused to its body that it has no other idea of itself and would never imagine a separation from it possible, if it were not that sickness and death forced it to. All the people we have loved we have loved *in* and *through* the body, and if we have a trusted friend, male or female, we read better and deeper things in their eyes and countenance than the scholars read in all the stars. We find on their lips the kiss of not only the body but also the soul in the rich words of the heart's abundance of love. So the hope of an eternal life from which the body is *excluded* comforts no human heart in need of comfort over and against death. That is why He who knew that it was not the healthy but the sick who need a doctor also gave His believers a hope of eternal life that embraces *all* of human life and crowns it with the glory of God. Especially, He gave us the great hope – with the rich and powerful comfort over death – in Himself, in His *bodily* resurrection, proving that He is the resurrection and the life, and by His faithful promise that we shall have fellowship with Him as He has with His Father. We shall become like Him and see

---

790. 1 Cor 15: 42-44.

Him as He is; our debased body will be formed in the likeness of His body in glory, which is the eternal mansion, the complete instrument and translucent mirror of His divine soul.

When therefore our hearts grow weak and we mourn for a time like others who have *no* hope, we feel the first reminder from the soul that this is only because we *forgot* the hope of God's glory and became frail in our faith in our crucified but risen Lord and in the power of His resurrection which lasts for ever. Then we feel the comfort that our soul derives from this faith, even though it is not as rich and strong for us as the faith that is given to the Church. And we pray to the Father in Jesus' name that His Spirit may strengthen us in the faith, so that the hope of God's glory may triumph within us. Then we may be found abundantly comforted against death and the perishable, and when the Lord calls us we can each gladly sing in our hearts:

Alleluia, alleluia!
God's Son is mine, I leave this place bound straight with Him for heaven.

49. Beside my Marie's Coffin (1854)

17th July 1854, Vartov Church

She is dead to this world, she who was not only the desire of my eyes but she to whom my heart and my soul clung with all their might; and the sorrow speaks for itself. The true language of sorrow is sighs and tears, and they cannot be grasped for as long as the old man wanders this earth whose support she was in his old age, in her eyes, in my eyes and in the eyes of all. But the Lord lives, praise be to my rock and to my God of glory! For the Lord was and is her rock and God of her salvation, this Christian woman whose dust has been lowered into the earth from which it was taken. She knows far better than I how firm the rock and how sweet the salvation is in the Lord Jesus Christ, the God of our salvation, in whom there is an escape from death. For truly:

Christ is risen from the dead
this Easter morning glowing red!
His people now in ev'ry place
with joyful song their Lord embrace:
Glory be to God in the highest![791]

791. For the full text of Grundtvig's hymn 'Christ is risen from the dead', see no. 22 in *Living Wellsprings* (2015).

So my sorrow must be silent before the Lord in this place, for here we met as those who would seek the Lord, here we so often entered together as we did the house of the Lord to tell of His wonderful deeds and sing His praises. And here is where she came for the last time outside her home to hear the blessing on our infant son that the Lord gives the little children when we bear them to Him in truth.[792] Here indeed sorrow must be silent, here only memory and hope must speak, both of which have beautiful and joyous things to relate, and far better things to promise. I venture to say that there have been very few married couples of whom it was truer what we read in the Book of the Old Covenant[793] about the two friends who met in contentious and troubled times and the one said to the other, "Is not your heart sincere towards my heart, as mine is towards yours?" and he said, "Yes it is." And the first one said, "Then give me your hand! For truly we only gave each other our hands because our hearts were sincere towards each other."[794]

My friends, there was such a rare similarity between our hearts and souls, our thoughts and feelings, our view of human life in this world, its purpose, its struggle, its victories. So from the very first moment to the last we could speak of these out of each other's hearts like two childhood friends, created to live and die with each other. That is why we rarely knew which of us would put into words what we both were thinking and that is why we could walk so happily together on all our paths and especially, God be praised, on the path that we both acknowledged to be the path to eternal light and salvation in the light of our Lord Jesus Christ and in truth in Himself who is the Truth, the Way, and the Life.

And because we walked together as kind and close friends on this blessed way to the eternal mansions, however great and irreplaceable the loss of such a companion – a wife from the Lord who is an unutterably good gift and delight – it cannot embitter the memory, the rich and blessed memory of our walking together to the House of God, for bitterness is removed by hope, the hope that cannot be put to shame, the sure and blissful hope that soon we shall meet again in the house on the eternal height, meet in far happier and closer agreement about the way of the Lord on earth and about His word of salvation to all people, far happier and in closer agreement than when we met and travelled together here on earth, even though that was already wonderful enough. Then we shall for ever be one soul and one heart in two transfigured bodies. And the little blessed child whom the Lord gave us before we were parted, whom in holy Baptism He has adopted as His child and will take the place of both mother and father, he is a living image of the great and imperishable hope that grows to comfort

---

792. Frederik and Marie's son, Frederik, was born on 15th May 1854. Marie died 53 days later, on 9th July 1854, following complications following childbirth.

793. i.e. the Old Testament.

794. 2 Kings 10:15, where Jehonadab and Jehu greet each other.

us over all temporal loss and is illuminated to prophesy the glory of eternity. He, together with his child-angel, who always sees his father's face in heaven, is to me a little angel from God who will always let me see his mother's face, as in Paradise, and he will accompany me to the gates of Heaven. Then I can, and I shall, always with a sad joy, dwell on her memory here with two short but deep sighs which I know will be ever memorable for all loving Christian hearts. On her final sickbed, as she fought to sever herself from all that she held dear in this world – and that was much, and it was hard, for everything she loved she loved with all the power of her strong soul – she called me and whispered, "I have suffered much and had a hard fight, and I have found that faith and Baptism stand firm, they are the rock." And she called me a second time and whispered, "I lay for a long time and said to myself, 'In the name of Jesus'. But it still seemed to me that something was missing that I could not remember. Then at some point I realised, 'In the name of our *Lord* Jesus', and then it was alright."

I cannot think of this without smiling through the tears, for I am sure that God's angels smiled at these deep words. They are not difficult to speak in healthy, calm days, but on the edge of the grave they can only be spoken out of the faith that overcomes the world. So may also *our* faith be witnessed and raised, our childhood faith in our Lord Jesus Christ, which in the soul of my female friend and innumerable others has overcome the world and shall with God's help and the Holy Spirit's aid also overcome the world among us and our children from generation to generation! In the power of this faith by which we are reborn in a heavenly Baptism to the rich blessing, peace be with the soul in God's house, where no pain can touch it, and peace to the dust which no power can prevent from being raised transfigured from the earth when the Lord comes again to transform our abased bodies to be formed like His blessed body in glory! Amen, in the name of our Lord Jesus, Amen!

50. Speech at the Friends' Meeting

9th September 1863, at Grundtvig's home, 'Gladhjem'

The Peace of God be with you!
This has been the popular greeting among us from time immemorial, and we know that it is also the Christian greeting with which, both at the beginning and at the end, our Lord Jesus Christ sent out his disciples. It is the greeting He Himself used to them when He returned from the kingdom of the dead bringing life and imperishability[795] into the light for the children of humankind, the new life of humankind in the im-

---

795. 1 Cor 15:42-44.

age of God which in the Lord's Church will walk towards transfiguration. In wishing God's peace upon this meeting in the name of our Lord Jesus, I am both acknowledging my faith in the Word of God's mercy as a true Gospel of peace, even though in a sinful world it cannot raise its voice without arousing its enemy to conflict, and I am expressing my regard for the Friends' Meeting as a step forward on the path of peace. The aim is to keep the peace not only with one another among ourselves but as far as possible with all people and with all that is human in thought, word, and deed.

In a little while you will see me no more in this world,[796] you who have a friendly regard for me today. At my advanced age that gives me pause for thought, so I have looked forward to meeting friends here from the whole circle listening to the voice in the wilderness which the spirit of the Lord has allowed to sound through me for a half-century now. It cannot do otherwise than make me feel at heart that before my demise I must do all I can by way of renewal, enlightenment, and confirmation of the life of the Christian Church which has awakened among us and with God's help will now flourish and bear fruit until the end of the world. This was the hope with which our first evangelist, the holy Ansgar,[797] went home, and with which God will also let me go home to Him who sent us out.

First and foremost I wish to speak as openly and plainly as I can about the heart and the soul of the movement of spirit and heart that for almost 40 years now, through me and from me, has been disseminated and applauded, or combatted, praised or censured under the name of my 'church view' or 'Grundtvigianism'.[798] However, from the very outset I have argued and continue to argue that this should really be called the 'Lutheran Christian enlightenment', which 300 years ago was nearly strangled at birth but which, with the dissolution of the State Church, is now breaking through and claiming its freedom to a living expansion. I know from within that it was in deep agreement with Martin Luther on the question of salvation that I came to the clear realisation about the Words of Institution at Holy Baptism and Holy Communion as being the Word of eternal life to us *from the mouth of our Lord Jesus Christ Himself.* They have imparted to us – and will continue to do so until the end of the world – the heavenly Christian light and the spiritual life of man, or the light of life, and the life of light, on earth. It will also become clear among the Christian reading public that Luther and I place the same emphasis on Baptism and Holy Communion as being

---

796. Jn 16:16.

797. The Benedictine monk Ansgar (801-65) is credited with bringing Christianity from Bremen to both Sweden and Denmark and is therefore known as 'the apostle of the North'. He is also credited with building the first Danish church in Hedeby.

798. 'Grundtvigianism' denotes the movement that built on Grundtvig's view of life as a gift from God for which we should be actively grateful and glad. The movement led to the building of parish halls for lectures and meetings, to the innovative people's high schools and free schools, to the establishment of free churches within the national church, and to the co-operative movement within agriculture.

the only Christian means of salvation. This is not because of their visible content but solely with regard to their *invisible* content from the Lord Himself as a living Word of God with the Holy Spirit. Both of us, however, not only admit but also assert that all visible things – in their indissoluble coinherence with the Word of God in the Lord's mouth – play their part in the secret working towards our Christian rebirth and full readiness for an eternal life. Anything in our preaching or writing that does not harmonise with this is a self-contradiction which in our human weakness has unwittingly remained part of our ingrown prejudice or has sneaked in through misunderstanding. Our opponents will always use it to challenge our Christian enlightenment and our fundamental agreement on the question of salvation, but in the long run it can never hurt or confuse our friends in God's Church, which we shall always belong to, and will serve, stand, and fall by, all our days.

What may at first glance appear to be a source of *dispute* between Luther and myself – and one that our opponents proclaim as its core – is, as you know, our Holy Scripture and the doctrines based on it that are essential for salvation. But the Christian reading public will soon realise that there is great *agreement* between Luther and myself on the relation between Holy Scripture and Christian salvation, and I know this to be a certainty, for over a number of years as a pastor (1811-25) I thought, spoke, and wrote about Scripture and its correct use very much as Luther did. On this I am in total agreement with myself, even though these days I must express myself even more clearly and more carefully. As the Apostle Paul, the master writer of the book of the New Testament, confessed: "However, I admit that I worship the God of our ancestors as a follower of the Way, which they call a sect. I believe everything that is in accordance with the Law and that is written in the Prophets."[799] Yet he never said that he had received the faith or expected eternal life through *Scripture*.

Luther and I agree first and foremost that we believe all that is written in the words of the prophets and the Apostles, but never that we have received the faith and the Spirit just by *hearing* the Word of God. We expect eternal life solely through *our faith in Jesus*, the only-begotten Son of the Father, with Baptism and Holy Communion according to His own Words of Institution. It is certain, as will be known to all informed Christians, that Luther and I simply believe through the Word of the Lord that the secret of salvation has not been revealed to the learned but to the deprived, and to minors, so that women and children who can neither write nor add up in a book can nevertheless not only be true Christians but much better Christians than all the learned scholars. From this it follows that no *book* whatsoever must form the basis of Christian salvation, nor must any other faith be required of the Church for salvation than our shared faith confessed at Baptism and at confirmation of our Baptismal Covenant.

799. Acts 24:14.

Scripture and everything else must be left to the judgement and free use of the Holy Spirit. Finally, by the 'Holy Spirit' we must understand the Spirit of our Lord Jesus Christ and all His Church, which we confess at Baptism and which is imparted to us not through reading and lectures by professors but through hearing the Word of God and through the grace of Baptism.

Therefore, when I was recently attacked for being too 'Lutheran', my opponents doubtless disagreed just as much with Luther as with me. They have only thought that I disagreed strongly with the Lutheranism that the so-called Lutheran professors in Germany produced, especially in the 17th century, and which also among us was parroted, spiritually dead and impotent, and in a so-called Lutheran 'house of correction'. This is as certain a truth as the fact that every hair on my head is inimitable now and forever! Otherwise it is a great aberration to think that the scholars of the kingdom of God have a greater right to be Lutherans than Grundtvigians as regards enlightenment. For if there is *life* in enlightenment, as there always is in *life*-enlightenment, it cannot stand still but must always move forward from one step of clarity to the next, and that is clearly the case with what can be called the Reformation enlightenment in Christianity. I am referring to how the life of the Christian Church – which from the days of the Apostles to those of Martin Luther became so wasted and darkened that it could barely be glimpsed or transmitted – could be gradually raised and strengthened so that:

> Lebanon and Carmel glow,
> Sharon's two-fold glory.[800]

In Luther's day they could glimpse how this – rather than the mere renewal of the Apostolic teaching – should be the goal of the long and strangely complex life-path of the Church as the spiritual people of God. But it was no more than a vague glimpse of the ancient prophecies. Luther was too clear-sighted to think that the goal was achievable, whether in a compulsory state church with more unbelievers than believers, or even in the purest free church with mere scholarly wisdom and church discipline, and he seems to have totally relinquished this hope. But that is not possible for the scholars of the kingdom of God in our day, for even if all the prophecies were doubtful or ambiguous, it is still certain that the God who redeemed humankind rather than create it in vain will also *glorify* mankind in His Church rather than have *redeemed* it in vain. The question among informed Christians can therefore only be when and where, and in what circumstances and with what means, God will glorify His Son in

---

800. For the full text of Grundtvig's hymn from which these lines are taken, 'Then the wilderness shall bloom' see no. 73 in *Living Wellsprings* (2015). The original text is from Isa 35:2: "The glory of Lebanon will be given to it,/the splendour of Carmel and Sharon."

His Church as the bride who prepares herself for her royal homecoming as the Queen of the kingdom.[801]

The answer in our day came simply to me when I saw that it is through our Lord's own institution in the words from His mouth to His Church that His light shines for all those within that house. That is where His quickening Spirit is imparted and His life transmitted, experienced, and glorified. Wherever and whenever one has this view, the Church must also feel itself called, enlightened, and strengthened to close in on the goal. With the very first step it must feel that freedom of the spirit and the heart are absolutely necessary, for the Lord's Spirit works only on the *heart*, and the human heart is only enlightened spiritually when it is *free*. So wherever a relatively enlightened Church cannot gain such freedom within the state-church or the church-state that encloses it, it must seek freedom *outside* it.

When the light over the Word of Life first arose for me almost 40 years ago and I conceived the bold hope, not on the path of learning but first and last on the path of life, to bring us closer to the church of the Apostles, I had not the slightest prospect of gaining within our State Church the free movement that is indispensable to this goal. I therefore endeavoured without animosity to be allowed to leave it, together with the few that wished to follow me. I had no fear that the Lord would wash His hands of us, even if we had been only two or three who wished to unite in His name and glorify it in the world through His Spirit. However, it was not to be, for like other prisons our State Church was equipped with bolts and bars which I had no desire to break open by force and no wish to lead the soft Danish heart into temptation thereby. In England,[802] the only home of civil freedom in Europe at the time, I had become better informed about the necessity of freedom for the development of human life in general. But being aware of the great danger that always accompanies a breakaway from a not obviously heretical state, for a number of years I settled for an intermediate state. I was allowed to hold services as I wished with all who wanted to attend, on condition that I did not administer the Sacraments and only sang from the current, wretched hymnbook.[803] My thinking was that in this way a free and peaceful separation from the State Church could best be prepared on both sides. But at this juncture it struck me that in our exceptionally peaceful Denmark perhaps also the *exception* could succeed! Perhaps here the sharp separation from the State Church could at least be avoided for a good while if we dissolved the parish-tie and if the self-assumed freedom of our

---

801. Eph 5:25-26: "Christ loved the church and gave himself up for her to make her holy, cleansing her by the washing with water through the word, and to present her to himself as a radiant church."

802. Grundtvig made four lengthy trips to England – in 1829, 1830, 1831, and 1843 – all of which had a great influence on his thinking.

803. *Evangelical-Christian Hymnbook for Use in Church and Home* was published by Ove Høegh-Guldberg in 1798. Grundtvig disliked the Enlightenment ideas he believed it contained.

pastors from the end of the previous century became law. In order to test this solution I again took up an office in the State Church, in which for almost 25 years now I have been free to administer the Lord's means of salvation and in recent years to sing hymns according to the desires of the heart. No pastoral calling has been freer since the days of the Apostles, and it has clearly proved that the freer we are, the better it is for all Christian relations.

However, despite the fact that the parish-tie has now been broken throughout the kingdom, it is far from being the case that all Christian pastors use their freedom as I do, with regard either to the great importance of hymn-singing or to the very condition of existence that the Lord's means of salvation constitute; for this freedom is only granted to such hospital chaplains as the Pastor of Vartov.[804] And yet all Christian pastors must enjoy at least as much freedom if they are to be proper instruments of the Holy Spirit and in their calling contribute to the edification of the Body of Christ – in other words the sincere growing together of the Church in Christ. It is a major issue whether the worldly authorities, even in Denmark, will allow such freedom to its parish pastors. But since the parish-tie, despite all the opposition from bishops and pastors, truly *has* been broken for all parishioners, I have the hope that soon it will also be dissolved for the pastors, just as soon as all Christian pastors genuinely wish this to be the case.

I must solemnly state here that I have only advised and continue to advise against anyone *voluntarily* leaving the State Church, in the hope that all my Danish fellow-servants of the Word will soon share my wish for this pastoral freedom, even though it cannot be achieved without our opponents also deriving benefit from it. That this has not so far been the case but that on the contrary pastoral freedom has found its most ardent opponents among my pastoral *friends* is the greatest sorrow I have faced in recent years. It is the only painful thing that I feel about my departure, which is close at hand without freedom yet being won. If the party of Christian friends that the Holy Spirit has created among us were to remain in the State Church *without* their pastoral freedom, it would die out in a generation, just as it did in Martin Luther's time, instead of growing up in mutual love and sincere separation from the world into a free Church of the Apostles with the full blessing of the Gospel of Christ. The reason why I do not break ranks at the last moment and leave the State Church with as many or as few as the Lord would move to follow me to build the New Jerusalem is only because I still have left a morsel of Abraham's hope. My overriding hope is that the Danish pastors will allow Him who has begun His good deed to complete it among them and through them until the day of our Lord Jesus Christ!

---

804. i.e. Grundtvig himself. He was pastor of Vartov Church for 33 years, from 1839 until his death in 1872.

Sources

Key:

VU 1-10	*Værker i Udvalg*, ed. Georg Christensen & Hal Koch (Gyldendal 1940-49)
US I-X	*Udvalgte Skrifter*, ed. Holger Begtrup (Gyldendal 1904-09)
GV	www.grundvigsværker.dk, website for Grundtvig's annotated works online
Holm I-VIII	*Grundtvigs Prædikener i Vartov* ed. Jette Holm & Elisabeth A. Glenthøj (Vartov 2007)
Thodberg	*N.F.S Grundtvigs Prædikener 1822-26 & 1832-39*, ed. Christian Thodberg (Gad 1985)
Clausen-Bagge	*Om Forsoning og Efterfølgelsen: Prædikener 1840-60*, ed. N. Clausen-Bagge (Kirkeligt Samfund 1927)
Lindhardt	*Konfrontation: Grundtvigs prædikener 1854-55*, ed. P.G. Lindhardt (Akademisk 1974)
KL	*Kirkelige Lejlighedstaler*, ed. C.J. Brandt (Schønberg 1877)
SP	*Sidste Prædikener*, ed. C.J. Brandt (Schønberg 1880)
Breve I-II	*Breve fra og til N.F.S. Grundtvig*, ed. Georg Christensen & Stener Grundtvig (Gyldendal 1936)
GS	Grundtvig Studier (Gyldendal 1952)

1.	The Church's Retort: Kirkens Gienmæle	VU II 321-342
2.	On Godly Assemblies: Om gudelige Forsamlinger	VU II 307-316
3.	Should the Lutheran Reformation Really Be Continued:	
	Skal den lutherske reformation virkelig fortsættes	VU V 278-355
4.	On the Clausen Libel Case: Om den Clausenske Injurie-Sag	VU III 294-302
5.	An Impartial View of the Danish State Church:	

	Den Danske Stats-Kirke upartisk betragtet	GV online
6.	The Christian Church and German Theology:	
	Den Christne Kirke og den tyske Teologi	US VIII 161-169
7.	On Religious Persecution: Om Religions-Forfølgelse	US VIII 460-473
8.	On the History of the Church: Om Kirkehistorien	VU V 233-242
9.	A People's Identity in Relation to Christianity: Folkelighed og Christendom	VU V 242-251
10.	The People, the People's Church, and Popular Belief in Denmark	
	Folket, Folke-Kirke og Folke-Tro i Danmark	VU V 378-394
11.	On a Christian Separation from the People's Church: Om en christelig Skilsmisse fra Folkekirken	GV online
12.	My Relation to the People's Church: Mit forhold til Folke-Kirken	GV online
13-27.	Basic Christian Teachings: Den christelige Børnelærdom	VU VI 003-153
28.	3rd Sunday in Advent: 3. søndag i Advent 1843	Holm 6 20-26
29.	Christmas Day: 1. juledag 1843	Holm 6 32-37
30.	New Year's Day: Nyaarsdagen 1838	Thodberg 11 103-09
31.	1st Sunday after Epiphany: 1. Søndag efter Helligtrekonger 1841	Holm 2 58-65
32.	2nd Sunday in Lent: 2. Faste-søndag 1837	Thodberg 10 136-140
33.	2nd Wednesday in Lent: 2. onsdag i Faste 1848	Clausen-Bagge 63-66
34.	The Annunciation: Maria Bebudelsesdag 1837	Thodberg 10 151-156
35.	Palm Sunday: Palmesøndag 1855	Lindhardt 079-081
36.	Easter Sunday: Paaske-Søndag 1837	Thodberg 10 171-176
37.	Pentecost: 1. Pinsedag 1824	US V 205-14
38.	10th Sunday after Trinity: 10. søndag efter Trinitatis 1855	Lindhardt 147-149
39.	27th Sunday after Trinity: 27. søndag efter Trinitatis 1837	Thodberg 10 368-373
40.	Sermon Before Parliament: Rigsdagsprædiken i Slotskirken 1856 4.okt.	KL 529-533
41.	Three Last Sermons: Tre sidste prædikener 1872	SP 502-506
42.	Letter to a Bishop: Brev til en biskop	Breve II 057-059
43.	Letter to Christen Olsen: Brev til Christen Olsen	Breve II 122-124
44.	Letter to the King 1831: Brev til Kongen	Breve II 202-204
45.	Letter to the King 1833: Brev til Kongen	Breve II 232-234
46.	Two Letters from the England Trip: To breve til Lise fra Englandsrejsen 1843	GS 1952 53-55, 59-61
47.	Letter to Elise Stampe: Brev til Elise Stampe 1857	Breve II 590-92
48.	Beside my Lise's Coffin: Talen ved Lises Kiste 1851	KL 87-90
49.	Beside my Marie's Coffin: Talen ved Maries Kiste 1854	KL 104-107
50.	Speech at the Friends' Meeting: Talen ved Vennemødet 1863	VU VI 391-407

Bibliography

Titles are listed alphabetically by author.

1. Other Translations of Grundtvig's theological works not included in this volume

Knudsen, J. (1976) 'Writings on the Church, Christian Life, and Human Living' & 6 Sermons. Philadelphia: Fortress Press, pp.9-112.

Lyhne, N.L./Broadbridge, E.J. (1984) 'Sermons for 16th Sunday in Trinity, 1823 & 1836' in *A Grundtvig Anthology*. Cambridge: James Clarke and Aarhus: Centrum.

Nielsen, E.D. (1985) *What Constitutes Authentic Christianity?* (*Om den sande Christendom*, 1826 + *Om Christendommens sandhed*, 1826-27). Philadelphia: Fortress Press.

2. Biographies and Essay Collections

Gregersen, N.H., Uggla, B.K, Wyller, T. (eds.) (2017) *Reformation Theology for a Post-Secular Age: Løgstrup, Prenter, Wingren, and the Future of Scandinavian Creation Theology*. Göttingen: Vandenhoeck & Ruprecht.

Allchin, A.M., Jasper, D., Schjørring, J.H., and Stevenson, K. (eds.) (1993) *Heritage and Prophecy: Grundtvig and the English-Speaking World*. Aarhus: Aarhus University Press.

Allchin, A.M. (1997, repr. 2015) *N.F.S. Grundtvig: An Introduction to His Life and Work*. Aarhus: Aarhus University Press.

Allchin, A.M., Bradley, S.A.J., Hjelm, N. & Schjørring, J. (eds.) (2000) *Grundtvig in International Perspective: Studies in the Creativity of Interaction*. Aarhus: Aarhus University Press.

Allen, E.L. (1947) *Bishop Grundtvig. A Prophet of the North*. London: James Clarke.

Bradley, S.A.J. (trans. & ed.) (2008) *N.F.S. Grundtvig / A Life Recalled*: An anthology of biographical source-texts. Aarhus: Aarhus University Press.

Davies, N. (1931) *Education for Life: a Danish Pioneer*. London: Williams & Norgate.

Davies, N. (1944) *Grundtvig of Denmark: a guide to small nations*. Liverpool: The Bryerthon Press.

Hall, J.A., Korsgaard, O., Pedersen, O.K. (eds.) (2015) *Building the Nation. N.F.S. Grundtvig and Danish National Identity*. Canada & Denmark: McGill-Queens UP and Djøf Publishing.

Knudsen, J. (1955) *Danish Rebel. A Study of N.F.S. Grundtvig*. Philadelphia: Muhlenberg Press.

Koch, H. (1952) *Grundtvig* (trans. & ed. Jones, L. from orig. Danish by Koch, H.) (1943) Yellow
   Springs, Ohio: Antioch Press.

Larson, P.M. (1986) *A Rhetorical Study of Bishop Grundtvig*. Evanston, Illinois: Northwestern
   University.

Lindhardt, P. (1951) *Grundtvig, an Introduction*. London: SPCK.

Martin, G.O. (1950) *N.F.S. Grundtvig: the Man and his Theology*. New York: Columbia University.

Nielsen, E. (1955) *N.F.S. Grundtvig: An American Study*. Rock Island, Illinois: Augustana Press.

Thaning, K. (1972) (trans. Hohnen, D.) *N.F.S. Grundtvig*. Copenhagen: Danish Cultural Institute.

Thodberg, C. & Thyssen, A. (eds.) (1983) *N.F.S. Grundtvig: Tradition and Renewal*. Copenhagen: Danish Cultural Institute.

Wen, G. (2013) *The Deep Coinherence: A Chinese Appreciation of N.F.S. Grundtvig's Public Theology*. PhD
   dissertation, Aarhus University (available online).

2. The Danish Lutheran Church and related subjects

Gregersen, N.H., Uggla, B.K. Wyller, T. (eds.) (2017) *Reformation Theology for a Post-Secular Age:
   Løgstrup, Prenter, Wingren, and the Future of Scandinavian Creation Theology*. Göttingen:
   Vandenhoeck & Ruprecht.

Iversen, H.R. (1987, repr. 2013) *Spirit and Life-form. The Home, the People, and the Church in Grundtvig's
   Time and Today*. Copenhagen: Anis & Impro Press.

Lausten, M.S. (2002) *A Church History of Denmark*. London: Routledge.

Marais, J.I. (1912 & 2016 repr.) *Bishop Grundtvig and the People's High Schools of Denmark*. London: Forgotten Books.

Veninga, J.E. (2014) *Secularism, Theology and Islam, The Danish Social Imaginary and the Cartoon Crisis of
   2005-2006*. London, Bloomsbury Academic.

3. English Articles in Grundtvig Studies
(an annual publication)

1989-90 Allchin, A.M. 'Grundtvig Seen in Ecumenical Perspective', pp.105-19.

1993 Bradley, S.A.J. 'Grundtvig's Palm Sunday 1867', pp.198-213.

1998 Allchin, A.M. 'The Holy Spirit in the Teaching of N.F.S. Grundtvig', pp.175-89.

2000 Lathrop, G. '"The Bath and the Table, the Prayer and the Word"', pp.104-17.

2003 Bradley, S.A.J. 'An Englishman in Vartov Church, 1872', pp.160-65.

2007 Wen, G. 'Grundtvig's eschatology and its realistic significance: Reflections from the Chinese
   Context', pp.198-216.

2015 Wen, G. 'The Deep Coinherence. An Attempt to Understand N.F.S. Grundtvig's Holistic
   Vision', pp.133-49.

2016 Bradley, S.A.J/Bugge, K.E. 'Grundtvig and the Descent into Hell', pp.95-182.

Biblical references

Index

includes adjectival forms e.g. Apostle/Apostolic

Personal names

Other

N.F.S. Grundtvig. Works in English

Translated and edited by Edward Broadbridge
Published by Aarhus University Press

"The world and scholarship have been done a great service with this edition of Grundtvig's works."

Linda Woodhead, Professor in the Department of Politics,
Philosophy and Religion, Lancaster University

"Scholars and general readers alike will find these translations to be not only invaluable sources for the study of the work of an influential modern genius, but also a very pleasurable reading experience, one that is inspiring and full of surprising insights."

Mark Bradshaw Busbee, Department of English
Chair, Samford University, Alabama

Vol. 1. The School for Life. N.F.S. Grundtvig on Education for the People (2011)

"Edward Broadbridge and his dedicated team have delivered a long-overdue English rendition of Grundtvig's educational ideas in a sensitive and highly readable translation that retains the power of Grundtvig's voice and moreover brings the "living word" alive in the accompanying audiobook."

Chris Spicer, Chair, Folk Education Association of America

"How wonderful to welcome Edward Broadbridge's remarkable new translation entitled *The School for Life*. The book draws together Grundtvig's most important works on education, both prose and poetry, representing a major addition to the English-language literature on educational philosophy."

Andrew Buckser, Dean of Arts and Sciences and Professor
of Anthropology at State University of New York

"This work has been long-awaited: a major translation of the Danish educationist, cultural philosopher, and theologian, N.F.S. Grundtvig. We can follow Grundtvig's theological foundational principle: "Human comes first, and Christian next" through his educational writings, which emphasise the need for a cultural self-awareness along with a radical tolerance for all forms of human expression in a cultural context."

Niels Henrik Gregersen, Professor of Systematic Theology, University of Copenhagen

Vol. 2. Living Wellsprings. The Hymns, Songs, and Poems of N.F.S. Grundtvig (2015)

"I expected a lot from this book and honestly, it is much more than I expected! The Grundtvig anthology of new translations presents the tremendous depth and breadth of Grundtvig's work in a highly accessible way. Songs and poems embracing Nordic sagas, Christian spirituality, education, democracy, wisdom, nature, as well as personal tributes to his wives, children and friends and even more can be found in *Living Wellsprings*."

Joy Ibsen, Church and Life, May 2015

"Students of historical hymn texts will find this a rich source of material. The translations are well done, reading quite naturally for the most part."

Lydia Pedersen, The Hymn Society in The Hymn, Vol. 67/2, 2016.

"A magnificent book."

Bertel Haarder, Former Danish Minister of Education (Letter to the Editor, 2015)

"One overarching characteristic of the translations becomes very clear after a reading of all the poems and reflecting on their collective effort. Broadbridge has produced translations that recapture Grundtvig's wonder at God's creation and man's place in it. Broadbridge's achievement is that his work bears the mark of Grundtvig's call for 'a plain and cheerful, active life on earth'."

Mark Bradshaw Busbee, Department of English
Chair, Samford University, Alabama